HUMAN FERTILISATION & EMBRYOLOGY

Regulating the Reproductive Revolution

HUMAN FERTILISATION & EMBRYOLOGY

Regulating the Reproductive Revolution

Robert G. Lee

and

Derek Morgan

BLACKSTONE PRESS LIMITED

Published by
Blackstone Press Limited
Aldine Place
London
W12 8AA
United Kingdom

Sales enquiries and orders
Telephone +44-(0)-20-8740-2277
Facsimile +44-(0)-20-8743-2292
e-mail: sales@blackstone.demon.co.uk
website: www.blackstonepress.com

ISBN 1 84174 119 1
© Robert G. Lee and Derek Morgan 2001
First published 2001

British Library Cataloguing in Publication Data
A catalogue record for this book is available from the British Library

Typeset in 10/11pt Times by Style Photosetting Ltd, Mayfield, East Sussex
Printed and bound in Great Britain by Antony Rowe Limited,
Chippenham and Reading

Contents

Preface

The past ten years have demonstrated that human fertilisation and embryology is one of the fastest moving and expanding areas of modern science. This book, which is derived from, but quite different in scope and ambition to, our earlier *Blackstone's Guide to the Human Fertilisation & Embryology Act 1990*, examines the consequent problems for public policy and continuing attempts through law and ethics to mediate and regulate in this area. However, trying to present a coherent account of developments in science, law and ethics is like trying capture in a photograph something that is flashing past on video or DVD.

There is one area that we have decided *not* to reflect on at length in this book: the completion of the introduction into UK law of the European Convention on Human Rights by the Human Rights Act 1998. This Act may prove to be a significant, indeed signal, event. There are references to the Act in the text, and, already, several attempts have been made to argue the provisions of the Act before the courts, notably in *R* v *Secretary of State for the Home Department ex parte Mellor* (31 July 2000). In that case, a life prisoner seeking judicial review of the Home Secretary's decision to refuse him facilities to 'export' sperm from prison to enable his wife to attempt insemination argued, unsuccessfully, that the decision breached the art. 12 Convention Right to 'marry and found a family'.

There is, of course, no reason why the HFEA will not come under 'rights' scrutiny within the provisions of the Act. A Department of Health briefing note on *The Human Rights Act 1988; European Convention on Human Rights Case Studies in Health and Social Care*, published in July 2000, advised that while it is 'unlikely' that the Act 'places a duty on the state to provide fertility treatment' it also cautioned that 'other potential issues include . . . the right to use the sperm of dead husband to conceive a child'. Indeed, it was always likely that the outriders of the reproduction revolution and the croupiers of the rights roulette would combine to find fertile ground in Human Rights Act challenges to the provision of assisted conception services. We debated a chapter on human rights' arguments but we have taken what might be called the 'Chou En Lai' approach to those issues here. The former Prime Minister of China was once asked what he thought had been the effects of the French Revolution nearly 200 years earlier in 1789. 'Too soon to say', he advised, 'too soon to say'. *Mutatis mutandi* 'reproductive rights'.

We have incurred the usual number of debts in preparing this book, which we are able to acknowledge here. We are grateful to the Department of Health for Permission to reproduce in Chapter 3 three figures from the Chief Medical Officer's Expert Advisory Group Report *Stem Cell Research: Medical Progress with Responsibility* (2000); to the Human Fertilisation & Embryology Authority for permission to reproduce as an Appendix the current 4th edition of its Code of Practice; to Deryck Beyleveld and Shaun Pattinson of Sheffield University, both for an early sight of a book manuscript and for their permission and that of Ashgate Publishing to incorporate information from their research into Tables found in Chapter 11; and to Helen Szoke and Federation Press for permission to reproduce a Table of Australian states' responses to assisted conception, also now found in Chapter 11. Other individuals who helped us in the preparation of the International Review are acknowledged in the notes to that Chapter.

Awen Edwards, Sarah Jones and Chantal Omer did some background research work funded by the Cardiff Law School Research Committee and we are grateful to them and the Committee for that assistance. The staff of the Cardiff University Law Library and the Legal Resource Unit at the Law School answered enquiries and chased references with extraordinary speed and accuracy. Unlike our earlier work, completed while one of us was in practice, we now enjoy the benefits of working in the same Law School and in the same building. However, we probably now see less of each other than was the case ten years ago. That we do collaborate from time to time is in large part due to the efficiencies of our secretaries Helen Calvert and Clare Pike in helping to plan schedules and switch drafts around on emails and discs.

We are delighted to be able to acknowledge debts of gratitude to Deryck Beyleveld, Angus Clarke, Erica Haimes, Anne Lee, Suzanne McCarthay, Shaun Pattinson, Helen Szoke and Celia Wells each of whom assisted, usually with written comments, in some cases extensively, on drafts that we asked them to review. Each improved this text with their contribution. Finally, we thank Alastair MacQueen, Heather Saward and the staff of Blackstone Press for handling the manuscript with their usual despatch and professionalism. The editor, Catherine Minahan, raised enough queries on our manuscript to fill a small portfolio of its own, and her work has saved this final text from a range of inconsistencies, inaccuracies and infelicities.

Robert G. Lee
Derek Morgan

Abergavenny
November 2000

Table of Cases

Table of Statutes

Table of Statutes

Chapter 1
Human Fertilisation and Embryology – Ten Years On

INTRODUCTION

Medical law is in large part a process of *naming, blaming, claiming* and *declaiming*. Naming – is this person ill, unwell, chronic, acute etc.; blaming – exploring the role of caring for oneself and one's responsibilities for health care, particularly whether we are responsible for our own health but also the state's responsibility for provision of health care and our collective responsibility for other nations' health; claiming – what are our entitlements to health care, of access to services; and declaiming – saying who we are and whom we want to become, giving a moral and symbolic emphasis to law.[1]

Medical concern is now inexorably seen as moral concern; medical politics is largely dominated by moral politics[2] as, indeed, it was from the mid-19th century embryonic development of 'medical ethics'; medical welfare was then as now equiparated with moral welfare. Across a broad range in the landscape of contemporary medicine, ethical choice and agency are now embedded as never before in a network of explicit rules and formal procedures and processes for making decisions. 'These rules stipulate (within certain limits) what types of decision may be made, how they may be made, by whom, and with the assistance of what resources.'[3] The increasing 'institutionalisation' of decision-making means that procedures, and to a limited extent prescriptions, are embedded in the organisational form of statutes, court opinions, administrative mandates and institutional protocols. It seems now almost extraordinary to recall that it is *only* 38 years since Patrick Devlin offered his 'pleasant tribute to the medical profession' that '. . . by and large it has been able to manage its relations with its patients on the basis of such an understanding [that conduct be regulated by a general understanding of how decent people ought to behave] without the aid of lawyers and law makers'.[4]

The intellectual origins of the 'reproduction revolution', of the debates leading up to and following on from the Warnock Report[5] – at least in the UK – were the death of social science, the imminent transformation of the biological sciences, and the social reform movements of the 1960s. There is a clear parallel between the abortion debates of the 1960s and 1970s and the embryo research and assisted conception debates of the 1980s and 1990s. These debates took place at a very specific historical moment, one in which a global concern with ethics appears to have become its defining stigmata.[6] The late 20th century saw an inversion of the mood that Orlando Figes has described as that of the immediate post-revolutionary period in Russia. Figes has characterised that as an 'age of optimism in the potential of science to change human life and, paradoxically at the same time, an age of profound doubt and uncertainty about the value of human life itself in the wake of the destruction of the first world war'.[7] In the late 20th century in contrast, we came to view scientific 'progress' with a profound scepticism – at least as to the human and economic costs entailed – while setting in place of the 'profound doubt' as to the value of human life a rededication, a reaffirmation, of its individual sanctity or sacredness.[8]

It is important to recall the historical place of the development of reproductive technologies so that we do not come to believe that the 'reproduction revolution' took place, as Christopher Hill has memorably remarked it sometimes appears to be thought that the first English revolution did, 'in a fit of absence of mind'.[9] Thus, we must locate the emergence of reproductive technologies in their modern form at the time that established social boundaries were decomposing. The nature and stability of the family and marriage were waining; the openness and acceptability of heterosexual partnerships without marriage and homosexual relationships without moment were waxing; and established social and legally enforced gender roles and stereotypes, both outside and inside the home, were being recast in the long shadows of feminism and the changing expectations of women and the demands that they were individually and collectively able and prepared to put on men. The institutional security (or domination) of established ethical concerns was under fundamental assault from feminisms, the collapse of traditional theological canons and the emergence of new questions in the methodology and epistemology of ethics and the nature of the philosophical enterprise itself. It is against these backgrounds that any examination of the regulation of reproductive technologies takes place, for they may then be seen as just one more assault upon the citadel of contemporary citizenship. As a popular song of the 1960s put it – a decade that perhaps more than any other epitomised many of the emergent metamorphoses – 'the times, they are a'changing'.

Internationally respected infertility practitioner Robert Winston has observed that from 1978 onwards, from the birth of Louise Brown as the first person conceived outside the womb, 'humans now had access to their very genesis and it caused a wave which still impacts on our understanding of ourselves'.[10] German philosopher Hans Jonas, in a different but compelling analysis, argued that modern technology, which has produced an ever-deeper penetration of nature and is propelled by the forces of market and politics, has enhanced human power beyond anything known or even dreamed of before.[11] According to Jonas, the enormously enhanced power which modern science and technology have helped to bring to human beings and their dominion of the world brings with it a change in *responsibility*; responsibility that is a 'correlate of power and must be commensurate with the latter's scope and that of its exercise'.[12] In his analysis, this means that we need to construct and identify a metaphysically based theory of responsibility – of humankind to itself, to distant posterity and to all terrestrial life. Assisted conception, as we shall illustrate throughout this book, brings at least those first two challenges to the fore in many of its applications; the regulation of assisted conception is no less than part of the story about who we say we are and how we describe ourselves.

The imperative requiring that we identify this theory of responsibility is to enable us 'to discriminate between legitimate and illegitimate goal settings to our Promethean power'.[13] The enlarged nature of human action – enlarged in magnitude, reach and novelty – raises moral issues beyond interpersonal ethics and requires reflection; responsibility is centre stage and calls for lengthened foresight – what Jonas calls 'a scientific futurology'.[14] This responsibility should be informed by fear – a 'heuristics of fear' – which will help to disclose what is possibly at stake, what values and traditions we may pass up, what approaches and opportunities we ought in all conscience to deny ourselves; 'what we must avoid at all cost is determined by what we must preserve at all cost'.[15]

Marilyn Strathern and her colleagues have shown how the deployment of reproductive technologies is affecting assumptions which we bring to understandings not only of family life but also to the family itself and cultural practice;[16] '. . . the way in which the choices that assisted conception affords are formulated, will affect thinking about kinship. And the way people think about kinship will affect other ideas about relatedness between human beings.'[17] And, we would add, the way in which we think about relatedness between human beings will affect the way in which we think about the relationship between individuals, groups and the state.

The most radical challenge to understandings of the family has been presented by assisted conception, or what Singer and Wells have called the 'reproduction revolution'.[18] The legal, biological and social constructs of parenthood have all faced vigorous re-examination, and new definitions and new family forms have become available. Even where families are created without assisted reproduction, parenthood is not a straightforward matter. As John Eekelaar has written, parenthood can be broken into three distinguishable elements – biological parenthood, legal parenthood and the holding of parental responsibility[19] – in such a way that 'the resulting structure of parenthood in English law is one in which a medieval land lawyer would have taken pride'.[20] John Robertson has characterised this as the 'decomposition' of parenthood.[21]

The role of the family and conceptions of personal identity and human nature are underlined in many ways by programmes of assisted conception, especially in the way in which rational women will use and pursue infertility programmes even when they know that the success rates are low.[22] This has been most critically studied by Lene Koch, who has observed that even where women entering *in vitro* fertilisation (IVF) programmes felt deprived of correct and realistic information, it did not seem to have affected their decisions to commence or to continue in an IVF programme after one or more failed attempts. In seeking to provide an explanation for this apparently 'irrational' behaviour, Koch reformulates the starting point of the rational inquiry not as one from an external, impartial observer, but as one which is taken from and constituted by the women's own experiences. Thus, as she pertinently observes, the wish to have a child is seen as part of what Helen Homans has in another context called part of the woman's reproductive career:

To want a child and to try to have it is an exercise of the reproductive freedom that the feminist movement has argued for since its very beginning. The decision to have a child at age 30 may be seen as a natural succession to the decision to contracept at 18, to have an abortion at 20; in other words to avail oneself of the medico technical services of the health system – first to avoid having a child, later to have one.

Thus she concludes, the wish for a child is an authentic wish and does not become less strong – or less authentic – because it is, as some critics of IVF and other reproductive technology programmes have argued, socially constructed. As Frances Price has commented, it is only after failing to satisfy the initial stages of socially sanctioned authentic wishes (unassisted conception) that the use of reproductive technology is introduced as evidence of inauthentic wishes.[23] As Koch comments:

> . . . the fact that infertile women want children, want to have a so-called normal family, is part of the explanation of why they do not hear the feminist critics. . . . infertile women do not consider prevention of infertility a relevant alternative to IVF. This is an option for future generations – not applicable to their situation.[24]

She then, in an important step, argues that the apparent irrationality of women in IVF programmes can be shown to make sense if the view of the 'infertile' woman is seen as belonging to a culture structured by its own rationality, one which is removed from, or supplements, any notion of 'universal rationality'.

From this it follows that women who experience infertility may view it as a loss of control, which is often reinforced by social stigmatisation. 'The decision to try IVF may be considered an attempt to liberate oneself from the powerlessness of infertility – if only to realise that a child of her own is no longer an issue.'[25] Hence the purpose of the IVF trials may be quite different for the infertile woman compared with that which an external, 'objective' or 'rational' observer might afford. Participating in an IVF programme may be one way of negotiating access to infertility; a woman is able publicly to admit to herself and to others that she is infertile once she has followed and exhausted all the acceptable rites of passage, including IVF, the choice for which, if seen solely as the choice for a child, would be regarded as an irrational one, given the paucity of the take home baby rate measure of success.

> IVF may be considered a way to prove to others that you are infertile – and is a precondition to a final resolution of infertility. . . . As each new reproductive technology enters the market, the definition of infertility changes. Infertility can only be defined as the condition that no reproductive technology can resolve. Thus, IVF virtually becomes an imperative, even for those women who might otherwise have been ready to accept their infertility. Human identity is closely affected by parental status and childlessness is an identity which is hard to obtain and must be fought for in a pronatalist society, since no doubt must exist as to the certainty of the condition.[26]

This is, of course, primarily a book about law. At one level, the clearest *legal* issues are the regulation of the uses of the fruits of scientific knowledge related to addressing infertility. Such fruits might come in at least two pallets:

(a)   changing or modifying existing practices or behaviour, whether in relation to individual human patients, their gametes or embryos, or gametes or embryos derived from a donor;

(b)   regulation of the circumstances in which embryos derived from these practices may be brought to conception, and the information later to be available to those individuals as to the circumstances of their conception.

These are the fairly standard concerns of lawyers who have addressed questions of the regulation of assisted conception. With them come several contributions (usually and necessarily derived from moral philosophy) to understandings of human dignity, 'personhood', and consequential matters relating to the medical or genetic interventions at the beginning of life.

At another level, however, are questions that are predicated upon a different understanding of the role and contribution of law. Here, law is seen not (just) as an autonomous body of knowledge but as a factor which contributes to; which in part translates and facilitates the so-called 'public understanding of science', but which also operates in a similar way in contributing to the less well-developed inquiry of the 'scientific understanding of the public'.[27] Of course, this may vary according to a number of discrete variables and modes of analysis; is law to be seen as only an instrumental response to assisted conception practices, or is there an ideological, a symbolic element to it as well, or instead?

While this is a book about law and not primarily a reflection upon the ethics of assisted conception and related technologies – still less an examination of their philosophical premises and problems – in this area of medicine almost above all other, what we might otherwise think of as these 'background' debates actually frame and determine so much of how the law is shaped. We may disagree about the extent to which that should be the case, the extent to which positive law does or should take its inspiration from moral philosophy, and how resolution of difficult questions in reproductive medicine are sometimes apparently resolved in the schools of political philosophy rather than in the clinic or laboratory. This is what Kenneth Clarke, then Secretary of State for Health, may properly be taken to have intended when he said, introducing the Human Fertilisation and Embryology Bill to the House of Commons in 1989, that this was probably the single most important piece of legislation which any government had brought forward in the last 20 years. It deals with matters which lie at the heart of the people that we say we are, and those whom we aspire to become.

THE LEGISLATIVE DEBATE

In 1989–1990, the debate which this book now retraces was about how and in what appropriate way(s) to respond to biological infertility and where, if judged appropriate, to bound the commons of assisted conception. Sections 13(5) and 30 and the definitional aspects of ss. 27–29 of the Human Fertilisation and Embryology Act 1990 were the clearest markers of what we originally said was to be the temporary marshalling of arguments reached at that point; the resultant expression of such barriers to entry to the reproductive quadrille. Remarkable metamorphoses in science and medicine have occurred at the same time as the rise of a global concern with ethics in the ten years from 1990. In that decade the news has been dominated by post-menopausal women[28] and posthumous pregnancies;[29] surrogate mothers[30] and homosexual fathers;[31] procreative tourism;[32] unintentional surrogacy;[33] abortion and sperm tourism;[34] sex selection[35] and genetics; virgin births[36] and multiple births:[37] the appearance of social infertility and, latterly, the cloning of sheep[38] and pigs.[39]

One of the striking features of the decade since 1990 has been the pace and nature of change and development in the reproductive and genetic technologies themselves; the science related to and derived from infertility treatment and its associated research has grown almost exponentially too. Three examples will suffice: the development of flow cytometry, which would make the determination of embryonic sex much easier and more difficult to regulate; the development and refinement of techniques of cloning; and the possibilities of embryonic stem cell work which could lead to treatments for a range of human diseases.

This has been mirrored, with the usual caveats, by the nature and pace of responses, ethical and legal ('limping behind and in the rear'[40]), regulatory and dismissive, which the developing technologies have themselves called forward. Yet once such a law is in place it is very hard to revisit; many of the issues raised are politicians' nightmares, and as essential from many perspectives as legislation is an authoritative body to regulate assisted conception and the associated and related research programmes. Trying to keep the face of the legislation up-to-date and properly reflective of (let alone anticipating) the science involved is the stuff of recurrent dreams.

Difficult and controversial areas with which 'regulators' internationally are grappling relate to eligibility for treatment, posthumous use of gametes, dealing with (i.e. disposing of) unclaimed embryos, embryo research and therapeutic cloning, genetic testing of embryos and storage of ovarian tissue, access to information about donation (where there appears to be a rapid shift even in the medical fraternity, to consider it to be a right for offspring to have access to this information), and surrogacy.

Surrogacy had strayed briefly on to the reproductive commons in 1984, but had been thought to have been adequately enclosed by the Surrogacy Arrangements Act 1985, which sought to place a tight regulatory fence around a market in reproductive services while leaving enough space within which this reproductive alternative could survive without thriving. Developments in the practices of surrogacy in the 1990s, as we shall see, brought about the establishment of a government inquiry to determine whether a whole sale reform of surrogacy law was appropriate. The Brazier Committee decided that it was.

Yet the introduction of a statutory regime is far from a panacea for resolving the public choice or legal issues in regulating reproduction. Indeed, some of the necessary complexities which statute introduces are that words do not interpret themselves, neither does science obligingly stand still, nor do 'patients' demands and expectations remain static. Attempting to paint a picture or take a snapshot of the relationship between law and aspects of medical science may distort what is its essentially fluid, dynamic nature; one which is metaphorically represented better by pentimenti than a fixed and unchanging portrait.

In concluding our overview of the 1990 Act we wrote, '. . . that the Human Fertilisation and Embryology Act is incomplete does not mean that it is unwelcome. But it will not be the last word on the subject'.[41] These words, written in the spring of 1989, have indeed come to bear some fruit just 11 years later; they were written before the name of Diane Blood had ever appeared on our computer screens. In turn, Mrs Blood has left the trail of her name in the corridors of the Human Fertilisation and Embryology Authority (HFEA) and the offices of its legal advisers, even before the coming into closer domestic effect of Articles 12 and 8 of the European Convention on Human Rights as provided in the Human Rights Act 1998. Article 12 provides that 'Men and women of marriageable age have the right to marry and found a family . . .'; and Article 8 that '(1) Everyone has the right to respect for his private and family life . . .', which may be abrogated only in limited circumstances.[42] A recent commentary on the Human Rights Act concluded one of its sections on 'future issues' by suggesting that:

> When Diane Blood sought to use her dead husband's sperm to conceive a child she succeeded on the basis of European Community free movement law. Had the Human Rights Act 1998 been in force she may have succeeded more easily by invoking Articles 12 and 8.[43]

There are problems and difficulties as much as solutions and opportunities with a rights-based approach to reproductive medicine. Margot Brazier reminds us that generally a right to *x* requires that there be a correlative duty on the part of some other person to supply *x*. 'Moreover, if a right to reproduce is a fundamental human right it must be gender neutral. If women have the a fundamental right to reproduce then so do men.'[44] She cautions: 'Consideration of a right to reproduce as shared by men and demanding a correlative duty on the part of someone else may prompt hesitation on the desirability for *women* of any such right at all.'[45] A similar point is made by Mrs Justice Hale in the concluding remarks to her Hamlyn lecture series, *From the Test Tube to the Coffin*, echoing the cautionary tale proposed by Hans Jonas:

> The new balances between choice and regulation are only slowly emerging. The law cannot impose a dictatorship, however benevolent, which insists that it knows best how people should conduct their private and family lives. . . . But that does not mean that everyone has to be supplied with the means of doing things differently. Nor does it mean that choices can be made irrespective of the consequences for the other people involved. New possibilities in human life and relationships are emerging all the time and the law will have to stay alert to develop in response to them.[46]

We introduce the example of Mrs Blood here for this important reason. Blood's case, along with post-menopausal women and egg-freezing litigation have shown that women are not prepared to take the state regulation of reproductive issues without at least some sort of challenge, whether legal, forum or otherwise. Immediately after the Blood case the Government commissioned a review from Professor Sheila McLean of the consents provisions of the 1990 Act.[47] Thereafter, Professor Brazier's committee reviewed the operation of the provisions of that Act and the Surrogacy Arrangements Act 1985.[48] The time may be approaching when it is right for a wider review of the Human Fertilisation and Embryology Act. This is necessary in an innovative field such as this anyway, but also better to be able to understand the nature and type of regulation which is properly called for in this sensitive area.

We are strengthened in this belief by the recent conclusions of the review by the Human Genetics Advisory Commission (HGAC) and the HFEA in their Consultation Report, *Cloning Issues in Reproduction, Science and Medicine.*[49] At para. 9.7 they observe:

> . . . because of the pace of scientific advances in the area of human genetics, the HGAC and the HFEA believe that the issues need to be kept under regular review to monitor scientific progress. We therefore recommend, that the issues are re-examined again in, say, five years time, in the light of developments and public attitudes towards them in the interim.[50]

Mutatis mutandi assisted conception as whole.

THE ACT AND THE REGULATORY BODY: KEEPING PACE WITH DEVELOPMENTS

It is opportune to review the operation of the legislation and the functioning of the regulatory body (the HFEA) and to offer a preliminary assessment of the place of the Act in the wider scheme of developments in reproductive science and medicine which have grown apace in the decade since it was enacted.

The Human Fertilisation and Embryology Act 1990

The role of the HFEA is to act as a buffer between those in the political arena and the often conflicting interests which they are supposed to serve. It is surprising that the work of the HFEA has drawn so little serious or sustained comment. Indeed, the only careful attempts at analysis of the work of the HFEA of which we are aware are Margot Brazier's recent essay on 'Regulating the Reproduction Business?'[51] and Michael Mulkay's *The Embryo Research Debate.*[52] Predictably, Robert Winston has offered some pertinent and searching observations and criticisms from his experiences as a world-renowned infertility practitioner,[53] while Comment on Reproductive Ethics (CORE), a group established soon after the 1990 Act was passed, has made a number of critical observations on the early work of the HFEA. For example, CORE has complained that:

(a)   the HFEA is unduly influenced by scientists 'working in the field', a situation exacerbated by the requirement that HFEA fund a large part of its operating costs by licence fees levied from those whose work it endorses and supervises;

(b)   the composition of the HFEA excludes those who are critical of or have reservations about the wisdom of the whole march of the 'reproduction revolution';

(c)   the Code of Practice cedes to clinics far too much control over the work that they do, it is vague and some centres comply only reluctantly with its imperatives;

(d)   the requirement in the Act to prioritise 'the welfare of the child' appears at best to be submerged in the Authority's workload;

(e)   the HFEA has become 'an arbiter' of fundamental ethical issues on which there is no widespread agreement.

Consequently its work as a whole is compromised.[54]

The extent to which these charges are made out can really be gauged only by a careful analysis of the Authority's own Annual Reports. We reserve that opportunity for another time. It is worth, in passing, however, drawing together the limited public comments that have been offered on the HFEA to see what sort of preliminary assessment they offer.

The HFEA is not bashful about the reach of its regulatory aspiration: 'Underlying all its activities is the HFEA's determination to safeguard all relevant interests – patients, children, doctors and scientists, the wider public and future generations.'[55] The Authority here identifies a diverse and potentially divided number of important stakeholders, some of whose interests may be in direct conflict with others, and not all of whom can be taken, unproblematically, to share the vision of the HFEA about its role, nor to understand or accept the alternative views which the HFEA must mediate. Whether the ambit of its formal powers under the 1990 Act enables it effectively to deliver the annual dividend which these diverse stakeholders might expect is something which needs careful study and reflection. Whether the Authority does – as a matter of judgment – always correctly make these difficult calls is a matter of public debate, political philosophy, practical ethics and *realpolitik*.[56]

One important preliminary question is to delineate the extent to which emergent 'innovative' health technologies could properly correspond to a 'market',[57] quasi-market[58] or 'moral regulation'[59] model, and what, if any, significant difference this might make either in regulatory terms, or to the ends to which such regulation might be directed.[60] Some commentators have argued that innovative health technologies give rise to new and pressing questions of social regulation and ethics,[61] including social identity and relatedness.[62] Others more sanguinely propose that developments in reproductive medicine and molecular biology either give rise to no new ethical questions,[63] or that, in so far as they do, the market may provide an appropriate[64] or the only[65] response.

The 1990 Act:

> provides the first attempt in English law to provide a comprehensive framework for making medical science democratically accountable. Its interest therefore arises both from the solutions it adopts for particular issues and from the model of regulation on which it builds. . . . The nature of the forum in which the debates about infertility treatment and embryo research are to be carried out is structured by a complex web of discretion, restraints, control and accountability.[66]

Margot Brazier has commended the British model of regulation adopted although she argues that no single, coherent philosophy underpins the Act's response to reproductive medicine. Yet pragmatism may have its advantages in regulating infertility treatment services and embryo research. Brazier suggests that the Act's model:

(a)   ensures public accountability in the development and delivery of both new treatments and research procedures;

(b)   promotes high standards of medical practice;
(c)   offers those lucky enough to benefit from reproductive medicine assurances
that their treatment is not likely to be marred by 'gross misadventure';
(d)   is built on and therefore promotes consensus between regulators, clinicians
and scientists which is to the benefit of patients; and
(e)   promotes British reproductive medicine.[67]

Statutory regulation might be thought to bring a number of significant advantages
and some possible disadvantages, which might include those set out in Table 1.1.
However, Brazier warns that there is a price to be paid for the 'pragmatic'
consensus that she identifies: '[A]ll too often crucial issues of individual rights, the
balance between rights and public policy, and issues of conflicting rights are skated
over.' Brazier concludes that there is 'little conceptual depth underpinning British
law,' with the result that 'again and again, as new medical developments emerge,
we debate the same issues in different guises'.[68]

This is a significant and troubling cost. It is one in which, as Matt Ridley has
suggested in a related field, we are condemned to play the role of the Red Queen,
forever rushing to stay in one place:

. . . 'in *our* country,' said Alice, still panting a little, 'you'd generally get to
somewhere – if you ran very fast for a long time as we've been doing.' 'A slow
sort of country!' said the Queen. 'Now, *here*, you see, it takes all the running
you can do, to keep in the same place. If you want to go somewhere else, you
must run at least twice as fast as that.'[69]

The problem with this is that it runs the danger – no more yet – of ignoring or
deflecting that distinctly important plea made by Jonas for a 'lengthened foresight'.

Table 1.1   Statutory regulation: advantages and disadvantages

Advantages	Disadvantages
Certainty, stability and consensus forming	Moral hazard and slippery slopes; legitimacy
Political advantages; democratic accountability and legitimacy	Definitional questions (e.g. what is a 'gamete'; cloning) and transitional problems (from self- or voluntary regulation to statutory regulation)
Statute with Code allows flexibility to respond to developments *after reflection*	Cost ('a tax on the infertile')
Remove or reduce 'procreative tourism' and 'forum shopping'	Legitimacy; conflicts of interest, 'capture' Adverse reactions (e.g. of patients) to compulsion (e.g. counselling) and or paternalism

We must remain aware that law is part of comparative public-policy making and represents one of our responses to the forces of globalisation; we must also focus on the negotiation of the movement from bioethics to biolaw (how and why laws and regulations come to be passed), or from bioethics to biopolitics (how and why some laws and regulations come to be passed and others not). This focus requires an account of the development and implementation of individual regulatory regimes and the way(s) in which those come to shape negotiation of European (and wider) policies, statements, or rules of international import which seek to address the global availability and impact of defined technologies in the art and practice of medicine. This is part of an examination of the role of law in regulating biotechnology in what Ulrich Beck has called 'the risk society'.[70]

Beck cautions against the dangers of uncontrolled or unregulated uses and developments of science and technology. He has suggested that while the latest research results constantly open up possible new applications, this happens at such a rapid, exponential rate that the process of implementation is practically uncontrolled. A variant on this that we would add is that where it is controlled, countervailing arguments are more easily marshalled on the basis of benign experience or supposed individuation of consequences. Accordingly, while medicine supposedly serves health, it has in fact 'created entirely new situations, has changed the relationship of humankind to itself, to disease, illness and death, indeed, it has changed the world'.[71]

One of Beck's interlocutors has recently distilled the concept of 'risk society' in an accessible fashion for a legal audience. Anthony Giddens has cautioned that the idea of 'risk society' might suggest a world which has become more hazardous, but this is not necessarily so. Rather, it is a society increasingly preoccupied with the future (and also with safety) which generates the notion of risk; the use of 'risk' is taken to represent a world 'which we are both exploring and seeking to normalise and control'.[72] In this understanding, 'risk society' suggests a society which increasingly 'lives on a high technological frontier which absolutely no one completely understands and which generates a diversity of possible futures'.[73]

> The origins of the risk society can be traced to two fundamental transformations that are affecting our lives today. Each is connected to the increasing influence of science and technology although not wholly determined by them. The first transformation can be called *the end of nature*; and the second *the end of tradition*.[74]

The 'risk society' is one that creates *manufactured risk*; 'science and technology create as many uncertainties as they dispel – and the uncertainties cannot be "solved" in any simple way by scientific evidence'.

The unprecedented speed of change in medical practices, and the radical uncertainty and anxiety which have been an accompaniment to this have produced new (self-producing) uncertainty:

> . . . we are living in a state of epistemological turbulence . . . It is as though Durkheim's motto has been reversed. Rather than studying social phenomena as if they were natural phenomena, scientists now study natural phenomena as if they were social phenomena.[75]

There are those who believe that work in present biotechnical research and associated infertility treatment services is like playing alchemy in the crucible of the genetic future. They suspect that the atoms will enter new, unforeseeable and dangerous trajectories and take on vectors and forces that cannot now be understood. In this vision, under the eye of the biotechnological clock we are moving towards some alchemical Armageddon in which the horsemen of the apocalypse become the cavalry charge of the chromosomal chemists. For some, the sanctioning of research on human pre-embryos signals that the orders for that charge have already been given, and that the slippery slopes of disaster and destruction have already been tested and will exercise an inexorable gravitational pull.[76]

In parallel with this are doubts that have consistently been voiced about the wisdom of investing resources so heavily in the 'reproduction revolution'.[77] Against a background of serious, if contested, concern about the continuing rapid population growth in certain quarters of the globe, and more explicit, feminist arguments that such technological fixes to the perceived problem of infertility and childlessness[78] are the wrong answers to the wrong questions, there are fears that present imperatives address at several levels the wrong problem and certainly propose the wrong solutions.

The challenge is to obtain all the benefits and advantages of these developments in reproductive technology, but to control these developments and guide them in the directions that we want. The major difficulties will be to agree upon and then identify the unwanted or unwarranted consequences; to consider how these are best to be avoided and minimised; and to determine the opportunity costs of having identified and chosen to regulate in one way rather than another.

The regulation of assisted conception

Sheila McLean has suggested that 'human reproduction is, in part, regulated by law because it is seen as more than a merely private matter'.[79] Most states have, on examination, concluded that some form of regulatory control (usually through specially framed and implemented legislation) is preferable to no regulation, although the nature of that regulation and review differs markedly. The types of control which could be envisaged include:

(a)   a private ordering approach, based upon individual control, responsibility and power;

(b)   professional self-regulation and control, through the medical profession, local research and institutional review committees, which has been a hallmark of medical regulation and supervision for many centuries;

(c)   community control, through national ethics committees and the courts;

(d)   legislative and regulatory control;

(e)   a combination or blending of one or more of these approaches.

Whichever is chosen will reflect the perceived judgment of the proper role of the state in assisted conception. Yet it is fascinating and remarkable that so few common law countries – in which we might also include the various jurisdictions of the US – have regulatory legislation dealing comprehensively with facets of assisted conception. The major jurisdictions of Canada, Australia, Japan and the US have no (federal) legislation (where that lies within the federal government's authority), and in the absence of that relatively few individual states have moved to fill that vacuum. Of course, it is true that wise government does not always legislate at the first opportunity, and the global nature of the reproduction revolution makes the lack of attention to concerted international legislation perhaps less surprising than would be its presence.[80]

Secondly, it is remarkable – with what seems to be increasing frequency – how often one reads of the 1990 Act as being viewed as the appropriate regulatory model to have introduced when comparative assessments of models of regulation are assayed. Some 11 years ago, when the Bill that was to become the 1990 Act was being debated, clinical freedom was then preyed in aid of relieving some aspects of assisted conception, such as gamete intra-fallopian transfer (GIFT), from the purview of the then to-be-created Human Fertilisation and Embryology Authority. As Lord Mackay of Clashfern, the Lord Chancellor of the day, said in debate:[81]

> . . . we think that licensing this technique [GIFT] except where it involves donated gametes when it does clearly fall within the scope of the licensing arrangements, would be to take a first step which could logically lead to a much larger degree of statutory regulation of medical treatment . . .

We thought that that judgment in that absolute form was wrong at the time and we remain unpersuaded that in this small field, this limited corner of medical practice, there is not room for greater oversight of further aspects of assisted conception. Indeed, Robert Winston has complained that 'one of the fundamental problems associated with the establishment of the HFEA [is that] the HFEA has no control over the great bulk of reproductive medicine'.[82] He concludes that 'after seven years of experience, I confess to having some nagging doubts about [the role of the HFEA]. . . . it does seem illogical to single out just one kind of medical treatment – not even the whole of reproductive medicine – for such careful, elaborate regulation'. IVF was singled out, Winston suggests, not to improve clinical standards, because standards of tubal surgery are much more variable and IVF is no more dangerous than other techniques. Indeed, 'stimulation of ovulation *without* IVF is almost certainly the most dangerous of any reproductive treatment, . . . [and] hyperstimulation has been more dangerous in those units with no IVF experience'.[83] Additionally, as Margot Brazier advises, 'it is instructive to ask what the Act does not do. It . . . does not apply at all to GIFT although GIFT is more likely than IVF to result in multiple pregnancy'.[84]

Part of the reason (if not the main one) sitting alongside clinical freedom, for excluding GIFT from the HFEA's regulatory remit was financial; to have brought such a potentially large aspect of reproductive medicine under statutory control would have been very expensive. As it is, Winston has observed that 'one has the very strong feeling that, ever since it was established, the HFEA has been chronically short of money'.[85] And this at a time when the past 11 years have seen the most profound changes in reproductive medicine, an increase in the role and range of treatment centres[86] and the 'dramatically increased role of commerce'.[87] Whereas the Warnock Report was based on the assumption that fertility services would be integrated into the NHS, 'the enormous commercial potential of developments in reproductive medicine' were unforeseen or unobserved. 'Yet debate on commodification and commercialisation is at the forefront of debate today.'[88] In times of reproductive recession, when the profit margins of all private treatments are being pressed from a number of points, the operation of fertility clinics in a private market is something that will need to attract special and sensitive review.

But more fundamentally Winston has observed what many clinicians echo privately, that the architects of the legislation made a fundamental mistake when calibrating the engine of the HFEA and setting up the inspectorate. It was decided that rather than follow the model of the Animals (Scientific Procedures) Act 1976, under which a full-time, salaried inspectorate is established to supervise experimental work with animals in the UK, the HFEA would work with inspectors who were also clinicians or scientists working with IVF. The HFEA currently employs 65 part-time inspectors, something that has been a cause of some comment and possible concern by clinicians questioning the wisdom of this type of inspectorate. According to Winston, this created

> . . . the first beginnings of a potentially serious conflict within the regulatory framework. . . . It has to be borne in mind that IVF has always had a strong commercial flavour. . . . the great majority of patients had to go for treatment on a fully private basis. This trend, already significant in 1991, has become much more serious in recent years, particularly with reforms in the funding of the NHS. Most IVF clinics required sufficient income to be viable, and by 1991, there was already increasing competition between clinics.[89]

Thus, empowering competing professionals to be part of the licensing (rather than regulatory) process 'was not particularly sound'.[90] It is difficult to see how it assists in fulfilling the requirement that the HFEA should seek to 'secure public confidence and the confidence of the centres'. Indeed, Winston suggests that 'there is clear evidence that inspections were inconsistent from the inception of the HFEA'.[91] The evidence supporting this particular charge is not perhaps as weighty as one might have wanted to sustain a charge of such gravity, but for Winston it clearly illustrates a serious lack of uniformity and objectivity on the part of HFEA inspection teams. This lack of uniformity – although it is not suggested that this exists in any serious or systematic way now – in such a commercially sensitive field, would be critical and leave the HFEA open to potentially damaging legal challenge if there was serious evidence of continuing in consistency.

Recent authoritative accounts of regulation[92] have had little to say about the emergence of 'new' health technologies and their social and statutory reception. Conceptually, there is nothing that necessarily dictates that access to and control over health technologies could not or should not be subject to the same or a similar analysis.[93] The work so far done has been of a predominately descriptive nature,[94] whether in the UK,[95] Europe,[96] or the common law world.[97] In so far as these accounts have considered seriously the emergence and expansion of health technologies, they have done so within discrete disciplinary boundaries; little work has sought to locate an account of *regulating* innovative health technologies, such as reproductive medicine and genetics, within changing constitutional frameworks, the responsibilities of holistic government,[98] related questions of social exclusion,[99] and the emergence of demands for supra-national regulation of bio-medicine and the identification of appropriate forums which have come to occupy the international community in the last decade.[100]

We are great believers that the field of medical law as much as medical ethics should conform so far as is possible with Bill Bryson's first rule of shopping: you should never buy anything which is too heavy to make the children carry home.[101] In other words, medical law, so far as is possible, should be simple and straightforward and capable of ready understanding in everyday use in the High Street as much as in the High Court. With assisted conception and embryology, the law is coming closer, we venture, to Flanders and Swann's view of the second law of thermodynamics than Bryson's more accommodating rule. It is becoming more and more complex and being made to dance upon the heads of embryological spindles.

Writing in 1990, we sought to offer an introductory commentary to the Act, trying to make the substance of the legislation comprehensible against the background philosophical, moral, scientific and political debates which had then framed its arrival on the statute book. As we then suggested, we only pared the surface of the rich seam of literature which assisted conception and reproductive technology had already generated. That is even more true a decade later. Rather than paring seams, we have for this text excavated, though again only superficially, one or two of the mines of professional and academic information, opinion and analysis, governmental and interest group reports which have been written and digested in that time. Our intellectual debts to that literature are clear.

NOTES

[1]   Clearly, this draws from and builds on Felstiner, W., Abel, R. and Sarat, A., 'The Emergence and Transformation of Disputes: Naming, Blaming and Claiming,' (1980–81) 15 *Law & Society Review* 631.

[2]   Hunt, A., *Governing Morals: A Social History of Moral Regulation* (Cambridge, Cambridge University Press, 1999).

[3]   Jennings, B., 'Possibilities of Consensus: Towards Democratic Moral Discourse' (1991) 16 *The Journal of Medicine and Philosophy* 447, at 450.

[4]   'Medicine and Law' in his *Samples of Lawmaking* (Oxford, Clarendon Press, 1962), at 103.

[5]   Report of the Committee of Inquiry into Human Fertilisation and Embryology (Cmnd 9314, 1984).

[6]   Hobsbawm, E., *Age of Extremes: The Short Twentieth Century 1914–1991*, (London, Michael Joseph, 1994), at 287.

[7]   *A People's Tragedy: The Russia Revolution 1891–1924* (London, Pimlico, 1996), at 733, 857n.

[8]   At least in individualised, westernised societies, and in respect at least of individual, westernised lives. This is not to imply that such concerns are exclusive to westernised societies: see, for example, Williams, N., *The Right to Life in Japan* (London, Routledge, 1997), esp. at 5–15 and 85–100; Jakobovits, Sir Immanuel, 'The Jewish Contribution to Medical Ethics' in Peter Byrne (ed.), *Rights and Wrongs in Medicine* (London, King Edward's Hospital Fund for London, 1986), at

115–26; and the papers variously collected in Fujiki, N. and Macer, Darryl R.J., *Bioethics in Asia*, (Tskuba Science City, Eubios Ethics Institute, 1998).

[9]   Hill, C., *Intellectual Origins of the English Revolution* (Oxford, Clarendon Press, 1965), at 1.

[10] *The IVF Revolution: The Definitive Guide to Assisted Reproductive Techniques* (London, Vermillion, 1999), at 137.

[11] Jonas, H., *The Imperative of Responsibility* (Chicago, University of Chicago Press, 1984), at ix.

[12] *Op. cit.*, at x.

[13] *Ibid.*

[14] *Ibid.*

[15] *Ibid.*

[16] Strathern, M. *et al.*, *Reproducing the Future: Anthropology, Kinship and the New Reproductive Technologies* (Manchester, Manchester University Press, 1993). And see Strathern, M., 'The Meaning of Assisted Kinship' in Meg Stacey (ed.), *Changing Human Reproduction* (London, Sage Publications, 1992), pp. 148–69. This essay is a succinct introduction to cultural and linguistic concepts deployed in arguments about the family, demonstrating in her use of examples the way in which what are taken as natural facts are themselves social and cultural constructs. For developments of this sort of argument, applied to various intellectual disciplines, see *inter alia*, Foucault, M., *The Order of Things* (London, Tavistock, 1970) and Thomas, K., *Man and the Natural World* (Harmondsworth, Penguin, 1983).

[17] Strathern, M., in Meg Stacey, *op. cit.*, at 149.

[18] Singer, P. and Wells, D., *The Reproduction Revolution* (Oxford, Oxford University Press 1984). A comprehensive consideration of the issues and questions involved is presented in the two-volume final report of the Canadian Royal Commission on the new reproductive technologies, *Proceed with Care* (Ottawa, Minister of Government Services, Canada, 1993).

[19] Eekelaar, J., 'Parenthood, Social Engineering and Rights', in Derek Morgan and Gillian Douglas (eds), *Constituting Families* (Franz Steiner Verlag, 1994), citing the Children Act 1989 for the introduction of the third important element.

[20] *Ibid.*

[21] Robertson, J., *Children of Choice* at 32.

[22] For an excellent analysis of this phenomenon, see Koch, L., 'IVF – A Rational Choice?', *Reproductive and Genetic Engineering: International Journal of Feminist Analysis*, 3, 1990, pp. 235–42.

[23] In Derek Morgan and Robert Lee (eds), *Birthrights: Law and Ethics at the Beginnings of Life*, 1989.

[24] Koch, *op. cit.* n. 22, at 239.

[25] *Ibid.*, at 240.

[26] *Ibid.*, at 241.

[27] A useful portmanteau phrase coined by Celia Wells; see her '''I Blame the Parents'': Fitting New Genes in Old Criminal Laws', in Brownsword, Cornish and Llewelyn, *Law and Human Genetics: Regulating a Revolution* (Oxford, Hart Publishing, 1998).

[28] For a valuable consideration of some of the main issues in this debate, see Fisher, F. and Sommerville, A., 'To Everything there is a Season? Are there Medical Grounds for Refusing Fertility Treatment to Older Women?' and

de Beaufort, I., 'Letter From a Post Menopausal Mother' in John Harris and Soren Holm (eds), *The Future of Human Reproduction; Choice and Regulation* (Oxford, Clarendon Press, 1998), at 203 and 238, respectively.

A retrospective data analysis of donor IVF and hormone replacement treatment given to 34 post-menopausal women considered the 'success rate' and complications arising from the treatments. The mean age of the women was 53 (50–62 years); the clinical pregnancy rate per transfer was 32.7% with no foetal or maternal mortality but some incidence of maternal morbidity (injury), especially in woman over 50, above and beyond what would be expected in the population group at large. ('Pregnancies in postmenopausal women over 50 years old in an oocyte donation program' (1995) *Fertility & Sterility* 63, 259.)

[29] A survey of over 300 fertility clinics in the United States and Canada found that more than a dozen had already 'harvested' sperm from dead men and stored them for possible after use. Three times as many had been asked to perform such a procedure: *New Scientist*, 30 November 1996. The New York Task Force on Life and the Law has recommended in its 1998 Report, *Assisted Reproductive Technologies: Analysis and Recommendations for Public Policy*, that 'in general gametes should not be retrieved without the subject's informed consent'. The case of Diane Blood was raised in the House of Commons by her MP; replying to Joe Ashton, Under Secretary of State for Health, John Horam reminded the House that the 1990 Act 'was passed after substantial public and parliamentary debate and is carefully drawn. It is therefore not an area in which either policy or legislation should be tinkered with on the spur of the moment' (*Hansard*, 30 October 1996, col. 584).

[30] In varying guises and disguises. A Californian couple are seeking a surrogate mother to carry a child for their dead daughter; she survived a brain stem tumour but developed lymphoblastic leukaemia two years later. She underwent fertility treatment, eggs were collected and fertilised by donor sperm and frozen. She died two years later, in late 1996. She had wanted at least one of her frozen embryos to be used to establish a pregnancy, and her parents were seeking to oblige (*Daily Mail*, 25 January 1997). A British woman, Edith Jones, became the UK's first 'surrogate grandmother' acting as a surrogate for her own daughter who has no womb (*Daily Mail*, 25 August 1998). Similar stories are reported from South Dakota, USA (*The Times*, 14 October 1991) and South Africa (Reid, S., *Labour of Love: The Story of the World's First Surrogate Grandmother* (London, The Bodley Head, 1988)).

[31] Sometimes surrogacy and homosexual parenting run together – witness the birth in late 1999 of Aspen and Saffron Drewitt-Barlow to their gay fathers, Tony Barlow and Barrie Drewett, who had found a surrogate mother in California to carry the pregnancy after a donated egg was fertilised with sperm provided by one of them. On arrival in Britain, the babies were refused entry at Heathrow airport (*Guardian*, 3 January 2000), and an immigration battle appeared imminent before the Home Office relented.

[32] The season of procreative tourism was publicly inaugurated by the birth to a 59-year-old British woman refused treatment services in the UK of twins in an Italian clinic. Health Secretary Virginia Bottomley lamented: 'We cannot stop people going to any country in the world for treatment but maybe we'll renew our efforts to have discussions with other countries as to the examples we set and how they can establish ethical controls over some of the dramatic achievements in

modern medicine.' Almost immediately following this the French junior Health Minister, Phillipe Douste-Blazy, announced the French government's intention to introduce legislation to prohibit IVF of post-menopausal women (*Guardian*, 5 January 1994), although this was followed immediately by protests from various parts of the political spectrum and different interest groups; and the Italian Health Minister Mariapia Garavaglia was quoted (*Guardian*, 6 January 1994) as saying that 'desires are not rights, and babies are not consumer goods' and announced the imminent establishment of a commission to establish 'controls over the treatment of sterile and post menopausal women'. See *The Independent*, 28 December 1993, p. 1; *Guardian*, 28 December 1993, p. 2, reporting an interview on the BBC's 'Today' programme, 27 December 1993. For a careful consideration of some of the possible consequences of treating reproduction and issue as if they *were* items of the consumer market, see Radin, M.J., *Contested Commodities: The Trouble with Trade in Sex, Children, Body Parts, and Other Things* (Cambridge, Mass., Harvard University Press, 1996).

[33] One particular case from a Manhattan IVF clinic concerns Donna Fasano and Deborah Rogers who attended the clinic on the same day. Mrs Fasano became pregnant, with twins; Mrs Rogers did not become pregnant. Mrs Fasano later discovered that she had been an unintentional host surrogate to Mrs Rogers' child when she gave birth to the babies; one was white, the other was black. Mrs Fasano is reported to have handed the black child to his biological parents and lawyers have been consulted (*Daily Telegraph*, 31 March 1999).

[34] So-called 'transport IVF' – where sperm is collected from a donor in one centre and transferred for fertilisation use to another – occasionally gives rise to its own problems and might have provided an original and startling reason for train delays on the Great Northern line. A phial of frozen human sperm was dropped by the courier while passing through York station. The leaking liquid nitrogen – in which frozen sperm is stored – caused fire crews to be called and the station cleared for two hours. Attending firefighters eventually discovered what they were dealing with by reading the confidential details of the donors in the papers which the courier was carrying (*Sun*, 24 October 1991).

[35] See Morgan, D., 'Legal and Ethical Dilemmas of Sex Selection' in Templeton, A. and Cuisine, D., *Reproductive Technology and Law* (Edinburgh, Churchill Livingstone, 1990).

[36] For an illustrative example of this early furore, see (1991) *The Lancet* 337, at 559–60; commentator Paul Johnson is reported as having called the prospect of lesbian mothers (for that is what this is) a 'nightmare vision of the baby production line'. Cited in *Bulletin of Medical Ethics*, March 1991, at 7.

[37] Mandy Allwood, pregnant with eight foetuses which all died, paralleled by Zoe Efsthatiou, a Cypriot woman pregnant with 11 foetuses after fertility treatment, who decided that seven should be aborted by selective reduction (*Daily Telegraph*, 20 December 1996).

[38] 'Viable Offspring derived from Foetal and Adult Mammalian Cells' [1997] *Nature* 385, at 881; 'Dolly' the sheep, born following a technique which involved nucleus substitution into an *egg* and not an embryo. Dolly had been preceded at birth by Morag and Megan, but they had been born following the use of an embryonic or foetal cell. All had been preceded by over 270 unsuccessful attempts to perform the technique: see Wilmut, I., Campbell K. and Tudge, C., *The Second*

Creation: The Age of Biological Control by the Scientists who Cloned Dolly (London, Headline, 2000).

[39] Dolly has since gained a number of piglet cousins; the birth of Millie, Christa, Alexis, Carrel and Dotcom was heralded in the British press in March 2000.

[40] Windeyer in *Mount Isa Mines* v *Pusey* (1970) 125 CLR 383.

[41] Morgan, D. and Lee, R.G., *Blackstone's Guide to the Human Fertilisation and Embryology Act 1990* (London, Blackstone Press, 1991), at p. 32.

[42] Article 8(2): 'There shall be no interference by a public authority with the exercise of this right except such as in accordance with the law as it is necessary in a democratic society . . . for the protection of health and morals, or for the protection of the rights and freedoms of others.'

[43] Wadham, J. and Mountfield, H., *Blackstone's Guide to the Human Rights Act 1998* (London, Blackstone Press, 1999), at p. 108.

[44] 'Reproductive Rights: Feminism or Patriarchy?' in John Harris and Soren Holm (eds), *The Future of Human Reproduction: Choice and Regulation* (Oxford, Clarendon Press, 1998), at p. 72.

[45] *Ibid.*

[46] *From the Test Tube to the Coffin: Choice and Regulation in Private Life* (London, Stevens/Sweet & Maxwell, 1996), at p. 125.

[47] *Review of the Common Law Provisions Relating to the Removal of Gametes and of the Consent Provisions in the Human Fertilisation and Embryology Act 1990* (London, Department of Health, July 1998).

[48] *Surrogacy: Review for Health Ministers of Current Arrangements for Payments and Regulation* (Cm 4068) (London, Department of Health, October 1998).

[49] London, HFEA and HGAC, 1998.

[50] This is a device adopted by other European jurisdictions, for example Denmark and France, in their legislation concerning assisted conception procedures and their regulation. For a recent review of the French legislation of 1994 (Loi 94–654) as required by that Act, see *L'application de la loi no. 94–654 du 29 Juillet 1994* (No. 1407 Ass, National; No. 232 Senat; Office Parlémentaire d'Evaluation des Choix Scientifiques et Technologiques, 1999).

[51] Brazier, M., 'Regulating the Reproduction Business?' (1999) 7 *Medical Law Review* 166.

[52] *The Embryo Research Debate: Science and the Politics of Reproduction* (Cambridge, Cambridge University Press, 1997).

[53] *The IVF Revolution: The Definitive Guide to Assisted Reproductive Techniques* (London, Vermillion, 1999).

[54] Smith, S. and Sutton, A., 'The Human Fertilisation & Embryology Authority: A Critique of its First Reports (1992–94)' (London, CORE, 1995).

[55] 8th Annual Report, 1999, p. 1.

[56] Waller, L. and Mendelson, D., *Legal Issues in Medicine* (Clayton, Victoria, 1999).

[57] Brazier, M., 'Regulating the Reproduction Business?', *op. cit.* n. 51.

[58] Bartlett and Le Grand, 'The Theory of Quasi-Markets' in Le Grand and Bartlett (eds), *Quasi-Markets and Social Policy* (Basingstoke, Macmillan, 1993).

[59] Hunt, *op. cit.* n. 2.

[60] Black, J., 'Regulation as Facilitation: Negotiating the Genetic Revolution' in Brownsword, Cornish and Llewelyn, *Law and Human Genetics: Regulating a Revolution* (Oxford, Hart Publishing, 1998); Propper, 'Quasi-markets and

Regulation' in Le Grand, J. and Bartlett, P. (eds), *Quasi-Markets and Social Policy*, (Basingstoke, Macmillan, 1993).

[61] Beck, U., *Risk Society: Towards a New Modernity* (London, Sage, transl. Mark Ritter 1992; originally published as *Risikogellschaft. Auf dem Weg in eine andere Moderne*, Frankfurt, 1986), 204; Jonas, H., *Philosophical Essays: From Ancient Creed to Technological Man* (Englewood Cliffs, Prentice Hall, 1974), *The Imperative of Responsibility: In Search of an Ethics for the Technological Age* (Chicago, University of Chicago Press, 1984); National Science Foundation, 'Biology and Law: Challenges of Adjudicating Competing Claims in a Democracy' (Washington, NSF, 1992).

[62] Strathern, M., *et al.*, *Reproducing the Future: Anthropology, Kinship and the New Reproductive Technologies* (Manchester, Manchester University Press, 1993); Strathern, 'The Meaning of Assisted Kinship' in Meg Stacey, (ed.). *Changing Human Reproduction* (London, Sage Publications, 1992), pp. 148–69.

[63] Clothier, *Report of the Committee on the Ethics of Gene Therapy* (Cm 1788) (London, HMSO, 1992).

[64] Duxbury, N., 'Do Markets Degrade?' (1996) 59 MLR 331.

[65] Silver, L., *Remaking Eden: Cloning, Genetic Engineering and the Future of Mankind* (London: Pheonix, 1999) at 144.

[66] Montgomery, J., 'Rights, Restraints and Pragmatism: The Human Fertilisation & Embryology Act 1990' (1991) 54 MLR 524.

[67] Brazier, M., 'Regulating the Reproduction Business?', *op. cit.* n. 51, at 167.

[68] *Ibid.*

[69] 'Alice Through the Looking Glass' in M. Gardner (ed.), *The Annotated Alice* (Harmondsworth, Penguin Books, 1960), at 210. Ridley, M., *The Red Queen: Sex and the Evolution of Human Nature* (Harmondsworth, Penguin Books, 1994). It is instructive to recall Gardner's exploration of the end game in the chess game in which Alice and the Red Queen take part: 'Throughout the problem, Alice remains on the queen's file except for her final move when (as queen) she captures the Red Queen to checkmate the dozing Red King. It is amusing to note that it is the Red Queen who persuades Alice to advance along her file to the eighth square. The Queen is protecting herself with this advice . . .' (Gardner, *op. cit.*, at 170). Of course, in a real chess match the game would have been up long before, because the White King had earlier been placed in check by the Red Queen without either side taking account of the fact.

[70] Beck, *op. cit.* 61; Bauman, Z., *Postmodern Ethics* (Oxford, Blackwell, 1993); Bauman, Z., *A Life in Fragments* (Oxford, Blackwell, 1995).

[71] *Op. cit.* n. 61, at 211.

[72] Giddens, A., 'Risk and Responsibility' (1999) 62 MLR 1.

[73] *Ibid.*, at 3.

[74] *Ibid.*

[75] de Sousa Santos, B., *Toward a New Common Sense* (London, Routledge, 1995).

[76] Anthony Giddens has recently called this notion 'plastic sexuality'; this is a potentially important analytical dimension in examining assisted conception: see Giddens, A., *The Transformation of Intimacy* (Cambridge, Polity Press, 1992).

[77] A term coined by Peter Singer and Deane Wells, *op. cit.* n. 18.

[78] For an introductory survey to these various approaches, see 'Frameworks of Analysis of Feminisms' Accounts of Reproductive Technology' in Sally Sheldon

and Michael Thompson (eds), *Feminist Perspectives on Health Care Law* (London, Cavendish Publishing, 1998), at 189–209.

[79] McLean, S., 'Reproductive Medicine' in Clare Dyer (ed.), *Doctors, Patients and the Law* (Oxford, Blackwell, 1992), at p. 89.

[80] Cook, R., and Dickens, B., *Considerations for Formulating Reproductive Health Laws* (Geneva, World Health Organisation, 1998).

[81] HL vol. 516, col. 1089.

[82] *Op. cit.* n. 10, at 151.

[83] *Ibid.*, at 163.

[84] 'Reproductive Rights: Feminism or Patriarchy?', *op. cit.* n. 44, at 68.

[85] *Op. cit.* n. 10, at 145.

[86] As of 31 August 1999 there were 118 clinics licensed to carry out either IVF and DI (75); 0 IVF only, 32 DI only; 8 for storage of sperm only; 3 with research licences only. Between April 1997 and March 1998 26,685 patients received IVF; 34,638 cycles started, including frozen embryo replacements of which 29,014 reached embryo transfer. There were 6,864 clinical pregnancies (19.8% of all treatments started), leading to 5,687 live births (16.4%). The rise in the 'success' rate for IVF treatments over the last six years (since at least 1993/94) is attributed to the growth of the use of micromanipulation techniques, up by 40% in 1997–8 compared with the previous year. In 1997/98 4,905 patients received treatment involving DI or GIFT using donated gametes; 12,753 cycles resulted in 1,485 clinical pregnancies and 1,229 (9.6%) live births. The number of DI cycles carried out annually since 1992/93 has fallen by 50%, from 25,623 to 12,753 in 1997/98. IVF data in the Authority's reports include treatments involving micromanipulation, such as ICSI, SUZU and frozen embryo replacements. DI data include cycles involving GIFT and IUI (intrauterine insemination) using donor gametes. *HFEA 8th Annual Report* (London, HFEA, 1999).

[87] Brazier, *op. cit.* n. 51, at 191.

[88] *Ibid.*; for a particularly clear and cogent treatment of these sorts of issues, see Radin, M.J., *Contested Commodities: The Trouble with Trade in Sex, Children, Body Parts and Other Things* (Cambridge, Mass. and London, Harvard University Press, 1996). The US fertility clinic industry is estimated to be worth over $3 billion annually.

[89] *Op. cit.* n. 10, at 148.

[90] *Ibid.*, at 148.

[91] *Ibid.*, at 148–49.

[92] Ogus, A., *Regulation: Legal Form and Economic Theory* (Oxford, Clarendon Press, 1994); Baldwin, R. and Cave, M., *Understanding Regulation: Theory, Strategy and Practice* (Oxford, Oxford University Press, 1999).

[93] See Ogus, *op. cit.* n. 92, esp. chs 3 and 6; von Hayek, F., *Law, Legislation & Liberty* (London, Routledge & Kegan Paul, 1973 edn).

[94] For an outstanding recent exception, see Black, *op. cit.* n. 60.

[95] Morgan and Lee, *op. cit.* n. 41, Brazier, *op. cit.* n. 51; for an early historical evaluation see Gunning, J. and English, N., *Human In Vitro Fertilisation* (Aldershot, Dartmouth, 1993); an outstanding exception to the descriptive accounts of the debates is Mulkay, M., *The Embryo Research Debate: Science and the Politics of Reproduction* (Cambridge, Cambridge University Press, 1997).

[96] Morgan, D., and Bernat, D., 'The Reproductive Waltz: The Austrian Medically Assisted Procreation Act 1992' [1992] *Journal of Social Welfare Law* 420, Morgan,

D. and Nielsen, L., 'Dangerous Liaisons: Law, Technology, Reproduction and European Ethics' in Shaun McVeigh and Sally Wheeler (eds), *Law, Health and Medical Regulation* (Aldershot, Dartmouth, 1992); Morgan, D. and Nielsen, L., 'Prisoners of Progress or Hostages to Fortune?' (1993) 21(1) *The Journal of Law, Medicine and Ethics* 30, Morgan, D., 'Licensing Parenthood and Regulating Reproduction: Towards Consensus?' in Cosimo Marco Mazzoni (ed.), *A Legal Framework for Bioethics* (The Hague, Kluwer Law International, 1998); Nielsen, L., 'From Bioethics to Biolaw' in Cosimo Marco Mazzoni (ed.), *op. cit.*; Beyleveld, D., *The Ethics of Genetics in Human Procreation* (Aldershot, Ashgate, 2000).

[97] Skene, L., 'Why legislate on Assisted Reproduction?' in Freckelton and Peterson (eds), *Controversies in Health Law* (Sydney, The Federation Press, 1999); Szoke, H., 'Regulation of Assisted Reproductive Technology: The State of Play in Australia' in Freckelton and Peterson (eds), *op. cit.*

[98] Perri 6, *Holistic Government* (London, Demos, 1997).

[99] Koch, 'IVF – An Irrational Choice?' (1991).

[100] Chalmers, D., 'The Challenge of Human Genetics' in Freckelton, I. and Peterson, K. (eds), *op. cit.* n. 97.

[101] Bryson, B., *Notes From A Small Island* (London, Doubleday, 1995).

Chapter 2
Law, Morals and Assisted Conception

INTRODUCTION

The relationship between law and scientific investigation and between law and fundamental moral principles is always open for debate and examination. Within the 49 sections of the Human Fertilisation and Embryology Act 1990 are some of the most difficult, most intractable and fundamental moral questions of which any society becomes seized. What characterised the 20th century more clearly than any preceding is that we assumed the power to cause death on a hitherto unimagined scale and, increasingly, to take scientific control of life itself.[1]

The Human Fertilisation and Embryology Bill originally brought before Parliament the issues surveyed by the Warnock Committee Report published in 1984. The moral turbulence centred on embryos, particularly on embryos created outside the body, and especially on research with such embryos. This turbulence swept through the legislative process, and is reflected in the way in which the Act has been drafted, interpreted and debated inside and outside Parliament. The limited way in which the licensing authority may be able to discharge its supervisory role owes much to the perceptions of problems created by the Warnock Report. The Act is a Warnock Act. It represents a limited attempt to capture or to understand the exponential technological leaps since then. In that important sense, Warnock is not only the benchmark but also the workbench of the present legislation.

The Human Fertilisation and Embryology Act 1990, when first enacted, represented a marshalling of arguments after nearly two decades of scientific research and ethical and philosophical debate. It would have been be idle to suppose that the form in which the Act was framed represented anything more than a temporary statement on the morality of the issues under examination. As with abortion, the questions involved are of such importance to the moral health of society that the process of debate and decision will be constant. Perhaps that is much as it should be. Believing that such fundamental moral (and legal) issues can be 'solved' betrays a misunderstanding of what moral disagreement is about, as much as it does about the political process of legislating life or regulating reproduction. The 1990 Act will probably always be a temporary statement.

The moral skirmishes which followed publication of the Warnock Report in 1984 suggested that the debates on and eventual resolution of the questions involved would provoke bitter Parliamentary battles and even more intensive public lobbying.[2] The original report was debated in the House of Commons in November 1984.[3] That gave an early indication of the debate which had been joined, emphasised by consideration of the unsuccessful private members' Bills introduced by MPs Enoch Powell, Ken Hargreaves (twice) and Alistair Burt in 1985, 1986 and 1987. These Unborn Children (Protection) Bills failed to gain final Parliamentary approval, despite an initial, overwhelming majority vote for the first reading of the original Bill in the House of Commons. These Bills would have made it an offence to create, store or use a human embryo for any purpose other than to assist a specified woman to become pregnant. In each case, a registered medical practitioner would have had to apply in writing to the Secretary of State for consent to the fertilisation of a human ovum *in vitro*. That authority would only have been forthcoming if the Secretary of State was satisfied as to:

(a) the arrangements made for the procedure;
(b) the competence and experience of the medical and other personnel to be involved; and
(c) the suitability of the premises where the procedure would have been carried out.

But there comes a time when fundamental moral disagreement collides with public and professional demands for certainty or consistency, however illusory these eventually prove to be. The nature and moment of scientific work in the past 30 years has ensured that new questions arise for the moral and legal agendas. Moreover, they will not go away. Whatever Parliament had decided about, say, experimentation or research with human embryos, it would have been mistaken to assume that pressure for reform would not be immediately rejoined. We have, it seems, lifted some veils which can no longer be firmly held back. The Human Fertilisation and Embryology Act has perhaps always been a temporary marshalling of arguments, a transitory marker in continued moral reflection.

Concern with and demand for reproductive medicine has become a global matter. The existence of a few specialist clinics has revealed a global market for assisted conception services. And with the facilitation of travel and the phenomenon of speed, the ability to avail oneself of the services available at the reproductive tourist office makes the franking of the stamp on the ethical envelope more interesting. Where technological development results in the blurring of national boundaries, the increasingly difficult task of one country insulating itself from events elsewhere in the world has given rise to the possibility of what has been called 'procreative tourism' and 'ethical dumping'.[4]

But there is also an important sense in which science has crossed a Rubicon for which there is no return ticket. This was reflected in one of the contributions made by the Labour Party frontbench spokeswoman on health, Harriet Harman, to the Standing Committee debates:

Human fertilisation and embryology are an area of rapid change and continuous advances in our knowledge. When we came to debate the Bill there were many new issues on the agenda which were not considered by the Warnock Committee because they had not even been thought of just those few years before. It is wrong to suggest that passing a law – which we fully support – that says that in principle research should be allowed to go ahead within a legislative framework somehow marks the end of the debate. The matter will remain one of public interest and also of controversy.[5]

Reproductive technologies are complex. Anne Maclean has suggested of surrogacy that it is complex and difficult because it raises not one issue but a cluster of issues, and issues of different sorts at that. 'It is easy to confuse considerations relevant to one of these issues with considerations relevant to another, or to misunderstand the character of a particular claim or a particular objection.'[6] There is no single moral issue called surrogacy; and in much the same way, this is true of reproductive technologies generally. People's (moral) worries about surrogacy arrangements (or reproductive technologies) will vary greatly depending on the type of surrogacy (or technology) in question, the relationships of the parties involved to one another, whether it is a commercial transaction and in what circumstances, and so on. And this moral concern will engage a variety of wider concerns too; not just about the family and parenthood but about one's whole attitude to what life brings. This is also an important observation about reproductive technologies more generally. The sorts of worries, or objections, the 'issues of different sorts' as Maclean puts it, will carry different force in different circumstances. Thus, worries about resource implications (which can of course involve ethical concern) are very different sorts of worries from those deep, inarticulate (speech of the heart) worries about the basic legitimacy of an action or of a general attitude exemplified in an action.

Concerns with surrogacy, then, like reproductive technologies more generally, cluster around commerce, commodity, consumerism and community. Today, the belief is rife, if not reasonable (and perhaps not so novel), that anything can be bought; that money can buy not only love (or at least its counterfeit) but also anything else (or at least its counterfeit). But, as Margaret Radin points out, the double bind is that 'both commodification and non-commodification may be harmful'[7] and 'it should be clear that there are coherent feminist arguments on both sides of the general issue of baby-selling (commissioned adoption)', as on reproductive technologies more generally.[8]

Reproductive technologies, in their recent manifestations of the past 30 years at least,[9] and the legal accommodations and responses to them allow us to witness the architectural and engineering dimensions of the *constitutive* aspect of law, rather than, which is often the case, its archaeological and anthropological sitings. The importance of this interpretative dimension is that it proposes that law (like other social institutions) shapes how individuals conceive of themselves and their relations with others. 'The underlying assumption is that social institutions are actualised through a set of assumptions, categories, concepts, values and vocabularies that we have internalised so that we are not consciously aware of how they have affected our ideas and behaviour.'[10] Assisted reproduction has introduced a new vocabulary to, and challenged old philosophies of, families and family law. It has also demanded a new literacy of lawyers, laypeople and legislators. While the past 40 years have seen the meltdown of the nuclear family and its surrounding myths and ideologies – in less than ten years half of all children born in the United Kingdom will be brought up outside the 'conventional' family – new demons, chimeras and spirits have been summoned to haunt the new families which technological and personal upheavals have introduced. This has been accompanied by the rise of the 'want' society – one in which it has become fashionable to seek the fulfilment of wants and to accept far less readily, if at all, that some desires cannot, should not, or even must not be satisfied or satiated.

There is a sense in which children are an example of this, and assisted conception part of the response, which includes also adoption, surrogacy, and the sale or stealing of children and newborns, sometimes on an international scale. This, in its turn, has fed the arguments of clinicians who service those wants to seek the widest possible freedom.

Marilyn Strathern, as we have said, has argued that reproductive technologies affect assumptions which we bring to our understandings not only of family life but to the very understanding of family itself and cultural practice:[11] 'assisted conception . . . will affect thinking about kinship. And the way people think about kinship will affect other ideas about relatedness between human beings'.[12] Importantly, once 'coital conception' is joined by 'non-coital means of conception and the emphasis on quality' this 'will loop back to influence how we view "normal" reproduction itself'.[13] Thus, central assumptions about life and thought are challenged openly and become the subject of debate and ideological controversy.[14] The many individual exercises of procreative 'choice' or 'autonomy' will culminate in larger social changes that may well presently seem to be undesirable; freedom to act does not mean that we will act wisely, but restriction on that freedom carries costs as well.[15]

Even without the advent of reproductive technologies, family forms in the last few decades have become more varied than in the 18th, 19th and even early-to-mid 20th century.[16] The consequences of this we have hardly begun to hazard at. Strathern has cautioned that the new reproductive technologies and the legislative and other actions to which they have given rise seek to assist natural process on the one hand and the social definition of kinship on the other. But

> . . . this double assistance creates new uncertainties. For the present cultural explicitness is revolutionising former combinations of ideas and concepts. The more we give legal certainty to social parenthood, the more we cut from under our feet assumptions about the intrinsic nature of relationships themselves. The more facilitation is given to the biological reproduction of human persons, the harder it is to think of a domain of natural facts independent of social intervention. Whether or not all this is a good thing is uncertain. What is certain is that it will not be without consequence for the way people think about one another.[17]

The role of the family, and conceptions of personal identity and human nature are underlined in many ways by programmes of assisted conception, especially in the way in which rational women will use and pursue infertility programmes even when they know that the success rates are low.[18] Lene Koch has observed that even where women entering IVF programmes felt deprived of correct and realistic information, it did not seem to have affected their decisions to commence or to continue in an IVF programme after one or more failed attempt. As Frances Price has commented, it is only after failing to satisfy the initial stages of socially sanctioned authentic wishes (unassisted conception) that the use of reproductive technology is introduced as evidence of inauthentic wishes.[19] As Koch writes, 'the fact that infertile women want children, want to have a so-called normal family, is part of the explanation of why they do not hear the feminist critics. . . . infertile women do not consider prevention of infertility a relevant alternative to IVF. This is an option for future generations – not applicable to their situation'. And then in an important step she argues that the apparent irrationality of women in IVF programmes can be shown to make sense if the view of the 'infertile' woman is seen as belonging to a culture structured by its own rationality, one which is removed from, or supplements any notion of 'universal rationality'.[20]

Koch argues that women who experience infertility do so as a loss of control, which is often reinforced by social stigmatisation. 'The decision to try IVF – may be considered an attempt to liberate oneself from the powerlessness of infertility – if only to realise that a child of her own is no longer an issue.' Participating in an IVF programme may be one way of negotiating *access to infertility*; a woman is able publicly to demonstrate to herself and to others that she is infertile once she has followed and exhausted all the acceptable rites of passage, including IVF. Thus, if IVF is seen *solely* as the choice for a child, given the paucity of the take home baby rate measure of success,[21] it might otherwise be seen as irrational.

> IVF may be considered a way to prove to others that you are infertile – and is a precondition to a final resolution of infertility. . . . As each new reproductive technology enters the market, the definition of infertility changes. Infertility can only be defined as the condition that no reproductive technology can resolve. Thus, IVF virtually becomes an imperative, even for those women who might otherwise have been ready to accept their infertility.[22]

TYPES OF PHILOSOPHICAL ARGUMENT

Followers of previous political debates in this area will not be surprised to find that much of the moral argument about embryos has centred on 'personhood', with contributors looking for an absolute point at which something becomes a person. The unspoken assumption is that the way in which we decide on the dividing line, the criteria, is where the morally important work is to be done. There is no shortage of candidates here: moral philosophers, religious leaders, pressure groups and scientific contributors have all canvassed conception, nidation, the beginning of the primitive streak (or of the neural streak), quickening, viability and birth, in an effort to decide the point at which someone becomes a 'person' or is entitled to receive the respect owed to a person.

Nor does the argument end there. Some commentators have suggested that what matters is an ability to sense and value life, so that birth as such presents no logical stopping point at which the debates about personhood must end – or begin. It follows that the argument actually surrounds adequate notions of what it is to be a person.

There are alternative approaches to this question, which start from and bring an entirely different perspective. This reverses the 'criterial' approach, and holds that it is only possible to determine what a person is by using morality to find out how a person might arrive out of that. It suggests that we cannot define morality outside, by reference to external criteria, which can then be applied to tell us what our moral position is (or should be). This position holds that otherwise there is nothing that morality can tell us, or anything that human agency can achieve (i.e., there is nothing to distinguish between morality and law). This suggests that there will inevitably be disagreement because we are not looking for one criterion, for a definition of a person. Indeed, it suggests that there is no morally correct position to arrive at; there is no right moral answer. Who or what is a person depends not on a conclusion reached – through applying some criteria – but on a conviction shown.

There is a third type of position, close to the one which Warnock herself appears to have held, which posits that there is no absolute point at which a person arrives and has moral status, no absolute point at which a person 'materialises', but that a person emerges as a gradually present moral entity and one which is possessed of more and more rights as a juridical person. If we then want to make particular legal or political decisions, of course we do have to select a point or a series of points. This, although it does not presently represent the status of UK law, is, we suspect, the one to which it is moving, a position which we review in Chapter 3 when considering embryo research. At present, English law holds that a foetus can possess different rights as it moves towards birth. In fact after birth the sorts of rights that it possesses can differ. Our abortion law, with its present concepts of 'capable of being born alive' and 'viability', or our law on congenital injuries and pre-natal torts, family law disputes commencing prior to birth and now our laws on embryo experimentation, suggest strongly a differential rights approach. At no point do we accord the foetus special status. These different sorts of approach, although not clearly articulated as such, can be identified as approaches taken during the moral and political debates in the lead up to this particular legislation.

Two different conceptions of ethical inquiry are suggested by the various analyses of what we might call the arguments from 'reproductive rights' and those from feminism. Certainly in the latter forms, of feminisms, there is no uniformity of analysis, and while many feminists have been explicitly or implicitly critical either of assisted conception generally or specific technologies or the applications of specific technologies, some feminists have advanced cases that are more or less based upon rounded 'reproductive rights' arguments. The development of assisted reproduction programmes and the medicalisation of infertility 'raise some of the most difficult questions for feminist theory and practice'.[23] The techniques and trappings of assisted conception – AI, IVF, GIFT, cryopreservation of gametes, eggs and embryos, gamete and embryo donation, and surrogacy – also challenge traditional views of procreation and parenthood, a challenge which has legal as well as ethical implications. According to Lene Koch, 'One of the most difficult problems that have confronted feminist critics of *in vitro* fertilisation (IVF) and the other new reproductive technologies, is the great enthusiasm for IVF among involuntarily childless women'.[24] Carol Smart has even doubted that there can be a satisfactory feminist response to reproductive technologies; to argue that they contribute to and reinforce (male) dominant ideologies of motherhood and womanhood is to deny individual women's experiences and announced intentions, and may be to suggest that individual women are not able – autonomously – to choose for themselves, to weigh and balance the consequences of infertility treatments and the possible opportunity costs of the treatments and the very real costs of disappointment and 'failure' in conception. On the other hand, to argue that they contribute to and liberate women from the burdens of unlooked-for consequences of their infertility or that of their present partner is to suggest an uncomfortably determinist approach to mental and physical well-being and notions of person-hood.[25]

We look first at a brief review of arguments based on 'freedom of choice' which characterise – here we may say they are emblematic of – 'reproductive rights' arguments. Thereafter, we suggest what seem to us to be some of the most important readings of assisted conception and reproductive technologies that have emerged from the burgeoning feminist literature.

Reproductive rights

Many of the strongest arguments from the rights-based approaches have been elegantly summarised in an accessible way by British philosopher John Harris and by American academic lawyer John Robertson. First, we epitomise the arguments offered by Harris in his essay 'Rights and Reproductive Choice'.[26]

Harris, drawing explicitly and extensively on arguments developed in a more general context by Ronald Dworkin,[27] has defined and described 'a vital feature of an essentially democratic approach to reproductive choices' as lying in recognition and broad reading of the concept of 'procreative autonomy' involving much-needed and much-desired treatment as a legitimate extension of human choice.[28] This is a principle which, in a broad sense, is embedded in any genuinely democratic culture.[29]

Developments in reproductive technologies have demanded that questions about what ought and what ought not to constrain choice in reproduction (an idea 'that is respected more in the breach than in the observance'[30]) should be brought to the bar of procreative autonomy. Specifically, we should ask of reproductive technolo-gies, 'is their use ethical and should access to it, or use of it, be controlled by legislation, and if so how?'[31]

Framing these questions is the belief and the justification that those requiring medical or other assistance should not be asked questions, or obliged to fulfil criteria that we do not ask, or could not be justified in asking, of those who do not need such assistance. In this sense, arguments from reproductive rights based on respect for procreative autonomy demand shortly that people should be treated in a material way, as far as their procreative and parenting choices are concerned, the same as anyone else. Health (such as familial genetic disease), medical (such as 'primary' or 'secondary' infertility) or social reasons (same sex choice of partner) which interfere with the ability to exercise choices that others would be able to make should not be used as a means of discriminating between those who make one set of choices and those who make – or are forced to make – another set of choices.

Dworkin has defined the 'right of procreative autonomy' as 'a right [of people] to control their own role in procreation unless the state has a compelling reason for denying them that control',[32] and has argued that it is a protected interest under both the First and Fourteenth Amendments to the United States Constitution. The First Amendment guarantees the rights to freedom of religion and prohibits the government from establishing any religion. The Fourteenth Amendment, which incorporates the First Amendment, imposes the same responsibility on the individual states of the Union. Dworkin has argued that

> The right of procreative autonomy follows from any competent interpretation of the due process clause and of the Supreme Court's past decisions applying it. . . . These provisions also guarantee the right of procreative autonomy.[33]

Harris takes Dworkin's expression and examination of that right in the abortion debate and asks whether it might properly be interpreted to include the right of procreative autonomy in what might be thought of as a more positive way (in assisted conception) rather than in the context in which Dworkin originally developed his argument. For Harris, on this analysis the right of 'procreative autonomy' would need to encompass the right

> . . . to reproduce with the genes we chose and to which we have legitimate access, or to reproduce in ways that express our reproductive choices and our vision of the sorts of people we think it right to create.[34]

He argues that we can draw an analogy with the right of freedom of religion guaranteed in the amendments to the United States Constitution, in much the same way that the Supreme Court has done in its discussions of 'penumbral' rights in the Constitution itself; not those that are in terms spelled out in the language of the original document, but those that can properly be regarded as sufficiently adjacent to or proximate to those rights as to be within the bounds of a fair and defensible reading of the Constitution, as indeed *Roe* v *Wade* 410 US 113 (1972) – the Supreme Court's landmark 'abortion jurisprudence' decision – itself was. Harris suggests that the First and Fourteenth Amendments are about freedoms to choose one's own way of life and to live according to one's most deeply held beliefs, '[beliefs which] are also at the heart of procreative choices'.[35]

In order for the argument of procreative autonomy to be trumped – a condition of such autonomy being taken seriously in other words – it is necessary for *any* democratic society (whether one with a written constitution or not) to demonstrate that it has a *compelling* reason for denying individual citizens control over their own reproductive choices and decisions.

> In so far as the decisions to reproduce in particular ways or even using particular technologies constitute decisions concerning central issues of value, then . . . to establish [that the state had such a compelling reason] the state would have to show that more was at stake than the fact that a majority found the ideas disturbing or even disgusting.[36]

These reproductive decisions are a central, almost a defining, part of moral responsibility; the idea that 'people have the moral right – and the moral responsibility – to confront the most fundamental questions about the meaning and value of their own lives for themselves, answering to their own consciences and convictions'.[37]

What follows from this is not, necessarily, an untrammelled, uninhibited orgy of assisted reproductive excess. Rather it requires a close and careful examination and explanation of what we propose to do, what we hope to achieve, *through law*, than perhaps we have become accustomed to. The presumption, cautions Harris, should be against over-hasty prohibition. What is required and justified is dual caution: caution when considering the acceptability of scientific 'advance' and the *use* of reproductive technologies; but equally caution against the deployment of baseless charges of unethical practices and the enactment of restrictive legislation based on such charges.

In contrast Robertson, drawing from the place of reproductive debates in American constitutional law, has fashioned an account of what he has called 'procreative liberty'.[38] Robertson adumbrates and articulates a version of a reproductive rights thesis which is grounded in and built upon the notion of procreative liberty as a negative right against state interference, either to have children or to avoid having them (here we concern ourselves only with the former aspect of the argument). This 'liberty' is not coextensive with everything that concerns procreation, but it is a primary liberty because it is central to personal identity, dignity and the meaning of one's life.[39]

This vocabulary, perhaps first articulated in the United States Supreme Court in *Skinner* v *Oklahoma* 316 US 535 (1942),[40] has begun to take root in the United Kingdom. For example, in a recent case on a claim for damages for an unwanted pregnancy (*McFarlane* v *Tayside Health Board* [1999] 4 All ER 961), Lord Steyn advocated that his analysis was informed by a starting point which recognised the right of parents to take decisions on family planning and, if those plans fail, their right to make their own untrammelled decisions on how then to proceed: 'The law does and must respect these decisions of parents which are so closely tied to the basic freedoms and rights of personal autonomy.' Lady Justice Hale, writing extra-judicially, has expressed herself in similar language:

> . . . The rights set out in Articles 8 to 12 of the European Convention on Human Rights form a coherent and related group; the right to respect for private and family life, home and correspondence; the right to freedom of expression; the right to freedom of peaceful assembly and free association; and the right to marry and found a family. These are the very essentials of a free-thinking and free-speaking society.[41]

Of course, what follows from this may legitimately be a source of disagreement. Hale, for example, would hardly be in accord with the whole of the following résumé of Robertson's thesis. But the emergent parallels in language are striking. On one specific point they are *in tandem*: 'procreative liberty' or the 'basic freedoms and rights of personal autonomy' are *negative* rights. The fact that assisted conception techniques have separated conception and childbearing does not mean that the state has a duty to supply a service on demand.[42] Procreative liberty implies a negative right against state interference – and not against private interference (as in the two gestational parties disagreeing about the fate, for example, of frozen embryos) – but it is not 'a positive right to have the state or particular persons provide the means or resources necessary to have or avoid having children'.[43] Without doubt, social and economic circumstances impact crucially on the ability to access reproductive technologies; impact (in other words) on whether an individual is able effectively to exercise or enjoy his or her procreative liberty. But whether the state should alleviate those conditions 'is a separate issue of social justice'.[44]

Similarly, that a right to procreative liberty should presumptively be recognised does not mean that the fact that reproductive choices impact on others should be ignored, or that they should never be limited. It does mean, however, that those who would limit reproductive choice 'have the burden of showing that the reproductive actions at issue would create such substantial harm that they could justifiably be limited'.[45] This distinct echo of Mill, whose *dictum* as to harm is set out below, recalls Harris's claim that distaste or disgust are not in themselves proper grounds for state interference with this identified claim. In Robertson's view, being unmarried, homosexual, physically disabled, HIV positive or imprisoned are not sufficient grounds in themselves to override this liberty: speculation or 'mere moral objections'[46] would not suffice. (In the context of these claims it is worth reminding ourselves that a proposal in the debates of 1989 and 1990 to limit access to assisted conception in the UK to married couples was defeated by only one vote.)

Robertson also attempts to anticipate and respond to criticisms which he believes his 'procreative liberty' thesis will draw from feminists (arguing that it simply perpetuates the disadvantages of gender, from the class perspective), claiming that it does nothing to address – and may indeed exacerbate – fundamental socioeconomic differences and discrimination) and from communitarians (arguing that procreative autonomy is an essentially individualising, alienating approach to modern society).[47] In each case, says Robertson, there are important strictures to observe and insights to learn from these critiques, but that, fundamentally, they are properly aimed at a different, broader target which reproductive technologies can do nothing to alleviate and little to ameliorate. And in none of the objections raised, even if on the evidence the charges could be sustained, which Robertson disputes, would the case be strong enough to justify *the state* in overriding or limiting an individual's right to be free from interference in his or her reproductive choices and decisions.

It is appropriate now to consider what some of the main strands of feminist jurisprudence have offered in response to developments in assisted conception. A general fear of feminism is that reproductive technologies weaken women's control of the processes of reproduction generally, and that they are or have the clear potential to be a source of further oppression to and of women. Concerns with surrogacy have come to be almost emblematic of these fears, but we will here concentrate on the more general ambit of reproductive technologies.

Feminisms' responses to reproduction and regulation

It is possible to identify at least three main sorts of feminist analysis of reproductive technologies: the 'critical', the 'contextual' and the 'choice' models. None represents an exclusive boundary; each displays some unifying themes and each serves to expose 'perhaps the greatest philosophical achievement of feminism over the past twenty years' which is that 'in the practice of moral and political philosophy . . . the long absence of women's generic interests from the agenda of these subjects could not be innocently explained'.[48] Each shares a number of organising themes and is clustered around an identifiable core of concerns; these are, principally, concerns with procreation, parenthood, the nature of the family and personal identity. Of course, there are the wider concerns of feminisms, such as patriarchy, as the backdrop against which these particular issues are framed.

Feminisms' responses to reproductive technologies share a number of salient characteristics. First, there is a general scepticism or rejection of the biomedical model of medicine. Secondly, and possibly but not necessarily flowing from this, is a belief that whether reproductive technologies are the wrong sets of responses to the wrong sets of problems, or whether at best they promise a limited set of successful outcomes for a very limited set of questions for a limited set of people, there is nonetheless something to be understood about the appeal that they have. Third, there is a belief in most perspectives of feminism, that where reproductive technologies do properly have a place in present-day westernised societies' responses to the consequences of infertility, they should be free from explicit manipulation by the state to secure other, underlying policy goals which exist for the benefit of the state rather than for the benefit of the individual users of reproductive technologies. We address first the scepticism with the biomedical model of medicine before turning to review the main tenets of what, crudely, we have called the 'critical', the 'contextual' and 'choice' analyses of reproductive technologies.

The biomedical model   Based on the notion of Cartesian dualism,[49] this model holds that health and disease can be explained through an engineering metaphor in which the body comprises a series of separate but interdependent systems. Ill-health is the mechanical failure of some part of one or more of the components of this engine, and the medical task is to repair the damage. The mind is separated from the body, and the individual is separated from the social and cultural contexts of his or her life. 'Illness' is an objective, positivistic fact – a descriptive, not an evaluative, term. Such a model has, in fact, as many feminist scholars acknowledge, led to enormous successes in understanding different types of disease and exploring treatment, and it is mistaken to reject the powerful investigative force which the medical model suggests. However, what has followed from this as well has been a neglect of prevention, now thought to be a major factor in the incidence of infertility, and an overreliance on a curative model in explaining the causes of disease and the different ways in which illness might be experienced.[50] Medical and legal concern with issues of reproductive technology have generally strayed little beyond this biomedical model. And it is in the concentration of reproductive technologies with physical aspects of women's health that the biomedical model has had its greatest and potentially most harmful impacts. The Foucaudian identification of a new kind of power relationship, in which 'authorities who understand our bodies have gained the right to make and enforce rules about morality',[51] flows directly from this model. The most thoroughgoing critics of the biomedical model are also those most critical of the whole project of reproductive technologies.

The critics   Four central points of criticism have emerged from the early life-cycle of reproductive technologies, and they have remained unanswered as far as those opposed to any use of such technologies are concerned.

The first criticism relates to the fact that IVF, originally developed to address one specific cause of infertility in women, blocked fallopian tubes, moved rapidly from the experimental to the clinical. It is in this step that those who see some advantages to the development of treatment services to address the consequences of infertility are prepared to tolerate the availability of choice for individual women while remaining critical of the overall project of medically-assisted conception. More explicitly, the critics charge that reproductive technologies generally and IVF specifically are techniques which augment medical control over procreation generally, and over women's choices and preferences in procreation specifically. Social screening and medical assessment have become part of a new ability to license parenthood to those deemed by the medical profession fit for the burdens and responsibilities. Compared with embryonic matter, such as gametes and embryos, women's physical health has been neglected. Rita Arditti and Gena Corea in the United States, Renate Duelli Klein and Patricia Spallone in Australia and the United Kingdom focused at an early stage on what was being overlooked or left out of the context of reproductive technology. Thus in her interview programme with women who had *left* IVF programmes without a child, Duelli Klein recounts recurrent sentiments of abuse, misinformation and malpractice, resulting in their lives being 'wrecked by the trauma of being living laboratories'.[52] Seeing IVF as a 'cure' for infertility ignores the iatrogenic causes of women's fertility problems, such as the inter-uterine device (IUD) and excessive abdominal surgery, and the compromises to which reproductive health is subjected by poor health care, nutrition and other environmental factors.

Secondly, critics allege that IVF was also seen as an example of manipulating the female body to serve patriarchal needs. Whether in facilitating the surgical removal of ova from healthy women to help in overcoming the consequences of a partner's low sperm count or motility, or in encouraging infertile women to go to extraordinary lengths to satisfy a partner's desire for a child, 'IVF was viewed as another example of putting all the risk and responsibility for reproductive failure on the shoulders of the woman'.[53]

Thirdly, the fiscal and emotional costs of IVF, when compared with the likelihood of failure to conceive and deliver a child, would not be seen as a reasonable choice in a world in which childbearing was regarded as only one option in complex life-styles. The existence of the demand for reproductive technologies evidences western society's attachment to perceiving women as unfulfilled without children. The belief in chosen childlessness is disvalued or dismissed, or characterised as the choice of the sexual or relational deviant. Doubts have been expressed by many commentators, such as Christine Crowe, arguing that IVF does not in any event represent a proper choice, since other options, like chosen childlessness or adoption, are not open or available to all women.[54]

Fourthly, IVF has revealed a profound attachment to genetic lineage that cannot be shared equally between the sexes. Women gestate and deliver: men can only stand by and admire their own physical characteristics as reflected in their children. Attachment to genetic lineage, especially by and for men, has had a distorting effect on women's stated desires to circumvent the consequences of infertility.

The contextualists: 'no daughters to comfort her and no sons to support her'[55]   It might be thought that for any contextual account of reproductive technologies to be given this *necessarily* implies a commitment to a liberal, contingent, in parts rights-based model. We want here to show why we believe that that would be mistaken, although it is undoubtedly *one* of the contexts that is available.

To view infertility as a medical construction and the desire to have a biologically related child as a social product does not deny the consequences of such definitions. While it is essential to critique the process of medicalisation and to be continually wary of the development of technologies and interventions that aim to alleviate infertility, these 'treatments' do not determine totally the capacity of individuals to make choices. That the available options are limited, restrictive and may involve medical intervention does not deny some scope for negotiation, bargaining and resistance.[56]

Without good health, a person's ability to act upon at least some of the choices he or she makes or would wish to make is curtailed. Providing the means by which citizens may preserve and restore or secure their health may be thought to be a fundamental task of any modern state. So, when we come to speak of health we are of necessity required to address at least a package of *conceptual* questions;[57] *political* questions – the role and responsibility of the state in securing, promoting or damaging the health of its citizens and those whom it affects directly and indirectly intentionally and accidentally through the extraterritorial effects of its behaviour;[58] and those of *gender*. As Lesley Doyal has recently reminded us, many women's lives *are* severely constrained because they are denied the opportunity to make real choices about procreation. This inability to influence one of the most fundamental aspects of biological functioning can have profound effects on both physical and mental health.[59]

This has two aspects. First is the prevention of unwanted pregnancy and responding sympathetically and appropriately to the consequences of contraceptive failure. The second is the circumvention of unlooked-for childlessness and responding sympathetically and appropriately to the *sequelae* which may ensue. This does not necessarily mean that the functional equivalent of access to services for the termination of pregnancy must be mirrored in the provision of reproductive technology programmes. The equivalent of access to abortion services does not necessarily mean that there must be a corresponding 'right' to or access to infertility treatment services, much less that there must be or is a 'right' to have a child. Both are connected, however, to the basic notion of reproductive self-determination; 'infertility can be a major disability and its treatment should be seen as a basic element in reproductive self-determination, along with abortion, contraception and maternity care'.[60]

We do not want to be thought to imply that each or any of these different types of question – the conceptual question, the political question and the gender question – can or does stand independently of any one other or of all. There are cross-cutting intersections and intermixtures of all of them, and the points of intersection and interlayering will often be complex but interesting and important ones. Feminisms' accounts of reproductive technologies are part of feminisms' accounts of science and the reason, logic and technological certainty and neutrality that it celebrates.[61]

Lene Koch has centrally captured the difficulties which reproductive technologies cause for many critical feminist commentators: 'there is no doubt that IVF is a powerful transformer of women's reproductive consciousness and an irresistible technology that few women can refuse'.[62] The role of the family and conceptions of personal identity and human nature are underlined in many ways by programmes

;ted conception, especially in the way in which rational women will use and
: infertility programmes even when they know that the success rates are low.
K․․ ․, in interviews with a sample of women entering and participating in an IVF
programme in Copenhagen, observed that although in a number of cases women
felt deprived of accurate or realistic information, this did not seem to matter: 'it
did not seem to have influenced these women's decisions, neither to start IVF in
the first place, nor to continue after one or more failed attempts'. She argues that
to want a child and try to have it 'is an exercise of the reproductive freedom that
the feminist movement has argued for since its very beginning'.[63] This wish to have
a child – this authentic wish of the women concerned – 'does not become less
strong because it is socially constructed'. Given the information which is available
about the success rates of IVF programmes, why do these 'infertile' women appear
to persist with irrational hopes and beliefs in the outcome of their project? Koch's
conclusion is an important one: 'as each new reproductive technology enters the
market, the definition of infertility changes'. If it is acknowledged that 'human
identity is closely affected by parental status and *childlessness is an identity which
is hard to obtain*', a rational understanding of reproductive technologies is
revealed.[64]

What Koch here describes is what we have suggested might be called the
problem of *access to infertility*; whereas infertility used to be considered to be a
matter of fate, 'it is nowadays turning into a deliberate decision, at least in a certain
sense. Those who give up without having tried the very latest methods (an endless
series) have to take the blame. After all, they could have kept trying.'[65] The social
role of fertility will always in some sense be seen as chosen,[66] part of the 'noiseless
social and cultural revolution' in which the exponential development of science
and technology, while supposedly serving health, has in fact 'created entirely new
situations, has changed the relationship of humankind to itself, to disease, illness
and death, indeed, it has changed the world'.[67]

The decision to try IVF becomes independent of the efficiency of the technology,
because it is 'judged by the yardstick of another rationality'.[68] Koch is no
proponent of IVF programmes – far from it: IVF is a dangerous and expensive
technology, which changes motherhood in detrimental ways; and it is a high-risk,
low-efficiency technology the costs of which foreclose the development and
application of preventive, cheap, low-technology solutions that every woman can
afford to choose. IVF programmes deleteriously affect the priorities of the health
services, but that does not mean that rational women do not pursue them.

Lesley Doyal offers a similar analysis of the contexts of reproductive technology, in which some of the millions of infertile women are drawn by their desire
for a child into the 'epicentre of high technology gynaecology and obstetrics'.[69]
She is more concerned with the cultural contexts of fertility, in which the status of
mother is still a 'central' one for many women and for whom 'an inability to
become a biological parent may have a profound effect on women's sense of
themselves and their well-being', in which they may suffer a major life crisis, may
indeed be 'disabled'.[70] Reproductive technology may, then, be seen not just as a
response to infertility but more profoundly as a (bio)technological response to a
total life and social crisis *to the person as a whole*. In other words, infertility
treatments might on this view be recontextualised as something other than a
'medical model' response to particular cellular dysfunction in the reproductive

system; rather they are a response to a life-threatening position. The cruel irony, then, is that while reproductive technologies 'have recently been hailed as the miracle solution for all those who cannot conceive within their own bodies', the reality is that 'they are suitable for only a small percentage of infertile women and only a few of these can afford them'.[71] In an arresting phrase which recalls the culturally differentiated experiences of women, to which feminisms particularly have become more attentive, Doyal examines the severe handicaps of a woman unable to have children and who may have 'no daughters to comfort her and no sons to support her'.[72]

Reproductive 'choice'   Rosalind Petchesky has observed that the critical issue for feminists is not so much the *content* of women's choices, or even the 'right to choose', as the social and material conditions under which choices are made. 'The fact that individuals themselves do not determine the social framework in which they act does not nullify their choices nor their moral capacity to make them.'[73] The most visible complaint is that where access to reproductive technologies is permitted, the state should not discriminate against certain individual women because of their sexual orientation, marital status, their race or social status. And yet, almost universally, where legislation has addressed these questions, judgments about 'fitness to parent' are explicitly or implicitly made by the state on grounds which characterise some women as unfit to mother or to parent.

Reproductive technologies have provided some people who are 'infertile' with the hope and chance of having a child, and have opened up the possibility of new and exciting opportunities for the formation of families with the separation of genetic, gestational and social parenthood in ways that previously belonged to the realm of science fiction.[74] Even those enthusiastic about their advent remain conscious of the challenge to 'respect the reproductive rights of infertile people to have access to reproductive technology, while critically evaluating and seeking to transcend the narrow confines of the definition of "family" within which reproductive technology operates'.[75] And yet it remains the case that for most women infertility is a life sentence; new technologies are characterised by their exclusivity, reserved for the relatively more wealthy, 'suitable couple', who are eternal optimists – Koch's new rationalists, as we might call them. And the problem with technological solutions to circumventing infertility, with their high cost and low 'success' rates and abysmal side-effects, is that their very existence may be diverting resources away from broader strategies for responding to and preventing 'reproductive impairment'.[76]

THE ETHIC OF CARE

In part based upon a consideration of the different approaches within feminism discussed above, and specifically a melding of the soft version of reproductive choice with a more critically contextual approach to reproductive technologies, a Royal Commission, the Baird Commission, established by the Canadian government in 1989, presented a report entitled *Proceed with Care*,[77] which established and explained the vision of a quite different approach to the consideration of reproductive technologies than that which had commended itself, for example, to the Warnock Committee almost ten years earlier. Specifically, the Baird

Commission announced that it had reached three overall conclusions about the delivery of new reproductive technologies:

(a) that there was an urgent need for well-defined boundaries around the use of the technologies so that unethical use of knowledge is prohibited;
(b) that within those boundaries accountable regulation is needed to protect the interests of those involved and society as a whole;
(c) given the pace of change, a flexible and continuing response to evolving technologies involving wide community-supported input was an essential component of the responsible delivery of assisted conception.[78]

The Commission then set out the choices of methodology that it considered it had available in evaluating the matters referred to it. On the one hand there was the possibility of identifying one overarching ethical theory, such as utilitarianism, natural law or contractarianism, to establish a framework for and to guide its decision-making. Alternatively, it considered and adopted a 'broader ethical orientation' – the ethic of care – and a set of guiding principles 'to serve as a prism for our moral deliberations'.[79]

Broadly speaking, the ethic of care holds that moral reasoning is not solely, or even primarily, a matter of finding rules to arbitrate between conflicting interests. Moral wisdom and sensitivity consist, rather, in focusing on the interdependence of our individual interests and then trying to find creative solutions that can remove or reduce conflict rather than simply ranking interests and setting one person's in priority over anothers'. 'The priority, therefore, is on helping human relationships to flourish by seeking to foster the dignity of the individual and the welfare of the community.'[80] Should intervention then be necessary, its aim should be to ensure, so far as possible, that everyone is served and that adversarial situations do not arise. At the very least, intervention must avoid causing harm to human relationships.

Clearly, elaborating this thesis into a potentially workable solution to the problems and possibilities of reproductive technologies was never going to be easy, and indeed the Commission process and proceedings turned out to be rancorous and controversial. Nor, compared with the Warnock approach, is the voluminous report and the associated reasoning which produced the Commission's recommendations going to be easy reading for government ministers charged to implement some version of the proposed scheme or provide a detailed response to it, and this may in part account for the legislative quiescence which has so far followed the report. Nonetheless, it is an invaluable document and its 'guiding principle' for translating the ethic of care in to a scheme that a state could endorse and promote repays revisiting.

Baird proposed that in consideration of how to respond to reproductive technologies, eight main considerations should be weighed:[81]

- Any response should respect individual autonomy, recognising that people are free to choose how to lead their lives.
- The response must enshrine the principle of equality – that every member of the community is entitled to equal concern and respect.
- All forms of human life, and indeed tissue in general, should be treated with sensitivity and respect.

- The protection of the vulnerable is an inescapable principle of the ethic of care, especially the protection of children.
- Decisions about human reproduction should not be determined by profit; commercialisation and commodification are anathema.
- Recognising the existence of diverse needs and finite resources, it is imperative that resources be used wisely and effectively.
- Those who hold power, whether in government, the professions or in other fields, must be accountable for the use of that power.
- Both individual and collective interests are worthy of protection and individual interests do not *necessarily* take precedence over collective interests, nor vice versa; it is appropriate that they are balanced, and it must be recognised that that balance may shift over time or from case to case.

The Commission then, in its lengthy and scholarly (critics have suggested scholastic) report, enumerated how these principles and the ethic of care should guide an appropriate response to reproductive technologies in Canada. Canadian society is still waiting to see whether it is possible or desirable to translate this approach into a legislative framework.

Of course, this introduces us to another important but more familiar variable in the ethical debate: what is the proper basis for the relationship between morals and law, and how should that relationship be managed? We turn briefly to consider that question.

LAW AND MORALS

A further matrix of complicated relationships is that between morality and law. Once we have decided on the ethics or morality of a particular issue, it does not then follow necessarily that this has to be translated into legal language. That will depend on what we see to be the relationship, if any, between law and morals. Questions about whether an activity is right or wrong, morally innocuous or repugnant, and the arguments supporting those views, belong to moral philosophy. We have identified above only some of the many possible approaches that can then be brought to bear in this analysis. The question of whether we should then have laws governing any particular issue, and what shape and rationale those laws might take, belongs to legal and political philosophy. There is no necessary, simple connection to be made between the rightness, wrongness or moral indifference to an act or practice, and the propriety or desirability of having a law which requires, permits or forbids it. Of course, we may have a position that holds, for example, that any conduct that is morally repugnant should be and is unlawful. Similarly, we may hold that because conduct is prohibited by legal *fiat* endorsed with sanction – whether criminal or civil – it is therefore morally imperative not to break that law. We could hold this latter position simply because we felt that whatever was unlawful was necessarily immoral, or because, whatever our judgment of the morality of the particular law, we placed a particular moral primacy on obeying the law, even if we found it to be morally repugnant.

We can put this another way. That there is no general direct connection between law and morality can be tested straightforwardly. One may consider that an act may be wrong, and wrong *only* because it is against the law. If so then there would

be a direct connection between the morality and legality of an act. But generally
we do not believe that to be the case. We look for some background, justifying
moral reason for the law to be the way it is. Debate in legal philosophy then turns
on whether morals and law should be co-extensive and co-terminous, or whether
there should be, in the Wolfenden Committee's memorable phrase, some acts
which are 'not the law's business'.

> Unless a deliberate attempt is to be made by society, acting through the agency
> of the law, to equate the sphere of crime with that of sin, there must remain a
> realm of private morality and immorality which is, in brief and crude terms, not
> the law's business.[82]

Of course, while it does seem to follow from this that the scope of moral debate
need pay no necessary attention to law, the question for lawyers has been the extent
to which the law is, or should or indeed can be co-terminous with moral positions;
and if so, with which one(s).

A traditional starting point for lawyers and political philosophers has been the
statement by the 19th-century thinker John Stuart Mill, that

> The only purpose for which power can be rightfully exercised over any member
> of a civilised community against his will is to prevent harm to others. His own
> good, either physical or moral is not a sufficient warrant.[83]

We do not want to dwell here on the difficulties to which this *dictum* has given
rise: What is harm? Who count as others? Must force be used to prevent harm to
others, or is this merely a necessary condition? What is wrong with the parentalist
intervention of others to prevent one causing harm to oneself? In other words, is
Mill correct that the state must always misperceive the individual's interests or be
untimely in its intervention? But the responses to the Wolfenden Report, which
recalls Mill's harm principle, illustrate some of the fundamental differences in
contemporary thought about the relationship between law and morals.

We do need to consider briefly, however, the role of the public/private
distinction that commended itself to Wolfenden. Mill was not himself the author
of the distinction; rather, he argued that for something to be brought within the
moral sphere it had to involve definite harm to some assignable other. The issue
of public regulation arose from that. For Mill, there was no 'bolt-hole' labelled
'private' into which one could escape and claim immunity from public regulation.
In so far as Wolfenden appears to suggest that there is, the public/private spheres
of morality have to be traced back to some other source, of which Machiavelli in
The Prince is an early example. For Mill, it was appropriate to argue whether the
public sanction of the law was more or less appropriate than some less formal
mechanism, but this did not depend on a supposed distinction between private and
public conduct. Anything that fell within the moral realm properly understood, in
that it involved harm to another, was amenable to public regulation.

One of the core questions posed by a respondent to Wolfenden, Patrick Devlin,
was whether Wolfenden was correct in assuming and stating that society does not
have the right to pass judgment on all matters of morals. Are morals a matter, and
exclusively a matter, for private judgment, or is there a public morality? Hart, in

responding to Devlin, recharacterised the question that Devlin had asked as follows: 'Is the fact that certain conduct is by common standards immoral sufficient to justify making that conduct punishable by law? Is it morally permissible to enforce morality as such?' Devlin's response to these questions was broadly 'Yes', Hart's 'No'. In an important respect, Hart and Devlin were in agreement. Both believed that if one can establish an identifiable harm to society then the proper ground for intervention is established. Where they disagreed was in whether morality constitutes a seamless web from which was spun a common, shared morality.

For Devlin, this was a constitutive part of what a society was, such that equating sin and crime was what defined law. Devlin's view was that what makes a society is precisely its shared morality, and that creating a society without common agreement on good and evil is doomed to failure. The same would apply to a society in which the common agreement goes. The use of law to enforce such agreement is as justifiable as its use to ensure the well-being of anything else that is essential to the existence of that society. Devlin believed, however, that law should be used only in some cases. He suggested four principles of restraint in the extent to which it should be used to enforce even that commonly shared notion of good and evil:

(a)   that only what is beyond the limits of tolerance – and this means a real feeling of revulsion and not mere dislike – should be punished by law;
(b)   the extent of tolerance of departures from moral standards will vary over generations;
(c)   as far as possible privacy should be protected;
(d)   the law is concerned with a minimum and not a maximum standard of behaviour.

Hart's response evolves from Mill's harm principle. While he includes harm to oneself, which Mill would have disavowed, Hart argues that recognition of individual liberty as a value involves, 'as a minimum, acceptance of the principle that the individual may do what he wants, even if others are distressed when they learn what it is that he does unless, of course, there are other good grounds for forbidding it'. Hart criticised Devlin's approach as 'legal moralism'; he charged that on Devlin's own account it assumes a congruity between law and morality (rather than substantiating it). But more than that, he argued that it is difficult for Devlin to distinguish between a change in morality and a subversion of it. For Hart, Devlin was locked into an unchanging morality, in which any change was discernible only as a subversion of morality. This seems a particularly important exchange when put in the context of, say, abortion or embryo research.

Rosalind Hursthouse has suggested a third approach to this question of the relationship between law and morality. As she points out, the confusion of questions about morality and legislation is particularly common in arguments about abortion (and we would add embryo research, although for different reasons: see below). As she elaborates, one reason for the confusion is the oppositional tactics taken in debate:

Many people, particularly women, do think there is something wrong about having an abortion, that it is not a morally innocuous matter, but also think that the current abortion laws are if anything too restrictive, and find it difficult to articulate their position on the morality of abortion without, apparently, betraying the feminist campaign concerning legislation.[84]

There are many echoes of this in the radical and the liberal feminist writings on abortion.[85] This enables us to suggest different approaches to, say, abortion and embryo research, which recognise their ambiguity, as well as their complexity.

LAW AND MORALITY: ABORTION AND EMBRYO RESEARCH

The law on abortion touches directly upon aspects of assisted conception technologies, such as in selective reduction of multiple pregnancy. It also provides an important source of arguments and thinking about embryo research and we reflect upon that here.

Hursthouse is one writer who has addressed the confusions between questions of law, morality and legislation. She has argued that once the distinctions between the questions of law and morality are separated out, it becomes possible to identify four different positions on abortion.[86] We suggest that this analysis might conveniently be applied to the arguments surrounding embryo research and the other provisions of the Human Fertilisation and Embryology Act 1990.

Morality of abortion	Laws on abortion	Position
Wrong	Restrictive	Conservative
Innocuous	Restrictive	'Totalitarian'
Innocuous	Liberal	Liberal/Radical
Wrong	Liberal	Liberal/Moderate

The first position is the familiar one in which legislation about morality is based on a conservative moral view. This view is perhaps the most easily identifiable in the Parliamentary debates which have accompanied criticism of the reform implemented in the Abortion Act 1967, and was represented in the Parliamentary debates on the 1990 Act by MPs such as Bernard Braine, Ann Widdecombe, David Alton and the Duke of Norfolk.

The two liberal views are an innovative and challenging position introduced by Hursthouse. It is much more difficult, whether in the abstract or in the context of Parliamentary speeches and votes, to identify which of the alternative positions an individual holds. An alternative way of describing the positions might be the liberal/moderate as the 'lesser of two evils', where the death of the foetus (or destruction of the embryo) is compared with and transcended by the rights or interests of the individual woman (or society generally). This may be contrasted with the liberal/radical position, where it is the moral insignificance of abortion which facilitates the approach. In the embryo research debates, it is perhaps easier to distinguish those who believe that embryo research does not involve anything of moral worth (the pre-human embryo) and those who hold that it does attract moral worth (the human pre-embryo). For those of the latter position, the value which attaches to the embryo is not sufficient to outweigh the benefits which may be derived from research in terms of infertility treatments; the alleviation of suffering to future generations caused by the existence of genetically inherited diseases or chromosomal disorders; the search for improved methods of contraception or the better understanding of the causes of infertility and miscarriage.

Those who argue that the embryo or the foetus is not a person, or does not have personhood or is not a human being, hold that abortion (and hence embryo research) is morally innocuous. For them abortion is no different from the removal of cancerous tissue or an appendix. Hence, the desirability of liberal abortion laws does not depend on the present lack of safe and effective birth control, or the plight of a woman overburdened with children or with a child who is likely to suffer from a serious physical or mental handicap. It depends only on the argument that men and women should have the same access to appendectomies or cancer treatments.

If, however, abortion is not morally innocuous, there is a problem for those who believe that women should be allowed access to lawful abortion facilities on a straightforward basis. (It is sometimes inaccurately called a dilemma; a dilemma is a choice between two alternatives; we do not argue that.) It is important for the liberal/radical to consider, concerning morality, what sort of wrong he or she believes abortion to be, and concerning legislation, whether it is the sort of moral wrong over which the state may or should exercise formal control. If, as conservative thinkers believe, abortion is a form of homicide, no morally responsible person should be able to proceed without legal repercussion. If abortion, though not as wrong as homicide, is still nevertheless morally compromised, there remains the problem of whether a woman should be given the access to lawful abortion services (to do a wrong or inflict a harm, as Devlin might put it).

If an act is morally compromised, it is not obvious that a right to do it should be enshrined in and protected by law. This does not say that liberal legislation cannot be justified by those who think abortion is morally wrong. Their appeal, however, will lie beyond 'the right to choose':

. . . the 'fashionable and liberal' way of regarding abortion as a morally innocuous event is dangerous because of its tendency to harm women, a tendency which makes it almost as anti-feminist as that of the anti-abortion campaigners.[87]

WHAT IS INFERTILITY AND WHAT ARE ITS CAUSES?

Is infertility an illness or a disease that should be treated? For some, infertility is a 'disease' just as any other; like cancer, it is about pathological physiology and shares with cancer the pathology of cells having 'gone wrong'. The 'plight' of 'the infertile' has thus been seen as legitimating the time, technology and resources expended on it. For others, infertility is a grief, not a disease, and is, literally, something sent to try those unable to conceive.

There are a number of points that are pertinent here. First, fertility is closely allied to the general position of women and men in society, and infertility is as much a social construct as a biological fact; the facts of infertility are loaded with the values of society. Secondly, expenditure on the 'disease' of infertility represents costs foregone elsewhere. The value of assisted conception technology to the wider community has come to be more extensively debated. In a world where there is little shortage of people or children, although not all of them may be of the 'approved' colour or able-bodied and able-minded, it is legitimate to ask whether resources should be committed to infertility work at all. Such concerns prompted one MP, Sir Michael McNair Wilson, to observe during the original Parliamentary debates that

> . . . in a world that is suffering from overpopulation and that is still afflicted with so many curable illnesses, can the medical profession justify the huge expenditure of vast resources on the more esoteric aspects of medicine, when that money could buy immediate and more easily achievable relief for so many.[88]

Of course, it is possible to challenge both the assumptions that lie behind this sort of observation and the conclusion to which it is made to give rise. So, on the one hand, the 'myth' of overpopulation has been questioned as something more simply understood as a failure to distribute resources equitably. On the other hand, it may be just foolish to think that by hostaging people with fertility problems to their 'fate', the population policies of the globe will thereby be resolved. There seems to be an extraordinary argument that by punishing those with infertility the sins of omission in the political processes of the world will be absolved. While it is the case that infertility treatments remain costly and their success rates low, it is undoubtedly necessary to guard against the production of high expectations and the increased grief which a failure (often repeated failure) of those expectations often engenders.

Reproduction has come to occupy an increasingly prominent role in the theatre of the personal. It has moved downstage, from being seen as a minor bit part of personhood, to being cast as one of the essential characteristics of its successful production and realisation. Issues such as childbirth, childrearing and child care are thus more easily identifiable as raising core questions of social justice. Hence, although there is no area of health care practice where resources are committed with infinite guarantee, the decision about how resources are allocated to infertility treatments cannot be made on the basis of salving our conscience about misallocations that we make elsewhere. Family life, howsoever that is constructed, construed or conceived, continues to exert an important and a powerful hold over issues of personal identity, reproduction and responsibility.[89]

Estimates vary of the incidence of infertility, but most agreed figures suggest that at least one in ten couples are affected at some stage in their lives. In Britain this would mean something like 50,000 new cases of infertility each year, although other studies suggest that the figure is closer to 1:6.[90]

Whatever conclusion is reached on this point, further disputatious points arise. Suppose, for example, that we agree that resources should indeed be devoted to infertility treatments. The first question that then arises is whether all types of fertility compromise should be viewed in the same way? IVF, for example, was originally used for inoperably blocked fallopian tubes. In Denmark, which has a restrictive approach, it is largely confined to such treatment. In the United Kingdom, however, it is also indicated in endometriosis, ovulation disorders, anti-sperm antibodies and male infertilities, many of which, it is argued, are socially or environmentally caused.

Secondly, should non-clinical criteria be employed as a way of rationing access to the scarce resource which treatment services represent? For example, the Warnock Committee averred that:

To judge from the evidence, many believe that the interests of the child dictate that it should be born into a home where there is a loving, stable, heterosexual relationship and that, therefore, the *deliberate* creation of a child for a woman who is not a partner in such a relationship is morally wrong . . . we believe that as a general rule it is better for children to be born into a two-parent family, with both father and mother, although we recognise that it is impossible to predict with any certainty how lasting such a relationship will be.[91]

In other words, the Committee felt more comfortable with the idea of a child born into a home where the uncertainty of its parents' commitment to one another was mediated by the different sexes of those whom it assumed would be the child's primary carers. These assumptions have not gone unchallenged, and in individual infertility treatment centres the sentiments that informed them have, to all intents and purposes, been left to whither away. Originally, of course, they had the intention (and very possibly the effect) of rationing or restricting access to treatment services.

It is an aspiration of many of those who work in the field that the 'treatment' or care of those with infertility is but the first practical application of embryo research and IVF work. The additional benefits of contraceptive vaccine, the resolution of causes of miscarriage, and the detection of genetic and chromosomal abnormalities in pre-implantation embryos or early foetuses remain the longer-term goals of this branch of research as the HFEA have recently begun to explore.

A third area that needs comment is that such 'infertility treatments' as there are are not freely available to all who would wish to use them. Most services are available only in private clinics, and hence to those who can pay the fees that the clinics charge. Throughout the original Parliamentary debates the lack of available treatment services on the NHS was referred to as 'a tax on the infertile'. Latterly this has become known as post-code rationing, to which we return later. And even for those women or couples who can afford access, for whom assisted conception technologies and techniques open up a realm of choice about childlessness, the success is limited.

Section 16(1) of the 1990 Act enables the HFEA to levy a fee from any applicant for a licence; under s. 16(7) it is open to the HFEA to set different fees for different types of clinic, or fees may be limited to the levels of work undertaken by each centre. On the question of whether this lack of central funding was discriminating against those who used infertility services, Baroness Faithful in the House of Lords put the Government's position – 'money available in this area is open to abuse'[92] – although she did not go on to specify the Government's worries.

There is a wide range of professional, demographic and socio-political factors which may affect the construction of the results about the 'success rates' obtained from any given clinic following its provision of infertility services. This can vary according to a clinic's decision to treat only a certain number or type of infertility each year; the age structure of the client population; the professional skill and expertise of the clinicians, and so on. These points need to be appreciated in reviewing the so-called 'league tables' of clinic success rates (particularly pregnancy and live births) per treatment cycle. As Robert Winston has suggested:

. . . one of the problems about publishing a comparative table of results is that it encourages clinics to take these risks because clearly they want to be seen to be doing better than their rivals. [This] encourages some clinics unreasonably to exclude women whose prognosis is unfavourable. . . . A very serious problem with league tables is that their presence undoubtedly encourages a few clinics to be 'somewhat economical with the truth'.[93]

Concerns with infertility

Medical advance has identified more and more potential causes of infertility, and the group of patients whose lack of fertility cannot be attributed to any anatomical, physiological or pathological cause – whose infertility is 'unexplained' – now rarely exceeds 18% of 'infertility patients'.[94] Some of the causes are iatrogenic, arising from contraception, drugs, abortion, surgery or invasive diagnostic procedures. Other causes are environmental – including a wide range of factors such as alcohol, poor nutrition, stress and background toxins – although more research is needed to identify securely causal relationships. Infertility can also arise from physiological factors: undescended testes, endometriosis (the presence of endometriotic tissue – normal uterine lining – in abnormal locations, such as the fallopian tubes, ovaries or peritoneal cavity), lack of sperm motility and so on. It does seem that there is a concern with infertility that is unparalleled in earlier times (although we could not make the same observation with respect to fertility). We want here to suggest tentatively four reasons why that might be so.

First, there do seem to be more individuals or couples presenting with primary infertility. This may in part arise out of changing patterns of family planning, including delayed childbearing, careers, chosen childlessness and changing choices. For many (especially women) in the late-1960s and 1970s, while reproductive choices were changing alongside slow and gradual economic and employment liberation, they tended towards the redefinition of chosen childlessness. Coupled with this, the changing patterns of family unit and the increased acceptance of the dissolubility of them, led to changing patterns of relationship and family units. The combined effects of this are that many, especially women, found their reproductive choices changing. This led to an abandonment of earlier choices about reproduction and childlessness, with a consequent desire to become pregnant later in their reproductive lives and/or a desire to have children in a number of sequential partnerships. This produces a wish to remain (re)productive for a longer period. Hence childbirth became for some more condensed, through choice, and attendant on apparent improvements in reliable contraceptive options.

Secondly, it would seem that an increasing number of couples with primary infertility are seeking care. The importance of assistance may grow as fewer new-born babies are available for adoption. This arises from a combination of contraception, abortion and the acceptance of single women keeping children born to them rather than their being adopted, either with the active support and encouragement of the state through social welfare programmes, or at least not in the face of open state-sanctioned hostility. Greater toleration of illegitimacy has been reflected in legislative changes aimed at removing the remaining vestiges of stigma and the adverse consequences of illegitimacy. Heightened expectations concerning the way in which we can assert control over our lives may lead to a reluctance or refusal to accept an involuntarily childless state. This may be especially true with rising incomes, so that a higher percentage of infertile couples can afford to make their voices loudly heard and expect to be listened to.

Medical advance provides a third reason, as an increasing number of physicians offer more sophisticated techniques of diagnosis and treatment. The birth and evolution of the technology of assisted reproduction has been rapid, but even relatively low-tech methods, such as surrogacy, have become more prominent. On the other hand, it has to be said that demand for infertility treatment far outstrips supply.

Lastly, we cannot ignore the role of the media in reflecting shades of opinion, not simply upon issues of infertility but also on questions of family and sex. Coverage of questions of infertility by the media has ranged from stories of high-technology pioneers on the frontiers of science to stories of grandmothers having babies for their daughters and daughters having children for their mothers; from the human misery of those who have been 'trying for a baby' for years to fears of a Brave New World mentality to accompany the technology. This media attention has reflected and been reflected in public interest and attitudes.

Popular culture, which has always had at the centre of its concerns human dilemmas, personal tragedy and the ingredients of life – what Beck and Gernsheim Beck have called the normal chaos of love – has, not surprisingly, moved to reflect some of the new concerns which have come to accompany westernised life in the last few years. Some examples are: 'Forget Paris' (blocked fallopian tubes), 'Nine Months' (failed contraception), 'The Handmaiden's Tale' (surrogacy), 'Twins', (female egg and male sperm research splitting embryos), 'Big Business' (babies mixed up at the hospital), 'Junior' (male pregnancy, Schwarzenegger), 'Honey I Shrunk [and subsequently 'Blew Up'] the Kids' (crude genetic engineering), 'Frankenstein' (the movie remake, cosmetic surgery, or more and slightly less crude genetic engineering), 'Face Off' (advanced cosmetic surgery), 'Austin Powers; Man of Mystery' (cryogenic freezing), Woody Allen's 'Sleeper' (cryo-preservation), 'First Sight' (optical engineering), 'Patch Adams' (complementary medicine), 'While You Were Sleeping' (coma care), 'Maybe Baby' (anxieties of infertility treatment) and 'The Sexual Life of the Belgians' (!).

Why legislate?

Assisted conception techniques bring with them as many philosophical, moral and legal problems as the more outstanding cases of embryo research and abortion. And while they have not commanded the news coverage, the resolution of these issues into Parliamentary debates and the resulting legislation illustrates the enormous range which the 1990 Act addresses. It introduces statutory control of a new form of clinical practice; it brings to the forefront of attention questions as to the provision of and payment for assisted conception services. The Government's refusal to commit more resources to the area was repeatedly described as a 'tax on the infertile'. In parallel with this, these new reproductive techniques have been developed at a time of resurgence in expression of feminist thought and values. Important among the issues that this has disclosed has been the centrality of the views of women; and in the assisted conception debates, the way in which their interests, desires, plans and goals are accounted for, discounted, factored in or out, has assumed a major importance. But, of course, the conclusions to which this leads various commentators are not uniform, other than perhaps in the view that where such issues fundamentally affect the life, well-being, health and emotions of

women, men should take a back seat. This was most forcefully expressed during
the Parliamentary debates by Teresa Gorman, a backbench Conservative MP,
usually noted for her strong commitment to market individualism. In the debate on
abortion law reform she interjected with this analysis of the arguments of those
who sought to reduce the time limits, or the grounds on which access to lawful
abortion could be obtained:

> Although superficially we are talking about medicine, science and when, where
> and whether we should stop abortion, emotions and deep passions bubble up
> from underneath. . . . Those motives form one of the deepest, most misogynous
> strands in human society. For centuries theologians have equated sex with sin
> and celibacy with grace. They have regarded women as little more than flower
> pots in which future generations of children, preferably boy children, are reared.
> . . . I hope that the majority of my colleagues, perforce mainly male, who do
> not have to bear the responsibility of an unwanted birth and pregnancy and who
> do not have to make such decisions, will not have the temerity, arrogance,
> inhumanity and insensitivity to make those decisions for women.[95]

Although vigorously opposed by some women MPs, this view echoes a common
strand of feminist thought and philosophy: where decisions affecting women and
their reproductive health and interests are concerned, it is the individual woman
herself who should have the right, and hence the responsibility, of making such
fundamental decisions about the morality of what she does.

Not all of those who participated in the original debates were wholeheartedly in
favour of assisted conception at all. For example, Alan Amos argued that 'IVF is
inefficient, expensive, time consuming and dangerous for women. It can lead to
cysts, coagulation, strokes, heart problems, ovarian cancer and many other
problems'.[96] And objecting to the legislation in the House of Lords debate on the
Report, Lord Kennet complained that the Bill had been forced through in
ignorance. He said that in important respects the legislation had been pioneered
without full consideration. Parliament knew little or nothing of the prevalence,
causes and nature of infertility. Although the Office of Population Censuses and
Surveys was now to be charged with responsibility for collecting those data, they
did not presently exist.

The Act also seeks to regulate embryo research. In what began (at least until
abortion was added to its provisions) as the most controversial part of the
legislation, the Bill was introduced with two possible variants of the embryo
research clause. The eventual shape of the legislation would depend on the result
of the vote upon whether a permissive or restrictive line was to be taken on the
question of research. In the event, on a free vote the permissive line received
support, but with a 30% vote against. It was a complaint thereafter that the
Standing Committee considering the Bill had only two out of its 18 members who
were specifically and publicly committed to a 'pro-life' view.

In the original debates there were a number of very important deliberations on
the question of embryo research, to which we return in Chapter 3. Here, we may
recall that such questions considered whether research should be permitted only on
'spare' embryos created in the course of treatment services. This position was
adopted, for example, by Lord Jackobovits in the House of Lords, in an amendment

that was defeated. Jackobovits argued that it was surely repugnant to create human life solely for the purpose of destroying it in embryo experiments. He sought also to introduce an amendment to sch. 2 to the Act (which sets out a list of purposes for which embryo research may be permitted) in order to exclude 'eugenic or frivolous' motives. Here he argued that embryo research, for example, to satisfy a preference for sons, or for smaller humans who would reduce the payload of spaceships, should be addressed and arrested before it got under way. Similarly, he wished to prohibit the use of embryos for research into contraceptives, which was described by Jackobovits as an insufficiently urgent purpose.[97]

The listing of such amendments illustrates the difficulties in drawing boundaries around the margins of embryo research even once a decision, in principle, is taken by majority to allow it. In the debates, there were proponents of four schools of thought on embryo research:

(a)   those for whom any research was acceptable and permissible;

(b)   those who did not want any research at all;

(c)   those who did not want any form of destructive research but who were prepared to countenance therapeutic research for the benefit of each embryo; and

(d)   those who wanted research to be permitted, if at all, only on spare embryos created in the course of providing treatment services and which would otherwise be allowed to perish or be condemned to die if not implanted.

This final stance addresses Jackobovits' point. *In vitro* fertilisation usually produces surplus embryos that cannot be transferred to the woman's uterus. The argument, then, that they may be used in beneficial research, is that this does them no additional injury. However, this argument sharply focuses research on embryos created specifically and only for the purpose of research. Opponents of such creation were fearful of the development of 'embryo farms'.[98] Such fears, doubtless felt most strongly, dictated that the law could no longer remain silent on the questions of whether, how, why, where and when embryo research could be undertaken.

The legislation eventually enacted sought to ensure that these sensitive issues of moral and legal complexity were dealt with in a clear framework. It sought to balance what are the sometimes conflicting interests of the involuntarily childless and the children of the reproduction revolution. Similarly, it sought to mediate between the families who may benefit from research into the causes of genetically inherited disease or chromosomal abnormalities (who may suffer from what has been called 'reproductive blight'), and the human embryo or foetus. In all cases, the broader social, moral and philosophical interests which disclose fundamentally different ways of conceiving of the world and the ways in which it may be inhabited are brought into conflict. In short, the Act is one important manifestation of who we are and who we say we want to become; the question that it raises is: 'Whom to be or not to be?'

Briefly, the Act has three fundamental objectives:

(a)   to provide a statutory framework for the control and supervision of research involving human embryos;

(b)   to provide for the licensing of certain types of assisted conception practice, namely those which involve the creation of a human embryo outside the body, or partly inside and partly outside, and any treatment service which involves the use of donated gametes (egg and sperm) or donated embryos;

(c) to effect changes to the Abortion Act 1967.

Certain infertility treatments ('treatment services') are permitted only under licence from the HFEA. This body has the authority to issue three, and only three, types of licence: a treatment licence, a research licence and a storage licence. A treatment licence or a storage licence may be issued only for a maximum period of five years, after which a reapplication must be made. A research licence is valid only for a maximum of three years.

A treatment licence may authorise one or more of the following: bringing about the creation of embryos *in vitro*; keeping embryos; using gametes; testing the condition of the embryo for replacement; placing an embryo into a woman; using a 'hamster test' to determine the potency and normality of human sperm; and other practices which may later be specified by Authority. Hence, a licence will be necessary for IVF, AID, donor GIFT, egg donation and IVC. The Government does not intend that a licence should be necessary where fertilisation takes place within a woman's body using her egg(s) and her husband's sperm (AIH) or, where they are unmarried, her partner's sperm (AIP). AIH, AIP and non-donor GIFT are outwith the licensing requirement.

A storage licence will permit the storage of gametes or embryos, or both.

A research licence will permit the creation of embryos *in vitro* and their use for specified projects of research. The research (or experimentation; the choice of terms is apt to reflect in part one's moral judgment) must be directed towards one or more of a presently defined number of aims and will be permitted only where the HFEA is satisfied that the research is necessary or desirable. These aims are:

(a) the promotion of advances in the treatment of infertility;
(b) increasing knowledge about the causes of congenital disease;
(c) increasing knowledge about the causes of miscarriages;
(d) developing more effective techniques of contraception;
(e) developing methods for detecting the presence or absence of gene or chromosome abnormalities before implantation of an embryo.

The HFEA has recently proposed that two additional research aims should be introduced by Regulation, in relation to therapies for mitochondrial diseases and damaged tissues or organs.

In respect of abortion, the 1990 Act made some fundamental changes to the Abortion Act 1967. For the first time a specific time limit was written into legislation. In England and Wales, the time limit within which most lawful abortions must be performed is 24 weeks. In Scotland, where the common law and not statute (the Infant Life (Preservation) Act 1929) applied in relation to child destruction, it was previously thought by some commentators that lawful abortion could be performed at any time up to birth. Effectively, however, most abortions in Scotland were performed broadly in line with the position in England and Wales. The 1990 Act now introduces this new statutory time limit into that jurisdiction as well. Amendments made to the Bill at the Report stage in the House of Commons (21 June 1990) removed Northern Ireland from the scope of the abortion provisions, and saw defeated the attempts to amend the Bill to make access to abortion more straightforward. Also defeated was an attempt to reintroduce time limits in respect of abortion on the grounds of foetal handicap and the health of the woman.

There are other examples of the statutory control of medical treatment, such as abortion, female circumcision, human organ donation, and treatments for detained patients under the Mental Health Act 1983, but in none of these is the treatment regulated. In this respect the 1990 Act was a first.

There is a variety of other questions, as yet unframed, which will face us in the future. The Human Fertilisation and Embryology Act 1990 is a statute seeking to regulate certain aspects of reproductive medicine and not a comprehensive code. However, that the Act is incomplete does not mean that it is unwelcome. But it will not be the last word on the subject.

NOTES

[1]   Glover, J., *Fertility and The Family: The Glover Report on Reproductive Technologies to the European Commission* (London: Fourth Estate, 1989), at 1.

[2]   Cmnd 9314, *Report of the Committee of Inquiry into Fertilisation and Embryology*, subsequently republished with an introduction by Mary Warnock as *A Question of Life* (Oxford, Basil Blackwell, 1985).

[3]   See House of Commons, Official Report, 23 November 1984, coll. 528–43 and 547–90.

[4]   Knoppers, B. and Le Bris, S., 'Recent Advances in Medically Assisted Conception' (1991) 7 *American Journal of Law and Medicine* 329. For a critical analysis of one particular 'case' of globalisation and the effect of that on a national regulatory scheme, see Morgan, D. and Lee, R.G., 'In the Name of the Father? *ex parte Blood*: Dealing with Novelty and Anomaly' (1997) 60 *Modern Law Review* 840.

[5]   Official Report, Standing Committee B, 8 May 1990, col. 49.

[6]   *The Elimination of Morality* (London, Routledge, 1993), at 202.

[7]   Radin, M.J., *Contested Commodities: The Trouble with Trade in Sex, Children, Body Parts, and Other Things* (Cambridge, Mass., Harvard University Press, 1996), at 127.

[8]   *Ibid.*, at 149.

[9]   Duelii Klein, R., 'What's New about the "New" Reproductive Technologies?' in Corea, G. *et al.*, *Man-Made Women: How New Reproductive Technologies Affect Women* (London, Hutchinson, 1985), at 64–73.

[10]   Sarat, A. and Felstiner, W., *Divorce Lawyers and their Clients: Power and Meaning in the Legal Process* (New York and Oxford, Oxford University Press, 1995), at 13. We are grateful to Katherine O'Donovan for originally drawing this to our attention.

[11]   Strathern, M. *et al.*, *Reproducing the Future: Anthropology, Kinship and the New Reproductive Technologies* (Manchester, Manchester University Press, 1993). And see Strathern, M., 'The Meaning of Assisted Kinship' in Meg Stacey (ed.), *Changing Human Reproduction* (London, Sage Publications, 1992), at 148–69. This essay is a succinct introduction to cultural and linguistic concepts deployed in arguments about the family, demonstrating in the use of examples the way in which what are taken as natural facts are themselves social and cultural constructs.

For developments of this sort of argument, applied to various intellectual disciplines, see, *inter alia*, Foucault, M., *The Order of Things* (London, Tavistock, 1970) and Thomas, K., *Man and the Natural World* (Harmondsworth, Penguin, 1983).

[12] Strathern in Meg Stacey, *op. cit.* n. 11, at 149.

[13] Robertson, J., *Children of Choice: Freedom and the New Reproductive Technologies* (New Jersey, New Jersey University Press, 1994), at 6. Indeed, we think that it is possible to suggest that this has already begun; see Silver, L., *Remaking Eden: Cloning, Genetic Engineering and the Future of Mankind* (London, Weidenfeld & Nicolson, 1999), discussing the emergence of 'reprogenetics'.

[14] Dolgin, J., *Defining the Family: Law, Technology and Reproduction in an Uneasy Age* (New York and London, New York University Press, 1997), at ix.

[15] Robertson, *op. cit.* n. 13, at 42.

[16] Eekelaar, J., 'Parenthood, Social Engineering and Rights' in Derek Morgan and Gillian Douglas (eds), *Constituting Families: A Study in Governance* (Stuttgart, Franz Steiner Verlag, 1994), at 87, citing the Children Act 1989 for the introduction of the third component, parental responsibility. For a thorough and illuminating discussion, see Dolgin, *op. cit.* n. 14, esp. pp. 1–62 for her insightful discussions of the 'Transformation of the Family' and 'Family Law in Transition'.

[17] Strathern in Meg Stacey, *op. cit.* at 167–68. This essay is a succinct introduction to cultural and linguistic concepts deployed in arguments about the family, demonstrating in the use of examples, the way in which what are taken as natural facts are themselves social and cultural constructs.

[18] For an excellent analysis of this phenomenon, see Koch, L., 'IVF–A Rational Choice?' (1990) 3(3) *Issues in Reproductive and Genetic Engineering* 235.

[19] In Derek Morgan and Robert Lee (eds), *Birthrights: Law and Ethics at the Beginnings of Life*, (London Routledge, 1989).

[20] Koch, *op. cit.* n. 18, at 239.

[21] *Ibid.*, at 240.

[22] *Ibid.*, at 241.

[23] Anleu, S.R., 'Reproductive Autonomy: Infertility, Deviance and Conceptive Technology' in Kerry Peterson (ed.), *Law and Medicine* (Melbourne, La Trobe University Press, 1994), at 36.

[24] Koch, L., *op. cit.* n. 18, at 235.

[25] *Feminism & the Power of Law* (London, Routledge, 1990), at 223–24.

[26] In John Harris and Soren Holm (eds), *The Future of Human Reproduction* (Oxford, Oxford University Press, 1998), at 5–37.

[27] Especially in his books *Life's Dominion* (London, HarperCollins, 1993), *Freedom's Law* (Oxford, Oxford University Press, 1996), *Taking Rights Seriously* (London, Duckworth, 1997) and *A Matter of Principle* (Cambridge, Mass., Harvard University Press, 1985).

[28] Harris, *op. cit.* n. 26, at 5 and 37.

[29] Dworkin, R., *Life's Dominion*, at 166–67.

[30] Harris, *op. cit.* n. 26, at 5.

[31] *Ibid.*, at 34.

[32] Dworkin, *Life's Dominion*, at 148.

[33] *Ibid.*, at 160.

[34] *Op. cit.* n. 26, at 34.

[35] *Ibid.*, at 35.

[36] *Ibid.*, at 36.

[37] Dworkin, *Life's Dominion*, at 166–67.

[38] Robertson, J., *Children of Choice: Freedom and the New Reproductive Technologies* (New Jersey, New Jersey University Press, 1994). Robertson's book-length treatment of procreative autonomy also contains at pp. 220–26 his reply to anticipated criticism from class, feminist and communitarian critiques of procreative liberty.

[39] *Ibid.*, at 24.

[40] There are useful discussions of the 'right to procreate' in the British context and literature in Mason, K., *Medico-Legal Aspects of Parenthood and Reproduction*, 2nd edn (Aldershot, Ashgate, 1998), at 85–87, The Hon. Mrs Justice Hale, *From the Test Tube to the Coffin: Choice and Regulation in Private Life* (London, Stevens/Sweet & Maxwell, 1996), at 5–9, and in a characteristically early essay by Sheila McLean and Tom Campbell, 'Sterilisation' in S.A.M. McLean (ed.), *Legal Issues in Medicine* (Aldershot, Gower, 1981), at 178 *et seq.*

[41] *Op. cit.* n. 40, at 7.

[42] *Ibid.*, at 8.

[43] Robertson, *op. cit.* n. 38, at 23.

[44] *Ibid.*

[45] *Ibid.*, at 24.

[46] *Ibid.*, at 35.

[47] *Ibid.*, at 220–35.

[48] Frazer, E., Hornsby, J. and Lovibond, S., *Ethics; A Feminist Reader* (Oxford, Basil Blackwell, 1994), at 4.

[49] Descartes, R., 'Meditations on the first philosophy in which the existence of god and the distinction between mind and body are demonstrated' in Haldane, E. and Ross, G. (eds and transl.), *1 The Philosophical Works of Descartes* (Cambridge, Cambridge University Press, 1967), at 144–99. Descartes argued that the physical body, in line with emergent anatomical science, should be understood as a machine, but that there were other parts of the person that could not be accommodated within this vehicle. The expression 'mind' he used to identify aspects of human consciousness, which in almost all respects differed from the opposite characteristics possessed and exhibited by the body.

[50] The best short introduction to this subject of which we are aware remains Doyal, L. and Doyal, L., 'Western Scientific Medicine: A Philosophical and Political Prognosis' in Lynda Birke and Jonathan Silvertown, *More Than the Parts: Biology and Politics* (London, Pluto Press, 1984), at 82–109. Other accessible accounts are in Kennedy, I., 'The Rhetoric of Medicine' in his *The Unmasking of Medicine* (London, George Allen & Unwin, 1981), at 1–25. The importance of the *philosophical* enterprise on which Kennedy has engaged himself – the exposure of a philosophical misconception at the centre of modern medicine – and the problems which may be encountered in the ethical enterprise are carefully and cogently explored in Maclean, *op. cit.* n. 6, at 187–201; especially important in the present context is her elaboration of how all contemporary medical education and practice '*dehumanises* and *diminishes* the people with whose health and well being they are charged' (at 199).

[51] *1 The History of Sexuality* (transl. R. Hurley) (Harmondsworth, Penguin, 1978), at 146.

[52] Duelli Klein, R., *The Exploitation of Desire; Women's Experiences with In Vitro Fertilisation* (Victoria, Aus., Deakin University Press, 1989), at 7; Corea, G. and Ince, S., 'Report of a Survey of IVF Clinics in the USA' in P. Spallone and D.L. Steinberg (eds), *Made to Order: The Myth of Reproductive and Genetic Progress* (London, Pergamon, 1987).

[53] Alto Charo, R., 'The Interaction Between Family Planning and the Introduction of New Reproductive Technologies' in Kerry Peterson, *op. cit.* n. 23, 58 at 65–66, on which this paragraph draws.

[54] 'Women Want It: IVF and Women's Motivations for Participation' in Spallone and Steinberg, *op. cit.* n. 52, and 'Mind over whose Matter? Women, In Vitro Fertilisation and the Development of Scientific Knowledge' in Maureen McNeil, Ian Varcoe and Stephen Yearley (eds), *The New Reproductive Technologies* (Basingstoke, Macmillan, 1990), at 27–57.

[55] Doyal, L., *What Makes Women Sick: Gender and the Political Economy of Health* (New Brunswick, NJ, Rutgers University Press, 1995), at 147.

[56] Anleu, *op. cit.* n. 23, at 36.

[57] Boorse, C., 'On the Distinction between Health and Disease' (1975) *Philosophy & Public Affairs* 5; Oakley, A., *Essays on Women, Medicine and Health* (Edinburgh, Edinburgh UP, 1993); Nordenfelt, C., 'On the relevance and importance of the notion of disease' (1993) 14 *Theoretical Medicine* 15; Doyal, L., *op. cit.* n. 55.

[58] Townsend, P. and Davidson, N., (ed), *Inequalities in Health*, (The Black Report) (Harmondsworth, Penguin, 1982); Williams, B., 'The Idea of Equality' in Peter Laslett and W.G. Runciman (eds), *Philosophy, Politics and Society* (Oxford, Basil Blackwell, 1962), 2nd series, at 110–31; Nozick, R., *Anarchy, State & Utopia* (Oxford, Basil Blackwell, 1974), at 233.

[59] Doyal, *op. cit.* n. 55, at 93. Are there two problems with this: (a) the effects of environment and diet on men's reproductive health; and (b) recent (contested) changes in the legal regulation of the consequences of failing to control one's fertility?

[60] *Ibid.*, at 147.

[61] A good introduction to feminisms' accounts of science is Rosser, S., *Teaching Science and Health from a Feminist Perspective* (New York, Pergamon Press, 1986); especially useful in the immediate contexts are pp. 3–22, 38–61, and 77–89.

[62] Koch, *op. cit.* n. 18 at 236.

[63] *Ibid.*, at 237.

[64] *Ibid.*, at 241.

[65] Beck, U. and Gernsheim Beck, E., *The Normal Chaos of Love* (Oxford, Polity Press, 1995), at 126, and see esp. pp. 102–39.

[66] Katz Rothman, B., *The Tentative Pregnancy: Prenatal Diagnosis and the Future of Motherhood* (New York, Viking, 1986), at 29.

[67] Beck, U., *Risk Society: Towards a New Modernity* (transl. Mark Ritter) (London, Sage, 1992), at 204.

[68] Koch, *op. cit.* n. 18 at 241.

[69] *Op. cit.* n. 55, at 145.

[70] *Ibid.*, at 146.

[71] *Ibid.*, at 145.

[72] *Ibid.*, at 147.

[73] 'Reproductive Freedom: Beyond "A Woman's Right to Choose"' (1980) *Signs: Journal of Women in Culture and Society* 674, at 675.

[74] Bennett, B., 'Gamete Donation, Reproductive Technology and the Law' in Kerry Peterson, *op. cit.* n. 23, at 41.

[75] *Ibid.*

[76] Doyal, *op. cit.* n. 55, at 149.

[77] *Proceed with Care: Final Report of the Royal Commission on New Reproductive Technologies* (Ottawa, Minister of Government Services Canada, 1993). In contrast with the Warnock Committee's slim response of 103 pages, the Baird Commission's two-volume report occupies 1,300 pages of text, recommendations and appendices and was preceded or accompanied by a dozen research reports on various aspects of the subject. Seven years on the Federal government has not yet enacted a Bill (although it has been presented twice) to implement Baird's conclusions and recommendations, or indeed any others. Dealing with Warnock from publication to legislation took a little over six years.

[78] *Ibid.*, chapter 1.

[79] *Ibid.*, at 50.

[80] *Ibid.*, at 52.

[81] *Ibid.*, at 52–58.

[82] Wolfenden Report, *Report of the Committee on Homosexual Offences and Prostitution*, Cmnd 247, 1957, para. 257.

[83] McCallum, R. B., *On Liberty* (Oxford, Oxford UP, 1946).

[84] *Beginning Lives* (Oxford, Basil Blackwell, 1987), at 15.

[85] See, for example, Rich, A., *Of Woman Born*, (1976, at 273–4).

[86] Rosalind Hursthouse, *Beginning Lives*, (1987) Basil Blackwell, p. 15.

[87] Mira Dana, quoted in Hursthouse, *op. cit.* n. 86, p. 24. This seems a purposive recall of the arguments of Rich, *supra*.

[88] House of Commons, Official Report, 23 April 1990, col. 89.

[89] For an overview of the different approaches to the place and power of the family, see Gittins, D., *The Family in Question* (Basingstoke, Macmillan, 1985), and Morgan, D.H.J., *The Family, Politics and Social Theory* (London, Routledge, 1985). For two radically different perspectives compare Barrett, M. and McIntosh, M., *The Anti-Social Family* (London, Verso, 1982) with Council of Europe, Parliamentary Assembly, Report on Family Policy (Doc. 5870, 5 April 1988) and House of Lords, Official Report, 29 November 1990, coll. 425–94, debate on Motion – The Family.

[90] But one detailed study in 1985 of one single District Health Authority estimated that at least one in six couples need specialist help at some time in their lives, because of an average infertility of two and a half years (Hull, M.G.R., 'Population Study of Causes, Treatment and Outcome in Infertility' *British Medical Journal*, 14 December 1985); *cf.* the summary of the 'Dobson Report' – Mathieson, D., 'Infertility Services in the NHS: What's Going On: a report prepared for Frank Dobson MP, House of Commons' in Lesley Doyal's essay, 'Infertility – A Life Sentence: Women and the National Health Services' in Michelle Stanworth (ed.), *Reproductive Technologies* (Oxford, Polity Press, 1987), at 174–90, arguing that the problems of infertility services are not unique to the area and that they reflect the broader failure of the NHS to meet women's needs and expectations. Doyal elsewhere suggests that infertility services reflect the general insensitivity and sexism apparent in the inadequate health care provision for women: see Doyal, L., 'Women and the National Health Service: The Carers and the Careless' in E. Lewin and V. Olesen (eds), *Women, Health and Healing* (London, Tavistock, 1985)).

[91] Warnock Report, para. 2.11, and see paras 4.16 and 5.10.
[92] House of Lords, Official Report, 6 March 1990, col. 1109.
[93] Winston *op. cit.* chapter 1, n. 10 at 163.
[94] Edelmann, R. and Golombok, S., 'Stress and Reproductive Failure' (1989) 7 *Journal of Reproductive and Infant Psychology* 79.
[95] House of Commons, Official Report, 24 April 1990, coll 230–32.
[96] House of Commons, Official Report, 23 April 1990, col. 106.
[97] House of Lords, Official Report, 6 March 1990, col. 1059; and lost again in the Commons, see House of Commons, Official Report, 20 June 1990, col. 900.
[98] See Frank Field, House of Commons, Official Report, 20 June 1990, col. 936.

Chapter 3
Embryo Research

'Although the questions of when life or personhood begin appear to be facts
susceptible of straightforward answers, we hold that the answers to such
questions are in fact complex amalgams of factual and moral judgments.'[1]

Perhaps the most remarkable fact of the embryo research debate of the 1980s was
that six years after the publication of the Warnock Report in 1984, Parliament came
to approve, in the 1990 Act, of any embryo research at all. In his survey of the
embryo research debates, Michael Mulkay has provided a reminder of the hostility
with which the Warnock proposals to limit and control embryo research were
greeted in the scientific communities and the revulsion which they inspired in
oppositional houses of moral politics.[2] Immediately following the Warnock Report,
a private member's Bill, the Unborn Children (Protection) Bill, was presented first
by Enoch Powell and then by Ken Hargreaves to successive sessions of Parliament
in 1984 and 1985. Clause 1 would have prohibited the fertilisation of a human
ovum *in vitro* other than for the purposes of subsequent re-implantation, and then
only for implantation in a specific woman authorised by the Secretary of State, and
then only within a limited period of four months. Interestingly, however, the Bills
would have allowed for the Secretary of State to permit the disposal of embryos
not inserted, but whether this would have been by perishing was never determined.
In 1985, the Powell Bill achieved a 238:66 vote which would have ended all
embryo experimentation and halted much of the programme of IVF; scientists only
gradually came to realise that they would have to fight hard if research on human
embryos was to survive at all.[3] A different perspective is offered by Professor
Robert Winston, who comments that the 1980s saw 'rather ill-informed, emotional
debates' in Parliament. 'Some of the speeches opposing the technology when
reread some nine years later now seem remarkably cranky, unreasonably suspicious and containing antique argument.'[4]

Whereas in the 1970s and 1980s David Attenborough and the BBC brought us
deep and intimate knowledge of the plant and the animal worlds, the 1990s were
marked out by Robert Winston and the Internet as the decade in which the intimate
and early life of the embryo and its constituent parts emerged from the privacy or
obscurity which they might once have enjoyed. The intimate life of the embryo
and its generational ancestors, the sperm and the egg, is now one which needs to

be understood to read the legislative framework and the regulatory apparatus which controls and directs embryological research and the prohibitions first agreed upon in 1990. A better understanding of the early developmental phases of gametes is now also necessary fully to appreciate some of the reach of the legislation, both in terms of the research which may or may not lawfully be done, and in terms of the extent to which the present regulatory framework for treatment services remains adequate to address the scientific changes which have been made in the past decade.

THE TIMING OF EARLY HUMAN DEVELOPMENT

Cells, sperm and eggs[5]

The basic living unit of life is the cell, of which each adult human has about 100 trillion. The cell is surrounded by an ultra-thin skin called a plasma membrane, within which the cell is like an intricate piece of machinery with hundreds of thousands of working parts, each localised to a specific compartment and each communicating with its cellular components. The information required to produce every one of the cell's many components in the right numbers and to place them all in the right places is encoded within its genetic material, deoxyribonucleic acid (DNA).

All cells have two separate compartments called the cytoplasm and the nucleus. The nucleus has its own membrane and sits like a ball in the middle of the cell. It contains all of the genetic material within structures called chromosomes. Single-cell organisms can carry just a single chromosome, while normal human cells carry 46. Each chromosome contains a single DNA molecule. All the cellular material that lies outside the nucleus, and inside the plasma membrane, is called cytoplasm. The cytoplasm contains the machinery that interprets genetic information flowing from the nucleus and responds to it by building all the structures that make up the cell.

There are two steps in the process of cell reproduction. Cells must generate more of their component parts as they increase their size twofold. They must also make accurate copies of each of their DNA molecules. When both of these processes are completed, cell division can occur.

Sperm and egg cells (both also known as germ cells or gametes) are distinct from every other cell in the human body. All the other cells (somatic cells) carry the *same* genetic material distributed across 23 pairs of DNA molecules, stored within 23 *pairs* of chromosomes. Each of the sperm or egg cells, however, contains only one variety of the human genome within just 23 chromosomes, but that variety is *never* the same as the one a person receives from his or her mother or father. Early in the process that leads to the production of each individual gamete, the maternal and paternal editions of the human genome exchange random 'pages' and whole chapters with each other in a very precise way so that entirely new editions of the encyclopaedia are produced.

Every sperm cell of the billions produced during a man's life and every egg cell produced by a woman bears a different composition of genetic material, a different mixture of human genome editions. It is for this reason that, with the exception of identical twins or a child created by cell nucleus replacement (CNR), it is impossible for a human couple to have two genetically identical children.

Millions of immature eggs – called oocytes – are stored in a woman's ovaries, and every month or so during the fertile period of her life, hormonal signals cause one of these oocytes to ripen into an egg that is capable of being fertilised. When the ripening process is complete, the egg is released from the ovary – an event referred to as ovulation. Upon leaving the ovary the egg begins its journey down the fallopian tube, where it remains receptive to sperm for about 20 hours. If it encounters sperm before being expelled during the woman's period then conception may take place.

The embryo

Some understanding of the development of the early embryo is useful in comprehending both the philosophical and the scientific debates about embryo experimentation. A series of important events in the developments after fertilisation can be expressed in tabular form (see Table 3.1).[6] The same information may be expressed diagrammatically (see Figure 3.1).

Table 3.1 Development of the early embryo

$1\frac{1}{2}$ hours before ovulation	LH surge (Lutenizing hormone begins)
Ovulation	
$\frac{1}{2}$–1 day after ovulation	Chemotaxis; sperm moves up a concentration gradient towards the ovum which is attracting it, leading to:
Fertilisation	
36 hours after fertilisation begins	2 cells
48 hours after fertilisation begins	4 cells
3 days	Small compact ball of 16–32 cells
4 days	Hollow ball of 64–128 cells
4–5 days	Blastocyst stage (formation of basal cell mass)
6–7 days	Implantation begins
8 days	Amniotic cavity forms
7–12 days	Trophoblast proliferates
8–13 days	Extra-embryonic mesoblast develops
11–12 days	Embryo has invaded the uterine wall and become embedded in it
13–15 days	Chorionic villi form
15–18 days	Primitive streak develops
22–23 days	Neural tube begins to close
42 days	First sign of cerebral cortex
56 days	Foetal stage begins

Figure 3.1

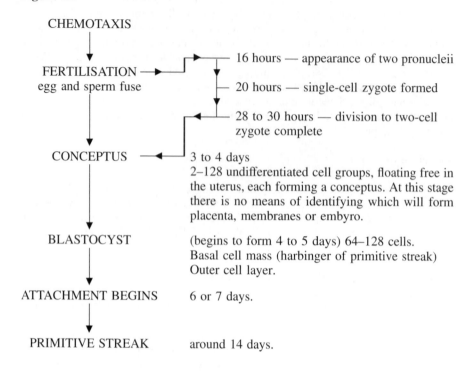

CHEMOTAXIS

↓

FERTILISATION ⟶   16 hours — appearance of two pronucleii
egg and sperm fuse

20 hours — single-cell zygote formed

28 to 30 hours — division to two-cell
zygote complete

↓

CONCEPTUS ⟵   3 to 4 days
2–128 undifferentiated cell groups, floating free in
the uterus, each forming a conceptus. At this stage
there is no means of identifying which will form
placenta, membranes or embyro.

↓

BLASTOCYST   (begins to form 4 to 5 days) 64–128 cells.
Basal cell mass (harbinger of primitive streak)
Outer cell layer.

↓

ATTACHMENT BEGINS   6 or 7 days.

↓

PRIMITIVE STREAK   around 14 days.

Figure 3.2   The reproductive process

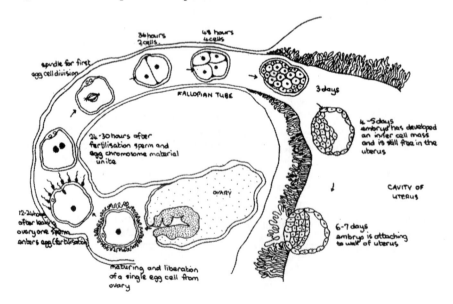

Figure 3.3   Genesis of the primitive streak

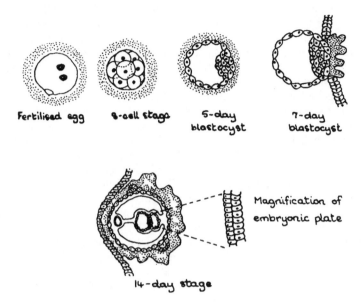

Figure 3.4   Early embryonic development

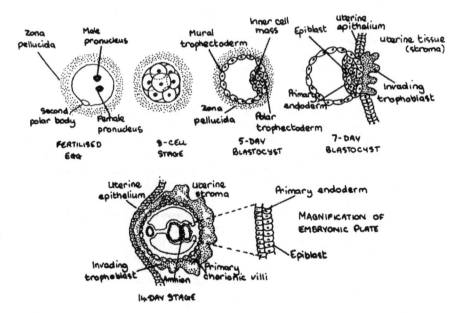

Sperm contain half the genetic information of their producer, and ova the full complement of 46 chromosomes (the carriers of genetic material, the DNA, made up of four nucleotide bases – adenine, guanine, cytosine and thymine – formed on a long chain comprising these four bases in many different sequences). The innumerable possibilities of sequences account for the variety that genetic material has shown itself capable of producing. In their famous two-page work of 1953, Watson and Crick proposed that DNA's structure was a double helix, a molecule composed of two coiled strands.[7] When DNA replication occurs as the cells divide and multiply, the two sides of the double helix separate. Then each single strand is used as the template to generate a new double helix, consisting of one molecule from the old double helix and one from the newly-generated, complementary strand. The new double helix is divided equally into two polar bodies (it is this complement which makes the possibility of inducing parthenogenesis – the development of the gamete without fertilisation – a theoretical possibility). Only one of these polar bodies takes part in the process of fertilisation, being retained in order to act as a means of disposing of surplus DNA in the newly-fertilised egg, and playing no further role in the development after fertilisation. The process by which this reduction in the chromosome number is achieved is termed meiosis.

Fertilisation is the process by which the sperm and the egg interact[8] to produce the zygote. The 1990 Act, s. 1(1) defines the end of this process: 'fertilisation is not complete until the appearance of a two cell zygote'. However, it leaves open the question when, as a matter of law, the process begins.

In an important article published as the Bill originally emerged from its Commons Committee stage, Peter Braude, Martin Johnson and John Aitken described the five stages of the interaction between the egg and the sperm. In the ovary a single mature egg is released and drawn into the egg duct about 9–16 days into the menstrual cycle. It passes into the Fallopian tube leading to the uterus. If it encounters and interacts with sperm, fertilisation will begin.

The first contact between the egg and the sperm will be as the sperm meets the cumulus cells that surround the egg. If there are few cumulus cells, they will be readily dispersed by the sperm. Alternatively, the clinician may promote fertilisation if there are few sperm by dispersing the cells either mechanically or using an enzyme. Secondly, the sperm encounters the zona pellucida, to which it binds through a zona glycoprotein. It is this contact which provides species specificity at fertilisation, and it can occur very rapidly *in vitro*. The third stage of fertilisation involves the absorption of the spermatozoon through the zona pellucida into the space between the zona and the egg itself. The sperm then attaches to the surface of the egg itself and fusion of the two cell membranes occurs, with the sperm passing through the corona radiata. It is here that the contents of the sperm enter the cytoplasm of the egg. Finally, the second polar body is ejected from the egg, and the approximation of the chromosomes of egg and sperm occurs. DNA is replicated, and after some 28–30 hours the process of fertilisation is completed and the two sets of chromosomes have come together on the new body's first metotic spindle (the structure on which chromosomes form before division) and genetic uniqueness begins.[9]

The product of this mixing is called a conceptus. During the whole of these stages the germ cells are genetically identical to all the other body cells of the parent. The process of cell division continues. Three to four days after the onset of fertilisation, the cells have increased in number from two to 128. At this stage there is no means of identifying which will subsequently form the membranes and placenta and which will create the primitive streak from which the embryo and foetus will ultimately arise; the cells are pluri or toti potential. Four or five days after fertilisation, when some 64–128 cells are present, the blastocyst begins to form, in which cells begin to differentiate and a small nodule or basal cell mass, the harbinger of the primitive streak, is identifiable along with an outer layer of cells which begin to be identifiable as the origins of the placenta and membranes. It is possible to remove a single cell from this outer layer and from which the placenta and membranes will develop without damage or detriment to the subsequent development of the remaining cells, and determine the sex of the conceptus about four or five days after the onset of the process of fertilisation. In normal human reproduction, about 80 per cent of blastocysts fail to implant, and so do not lead on to a pregnancy.

This is one of three sites from which it is possible to do embryo biopsy; another is the second polar body, which is merely a means of disposing of surplus DNA in the newly fertilised egg, playing no further developmental role after fertilisation. Because it represents spare maternal DNA, the second polar body cannot give information on the genetic contribution of the sperm. But it can be of use in some diagnoses. For example, in 80 per cent of all cases of Down's Syndrome the extra chromosome is in the egg and not from the sperm; whereas in normal development, one of the maternal chromosomal pair will end up in the egg and the other in the polar body. Another type of biopsy is possible where, in IVF, clinicians usually replace the pre-embryo in the uterus between the four- and 16-cell stages. A researcher could remove one to two cells at the eight- to 16-cell stage to test for genetic defects, using either (a) fluorescent in situ hybridisation (FISH) for chromosome disorders (most commonly where patients are at risk of transmitting an x-linked disorder, thus affecting only males, but also in patients with 'translocution', where all or part of a chromosome is misplaced or missing), or (b) polymerase chain reaction (PCR) for genetic errors that occur at the level of the gene (for example single-gene defects or triple-repeat disorders). The third, later stage, is the blastocyst stage, removing cells from the mural trophectoderm. For a fertile couple this would involve fertilisation after intercourse, followed four or five days later by recovery of the blastocyst from the uterus by lavage (washing the embryo from the uterus before it has begun the process of implantation into the uterine wall). This carries certain hazards such as damage to the blastocyst and the risk of causing ectopic pregnancy, where the blastocyst implants outside the uterus. But the flushing is said to be no more stressful for the woman than insertion of an IUD. Recovering blastocysts in this way and replacing them gives a good pregnancy rate. In addition, those who favour it argue that lavage is of great importance to research into pre-implantation diagnosis, and have successfully resisted attempts to prohibit the practice.[10]

Some people argue that work of this kind is the thin end of the wedge, leading inevitably to the application of genetic engineering to human beings. Anne McLaren, a member of the Interim Licensing Authority (ILA) and a prime scientific mover in the embryo research debate of the last ten years, argues that the opposite is true. At the moment it is impossible to replace a defective gene with a normal one. Any attempt at gene therapy would thus introduce more genetic problems than it solved. It would be pointless, therefore, to attempt gene therapy if we have effective methods of pre-implantation diagnosis.[11] In 1999, the HFEA issued a Consultation Paper on pre-implantation Genetic Diagnosis (PIGD), seeking public consultation on whether, and if so how, PIGD should be permitted and regulated beyond the four centres then licensed to carry out such work. The HFEA also asked respondents to make particular observations on the specific uses to which PIGD might be put, if more widespread use were to be permitted.

From the sixth or seventh day after fertilisation, about one in five blastocysts begins the process of attachment to the wall of the uterus. The basal cell mass begins to organise itself into a flat, oval two-tiered shape – the embryonic plate. It is still not possible to know whether the fertilisation process has produced anything that will develop beyond a cluster of cells. Each cell, being pluripotential, may go on to develop into an embryo, a hydatiform mole, or indeed, if biopsied at that stage, into many other (cloned) human embryos. Around the fourteenth day after fertilisation, if the cells have met no other unfavourable conditions in the uterus, there develops in the embryonic plate a groove – the primitive streak – into which a third layer of cells migrates. It is the development of this groove on which the Warnock Report fixed as the crucial transformation, when the Rubicon is crossed between molecular matter and potential human being. To this molecular matter scientists later gave the appellation 'pre-embryo'; biologically speaking, an important developmental event does occur at 14 days, although Silver has suggested that there are other important events that occur before that time and many more that occur later.[12]

THE MORAL STATUS OF THE EMBRYO

Jonathan Glover has, in our view quite rightly, observed that 'any right a pre-embryo may have is not diminished by calling it a pre-embryo rather than an embryo'.[13] More contentiously, he then goes on to argue that

> no one denies that [the pre-embryo] is alive, and that it is surely a member of our species rather than any other. . . . but . . . It is widely assumed that qualifying as a human being is sufficient to guarantee the possession of a right to life. But this assumption is questionable, and perhaps derives much of its plausibility from our thinking of 'human beings' in terms of our friends and neighbours. An embryo is not the kind of human being you can share a joke with or have as a friend.[14]

One difficulty with this argument is that there may be some of one's friends, and certainly many of one's colleagues, about whom one might say the same thing; in short, this objection shows us nothing of any moral substance. And notice what the argument entails: it is clear that we have a human being, 'but it is not clear that the status "human being" brings with it any moral rights'. That may be thought by many to be offensive and morally outrageous in itself. It is indeed widely assumed that qualifying as a human being is sufficient to guarantee the possession of a right to life. The history of the centuries shows us that when we think of the status 'human being' as being insufficient to guarantee a certain moral respect, many of our troubles and ills have begun.

Mulkay has recently advanced a new form of argument in relation to the 'pre-embryo': that the boundary implicit in the 14-day rule may be regularly ignored in clinical practice 'as would be parents respond to the living products of IVF technology'.[15] By this, of course, he does not mean that scientists or clinicians regularly ignore the provisions of the 1990 Act; rather, that whatever the Act says about stages of embryological development, some potential parents speak of early human embryos not as though they were 'unborn children', but rather as existing children. He cites two examples, one drawn from a television programme and one from a popular magazine, one from a woman, one from a man, both of whom suggested that they had already 'developed a strong parental relationship with their pre-fourteen-day embryos'.[16] Mulkay observes that

> . . . although the legal outcome of the parliamentary process embodies a rigid distinction between the human embryonic material deemed to exist during the fourteen days after fertilisation and the human individuals who appear subsequently, the medical practice deriving from embryo research actively fosters, at least for some participants, on some occasions, an image of the embryo as an individual person from the time of conception.

Attitudes to the embryo: ethical approaches[17]

A significant body of opinion holds that, as a moral principle, an embryo is a human being from the moment of its creation; any non-therapeutic use of any embryo is unethical and unacceptable on the grounds that an embryo is a human being entitled to full human rights from the moment of its conception, and in particular the right to life. Thus Lord Rawlinson in Parliamentary debate remarked:

> The question is asked: 'when does life commence?' Surely if it has commenced the killing is not acceptable. To those who reply 'after fourteen days' I say 'fourteen days after what?'[18]

In a similar vein, Alan Holland argued that embryo research should not be defended

> . . . by relying on the metaphysically dubious notion of the 'pre-embryo'. We should shun at all costs the capture of moral ground by verbal manoeuvres. You and me are human beings. There is only one concept of 'human being' – the biological one. . . . In contemplating embryo research we must describe accurately, honestly and without sentimentality what it is that we propose to do. We must not hide from ourselves (what we believe to be) the fact that when we experiment on human embryos we experiment on human beings.[19]

Indeed, Silver has argued that the term 'pre-embryo' has 'an alibi function'.[20]

Others argue that the embryo requires and deserves no appreciable moral attention whatsoever, that an early embryo is simply and nothing more than a collection of cells. Robert Edwards memorably once referred to the blastocyst at this stage as looking like a 'microscopic raspberry'.[21]

A middle ground between these positions recognises the special status of an embryo and accepts it as a potential human being, but argues that the respect due the embryo increases as it develops and that in the early stages, in particular, this developing respect may properly be weighed against the potential benefits arising from proposed research. This view accepts that it is justifiable to use early embryos for serious research purposes that may benefit others.

> . . . We found that the more generally held position . . . is that though the human embryo is entitled to some added measure of respect beyond that accorded to other animal studies, that respect cannot be absolute, and may be weighed against the benefits arising from research.[22]

The simple 'balancing' approach, which commended itself to the Warnock Committee when first charged to lay out ground rules for approaching human embryo research, is not the only possible approach and not indeed the only one to commend itself to those of the 'moral middle ground'. Some of the issues associated with the embryo are especially sensitive, and it has been suggested that they do not necessarily lend themselves easily to this form of balancing.

> In calibrating the proper approach to the imperatives and impetus of science and any fundamental moral and ethical objections to certain types of research it is – quite properly – observed that more needs to be shown.[23]

Hence a more restricted approach might be justified in this developing field of research science and a more cautious approach required. This approach would demand, for example, that research on those embryos created specially for research purposes, as with those created from cell nucleus replacement for use in therapeutic trials only for the possible benefits of others, would be justifiable, if at all, only if there are *no less morally problematic alternatives* for advancing this research. This would place a particularly heavy *ethical* burden on the scientific community to demonstrate clearly why this particular source of embryos for research is necessary and alone can satisfy the research questions which (to take an example) embryonic stem cell work suggests as a *required* step towards the development of therapeutic protocols.

Indeed, it may be thought that there is a new, moral objection in relation to the derivation of stem cells from embryos created either *in vitro* or by cell nucleus replacement *only* for the purposes of research, where there is never any question of the embryo itself being created in its own right. This may have an impact on the possible longer-term therapeutic opportunities suggested by cellular differentiation or reprogramming and tissue replacement treatments, particularly (in the first instance) for diseases of the brain, heart, liver or skin.

We return later in this chapter to review some of the legal doubts which the development of the technique of cell nucleus substitution disclosed in the 1990s. But in concluding this overview of the ethical positions and moral questions posed by the embryo, we introduce this further, novel question which the developments in science in the past ten years now cause us to address: what are Dolly, Millie, Christa, Alexis, Carrel and Dotcom? At one level they are, respectively, one sheep and five pigs. But, created as they were outwith the established fertilisation boundaries – either 'naturally' or 'scientifically' – sparked into life after an electrical pulse, have they been born from a *new kind of embryo*, morally speaking?

This argument comes from examining the stress previously laid by moral philosophers and theologians on the significance of fertilisation. Thus Leon Kass has argued that:

> While the egg and the sperm are alive as cells, something new and alive *in a different sense* comes into being with fertilisation . . . there exists a new individual with its unique genetic identity.[24]

This has drawn forth the following suggestion from Professor of Molecular Biology, Lee Silver:

> All non-religious objections to the cloning of human beings evaporate when a child is born through the fusion of cloned embryos. Such a child will not be genetically identical to either of her progenitor-parents and thus there cannot be any violation to her so-called 'right to genetic uniqueness'. . . .[25]

Silver's argument, while a good example of many of the *non sequiturs* which abound in this debate, illustrates clearly the role that will need to be assumed here by law in what we have called its declamatory function – marking out the boundaries (or merely a temporary fence) to the people whom we say we are and those that we want to become.

In fact, as we try to show later, the importance of the resolution of this moral debate has more than the usual significance for the legal regulation of embryo research; to paraphrase Margot Brazier, it is more than just an ethicist's tiff. Suppose that, morally, we conclude that an embryo created following cell nucleus replacement is not fundamentally a different *type* of embryo because, like all other embryos, it is (i) undoubtedly human embryonic life, and (ii) could develop into a human being. If indeed we regard this as a morally compelling reason for treating the cell nucleus replacement created embryo more or less like any other embryo, or certainly *sufficiently* like an embryo created either *in vivo* or following *in vitro*, this is to take what might be called a 'purposive' (or resulting) moral view of the embryo. That is, that the moral status of the embryo is given from what results and not (although some once thought and wrote differently) from the mechanisms or processes – or even some particular point in that mechanism or process – by which it comes into existence. If this moral point or argument is defensible then, contrary to Beyleveld and Pattinson, Brazier and Silver, the legal position based upon a purposive interpretation of the 1990 Act is similarly defensible.

Margot Brazier has aired her worries on this particular question: 'nuclear substitution challenges our understanding of what a human embryo is and what its moral claims may be'.[26] While this is one of the first essays in the UK in which this 'moral status' has been publicly raised, we suspect that it will not be the last. What Brazier means is that many opponents of embryo research centre their opposition to destruction of embryos on the view that from the creation of a zygote – after the process of fertilisation between the egg and sperm – a new genetic person comes into being. It is the fusion of egg and sperm which begins a new human creature. When the embryo is created by the cell nucleus replacement technique and not from the fusing of sperm and egg, *when fertilisation never takes place, in what (moral) sense* is an embryo as a genetically unique entity created?

The use of cell nucleus replacement to produce human embryos might be thought to create a new form of early embryonic life – one that is genetically virtually identical to the donor of the cell nucleus. This prospect goes further than that contemplated by either the Warnock Committee or Parliament when they debated these issues. As we shall later describe, the creation of embryos in this way is not ruled out under the 1990 Act, provided that any research use to which it is proposed to put the embryo is for one of the five existing purposes. Although these embryos differ in the method of their creation, they are undoubtedly human embryonic life, which, given the right conditioning, could develop into a human being. But are they the same kind of embryo – morally speaking – as that which deserves respect as a member of the human species as Warnock originally thought and as the 1990 Act decreed? As Brazier asks, 'what is the fundamental nature of cloned cell tissue or organs?'[27]

When did I begin: a moveable feast?

The philosophical argument is concentrated on the question 'Is this a human being?' Debate is joined about how it is possible to identify a human being: is it a matter of criteria, or of how we feel it is right to treat someone? That is, is it a conclusion reached or a conviction shown? The moral question, which is not disposed of by the answer to the philosophical question, is: 'Should we experiment on it?' We say that the question is not 'disposed of' here because, as was clear from the Nazi regime, some people thought, at least for some time, that it was morally permissible to experiment on human beings, and even to destroy them, in the supposed name of medical science. Of course, this assumes some intention to produce scientifically useful information and, further, that it might be ethical to use it if it was produced. But it would seem to suggest that the conclusion that 'as x is a human being, experimentation is unthinkable' is open to much deeper scrutiny, as are the reasons given for experimentation. Notice also that the conclusion 'x is not a human being' does not, of and in itself, make the conclusion that 'x may be experimented on and destroyed' necessarily any more straightforward. Some of the responses to animal research are sufficient to demonstrate that. Indeed, in their understandable zeal to apply a criterial approach to persons, some philosophers are led to argue and conclude that some animals should have more protection than some humans.

This was one of the answers given to the objectors to embryo experimentation, who pointed to the rigorous review procedures in respect of animal welfare safeguarded by the Animals (Scientific Procedures) Act 1986. Scientists argued that whereas with animals one was dealing with mature, sentient animals able to experience pain, with (at least some) embryos or foetuses that was simply not the case. And for some, the question of pain will dispose of the moral acceptability of research, whether it is carried out on a human being or not. Naturally, this will give rise to difficulties in relation to the ethics of researching upon those who are clearly human but who are unable to experience pain, such as the comatose. (Of course one might bring to them an additional series of protections or reasons, which do not apply so compellingly, if at all, to the embryo or to the pre-embryo.)

The weight that is to be attached to the fact that it is not possible to identify which cells will develop in which way(s), and that they appear to be pluripotential until the formation of the primitive streak, was one of the issues which gave rise to the moral disagreements about the significance (or otherwise) of these early stages of development. These scientific facts can only contribute to, and not adjudicate upon, the moral and philosophical disagreements, still less determine them. There is, however, an important way in which the assessment of those facts may determine the moral question of how it is right to treat the human conceptus. It may also be persuasive of the determination of the legal issue: what sort of protection, if any, should the early human embryo be given?[28]

Anne McLaren argues that the newly conceived embryo is not yet a human being not because it lacks the proper form of a human being, but because it has not yet become an individual human being. The point at which the total human being begins is at the formation of the primitive streak. 'If one tries to trace back further than that there is no longer a coherent entity. Instead there is a larger collection of cells, some of which are going to take part in the subsequent development of the embryo and some which aren't.'[29] This would seem to suggest that the pre-embryo does not have the wherewithal to count as an individual and does not stand in the required relationship to the subsequently developing human being for it to be counted as the same individual.

McLaren's argument depends on asserting that it is only when the primitive streak forms in the embryonic plate when we have 'a spatially defined entity that can develop directly into a foetus and thence into a baby, that we are for the first time justified in using the term embryo'.[30] The then Archbishop of York, John Hapgood, put it in what was to become a highly significant point of reference throughout the legislative debates in 1989:

> What is happening embryologically is the creation of persons through a process, which although it begins with genetic union, is not simply about a union of genes but also depends on a certain cellular identity which only becomes apparent at the time of the appearance of the primitive streak.[31]

And, in a passage which could serve as a metaphor not just for embryonic existence and human life but for the whole of the moral debates which these issues engendered, he said:

> By and large a biological approach to life is rooted in gradualism. . . . The same is true in the development of individual lives. They begin with chemistry and they reach their fulfilment in mystery. . . . Biologically speaking we are looking at a continuous process. Perhaps we can make the significance of this a little more clear by giving your Lordships an analogy. Exactly ten years ago a mathematician called Mandelbrot first discovered what is now called the Mandelbrot set. It is a set of points which can be mapped out as a computer graphic to form the most amazing, beautiful and complex structure that it is possible to imagine. It is a picture of literally infinite depth. If one magnifies the details of any part of the picture, one finds that in them are whole worlds of further detail which are always beautiful, which never repeat themselves and which always reveal more and more detail, on and on, *ad infinitum*. How is the Mandelbrot set made? It is made by the use of an absurdly simple equation with only three terms. The secret lies in the process. It is a process whereby the

answer to one use of the equation becomes the starting point for the next. In other words, it is a cumulative process, just like evolution in which one life form builds on another and just like embryology in which the development of one cell provides the context for the development of its neighbours and its successors.[32]

This analogy was supported and echoed by Gordon Dunstan, a theological member of the ILA, who was quoted by David Steele in the House of Commons debate:

For upwards of 2,000 years the embryo has been said to denote growth of the organism in the womb from the time of the first formation of the body parts until their completion followed by the fetal stage in which the completed baby grows to viability. Now that science has revealed a vital pre-embryonic stage of cellular activity before organogenesis can begin an appropriate name should be given to it. Pre-embryo seems a proper name to describe this stage in development.[33]

One response which has been made to these arguments is of the 'but I'm in there somewhere' type (i.e., that even though it is not possible to identify one, individual human being in the pluripotential cells, it is sufficient to be able to aver that an identifiable individual will in due course emerge from the cluster). Holland responds to this by arguing that 'we live forwards not backwards. The very question, "when did I begin?", encourages one to overlook this simple fact'.[34]

There is a stronger sense of this argument, which is that although no cell in the early stages of development is earmarked for a particular future role, cell commitment is a gradual process. The potency of a cell, the total of the things into which it can develop if put in the appropriate environment, becomes more and more restricted as development proceeds in response to external stimuli. McLaren's implicit allusion, to the lack of a spatially defined entity so far as the pre-embryo is concerned, may well be predicated upon and be a response to the 'I'm in there somewhere' sort of argument, but that argument itself proceeds on the basis of the whole embryo, and not just some special part of it. That many of the cells are destined to be extra-embryonic does not mean that the whole does not contain some very important part.

As we have noted, until the fourteenth day cells are pluripotential, and until the appearance of the primitive streak it is not known whether they will develop into a hydatiform mole; into twins; into one embryo; or degenerate into nothing. It is on this basis that the fourteenth day is said to be important. But the response often invoked is that the fact that the cells are pluripotential and that they have a unique genetic encoding from the end of fertilisation tells us only about the limits of our knowledge and nothing about the embryo. Certainly it tells us nothing about how it is right to treat the embryo. Indeed, in terms of selection of biologically relevant dates, the acquisition of further knowledge may affect our approach to research up to the fourteenth day, or even beyond it. For example, we might push backwards, towards the formation of the basal (or inner) cell mass in the blastocyst, around the fifth day after the onset of fertilisation. Or we may come to say (as some already do) that the formation of the primitive streak tells us nothing of moral significance. Here, the argument is that useful knowledge that might be gained can be acquired only from the onset of organogenesis, which will occur from about the fourteenth day or later. An example of this sort of reasoning is given by Williamson:

. . . organogenesis – whether we are studying limb formation . . . , the heart in septum defects, or the nervous system – for the most part occurs at between fourteen and twenty-eight days of embryonic development. It is this area of research, which is central to the understanding of congenital malformation, which in our view would be most inhibited were a strict fourteen-day rule to be implemented.[35]

In that sense, we may come to rely on the fourteenth day as being only the beginning of the process of fertilisation, whereas what we are (morally) interested in preserving is something beyond that stage.

Thus, we might characterise this sort of claim of pluripotentiality as a weak sense in which the claim to individuation is being made. There is, however, a strong sense in which this claim can be put. If it is the case (if the 'biological facts show') that in a two-, four- or eight- cell stage embryo, any one cell can be extracted and that it will itself divide in order to produce another embryo, and that such cells will sometimes themselves divide naturally, then individuation is not just a sufficient condition, it is a necessary condition for taking of a human life, as opposed to the life of a cell.

These opposing arguments can be rephrased by asking: 'What weight do we attach to this mass of undifferentiated cells?' In the weak sense (a state of ignorance argument) we can respond by saying that we have no means of knowing which cells are which and that it seems a matter of chance what will develop from which. This sort of argument is most characteristic of that deployed during the Parliamentary debates. It also characterises the scientific arguments on which they are based. However, Evans's suggestion is that there is a strong sense in which the lack of differentiation may be approached. In that, until the fourteenth day, it is not possible to say whether the cells will form a hydatiform mole; one embryo; two embryos; or even millions of embryos (if cells are progressively biopsied and encouraged to develop to the 16–32 cell stage when more are biopsied, and so on). In that sense, there is a strong logical difference in talking about a human being before, and speaking about one after, some time of organisation (whether at 14 days or some other time). The point of individuation (14 days or whatever) is when we can describe a human life. Before this, as long as the cells are genuinely undifferentiated, we cannot speak of a human life. There is no doubt that there is a fertilised ovum, nor that it may be the pre-embryonic stage of human life; but that is not the same as a pre-embryo, still less an embryo.[36] The particularly salient aspect of Evans's argument is that it acts as a stopper against the argument that what we are interested in is not the beginning of the formation of the primitive streak, but (some later point) its completion, in the same way that the beginning of the process of fertilisation is now held to tell us nothing. The attraction of the strong sense of individuation is that it delineates the outer ambit of that concept, and not some further moveable feast.

If then, we have spare embryos and no willing woman into whom they could be placed, there arises an important philosophical distinction between killing and letting die. If it is possible to do something about the saving of a life, it may be killing if we fail to do that. Where we are incapable of saving the life then all that can be said is that we have let it die ('allowed it to perish', see s. 14(1)(d)). If we concentrate only on the consequence (the embryo is dead) then we will find the distinction between the means of death irrelevant. If, however, we think that the distinction between killing and letting die describes the morally relevant difference between the two deaths – for one of which we are indeed responsible (and maybe culpable), but for the other of which we are not – then we may be morally justified in proceeding to treat the two deaths, and the two ways of dying, very differently.

THE PARLIAMENTARY DEBATES ON EMBRYO RESEARCH: THE 1990 BILL

Mulkay observes in the course of his analysis of these Parliamentary debates that

> the basic structure of moral argument was identical on both sides of the debate in that they both endorsed the principle of the sanctity of human life and both regarded research on human individuals as immoral. The critical difference between the two sides lay, not in their overall style or structure of argumenta-tion, but in their judgment of when the developing human embryo becomes an individual and, accordingly, when the moral principle requiring protection of the individual comes into effect.[37]

We turn now briefly to review how these philosophical and ethical positions were played out in the original Parliamentary debates.

Arguments against embryo research

The conservative position on embryo research was that it and assisted reproduction were radical departures which contravened fundamental human rights, threatened the long-standing structure of family life, and which could easily lead towards a world in which science intervened increasingly in human affairs and 'began to focus its amoral gaze upon the most intimate and morally sensitive areas of human conduct'.[38] Those who opposed all such research, regulated or not, argue that any such 'benefits' are bought at a price which is unacceptable. The fundamental point of objection is that from conception (when the process of fertilisation begins) a unique human being is created with exactly the same rights and interests as any other human being, whether adult or child. A variant is that this full protection attaches from the point of syngamy, when the process of genetic fusion of the sperm and the egg is completed, about 30 hours after the onset of fertilisation. Research which leads to the eventual destruction of the embryo is, on these views, morally no different from murder. Another variant holds that, being a human person, the embryo is unable to consent to research being undertaken on it. At the least, then, it is only research clearly and demonstrably for the therapeutic benefit of that embryo alone which might be justified. Others object to such research because they claim that animal studies can yield all the same information anyway, or because such 'experiments' with embryos put society on a slippery slope to even more awful possibilities, or because the whole development of embryology amounts to 'playing god' and interfering with human life in ways which recall the abhorrent regime of the Nazi concentration camps. Perhaps the most forceful exposition of this view was put by the Earl of Lauderdale in debate in the House of Lords. Opposing research on embryos he said:

My conscience requires that I say that I believe that this legislation is playing God in the most intimate and sacred centre of life itself. If the embryo were not human then experimentation would have little purpose. Thanks to what we have consented to here, life may now be created simply for laboratory experimentation, however noble the purposes of that experimentation may be. The ethics of human vivisection have been condemned ever since classical Alexandria, and I believe that they are implicitly at work here. In exchanging the ethics of the farmyard for those of the family, we believe that human debasement has plumbed new depths.[39]

A forceful argument which was heard occasionally in the Parliamentary debates concerned the extent to which 'destructive' embryo research represented a major derogation from the Helsinki Declaration of 1964 as amended in 1975. That Declaration, which is one of the governing instruments of ethical control of medical practice, provides in part that 'the interests of science and society should never take precedence over considerations related to the well-being of the subject'. Many made it clear that they were opposed only to research that caused the death or destruction of the embryo and not that which was intended for its therapeutic benefit. Even so, it was on the basis of the Helsinki Declaration that the use of the term 'pre-embryo' to describe the conceptus in its first 14 days was regarded as a neologism, a piece of linguistic engineering as dazzling as the reproductive engineering which it was supposed to serve.

Research with human pre-embryos, opponents charge, is not and has never been concerned with the treatment of genetic disorders or chromosomal abnormalities but with their prevention. It was accepted by supporters of research that embryo experimentation has neither identified or cured any genetic disease. But they responded by suggesting that this was to fail to understand or to have ignored all the arguments which favoured continued research: gene therapy is in its infancy, the ability to 'engineer' faulty genes so that the dysfunction may be overcome is at its dawn. Opponents responded by asserting that the 'fact' that it is only at the fourteenth day after fertilisation that an identifiable human embryo is present is a failure not of the genetic programming of that embryo but of our own human processes and procedures for assessing identifiable evidence. It is in both senses a failure of our vision.

It is now sometimes forgotten that three members of the Warnock Committee expressed their dissent from the majority:

> The beginning of a person is not a question of fact but of decision made in the light of moral principles. The question ['when does the human person come into existence?'] must therefore be refined further. It thus becomes 'At what stage of development should the status of a person be accorded to an embryo of the human species?' Different people answer this question in different ways. Some say at fertilisation, others at implantation, yet others at a still later stage of development. Scientific observation and philosophical and theological reflection can illuminate the question but they cannot answer it.[40]

Building on this approach, the dissentients held that the special status of the human embryo, to which all members of the Committee were committed, did not depend on the decision as to when it becomes a person. Before that point, its potential for development to the stage where everyone would accord it the status of a human person was sufficient to ensure that nothing should be done to reduce the possibility of a successful implantation of the embryo:

> . . . in the event of there being more embryos than it is judged [by the clinician] right to implant at any one time the remainder should be frozen with a view to implantation at a later date or allowed to die. They should not be used for experimentation. Still less should they be deliberately created for the purpose of experimentation.[41]

On this latter question, of embryos created specifically for the purposes of research, a further four members, while permitting research on 'spare' embryos created during the provision of treatment services, joined in dissenting from the acceptability of embryos created specifically for research purposes.[42]

In debate, an amendment in the House of Lords limiting research to those 'spare' embryos donated by a woman who no longer had any need or desire for them and criminalising any other matter of research, was defeated by 214 votes to 80. Lord Bridge, opposing the amendment, argued that the 'moral scrupulosity' which distinguishes between the propriety of research upon a spare embryo and the iniquity of research upon a specifically created embryo 'may be an admirable subject for debate in the senior common room but it has no place at all in the dock of the Old Bailey'.[43] This lacklustre approach was countered more forthrightly by Lord Robertson,[44] who argued that it would be unthinkable to grow a person through birth to adult life solely for the purpose of carrying out research on her or him: 'The principle is surely the same and the difference is one of degree when one is dealing with an embryo.' Similar arguments were rehearsed in the House of Commons, both in Committee and on the debate on the Report, where further unsuccessful attempts were made to limit the practice of research to embryos obtained during the course of treatment services which were 'spare' to that treatment and which otherwise would have perished.

Perhaps the most consistent approach of those opposed to embryo research, admitted no concessions in terms of the potential benefits or the lack of specificity with possible alternatives to such research. Proponents of this view hold that from the beginning of the fertilisation process the embryo is a new human life – the fusion of the sperm and egg introduces an 'intrinsic organising power'[45] – which independent of further outside stimulus represents a small, developing human being. This fact alone should govern its status, dignity and rights under the law. No wrong could justifiably be done to this life, even for the right reasons or for a noble cause. To research destructively on it is to discriminate against it on the basis not of its humanity but of its size. In debate this point was most clearly put by Michael Alison:

> . . . the embryonic human individual . . . has been imperceptible, invisible and not in evidence but essentially, logically and potentially there from the moment of fertilisation.[46]

Bernard Braine argued that the human embryo is growing and developing at a tremendous rate. It has an orientation towards growth and is thus different from the previously inert sperm and egg. The simple fact is that the human embryo is a tiny human being, which has all the potential to become a foetus, a baby, a child and an adult, given a favourable environment and appropriate nutrients. He summed up these arguments by arguing that

> when one bases decision making on the proposed benefits of a type of research, rather than its morality, one will always be under pressure to extend that limit when greater benefits are envisaged. That is no way to make law. The anticipated benefits seem compelling but they are misleading.[47]

And in the House of Lords, Lord Kennet had objected to seeing the beginning of moral worth at 14 days because, he said, it encapsulated a typical reductionist myth: it may be true, but it was not important.[48]

There were several other types of argument against the use of embryos for research purposes which were deployed. First was that rehearsed by Dale Campbell Savours. Perhaps surprisingly, he was the only MP to refer explicitly to any radical feminist views. When he did so, he quoted from the arguments put forward by the Feminist International Network of Resistance to Reproductive and Genetic Engineering (FINNRAGE), formed in Vellinge, Sweden in 1985. FINNRAGE, while pro-abortion, is opposed to research on embryos and the development and application of technologies derived from embryo research. They argue that reproductive and genetic technologies are harmful to all women: they destroy women's physical integrity; exploit their procreativity; and attempt to undermine women's struggle for control of their own reproduction.

A second line of argument and dispute concerned the adequacy of other sources of research, such as the human egg or animals. On the latter, it was argued that it is not possible to extrapolate the results of animal studies to humans because human embryos react differently to other mammalian embryos under various conditions. The differences in their physiological make-up were also stressed.

Third, opponents of embryo research pointed to the experiences of other countries in which research has already been prohibited. For example, in Australia in both South Australia and Victoria, IVF programmes claimed increased success rates since prohibition, citing 17–18% better success rates than those suggested by the figures for the UK in the ILA fourth report in 1989. Critics of this argument responded by pointing out that South Australia had not banned therapeutic research, and also questioned the age (and hence the fertility) of the patients involved in the IVF programmes when compared with UK clinics.

A similar disagreement surrounded claims that embryos were unnecessary for research into genetic disease. Opponents argued that recent US reports had suggested that techniques of molecular biology used to diagnose genetic disorder would be better applied to gametes than to the early embryo. The necessity of embryo research was also questioned by pointing to the development and deployment of laboratory-based molecular biology and DNA recombinant technology. This, it was said, has been applied recently on blood and tissue samples from consenting human subjects, leading to the identification of the exact chromosomal localisation in the human genome of the abnormal genes responsible for diseases such as cystic fibrosis (the gene for which was discovered in Toronto from research on DNA taken from an ordinary cell); Huntington's chorea; haemophilia; myotonic muscular dystrophy; one form of peroneal muscular atrophy and Duchenne muscular dystrophy, the gene for which was identified in December 1987 at Boston Children's Hospital. In addition, research not involving embryos has produced advances as diverse as those on auto-immune disease (Cambridge, Mass.); sickle cell anemia (at the National Institute of Medical Research); and retinitis pigmentosa (Trinity College, Dublin). Kay Davies, head of the molecular genetics group at the Institute of Molecular Medicine in Oxford, was quoted in the debates as suggesting that during the 1990s tests would be discovered and developed for the defective genes that cause the most common severe genetic disorders. Indeed, it was argued that the benefits are overstated, in that even if every embryo with cystic fibrosis were discarded, it would take 1,250 years to halve the frequency with which the gene occurs. It was also said that a very high incidence of congenital defects and gene mutations occur in families with no history of disorders and no high-risk factors. Hence, screening of all potential parents might be necessary if the effect on disease was to be other than marginal.

Lastly, opponents of embryo research pointed to the increasing study of seminal fluids and the functioning of the female immune system, both of which appear to hold out prospects equal to those of the development of IVF, as an alternative approach to the understanding of infertility. Other alternative approaches to infertility treatment, including microsurgery, gene therapy and IVF without superovulation, were also highlighted. One clinic, the Jessop in Sheffield, reports that one in four of their patients who are not superovulated and who finally receive an embryo become pregnant, although not all of them run to term.

These alternatives to experimentation were supplemented by appeals to international legislative comparisons; several European countries had already banned research and the European Parliament, following a debate on the Rothey Report, had voted for an eventual ban. Indeed, even if the 'restrictive' provisions of the Bill had been enacted and embryo experiments had been prohibited, it would still have been permissible under sch. 2, para. 1(d) to screen embryos for genetic defects before implantation.

Arguments in favour of embryo research

Two different types of arguments can be discerned from those who were in favour of embryo research: a response to the criticisms made by those opposed to research; and advocacy of the value of research. We consider each type of argument separately, although there is some overlap.

Responses to critics   Those who argued that embryo research was permissible did so on a number of grounds. Suppose that we refocus on the question of whether, whatever its status, it was right or permissible to experiment on the human person in embryonic form. Here the question of whether we are speaking of a human pre-embryo or a pre-embryo human becomes important. And here, scientific evidence might enable us to reach a conclusion with which we felt more comfortable; a conclusion with which, quite literally, we thought we could live. That, for example, the embryo is incapable of experiencing pain might be thought to be quite relevant. That it could not envisage its history or its future, for example, or that others to whom it is most closely related, such as its genitors, felt that it was right (not just all right, but morally permissible) to subject it to non-therapeutic research for the benefit of others, might be thought to be highly relevant (if not of itself conclusive). An appeal might here again be made to the 'scientific facts', for reassurance as to what was being experimented on. Fears of the 'slippery slope' kind would be prevented, because the foetus, the neonate, the baby, the child and the adult all differ from the embryo in important and morally significant ways.

The argument was advanced that we accept post-coital contraception, such as the IUD, which acts to prevent implantation of the fertilised ovum. Indeed, the Attorney-General has gone so far as to advise that this and other techniques which prevent the implantation are not abortifacients.[49] The argument proceeded that if this practice was condoned, the same entity – the fertilised ovum – could not be given a different status here. Of course, that argument ignores the different sorts of reasons that one might want to give for favouring, tolerating or opposing abortion and embryo research. Concern to set limits to embryo research is sometimes dismissed on the basis that if abortion is allowed then concern for the embryo is misplaced. But if there is no metaphysical frontier, there is 'the possibility that abortion and embryo research should be treated differently, perhaps because the reasons supporting them are of different weight'.[50]

Responding to some of the charges made in the attempt to limit research to 'spare' embryos alone, and not to have embryos created specifically for the purposes of research, Lord Walton argued that research into the mechanisms of fertilisation and on chromosomal abnormalities which cause miscarriages or malformations could be done only by investigation of deliberately fertilised normal eggs from normal donors with no intention of providing a treatment service.[51] A further line of research, known as polar body biopsy, which involves the removal of chromosomal material from the egg before fertilisation and which may eventually be an effective way of avoiding embryo biopsy, could never be justified ethically unless prior validation had been made by deliberately fertilising such biopsied eggs not in the course of providing treatment services but to see how the biopsy affected their development. The improvement in IVF techniques and the development of freezing techniques will, in any case, mean that the numbers of 'spare' eggs and embryos available will be reduced. Nonetheless, according to Walton, it remained important that embryos donated in the course of treatment services should be available for research. The small number of 'spare' embryos would not be sufficient on their own to allow for the study of the metabolism or the chemical behaviour of the dividing embryo in its early stages, and study of the development of its chromosomes as well as the production of the pre-implantation hormone which promotes implantation in the uterus would be compromised. And in relation specifically to research into Duchenne muscular dystrophy and cystic fibrosis, he argued that while it is already known that embryo biopsy is possible, the next crucial step is to extract DNA from the single biopsied cell to determine whether or not the dystrophic gene is present. More research would be needed to perfect this technique.

In summary, Walton argued for the preventative approach to genetic disease through continued research. It was surely preferable, he said, to identify within that group of cells resulting from fertilisation the presence of a harmful gene, and to allow that group of cells to degenerate naturally, than for a woman to carry a child with a major, fatal, crippling disease. He pleaded that it must surely be preferable to undertake such screening than to allow the pregnancy to proceed to ten-12 weeks and then to see whether or not the gene is present and carry out an abortion. And of alternatives to embryo research, such as examining the chromosomal material in the polar body that is discarded by the egg and plays no further part in its development, despite advances in DNA technology, studies on the discarded polar body are said to be unreliable as a means of detecting genetic abnormality with any degree of confidence. This work requires the removal of the polar body before it is naturally discarded, and there are fears that such manipulation of the ovum prior to fertilisation might impair fertilisation or produce foetal abnormalities.

Advocating embryo research   Everyone in Parliament was in favour of banning embryo research and making it subject to the criminal law. The matter of difference, when it arose, was at what stage it should be banned. Some of the commentators in the debates pointed out that if for some reason the Bill should not pass, embryo research would continue in its statutorily unregulated fashion and ostensibly subject to no law. Indeed, it seemed to be accepted on all sides, and the debates proceeded on this basis, that as the law stood it was entirely up to an individual researcher when research was to be terminated because there was no express legal provision against it.

Given the scheme of protection afforded by the common law and by statute, it would have been surprising if an alternative conclusion had been advanced. Although John Keown has argued that there is nothing in principle to prevent the courts exercising wardship jurisdiction over a fertilised egg or embryo, this is not a popular view. Keown is correct to the extent that he shows that the courts' reluctance to countenance the wardship of an unborn foetus in the uterus – as attempted in *Re F (in utero)* [1988] 2 All ER 193 – proceeded on the basis that the courts have no power to direct the life of the pregnant woman. This constraint does not apply to the embryo outside the body. Nonetheless, the courts have refused to expand the ambit of the common law to include a foetus (as we discuss below). Therefore, it was always unlikely that the law in 1990 would operate to protect an embryo from research.

When the Parliamentary speeches in favour of embryo research are further analysed it is interesting to observe, as Mulkay has done, that those made by the representatives of the scientific community were much more restrained in their assessment of the role of scientific evidence than those of more enthusiastic supporters: 'Scientists themselves never maintained that [facts about early embryological development] could be used unequivocally to decide the moral issues under examination; nor did they endorse the suggestion that those arguing the case for embryo research had special access to the realm of rational thought.'[52]

Of course, the issues involved here are fundamental to any society and the way in which it orders its moral thinking, argumentation and boundaries. The claimed benefits for continued research are great. It is held to offer potential for improvements in assisted conception (with one contention that it could increase the 'successful' outcomes in IVF from around 10–20% to nearer 70%) and better understanding of causes of unexplained infertility (thought to affect 40,000 couples in the United Kingdom) and repeated miscarriages (with 75,000 miscarriages a year in the UK this accounts for more than one in five of all pregnancies).

Additionally, it is argued that continued research will assist in the development of newer contraceptive techniques – one project has sought to develop a vaccine which would enable the egg to repel sperm from seeking to fertilise it. (As we have seen, amendments which sought to prevent such research as 'frivolous' were defeated.) However, the greatest potential for continued research is in the development of safe and reliable techniques for pre-implantation diagnosis of genetic abnormalities. Approximately 14,000 infants (2% of all babies) are born each year with a genetic defect, and half of those are born with an obvious single gene inherited defect, of which there are over 4,000. Imminent 'breakthroughs' in relation to cystic fibrosis, muscular dystrophy and thalassemia fuelled the 1990 debate.

The belief by laypersons that scientists would be able to deliver effective control over a wide range of genetic diseases in a form that would benefit the population at large 'was critical in establishing a substantial parliamentary majority in the Lords in favour of embryo research'.[53] And yet many of those who had participated in the long process of moral appraisal 'remained unconvinced and deeply disturbed . . . about the future'. For them, Parliamentary approval of embryo research marked not '. . . the resolution of a passing legislative difficulty, but an ominous shift in the balance of power between science and society which would have lasting repercussions in the years to come'.[54]

Mulkay's invaluable review and examination of the Parliamentary debates leads him to the following evaluation of the way in which they were structured and conducted. Those opposed to embryo research and those in favour did not differ significantly on their use of reasoned argument, in their dependence on authoritative pronouncement, in their reliance on established moral principle or in their recourse to dogmatic assertion. 'Opposition to embryo research was weakened by the absence of consistent religious leadership and by divisions within religious opinion which made religious condemnation of research on human embryos appear increasingly arbitrary.'[55]

The triumph of the pro-research lobby was based on three cardinal factors; three critical changes in parliamentarians' conception of embryo research:

(a) the transformation of participants' understanding of the experimental subject of embryo research;

(b) the increasing emphasis on the possibility of controlling genetic disease without altering the genetic make-up of human individuals; and

(c) replacement of its opponents' rhetoric of fear concerning the long-term impact of embryo research with an alternative rhetoric of hope.[56]

It was not the superior rationality of the supporters of embryo research, nor indeed their detached assessment of the facts which carried the day, but rather the fact that they were successful

. . . in imposing on the debate the cultural authority of science, and of generating thereby a sufficient degree of dogmatic conviction and unquestioning faith about the morality and benefits of embryo research among the decision-makers in Parliament.[57]

THE LEGAL STATUS OF THE EMBRYO

We shift the focus now away from the moral and the Parliamentary debates which led up to the enactment of the embryo research provisions of the 1990 Act and turn to what is, in the whole reproductive technology debate, probably the most contested yet difficult question, of the *legal* status of the *in vitro* embryo. Sheila McLean has suggested that although the status to be given to the human embryo/foetus 'may seem like an unnecessarily esoteric question,' it is 'one of increasing practical relevance to women, doctors and the law'.[58]

In the United Kingdom

The main questions with which a lawyer confronted with determining the status of the embryo will be concerned are:

(a)   Who has control over the *frozen* embryo?
(b)   In what way if at all is that control restricted?
(c)   What limits apply to the way in which gametes and embryos can be used?

The Human Fertilisation and Embryology Act 1990, although not commonly seen in this way, was a major piece of restrictive legislation. It imposed limits on the use and control of embryos where none had effectively operated before. The limitations on the research use of the embryo, the restrictions on their use in the provision of treatment services and the protection given to children subsequently born alive who can show that they have suffered injury as a result of the negligent handling of gametes or embryonic material, are all major steps in the *legal* protection given to the embryo. But what status is being recognised?

Before the 1990 Act there were a number of cases which might have arisen where the legal *status* of the embryo would be critical in determining its fate. Some of these conundrums may have survived the legislation. First, suppose that in a fire at an IVF clinic a clinician deliberately destroys an embryo created from A's and B's gametes:

(a)   Does he or she kill the embryo?
(b)   Does he or she convert it?
(c)   Is the claim on any insurance policy for damage to goods or for loss of life?
(d)   Can A and B claim for post-traumatic stress disorder caused by the loss of an embryo formed from their gametes?

The point of this example is that the clinician's act operates against the genitors, but especially against the woman's interests. Thus recognising the embryo as a 'person' would hardly interfere with any interest which she has; on the contrary, it would serve to protect or preserve it. Additionally, the clinic would be likely to carry insurance against the loss.[59]

These two remarkable features – that allowing the claim would not interfere with any interest of the woman and that liability insurance would cover any general damages recoverable – are the salient features of the *single* current exception to general maternal immunity to suit from a foetus and 'furnishes a rare instance of a legal duty owed directly to the unborn infant'. In this hitherto unique case a child born with congenital disabilities as a result of injuries incurred as a result of its mother's negligent driving has a direct cause of action against her; in reality, of course, against the company with which she has placed the risk against which she must by law insure.[60] While we may conclude that even in our hypothetical case the law would not recognise the embryo as a 'person', this is merely symptomatic of the blindness of English law to the need to make supportable distinctions based on the sort of interest which requires protection.[61]

Andrew Grubb has suggested that:

> When a court is seized of a case . . . [it] would have no choice but to treat an extra-corporeal embryo as either a person or a chattel. The likely outcome is that it would be held to be a chattel. Such law as exists points in this direction and the pragmatism of the common law would see that to treat an extra-corporeal embryo as a chattel is more consistent with common sense than for it to be given the rights of a person.[62]

How does this conclusion come about?

Early attitudes to the foetus   Legal attitudes to foetuses and new-borns have varied over time; some cultures proscribing abortion and infanticide, some early codes giving the foetus indirect protection by prohibiting the striking of a woman so as to cause the death of her unborn child. In other cultures abortion and infanticide were seen as acceptable resolutions of dilemmas posed by scarce resources, birth defects or sexual balance.[63] Neither ancient Greek nor early Roman law forbade abortion, the latter not regarding the unborn child as a living human being. The common law has long drawn a fundamental distinction between the foetus and the child following birth. Recent developments in common law jurisprudence have, however, seen the recognition of interests – notice the importance of that term, interests, not rights – against harm to the child before its birth.

That a foetus is not a person within the common law has been reiterated on a number of occasions when the issue has arisen in a variety of ways in common law courts. Under UK law the foetus has no legal existence separate from its mother. This has been affirmed in such disparate cases as:

- where a husband attempted to prevent his wife from having an abortion: *Paton v Trustees of the BPAS* [1979] 1 QB 276;
- where, suing on behalf of the foetus, a man attempted to prevent his former girl-friend from having an abortion: *C v S* [1988] 1 QB 135;
- where, supposedly for the benefit of the foetus, an attempt was made to have the foetus made a ward of court so as to control the behaviour of a woman who was 36 weeks' pregnant: *Re F (in utero)* [1988] Fam 122;
- where a claim was made in respect of congenital disabilities before the coming into force of the Congenital Disabilities (Civil Liability) Act 1976: *Burton v Islington Health Authority* [1992] 3 All ER 833; *de Martell v Merton and Sutton HA* [1992] 3 All ER 820 and *de Martell v Merton and Sutton HA* [1992] 3 All ER 833 CA;

- where the right of a woman to refuse treatment was upheld even where that would lead to her death and that of the viable foetus that she was carrying: *S v St George's Healthcare NHS Trust* [1998] 3 WLR 936, at 957A;
- where a defendant had stabbed a pregnant woman whose child later died, the House of Lords held that the foetus is not a person for the purposes of the law of murder and manslaughter: *Attorney-General's Reference (No. 3 of 1994)* [1998] AC 245; and
- in a common law jurisdiction with a Bill of Rights and a Constitution, the Canadian Supreme Court has held that the common law does not recognise the foetus as a legal or juridical person possessing rights: *Winnipeg Child & Family Services (Northwest Area)* v *G* [1997] 3 SCR 925. A similar outcome has been endorsed by the High Court of Australia: *Attorney General (Qld) (ex rel. Kerr)* v *T* (1983) 57 ALJR 285.

Some examples of *dicta* drawn from these cases will illustrate the point at issue:

(a)   In *Paton* v *BPAS*, Sir George Baker said: 'A foetus cannot, in English law, in our view, have any right of its own at least until it is born and has a separate existence from the mother.'

(b)   In *Re F (in utero)*, the Court of Appeal held that an unborn child lacks legal personality to be made a ward of court because it would be incompatible with the rights of the mother.

(c)   In *C* v *S*, (putative father attempts as next friend of the foetus to prevent his former girlfriend having an abortion), Mrs Justice Heilbron at first instance, in holding that a child injured while in the womb may be the subject of a legal action by the child once it is born, said that 'the claim crystallises on the birth, at which date, but not before, the child attains the status of a legal persona, and thereupon can then exercise that legal right'.

(d)   In *Attorney-General's Deference (No. 3 of 1994)*, Lord Mustill said that 'The emotional bond between the mother and her unborn child was also of a very special kind. But the relationship was one of bond, not of identity. The mother and the foetus were two distinct organisms living symbiotically, not a single organism with two aspects. The mother's leg was part of the mother, the foetus was not. . . . It is sufficient to say that it is established beyond doubt for the criminal law, as for the civil law that the child *en ventre sa mère* does not have a distinct human personality, whose extinguishment gives rise to any penalties or liabilities at common law.'

(e)   At first instance in *de Martell*, Mr Justice Phillips observed that: 'The human being does not exist as a legal person until after birth. The foetus enjoys no independent legal personality. . . . An unborn child lacks the status to be the subject of a legal duty.'

This classical view was restated by the Warnock Committee in their Report:[64]

> We examined the current position of the *in vivo* embryo in law. The human embryo *per se* has no legal status. It is not, under law in the United Kingdom accorded the same status as a child or an adult, and the law does not treat the human embryo as having a right to life. However, there are certain statutory provisions that give some level of protection in various respects.

The Committee concluded that the embryo of the human species was entitled to special consideration and yet recommended that the couple who have stored an embryo should have rights to use and dispose of it;[65] that there be rights of sale of gametes and embryos where licensed[66] and limited circumstances where drug testing may be carried out on embryos created specifically for that purpose.[67] This led Ian Kennedy and Andrew Grubb pointedly to ask:

> What special status does an embryo have if it may be the object of research during the first fourteen days of gestation and thereafter destroyed? What is ownership if it is not the right to control, including to dispose of by sale, or otherwise?[68]

An embryo *in vitro* is never carried by a woman and hence it falls outside the law's ambit in this regard. As Margot Brazier wrote of the embryo before the passage of the 1990 Act, 'it exists and dies in a legal limbo'.[69] It has been suggested by John Keown that these cases establish nothing about the forms of protection which could have been made available to the *in vitro* embryo before the 1990 Act. In particular, he suggested that because it was *in vitro*, no question of conflict with the mother's rights arose, and hence it could be possible to make such an embryo a ward of court.[70] This view is strongly challenged by Andrew Grubb, according to whom:

> . . . it would be quite wrong to see the cases as only failing to recognise the legal status of the unborn child because to do so would lead to a certain conflict with the pregnant mother's interests. . . . if an unborn child is not a legal person, it cannot seriously be argued that a frozen two-, four- or eight-cell embryo is a legal person with all the legal consequences stemming from such recognition by the law.[71]

In the only legal pronouncement that we are aware of dealing specifically with the status of the (frozen) embryo (as quite distinct from the foetus), the Official Solicitor refused to intervene to prevent the destruction of over 3,000 embryos already in storage whose genitors could not be traced to discover if they would consent to extended storage, as the embryos had no legal rights until born alive.[72]

The European Convention on Biomedicine and Human Rights, to which the United Kingdom is not however a signatory, does provide some form of protection for the human embryo. Thus, Art. 18(1) provides that 'Where the law allows research on embryos *in vitro*, it shall ensure adequate protection of the embryo', and Art. 18(2) that 'The creation of human embryos for research purposes is prohibited.' Under Art. 36, countries – such as the United Kingdom – which have a pre-existing law may make a reservation to the Convention based on that existing law. Those countries which have no pre-existing law on the embryo and which sign the Convention will be hindered or prohibited from sanctioning embryo research, unless they formally withdraw from the Convention, pass the new permissive law and then re-sign (as has happened possibly with Finland and certainly with Greece).

The enactment of the Human Rights Act 1998 bringing the provisions of the European Convention on Human Rights closer to UK domestic law has provoked some commentators to focus on the provisions of Art. 2 of the Convention as having potentially significant effect on domestic abortion and embryo status law. Article 2 provides: 'Everyone's right to life shall be protected by law.' Whether this will afford any greater degree of recognition, let alone recognition itself, to the foetus, let alone to the embryo, is unlikely.

No European consensus exists on *abortion* (or as Table 3.2 below shows, embryo research) and the Commission and European Court of Human Rights have been reluctant to pronounce substantively on whether the protection in Art. 2 extends to the foetus. In the light of these differing laws, a state will have what is called under European human rights legislation a wide 'margin of appreciation' with regard to the Convention on the issue of abortion, and thus, we believe, embryo research. (See *Application 17004/90 H v Norway* 73 DR 155 (1992) E Com HR.)

Again, the attitude of the Commission and the Court can be traced through a short series of cases:

- *Paton* v *UK* (1981) 3 EHRR 408: termination of a ten-week-old foetus to protect the health of the woman did not breach Art. 2, although it is not clear if this is because the foetus was not included in the word 'everyone' or because, if included, its rights were not absolute and on the facts subject to permissible limitations;
- *H* v *Norway* (above) the Commission noted that the laws on abortion differed considerably and accorded the state a degree of discretion in determining its obligation to protect life in the context of abortion;
- *Poku* v *United Kingdom* (Application 26985/95 15 May 1996): on an application made under Art. 2 on behalf of a third trimester foetus whose life was threatened by the woman's imminent deportation from the UK because of a risk to the pregnancy from severe complications, the Commission found an Art. 2 claim to be inadmissible because the woman had not been deported and the child had been born alive, and the Commission found it unnecessary to rule as to the admissibility of a complaint issued by a foetus.

The European Court of Human Rights has yet to rule on whether the term 'everyone' includes a foetus. In *Open Door Counselling & Dublin Well Woman* v *Ireland* (1992) 15 EHRR 244, the Commission had recognised the possibility that Art. 2 might in certain circumstances offer protection to a foetus, but took the point no further and the Court offered no guidance.

European approaches to embryo research

We may distinguish four approaches to the question of the legality or otherwise of embryo research in the member states of the European Union as set out in Table 3.2: first, those jurisdictions where it is specifically prohibited; secondly, those where it is specifically permitted by law, although subject to conditions, which in the case of France are particularly exceptional ones; thirdly, those jurisdictions which have no specific law but where we may say from the generic law or domestic constitutional provisions that embryo research is implicitly prohibited; and fourthly, those which have no specific law but where we may say that embryo research is implictly permitted.

The relevant legislative provisions and in some cases their conditions are set out in Table 3.3.

Table 3.2   Embryo research in the EU

Permitted (with conditions)	Prohibited unless therapeutic	Permitted by default	Prohibited by default
Denmark Finland France (exceptionally) Spain Sweden UK	Austria Germany	Belgium Greece Italy The Netherlands Portugal	Ireland Luxembourg

Table 3.3   Member states' legislation on embryo research[73]

Country	Legislation	Provisions
Austria	Act on Procreative Medicine 1992	ER prohibited other than for therapeutic use
Belgium	under discussion	ER permitted by default
Denmark	Law 460, 1997	ER permitted to 14 days in some cases; research to improve IVF
Finland	An Act on Medical Research (488/1999) entered into force 1 November 1999	ER permitted where the research institution has been approved by the National Authority on Medicolegal Affairs in circumstances similar to the UK
France	Law 94–654 and Decree 1997	Exceptionally, therapeutic research is permitted up to seven days after fertilisation; *in vitro* conception of embryos for research prohibited
Germany	Embryo Protection Act 1990	Non-therapeutic ER prohibited
Greece		ER permitted by default, although Greece, with Act 2619/1998 (*Official Gazette* A'132), has already ratified the European Convention for the Protection of Human Rights and Dignity of the Human Being with regard to the Application of Biology and Medicine: Convention

Country	Legislation	Provisions
Greece (*continued*)		on Human Rights and Biomedicine (ETS No. 164), and has recently established a National Bioethics Committee. The role of the Committee is to address the problems pertaining to the applications of genetic technology and to investigate their moral, legal and social aspects and impacts (Art. 10 IV of Act 2667/1998, *Official Gazette* A' 281)
Ireland	8th Amendment to the Constitution (40.3.3)	ER implicitly prohibited
Italy		ER permitted by default; law proposed to prohibit creation of embryos for research and all non-therapeutic research
Luxembourg		ER not performed
Netherlands		ER permitted by default; permissive law under consideration
Portugal		ER permitted by default
Spain	Law 35 1988; constitutional challenge	ER permitted by default; the object of the challenge was to argue that this law was not enacted according to the appropriate procedure; being concerned with fundamental rights and the right to life, the 1988 Law should have been enacted as a '*Ley orgánica*' and not just a '*Ley ordinaria*'
Sweden	Law 115, 1991	In 1991 a Law concerning embryo research was enacted. Research is forbidden if it takes place later than two weeks after fertilisation. In addition, the research must not have the intention of developing methods of creating genetic effects which can be hereditary. A fertilised egg which has been subject to research must be destroyed without delay after the expiration of the two weeks

Country	Legislation	Provisions
UK	1990 Act	ER permitted up to 14 days; research must be necessary or desirable for five permitted purposes (see below)

The embryo and the 1990 Act

General prohibitions   Section 3 of the 1990 Act defines activities which it is beyond the power of the HFEA to license. For example, the Authority may not authorise the use or retention of a live human embryo after the appearance of the 'primitive streak' (s. 3(3)(a)). Unless the embryo is stored by way of freezing (see below), this is taken to be 'not later than the end of the period of fourteen days beginning with the day when the gametes are mixed' (s. 3(4)). This much-criticised pragmatic solution was adopted by the Warnock Committee as the point when human life begins to matter morally.[74]

Similarly, the Authority may not authorise the placing of a human embryo in any animal, the keeping or use of an embryo where regulations prohibit this or nucleus substitution (sometimes referred to as cloning). Nucleus substitution occurs where the nucleus of the cell of an embryo (which contains the hereditary genetic material) is removed and replaced with the nucleus taken from a cell of another person, embryo or later developed embryo (s. 3(3)(b), (c) and (d)). This latter technique has been claimed to hold important prospects for work with genetically inherited disease and the production of immunologically identical organs for transplantation purposes. But it raises the spectre of the production of genetically identical humans, clones, or humans with specific characteristics. The HFEA is not presently be able to license such work. For further details, see below.

Section 3(3)(b) prohibits 'placing an embryo in any animal'. There is, on the face of it, no similar prohibition in respect of placing human sperm and egg together in the uterus of another animal. Section 4(1)(c) prohibits the mixing of human gametes with the live gametes of any animal except in pursuance of a licence, but that is not what is contemplated by placing human sperm and egg in an animal. Such experiments have in fact been reported in Australia, by Carl Wood and Anne Westmore. In their book, *Test-Tube Conception*,[75] they recount an experiment in which they introduced human eggs and sperm into the fallopian tube of a sheep. They comment, on the failure of the fertilisation:

> In some ways we were relieved at the failure of this experiment as it may have been difficult to convince the community that the sheep was an appropriate place for human fertilisation and early human development.

Under the Act, it seems that such an experiment would not be totally prohibited. It could, it appears, be done, but only under licence. A licence would be required because the experiment might amount to 'storing' gametes under s. 4(1)(a). Section 2(2) provides that references to 'keeping, in relation to embryos or gametes, include keeping while preserved, whether preserved by cryopreservation *or in any other way*' (emphasis added) and s. 1(3) provides that 'This Act, so far as it governs the keeping or use of an embryo, applies only to keeping or using an embryo outside the human body'.

But notice the two important limitations to this argument. Section 1(3) applies only in respect of embryos, and although s. 1(1)(b) defines that to include an egg in the process of fertilisation, the point of the experiment is to see whether fertilisation will occur or not. And, secondly, the extended meaning given to 'keeping' in s. 2(2), actually applies to 'keeping while preserved'. Unless the gametes in the sheep uterus are regarded as 'preserved' while there, s. 2(2) does not straightforwardly determine whether such an experiment can proceed only with a licence. The problem here is that the outcome or likely outcome of the experiment is determining the need for a licence under the Act. Moreover, s. 2(2) does not purport to give an exhaustive definition of 'keeping'; it merely provides some instances which are included. Thus a s. 4(1) licence would be necessary for the storage of gametes in such an experiment. It is possible that regulations will prohibit such an experiment altogether, in which case no licence could be issued to endorse it (s. 4(2)).

Schedule 2 'treatment licences' may authorise a variety of practices designed 'to secure that embryos are in a suitable condition to be placed in a woman or to determine whether embryos are suitable for that purpose' (para. 1(1)(d)), which may in practice look uncommonly like research.

Section 4 provides more contentious reading. Section 4(1)(a) and (c) provide for offences of storing gametes (ova or sperm) and cross-species fertilisation using live human gametes without an HFEA licence.

Licensing human embryo research   To June 1990 the ILA had licensed 66 research projects; 13 new projects in 1989–90, having started with 22 in 1985–86. (It is difficult to make the ILA annual figures tally with the overall figure and the data for 1986–87 are not clearly presented; the ILA appears to have approved an additional ten projects compared with their first report but only received seven applications.) The aims of these projects were either the improvement of existing IVF provision (on average only one in ten IVF cycles successfully results in a live birth), or the treatment of infertility (an estimated one in eight couples experience difficulties with conception) including the causes of miscarriage (of which there are some 75,000 annually in the UK). These activities were not themselves uncontroversial, but they were the first practical results of the research work which has been done in the previous 25 years. Other applications to which research may be put include the diagnosis of genetic abnormalities in an embryo before implantation[76] and the discovery of improved methods of contraception. The ILA had established voluntary guidelines for such research work, which included provisions for donor consent and prior ethical committee approval of the work. Prior to the 1990 Act, only one projected protocol had been refused a licence, and that because the procedure involved the transfer to the uterus of a woman of an embryo on which no check had been made as to its chromosomal content following research.

Between 1991 and 1998, 765,509 embryos were created in total. Of those, 351,617 were used in infertility treatments and a further 183,786 were stored for use in future treatment cycles; 237,603 embryos were not used for any purposes at all and were destroyed. Of the remainder, 48,444 were excess to couples or women in fertility programmes and were given for use in research; 118 were specifically created over that period only for the purposes of research.[77]

Originally, there was nothing in the Bill which would have prevented unlicensed 'research' up to the point of syngamy. Section 1 was amended to deal with this point; it adopts a scientific understanding as its definition of an embryo. Section 1(1) provides that references to an embryo are to a live human embryo 'where fertilisation is complete', but that references to an embryo 'include an egg in the process of fertilisation'. Fertilisation is not complete 'until the appearance of a two cell zygote'. The difficulty with this definition, providing as it does a clear indication of when, for legal purposes, fertilisation ends, is that it does not provide when 'an egg in the process of fertilisation' begins. The difficulties to which this gives rise in the determination of whether an embryo has been brought about partly inside and partly outside the human body for the purposes of s. 1(2) are discussed in Chapter 5.

A licence authorising specific research under the 1990 Act may be granted by the HFEA for a maximum period of three years (sch. 2, para. 3(9)). Any research licence may be made subject to conditions imposed by the HFEA and specified in the licence (sch. 2, para. 3(7)), and any authority to bring about the creation of an embryo, to keep or use an embryo or mix human sperm with a hamster or other specified animal's egg may specify how those activities may be carried out (sch. 2, para. 3(8)). Each research protocol must be shown to relate, broadly, to one of the existing categories of research aim (sch. 2, para. 3(2)), and even then the HFEA may, grant a licence only if it is satisfied that the proposed use of embryos is 'necessary for the purposes of the research' (sch. 2, para. 3(6)).

The categories of research set out in s. 3(2) are as follows:

(a)   promoting advances in the treatment of infertility;

(b)   increasing knowledge about the causes of congenital disease (an amendment seeking to limit this to life-threatening or severely disabling conditions was withdrawn);

(c)   increasing knowledge about the causes of miscarriage;

(d)   developing more effective techniques of contraception (an amendment condemning this as 'frivolous' was defeated);

(e)   developing methods for detecting the presence of gene or chromosome abnormalities in embryos before implantation; or

(f)   more generally, for the purpose of increasing knowledge about the creation and development of embryos and enabling such knowledge to be applied.

The 'hamster test' referred to in sch. 2, para. 3(5) is used to test the motility and normality of sperm. The hamster is at present the only known animal amenable to such a test. The zona pellucida of the ovum and the tip of the sperm are species specific. Whereas very closely related species such as the horse and the donkey can interbreed, the hamster is the only known exception to possess a removable zona pellucida which would otherwise repel the sperm from another species. The hamster zona can be removed following treatment with an enzyme, and what has become known as the zona free hamster oocyte penetration test performed. The test requires the mixing of 40 hamster eggs with sperm. After three to four hours, a judgment is made as to the percentage of the eggs that have been penetrated by the sperm, on the basis of which judgment is made as to the fertility of the sperm. No embryo is formed and the result is immediately destroyed. The provision in sch. 2, para. 3(5) to extend this test to other animals specified in directions (sch. 2, para. 1(1)(f), sch. 2, para. 3(5) and s. 24(11)) subject to the report of the proposed directions to each House of Parliament by the Secretary of State, anticipates the discovery of any other suitable source of testing. Anything which forms must be destroyed when the research is complete, 'and in any event, not later than the two cell stage' (sch. 2, para. 3(5)). The importance of the test, introduced in the United States in 1976, is its value in studying the chromosomal constitution of human sperm, and hence the male contribution to genetic abnormalities, and to infertility, thought to affect one in 16 of the male population. It is said also to be a key part in researching the development of a male contraceptive agent, including in particular a contraceptive vaccine. Lord Houghton enlivened Parliamentary proceedings on debate when he announced that he had 'a small constituency in the animal world' and declared that 'I must stand up for the hamster. . . . I am simply asking, on behalf of the hamsters of this world, what happens to them when the embryos have been taken away and immediately destroyed'.[78]

The HGAC and the HFEA in a consultation paper on cloning and the subsequent report (*Cloning Issues in Reproduction, Science and Medicine*, (1998)), recommended that two further purposes might be added to the existing sch. 2 purposes by way of regulations. These purposes would additionally permit the HFEA to license a research protocol within the terms of sch. 2 where it was proposed:

(a) to extract *embryonic stem cells* for research on the possible treatment benefits in a wide range of disorders by replacing cells that have become damaged or diseased; and

(b) to conduct research into the treatment of some rare but serious inherited disorders carried in maternal mitochondria.

These recommendations were later endorsed by an Expert Group chaired by the Chief Medical Officer in a report entitled *Stem Cell Research: Medical Progress with Responsibility* (London, Department of Health, 2000).

Mitochondria are small organelles in the cytoplasm of all cells, whose main purpose is the production of energy. They have their own single, circular chromosome, such that it replicates independently of the 46 regular chromosomes in the human genome. Several mitochondrial diseases produce severe and widespread neurological diseases which are hereditarily transmitted through the maternal mitochrondria at fertilisation. The sperm pronucleus does not carry any mitochondria with it and inheritance comes exclusively from the mother. While she may have insignificant disease, her children may be very badly affected. It may be possible to prevent a child inheriting damaged mitochondria from the mother by inserting the nucleus of the mother's egg into a donor egg with healthy mitochondria which has had its nucleus removed. This would be a form of cell nucleus replacement. In other words, it may be possible[79] to effect an exchange of the cytoplasm by taking a cell nucleus from a pre-implantation embryo and transferring this via the cell nucleus replacement technique to an enucleated egg donated for the purpose, i.e. an egg from which the nucleus has been removed leaving the healthy mitochondria to 'transport' the nucleus.

Nucleus substitution Licences may not authorise the nucleus substitution (re-placement) of an embryo (s. 3(3)(d)). A licence is required for the creation of an embryo outside of the body (ss. 3(1)(a) and 1(2)), where an embryo is defined as a live egg that has been fertilised or is in the process of fertilisation (s. 1(1)(a) and (b)). Quite clearly, this prohibits cloning, where the technique involves replacing the nucleus of a cell of an embryo *with a nucleus taken from elsewhere*, such as a person or another embryo.

A licence cannot authorise . . . (d) replacing a nucleus of a cell of an embryo with a nucleus taken from a cell of any person, embryo or subsequent development of an embryo. (s. 3(3)(d))

Until recently, it was assumed that any cloning by nuclear substitution would entail such a replacement of the *nucleus* of an embryo, or replacing the nucleus of an egg with a *nucleus* from an embryonic cell. Indeed Dolly had been preceded at birth by Morag and Megan, but they had been born following the use of an embryonic or foetal cell. The Dolly technique, however, involved nucleus substitution into an *egg* and not an embryo. A donor cell *was taken from an adult animal* (here, an udder cell) and cultured in a laboratory. A donor *cell* was taken from the culture and 'stored' in a medium which kept it just alive; the reason for this was to slow down or shut down the activities of the cell and send it into a period of dormancy (or 'quiesence', scientifically called the G0 or Gap Zero cell stage). The G0 cell was then placed alongside a sheep *egg cell* (an oocyte; *not an embryo*) from which the nucleus had been removed. An electric pulse was used to fuse the two cells and activate embryo development, which after five to six days' further development in a laboratory was implanted in the surrogate mother ewe, Dolly's 'mother'. Some 150 days later, to public astonishment and incredulity, Dolly's birth was announced in the scientific literature.[80]

The 'Dolly technique' not only stormed the popular imagination and gave the *Boys from Brazil* their greatest exercise in the last 15 years, it again appeared to shake the foundations on which the 1990 Act had been built; the scientific rocks on which the legislative house had laid its foundations were being battered by the waves of scientific endeavour and coming increasingly to resemble the shifting sands on which public policy's slippery slopes have their first outing: law was surfing again the turbulent seas of chaos theory.

A team of scientists in South Korea later reported in 1998 that they had achieved nuclear replacement in a human ovum and then cultivated the fertilised egg to an early embryonic stage, and while other scientists doubted the veracity of this report, many later confirmed their belief that human reproductive cloning would occur before 2010.[81]

The Warnock Committee made the assumption that the vast majority of embryos used in research would be spare embryos, created in the course of *in vitro* fertilisation treatment but no longer required for that purpose. The tiny minority of embryos created specifically for research would have been produced by similar techniques (i.e. mixing sperm and egg in the laboratory to achieve fertilisation outside the body). The creation of embryos by means other than by fertilising an egg with sperm was not possible when the issues were debated by the Warnock Committee and in Parliament.

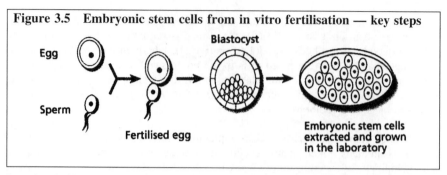

Figure 3.5   Embryonic stem cells from in vitro fertilisation — key steps

Egg

Sperm

Fertilised egg

Blastocyst

Embryonic stem cells extracted and grown in the laboratory

Reproduced with permission from *Stem Cell Research: Medical Progress with Responsibility* (London, Department of Health, 2000)

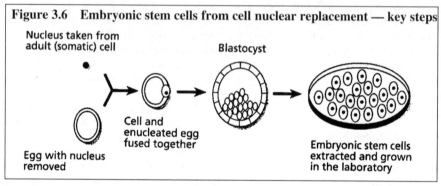

Figure 3.6   Embryonic stem cells from cell nuclear replacement — key steps

Nucleus taken from adult (somatic) cell

Blastocyst

Cell and enucleated egg fused together

Egg with nucleus removed

Embryonic stem cells extracted and grown in the laboratory

Reproduced with permission from *Stem Cell Research: Medical Progress with Responsibility* (London, Department of Health, 2000)

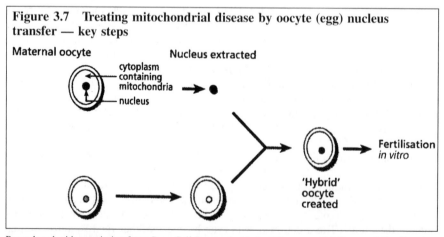

Figure 3.7   Treating mitochondrial disease by oocyte (egg) nucleus transfer — key steps

Maternal oocyte

Nucleus extracted

cytoplasm containing mitochondria

nucleus

'Hybrid' oocyte created

Fertilisation *in vitro*

Reproduced with permission from *Stem Cell Research: Medical Progress with Responsibility* (London, Department of Health, 2000)

It is important here to observe four things:

(a)   *cell nucleus replacement* is not specifically prohibited by the 1990 Act;

(b)   the same is true of 'embryo splitting'. Embryo splitting occurs naturally at a very early stage of embryonic development in the formation of identical twins. This can also be done *in vitro* in some species at the eight-cell stage and identical 'cloned' embryos may develop;

(c)   the HFEA gave careful consideration to embryo splitting as an additional possible form of infertility treatment in 1994, when its potential use at the two- or four-cell embryonic stage was discussed. After considering the social and ethical issues involved the HFEA decided to ban embryo splitting as a possible fertility treatment and additionally indicated that it would not license research towards the development of cloning as a form of treatment. However, the Authority did not then make a similar prohibition in respect of cell nuclear replacement research;

(d)   the so-called 'Dolly' technique, where the nucleus of an egg cell is replaced with a nucleus of a somatic cell taken *from an adult* was beyond the bounds of scientific credibility, at least when the 1990 Act was passed.

Somatic cell nuclear transfer, then, raised at the very least a new legal question on the ambit of the 1990 Act: as the technique involves nucleus substitution into an egg and not an embryo, and this is not specifically covered by the wording of s. 3(3)(d) of the Act, is it prohibited? And as fertilisation is not then involved, such that s. 3(1) ('No person shall . . . bring about the creation of an embryo . . . except in pursuance of a licence') does not apply either, is it regulated at all by the Act?

The HGAC and the HFEA in their Consultation Paper on cloning and the subsequent report, *Cloning Issues in Human Reproduction* (1998), together with the Chief Medical Officer's Report, *Stem Cell Research (2000)*, rejected the arguments implicit in both of these questions, which would have left cell nucleus substitution outside the regulatory ambit of the Act. Rather, following counsel's advice, they declared that, depending on the method used, cloning is either prohibited, or subject to licensing. The Report observed that while 'embryo splitting and the nuclear replacement of eggs are not expressly prohibited . . . both involve the use or creation of embryos outside the body'. Hence, they concluded, 'they fall within the . . . Act and therefore come under the jurisdiction of the HFEA'.[82] Clearly, this relies on taking a 'purposive' rather than a 'literal' interpretation of the 1990 Act and the meaning assigned in the legislation to the term 'embryo', and the HFEA has made it clear that it will not issue a licence for any research 'which has reproductive cloning as its aim'.[83]

It has not been (indeed it is far from) settled that the application of the 'Dolly technique' to humans would fall within the narrowly drafted provisions of the HFEA. At least three objections have so far been publicly registered: from Deryck Beyleveld and Shaun Pattinson, from Margot Brazier and from the All-Parliamentary Pro-Life Group. First, Beyleveld and Pattinson have insisted that using the Dolly technique does not involve the creation of an embryo at all, because an embryo is defined under the Act in s. 1 as 'a live human embryo where fertilisation is complete', including 'an egg in the process of fertilisation'. Indeed, as they aver, Wilmut has himself suggested that '[t]he oocyte is an egg but it has not been fertilised and it *never is fertilised* because the nucleus is transferred to it' (emphasis

ugh they do add their belief that 'in practice, it is very unlikely that
ilisation' will not be judicially construed to include the nuclear
an egg, especially since the HFEA seems to be acting according to
on of this term'.[85]

Margot Brazier has offered a similar interpretation: 'I would contend
that nuclear substitution into an egg cell is unregulated in the United Kingdom
today.'[86] Using the analogy of plant breeding, she avers that cell nucleus
substitution constitutes propagation not fertilisation. Section 3(1), requiring a
licence from the HFEA to bring about the creation of an embryo, is subject to the
definition of an embryo in s. 1, which provides that 'embryo means a live human
embryo'; and if that is all that it said, then cell nucleus replacement would clearly
be within the statutory scheme of the 1990 Act.

Thirdly, the All Parliamentary Pro-Life Group have taken up and challenged the
interpretation offered by the joint Consultation Paper of April 1998, issued by the
HFEA and the HGAC. Repeating the Authority's and the Commission's view that
embryo splitting and nuclear replacement of the eggs fall within a purposive
interpretation of the legislation, the Parliamentary group object that the Act defines
an embryo as 'a live human embryo where fertilisation is complete' and observe
that:

> . . . the clear intention of Parliament was to prohibit the creation of cloned
> human embryos, both for research and reproductive purposes. . . . since a cloned
> embryo has not undergone fertilisation, it might be argued that a cloned embryo
> is not an embryo for the purposes of the Act. If the courts were to adopt this
> interpretation, it would follow that the HFEA has no power to regulate the
> creation or keeping of embryos.[87]

They conclude that it is questionable that 'work which would create cloned human
beings cannot lawfully be carried out', as the Government had concluded, and
called for the Act to be clarified to ensure that such a prohibition was unassailably
in place.

Let us add to this our own view, shortly. Recall that we have already argued
that, at least from a moral point of view, and taking what we might call a purposive
or result-orientated approach, it may be possible to reconcile the cell nucleus
substitution embryo with embryos created *in vitro* in what, astonishingly, we might
now call 'the ordinary way'. From this it would follow, contrary to Brazier and
Beyleveld, that there is no particular difficulty in accepting the view to which the
HFEA works, that the creation of embryos by cell nucleus substitution is *already*
brought within the scheme of the Act by an extended interpretation of s. 1.

So far what we have quoted from s. 1 might throw doubt on the advice received
by the HFEA and HGAC, which is the advice received by and acted upon by the
Department of Health. But that is not all that s. 1 says. It is limited not just in the
one way that Beyleveld and Brazier have pointed out, but (we believe) in an
additional way too. Correctly, they have reminded us that an embryo in s. 1 means
'a live human embryo where fertilisation is complete'. Where, as with an embryo
created by cell nucleus substitution, fertilisation never has taken place it is difficult
to accept that an embryo within the meaning of the Act has been created. And
herein lies the second difficulty.

Section 1(1)(a) in full reads:

> (1)   In this Act, *except where otherwise stated—*
>   (a)   embryo means a live human embryo where fertilisation is complete,
> . . .

The emphasised words make it plain that the legislators could have provided for embryos created other than by *in vitro* fertilisation to be included within the statute, but evidently they did not. To read the statute as providing for embryos created by cell nucleus replacement is to read it as providing that an embryo means a live human embryo where fertilisation is complete, *unless the context otherwise requires.* And that decidedly, the Act does not do.

The fundamental problem with adopting the purposive approach to the interpretation of s. 1 which has been commended to the HFEA is that as a matter of statutory interpretation practice the purposive approach can only be relied upon when there is an ambiguity produced by a literal interpretation of the provision in question. On the face of the Act, there does not appear to us to be any such ambiguity. However, we do suggest that the way in which a court might be persuaded to approach this difficult question might well depend on *context.* We can foresee at least two cases in which this question of the legal status of the cell nucleus replacement embryo and the ambit of the 1990 Act might come to be argued.

First, suppose that an embryologist advised of the 'literal interpretation' argument decides, without more, that he or she will proceed to create such embryos without reference to the HFEA. He or she does so, and conducts experiments on those embryos without applying to the HFEA for a licence, and is then prosecuted under ss. 3(1) and 41(2) for carrying on without a licence an activity for which it is said a licence is necessary. Conviction on indictment on such a charge carries a possible term of imprisonment of up to two years. The usual rule in a criminal prosecution would enable the embryologist to claim the benefit, and here the protection, of the literal interpretation of the 1990 Act argued for above. A court might be somewhat more reluctant to adopt this sympathetic approach with an embryologist who had kept (and perhaps even conducted experiments that entail keeping) the embryo long beyond the appearance of the 'primitive streak' (the '14-day' rule) as provided for in s. 3(3)(a) and (4) but if this 'literal' argument is correct such experiments would not be unlawful *under the 1990 Act.* Whether the embryologist might commit an offence under another enactment is a moot point.

Suppose, however, in a second example, that a case comes before the High Court by way of an application for judicial review, the HFEA having refused to grant a (particular) licence on application to conduct experiments set out in a research protocol on cell nucleus replacement embryos or, perhaps more realistically, attaching conditions to a licence providing that such embryos are not be used in the project or that such an embryo is not to be kept beyond the statutory period. Here the embryologist's argument is that he or she is being unlawfully deprived of a research opportunity by the HFEA, which it is alleged is acting beyond its powers. The strength of the case for a literal rather than a purposive interpretation of the Act is far less compelling.

It may seem less than extraordinary that a provision such as s. 1 of the 1990 Act might be open to competing interpretations; it is the essence of statutory *interpretation* that, as we have said earlier, words do not interpret themselves. What is more unusual is that the interpretation to be settled on might depend on the circumstances of the case first bringing the question to the court. But this *contextual* argument has some weight of legal experience behind it (see *Coventry Waste Disposal* v *Solihull BC* [1999] 1 WLR 2093).

Pressure for a global legal ban on the development and use of cloning human beings has led ten of the 15 EU countries to sign the European Convention on Human Rights and Biomedicine and its additional protocol on the prohibition of cloning human beings.[88] This protocol makes what was implicit in the Convention explicit by declaring in Art. 1(1) that: '[a]ny intervention seeking to create a human being genetically identical to another human being, whether living or dead, is prohibited'. Since 'genetically identical' is defined as 'sharing with another the same nuclear gene set' (Art. 1(2)), somatic cell nuclear transfer is included within this prohibition.

The Netherlands, when it signed the Convention and its protocol, added an interpretative statement that:

> . . . [i]n relation to Article 1 of the Protocol, the Government of the Kingdom of The Netherlands declares that it interprets the term 'human beings' as referring exclusively to a human individual, i.e., a human being who has been born.[89]

LAW, SCIENCE AND PUBLIC POLICY

Here, then, there is a real tension between science and law. Not in what science was able to tell the draftsman of the Act in 1990, but what, respectively, science and law have to contribute to the interpretation of laws seeking to regulate science. It is as well to be clear here what we mean by what we say, for as Humpty Dumpty would well have recognised: 'Words mean what I want them to mean; and the question is, who's in charge?'

> The examination of the rights and wrongs of embryo research in Britain during the 1980s was highly unusual in the degree to which it subjected a particular branch of scientific inquiry to sustained, collective appraisal. . . . The public debate over embryo research led people to assess the morality of scientific research in its approach to such fundamental concerns as birth, death, disability and respect for human individuals. In the course of the debate, people's hopes and fears about this area of scientific investigation and their conflicting ideas about the place of the life sciences in present day society were publicly formed and displayed as they struggled to respond to the challenge posed by embryo research, and by the associated technology of controlled human reproduction.[90]

But, as Brazier intimates, this is more than just a lawyer's tiff. It may be argued that broadening out the research purposes to promote understanding of a broader range of diseases through the extraction of stem cells, treats the embryo as no more than a convenient source of research material and thus removes any respect for the embryo as an entity in itself. The moral objection to the use of embryos might increase for some people if embryos were to be produced in a laboratory for the specific purpose of extracting stem cells for experimental purposes, even though the ultimate benefit might be understanding of disease or its treatment. Such an approach, some would argue, does not retain any sense of the respect for the embryo, used by the Warnock Committee to justify research on embryos.

A contrary moral view is that, provided the research is necessary to secure benefits to human health in the future, the use of embryos at a very early stage in their development is not lacking in respect. Taking this view, it might be argued that the use of embryos to increase understanding of disease does not differ so fundamentally from the purposes of currently permitted research, even though conceptually the embryo is more closely associated with the reproductive process. In particular, research leading to potential treatments for major diseases of tissue or organs may not be any less respectful of the embryo's moral status than research on congenital disease, for example. Indeed, if there is greater potential for the research to benefit a wider range of people or treat a wider range of disorders such research may be more ethically justified.

The current research purposes specified in the 1990 Act relate only to research which could be envisaged at that time. It is, however, difficult to argue that they were based on immutable moral criteria. The existence in the 1990 Act of the power to broaden the research purposes in due course supports this view. In all types of embryo research under consideration it has to be accepted that the embryo cannot itself receive any benefit. It *is* used instrumentally – as a means to an end – and will be destroyed. This is, in any event, an inevitable outcome for all spare embryos, whether donated for research under the currently allowed research purposes or no longer required for treatment. If the arguments of the Warnock Committee are accepted the issue to be considered is one of balance – whether the research has the potential to lead to significant health benefits for others and whether the use of embryos at a very early stage of their development in such research is necessary to realise those benefits.

This episode so clearly and cogently illustrates an evaluation of the approach of the legislation that it is worth repeating our earlier use and assessment of it here. Recall that Margot Brazier commended the British model of regulation adopted and enacted in the Human Fertilisation and Embryology Act, but cautions that 'again and again, as new medical developments emerge, we debate the same issues in different guises'.[91] As with the Red Queen, public policy in regulating biotechnology is forever rushing to stay in one place: 'you see, it takes all the running you can do, to keep in the same place. If you want to go somewhere else, you must run at least twice as fast as that.'[92]

As we have seen earlier, this runs the danger of ignoring Hans Jonas's plea for what he called a 'scientific futurology' – a 'lengthened foresight' – which will help to disclose what is possibly at stake, what values and traditions we may pass up, what goals and opportunities we ought in all conscience to deny ourselves: 'what we must avoid at all cost is determined by what we must preserve at all cost'.[93]

NOTES

[1]   Warnock Report (Cmnd 9314), *Report of the Committee of Inquiry into Fertilisation and Embryology*, republished as *A Question of Life* (Oxford, Basil Blackwell, 1985), at 60.

[2]   *The Embryo Research Debate: Science and the Politics of Reproduction* (Cambridge, Cambridge University Press, 1997).

[3]   *Ibid.*, at 58.

[4]   *The IVF Revolution: The Definitive Guide to Assisted Reproductive Techniques* (London, Vermillion, 1999), at 141, 144.

[5]   This present characterisation of germ cells (sperm and eggs) and somatic cells (all other cells in the body) is taken from Silver, L., *Remaking Eden: Cloning. Genetic Engineering and the Future of Mankind* (London, Weidenfeld & Nicolson, 1999), at 41–47. Almost every embryology and genetics textbook carries a similar description, and there are some excellent websites which allow further study of the components of cellular life and the processes of conception and fertilisation, whether *in vitro* or not.

[6]   From McLaren, A., 'Prelude to Embryogenesis' in The CIBA Foundation, *Human Embryo Research: Yes or No?* (London Tavistock Publications, 1986), at 15.

[7]   Watson, J.D. and Crick, F.H.C., 'A Structure for Deoxyribose Nucleic Acid' (1953) 171 *Nature* 737.

[8]   Contrary to popular belief, the sperm and egg never fuse; the DNA molecules from the mother and the father do not even meet or touch each other, they are merely closer than they were before: see Silver, L., *op. cit.* n. 5, at 45–50.

[9]   'Human Fertilisation and Embryology Bill goes to report stage' (1990) 330 *British Medical Journal* 1410.

[10]   House of Lords, Official Report, 6 February 1990, col. 805 (Lord Walton).

[11]   See *New Scientist*, 10 December 1987.

[12]   For accessible overviews of the scientific literature at the time of the original debates on the Bill, see Warnock Report, paras 11.2–7; Leach, P., 'Human In Vitro Fertilisation' Annex 3, Voluntary Licensing Authority, First Annual Report, 1986, at 39–40; McLaren, A., 'Can we Diagnose Genetic Disease in Pre-Embryos?' *New Scientist*, 10 December.

[13]   Glover, J., *Fertility and the Family; The Glover Report on Reproductive Technologies to the European Commission* (London, Fourth Estate, 1989), at 94.

[14]   *Ibid.*

[15]   *Op. cit.* n. 2, at 137.

[16]   *Ibid.*

[17]   We are grateful to Alistair Campbell, Professor of Ethics in Medicine, University of Bristol, for permission to draw on unpublished work in drafting this section.

[18]   House of Lords, Official Report, 8 February 1990, col. 953.

[19]   'A Fortnight of My Life is Missing: A Discussion of the Status of the Pre-Embryo' (1990) 7 *Journal of Applied Philosophy* 25, at 35–6. Mulkay has castigated the use of the term 'pre-embryo' as a 'dubious neologism': *op. cit.* n. 2, at 32.

[20]   *Op. cit.* n. 5, at 46 and 328.

[21]   See *Life Before Birth: Reflections on the Embryo Debate* (London, Hutchinson, 1989), at 50.

[22]   Warnock Report, para. 11.15.

[23]   US National Bioethics Advisory Committee, 1999.

[24]   Kass, L., 'The Meaning of Life – in the Laboratory' in K.D. Alpern (ed.), The *Ethics of Reproductive Technology* (New York, Oxford University Press, 1992), at 98–116, emphasis in original.

[25] *Op. cit.* n. 5, at 305.

[26] Brazier, M., 'Regulating the Reproduction Business?' (1999) 7 *Medical Law Review* 166 at 189.

[27] *Ibid.*

[28] For this form of distinction between law and morality, see Hurthouse argument pp. 12–25, dealing more specifically with the issue of abortion, which we discussed in chapter 2.

[29] CIBA, *op. cit.* n. 6, at 22.

[30] *Ibid.*

[31] House of Lords, Official Report, 8 February 1990, col. 956.

[32] House of Lords, Official Report, 7 December 1989, col. 1020.

[33] Quoted in House of Commons, Official Report, 2 April 1990, col. 936.

[34] *Op. cit.* n. 19, at 31.

[35] 'Research Needs and the Reduction of Severe Congenital Disease' in The CIBA Foundation, *Human Embryo Research: Yes or No?* (London, Tavistock Publications, 1986), at 108–09.

[36] See Evans, D., *Making and Taking Life* (London, Macmillan, 1991).

[37] *Op. cit.* n. 2, at 101.

[38] *Ibid.*, at 50.

[39] House of Lords, Official Report, 20 March 1990, col. 247.

[40] Warnock Report, 'Expression of Dissent', at 90.

[41] *Ibid.*, para. 5.

[42] *Ibid.*

[43] House of Lords, Official Report, 6 March 1990, col. 1072.

[44] *Ibid.*, col. 1080.

[45] Lord Harrington, House of Lords, Official Report, 7 December 1990, col. 1070.

[46] House of Commons, Official Report, 23 April 1990, col. 67.

[47] House of Commons, Official Report, 2 April 1990, col. 934.

[48] House of Lords, Official Report, 7 December 1990, col. 1026.

[49] Although this view has not gone unchallenged: see the survey of these arguments in Mason, J.K., *Medico-Legal Aspects of Reproduction and Parenthood*, (Aldershot, Ashgate, 2nd edn 1998).

[50] Glover, *op. cit.* n. 13, at 101.

[51] House of Lords, Official Report, 6 March 1990, col. 1065.

[52] *Op. cit.* n. 2, at 105.

[53] *Ibid.*, at 111.

[54] *Ibid.*, at 68.

[55] *Ibid.*, at 113.

[56] *Ibid.*, at 132–33.

[57] *Ibid.*, at 115.

[58] McLean, S., *Old Law, New Medicine* (London and New York, Rivers Oram Press, 1999), at 50–51.

[59] These examples are derived from and discussed in 'The Legal Status of the Embryo and the Fetus' in Leonard Barron and D.F. Roberts (eds), *Issues in Fetal Medicine: Proceedings of the 1992 Galton Symposium* (London, Macmillan, 1995), at 142–62.

[60] Brazier, M., 'Embryos' ''Rights'': Abortion and Research' in M. Freeman (ed.), *Medicine, Ethics and the Law* (London, Stevens, 1988), at 21.

[61] For this argument, see Wells, C., and Morgan, D., 'Whose Fetus Is It?' (1991) 18 *Journal of Law and Society* 431.

[62] Grubb, A., 'The Legal Status of the Frozen Human Embryo' in A. Grubb (ed.), *Challenges in Medical Care* (Chichester, John Wiley & Sons, 1991), at 72.

[63] Codes: Summerian 2000 BC, Assyrian 1500 BC, Hittite 1300 BC and Persian 600 BC.

[64] Warnock Report, para. 11.16–17.

[65] *Ibid.*, paras 10.11 and 10.12.

[66] *Ibid.*, para. 13.13.

[67] *Ibid.*, para. 12.5.

[68] Kennedy, I. and Grubb, A., *Medical Law: Text and Materials* (London, Butterworths, 1989), at 682.

[69] *Op. cit.* n. 60, at 10.

[70] Keown, J., 'Creative Criminals', paper presented at 'Assisted Conception and the Law: A Medical/Legal Forum', Royal Society of Medicine, London.

[71] *Op. cit.* n. 62, at 75.

[72] Consequent upon the coming into force of the Human Fertilisation and Embryology (Statutory Storage Period for Embryos) Regulations 1996 (SI 1996 No. 375).

[73] This table has been adapted from (and supplemented in the case of later provisions) Beyleveld, D. and Pattinson, S., *The Ethics of Genetics in Human Procreation* (Aldershot, Ashgate, 2000). We are grateful to the editors for an early sight of their completed manuscript, and the opportunity to incorporate their research into this chapter.

[74] Warnock Report, para. 11.2–9.

[75] (Sydney, George Allen & Unwin, 1984).

[76] There are 14,000 births annually of babies with genetic abnormalities: see the Royal College of Surgeons' Report, *Prenatal Diagnosis and Genetic Screening* (1989).

[77] HFEA, as reported in the Chief Medical Officer's Report, *Stem Cell Research* (London, Department of Health, 2000), Table 2 at 32.

[78] House of Lords, Official Report, 13 March 1990, col. 1505. It has not been possible to trace a satisfactory reply.

[79] And indeed, an American gynaecologist Dr Jamie Grifo reported in 1998 that he had done this with two women patients – one successfully. See *The Times*, 10 October 1998.

[80] 'Viable Offspring Derived from Foetal and Adult Mammalian Cells' *Nature* (385, 881: 1997).

[81] *Guardian*, 17 December 1998; *Independent*, August 2000.

[82] HGAC and HFEA, *Cloning Issues in Reproduction, Science and Medicine* (1998), para. 3.4.

[83] *Ibid.*, para. 5.4.

[84] Beyleveld and Pattinson offer a second example of difficulties with legislative interpretation. The German Embryo Protection Act (*Embryonenschutzgesetz*) 1990, is clearly intended to prohibit cloning; Section Six renders it an offence to create an embryo that is genetically identical to another embryo, foetus, or any living or dead person; but the Act does not define the term 'genetically identical', so it is questionable whether it is wide enough to encompass a clone produced by somatic

cell nuclear transfer whose mitochondrial DNA will not be identical to that of the nuclear DNA donor.

[85] *Op. cit.* n. 73, at 233.

[86] Brazier, M., 'Regulating the Reproduction Business?' (1999) 7 *Medical Law Review* 166, at 189.

[87] All Parliamentary Group (1998) para. 1.3.2–3.

[88] *Council of Europe, Additional Protocol to the Convention for the Protection of Human Rights and the Dignity of the Human Being with regard to the Application of Biology & Medicine, On the Prohibition of Cloning Human Beings* (Strasbourg, 1997).

[89] Beyleveld and Pattinson, *op. cit.* n. 73.

[90] Mulkay, *op. cit.* n. 2, at 2.

[91] *Op. cit.* n. 86, at 167.

[92] 'Alice Through the Looking Glass' in M. Gardner (ed.), *The Annotated Alice* (Harmondsworth, Penguin Books, 1960), at 210. Ridley, M., *The Red Queen: Sex and the Evolution of Human Nature* (Harmondsworth, Penguin Books, 1994).

[93] Jonas, H., *The Imperative of Responsibility* (Chicago, University of Chicago Press, 1983).

Chapter 4
The Human Fertilisation and Embryology Authority

The Human Fertilisation and Embryology Authority (HFEA) is established as a statutory corporation by virtue of s. 5 of the 1990 Act. It is a non-departmental independent governmental agency and, in the words of its chairman, Ruth Deech, is able to carry out regulation with the purpose of maintaining 'respect for human life at all stages'.[1] The principal statutory functions of the authority include the licensing and monitoring of clinics which carry out certain artificial reproductive procedures for research and treatment purposes, and the regulation of the storage of gametes together with the policing of activities relating to gametes and embryos. It also has several other important roles under the law, including the formal registration of information concerning assisted conception. The Authority operates under a Code of Practice which guides the conduct of licensed activities. It both crafts and applies this Code, although this is subject to the approval of the Code by the Secretary of State (ss. 25 and 26). The HFEA also acts as a source of information and advice to the general public about assisted conception to potential patients and to donors.

The Warnock Committee[2] was charged with considering 'recent and potential developments in medicine and science related to human fertilisation and embryology' but human foresight is persistently outstripped by the exponential rate of scientific advance in reproductive technology. Nonetheless Warnock proposed a regulatory structure, the case for which, in the modest wording of the HFEA's quinquennial report, remains valid.

THE COMPOSITION OF THE HFEA

There are 21 members of the Authority, chosen to bring to their office a broad range of medical, scientific, social, legal and religious knowledge and experience. Schedule 1, para. 4, of the Act provides that the Secretary of State shall make appointments to the Authority, ensuring that it is informed of the views of both men and women. Paragraph 4(4) provides that the Secretary of State has to appoint at least a third but not more than half of the membership from the specifications in para. 4(3):

> (a)   any person who is, or has been, a medical practitioner registered under the Medical Act 1983 (whether fully, provisionally or with limited registration), or under any repealed enactment from which a provision of that Act is derived,

(b) any person who is, or has been, concerned with keeping or using gametes or embryos outside the body, and

(c) any person who is, or has been, directly concerned with commissioning or funding any research involving such keeping or use, or who has actively participated in any decision to do so.

At least one member must fall within the requirements of subparas (a) and (b). When it comes to the appointment of the chairman and the deputy chairman, persons falling within para. 4(3)(a)–(c) (above) are disqualified from being appointed. This is to ensure that the overall direction of the Authority is independent of the medical-scientific view. As an extra restriction, it seems that members of the House of Commons are not eligible to become members of the Authority, although there seems to be no such restriction when it comes to members of the House of Lords (see sch. 1, para. 6). In accordance with the Nolan guidelines, appointments have to be made with the overriding principle of appointment on merit, appointees being selected not as representatives of any particular group but because of their personal expertise and knowledge (this is seemingly something which the Act pre-empted in its provisions pertaining to the appointment of Authority members). Appointments to the HFEA are widely advertised and are said to attract both numerous and strong applications.

Given that under the terms of tenure in sch. 1, para. 5, a person shall not be appointed as a member of the Authority for more than three years at a time (although he or she shall be eligible for reappointment), it is hardly surprising that the current membership of the Authority bears little resemblance to the original roll-call, with only one member still sitting. At the end of December 1994, Ruth Deech, Principal of St Anne's College, Oxford, took over from Professor Sir Colin Campbell (another academic lawyer) as chairman of the Authority. The recent successor to Diane Britton as deputy chairman is Jane Denton, Director of the Multiple Births Foundation, Queen Charlotte's and Chelsea Hospital London. At the time of writing, the other 19 members continue in the tradition of diversity and include individuals from science, religion, academia and so forth:

- Professor Brenda Almond – Professor of Moral and Social Philosophy at the University of Hull
- Dr Sue Avery, clinical embryologist, Bourn Hall Clinic, Cambridge
- Professor David Barlow – Nuffield Professor of Obstetrics and Gynaecology and Head of Department, University of Oxford. Clinical Director, Assisted Reproduction Unit, John Radcliffe Maternity Hospital, Oxford
- Professor Peter Braude, consultant obstetrician and gynaecologist, Guy's, King's and St Thomas's Hospitals, London.
- Moira Coath – Solicitor, Non-executive Director of Dorset Health Care NHS Trust
- Professor Christine Gosden – Professor of Medical Genetics, University of Liverpool, Liverpool Women's Hospital
- Professor Andrew Grubb – Professor of Medical Law, University of Cardiff
- Professor Martin Johnson – Professor of Reproductive Sciences, University of Cambridge
- Professor Henry Leese – Professor of Biology, University of York

- Professor Stuart Lewis – Professor of Psychology Applied to Medicine, The Queen's University, Belfast
- Dr Anne McLaren – Principal Research Associate, Wellcome CRC Institute, Cambridge
- Dr Sadia Muhammed – General Medical Practitioner at York and forensic medical examiner to the North Yorkshire Police
- Sara Nathan – Until recently Editor of Channel 4 News
- The Right Reverend Dr Michael James Nazir-Ali – Bishop of Rochester
- Sharmila Nebhrajani – Head of corporate planning at the BBC, a chartered accountant and former management consultant
- Dr Francoise Shenfield, clinical lectures in fertility, UCL Medical School, London
- Professor Allan Templeton – Professor of Obstetrics and Gynaecology, University of Aberdeen
- Julia Tugendhat – Family therapist
- Ms Liz Woods, former civil servant (Commissioner), HM Customs and Excise

Schedule 1, para. 5(3) allows for a member to resign his or her office at any time by giving notice to the Secretary of State. The Secretary of State may also decide under para. 5(5) that a member should vacate his or her position. An appointed member may be removed from office if he or she:

(a) has been absent from meetings of the Authority for six consecutive months or longer without the permission of the Authority; or
(b) has become bankrupt; or
(c) is unable or unfit to discharge the function of a member.

Arrangements for the remuneration of the person who chairs the HFEA and for the payment of pensions, allowances, fees, expenses or gratuities of any members may be made by the Authority in accordance with the Secretary of State's determination and with the approval of the Treasury (sch. 1, para. 7(1)).

When it comes to the hiring of employees as set out in sch. 1, para. 8, the Authority may appoint employees upon the terms and conditions set down by the Authority, which have had the approval of the Secretary of State and the consent of the Treasury. With regard to inspectors, the Authority has to ensure that any person employed is of such character, 'and is qualified by training and experience, as to be a suitable person to perform that function' (sch. 1, para. 8(2)). This is especially important, as it is the job of the inspectors to report on the licensed premises and decide whether or not prohibited or unlicensed activities are being carried out. As of 31 July 1998, the HFEA had clinically qualified inspectors who are consultant obstetricians and gynaecologists, a high percentage of the others being senior registrars, senior lecturers or specialists in the appropriate field.

THE HFEA AND INFORMATION

Apart from the Authority's duties under s. 9 of setting up a 'licence committee' with the purpose of granting, varying, suspending and revoking licences and arranging inspections of the licensed activities (see below), the Authority has a number of other statutory duties and functions. Section 8, for example, requires the Authority to keep under review information about:

(a)   embryos and their subsequent development;
(b)   the provision of treatment services; and
(c)   prohibited activity relating either to embryos or gametes.

The HFEA may be called upon to advise the Secretary of State if asked to do so on any of the functions listed above. These functions are widely drafted; for example, reviewing information about embryos and their subsequent development could include a statutory review of abortion services provided under the Abortion Act 1967. However, the power has yet to be so interpreted. The Authority seems to have taken a restricted view and limited itself to the development of the embryo created as a result of regulated reproductive techniques.

There is a variety of sources of information concerning the workings of the Authority. For example, there is a statutory duty on the Authority to produce an Annual Report. The HFEA must provide the Secretary of State with such a report detailing activities in the 12 months covered and proposed activities for the 12 months following the publication (s. 7). At time of writing there had been eight such reports published and laid before the Houses of Parliament. An ethos of openness and accountability is demonstrated in the Annual Reports, which provide comprehensive information on many issues. The content and style of the reports is beginning to assume a set pattern, including:

(a)   a provision and account of the structure and the functions of the Act;
(b)   information on the licensing procedure, any additions or losses of licences;
(c)   progress reports on the inspection process;
(d)   annual updates on the Code of Practice, highlighting issues that are to be subject to possible revision;
(e)   information on new developments, and particularly on research being undertaken, together with social and ethical responses;
(f)   registered data;
(g)   the finances of the Authority;
(h)   issues that are going to be addressed by the Authority in the forthcoming 12 months; and
(i)   comprehensive lists of membership, inspectors, clinics undertaking treatment, research projects, etc.

The Annual Report and Accounts is a particularly useful document given that the proceedings of the HFEA in its meetings are available only in summary form on the HFEA website.[3] Pressure for public hearings or an available record of proceedings at the time of the Bill was resisted on the basis that treatment records and services considered by the Authority would inevitably involve personal or confidential information which it would be improper to disclose.

Further, in relation to information sources, the Authority has a duty to collect data from licence treatments and keep a register of them. Section 31(2) provides that the register shall include information relating to:

(a)   the provision of treatment services and any resultant births; and
(b)   the keeping or use of the gametes or embryos.

The purposes of the register are threefold. The first purpose is to provide information to children born as a result of such treatment; 'the applicant' may, after reaching the age of 18 (or 16 if they are planning on getting married) and after receiving appropriate counselling (s. 31(3)), be given information pertaining to genetic background.

A second purpose is to monitor the provision of treatments. For example, the records ought to ensure that a gamete from a single donor will not be used for more than ten inseminations, as set out in the Code of Practice.

Lastly, there are wider purposes in providing information to the Government, patients, clinics and the general public. For example, although the information contained in the register is confidential under s. 33 and its disclosure is restricted to certain situations, it might be sought by the Registrar General (s. 32), or used to serve the interests of justice (s. 34) or to reveal a congenital disability (s. 35).

Although the accounts of the HFEA are not open to public inspection as such, the full accounts are audited by the Comptroller and Auditor General and a copy of that official's report is laid before Parliament (s. 6). Financial provisions also control the functioning of the Authority in two ways. First, the HFEA must bring many of its plans back to the Secretary of State for approval and Treasury ratification; and, secondly, the public funding of the whole project necessarily limits and shapes the entire regulatory processes administered by the Authority.

With regard to finances, the Authority has an obligation under s. 6 to keep proper accounts and proper records in relation to the accounts, and to prepare a statement of accounts each accounting year. A copy of the accounts must be sent to the Secretary of State and the Comptroller and Auditor General, who has to certify and report on the statement of accounts and lay this report before Parliament.

The HFEA can seek to gather information or gauge opinion on policies or developments; all of its publications are available on the HFEA website at www.hfea.gov.uk. In February 1998, for example, the HFEA issued a circulation paper asking for views on the best way to implement a policy of non-payment for sperm and egg donations (although this was subsequently withdrawn). It established a joint working group with the Advisory Committee on Genetic Testing and prepared a public consultation document on the use of pre-implantation genetic diagnosis. More famously, it has produced a report with the HGAC,[4] reaching the conclusion that the HFEA and the Act were adequate to ensure that human reproductive cloning would not be allowed.

DIRECTIONS

Section 23 of the 1990 Act gives the Authority power to make directions, thereby imposing additional conditions on licensed activities – an ability to 'fine-tune its controls'.[5] This flexibility might be justified by reference to the need for regulatory flexibility in view of the pace of scientific advance and changes in the underpinning social acceptance of reproductive techniques. Table 4.1 sets out the matters in respect of which the HFEA can issue directions. Once given, directions can be varied or revoked (s. 23(1)). Directions may apply generally, or to a specific person or clinic by the service of a notice (s. 23(4)); and failure to comply with such directions may lead to the revocation of a licence regardless of the seriousness of the breach (s. 18(1)(c)). Quite separately, s. 9(4) provides that any person, committee, or subcommittee discharging the functions of the HFEA shall do so in accordance with general directions of the Authority.

Table 4.1   Matters on which the HFEA may issue directions

Sections	Providing for
12(d)	Maintenance of proper records by licensed persons in a form specified by HFEA
12(e)	Authorisation of payment or other benefit for gametes or embryos unlawful under s. 41(8) unless in accordance with such directions (the intention is that only expenses should be authorised and that a commercial market in gametes or embryos prohibited)
12(f)	Information to be supplied to the licensed recipients of gametes or embryos
13(a)–(f)	Information to be recorded in pursuance of a treatment licence (see below s. 24(2))
13(4)	Length of time for which information must be kept (subject to s. 24(1), information to be kept for at least 50 years if the provider of treatment services does not know whether a child was born)
14(1)(d)	Records dealing with the storage of gametes or embryos to include the consents required for their storage under sch. 3, the terms of those consents and the circumstances of the storage, and (sch. 3, para. 2(3)) any other matters which HFEA specifies
14(2)	Length of time for which information about the storage of gametes or embryos must be preserved
15(2)	Information to be maintained in research licence records
15(3)	The length of time for such information to be held
24(2) and 13(2)(a)–(e)	In respect of every treatment licence under sch. 2, para. 1 which involves either:

    (a)   bringing about the creation of an embryo *in vitro,*
    (b)   keeping embryos,
    (c)   using gametes,
    (d)   any therapeutic practice with an embryo to ensure it is in a suitable condition for transfer to a woman,
    (e)   placing any embryo in a woman,
    (f)   using the hamster or other specified test to determine the fertility or normality of sperm, or
    (g)   any other specified practice

Information be recorded and given to HFEA in respect of:

Sections	Providing for
24(2) and 13(2)(a)–(e) (*continued*)	(i) the persons for whom any of those services have been provided, (ii) the services provided, (iii) the persons whose gametes are kept or used for those purposes or the bringing about the creation of an embryo, (iv) any child appearing to the person responsible to have been born as a result of the licensed treatment service, and (v) any mixing of egg and sperm or taking of an embryo from any woman or other acquisiton of an embryo from another licensed person, whether inside or outside the United Kingdom.
24(4)	The receipt or despatch of embryos or gametes from or to outside the United Kingdom to be subject to specified conditions and that the provisions of ss. 12–14 be modified accordingly
24(5)–(7)	Licence committees to direct what is to happen when a licence is to be varied or cease to have effect because it has expired, been revoked, suspended, or otherwise (including surrender). It is an offence under s. 41(2)(d) to fail to comply with a direction under s. 24(7)(a), requiring the continued discharge of duties under a licence which has expired, been suspended, revoked or surrendered. A person guilty of such an offence is liable to a maximum penalty of two years' imprisonment or an unlimited fine or both, if tried on indictment or, if tried summarily (i.e. before magistrates), to a maximum of six months' imprisonment or to a fine not exceeding the statutory maximum (presently £2,000), or both
26(5)	The draft code approved by the Secretary of State shall come into force as laid out in the directions
24(11), sch. 2, para. 1(1)(f), sch. 3, para. 2(4)	The egg of an animal other than the hamster not to be used under a treatment or a research licence to test the fertility or normality of sperm until proposed directions have been reported by the Secretary of State to each House of Parliament.

As Table 4.1 demonstrates, directions can be made for a wide variety of regulatory purposes. In 1991, for example, the Authority issued directions concerning the payment of egg and sperm donors (under s. 12(e)). They stated that clinics could pay donors up to £15 per donation plus reasonable expenses, or offer free treatment or sterilisation. In 1996 these directions were amended to cover payments from third parties – clinics are not allowed to accept 'donations' from donors where it is known that payments exceed the limit in the directions. The directions would have had to have been amended to take account of the Authority's decision not to allow any additional payments (except reasonable expenses) for donations, although this resolution was later withdrawn following a particularly hostile reception from clinicians involved in providing treatment services. The background to this, one of the HFEA's longest-standing policy proposals, is discussed in the *Annual Report* for 1996, s. 6, and probably represents the most significant rebuttal for its policies since the Authority was established. In February 1999, the Authority considered whether directions should be made allowing the injection of human sperm into mouse oocytes for research purposes. Such directions could be made under para. 1(1)(f) of sch. 2, but the proposed directions would have to be reported to the Secretary of State who would then decide whether to lay a copy of the report before both Houses of Parliament in order that the directions could become effective (s. 24(11)).

Where there has been an alleged or apparent breach of directions, the HFEA may make preliminary inquiries to establish whether there is *prima facie* evidence of a breach, referring its findings to a licence committee who will decide what further action needs to be taken, if any. In the event of a possible criminal offence, the decision has to be made whether to refer the matter to the Director of Public Prosecutions. Any decision could result in the licence being revoked or suspended, but subject to appeal to an appeal committee. There is then a further right of appeal to the High Court on a point of law (see below).

REGULATIONS

In keeping with the generally flexible framework of the legislation, there are enabling provisions under s. 45 for the Secretary of State to make changes by way of regulations. However, some provisions of the Act are regarded as providing protections so fundamental to the integrity of the scheme agreed on that they may not be changed without Parliamentary scrutiny. Scrutiny of secondary legislation takes two forms: the 'negative' and the 'affirmative' resolutions of the Houses of Parliament. Under the former, the statutory instrument will be laid before Parliament and will take effect unless there is a 'prayer for annulment' which then receives a favourable vote. This seldom happens. Under an affirmative procedure, the draft statutory instrument will not take effect until approved by affirmative resolution, and Parliamentary time must be found for this.

Three activities fall within the affirmative resolution procedure. Section 45(4) provides that the Secretary of State may not make regulations which would permit the hitherto prohibited keeping or use of an embryo (under s. 3(3)(c)) without the opportunity for full Parliamentary consideration secured by the affirmative resolution procedure. A similar reservation is made in respect of any proposal to relax regulations prohibiting the storage or use of gametes (s. 4(2)) or any changes proposed under sch. 2, para. 1(1)(g) or (4). These last provisions concern, respectively, the practices which may be authorised in a treatment licence and a condition in a research licence which authorises the alteration of the genetic structure of an embryo cell. If any amendment is proposed to either of these provisions it must be the subject of affirmative Parliamentary scrutiny.

There is a further range of matters which, while important, it was thought suitable to leave to the less stringent safeguard of the 'negative' resolution procedure (s. 45(5)). This provides that where regulations are made which have not been subject to prior scrutiny and approval, a copy should be lodged in the office of the clerk to each House and the regulations will come into force 40 days after lodging if they have not been made subject to a resolution for annulment passed in either the House of Commons or the House of Lords. There are five sorts of amendment subject to this kind of review. They concern any additional functions to be undertaken by the HFEA (s. 8(d)); the composition of the HFEA licence committees (s. 9(5)); changes in the licensing procedure (s. 10(1), (2)); any proposed increase or decrease in the permitted period for the storage of eggs or embryos (s. 14(5)); and any changes in the information which the HFEA is obliged to disclose to an applicant under s. 31 of the Act (ss. 31(4)(a), 45(4)). In February 1996, for example, the Human Fertilisation and Embryology (Statutory Storage Period for Embryos) Regulations 1996 (SI 1996 No. 375) were laid before Parliament. They took effect in May 1996 and extended in certain circumstances the statutory storage period for embryos in the 1990 Act from five years to ten years under s. 14(5) (above).

THE CODE OF PRACTICE

A significant part of the HFEA's supervisory function is the requirement to draw up and maintain in force a Code of Practice for licensed centres and individuals. The Code relates to the proper conduct of licensed activities and to the discharge of the functions of the individual under whose supervision those activities are carried on and of any other persons to whom a licence applies (defined in s. 17(2)). In particular, s. 25(2) states that the Code must give guidance to those licensed to provide treatment services about the account which is to be taken (under s. 13(5)) of the welfare of children born following treatment services. The Code also determines the account which is to be taken of the welfare of any other children affected by the birth of children of assisted conception. (See further, below.)

The 1994 Annual Report referred to the Code as the 'backbone of the Authority's work', setting the standards – professional, ethical and legal – that centres should adopt. The object of the Code, as specified in the introduction to the fourth edition (see Appendix 2), is:

. . . wider than to secure the safety or efficacy of particular clinical or scientific practices. It is concerned with areas of practice which raise fundamental ethical and social questions. In framing it, we have been guided both by the requirements of the Human Fertilisation and Embryology Act and by:

- the respect which is due to human life at all stages in its development;
- the right of people who are or may be infertile to the proper consideration of their request for treatment;
- a concern for the welfare of children, which cannot always be adequately protected by concern for the interests of the adults involved; and
- a recognition of the benefits, both to individuals and to society which can flow from the responsible pursuit of medical and scientific knowledge.

Since the original Code, which was received by the Secretary of State in July 1991, there have been three further editions, each with amendments pertaining to advances and issues that have come to be tackled by the Authority. In the second edition, for example, changes were made to take account of the Human Fertilisation and Embryology (Disclosure of Information) Act 1992, legislation relaxing the confidentiality rules between different doctors and between lawyers and patients.

The third edition took account of the coming into effect of parental orders under s. 30, which would allow the transfer of legal parental responsibility to the commissioning parents from the surrogate parents without the need for the full adoption procedure. The fourth edition (third revision) incorporates the Human Fertilisation and Embryology (Statutory Storage Period for Embryos) Regulations 1996, which allow in certain circumstances an increase in the storage period of embryos. The procedure for changing the Code of Practice is contained within s. 26 of the Act. A draft revision of the Code is sent to the Secretary of State, and when he approves the revision he shall lay it before Parliament. It will then come into force in accordance with directions. If the Secretary of State does not approve of the revision he can send it back to the Authority for redrafting together with reasons for the rejection.

Throughout each revision the basic format and content of the Code have remained the same. In particular, the Code provides guidance on the assessment of the welfare of the child. This is a statutory requirement under s. 13(5) of the Act which is expanded and explained in Part 3 of the Code. It pin-points factors which the clinics should take into account before providing treatment to an individual or a couple. They include such matters as: their commitment to having and bringing up a child or children; their ability to provide a supportive environment; medical histories; their ages and future likely ability to look after any children born as a result of treatment; the possible effect on any existing children in the family. The most recent edition includes considering the position of HIV positive parents and the effect on any resultant child. Since the need of the child for a father is singled out in the welfare considerations in s. 13(5), this consideration is repeated in the Code. Where, however, a child would be born with no legal father (not falling within s. 28), the clinic should pay particular attention to the mother's ability to meet the needs of the child throughout its childhood, and whether there is anyone else within the patient's family and social circle who would be willing and able to share the responsibilities of bringing up and maintaining any child born. The Code also highlights the requirements for the qualifications of staff; the need and procedure to obtain consent; the requirements for counselling and the types of counselling that should be available to the prospective patients or donors. The specifics of the Code are discussed further throughout the book.

Failure by any affected person to observe a provision of the Code is not, of itself, sufficient to render that person liable to civil or criminal proceedings; but a licence committee may take into account the provisions of the Code and their observance or breach when it is considering whether or not to vary or revoke a licence under s. 18 (s. 25(6)(b)). In addition, a licence committee must, when considering whether there has been a failure to comply with licence conditions (a breach of the duty which is imposed on the person responsible by s. 17(1)(e) for which a committee many revoke or vary a licence (under s. 18(1)(c), (3)), take account of any relevant provision of the Code, especially where those licence conditions require anything to be 'proper' or 'suitable' (s. 25(6)(a)).

The Code has not been without its critics. Savas and Treece,[6] for example, carried out empirical research into how clinics interpret the Code and found that the discretion allowed to clinics in deciding who were and were not to become parents was leading to ambiguity and inconsistent decisions. They refer to controversial cases such as Liz Buttle, for example, and Diane Blood, pointing out that despite the guidelines there is still a lot of room for variation between clinics on treatment decisions. On this analysis terms such as 'bear in mind' and 'suitable opportunity' open the way for assessments by the doctors and their teams in areas in which they are not trained or at the very least should not be attempting. How, for example, is a doctor supposed to make an assessment on parenting skills in the brief time treatment will take, especially as GPs' notes will generally contain only medical histories? Savas and Treece reach the conclusion that there is a wide array of possible interpretations of the Code, and as such it is of questionable legal value: 'The process of deciding who should and should not benefit from fertility treatment will effectively exclude certain people from parenthood. Therefore it should only be done on a transparent basis and applied consistently.'[7] They believe that unless the system is changed, there is too much scope for an elitist view to prevail and that there is the possibility of 'shopping around' to find a clinic that will offer treatment.

Against this, it must be remembered that there are local ethics committees and that there is a hierarchy of regulatory mechanism, with the Code ranking lowest in terms of its prescription. Arguably some autonomy should be allowed to treatment centres in offering reproductive therapies, both because of their direct contact with those seeking access to treatment and to allow some room to develop clinical practice.

A fifth edition of the Code is promised, probably in early 2001. The HFEA has said that it consults with the clinics on how to make the Code more organised and easier to use, and will attempt to recast the structure of the Code. Issues that will need to be included or expanded are genetic testing and egg sharing. Later versions will probably be required to deal with donors, both in terms of their remuneration and, as will surely come sooner or later, how to manage the process of revealing identifying information to children born following treatment services.

The significance of the Code should not be underestimated either in terms of its status, or of its role in embellishing the skeletal framework of the Act. The language of the Act makes free use of loose adjectives. These include 'proper records' (s. 12(d)); 'proper counselling' and 'relevant information as is proper' (s. 13(6) and sch. 3, para. 3(1)(a) and (b)); 'suitable opportunities for counselling' (s. 13(6) and sch. 3, para. 3(1)(a)); and 'suitable procedures' (s. 13(7)(a) and (b)) for determining the matters there referred to. We do not include among these loose adjectives 'suitable person' (s. 16(2)(b)(ii)) or 'suitable premises' (s. 16(2)(d)) because they relate to a condition for the grant of a licence and not a licence condition, nor similar words used in s. 18 which deal with the conditions for revocation or variation of a licence. But we might include the duty imposed under s. 17. If the discharge of the duty imposed on the person responsible under s. 17(1) is regarded as a condition of a licence, then these must be taken into account under s. 25(2)(a). Such duties may include those to ensure: the employment of 'suitable persons' (s. 17(1)(a)) and the use of 'suitable practices' in the course of licensed activities (s. 17(1)(d)); that 'proper equipment' is used (s. 17(1)(b)); and that 'proper arrangements' are made for keeping gametes and embryos and disposing of those which have been allowed to perish (s. 16(1)(c)).

In addition to the reliance on the Code by the licence committees, it may be utilised by both the civil and criminal courts as an appropriate evidential yardstick. This may be in the context of the judicial review of, for example, the reasonableness of a decision to refuse or revoke a licence. In relation to the criminal law provisions of the Act, the Code may be taken as a measure of the appropriate standards of conduct. The reliance on codes published under statutory authority by statutory bodies has grown considerably in recent years. It is clear from either context that Codes of Practice have an effect such that for practical purposes they can be regarded as statements of the requirements imposed both by the tribunals and the courts.

LICENCES

Section 11 of the 1990 Act allows the Authority to issue three different types of licence, specifically those providing for:

(a) treatment services;
(b) the storage of gametes and embryos;
(c) work upon a research project.

The number of licences issued by the licence committee as of 31 August 1999 can be found in the 1999 Annual Report and were as follows:

HFEA licensed clinics

IVF and DI	75
IVF only	0
DI only	32
Storage of sperm only	8
Research licences only	3
Total	**118**

The first Annual Report of the Authority in 1992 considered the licensing procedure to have four main objectives:

(a) to ensure that no prohibited activities take place and that no activities for which a licence is required are undertaken except under licence;
(b) to secure public confidence and the confidence of centres that the Authority is maintaining a fair and consistent framework for licensing;
(c) to ensure the public and Parliament that the research work which is undertaken under licence is necessary, within the conditions set out in the Act; and
(d) to assure the public that centres operate to certain minimum standards.

A licence granted by the HFEA can authorise the specified activities only under supervision of an individual named in the licence and to be carried on only on premises which the licence specifies (s. 11(2) and sch. 2, para. 4(1)). No licence can authorise more than one research project – each proposed project requires a separate licence (s. 11(2) and sch. 2, para. (2)(b)). No licence can authorise more than one individual who is to be responsible for the licensed activities (s. 11(2) and sch. 2, para. 4(2)(c)), or apply to premises in different places (s. 11(2) and sch. 2, para. 4(2)(d)). A licence authorising treatment services or a licence authorising research can also permit the storage of embryos or gametes, but a treatment licence cannot authorise research, nor a research licence treatment; each activity must be considered in a separate licence application (s. 11(2) and sch. 2, para. 4(2)(a)).

The legislation precludes the granting of licences for certain types of activity. Under s. 3(3) a licence cannot authorise:

(a)   keeping or using an embryo after the appearance of the 'primitive streak', taken to be not later than 14 days after gametes have been mixed, but excluding any time when the resulting embryo has been preserved by freezing (s. 3(4));

(b)   placing a human embryo in any animal;

(c)   keeping or using an embryo in contravention of regulations;

(d)   nucleus substitution, sometimes called cloning.

The licensing process also helps the HFEA to keep informed about current and developing practices, which in turn helps it to gather and disseminate information constantly upgrading standards. Each type of licence has its own procedures and rules which will be discussed further below.

THE LICENCE COMMITTEE

Licence committees were set up under s. 9(1) of the 1990 Act. They have the mandate of discharging the Authority's functions relating to the grant, variation, suspension and revocation of licences. A licence committee consists of five members of the Authority, operating with a quorum of three. Section 9(5) requires that at least one member be present who is not authorised to carry on or participate in any activity under the authority of a licence and would not be so authorised if any application he or she had made were approved. The licence committee is the only committee that cannot delegate to a subcommittee (s. 9(3)) neither can it co-opt members other than existing members of the HFEA (sch. 1). Schedule 1, para. 9(1) allows the committee to run its own procedures in whatever way it sees fit, although s. 10 allows the Secretary of State to make such regulations as appear 'necessary or desirable' pertaining to the procedure of licence committees and of the Authority in its appeals capacity. These regulations may include provisions to give evidence or produce documents and about the admissibility of evidence.

Schedule 1, para. 10(1) contains another restriction on the membership of the licence committee. In line with general public law policy, a member of the Authority who is in any way directly or indirectly interested in the licence granted or proposed to be granted shall disclose the nature of this interest to the Authority. The member shall then not be permitted to sit on any such committee and any deliberations or decisions made in breach of this rule shall have no effect. In setting its procedural rules the committee should have regard to this principle, breach of which would surely be grounds for challenge by way of judicial review of any decision taken.

The Authority has developed a strategy to ensure that it maintains a consistent approach to licensing. This is as follows:

(a)   It is usual to attach additional conditions to licences where breaches of the Act or the Code of Practice have been found by an inspection team. Setting time limits means that such conditions are used as means to apply pressure for speedy compliance with the necessary standards.

(b)   Licences are usually issued for a period of 12 months, but shorter periods may be deemed necessary when licences have particular (often clinic-specific) conditions which have to be closely monitored.

(c)   Letters may be sent to centres which include specific recommendations – usually practical advice based on the Authority's experience.

(d)   Commendations for good practice and particularly high standards in procedure and method are delivered and used as examples to other clinics.

By using this approach, the aim is to achieve consistent and high standards throughout the licensing procedures. Licence committees also have to deal with appeals made against its decisions. Details of the appeals structure are given below.

Applicants for licences have the help and guidance of the Code of Practice and the Manual for Clinics which are both updated regularly. Licence application forms are produced with the requirements of the Act and the Code of Practice in mind; they have the purpose of gathering a comprehensive set of information on the centre before the licensing deliberation begins. Information requested includes that about the centre's staff, premises, patient information leaflets, consent forms, record forms, charges and, where appropriate, the ethics committee.

THE LICENSING PROCEDURE

Introduction

Once the application form has been received by the HFEA there follows a site visit by a team of inspectors. Thereafter the licence committee considers both the application and the results of the inspection. The outcome of these deliberations is then notified to the applicant.

The statutory requirements that the licensing committee must take into account can be found in ss. 16 and 17 of the Act. Section 16(1) provides that a licence may be granted to any person who makes an application to the Authority together with the initial fee as long as that person fulfils the requirements of s. 16(2). The initial fee is decided by the Authority under s. 16(5) with the approval of the Secretary of State and the Treasury. At present the Authority strives to find 70% of its expenditure through licence fees, made up of the initial fee and thereafter additional fees for treatment licences. The HFEA budget was £1,559,000 for 2000–01 and as from October 2000, the initial fee was raised to £200 (from £100) for research-only and storage-only licences, and £500 (from £250) for treatment licences. The s. 16(2) requirements provide that the application for a licence has to specify a designated individual (who must be a named natural person, not a body corporate or other legal person) under whose supervision the activities that are authorised will be carried on (s. 16(2)(a)). Either this individual must be the applicant, or the application has to be made with the consent of this person. In this event the actual applicant must be someone who is, in any case, a suitable person to hold a licence (s. 16(2)(b)). The licence committee also has to be satisfied that the proposed individual has such character, qualifications and experience to carry out the requirements of s. 17 (s. 16(2)(c)). This is used as a mechanism to ensure that fit and proper persons hold the licence and is a common form of regulatory provision.[8]

Section 17 details the responsibilities of the 'person responsible', the individual under whose supervision the activities authorised by licences are carried on. This person has to secure that the other persons to whom a licence applies are of suitable character, hold suitable qualifications and training and experience to participate properly in the licensed activities. These people are those specified in s. 17(2) as any person designated in the Act or to whom the licence applies after notice has been given to the Authority. It also includes any person acting under the direction of the person responsible, or any person designated such as staff involved in counselling, nursing and so on. The responsible person has to ensure also that proper equipment is used, that proper arrangements are made for the keeping and disposal of gametes and embryos and that the conditions of the licence are met. The licence committee must be satisfied that the premises specified are suitable for the licensed activity and that the other requirements in the Act relating to the grant of a licence are fulfilled (s. 16(2)).

If the above information is deemed insufficient by the licence committee to determine the application, s. 16(4) allows the Authority to require the applicant to provide further information until such point as the application can be determined. The licence cannot be granted unless a copy of the conditions that will be imposed in the licence have been acknowledged in writing by the applicant, or the person responsible if he or she is not the applicant.

We now discuss in greater detail some of the stages of the licensing mentioned above.

Inspection

When an application for a licence is received by the HFEA, a licence committee must arrange for an inspection of and report in respect of the premises for which the licence is sought (s. 9(7)). This applies where an application is made to carry on activities not already licensed, or to carry on previously licensed activities in as yet unauthorised premises. Where the application comes from a licensed person and the premises have been inspected within the previous 12 months, the licence committee may dispense with a second inspection. This could occur if a further licensed activity is proposed at existing licensed premises, since different licences must be applied for and granted in respect of research, treatment or storage. Equally, an inspection may be necessary if premises change ownership and a previously unlicensed person makes an application. The HFEA is required to ensure that licensed premises are inspected once in each calendar year (s. 9(8)), unless a licence committee considers that an inspection is unnecessary. This might be the case where, for example, research or storage or treatment services have for some reason been suspended and work is not actively in progress for that year or a large part of it.

The Authority has recently changed the inspection process. Before 1994 it would fully inspect all premises once a year, looking into all the areas covered by the Act. This included investigating areas such as: the qualifications and experience of staff employed; the standards of the facilities and laboratory conditions; the method used in assessing clients' medical and social investigations to determine the welfare of the child; the screening procedure for donors; information given, especially that leading to consent; counselling provisions; the techniques used for the handling and storage of embryos and gametes used; confidentiality of records and so on. This procedure did not allow for focused attention on any one area. The Authority decided, therefore, that the process should become more 'focused, flexible and efficient'.[9] Under the redesigned licensing system the Authority has introduced a three-year licensing cycle. All clinics will receive one broad-based general inspection (as detailed above) at least once every three years with highly focused inspections in the intervening years, the focus to be determined by the licensing committee. The HFEA has also advocated more surprise visits by the inspectors. This system started in May 1997 and has the benefit of being more cost efficient, in line with the new public management requirements of modern government.

Full inspections require four team members, normally comprising:

(a) a clinician;
(b) a scientist;
(c) a 'layperson', who should have an interest in a related area such as counselling; and
(d) a member of the HFEA executive staff.

One of the team may also be an Authority member, or a member may merely act to chair the inspection team. The inspection team's composition for a more focused inspection will be determined by the licence committee as and when required. When the Authority choose its inspectors it has to ensure that they have the depth of knowledge and experience required for the HFEA to fulfil its statutory requirements. In 1995 the Authority carried out a recruitment exercise to ensure that it had an inspection team capable of carrying out the new focused inspections. Nominations were made and a subcommittee chose a new, highly qualified and objective team of inspectors to seek to ensure compliance with HFEA policies.

Licence conditions

General conditions When it comes to the actual content of the licences, s. 12 details what each and every licence should contain, regardless of its purpose. The general conditions are as follows:

(a) As mentioned above, the activities specified in the licence can be carried out only on the premises specified in the licence under the supervision of the person responsible (s. 12(a)). The person responsible is that person who carries out the duties in s. 17. He or she is the individual under whose supervision the activities authorised in the Act are conducted.

(b) Any member of the Authority shall, at any reasonable times and on the production of documentation identifying that person, be permitted to enter the licensed premises and inspect them, as well as inspect any equipment or records or observe any activity (s. 12(b)). In addition to this licensing procedure, s. 39 gives such employees entering and inspecting premises the right to take possession of anything they have reasonable grounds to believe may be required for the purpose of the licensing functions of the Authority or as evidence of an offence under the Act. This includes information in any form. Section 39(3) even allows a member of the Authority to keep an embryo or gamete in pursuance of the Authority's functions without a licence, even an embryo past the primitive streak. Under s. 40, a justice of the peace (sheriff in Scotland) has the power to issue a warrant to enter any premises if there are reasonable grounds for suspecting that an offence under the Act is being, or has been, committed.

(c)   The consent requirements detailed in sch. 3 must be complied with (s. 12(c)). (See Chapter 7 for details.)

(d)   Proper records must be maintained in a form specified by the Authority in directions (s. 12(d)). The details of the requirement can be found in Part 11 of the Code of Practice, outlining confidentiality requirements and so on (see Appendix 2). (See below for details of the new clinical data audit procedure.)

(e)   No money or other benefit shall be given for the supply of gametes or embryos unless authorised by directions. As mentioned above, originally directions allowed for £15 payment and reasonable expenses, but this is now in the process of being stopped to encourage altruistic donation. Reasonable expenses will still be allowed. Any payment given outside of these directions comes under the remit of s. 41(8), whereby the person responsible or the nominal licensee is guilty of an offence if he or she gives or receives money for the supply of gametes or embryos. Such persons would be liable to a term of imprisonment not exceeding six months, or a fine not exceeding level five on the standard scale or both. A nominal licensee is a person holding a licence but is not the person responsible for the licence (s. 17(3)).

(f)   Where gametes or embryos are supplied by one licence holder to another, the supplier shall give to the recipient such information as the HFEA specifies in its directions. This is to ensure that where gametes or embryos are moved around, the information held by one centre about the genetic identity of the donor, the nature and extent of the consents given, and the purposes for which the gametes or embryos are to be used, will be passed from the first to the subsequent custodians of the gametes or embryos. It should also be possible for the donor or gestator to contact the new holders of their gamete or embryo quickly in case they want to vary their consent within sch. 3.

(g)   In addition to such conditions the Authority can issue directions specifying that it shall be provided in such form and at such intervals with copies or extracts from the records or any such other information as it may specify.

Note that the above list represents conditions which *must* be imposed. The HFEA will decide to impose further conditions where appropriate. These can be specific to the centre and can relate to a wide range of other issues, from security to counselling functions.

Treatment licences   The provisions for treatment licences (sch. 2, para. 1) specify what can come under the umbrella of a treatment licence, which includes such activities as:

(a)   bringing about the creation of an embryo *in vitro*;
(b)   the use of gametes;
(c)   keeping embryos;

(d)   placing embryos in a woman;

(e)   practices designed to ensure that embryos are in a suitable condition to place in a woman;

(f)   the testing of the fertility and normality of sperm; and

(g)   other specified activities.

The licence committee can authorise licences of this nature only if it appears to the Authority to be 'necessary or desirable' for the purpose of providing treatment services (sch. 2, para. 1(3)), and then they cannot be granted for a period which exceeds five years (sch. 2, para. 1(5)). The Authority in 1995 advocated a shortened renewal period for licences if it believed that the clinic had not radically changed since the last inspection or committee decision.

The licence may contain conditions, or may specify the manner in which treatment activities are to be carried out. Section 13 contains conditions which are specific to every treatment licence issued. It details the information that has to be kept by the clinic when carrying out treatment services, such as the name of the person being provided with the treatment, the treatment they had, and any child or children born as a result of the treatment and so on (see Chapter 9). The section also highlights the obligation on clinics to make assessments such as the welfare of the child when determining the potential beneficiaries of their treatment (see Chapter 6 for details).

As new techniques are discovered and marketed, the Authority has to consider whether its controls are adequate to guarantee the safety and respect of all persons and potential persons involved. This was the case with the relatively new Intra Cyptoplasmic Sperm Injection (ICSI) technique. This is a technique whereby a single sperm is injected into the cyptoplasm of an egg using a very fine glass needle. It can be particularly valuable in cases of male sub-fertility as only a single sperm is required, although the success is dependent on the skill and experience of the practitioner. With this in mind, the Authority set up the Working Group on New Developments in Reproductive Technology which established an alternative licensing procedure. Under this system a clinic applying for a licence to practise ICSI must provide both clinic- and practitioner-orientated information. The clinic information would detail such areas as patient selection criteria for the new technique, consent forms and laboratory protocol. Practitioner information depends on the status of the embryologist. Where the practitioner is recognised as competent in the technique by the Authority clinical records for the past years are examined. If a practitioner is not so recognised, a CV and training record are required together with a report by an HFEA inspector, skilled in the new technique, assessing the suitability of the practitioner to carry out the procedure. All the information is then considered by the committee and a decision made. Monitoring progress is then fundamental. In addition to checks on an annual basis, new practitioners are monitored three months after commencing the clinical technique. This is not to say that all aspects of a new technique will be given approval. In 1995, for example, the possible use of spermatids (immature sperm) in ICSI was shelved until further research could be carried out to convince the Authority as to the safety of the procedure, whnich it has still not licensed.

Research licences   Research licences cover the creation of embryos *in vitro* and the keeping or use of embryos for the purposes of a research project (sch. 2, para. 3). This project must be specified on the licence. The Authority cannot issue a licence unless it appears to it to be 'necessary or desirable' for at least one of a number of specified purposes; and even then the Authority must be satisfied that the use of an embryo is necessary for the purposes of the research (sch. 2, para. 3(2) and (6)). The specified purposes are:

(a)   promoting advances in the treatment of infertility;
(b)   increasing knowledge about the causes of congenital disease or about the causes of miscarriages;
(c)   developing more effective techniques of contraception; or
(d)   developing methods for detecting gene/chromosome abnormalities in embryos pre-implantation.

Annex 4 of the 1999 Annual Report contains a list of all licensed research projects. They include research improving methods for the biopsy and diagnosis of inherited genetic disease of human pre-implantation embryos licensed at St Thomas's Hospital, London, and a comparison of human oocyte cyropreservation methods on the outcome of *in vitro* fertilisation methods conducted at the University of Aberdeen. As of August 1999, some 124 licence applications had resulted in 102 research licences, 12 of which were refused on renewal.

Parliament decided that certain activities involving human embryos were not to be allowed, regardless of the curtailment this would mean to research in the UK. These prohibitions are as follows:

(a)   keeping or using an embryo after the appearance of the primitive streak or after 14 days, whichever is the earlier;
(b)   placing a human embryo in an animal;
(c)   replacing a nucleus of a cell of an embryo with a nucleus taken from the cell of another person, another embryo, or subsequent development of an embryo;
(d)   altering the genetic structure of any cell while it forms part of an embryo; and
(e)   using embryos for any other purpose except in pursuance of a licence.

In addition, the Code of Practice states that it is the policy of the HFEA not to license research projects involving embryo splitting with the intention of increasing the number of embryos available for transfer (para. 10.5).

The procedure for obtaining a research licence is more elaborate than that for treatment licences. Prior approval of the research topic by an external ethics committee is a necessary prerequisite to an application. If the centre is part of the NHS then proposed projects should be sent to the Local Research Ethics Committee (LREC), or to a Multi-Centre Research Ethics Committee[10] if five or more centres are involved (para. 10.8). For centres outside the NHS the Code of Practice details the necessary procedure. It states that such centres may send a proposal to an LREC by prior arrangement, or they can set up their own ethics committee. Such a committee should be an independent body of no fewer than five members, no more than a third of whom should be employed by or have a financial interest in the centre. The chairman should be independent and membership composition should be approved by the HFEA.

Applications must include information concerning the objectives and duration of the proposed research (research licences can be granted only for a period not exceeding three years: sch. 2, para. 3(9)), the reasons why the use of gametes and/or embryos is essential and a full account of the methodology and relevant protocols. In addition to all this the application must be submitted for peer review. The peer reviewers, chosen by the Authority, comment on the proposal, including the originality of the work, its methodology and the justifications for it. A list of the current peer reviewers chosen for their knowledge and experience can be found in Annex 5 of the 1999 Annual Report. The findings and recommendations resulting from the peer review are then sent to the licence committee which decides, after having regard to all the information before it, whether or not a research licence should be granted.

As with the treatment licence, conditions may be specified by the committee as part of the licence. Section 15 contains the conditions with which all research licences must comply. Again these include the recording of information, but also provide that no other use shall be made of the embryo except for the purpose specified in the project (s. 15(4)). This prohibits another avenue of research being carried out under the guise of the original research licence (sch. 2, para. 4(2)(b)).

Storage Storage licences form an integral part of treatment and research licences, storage being a necessary prerequisite for the efficient running of research and treatment procedures. Such licences can also be issued in their own right. In line with treatment, storage licences which may authorise the storage of both embryos and gametes can be issued for a period not exceeding five years (sch. 2, para. 2(3)). Section 14 deals specifically with the conditions of such licences. Statute allows for the storage and freezing of gametes for up to ten years (s. 14(3)) and embryos for five years (s. 14(4)), after which time they should be allowed to perish. By the end of 31 July 1996 the original five-year storage periods were terminated. In the absence of consent to use the embryos for treatment or research the embryos had to be allowed to perish. However, using powers under s. 14(5) of the Act the Secretary of State has since issued the Human Fertilisation and Embryology (Statutory Storage Period for Embryos) Regulations 1996 (SI 1996 No. 375). These Regulations allow for the extension in certain circumstances of the statutory storage period of embryos from five years to ten years. This may arise in the case of a woman about to go through intensive cancer treatment who may wish one day to have a child and siblings some years later. Without an extension of the statutory storage period genetically related children would not be an option. Thus, an embryo created from gametes which have been stored for say, eight to nine years, or right up to the ten-year limit, may then be frozen and stored for the maximum allowed for the storage of embryos. In this way an embryo could be used in the provision of treatment services for a maximum period of up to 20 years after the egg or sperm from which it derives was donated.

No gametes or any embryo which was created *in vitro*, or any embryo obtained by lavage may be stored unless there is effective consent by, respectively:

(a) the person whose gametes they are;
(b) the people whose gametes were used to create the embryo or the woman from whom the embryo was obtained, and unless;

(c) the gametes or embryos are stored in accordance with those consents (s. 12(c), sch. 3, para. 8(1)–(3)).

Section 14(1) envisages four types of provider for embryos or gametes which may then be stored:

(a)   sperm donation;
(b)   egg donation;
(c)   an embryo created *in utereo* and obtained following lavage;
(d)   an embryo created *in vitro*.

In respect of (a), (b) and (c), the gametes or the embryo may be placed in storage only if received from a consenting donor or from another licensed centre (s. 14(1)(a)).

Embryos created *in vitro* by someone other than the licence holder (a storage licence may also authorise bringing about the creation of an embryo under sch. 2, para. 1(1)(a)) may be stored only if they are acquired from another licensed person. Section 14(1)(a) is ambiguous on the point of whether that licence must be one which authorises the creation of embryos *in vitro*, or, as the section provides *ex facie*, whether it can include only for the purposes of storage, or for providing treatment services or research, either of which may authorise the bringing about the creation of an embryo *in vitro* (sch. 2, paras 1(1)(a) and 3(1)(a)). The wording of s. 14(1)(a) seems to contemplate that an embryo may be placed in storage by a duly authorised person even if it is created by someone who is not licensed to bring about the creation of an embryo, as long as he or she is 'a person to whom a licence applies'. The section contains no limitation such as 'a relevant licence', neither does it say that an embryo created *in vitro* may be placed in storage only if received from a person who is licensed to bring about the creation of embryos *in vitro*. It is true that it would be more consistent with the general scheme of the Act for the section to be read in the more restrictive way, and for an embryo to be stored only if it is received from a person who is licensed to bring about the creation of embryos. The other interpretation contemplates the storage of embryos even if they are received from a person who is not licensed to create them, and who may indeed commit an offence if that creation is done deliberately.

However, s. 41, which makes further provision with respect to offences, ensures that a person accused of an offence of unlicensed creation of an embryo (under s. 3(1)) has a defence of showing that he or she took all such steps as were reasonable and exercised all due diligence to avoid committing the offence (s. 41(11)(b)). So the wider interpretation of s. 14(1)(a) may be to make provision for a person who is licensed to provide treatment services, but who does not have the necessary facilities or personnel to carry out proper *in vitro* fertilisation, and who mistakenly produces an embryo which may then lawfully be passed on to a licensed storage facility. The storer may later pass on the embryo to another treatment facility, and the embryo may be lawfully used for the purpose of assisting a woman to become pregnant.

Embryos may not be placed in storage at all if they have been created *in vitro* by an unlicensed person (s. 14(1)(a)), and an embryo which has been 'appropriated' for the purposes of any project of research may not be kept or used other than for such a project (s. 15(4)), whether it has in fact been used in such research or not.

REVOCATION, VARIATION AND SUSPENSION OF LICENCES

A licence committee may revoke a licence, or vary any terms of a licence which it would otherwise have the power to revoke (s. 18(1), (3)). The circumstances in which a licence may be revoked are set out in s. 18(1), and the procedures to which a committee must adhere in either refusing, revoking or varying a licence are set out in s. 19. The Act also gives limited grounds upon which a licence holder may apply for changes to the licence. Sections 19 and 20 provide mechanisms whereby parties interested in revocation or variation of a licence may be entitled to be heard before a committee determines the application. It would seem clear on the principles of *Ridge* v *Baldwin* [1964] AC 40 that the licence holders at least would have this right, but so too might interested third parties in appropriate cases (see *R* v *Hendon RDC ex parte Chorley Taxi Fleet Operators' Association* [1972] 2 QB 299). Sections 19 and 20 provide limited grounds upon which an appeal from such a determination can be taken, in the first instance to a review committee of at least five members of the HFEA and thence, on a point of law, to the High Court (see further below).[11]

The grounds for revocation or variation under s. 18(1) are that:

(a)   any information given in a licence application was false or misleading in a material respect;

(b)   the licensed premises are no longer suitable for the licensed activities;

(c)   the person responsible has failed to discharge, or is unable because of incapacity to discharge, the s. 17 duty, or has failed to comply with any directions given in connection with any licence;

(d)   there has been a material change of circumstances since the grant of the licence.

In addition, a licence committee may revoke or vary a licence if there has been an application by the person responsible or the nominal licensee (s. 18(4)).

A licence can be varied only to the extent that it affects activities authorised by licence, by changing the manner in which the licensed activities are conducted or by changing or removing conditions which a licence committee has attached to a licence (s. 18(6)(a)). To the extent that the licence authorises the conduct of activities on licensed premises, the licence can be varied only so as to extend or restrict the premises to which the licence relates (s. 18(6)(b)). In other words, an application to vary a licence cannot seek to add new, previously unlicensed premises to the licence, nor to add new services to an existing licence, nor to authorise the conduct of an activity which needs a separate application for a new licence. There is one exception to this provision, which is where a nominal licensee applies to vary a licence to designate another individual in place of the present person responsible for overseeing the licensed activities and securing the discharge of the duties under s. 17. Here, as long as the application is made with the consent of the person responsible and the committee is satisfied as to the person's character, qualifications and experience to supervise the licensed activities and discharge the duty, the committee may vary the licence as requested (s. 18(5)).

Section 18(2) provides three additional grounds for revocation only, and not variation. These are, first, where the committee ceases to be satisfied that the character of the person responsible or the nominal licensee (see s. 17(3)) is such as is required for the supervision of the licensed activities. It could be, for example, that such a person is convicted of an offence unrelated to the Act but which casts general doubt on that person's continuing suitability (s. 18(2)(a)). The second and third grounds may occur either where a person responsible dies, or where he or she is convicted of an offence under the Human Fertilisation and Embryology Act 1990 (s. 18(2)(b)).

In any case where a licence committee has reasonable grounds to suspect that revocation of a licence would be warranted under s. 18 and believes that matters are sufficiently serious to warrant an immediate suspension, it is given power in s. 22(1) to suspend the licence immediately for a period not exceeding three months. Section 22(2) provides that such a suspension is to be effected by giving notice either to the person responsible or, if he or she has died or appears to the committee to be incapable of discharging the s. 17 duties, to the nominal licensee or to any person to whom the licence applies (as defined in s. 17(2)(a)–(c)). A suspended licence, which may be further suspended for periods not exceeding three months (s. 22(2)), is of no effect (s. 22(3)), but while it is suspended an application may be made by the nominal licensee under s. 18(5) for the new person to be designated as the person responsible (s. 22(3)).

Section 19 details the procedures to be followed where a licence committee proposes either:

(a) to refuse a licence or to refuse to grant an application for variation to designate a new 'person responsible' (s. 19(1)); or
(b) to vary or revoke a licence (s. 19(2)).

In the first case the committee must give notice of the proposal to the applicant and include the reasons for its proposed refusal (s. 19(1)). In the second case the committee must give notice of its proposal and the reasons for it to the person responsible under s. 17 and the nominal licensee (but not to anyone, such as a member of the public, who has applied for the variation or revocation) (s. 19(2)). In both cases the notice must indicate that the recipient may within 28 days give notice to the committee of his or her intention to make representations (s. 19(3)). If such a wish is expressed, the committee is obliged to give the person or someone acting on his or her behalf an opportunity to make oral, or written representations or both at a meeting of the committee before it reaches its determination (s. 19(3), (4)). The licence committee must give notice of its determination and reasons for it to the relevant parties (s. 19(5)(a)–(c), (6)). This provision may be significant, for it has been said that there is no general legal principle stating that reasons must be given (*Payne* v *Lord Harris of Greenwich* [1981] 1 WLR 754, at 765). Having said that, the more judicial the setting, the more likely the requirement for reasons, simply because the basis of appeal is the duty to act fairly (see further below).

In any case where the committee proposes to suspend, revoke or vary a licence, or where a licence has been varied, has expired, been suspended, revoked or otherwise ceased to have effect, the committee may make directions ensuring the continued discharge of the duties of the person responsible under the 'old' licence

(s. 24(6), (7)). In particular, such directions may require anything kept under the old licence to be transferred to the HFEA or to any other person. This could include instruments, gametes, stored embryos or information generated under the terms of the old licence (s. 24(7)(a)). In addition, the HFEA may secure through directions the continued discharge of the duties under the Act by the person taking over from the person responsible. The HFEA must be satisfied that that other person fulfils the requirements that would be demanded if he or she were an applicant to be a person responsible under a licence. That person must consent in writing to taking over (s. 24(7)).

AUDIT

The newest remit (although not technically part of the licensing procedure) is the Audit of Clinics' Data. The National Audit Office (NAO) strongly recommended when inspecting the HFEA that it should employ its own auditor to ensure the accuracy and completeness of the data collected from the clinics. This is a function that the NAO would normally carry out itself, but due to the highly sensitive and confidential nature of the information it is restricted by statute from carrying out such function. With this in mind, a Systems and Data Auditor (SDA) was appointed in April 1996. The SDA extracts, using random samples, a data set from the Authority's register which is checked against patient/donor records at the centre. When auditing a centre the process is reversed – a set of the centre's records is taken and checked against the data held on the register. Every centre is subject to such audits, although new centres will be incorporated only after they have been licensed for three years. This gives them a chance to develop their systems and become familiar with procedure. As of 1 October 1999, approximately 60 such audits had been carried out. Every audit leads to clinic feedback and a formal audit report which is considered by the licence committee and can be used as relevant information in deciding licensing issues for a particular clinic. Clinics are given the opportunity to respond to these reports.

APPEALS AND JUDICIAL REVIEW

Appeals

A person may seek to challenge the exercise of the statutory powers laid upon the licence committees by the Act. One possibility is that the committee has imposed a licence condition which the applicant is reluctant to accept. Here a further application to vary the condition in question may provide a possible remedy (see s. 18(4) and 18(6)(a)). However, the wording of ss. 19(1) and (2) and 20(1) and (2) is such that there would then be no further right of appeal to the HFEA as a whole if the committee rejected that application for variation. Although the HFEA does have the power to hear appeals concerning the refusal of a variation, this is only in the context of variation to designate another person as the responsible person under the licence (s. 18(5)). A licence holder who dislikes any other condition imposed by the committee, which the committee refuses to vary, must rely on the second and doubtless more expensive and time-consuming method of seeking judicial review (see below). However, under s. 20(2), where a committee determines to allow a variation of a licence, an appeal lies at the suit of any person on whom notice of the determination was served. The appeal may be against the extension or the limitation of a current licence. This means that although a concerned member of the public may bring to the Authority's attention the existence of grounds for investigating a licence holder, he or she may not appeal against the committee's determination to vary the licence. Where an appeal does lie, 28 days' notice of the intention to appeal must be given to the committee and the HFEA.

More straightforward is the situation in which an application for a licence, or to vary the responsible person under the licence, is refused by the committee. Here the applicant may appeal to the HFEA, on giving notice to the committee, within 28 days of the service of the committee's determination. Any appeal under s. 20 must be heard by a committee of at least five members of the Authority; the appellate function cannot be delegated to a committee, member or employee of the HFEA. The quorum for an appeal is five members of the Authority (s. 20(6)) and any member who took part in the work of the licence committee which resulted in the determination under appeal is disqualified from sitting on the appeal (s. 20(3)). This accords with administrative law principles relating to administrative fairness (see *McInnes* v *Onslow Fane* [1978] 1 WLR 1520; *R* v *Barnsley MBC ex parte Hook* [1976] 1 WLR 1052 and *Huntley* v *AG for Jamaica* [1995] 2 AC 1). An appeal takes the form of a rehearing (s. 20(3)) and the appellant is entitled to representation (s. 20(4)(a)), as are the members of the licence committee (s. 20(4)(b)). The HFEA is charged to consider any written representations made by the appellant or any licence committee member and to take into account any matter which the licence committee could have taken into account. The HFEA is precluded from taking into account anything adduced by a member of the public, other than the grounds for his or her original complaint. The Authority must give notice of the determination to the appellant; and where the appeal has concerned an unsuccessful application for a licence under s. 16 or an unsuccessful application to vary a licence under s. 18(5), the HFEA must give reasons for its decision (s. 20(5)).

The provision that an appeal takes the form of a rehearing dictates the function of the HFEA as an appellate body. Without this provision, it might be assumed on general principles that the HFEA should review only the legality of the decision. Appeal by way of rehearing allows consideration of all relevant and available evidence with a right of the appellate body to reach its own conclusions (see *Sagnata Investments* v *Norwich Corporation* [1971] 2 QB 614). Thus, although the Authority can have in mind its broad policy, it must not apply that policy inflexibly or with a closed mind (*R* v *Secretary of State for the Home Department ex parte Venables* [1997] 2 WLR 67).

Judicial review

In any case where the Authority decides under s. 20 to refuse a licence, to refuse to vary a licence under s. 18(5) or to vary or revoke a licence, an appeal on a point of law lies to the High Court, or in Scotland the Court of Session (s. 21). This is to ensure that a statutory body such as the HFEA is subject to public law scrutiny in exercising the power to grant licences without which wide forms of clinical practice are not permitted. The courts must ensure that it does not abuse its licensing powers, while, at the same time ensuring that the power that Parliament has granted to such a body is not usurped by the courts.

Grounds for judicial review basically fall within two broad headings: substantive and procedural. As these terms suggest, substantive grounds generally concern the substance of the decision itself, while procedural grounds cover the administrative background of any such decision. One of the most important grounds is that of reasonableness; in the current context, for example, the HFEA is subject to a duty to impose only such licence conditions as could be considered 'reasonable' under the test established in *Associated Picture Houses* v *Wednesbury Corporation* [1948] 1 KB 223. This is not, as Wade explains[12] the negligence standard of the reasonable passenger on the Clapham omnibus, but it is the standard indicated by the true construction of the Act in question. It distinguishes between the proper and improper use of the power. The formulation of the *Wednesbury* principle was given by Lord Greene (at p. 229):

> . . . a person entrusted with a discretion must, so to speak, direct himself properly in law. He must call his own attention to the matters which he is bound to consider. He must exclude from his consideration matters which are irrelevant to what he has to consider. If he does not obey those rules, he may truly be said, and often is said, to be acting 'unreasonably'.

So, the sorts of conditions that a licence committee may lawfully impose on an applicant or person responsible are wide-ranging but not without limit. In considering whether a condition is unreasonable, regard has to be had to the statutory background and purpose; but that considered, the ability of the licence committee to impose rigorous limiting conditions is wide, and the ability of an applicant to object to them is available only through judicial review. A sense of the legal standard of reasonableness may be understood from a review of the judgments and speeches in the case of *Secretary of State for Education and Science* v *Tameside Metropolitan Borough Council* [1977] AC 1014. There, judges in the Court of Appeal and the House of Lords discussed the error of confusing differences of opinion with unreasonableness on the part of one side or the other. To exceed a statutory power, a party must be 'so wrong that no reasonable person could sensibly take that view' (Lord Denning, at p. 1023). Lord Diplock said that 'The very concept of administrative discretion involves the right to choose between one or more possible courses of action upon which there is room for reasonable people to hold differing opinions as to which is the preferred' (at p. 1064). Equally, where the Authority can be shown to act irrationally, where its response is lacking in proportion to the underpinning purpose of the legislation or where irrelevant considerations have been taken into account, the decision may be open to challenge. This is apart from challenges based also on bad faith (see further, below) or improper motive shown by the Authority, or review of a decision which is *ultra vires* being in excess of delegated powers or outside its jurisdiction.

Consequently, the HFEA licence committee may lawfully write into a licence conditions which relate to such matters as:

(a)   the procedures to be adopted in determining the quality of sperm received from a donor;

(b)   the frequency with which donated sperm may be used;

(c)   the types of emergency resuscitation measures which must be available in a centre;

(d)   the number of eggs or embryos which may be transferred in the course of any given treatment cycle, or indeed the number of treatment cycles to which a woman may expose herself overall;

(e)   the frequency with which treatment services may be offered;

and so on, but perhaps not the size of the bed which a person receiving treatment services must occupy, or the number of television sets which should be available for patients admitted to the licensed centre during the course of a service. Other examples can be given which would illustrate the general point, that as long as a condition is properly related to the aims and scheme of the regulatory statute then it will be difficult to persuade a court by way of judicial review that a licence committee has exceeded its powers (*McEldowney* v *Forde* [1971] AC 632).

Thus far, what has been said is that in the context of the parent Act, irrelevant considerations, errors of law and unreasonable conditions may be such as to render administrative decisions by the Authority *ultra vires*. In such instances the substantive provisions of the regulations would fail to fulfil the general purpose(s) of the statute. There are a number of other types of substantive *ultra vires* which might be relevant. A clear example would be bad faith, although instances of successful claims of bad faith are rare, and the burden of proof upon those making such allegations is stringent: see *Cannock Chase DC* v *Kelly* [1978] 1 WLR 1.

Another obvious example of substantive *ultra vires* arises out of the improper exercise of discretion. A good example of this in the present context arises from the provision, in s. 9(3) and (5), that the licence committee cannot delegate its work to a subcommittee. Such statutory requirements will be rigorously upheld by the courts, and even without the express prohibition of statute, the general line of administrative law would be that a body given a discretion under statute must exercise that discretion (see *Vine* v *National Dock Labour Board* [1957] AC 488, *R* v *Tower Hamlets LBC ex parte Khalique* (1994) 26 HLR 517). Another method by which the Authority might neglect the true exercise of its discretion would be continually to fetter its discretion. This might be so, for example, if a licence committee took an early decision that a certain category of research laid down in sch. 2, para. 3(2)(a)–(e) could never be appropriately pursued using embryos. In such cases the courts generally take the view that the person exercising the power should always be willing to hear representations before making a decision (*R* v *Secretary of State for the Environment ex parte Brent LBC* [1982] QB 593). The courts may uphold general policies for administrative convenience, but only if the body in question can show that it is willing to hear from particular applicants on why the policies should not apply in the instant case (see *British Oxygen Co Ltd* v *Board of Trade* [1971] AC 610 and *Findlay* v *Secretary of State for the Home Department* [1985] AC 318).

In a piece of legislation which is so detailed in the procedures which it lays down, it is important to consider not merely the substance of the decision but also errors in procedure which may lead to challenge for procedural *ultra vires*. In this context, procedural *ultra vires* lies in the failure to follow the mandatory directions of the Act. However, a failure to meet wider principles of administrative fairness constitute a ground for judicial review of action taken.

As regards directions under the statute, there are both mandatory and directory provisions governing the action of the Authority. The distinction between the two is crucial. Where the statute lays down that a licence committee must follow a particular procedure then this is a mandatory requirement, failure to comply with which will render the decision invalid (*O'Reilly* v *MacKman* [1983] 2 AC 237). Examples of this might include: a determination by a licence committee which is improperly constituted in breach of the regulations that determine the composition of such committees (see s. 9(5)); or where a licence committee fails to give notice of a determination of a licence application contrary to s. 19(5). Where proceedings are merely directory, however (for example, where a licence committee may by notice suspend a licence under s. 22(1)), the courts will not necessarily find committees bound by such directory provisions and failure to meet the procedural requirements may not be fatal to the validity of the action (see *London & Clydeside Estates* v *Aberdeen DC* [1980] 1 WLR 182, at 188).

It should be noted that action on the part of the committee may be enforceable, even where dealing with directory provisions. For example, under s. 9(8), the HFEA is required to ensure that licensed premises are inspected once each calendar year. This inspection may be forgone if the licence committee considers it unnecessary. It is possible, however, that someone with sufficient standing could seek to require the remedy of mandamus to cause the Authority at least to consider whether it ought to inspect where it appears that it has not directed its mind to the problem.

There are certain classes of procedural requirements which the courts are vigilant to uphold. Thus, for example, where licensed premises change ownership and a previously unlicensed person makes an application for the transfer of the licence, there is little doubt that a decision by the licence committee without consultation or hearing to refuse to transfer the licence would be reviewable (*R* v *Commission for Racial Equality, ex parte Hillingdon LBC* [1982] AC 779). This is because, in practice, provisions to consult, inform or offer hearings are treated as though they were mandatory requirements (see *Agricultural Training Board* v *Aylesbury Mushrooms* [1972] 1 WLR 190). Here the procedural requirements of the statute slowly merge with the background principles of 'natural' justice and a broad duty to act fairly. Many of the principles of natural justice, such as the right to be heard, are encompassed within the procedures of the Act itself or in regulations (s. 10(2)). There are similar protections within the statute against bias. For example, sch. 1, para. 10(1) states that a member of the HFEA who is directly or indirectly interested in a licence must disclose that interest to the Authority.

In the GCHQ case, *Council of the Civil Service Union* v *Minister for the Civil Service* [1985] AC 374 at 414, Lord Roskill proposed that the phrase 'natural justice' be 'replaced by speaking of a duty to act fairly'. It is true to say that it is now more common to talk of broad duties to act fairly rather than strict principles of natural justice (see *R* v *Bartle and the Commissioner of Police for the Metropolis, ex parte Pinochet* [1999] 2 All ER 97). In particular, the courts will be prepared to uphold broad principles of fairness in situations in which persons have legitimate expectations (such as that a licence may be renewed in the absence of changed circumstances; and see *R* v *Rochdale MBC, ex parte Schemet* [1974] ELR 90) and where what is vested in a person is a particular right or privilege which the holder might expect would be safeguarded by clear principles (*R* v *Jockey Club, ex parte RAM Racecourses* [1993] 2 All ER 225). This is all the more true where statute gives a clear inference (as is the case with the 1990 Act) that it wishes strict and fair procedures to apply (*R* v *Commission for Racial Equality, ex parte Hillingdon LBC*, above). In the context of other sorts of licence holders, there are clear examples of the strict application of such principles: see *R* v *Barnsley MBC, ex parte Hook* [1976] 1 WLR 1052; *Wheeler* v *Leicester City Council* [1985] 3 WLR 335; and *Congreve* v *Home Office* [1976] QB 629.

One important remaining question in relation to judicial review is precisely who may have standing to bring a case. This is because 'the law does not see it as a function of the courts to be there for every individual who is interested in having the legality of an administrative action litigated' (*R* v *Secretary of State, ex parte Rose Theatre* [1990] 1 All ER 754, at 768). Under the judicial review procedure (contained in RSC Ord. 53, see CPR 1998, sch. 1), for the applicant to have standing he or she must hold 'sufficient interest in the matter to which the application relates'. No application for judicial review can be entertained without leave of the High Court, and a major element of the leave hearing is the question of standing. In *IRC* v *National Federation of Self-employed and Small Businesses Ltd* [1982] AC 617 the House of Lords decided that rather than have a rigid test of *locus standi* which would be unconnected with the precise facts of each case, the courts should use their general discretion to determine the applicant's status in accordance with the strength of the case in all respects. The courts have been traditionally restrictive as to whom they allow standing, so that pressure groups such as that in the *Rose Theatre* case were not allowed standing lest this would deprive the phrase 'sufficient interest' of all meaning. More recently, however, the courts have been considerably more liberal in recognising the standing of public interest groups. In *R* v *Inspectorate of Pollution, ex parte Greenpeace* [1994] 4 All ER 348, for example, the applicants Greenpeace were found to have sufficient interest to bring their case. It was held that account should be taken of 'the nature of the applicant, the extent of his interest in the issues raised, the remedy which he sought to achieve and the nature of the relief sought'. The court found that Greenpeace was an entirely responsible and respected body with a genuine interest, and 2,500 members living in the relevant area who 'might not otherwise have an effective means of bringing their concerns before the court'. In *R* v *Secretary of State for the Foreign and Commonwealth Office, ex parte World Development Movement* [1995] 1 WLR 386, concerning the public interest in the funding given to the Pergau Dam, it was said (at 395, 396) that:

> having regards to the merits of the challenge, the importance of vindicating the rule of law, the importance of the issue raised, the likely absence of any other responsible challenger, the nature of the breach of duty against which relief was sought and the prominent role of the applicants . . . in giving advice, guidance and assistance with regard to aid . . . the applicants do have sufficient interest in the matter.

A similar liberalisation may be found in relation to individual applications (*Gillick* v *West Norfolk and Wisbech* [1986] AC 112), and a direct pecuniary interest is by no means necessary since 'grievances are not measured in pounds and pence' (*Arsenal FC* v *Ende* [1979] AC 1, at 24 *per* Lord Morris). Such liberal application of the *locus standi* rule has obvious significance in the context of the background debate on embryo research, for example. Clearly, there are many interest groups and individuals which might seek to challenge the decisions of the licence committees. Given the widening approach toward interest groups demonstrated in the cases above, there seems to be ample scope for the right body to appeal against the decisions of the Authority on the grounds of public interest.

The situation as to standing would be different if the complainant were a party in some way connected to the provision of infertility treatment, as indeed was the position in the now infamous case of *R v HFEA, ex parte Blood* [1997] 2 All ER 687. The facts of the case are sufficiently well known not to need reiterating. Mrs Blood claimed that the Authority had applied the law wrongly in claiming that she and her husband were not undertaking treatment together, and that it had not applied its discretion properly in refusing to allow the stored sperm to be exported abroad. Sir Stephen Brown P, in the first instance, held that it was 'simply a matter of construction' of the statutory provisions and the Code of Practice whether Mrs Blood and her unconscious husband (who had not made any indications of his consent for the use of his sperm in this way), could not be taken as treated together for the purposes of s. 4(1). It had been a unilateral act to take the sperm of the unconscious husband such that that could not constitute the husband and wife receiving treatment together. Moreover, the storage of the sperm in the first place was not allowed as the consent provisions of sch. 3 were not complied with. Although, on appeal, Lord Woolf accepted that the consent provisions had been breached, his Lordship directed the Authority to reconsider its position in the light of Art. 59 (now 49) of the EC Treaty and the directly enforceable right of the applicant to receive medical treatment elsewhere in the European Union:

> Parliament has delegated to the Authority the responsibility for making decisions in this difficult and delicate area, and the court should be slow to interfere in its decisions. However, the reasons given by the Authority, while not deeply flawed, confirm that the Authority did not take into account two important considerations. The first being the effect of Art. 59 [now 49] of the treaty. The second being that there should be, after this judgment has been given, no further cases where sperm is preserved without consent. The Authority is not to be criticised for this because, in relation to the law, it was dependent upon the guidance it received. However, the fact remains that having not received the appropriate guidance, the Authority did not take into account two matters which Mrs Blood is entitled to have taken into account. (at p. 702)

The Authority did indeed go on to authorise Mrs Blood to export the sperm several weeks after the Court of Appeal's judgment amidst a background of overwhelming public support for Mrs Blood. (See further the discussion of *Blood* in Chapter 9.)

It even seems that general members of the public are being granted *locus standi* to contest decisions of a public body. In *R v Somerset County Council and ARC Southern Ltd, ex parte Dixon* [1997] COD 323 (*cf. R v Secretary of State for the Home Department, ex parte Rees-Mogg* [1994] 2 WLR 115). Sedley J traced a long line of old (as well as modern) precedent allowing applications for judicial review where the applicant was neither a busybody nor a mere trouble-maker and there was a wide public interest in the matter subject to review: 'He is, on the evidence before me, perfectly entitled as a citizen to be concerned about, and to draw the attention of the court to, what he considers is an illegality . . .' (at p. 331).

The Human Rights Act 1998

As a final point, the effect of the Human Rights Act 1998 will need to be considered, since this provides for the first time that identifiable rights under the European Convention on Human Rights may be argued before domestic courts. The HFEA being a public body falls within the s. 6 requirements of the 1998 Act, and as such it would be unlawful for it to 'act in a way which is incompatible with convention rights' (s. 6(1)). This opens the way for various potential grounds of appeal against the Authority once the s. 7 requirements of standing are met. Standing here, however, is a narrower test than that put forward by the courts in recent years for judicial review, since in line with the Convention a 'victim' test is adopted (s. 7(1) as set out in Art. 34 of the Convention). This would seem to outlaw more abstract legal challenges (*F* v *Switzerland* (1988) 10 EHRR 411) to the disadvantage of organisations such as the SPUC or LIFE that might wish to bring actions under the Art. 2 – right to life – provision. In reality, however, it would be rare if such organisations could not find a willing individual to play the victim, with the organisations providing the essential funding and support to him or her. In *X* v *UK* ((1981) 19 DR 244), a 'potential father' was considered to be a victim for his Art. 2 case claiming a right to life for a foetus following the termination of his wife's pregnancy. In *Bowman* v *UK* (1998) 26 EHRR 1 Ms Bowman was held to be a victim when the UK Government stopped the publication and distribution of anti-abortion leaflets detailing the opinions of Parliamentary candidates. Following such examples, there seems no reason why the HFEA could not come under attack within the provisions of the Act, especially before courts applying the Convention that have moved to have liberal standing rules in administrative law.

NOTES

[1]   Deech, R., 'Infertility and Ethics' (1997) *Child and Family Law Quarterly* 9(4) 337, 339.
[2]   Committee of Inquiry into Human Fertilisation and Embryology, Cmnd 9314 (London, HMSO, 1984).
[3]   Though this may change over time following reform of freedom of information – see the Freedom of Information Bill, 18 November 1999. Althnough there is an HFEA Annual Conference it is the practice to invite delegates.
[4]   *Cloning Issues in Reproduction, Science and Medicine*, available on the HGAC website www.hgac.gov.uk.
[5]   'The Role of the HFEA' (1997) 3 *Medical Law International* 1.
[6]   'Fertility Clinics: One Code of Practice?' (1998) 3 *Medical Law International* 243.
[7]   *Ibid.*, at 256.
[8]   See, for example, Animals (Scientific Procedures) Act 1984, s. 4; or in an entirely different context, Environmental Protection Act 1990, s. 74.
[9]   1995 Annual Report, p. 9.
[10]   Under Health Service Guidelines (97) 23.
[11]   Section 6 of the Human Rights Act 1998 makes it unlawful for a public body to act in a way that is incompatible with a Convention right, and this would include

Art. 6 of the ECHR which states that civil rights and obligations should be determined by a hearing of 'an independent and impartial tribunal' – see *County Properties* v *The Scottish Ministers* (*The Times*, 19 September 2000).

[12] Wade, W.H., and Forsyth, C., *Administrative Law*, 8th edn, (Oxford UP 2000).

Chapter 5
Regulating Clinical Practice

INTRODUCTION

In this chapter we turn to consider the areas of clinical practice relating to assisted conception that the Act seeks to regulate, together with those which it is suggested are excluded from review. We also consider the statutory limitations on access to licensed centres introduced by s. 13(5), and the the requirement of s. 13(6) that before certain treatment services are offered to a woman or a couple they should be provided with the opportunity to receive counselling. We examine the question of consent to which all assisted conception services give rise, including the requirements of the consent schedule (sch. 3) and the background common law of consent which is relevant to a proper understanding of the law on assisted conception. The scope and nature of clinical regulation under the Act is a matter increasingly likely to occupy the courts.[1]

This chapter begins by exploring the extent of regulation by reference to the crucial definition of 'treatment services'. Later in the chapter we consider the centrality of the definition of 'treatment services' by reference to certain types of medical interventions which may fall outside the Act. In between there is a discussion of why these matters should be the subject of regulation and a review of the chosen regulatory form. The chapter concludes with a consideration of the scope and content of treatment licences, and by considering the criminal law provisions which relate to unlicensed activity, or clinical practice in breach of licence provisions.

WHAT ARE TREATMENT SERVICES?

Treatment services are medical, surgical or obstetric services provided to the public or a section of the public for the purpose of assisting women to carry children (1990 Act, s. 2(1)). A treatment service may be provided to a woman only when 'account has been taken' of: (i) 'the welfare of any child who may be born as a result of the treatment'; and (ii) 'any other child' who maybe 'affected by the birth' (s. 13(5)). It is difficult to interpret these provisions other than as an attempt to place a restraint on the provision of certain modes of assisted conception to certain groups or types of women or couples. Nonetheless, the actual wording of subsection 13(5) gives rise to considerable levels of ambiguity which we address in our discussion of access to treatment services (see Chapter 6).

There are many different ways in which one might try to address problems caused by sub-fertility, and not all of these will require medical intervention. Even where medical intervention is required, the Act does not necessarily regulate that activity. Thus, to take an obvious example, hormone therapies would not of themselves be regulated. At heart what is regulated is treatment involving donated gametes and/or the creation of embryos outside the body. Thus certain types of 'infertility treatment' – or as we term it, assisted conception – can be included within the regulatory framework. This can cover: artificial insemination by donor; egg donation; embryo donation; and *in vitro* fertilisation (IVF) where an embryo is created outside the human body. Intra cytoplasmic sperm injection (ICSI) is also regulated. This involves the injection of a single sperm directly into an egg, followed by the transfer back to the womb of the embryos so created. The success rate for ICSI seems to be rising above that for IVF, with an average live birth rate of 22% per embryo transfer compared with an average of 17% for IVF. The definition of 'treatment services' has been taken to mean also that gamete intra-fallopian transfer (GIFT) will not be the subject of regulation provided that neither the sperm nor the egg being used has been donated. It also follows that the artificial insemination of a woman with the sperm of her husband (AIH) or partner (AIP) is also excluded from the ambit of the Act where such treatment does not involve the use of donated gametes from outside the treated couple. This new lexicon of life has given rise to the need to provide a quick guide to the treatments considered and related matters. We have done this at Appendix 3. It is common to refer to artificial insemination, whether by donor or husband or partner, simply as AI, but we have retained the more precise formulations in this chapter.

The inclusion and exclusion of certain types of treatment is ensured by the wording of ss. 1(2) and 4(1)(b). These provide respectively as follows:

1.—(2)   This Act, so far as it governs bringing about the creation of an embryo, applies only to bringing about the creation of an embryo outside the human body; and in this Act—

(a)   references to embryos the creation of which was brought about *in vitro* (in their application to those where fertilisation is complete) are to those where fertilisation began outside the human body whether or not it was completed there

. . .

4.—(1)   No person shall—

. . .

(b)   in the course of providing treatment services for any woman, use the sperm of any man unless the services are being provided for the woman and the man together or use the eggs of any other woman . . .
except in pursuance of a licence.

Hence, the intention is to regulate IVF (s. 1(2)) and IVC (s. 1(2)(a)), though not GIFT unless it involves the use of donated sperm or eggs (ss. 1(2), 4(1)(b)). The omission of GIFT was not without controversy, and at the time of the passage of the Act a specific amendment to include GIFT within the regulation failed. Similarly, where artificial insemination is undertaken by a couple privately, notwithstanding the use of donated gametes, provided these have not been stored, such activity falls outside the Act.[2] Consequently, it is apparent that this Act is not meant to be a comprehensive code covering all the legal and ethical issues to which the 'reproduction revolution' has or may give rise. This was recognised by Lord Mackay when he said that this was a limited measure when set in the context of infertility treatment as a whole.[3] Most obviously, this point is made by the separate, limited regulation of surrogacy arrangements under the provisions of the Surrogacy Arrangements Act 1985 (as amended). Of course it may be that the surrogate birth is achievable only by the use of donated gametes or through some form of medical intervention such as IVF, which itself will be regulated by the 1990 Act. More broadly speaking, the general civil law will apply, which would include such matters as negligence, strict product liability, the wider regulation of the supply of goods and services, probate and property rights, contract law, and family law provisions. In perhaps the most (in)famous case under this legislation, *R v HFEA, ex parte Blood* [1997] 2 All ER 687, much turned upon provisions of EC law.

WHY REGULATE TREATMENT SERVICES?

In the Foreword to the 5th Annual Report of the Interim Licensing Authority (ILA), established by the Royal College of Obstetricians and Gynaecologists and the Medical Research Council, Mary Donaldson, the Chair, wrote (at p. 2):

> We have been disturbed at the increase in the number of small IVF centres seeking to establish themselves without the necessary facilities, adequately trained staff or the requisite specialist supervision. We are also aware of the poor success rates in a number of established and licensed centres. In the interest of women seeking treatment the Authority has decided that those centres whose pregnancy and 'take home' baby rates show little or no success over the next 12 months will be warned that their licences might be withdrawn.

Mary Donaldson here identifies two separate problems. The first is the standards – physical and professional – of those engaged in the provision of treatment services, and of the plant and associated services which they can offer. The second is the whole enterprise of assisted conception itself. It has, indeed, a low 'success rate' – the rate of clinical pregnancies was 21%, and the live birth rate for IVF is 17% of treatment cycles,[4] down to 12% for frozen embryo transfer. The rates per clinic varied enormously. One has to be careful of reading too much into these figures, however, given the age of many of the women presenting themselves for treatment. It must be healthy that the provision of assisted conception is a matter of discussion and debate. Prior to the Act, little was known or discussed outside a very limited circle. The fundamental issues which lie behind treatment services, such as embryo research, were not generally the subject of exhaustive and thoroughgoing examination and debate. Much of that has changed since the passage of the legislation, and the development of a system of regulation operating as a mediating institution in informing the general public of scientific developments is a significant by-product of the legislation.

In the ten years after the birth of the first 'test-tube' baby, Louise Brown, in 1978, various national governments began to address the legal, social and moral

issues at stake in the 'reproduction revolution'. The provision of assisted conception treatments was taken to be an unqualified human good; and in particular the
debate about the use of human embryos for the purposes of non-therapeutic
research was strongly contested (see Chapter 3). But for a long time, the major
questions about the provision of 'treatments' for or to circumvent 'infertility' were
conducted, at an official level at least, with an air of critical indifference. Feminist
analysis was both most sympathetic and most questioning of the nature, methods
and rationale of assisted conception.[5] Established religious responses, while not
uniform, were not overtly sympathetic to the project. This is clear from a review
of the contrasting approaches of the Roman Catholic Church[6] and of the Church
of England.[7]

One reason to regulate the provision of assisted conception might be the risks
which can attach to treatments such as IVF. Unlike many medical procedures this
must include risks which could attach a third party, i.e. the child born as a result
of treatment. IVF treatment depends upon the collection of ova through hormonal
stimulation. Ovarian hyper-stimulation can give rise to the development of ovarian
cysts, with accompanying abdominal discomfort or severe pain. Ovarian cysts may
rupture, resulting in bleeding into the abdominal cavity which may require surgery
and the removal of all or part of the affected ovary. Ovarian hyper-stimulation can
also lead to temporary or permanent ovarian dysfunction. However, miscarriage
rates for those pregnant as a result of IVF are apparently no higher than for
pregnancies generally.[8] These risks must be assessed against the background of the
limited chances of a live birth resulting. In addition to these risks to the women
are those attaching to multiple order births which are more likely to result from
assisted conception. There are social as well as medical consequences to be
considered here.

It is necessary also to evaluate risks which are not fully encapsulated by medical
notions of side-effects or the immediate adverse consequences of treatment.
Giddens has suggested that modern perceptions of risk arise out of uncertainties
which can attach to scientific advance.[9] Here, the risk lies in the unknown, and the
fear is not of particular anticipated consequences but of the consequences that no
one can foresee. Recent examples of the HFEA regulating in the face of uncertainty
include the prohibition of treatment services by spermatids, immature sperm which
is unable to develop fully, even though research licences are granted, and the row
which broke out when, having allowed women undergoing treatment for cancer to
store eggs, treatment using those eggs was not then initially sanctioned, as the
Authority remained to be convinced that the procedure is sufficiently safe.[10]

Costs and benefits arise in terms of monetary factors as well as medical factors.
If reproductive treatments are to be provided as part of the fabric of the National
Health Service, these are in inevitable competition with other forms of medical
provision. Indeed, it is argued that given the limited prospects of childbirth arising
out of infertility treatment, resources would be better deployed by investigating and
eliminating the causes of infertility.[11] One difficulty in this equation lies in knowing
what weight to give to the birth of a healthy child to an otherwise childless couple.
Where NHS provision is available, it will also be subject to the general process of
waiting lists that govern most forms of treatment in the public sector. This in a
situation in which many couples will realise that their chances of parenthood are
declining with age.

In fact, although some provision of treatment is available through the NHS, it is not routinely granted, and for most people ready access is available only through private clinics. The prevalence of private provision may add to the arguments favouring regulation. Outside of the confines of the NHS, regulation would otherwise be left to the market. Many would be unhappy with this, especially since informational asymmetries might make it difficult to balance factors of risk and success. As to whether it might be better to provide the treatment through the NHS, this would not of itself rule out private provision, and it seems unlikely that a stretched national system could easily incorporate assisted conception services. Whether the NHS ought to do so is a difficult question. It might be possible to argue that we have already gone far enough down the road of the medicalisation of infertility and the commodification of children. However, it is not clear that present, largely private arrangements do much to reverse these trends. And against this argument is the enormous desire of the childless for children.

Rationing problems within the NHS often concern the filtering out of relative need from a considerable demand for treatment. It can be argued that the desire for children cannot be described as a form of medical need since the couple may be healthy other than for the subfertility which affects them. This might mean that they should be afforded the facility to diagnose and treat the condition of infertility. In reality, the picture is not so simple. Although assisted conception is largely palliative and may not be aimed at or capable of curing an underlying problem, the technologies employed have done much in allowing an understanding of the causes of infertility.[12] Moreover, the division between treating and assisting conception is simplistic without a much more detailed consideration of the techniques employed and the nature of the medical problems concerned.

One undoubted problem in questions of allocation of assisted reproductive therapies is that of how to select patients for treatment. In any process of allocation of scarce medical resources there is a danger that extraneous social factors may creep into the judgment even though they have little to do with the success of the treatment sought.[13] A challenge to a decision said to have been made in this way within the NHS has already occurred in *R* v *Ethical Committee of St Mary's Hospital, ex parte Harriott* [1988] 1 FLR 512. Moreover, as is shown below, there are particular stances taken by the legislation in relation to access to treatment. These are not uncontroversial, and some are heavily contested. However, given the capacity for unrestricted access to assisted conception to cause harm to human health and to transgress the boundaries of the natural order with unforeseen and perhaps unforeseeable consequences, few would argue for such access. Against this there is an argument that licensing activity in the longer term is a form of facilitation rather than of restriction.

What is clear is that assisted reproduction is a dynamic field of activity, not only in terms of the pace of technical development, but also in terms of the complex social problems that result from the possibilities that the technologies allow. These go to the heart not only of central social structures such as the family, but also to our understandings of and respect for humanity. There are some who are not merely suspicious of the technology but who regard it as fundamentally wrong. With an estimate of over 100,000 children born worldwide as a result of IVF,[14] however, there is a growing acceptance of assisted conception alongside regular and well-publicised concerns about new technologies or the novel application of existing techniques.

Against this background, it may be argued that, without unduly restricting scientific advance, clinicians have been offered a structure within which they can pursue both research and treatment without widespread public alarm. Indeed, there seems some truth in the statement by Ruth Deech, Chair of the HFEA, that 'scrutiny from the press has shifted from the clinics to the HFEA'.[15] Rather than continual wrangling regarding the advance of reproductive technologies, or, worse still, no debate about what clinicians do, there are lines of demarcation within the Act itself, and a forum for determinations which is public and in which the public may play a part. Moreover, it is worth remembering that not all of the Act is concerned with the regulation of scientific developments. Large parts of the Act and the regulations concern the quality of provision which those seeking treatment receive in terms of such matters as counselling, consent, confidentiality and the like. Such rules seek to protect not only the couple seeking treatment, but also any child born as a result of assisted conception.

WHAT FORM OF REGULATION?

This is not to accept unthinkingly the structure of the regulation, which is curious indeed. To begin with, there are significant areas of discretion allowed to the HFEA, even though it might be thought easy enough to have left certain matters to Parliament. Take one example. In the course of debate an amendment sought to lay down a limit to the number of occasions on which donated gametes could be used. The Warnock Report had suggested an upper limit of ten donations.[16] The fear was that of unwitting incest, and in the House of Lords an article from the *Los Angeles Times* was produced[17] in which a man was reported as having discovered that his intended bride was his own genetic daughter following his sperm donation 20 years earlier. This was used not as a moral warning about cross-generational marriage but to illustrate the point at issue (or issue in point) that the risk of such happenings must be reduced. Nonetheless, the Government resisted any amendment and the Act is silent on the matter of how many donations might be permitted. In the end the HFEA's Code of Practice followed the Warnock line and ruled that, save in exceptional circumstances, no more than ten children should be fathered by one donor.

One might well ask why the Government should resist the adoption of a simple rule which followed earlier guidance from a committee constituted to examine such matters. There are two answers to such a question. The obvious one is that the Government appreciates the flexibility of a Code of Practice that can be quickly and easily amended in the future. This might be because a greater or more informed insight into the feared consequences becomes available, suggesting an amendment upwards or downwards. Or it may be that some other change in policy (such as the payment of donors) necessitates revision of the number of permitted inseminations. But this notion of regulatory flexibility can only be part of the story, for we are dealing with what Hunt has described as moral politics.[18] By this he means that these types of decisions are at the interface of the political and the moral. This is an obvious truth in so far as the politicians could have made a decision involving questions of morals but left that decision to others. In a wider sense, then, much of what is expected of the HFEA has not only a moral dimension but also a political one. Decisions are political in that they relate to much wider questions of governance. This is because of the capacity of assisted reproductive technologies to alter our relations with each other. As Marilyn Strathern has written (as we quoted in Chapter 1): 'the way in which the choices that assisted conception affords are formulated, will affect thinking about kinship. And the way people think about kinship will affect other ideas about relatedness between human beings'.[19] It is political also in the capacity to generate argument between interest groups with strong affiliations to particular sides of the argument and government.

A second answer to the question raised above concerning the generality of the legislative framework would seem to be that there are limits as to how far government wishes to stray into the realm of moral politics. A striking example of this came when decisions had to be made concerning frozen embryos created and stored prior to the coming into force of the Act. Approaches by the HFEA for guidance from Health Minister Bottomley were effectively rebuffed as the matter was referred back to the HFEA as the appropriate decision-maker. At one level this extends the power and independence of the HFEA, and in recent times it would seem to be the courts rather than the Government which is more likely to supervise and check this power. It is worth remembering, however, that ultimate control lies with the Government and that an Authority falling into discredit in handling the moral politics could find itself quickly wound up. Hence sensitivity to the political as well as to the moral dimension is vital to the continued existence of the HFEA.

The mechanisms employed here can be seen as a part of a wider and well-documented move towards discretionary regulation. We see a reversal of what Weber claimed a century ago. Now, rather than formal rationality there is an obvious shift to substantive rationality with ever-more discretionary regulation pursuing policy goals. Not surprisingly judges have reacted to this tendency to replace formal rules with a wider administrative discretion to act by an increasingly active commitment to the development of powers of judicial review. We would not claim that the regulation of assisted conception is at all unique or unusual in this respect, but there are some interesting insights into this change which study of the HFEA can offer.

Perhaps the first of these relates to a phenomenon pointed out by Unger,[20] who, having pointed to the generality of legislation and the open-ended nature of the standards permitted to administrative bodies, argues that such regulation will have the tendency to erode the barriers between private and public law, and indeed between the very spheres of the private and the public. We would argue that this is very much the case in relation to the regulation of assisted conception. In so far as the Act chooses to regulate the essentially private domain of human reproduction, it inevitably intrudes on private ordering and asserts a public interest in issues such as who might be born and to whom. It focuses not just on if but also on how conception will be achieved.

At the same time the move to discretionary regulation in this area represents an extension of the ambit of state power and a retreat from formal processes of governance. Thus we see an attempt to regulate forms of medical and technological advances which have the capacity to disrupt the social and political order. The regulation required is much more particular, precise and requires extraordinary flexibility if it is to fulfil this objective in the face of rapid scientific advance. Yet at the same time the Government shows little desire to impose rules directly. We are left with an amalgam of legal authority, administrative process and policy development that heralds a decline in legal autonomy.[21] And the HFEA seems a particularly British institution. The Act invested regulatory tasks in a body in which up to half of the members can be selected from the scientific community which is the subject of regulation, and where the remainder have tended to be notable academics, religious leaders and public officials of some standing.

Chairs of the Authority, both academic lawyers, have shown some confidence in the structure and process. Sir Colin Campbell wrote of the HFEA:

> It seeks to balance the views of the scientists with those of the patients, ethicists, members of the public and others . . . Whatever the future of reproductive medicine and law, the HFEA has clearly demonstrated that complex science and ethics can be considered impartially and the public reassured that social policy controls science and not vice versa.[22]

In spite of this confident assessment, it must be clear that in wider terms the move to this form of regulatory structure represents law becoming more dependent on scientific opinion. Rather than a more traditional, normative structure of legal rules based upon some shared community ethic, the discretionary regulation involves the exploration of science and pursues wider issues of risk, of commerce, and of promotion of technology. Scientific claims are interpreted through an increasingly technical process which may render any underpinning moral values more difficult to locate. In the end the advance of technology drives the agenda and presents the regulatory problems with which the HFEA is charged, and any model based on notions of the rule of law must concede territory in the face of the growth of this discretionary technical regulation.

Certainly, the HFEA is a long way from the Diceyan Elysium that the House of Commons interferes in matters of administration.[23] However, Craig[24] pointed out that even in the 18th and 19th centuries the Board system possessed a significant degree of independence from direct Parliamentary control. This allowed a greater continuity of policy which proved adaptable to administrative need. It also allowed a useful form of patronage. According to Craig, the decline followed a growth in Parliament's own sense of desire and responsibility to control governmental activity, following the widening of the franchise. Here, in the absence of strong desire to encroach upon the private and public conscience, we find a model of highly independent regulation.

By this we mean independent from government. The extent to which it is independent from the scientific community which it regulates is a much thornier issue. As Montgomery states,[25] the Act is remarkable in that it provides 'the first attempt in English law to provide a comprehensive framework for making medical science democratically accountable'. The inroads that the Act has made into traditional notions of clinical freedom should not be overlooked, although this development coincided with the retreat of such freedom on a number of fronts in the face of managerial advance within the British NHS. There is no doubting the capacity of the HFEA to dictate what is permissible and what is not; what is good practice and what cannot be tolerated. The HFEA may give directions with which clinicians must comply, and these may be individually addressed or of a general nature. Similarly, a licence committee may issue directions upon the variation or cessation of a licence requiring that an individual (subject to written consent) discharge particular duties. Failure to meet mandatory directions can constitute an offence, and will provide grounds upon which the licence can be revoked by the HFEA. These formal statutory powers should be considered alongside other forms of intervention in the form of, e.g., the Code of Practice, which inevitably drive clinical practice.

In practice, however, it has not been the style of the HFEA to operate by processes of command and control. The picture that emerges is one of a continual dialogue between the regulator and the regulated. This inevitably produces a closeness of relationship, especially given that there are only 75 centres licensed for both IVF and DI treatment, and, often, negotiated rather than mandated solutions. There is no reason on this account to doubt the effectiveness of the HFEA. Stanley de Smith once wrote that there is little sense in judging a watchdog by the number of people that it bites. It is hard to know in any case how one might judge the HFEA to be effective. But in such heavily contested territory, to hold the peace between factions committed to very different principles and purposes is no small task. Yet we must be careful here. It may be that compromise is achieved by the exclusion of groups from effective participation in debate. Whether one believes that depends on the extent to which the composition of the HFEA itself reflects the main protagonists in the debate, and whether, even then, the structure of the Authority allows for participative and transparent processes with which those protagonists can engage.

In the text that follows we present three case studies of the relationships between the clinical community, the legislature and the HFEA in contexts in which the regulation of clinical practice is contested. These debates concern not only questions of the interpretation of the legislation, but also questions of legal regulation beyond the confines of the Act. In each case there is a rich political vein to the arguments concerning the capacity for legal intervention.

LIFE AT THE REGULATORY BOUNDARIES: THE CASE OF GIFT

There were several attempts during the Parliamentary debates to amend the Bill and bring GIFT within the purview of the Authority. An amendment at Committee stage in the House of Lords seeking to achieve this was withdrawn on assurance that the question would be reconsidered. Following that, in a division on a Commons amendment in Standing Committee to include GIFT, the amendment was defeated only on the casting vote of Michael Shersby, the Chair, after the Committee divided 8:8.[26] The Government announced its intention to resist these pressures to amend the Bill. When the Bill went to the Commons, Health Minister Virginia Bottomley reiterated the Government's aim to exclude GIFT.

In the House of Lords, Lord Mackay claimed that to regulate GIFT using couples' own gametes would be the first step which could logically lead to a much greater degree of statutory regulation of medical treatment than envisaged in the White Paper.[27] He added that to license GIFT would be the first step to licensing the use of the superovulatory drugs themselves. These arguments were not only a flawed appeal to the 'slippery slope', they ignore crucial aspects of GIFT itself. GIFT differs fundamentally from the use of such drugs alone because large numbers of eggs are removed from a woman and a decision is taken as to how many to return in a treatment cycle. The use of superovulatory drugs alone involves neither the manipulation of gametes nor clinical decisions as to their use.

A woman will usually have been on a regime of superovulatory drugs in order to stimulate the production of eggs, occasionally producing up to 20 in one menstrual cycle. Such drugs are not always used, since some clinics prefer to use eggs produced naturally in an unstimulated cycle. GIFT involves obtaining ova (the female gamete or egg) or oocytes (female cells which have not yet developed into an ovum) from a woman using ultrasound imaging. The gametes are then injected, with the husband's or donor's sperm, directly into her fallopian tube, where fertilisation takes place. The most common use of GIFT is in the treatment of women who are infertile because sperm is prevented from fertilising naturally produced ova by a blockage of mucus in the cervix of the uterus or womb. Where GIFT is practised using donated gametes, it is within the ambit of the Act. But it is argued that GIFT using the couple's own gametes is not.

This is a policy which the HFEA has promised from the outset to keep under review. Certain other countries, such as Spain, already regulate GIFT. Interestingly, in Victoria, under the Infertility (Medical Procedures) Act 1984,[28] GIFT was not regulated at the outset but brought into the regulatory framework after a number of years. There are two distinct types of reason for arguing that GIFT should be subject to the same sort of statutory regulation as IVF. The first concerns problems which surround GIFT procedures and which are virtually indistinguishable from those attendant upon IVF. We here identify three. Secondly, there are dangers associated with multiple order births resulting from the use of GIFT which render professional self-regulation inappropriate.

First, then, the similarities with other, regulated, assisted conception treatments:

(a)   The critical issue at stake here is not only a concern with the embryo or foetus which is produced, but with the welfare and interests of the woman or the couple using this form of treatment service. The 'infertility work up' which a woman has to undergo is similar in GIFT to that in IVF. Both involve the use of superovulatory drugs to stimulate the production of multiple eggs. This carries with it a small risk of ovarian hyperstimulation syndrome, which might well be missed in a small clinic providing few treatment services on an annual basis, compared with the many hundreds provided in a duly licensed centre which offers both IVF and GIFT.

(b)   The only real difference between GIFT and IVF is that the sperm and the egg mixes to form a fertilised egg inside (for GIFT) rather than outside (for IVF) the body. While it is true that this does not give rise to exactly the same problems with respect to the embryo, it does involve the same sort of clinical manipulation of gametes. The similarity is striking, with attendant risks for the health of a resulting embryo and for the continuing health of the woman. On this basis it could be argued that the monitoring, supervision and licensing, the keeping of records and making of returns, and the assessment of the fitness of the clinicians running such programmes, should fall within the licensing scheme.

(c)   Lastly, there is the broad question of the proper maintenance of clinical standards. In the Fourth Report of the ILA, published in 1989, the Authority expressed its view that GIFT treatments should be included in any regulatory scheme and that at that time GIFT was not always practised 'in a satisfactory setting with the necessary back-up facilities'.[29] It is worth bearing in mind that there is much in the statutory scheme in terms of issues of consent, counselling, record-keeping, etc. which could either be extended to GIFT or left to the vagaries of the common law. The decision to omit GIFT from this framework smacks of pragmatism, and of a political compromise reached with the clinicians.

The history of this is also significant in relation to the multiple transfer of eggs and the consequent increased risk of multiple order pregnancy. In particular, at the time of the Act these higher order transfers were being undertaken in anticipation of increasing the 'success rates' of clinics' treatment service programmes. Multiple pregnancy was then either maintained, with increased risks to the pregnant woman, or some of the foetuses were aborted in a procedure which has become misleadingly known as selective reduction and which is more accurately called 'random reduction'. This carries risks for the pregnant woman, and for the remaining foetuses which are not aborted.

Higher order pregnancies are attended by major risks of morbidity and mortality. For example, the risk of stillbirth is six times higher than for a single pregnancy and the risk of death in the infant's first year is about ten times higher. The rate of death below the age of one is 8.5 per 1,000 for single infants. With twins this rises to 44.7 per 1,000, and for triplets and other higher order births the rate is 92.5 per 1,000. Compared with single births, twin, triplet or higher order pregnancies have greatly increased rates of congenital malformations visible from birth. And in addition to the demands made by such births on chronically stretched neonatal intensive care facilities, the ongoing financial costs to the health services are considerable. But most poignant are the costs, usually hidden, to the erstwhile hopeful and expectant parents. Triplet and other higher order births carry considerable financial and social consequences.

In relation to embryo transfer governed by the HFEA, a clinic can now transfer up to a maximum of three embryos. Evidence seems to show that the chances of a live birth do not improve beyond this figure, and may even decline. The Royal College of Obstetricians and Gynaecologists (RCOG) now advise in their guidelines that a maximum of two embryos only be transferred in women aged less than 40. There are some suggestions that over that age the chances of a live birth may increase by the transfer of more than two embryos. However, the guidelines state that every attempt should be made to avoid multiple births, especially triplets, and that the chances of a triplet pregnancy in a woman aged over 40 are still significant. This discrepancy between the HFEA rule and the RCOG guidelines may be subject to future review, but it indicates the anomaly of leaving a common form of infertility treatment outside the statutory mechanism, when the risks of the activity of assisted reproduction are so obviously a matter of debate and concern within the professional community.

Unless GIFT is included in the statutory scheme, couples opting for, or being directed towards, GIFT will enjoy no statutory right to counselling. Arguably, these are the very people who are most likely to benefit from it. They would have a structured opportunity to consider the risks of the procedures and their possible consequences. It would provide a brake also on the unthinking promotion of a technique which may otherwise be adopted as a treatment of last resort in cases of unexplained infertility. Again, the RCOG support counselling for all stages of infertility investigation and treatment, emphasising the significant psychological stress attaching to these procedures. These recommendations apply equally to GIFT, so that again it is odd that no statutory backing is available.

All of this assumes that GIFT does fall outside the ambit of the legislation in the manner in which those framing it hoped. This is not so readily obvious as might be supposed, as the following argument seeks to demonstrate. The Act prohibits several activities in the absence of a licence from the HFEA. It is an offence to provide 'treatment services' without a licence, unless the gametes are those of the couple being treated. And it is an offence to 'bring about the creation of an embryo' without an HFEA licence. The Bill as originally drafted provided no 'protection' to the developing conceptus until the end of the process of fertilisation, some 30 hours after its commencement. This caused concern and consternation, particularly amongst those implacably opposed to research of any kind. The Bill was consequently amended, and s. 1 now defines an embryo as including 'an egg in the process of fertilisation'. The wording of the amendment is unfortunate. The section begins with a definition of 'embryo' as a 'live human embryo where fertilisation is complete'. However, to this is added that any reference to an embryo should be taken to include 'an egg in the process of fertilisation'. Thus we are asked to assume that an egg in the process of fertilisation is included as a completely fertilised embryo. There is then a proviso, that for the purposes of s. 1(1)(b) fertilisation is not complete 'until the appearance of a two-cell zygote'. Thus at the same time an egg in the process of fertilisation must be assumed to be both a complete embryo and not so.

In comparable Australian (Victorian) legislation, fertilisation is defined as complete on the coming together on the first meiotic spindle of two sets of chromosome.[30] This 1987 amendment was introduced to bring GIFT within the ambit of the Standing Review Committee and to allow research on the process of fertilisation before syngamy on eggs not destined to be replaced. (Syngamy being defined to mean 'the alignment on the meiotic spindle of the chromosomes derived from the pronuclei'.)

In spite of the unfortunate wording of the British legislation, it is clear that an egg in the process of fertilisation must be considered an embryo. This gives rise to an intriguing possibility, discussed by Johnson, Braude and Aitken,[31] who argue that with GIFT the beginning of the process of fertilisation often occurs, or may occur, while the embryo is outside the body. This is so even though the process is completed after the transfer to the woman's fallopian tubes. This possibility occurs because the putting of sperm and egg together in a catheter ready for transfer to the woman raises the possibility of initiating fertilisation. Their argument is that as the sperm very rapidly binds to the zona pellucida of the egg, and separation in the catheter by an air bubble is 'functionally incomplete', fertilisation may be under way before the gametes are transferred to the fallopian tube. It is difficult for the clinician to be sure that the egg is not 'in the process of fertilisation' while still outside the body. Section 1(2) of the 1990 Act provides that 'references to embryos the creation of which was brought about in vitro' include those whose creation was brought about partly in the human body and partly in vitro. If this view is correct, GIFT may indeed be within the remit of the HFEA.

All of this is interesting only at a theoretical level given that it is not the practice of the HFEA to regulate GIFT. Section 4(3) and (4) allow the Secretary of State to lay before Parliament regulations which would incorporate GIFT into the regulatory framework. If correct, the analysis above would suggest that the HFEA could regard GIFT as falling within the definition of treatment services and claim the capacity to regulate GIFT without the requirement of additional regulations. This possibility appears remote given the express debate at the time of the passage of the legislation. In the absence of this, it would be wrong to suppose that GIFT is entirely unregulated since alongside the professional guidance of the Royal College of Obstetricians and Gynaecologists sits the common law. GIFT, as with other assisted conception techniques, is subject to the law of consent. Consent at common law is considered in Chapter 7.

There would seem to be two important lessons to learn from the situation of GIFT. The first is that in responding to the technological challenges of the era immediately prior to the passage of the Act, Parliament was concerned, perhaps overly concerned, to defer to professional interest groups in order to secure support for the wider principle of clinical regulation in this area. This compromise hardly left the new regulatory body in the strongest position from the outset. Secondly, the struggle over the exclusion of GIFT reminds us that there are real commercial considerations at stake, which it is easy to overlook when focusing on the moral dimensions of regulation. Costs attach to licensing, and benefit lies in taking procedures out of the regulatory regime. These come in the form of cost savings which convert into market advantage for technologies which escape regulation. This can allow the perplexing pattern in which it is the unsupervised technologies which hold the strongest appeal to the consumer.

THE LEGALITY OF TAKING AND STORING OVARIAN TISSUE AND GAMETES

In *Blackstone's Guide to the Human Fertilisation & Embryology Act 1990*, we pointed in the Introduction to a number of matters, not included in the Act, which we suggested might cause difficulty. The first of these was as follows:

> 1.   The Act nowhere deals with the special position of minors and gamete donation. It is presumably left to the common law, or to any guidance which [HFEA] is minded to offer in the Code. There may be good reason to distinguish between the donation of sperm and the donation of eggs, particularly in relation to minors. . . . A specific exception could perhaps have been considered in the course of therapeutic surgery . . .

The relevant provisions to consider here are those of the Human Fertilisation and Embryology Act 1990, ss. 4(1), 12, 14 and sch. 3 (consents); s. 2(2), sch. 3, para. 8(1) (storage) and the HFEA Code of Practice, paras 3.39–3.42.

The general rules in relation to the removal and storage of ovarian tissue and testicular tissue are set out in guidance from the HFEA, given its understanding of the common law and the provisions of the 1990 Act. It is possible to summarise the position relating to oocyte preservation and ovarian tissue storage as follows:

(a)   A person who keeps or uses gametes in contravention of the Act is guilty of an offence.

(b)   If ovarian tissue contains gametes as understood by the HFEA then the licensing provisions of the Act apply and a storage licence is generally required.

(c)   Gametes are understood by the HFEA to be:

. . . a reproductive cell, such as an ovum or a spermatozoon, which has a haploid set of chromosomes and which is able to take part in fertilisation with another of the opposite sex to form a zygote.[32]

(d)   If the ovarian tissue which is taken does *not* contain gametes as understood by the HFEA (and a practical difficulty is that the best results appear to be obtained using oocytes taken from the largest follicles which are therefore already the most mature *in vivo*[33]) then it may be stored (as an non-licensable activity), in, say, prospective oncology treatment, as a form of 'fertility insurance'[34] (if the HFEA is correct):

(i)   with the consent of the woman if over 18, as with any other adult;
(ii)   if 16–18, with consent by the adolescent woman herself;[35]
(iii)   with the consent of the adolescent woman herself if she is under 16 and '*Gillick* competent'[36]; or
(iv)   if not *Gillick* competent then with the consent of her parent(s) or another person with parental responsibility.[37]

(e)   It is possible that autografting pieces of ovarian tissue which have been excised and cryopreserved would enable a woman to attempt to conceive without IVF. However, if the immature gametes are later taken from the tissue and matured *in vitro*,[38] the Act will apply *even if the oocytes are to be used for the woman's own benefit*. Ovarian tissue grafting carries a risk, of course, which is not present with use of frozen mature oocytes, of reintroducing the cancer cells with the transplant.

Public Health Minister Yvette Cooper announced in August 2000 that the common law requirement that a person's consent should be obtained before sperm or eggs are recovered will, as recommended by the McLean Review of the Consents' Requirements (published in 1998), be retained. The result is that where a person is incapacitated and unable, for whatever reason, to give consent to the removal of sperm or eggs, and that person is likely to recover but his or her fertility is likely to be affected, it will be lawful to recover gametes *only* if it is in that person's 'best interests' to do so under the *Re F* test ([1990] 2 AC 1). In case of any doubt as to whether that test is satisfied, the matter should be taken to court.

The Government has also decided that the Human Fertilisation and Embryology Act 1990 should be amended to provide the HFEA with the power to waive. The requirement for consent to the *storage* (but not use) of gametes where they have been removed lawfully. Presently, as we have explained, the HFEA has no power, even where gametes have been lawfully recovered, to authorise *storage* unless consent has been given – a provision which, as McLean had alerted, might be vulnerable to a Human Rights Act challenge. This limited change, which will provide for storage only for as long as necessary to enable the person to recover and to provide for what is to happen to the sperm or eggs, will also benefit that small number of children who are about to undergo treatment which might affect their future fertility. In some cases, children might not be able to give an 'effective' consent under Sch. 3 because they do not fully understand the procedure. An amendment will seek to enable storage until the child achieves capacity to make her or his own decision about continued storage.

Once again, merely because the tissue is stored in the course of an unlicensed activity does not mean, however, that it is free from legal control, especially not at the behest of the tissue provider. Thus, where the unlicensed activity takes place in a clinic outside the NHS, there will be an express or implied contract between the gamete provider and the clinic. The contract might expressly provide what is to happen to the tissue, although the enforceability of a detrimental term against a *minor* would be highly unlikely. More likely might be a claim *against* a clinic for wrongful disposal of the tissue, including a claim that the tissue disposed of belonged – in a proprietary sense – to the provider. Any such (contractual) claim could include a claim for damages for any personal distress caused to the provider by the dealing with the tissue (for example, apparent use or disposal of the tissue without the provider's consent or in breach of the implied terms of the contract). (See *Bliss* v *South East Thames RHA* [1987] ICR 700; *Hayes* v *Dodd* [1990] 2 All ER 815.)

What would need to be shown to establish a proprietary interest is that there is 'some practical value or possible sensible purpose in retaining the specimen for future use such that it makes sense to recognise a proprietary or possessary interest' (see *Dobson* v *North Tyneside Area Health Authority* [1996] 4 All ER 464). A cryopreserved or otherwise stored immature gamete probably comes as close to illustrating such a consideration as any other tissue is likely to do. The consent provisions here are particularly problematic, but we return to these in Chapter 7.

TREATMENT LICENCES AND BREACH OF LICENCE

The licensing functions of the HFEA are considered in Chapter 4. There are certain features of treatment licences which are worthy of consideration here. A treatment licence provides for the monitoring of 'treatment services'. It is worth reiterating that there are certain activities relating to treatment that the HFEA cannot licence, since specific prohibitions appear in the Act. Thus the placing in a woman of live gametes other than human gametes is forbidden and could not constitute licensed activity (s. 3(2)). Also prohibited is the use of female germ cells derived from an embryo or foetus 'for the purpose of providing fertility services for any woman'. Thus infertility treatment (though not, apparently, research) using cells from an aborted foetus in an attempt to create an embryo cannot be lawfully licensed. This 1994 amendment to the Act (s. 3A, as added by the Criminal Justice and Public Order Act 1994, s. 164) overcomes the problem that as foetal eggs are not gametes, as originally drafted the storage and use of foetal cells or eggs fell outside the control of the Act. Similarly treatment licences cannot authorise the altering of the genetic structure of any cell while it forms part of an embryo (s. 11 and sch. 2, para. 1(4)).

Where 'treatment services are subject to licensing, the general (s. 12) and specific (s. 13) licence conditions (see Chapter 4) will be incorporated into the licences. The responsible person under the licence will then be charged with ensuring that treatment at the centre accords with the conditions of the licence (s. 17(1)(e)). In the event that this responsible person has failed or is unable to discharge this responsibility then the licence may be revoked or its conditions varied (s. 18(1)(c) and 18(3)). Otherwise treatment licences can be granted for a period of up to five years (s. 11 and sch. 2, para. 1(5)).

A treatment licence granted in this way will be subject to the provisions of s. 13 and sch. 2, para. 1 of the Act. These allow certain activities to be licensed in the course of treatment, including: the 'bringing about of the creation of' an embryo *in vitro*; the keeping of embryos; the use of gametes; and the placing of an embryo in a woman. Also included are two types of activity prior to treatment. The first is the testing of sperm fertility by assessing its ability to penetrate the eggs of another species, but always on condition that anything which forms is destroyed by the two-cell stage. Secondly, the therapeutic screening of embryos for subsequent re-implantation to ensure that they are in a 'suitable condition' may be permitted by licence. This provision is discussed more fully in Chapter 5, but for now it can be noted that this was said at the time of the Act to refer to medical suitability such that a defective embryo was not re-implanted. However, the term 'suitable condition' is not defined, and an amendment to the Bill designed to restrict this to tests that would do no more than ensure the survival of the embryo was withdrawn. It remains to be seen whether testing to fulfil some particular criteria demanded by the commissioning couple would fall within 'licensed activity'.

In each of the cases of permitted activity discussed above, there is an overriding requirement that the HFEA must be satisfied that that activity is necessary or desirable, thus giving the Authority a wide discretion to deal with problems such as that raised by the term 'suitable condition'. This discretion might prove difficult to challenge if the HFEA has taken appropriate steps to satisfy itself as to the necessity or desirability of the proposed activity. Note that although this refers to licensed activity, there is a provision in s. 13(7)(b) that requires a licence holder to maintain procedures which will ensure that consideration is given to all clinical practices even though these may not require the grant of a licence. Thus some of the activities referred to earlier in the chapter, such as GIFT, ought to be the subject of processes of monitoring and review.

Many of the other conditions attaching to treatment licences relate to issues of what might be termed quality control and scrutiny of techniques of assisting conception, especially through record-keeping. For example, s. 13(7)(a) requires the licence holder to ensure suitable procedures for determining the gamete and embryo donors. Information must then be kept on the source of gametes retained or used for providing licensed services and/or from which embryos derive where those embryos are kept or used in pursuance of a licence (s. 13(2)(c)). This is so whether gametes are donated or provided for one's own use. Similarly, records must be kept of the taking of an embryo from a woman and any mixing of sperm and eggs (s. 13(2)(e)). Both ss. 14(1) and 12(f) envisage that embryos may be 'acquired' or 'supplied' by a licence holder. Where this occurs, again that information must be recorded. Records must be kept of people treated at a licensed clinic (s. 13(2)(a)) and of the services with which they were provided (s. 13(2)(b)). Lastly, information must be recorded about any child who the responsible person under the licence believes has been born following licensed treatment services (s. 13(2)(d)). To this long list can be added any other matter specified by the HFEA following directions made under s. 23 of the Act (s. 13(2)(f)).

Where the Act demands that records be kept, the HFEA is free to specify the time over which such records should be preserved (s. 13(4)). Records of that class cannot then be removed before the expiry of the period set. Where a licence holder does not know whether a child has been born as a result of treatment then the information demanded by s. 13 must be retained for a period of 50 years from first recording (s. 24(1)). If the reasoning here is that someone born as a result of assisted conception might find out only later in life that this was the case, the provision is slightly curious. The object then would be to allow this person to make inquiries in line with s. 31(3)–(6) of the Act. But why restrict the storage of this information to 50 years? It is possible to imagine that someone could come by such information, say, on the death of a parent. If the treatment centre did not know of a child born as a result of treatment services, important information could date back before the birth of the person then exploring his or her genetic background. Sweden has a comparable provision requiring retention of recorded information for a period of 70 years – admittedly still arbitrary, but perhaps a longer period is preferable.

There is an additional requirement to meet the provisions of sch. 3 of the Act as a 'licence condition' (s. 12(c)). It follows that record-keeping on consents is required, and this is independently demanded by s. 13(3). Alongside these requirements on consent (considered more fully in Chapter 7) are also requirements as to counselling. Section 13(6) requires that persons seeking treatment are given access to a 'suitable opportunity' for 'proper counselling' on the implications of treatment services. The circumstances in which such counselling should be provided are considered in greater detail in Chapter 7, but for now it is necessary to note that such services are required as a condition of a treatment licence. Similarly, and perhaps more controversially, a woman cannot be provided with treatment services unless account has been taken of the welfare of any child born as a result of treatment services. Since this consideration notoriously includes 'the need of that child for a father', this particular licence condition is also subject to more detailed scrutiny elsewhere (see Chapter 6). Note, however, the capacity of the treatment licence conditions on consent, counselling and welfare to restrict access to assisted conception services.

CRIMINAL OFFENCES

In any regulatory system, a licensing procedure will generally be backed by criminal sanctions for operating without a licence or in breach of conditions attaching to it. Having said that, powers to revoke or vary the licence can often mean that resort to criminal charges is unnecessary. The threat of revocation, where departures from licence conditions are discovered, may be sufficient to ensure future compliance. Much of this is true for the HFEA. Although the HFEA does seem to have withdrawn licences, there seem to have been no prosecutions under the 1990 Act. The operation of the powers of the HFEA, together with the enforcement powers in ss. 39 and 40, have already been considered in Chapter 4. Here we consider the potential criminal offences together with related issues of enforcement. Note that by virtue of s. 42 of the Act, no prosecution may be instituted in England and Wales without the consent of the Director of Public Prosecutions, or, in Northern Ireland, the Director of Public Prosecutions for Northern Ireland.

As shown above, there are various activities which are prohibited and cannot be authorised by licence. Thus the most serious offences relate to these types of activity.[39] These offences are far more likely to relate to research rather than infertility treatment as such, but included here are the following:

(a)   acting in contravention of s. 3(2) or s. 4(1)(c) by placing in a woman a live embryo other than a human embryo, or live gametes other than human gametes, or by mixing human gametes with live animal gametes without a licence is an offence punishable on indictment with up to ten years' imprisonment, or an unlimited fine or both (s. 41(1)(a));

(b)   anyone who keeps or uses an embryo after the appearance of the primitive streak, places a human embryo in an animal, keeps or uses an embryo in contravention of regulations or engages in nucleus substitution commits an offence punishable as in (a) (s. 41(1)(b)).

Section 41(11) provides a statutory defence to all offences charged under this Act, in favour of a person to whom a licence applies or a person to whom statutory directions had been given. Where such persons show that they took all such steps as were reasonable, and exercised all due diligence to avoid committing an offence, they will be entitled to acquittal. Section 41(10) provides for an additional defence in respect of the offence under ss. 3(1) and 4(1)(c) of unlicensed mixing of gametes, where the defendant can show that she or he was acting under the direction of another whom he or she believed on reasonable grounds:

(a)   to be the person responsible under a licence, a person designated as one to whom a licence applies under s. 17(2)(b) or a person to whom statutory directions had been given under s. 24(9); and

(b)   that she or he was authorised by virtue of the licence or directions to do the activity now complained of.

The second set of offences relate to activity which might be the subject of a licence but which is carried out otherwise than in accordance with a licence. Included here is:

(a)   the unlicensed keeping, using or bringing about of the creation of an embryo (but falling short of either keeping or using it after the appearance of the primitive streak, placing it in an animal, keeping or using it in contravention of regulations or practising nucleus substitution with it) contrary to s. 3(1);

(b)   the unlicensed storage of gametes or provision of treatment services involving the use of donated gametes contrary to s. 4(1)(a) and (b);

(c)   the unlicensed placing of sperm and eggs in a woman in any circumstances specified in regulations (s. 4(3)); or

(d)   failure to comply with directions given by the HFEA under s. 24(7)(a) to provide information when a licence committee proposes to take certain specified action.

Each of these four activities is an offence (s. 41(2)) triable either way and punishable on conviction on indictment by a maximum of two years' imprisonment or an unlimited fine or both; or on a summary conviction, by a maximum of six months' imprisonment or a fine not in excess of the statutory maximum or both (s. 41(4)).

In addition to the statutory defence of s. 41(11) which applies to all these offences, persons tried in respect of an offence under ss. 3(1) or 4(1) (keeping or using gametes or embryos in contravention of the Act) may seek to avail themselves of the additional statutory defence under s. 41(10), discussed above. The same penalties are provided by s. 41(4) for offences under s. 41(3) of knowingly or recklessly providing information for the purposes of the grant of a licence which is false or misleading in a material particular. A misstatement of the experience and qualifications of a laboratory technician employed to prepare culture fluid might not be material for these purposes, whereas a similar misstatement in respect of the person to be the 'person responsible' under the licence would be.

Since, according to s. 12(e), no money or other benefit may be received in the supply of gametes or embryos except under the authorisation of directions, s. 41(8) of the Act creates a corresponding offence. This is committed where any person to whom a licence applies or the nominal licensee gives or receives any money or other benefit, not authorised by directions, in respect of the supply of any gametes or embryos. This restriction on payment is considered further at pp. 107–8. The unauthorised disclosure of information by a member, employee, former member or former employee of the HFEA in contravention of s. 33 of the Act is an offence punishable following conviction on indictment with up to two years' imprisonment or an unlimited fine or both; and following summary conviction by imprisonment for up to six months or a fine not exceeding the statutory maximum or both (s. 41(5)). The s. 41(11) defence is available.

Section 41(9) provides a similar scale of penalties for five offences under s. 41(6) and (7), all of which relate to the obstruction of the HFEA and the enforcement process. These offences may be tried only before a magistrates' court and on conviction a person is liable to imprisonment for up to six months or a fine not exceeding level 5 on the standard scale or both. In respect of each of the offences, the statutory defence under s. 41(11) applies. The offences are:

(a)   failure to comply with a requirement made under s. 39(1)(b) (for reasonable assistance to be rendered to any member or employee of the HFEA entering and inspecting premises and seeking to preserve or prevent interference with anything which may be necessary as evidence for an offence under the Act or in connection with the grant, variation, suspension or revocation of a licence);

(b)   failure to comply with a requirement made under s. 39(2)(b) (request to produce copy of information to a member or employee of the HFEA);

(c)   failure to comply with a requirement made under s. 41(2)(b)(ii) or s. 40(5)(b) (request to produce copy of information to someone entering premises under warrant);

(d)   intentional obstruction of the exercise of rights conferred by a warrant issued under s. 40;

(e)   failing, without reasonable excuse, to comply with requirements imposed by regulations made under s. 10(2)(a) (requiring persons to produce documents or give evidence).

Powers of policing and enforcement of the provisions of the Act are given in ss. 39 and 40. Any member of the HFEA, or any employee entering and inspecting licensed premises, may take possession of anything which she or he has reasonable grounds to believe may be required as evidence of an offence or may be necessary in the HFEA's discharge of its licensing functions (s. 39(1)(a)). Such a person is given power to take such steps as appear to be necessary to prevent interference with the evidence or to preserve it (s. 39(1)(b)), and may request anyone having the power to do so to provide assistance with the preservation or prevention of interference. Anything taken may be kept for as long as necessary for the purpose in question (s. 39(1)).

The 'things' referred to in this section clearly contemplate embryos kept beyond the appearance of the primitive streak, the creation of hybrids, nucleus substitution and so on; but it also extends to cover information kept at licensed clinics. There is a saving in s. 39(3) to protect members or employees of the HFEA; nothing in the Act makes it unlawful for them to keep embryos or gametes in pursuance of their functions.

Section 40(1) provides for the issuance to a member or employee of the HFEA of a warrant to enter and inspect premises and to search premises. The usual allied powers of calling on the assistance of constables and the use of reasonable force are also granted (s. 40(2)). Anything taken under authority of a warrant must be returned within six months, unless proceedings for an offence are instituted, in which case the evidence may be retained until the conclusion of the proceedings.

NOTES

[1] *R v Human Fertilisation and Embryology Authority ex parte Blood* [1997] 2 All ER 687.

[2] This view is reinforced by the definition in s. 2(1) of 'treatment services' which relates to 'medical services . . . provided to the public or a section of the public'.

[3] House of Lords, Official Report, 7 December 1989, col. 1004.

[4] HFEA, *Sixth Annual Report* (1997); the figure for pregnancies is based upon the re-implantation of three embryos.

[5] For a selection of this voluminous literature, see Klein, R.D., *Infertility* (London, Pandora Press, 1989); Spallone, P., *Beyond Conception* (Macmillan, 1989); Corea, G., *The Mother Machine* (London, The Women's Press, 1988).

[6] Best expressed in *Instruction on Respect for Human Life in its Origin and on the Dignity of Procreation*, 1987.

[7] See *Personal Origins*, The Report of a Working Party of the Board for Social Responsibility on Human Fertilisation and Embryology, 1985.

[8] Raymond, C.A., 'In Vitro Fertilisation Enters Stormy Debate as Experts Debate the Odds', *Journal of the American Medical Association*, 22–29 January 1988, pp. 464–65; for further catalogues of the physical and emotional costs of IVF, see Williams, L.S., 'No Relief Until the End' in Christine Overall (ed.), *The Future of Human Reproduction* (London, The Women's Press, 1989), at 120–38 and, importantly, Brown, L. and Brown, J., with Freeman, S., *Our Miracle Called Louise* (London, Paddington Press, 1979). It is often forgotten that the Browns had a child of his first marriage. We discuss other health risks to which a woman undergoing assisted conception may expose herself in Chapter 7, abortion at p. 241, and in this chapter at p. 137.

[9] Giddens, A., 'Risk and Responsibility' (1999) 1 *Modern Law Review* 62.

[10] See *Daily Telegraph*, 19 December 1999.

[11] See Wagner, M. and St Clair, P., 'Are IVF and Embryo Transfer of Benefit to All?' *The Lancet*, 28 October 1989, p. 1025. In the course of debate on the Bill, Ann Winterton MP argued that resources could be better used to assist the infertile by 'highlighting the problems of promiscuous sexual activity and abortion so as to prevent the occurrence of infertility in the first place' (126 *HC Debates*, col. 1240).

[12] A point made by McLean, S., 'Reproductive Medicine' in C. Dyer (ed.), *Doctors, Patients and the Law* (Oxford, Basil Blackwell, 1992); see also S. Elliston and A. Britton, 'Is Infertility an Illness?' (1994) 145 *New Law Journal* 1552.

[13] See Lee, R., 'Legal Control of Health Care Allocation' in M. Ockelton, *Medicine, Ethics and Law* (Proceedings of ASAP 13th Annual Conference) (Stuttgart, Steiner, 1987).

[14] This figure is taken from Deech, R., 'Infertility and Ethics' (1997) 9 *Child and Family Law Quarterly* 337, which considers the necessity for regulation.

[15] *Ibid.*, at 339.

[16] Warnock, para. 4.26.

[17] By Lord Jackobovits, see House of Lords, Official Report, 7 December 1989, col. 1074.

[18] Hunt, A., *Governing Morals: A Social History of Moral Regulation* (Cambridge, 1999, Cambridge U.P.).

[19] Strathern, M., 'The Meaning of Assisted Kinship' in M. Stacey (ed.), *Changing Human Reproduction* (London, Sage, 1992), at 148–9.

[20] Linger, R., Law in Modern Society: Toward a Criticism of Social Theory (New York, Free Press 1976).

[21] See Nonet, P. and Selznick, P., *Law and Society in Transition: Towards Responsive Law* (New York, Harper, 1978).

[22] Campbell, C., 'Legislation and Regulatory Bodies: The Interface between Law and Ethics' (1995) 46 *Northern Ireland Legal Quarterly* 365.

[23] Dicey, A., *Law of the Constitution*, at 156.

[24] Craig, P., *Administrative Law* (4th ed., London, 1999, Sweet and Maxwell).

[25] Montgomery, J., 'Rights, Restraints and Pragmatism: The Human Fertilisation and Embryology Act 1990' (1991) 54 *Modern Law Review* 524.

[26] House of Commons, Standing Committee B First Sitting, 1 May 1990, coll. 3–25.

[27] House of Lords, Official Report, 6 March 1990, col. 1089.

[28] See now the 1995 Act discussed in Chapter 11.

[29] Interim Licensing Authority *Fourth Report* (1989), at 2; and see p.13, para. 5.2 and pp. 17–18, Table II.

[30] See the Infertility (Medical Procedures) Act 1984, as amended by the Infertility (Medical Procedures) (Amendment) Act 1987 and now consolidated in the Medical Procedures Act 1995; see further Chapter 11.

[31] Braude, Johnson & Aitken, (Letter) *The Lancet* (2 December 1989).

[32] 'Storage and Use of Ovarian Tissue' (London, HFEA, 1998). Section 1(4) of the 1990 Act is the closest that the legislation itself comes to a definition: 'references to gametes or eggs do not include eggs in the process of fertilisation'.

[33] Health Council of The Netherlands, Committee on *in vitro* fertilisation, *IVF-Related Research* (Rijswijk, 1998), at 41, para. 3.2.2.

[34] Because s. 2(2) does not apply by virtue of s. 1(4); for the notion of 'fertility insurance', see Health Council of The Netherlands, *op. cit.* n. 33, at 47, para. 3.4.3.

[35] Family Law Reform Act 1969, s. 8 provides:

'(1)   The consent of a minor who has attained the age of sixteen years to any surgical, medical or dental treatment which, in the absence of consent, would constitute a trespass to his person, shall be as effective as it would be if he were of full age; and where a minor has by virtue of this section given an effective consent to any treatment it shall not be necessary to obtain any consent for it from his parent or guardian.'

[36] See *Gillick* v *West Norfolk and Wisbech Area Health Authority* [1985] 3 All ER 402.

[37] For the concept of 'parental responsibility', see Children Act 1989, s. 3.

[38] Ivm (*in vitro* maturation of oocytes).

[39] Although one such activity, the mixing of gametes with the live gametes of any animal under s. 4(1)(c), is capable of being authorised without a licence.

Chapter 6
Access to and Delivery of Treatment Services

ACCESS TO TREATMENT AND QUESTIONS OF RESOURCES

In Chapter 2 we considered the question (which we do not intend to revisit here) of whether infertility is an illness and also the location of infertility treatment within a system of national health care provision. That system has been built on the nationalisation of the assets of the health care industry, so that it can be funded through taxes to pay for treatment free to the patient at the point of consumption. Yet alongside this free provision of health care has grown up a health care industry in assisted conception that is largely private and which operates outside the NHS provision. This business interest should not be overlooked since it lies at the heart of the legislation for the following reason.

Had provision for assisted conception been widely available within the NHS, the 1990 Act would have been a very different piece of legislation and may have arrived somewhat later. It was in no small part activity within private clinics that prompted the Warnock Report, and from there the Act. The internal controls through guidelines and circulars ordinarily available within the NHS proved of little use in relation to the largely private provision of infertility treatment. Yet, the Act having been passed, there is a level at which the activities of these clinics are not only state licensed but also state endorsed. And it is undeniable that the very passage of the Act, and thereafter the constitution and workings of the HFEA, gave a prominence to the availability through the clinics of assisted conception.

Ordinarily one might expect that this sort of private activity would be regulated through the market, and to some extent it still is. People express their demand for these particular medical services in unequivocal terms, and, as businesses, one imagines that clinics are for the most part ready to supply the services. It is not true to say that matters were unregulated prior to the passage of the Act. As suppliers of professional medical services, the relevant professional bodies were not slow to seek to supervise the activity of their members, and indeed to move towards voluntary licensing.[1] However, regulation through the market, or even via professional bodies, was never likely to be an adequate response in the face of concern and disquiet at the sorts of uses to which it was feared the technologies might be put. Nevertheless, as we shall see, to articulate these fears sufficiently strongly to support legislation is the easy part; to identify those fears sufficiently precisely to shape the regulation was much more difficult. This is the case particularly in relation to access to treatment.

In general terms judges have proved highly resistant to the notion that they should rule on access to health care resources or decide priorities for treatment. This has been true for decisions at the macro level, such as whether facilities should be built (see *R* v *Secretary of State for Social Services, ex parte Hincks* (1992) 1 BMLR 93[2]); at the meso level, in terms of whether certain specialisms were adequately resourced (see *R* v *Central Birmingham Health Authority, ex parte Walker* (1992) 3 BMLR 93); and at the micro level, in terms of whether particular patients should receive treatment (see *R* v *Cambridge District Health Authority* [1995] 2 All ER 129). This judicial reluctance is considered elsewhere,[3] but it is relevant to questions on access to assisted conception for a number of reasons. The first is that access here is not presented as a resource question but as a welfare question. As we shall see, the relevant provision does not ask the judges to look at the relative need for treatment services. Presumably it was thought that need can find its best expression in the money expended to pay for treatment. The fact that each pound has a different value to the persons spending it is an incident of everyday life and not one with which the legislature chose to concern itself.[4] Judges are asked instead to look at the welfare of children involved in assisted conception.

Given the historic reluctance of judges to involve themselves in questions of treatment, and their ready involvement of questions of child welfare, the expression of the legislation in relation to access is most convenient. In addition, the first inroads into the stand-off of judges in relation to health care resource allocations have recently been noted. In *R* v *North Derbyshire Health Authority, ex parte Fisher* (1997) 8 Med LR 327 Dyson J found that a health authority had behaved in an unreasonable manner in failing to take adequate account of NHS guidelines relating to the administration of the drug beta interferon, and he quashed the authority's decision, making an issued order for mandamus requiring it to re-consider and make a new policy in line with the guidelines. Even here, though, once this had been done, whether the applicant would gain access to the treatment would depend on matters of clinical judgment and the availability of resources in the authority. *Fisher* is an important case since it is clear that Dyson J goes further than before in questioning the policy of the authority and opening it up to scrutiny (and at times severe criticism).[5] But the tool which allowed this was the NHS Executive letter containing policy guidelines for the drug administration.

In the course of giving judgment in this case, Dyson J considered the status of this type of guidance and drew a distinction between directions which an authority must follow and mere guidance which will not be mandatory:

> The difference between a policy which provides mere guidance and one which the health authority is obliged to follow is crucial . . . If the circular provided no more than guidance, albeit in strong terms, then the only duty placed upon the health authority was to take it into account in the discharge of their functions. That would be susceptible to challenge only on *Wednesbury* principles if they failed to consider the circular or they misconstrued or misapplied it whether deliberately or negligently. (at 331)

The greater force of directions over guidance proceeds from the statutory requirement to comply with directions contained in s. 17 of the National Health Service Act 1977. This distinction is relevant under the 1990 Act, which makes provision both for directions (ss. 23 and 24) and for guidance (ss. 25 and 26). To take examples, the HFEA could specify in directions that clinics must keep particular records on persons for whom services are provided (s. 13(2)) in order to police access in line with s. 13(5) (considered below). This would become mandatory. On the other hand, a failure to meet a requirement in the Code would be a failure to follow a guideline, and while a licence committee might consider such a failure as a licensing issue it would be more difficult for a patient feeling that her interests had been harmed by a breach of the Code successfully to challenge the action of the clinic. Nonetheless, even here the presence of guidelines (in the form of the Code) makes it easier rather than harder for a patient (or some other person with sufficient standing) to seek to review the action of a clinic where the Code appears to have been disregarded.

This assumes, however, that the treatment centre will be susceptible to judicial review. Where a treatment centre operates within the NHS this is likely to be the case. Public authorities are assumed to be answerable in public law for alleged wrongdoing unless specifically exempted in some way (see Lord Wilberforce in *Davy* v *Spelthorne BC* [1984] AC 276). However, if the matter complained of is essentially private then it will not avail the claimant that it is a public body involved. This was a central area of disagreement in the *Gillick* case (*Gillick* v *West Norfolk and Wisbech Area Health Authority* [1986] AC 112; contrast Lord Bridge's notion that the claim was 'in public rather than private law . . . [she] has no private right' with Lord Scarman's belief that Mrs Gillick was pursuing 'rights as a parent under private law', at pp. 192 and 178 respectively). However, to be amenable to judicial review, not only the activity but also the body must be public in nature. Thus in *R* v *Panel on Takeovers and Mergers, ex parte Datafin Plc* [1987] QB 815, at 848, it was said that the emphasis should be on the duty placed on the body in question: '. . . if the duty is a public duty then the body in question is subject to public law'. Here, however, the body in question was one whose functions were largely regulatory in nature. It is one thing to state that the HFEA may be amenable to review (seen as no problem in the *Blood* case), but quite another to imagine that private clinics selling medical services might be.

However, this analysis of current administrative law should be read in the context of the Human Rights Act 1998 and the proposal to incorporate the European Convention on Human Rights into English law. The Convention extends to acts or omissions of public authorities. Quite clearly this will include statutory regulatory authorities (such as the HFEA). However, there is an intention in the Act (s. 6) to include other persons or bodies that exercise both private and public functions. The 1998 Act does not contain a complete definition of 'public authority'. The intention is to leave the ambit of this to the courts. The courts may wish to do no more than extend the Convention to the activities of self-regulatory bodies (for example, the Royal College of Obstetricians and Gynaecologists). It is possible to argue, however, that in the context of national provision of health services generally, clinics making allocation decisions can be seen as hybrid bodies within the 1998 Act. This may seem somewhat unlikely, but the point needs to be made that earlier case law on judicial review needs to be treated with care.

There may be some advantages if judicial review is available, especially in terms of speed and perhaps of expense since cases can be weeded out at the leave stage. However, until it is clear that the European Convention on Human Rights does extend to licensed clinics, the disappointed patient refused access to infertility treatment might have to look for some private remedy against the clinic. In the absence of a contract offering treatment services, this is most likely to be found in laws on discrimination. In *R v Ethical Committee of St Mary's Hospital, ex parte Harriott* [1988] 1 FLR 512 (a judicial review case involving an NHS hospital), Schiemann J expressed the view that a blanket policy to exclude Jewish or coloured people might be illegal. This seems to be an understatement of the position. Here we can forget about private and public law issues and state that such policies, in so far as they relate to race, *are* illegal under the Race Relations Act 1968.

The other available route might be to complain to the HFEA. Where the policy being pursued by the clinic breached the Code, it would be open to the Authority to take action under the licence. If the Authority then refused to do so, it could find itself subject to an application for judicial review of this decision. One facet of modern regulation is that it becomes ever easier to work either side of the procedural boundaries of public and private law in this way. For example, it is not obvious that Diane Blood should choose to proceed against the HFEA. Had the clinic not involved the HFEA at an early stage, it is equally possible that this could have become a seminal case involving Mrs Blood's property rights as against the clinic. In fact, as we will show below, the practical remedies for exclusion from treatment are much less than clear, especially because the primary provision relating to access put in place by s. 13(5) of the Act seeks to limit rather than facilitate the availability of treatment.

LICENSING PARENTS? THE BACKGROUND TO THE WELFARE PROVISIONS

Section 13(5) of the 1990 Act provides that:

A woman shall not be provided with treatment services unless account has been taken of the welfare of any child who may be born as a result of the treatment (including the need of that child for a father), and of any other child who may be affected by the birth.

This section raises (but does not directly address) a question in respect of assisted conception which might be seen as increasingly important following the passage of the Human Rights Act 1998. Even if all the many financial, psychological and other hurdles pointed out in this text are overcome, does everyone have a right to 'found a family' (European Convention on Human Rights, Art. 12), by access if necessary to treatment services? In fact the words of Art. 12 refer to the right to 'marry and found a family' and the issue raised by s. 13(5) concerns the grounds on which persons may be rejected when seeking treatment services, and more particularly whether the regulation of assisted conception can become an excuse to promote values and limit persons to relationships seen worthy of support by the state. Warnock clearly thought that such a 'right' would be undesirable:

. . . many believe that the interests of the child dictate that it should be born into a home where there is a loving, stable, heterosexual relationship and that, therefore, the deliberate creation of a child for a woman who is not a partner in such a relationship is morally wrong . . . we believe that as a general rule it is better for children to be born into a two-parent family, with both father and mother, although we recognise that it is impossible to predict with any certainty how lasting such a relationship will be.[6]

At the time of the Act there were other leads available, however. For example, the comprehensive report by the Ontario Law Reform Commission[7] considered the constitutionality of excluding single or unmarried people from access to assisted conception and concluded that eligibility to participate in an artificial conception programme should be limited to 'stable single women and to stable men and stable women in stable marital or nonmarital unions'. The Commission concluded that criteria for participation in an assisted conception programme should be set out in provincial regulations. The Canadian Law Reform Commission[8] was to reconsider access in 1992, and concluded that 'with regard to artificial insemination, protection for the traditional family should not be incorporated into the legislation at the expense of the right to equality'.[9] On the other hand, the Infertility (Medical Procedures) Act 1984 (Victoria, Australia)[10] provided in respect of eligibility for treatment that a 'married woman' could include a woman who was living with a man as his wife 'on a bona fide basis' although not married to him, but would exclude single women from eligibility for treatment services. Sweden had vague criteria for the consideration of 'the medical, psychological and social circumstances of the couple' by the physician, though at least there was a right of appeal against refusal.[11]

Those tempted to view restrictions to couples only as a dated and odd requirement in the biotechnological world of the 21st century would do well to revisit the history of the provision. A House of Lords amendment to restrict the provision of services to married couples – which would have made it an offence to provide treatment services (but not to receive them) for an unmarried couple, and hence, for a single woman – was defeated by 61 votes to 60. Lord Ashbourne supported the amendment by arguing that the full impact of ss. 3 and 4 of the Act would be that 'national resources may be used legally to encourage single parenthood and that children . . . would obviously have no statutory father.'[12] And in the House of Commons Standing Committee B, David Wilshire argued that the deliberate creation of one-parent families through assisted conception offended against the rights of the individual born as a result of the treatment services, the values and standards of society and the 'biological facts of life'. He argued: 'Science cannot stop us being social animals in the animal kingdom and . . . it cannot stop us reproducing by means of a mother and a father'.[13] The statement represents a common conflation between woman and mother, and father and man.

In the debates Lord Mackay, the then Lord Chancellor, set out the cautionary note which the Government would sound throughout the debates. It would 'clearly be unfortunate', he said, if the Act was seen in any way to be conflicting with 'the importance which we attach to family values'. In particular, he thought that the HFEA would want to give general guidance to clinics in the Code of Practice to be prepared and 'approved by Ministers' under s. 25 in respect of 'this sensitive aspect of their work'.[14] Against this, Lord Ennals sought to present an alternative view:

Having children is a private area of human affairs. I believe that it is really not for the state to decide who should or should not be allowed to bear children . . . Parenting, in any case, is a high risk activity . . . The question of whether a couple has gone through a form of marriage vows is hardly relevant to the quality of parenthood.[15]

As it turned out, the Act does what it can to ensure that if it is possible for unmarried couples to receive treatment services then both partners should have the responsibility for any resulting child. This is achieved by s. 28(3) (reviewed in Chapter 9). Accordingly, where an unmarried woman and her partner together undergo a treatment service using donor sperm (whether embryo transfer, IVF, GIFT or AID), he (and no other: s. 28(4)) is to be treated as the father of any child. The provision extends the general scheme of s. 28 to treat an unmarried couple in a similar way to a married couple. There is a saving in respect of 'any child who, by virtue of the rules of common law, is treated as the legitimate child of the parties to a marriage' (s. 28(5)). There are some particular benefits for the child in this approach. First, if the woman dies, whether during childbirth or later, the child will have a legally recognised 'family' which may serve as an alternative to the child being taken into care. Secondly, it will enable the child to seek support from the man's estate following his death, or indeed the woman to seek child support during his lifetime.[16] A hint of this is given in the statement of Lord Mackay that the formal recognition of fatherhood may help to 'cement and strengthen the relationship with the informal family and reduce the risks of breakdown with its consequences for the child and, indeed, the taxpayer'.[17] This approach also removes the spectre of large numbers of legally 'fatherless children' from the legislation, a possibility which had troubled commentators on the original draft of the Bill. As we shall see, though, it does not go the whole way and remove it altogether.

It is interesting to revisit the views expressed by Lord Mackay in presenting the Bill, and these can be repeated in summary without parody (although sometimes it may seem otherwise). The importance of the family is manifest; and it is vital that children are born into a stable and loving environment. The family is a concept the health of which is fundamental to the health of society in general. Hence, the fundamental principle of law relating to children, that their welfare is the paramount consideration, had a necessary place in legislation dealing with assisted conception. The concept of the welfare of the child is broad and all-embracing. A very wide range of factors must be taken into account when considering the future lives of children who may be born as a result of the licensed treatment services. Then, quoting from a discussion of the 'welfare concept' by Hardie Boyce J in *Walker* v *Harrison* (1981) 257 New Zealand Recent Law Lord Mackay said that:

'Welfare' is an all-encompassing word. It includes material welfare, both in the sense of an adequacy of resources to provide a pleasant home and a comfortable standard of living and in the sense of an adequacy of care to ensure that good health and due personal pride are maintained. However, while material considerations have their place, they are secondary matters. More important are the stability and the security, the loving and understanding care and guidance, the warm and compassionate relationships, that are the essential for the full development of the child's own character, personality and talents.[18]

When considering the political statements relating to s. 13(5), it is important to bear in mind the wording of the subsection and its width. First, it is not limited to the provision of donated gametes or to embryos created outside the body. It extends to any treatment service, defined in the Act to mean 'medical, surgical or obstetric services provided to the public or a section of the public for the purpose of assisting women to carry children' (s. 2(1)). In so far as it is not limited by either s. 1(2) or s. 4(1)(b), this provision clearly applies to GIFT, to AID (in both cases where the couple's own gametes are used), and arguably to a much wider range of services not otherwise covered by the Act.

Secondly, s. 13(5) clearly applies to surrogacy, for the welfare criterion is not limited to any child who may be born as a result of the treatment for the woman to keep, but merely provides for any child. In all cases, including perhaps most importantly the surrogate-mother case, the welfare of 'any other child' who may be affected is to be taken into account. Thus, the welfare of any existing child of the putative surrogate mother will fall to be considered, and this may pose an additional obstacle to the provision of formal services to an intending surrogate and the couple for whom she proposes to carry a child (we deal with further provisions of the Act with respect to surrogacy in Chapter 8).

Thirdly, what does it mean to say that 'account has been taken' of the future child's welfare and that of 'any child who may be affected by the birth'? What must be shown in order to demonstrate that the statutory duty has been discharged? This gives rise to the additional difficulty, not addressed in the Act, of who takes account, and what is to happen if services are provided in breach of the duty. Presumably there may be licensing implications, but how might the HFEA show that the equation has been wrongly calculated? Similarly, the Act itself is silent on who may have *locus standi* (standing to bring proceedings) either to determine that 'account has [not] been taken' or to challenge the account which has been taken and the conclusions arrived at. The Government expressed the view that the ultimate decision of whether to proceed with the treatment in accordance with the conditions laid down by the HFEA will be made by the clinician, subject to such review by the High Court as it is prepared to allow (see above).

The substance of such review is an important consideration. Bear in mind that the relevant criteria include the welfare of any other child affected by the birth. Suppose that a particular NHS clinic decides that it would not be in the interests of the daughter of a woman seeking treatment services to provide these services. May the woman challenge this decision? And if so, on what public law principles? On the basis of *R v St Mary's Hospital Ethics Committee, ex parte Harriott* [1988] 1 FLR 512, would seem that challenge *is* possible, but that successful challenge may prove problematic short of manifest unreasonableness. Or take an example that might almost prove more realistic: suppose that a private clinic has a policy of open access for those who can afford the treatment, with few questions asked. Belinda's aunt and uncle think that Belinda's interests will not be best served by the arrival of a sibling now that Belinda's mother lives with a nasty but impotent new boyfriend. Can they challenge the clinic's decision to provide treatment services using donated sperm? Can they seek a declaration that it would not be in their niece's interests for the child to be born?[19] Suppose that the argument is that it would not be in Belinda's interests because she would inherit only a fraction of the estate that she would otherwise inherit, and that this is a particular problem allowing for the propensity of multiple order births?

It is not hard to think of other circumstances in which difficulties of interpretation and application of the section's requirement may arise. In the 1991 book, for the purposes of inquiry, we canvassed the following, some of which doubtless seemed far-fetched:

- a couple who already have children but who cannot reproduce as a couple (most famously, Lesley and John Brown)
- a woman who wants to become pregnant in order to produce an abortus which could provide foetal tissue for use in a therapeutic operation to save her husband's life or the life of her three-year-old daughter (in the *Ayala* case referenced in Robertson[20] a child was conceived and brought to term to provide bone marrow for an existing child suffering from leukaemia)
- a woman (or a couple) who only wants a child of a particular sex (see the Masterton example, *Guardian*, 16 October 2000)
- a woman who suffers from Munchausen's syndrome, in which sufferers present with imagined or induced medical problems, and in whom the existence of 'Munchausen's syndrome by Proxy' is a real possibility (such a patient was indeed treated)
- a woman who has formerly worked as a prostitute (refused treatment in *R v St Mary's Hospital Ethics Committee, ex parte Harriot* [1988] 1 FLR 512)
- a woman whose partner has low sperm motility because of the excessive alcohol which he consumes (probably treated all the time?)

To this list we might now add:

- two homosexual men hoping for a baby (as in Barlow and Drewitt, who brought twins born of a surrogate mother into the UK from California)
- woman who is, or a woman and a partner both of whom are, +HIV. The risk of a woman passing the HIV virus to her foetus is between 14 and 35 per cent. There has been no case of a +HIV baby being born if her mother is negative and the father positive. The risk of transmitting HIV to the foetus comes, therefore, exclusively from the mother. In treatment services, where one or both partners are +HIV, the risk of transmitting the HIV virus to the foetus can be reduced to 1 to 2 per cent if (i) the sperm is 'washed' to remove possible +HIV; (ii) the woman receives triple therapy; (iii) the baby is delivered by Caesarean section; (iv) the baby is not breast-fed
- a woman who is a cystic fybrosis carrier whose partner is also a carrier and has a condition known as vasa aplasia (therefore needing sperm recovery); many clinics would admit for treatment services, yet the risk of transmitting the cystic fybrosis gene in such a case is over 50 per cent
- a virgin birth for a woman with no wish to engage in, or with a fear of, sexual relations (see a report in the *Guardian*, 12 March 1991, for a report of a clinic counselling a patient in this situation)
- treatment for a woman who has a partner in prison (refused in the USA, see Robertson, above; but may happen frequently if sperm can be smuggled out of prison)
- treatment for a long-term female prisoner who would need to raise the child in prison, or who asks to have oocytes frozen so that she can have children in later life having served her sentence

Faced with such possibilities, s. 13(5) is not a great deal of help, neither is the message from the Parliamentary discussions clear. But not surprisingly, it has all the hallmarks of a pro-family ideology. Assisted conception is to be, for the most part, for the married, mortgaged middle classes; a conclusion which is entirely consonant with infertility services being unavailable on any scale through the NHS. One (defeated) amendment in the House of Lords sought to limit treatment services to married couples using their own gametes, i.e. to AIH and not AID. The Earl of Lauderdale described the former as embodying the ethics of the household, while the latter embodied the ethics of the farmyard.[21] This sort of argument makes the debates on the status of children born following assisted conception seeking to succeed to various hereditary titles at least comprehensible, if nonetheless anachronistic.

At least s. 13(5) has avoided mention (which some would have preferred in debate) of any requirement that the welfare of that child be considered as paramount. This at least saved the workings of the section from a philosophical appreciation of existence against non-existence.[22] Nonetheless, it introduces a 'social' conscience clause, whereby consideration of the 'fitness to parent' of prospective applicants (and the use of the plural here is deliberate) could amount to a licensing system for parenthood. That it has not done so – and, on the contrary, has largely been ignored by clinics – may owe more to commercial pressures to provide treatment services than to any act of rebellion on behalf of the providers. This is not to suggest that there will never be any screening mechanisms for good or for bad (see *R* v *Ethical Committee of St Mary's Hospital, ex parte Harriott* [1988] 1 FLR 512 and *R* v *Sheffield Health Authority, ex parte Seale* (1996) 3 Med LR 326).

The extraordinary facet of this debate is that the evidence which would enable the negative conclusions to be drawn about single or lesbian-couple parenting is in scant supply – both then and now.[23] Even if one establishes a correlation between one-parent families and emotional or behavioural deprivation, that does not lead straight to the conclusion that it is the single parenting which causes the problem. It may tell us more about some of the priorities in social welfare spending. While it remains possible that there are effects on development of being brought up in a home that lacks any contact with men, these have yet to be demonstrated. Indeed, it would be idle to think that all one-parent (or indeed lesbian) households are likely to offer the same experience of care and loving for the child any more than a married relationship will offer a uniform experience of parenthood or family life. Surely in the aftermath of scandalous abuse of children in some children's homes in the UK, we might be permitted to venture that it may make more sense to focus on the quality of relationships and the pattern of loving care during upbringing than on the sexual orientation of the mother.

In the years since the Warnock Report, little has happened to restore the stability of marital relationships. Modern relationships as a whole may have a failure rate as high as 50%. If families need fathers then a time bomb is slowly ticking. Yet the legislation persists with the notion that the two-parent, heterosexual family is the norm and that any deviation from this ideal is bound to cause problems for the child. Around 1:8 families with children in Britain are one-parent families. The majority are headed by women, and a growing percentage of those are unmarried. Is it really sensible to suppose that one and a half million children will be damaged by this experience? And does it make any sense to suppose that the social and emotional development of AID and IVF children in fatherless families would be different from that of children who find themselves in heterosexual one-parent families or in lesbian families after they reach the age of two or three years?[24]

THE WORKING OF THE WELFARE PROVISION

It is worth noting that there are many issues in relation to access to treatment that s. 13(5) does not resolve. For example, it says nothing of the need of the woman (and it is the woman who is singled out) for treatment services. It may be that certain issues relating to whether the woman is in need will also be relevant for the application of the s. 13(5) test, as with so-called 'virgin births'. Nonetheless, there will be many instances in which, quite apart from any application of s. 13(5), the clinician will have to decide in infertility treatment, as with many other forms of treatment, whether the patient is in need of the services. This may involve simple issues such as how long a woman ought to try to conceive through sexual intercourse prior to undergoing some of the risks inherent in assisted conception; or it may involve more complex questions as to whether a woman is now too old for treatment, perhaps having met a partner late in life and finding pregnancy hard to achieve. As we will see, and as will be apparent from the case of *R* v *Sheffield Health Authority, ex parte Seale* (1996) 3 Med LR 326, age is an important factor in allocating assisted conception services.

It might be thought that given that, this is largely a private activity, few applicants for treatment would be refused. This is not the case, however, where success rates in achieving pregnancy and live births are used as performance indicators. This is important not merely in relation to the marketing of clinics' services, but it also becomes part of the information gathered through the regulatory process, and which may be relevant to decisions regarding licensing. Moreover, once again, this is not purely a business. It involves qualified professionals who wish to act in their patients' best interests. In fact, one of the curiosities of s. 13(5) is the invasion of this territory of clinical judgment. The problem with the provision is twofold: it dictates to the doctor the manner in which judgments should be made about patients, but it does so by insisting that the doctor takes into account issues which are primarily medical but largely social. It may be, of course, that much of the time doctors are making decisions about allocation of scarce resources which involve questions other than the purely medical. Certainly, there seems to have been relatively little overt resistance from doctors disclaiming the capacity to make the social assessments required by s. 13(5).

These assessments are also required from anyone offering 'treatment services' within the definition in s. 2(1) of the Act. This means that anyone providing medical, surgical or obstetric services to (say a section of) the public for the purpose of assisting women to bear children ought to be asking, in advance of the delivery of that service, questions concerning the welfare of any child who might be born as a result of treatment. This could apply, therefore, to a woman seeking investigation into causes of thus far unexplained infertility. It seems difficult to imagine a doctor, knowing that the woman is single, refusing even to begin the process of investigation. Freeman goes much further than this, stating:

> . . . in theory ante-natal services could be denied to a lesbian woman on the ground that it would be better for the child if she miscarried. No one, it is

assumed, would put this construction on s. 13(5) but extraordinarily it is capable of bearing this meaning.[25]

Freeman goes on to point out that the provision applies to surrogacy. Thus it involves even more complex judgments on the part of any clinician who assists in a surrogacy arrangement. Lastly, there is a wide range of circumstances in which the requirement of 'the need of that child for a father' could perplex the clinician. There is something really rather remarkable about a piece of legislation that legislates to create fatherless children and yet at the same time includes this provision. As we have pointed out earlier, what is demanded here is not so much a father, since surely the child will have one, but a man. Perhaps the doctor should become involved in considering what sort of a man: homosexual or heterosexual? rich or poor? living at home or working abroad? divorced with other children or a first-time father? in and out of prison? or just a City workaholic?

Our colleague, Gillian Douglas, reviewed the working of s. 13(5) in practice in the early years of the application of the 1990 Act.[26] She concluded that the passage of the Act had made relatively little impact on the attitudes or practices of those offering infertility treatments.[27] In general, where a patient was considered not suitable for treatment, she would be ruled out at a very early stage, and probably prior to any formal consultation. Thus it seemed that clinicians were in a position to reject people on principle (whether on the grounds of marital status or on the grounds of age) without requiring further investigation and without offering any justification for refusal to admit to treatment. Where patients were then admitted to treatment, however, there did seem to be little effective assessment of individual fitness to promote the welfare of the child. On the whole it seemed that the decision was taken on the basis of a narrow range of information, and generally (in about two-thirds of the cases) by the individual clinician alone.

This was an early study of the workings of the welfare provisions, but it seems doubtful whether such practices meet the requirements of the Code that 'people seeking treatment are entitled to a fair and unprejudiced assessment of their situation and needs' (para. 13.6). At this point the Code goes on to state that such assessments should be conducted with 'the skill and sensitivity appropriate to the delicacy of the case and the wishes and feelings of those involved.' However, the Code, as it is required to do, follows the Act in demanding that attention be paid to the child's need for a father and stresses the prospective mother's ability to meet the child's needs through childhood. When this factor is added to certain others listed in the Code, it may seem that some of the odds are stacked against the single woman receiving treatment. Thus the Code suggests that account be taken of the prospective mother's:

(a)   ability to provide a stable and supportive environment;
(b)   health and consequent future ability to look after or provide for a child's needs;
(c)   age and future ability to look after and provide for a child's needs;
(d)   ability to meet the needs of any child or children who may be born as a result of treatment, including the implications of any possible multiple births; and

any possibility known to the centre of a dispute about the legal fatherhood of the child. Indeed, centres are asked to consider whether there are others within the prospective mother's family and social circle willing and able to share responsibility for meeting the needs of the child (and presumably this includes the child's need for a father) and for bringing up, maintaining and caring for the child.

Such welfare provisions also arise in the case of surrogacy arrangements. Clearly, licensed clinics may become involved in surrogacy arrangements, not least because it offers the only possible solution to infertility for certain couples. The Code of Practice does not rule out this involvement, but it does place certain obligations on the centres if they are to assist in a surrogacy arrangement. Thus the Code points out that the eventual percentage of the child cannot be certain at the outset of a surrogacy arrangement. In consequence, many of the factors considered above have to be applied in relation to all parties involved if the welfare of the child is fully to be taken into account. In addition to this the Code stresses 'any risk of disruption to the child's early current upbringing should there be a dispute'. Centres are also asked to take into account the effect of any proposed arrangement on any child of the carrying mother's family, as well as any effect on any child of the commissioning parents' family. Lastly, the Code states that the application of assisted conception techniques to initiate a surrogacy pregnancy should be considered only where it is physically impossible or highly undesirable for medical reasons for the commissioning mother to carry the child (para. 3.20).

Note that the conditions set out in the Code apply to all licensed centres. They apply whether or not the services offered by way of assisted conception themselves require a licence. Thus, a clinic offering GIFT might need to take into account the same considerations in relation to the welfare of the child as would a clinic providing treatment through IVF. The Code does, however, state that the degree of consideration necessary will be greater if the treatment required is licensed, and especially if it involves the use of donated gametes.

CONSCIENCE CLAUSES

The majority of issues relating to the provision of treatment services are dealt with elsewhere in this chapter. There is, however, one remaining matter relating to the provision of services which is covered by the 1990 Act, but with which we have yet to deal. Individuals asked to assist with licensed treatments or experimentation under the 1990 Act may be able to take advantage of a statutory provision (s. 38(1)) which allows them to opt out on grounds of conscience. This is modelled on s. 4 of the Abortion Act 1967, which provides that:

> No person shall be under a duty, whether by contract or by statutory or other legal requirement, to participate in any treatment authorised by this Act to which he has a conscientious objection.

The remainder of s. 4 goes on to state that, in legal proceedings, the burden of proof in conscientious objection shall rest upon the person claiming to rely on it. It is also made clear that the section is not intended to affect any duty of practitioners to participate in treatment which will be necessary to save the life of or prevent grave permanent injury to the physical and mental health of a pregnant woman.

Surrounding this statutory requirement is a long-standing agreement between the Department of Health and the medical profession to the effect that no reference to termination duties will be included in the advertisement of hospital posts. However, if posts involve such duties, mention of them should be made in job descriptions so that doctors who do not want to be involved in termination duties are aware of the position. Amongst other things, the guidelines[28] state that unless the job description specifies that there are likely termination duties, candidates should not be asked whether they would be prepared to undertake such duties. Even where job descriptions do state that termination duties are necessary, questions should be confined to professional intentions and should not seek to elicit candidates' personal beliefs. It should be noted, however, that in the case of junior medical staff it is thought inappropriate for termination responsibilities to be included in the job description. This is because it is thought unnecessary for training purposes to require all junior staff in training grades to undertake such duties.

As regards nursing staff, the requirements of s. 4 of the 1967 Act apply equally to nurses and midwives. It is important to note also that the statute applies both to the NHS and to the private sector. This is of particular importance in considering the equivalent conscience clause in the 1990 Act, given the preponderance of private centres offering assisted conception services. The provisions in relation to nursing staff are similar to those applying to doctors; there may be no mention of the duties in the advertisement, but the job description may include reference to terminations.

Around the time of the passage of the 1990 Act, the workings of the conscience clause under s. 4 of the Abortion Act 1967 were reviewed. The views of those giving evidence to the Select Committee[29] seem remarkably varied. On one hand, there did not seem to be wide use made of the clause, but possibly this is because the doctors likely to invoke it avoided the relevant specialties. On the other hand, some doctors felt that the clause was vital but was working inadequately, allowing possible discrimination against those doctors likely to invoke it. Nonetheless, when asked, the Department of Health representatives before the Committee thought that it was reasonable to reproduce the 'conscience clause' in the Human Fertilisation and Embryology Bill. This was because certain people would clearly have conscientious objections to some of the treatments for infertility which the Act would license. In the Department's view there was 'no evidence to suggest that "Conscience Clauses" were causing sufficient problems' to the point that it would be unwise to include one within the legislation on human fertilisation and embryology.

Section 38(1) of the 1990 Act creates a provision on conscientious objection that is phrased rather differently from the one contained in the Abortion Act. It retains the burden of proof on the objector (s. 38(2)), but it simply says that 'No person who has a conscientious objection to participating in any activity governed by [the] Act shall be under any duty, howsoever arising, to do so'. It does not repeat s. 4(2) of the Abortion Act 1967, to the effect that a duty to participate in life-saving treatment is retained. This may be because it is assumed that participation in the activities governed by the 1990 Act will not generally give rise to life-threatening or seriously disabling conditions. This, of course, was frustrated at the point where abortion was included as an activity governed by the 1990 Act; and indeed, there is now an implicit conflict between s. 38 of the 1990 Act and s. 4 of the Abortion Act 1967. To the extent that any activity governed by the 1990 Act might give rise to a life-threatening condition, it should be stated that, in spite of the absence of any proviso relating to this within the statute, at common law once a doctor had commenced treatment on a patient, the doctor would be under a duty to intervene in order to arrest conditions which are life-threatening or causing grave physical injury (see *F v Berkshire Health Authority* [1990] 2 AC 1). Such duty may arise both out of negligence and the criminal law.

There is also a body of law on the scope of the conscience objection allowed by s. 4 of the 1967 Act, which may be relevant here. This concerns the question of what might amount to participating in treatment (see *Royal College of Nursing v Department of Health & Social Security* [1981] AC 800). This case concerned a circular dated 21 February 1980 from the Department of Health & Social Security, which purported to explain the law relating to abortion in connection with the termination of pregnancy by medical induction. The Royal College of Nursing sought a declaration that the circular was wrong in law in so far as it allowed that important parts of this process would be performed not by a registered medical practitioner, but by a nurse acting under instruction. The issue arose as to whether the actions of the nurse were unlawful, and it was held that they were not. The grounds given were that what was authorised by the Act was the whole medical process which would result in the termination of pregnancy. Provided that process was carried out by a registered medical practitioner, procedures done under her or his supervision and in accordance with those instructions could be lawful. The declaration was refused. In the course of the judgment in the House of Lords, Lord Roskill considered the application of s. 4 and the words 'participate in any treatment'. The importance of the provision, in Lord Roskill's view, for the purposes of the case, was that unless it was anticipated that nursing staff would from time to time become involved in the treatment procedures for terminating pregnancy, it was difficult to see why conscientious objection might be permitted.

A case more directly in point is *Janaway v Salford Area Health Authority* [1988] 3 All ER 1079. In this case the applicant was employed by the local health authority as a doctor's receptionist and secretary. She refused to type a letter of referral for an abortion on conscientious grounds. She was then dismissed by the authority. The applicant sought judicial review of this decision, contending that she was entitled to refuse by virtue of s. 4(1) of the 1967 Act. The House of Lords, however, applied the ordinary and natural meaning of the word 'participate', to mean that the objector had to be required actually to take part in administering treatment in a hospital or other approved centre for the purpose of terminating a pregnancy. Consequently, arrangements preliminary to the termination, such as typing letters of refusal, would not be included. Unfortunately, this does not resolve all the questions concerning what amounts to 'participating'.

Under the Abortion Act, it is usual for a form of certification (the green form) to be signed by two registered medical practitioners in pursuance of s. 1(1)(a) of the 1967 Act. It is well known that certain medical practitioners will not sign the green form as a matter of practice, and request that other practitioners be found. In *Janaway*, Lord Keith in the House of Lords considered the question whether or not in the light of their decision, s. 4(1) would extend to practitioner refusals to sign the green form. Unfortunately, he then concluded that: 'The fact that during the twenty years that the 1967 Act has been in force no problem seems to have surfaced in this connection may indicate that in practice none exists. So I do not think it appropriate to express any opinion on the matter' (at p. 1083).

Given the repetition of s. 4 of the 1967 Act in the 1990 legislation, it is unfortunate that the House of Lords did not take the opportunity presented in *Janaway* to express a clearer view upon the operation of the conscience clause. There is apparent uncertainty as to the extent of the clause in relation to participating in treatment. In written evidence to the Social Services Committee it was averred that 'the status of others such as anaesthetists who help the practitioner provide the treatment is uncertain'.[30] In the nature of things, it would seem that if the anaesthetists help to provide the treatment, by definition they participate in it and must be covered by the 'conscience clause'. It might be thought that the guardian of the conscience clause would be the HFEA in its role of licensing authority, but the Annual Reports of the Authority give little indication that it oversees the workings of the Act in this respect.

There has been some debate in the context of the Act concerning what might amount to a matter of conscience. In particular, it has been suggested that a person may invoke the benefit of the clause because he or she objects to providing treatment services for lesbian mothers.[31] At first sight this might seem attractive. After all, a conscientious objection is one made on the grounds that something seems morally repugnant. Freeman[32] argues that this instance would amount to a matter of prejudice rather than conscience. This seems unpersuasive, since however misconceived the objection, if it is a genuinely felt objection on grounds of conscience then it must surely be open for the person to demonstrate this and rely on it. To begin to look behind the reasons for the objection would lead into very tricky territory. A better reason may be that the wording of the Act demands that the objection be to the participation in the activity. If by 'activity' one means the service provided, one surely must have an objection to that service itself rather than its provision to particular persons.[33]

NOTES

[1]   Gunning J. and English, V., Human In Vitro Fertilisation: A Case Study in the Regulation of Medical Innovation (Aldershot, Dartmouth, 1993).
[2]   Newdick, C., 'Rights to NHS Resources After the 1990 Act' (1993) 1 *Med L Rev* 53; Parkin, A., 'Public Law and the Provision of Health Care' (1985) 7 *Urban Law & Policy* 101.
[3]   Lee, R.G., 'Judicial Review and Access to Health Care' in Buck, T., *Judicial Review and Social Welfare* (London, Pinter, 1998).
[4]   These points owe much to the work of Calebresi, G. and Bobbit, P., *Tragic Choices* (New York, Norton, 1978).
[5]   As Laws J would have done at first instance in *R* v *Cambridge HA ex parte B* [1995] 2 All ER 129.
[6]   Warnock Report, para. 2.11.
[7]   *Report on Human Artificial Reproduction and Related Matters* (Ministry of the Attorney General, Toronto, 1985). See Recommendation 5, p. 275, and see pp. 45 *et seq.* and pp. 153 *et seq.*
[8]   Royal Commission Report of 1992.
[9]   Canadian Law Reform Commission, *Medically Assisted Procreation* (Working Paper No. 65, 1992).

[10] See now the 1995 Act which is fully explained in Chapter 11.

[11] Article 3 of the Law on Insemination (No. 1140 of 20 December 1984).

[12] House of Lords, Official Report, 6 February 1990, col. 757. This issue is further discussed in Chapter 2.

[13] House of Commons, Official Report, 15 May 1990, coll. 145–146.

[14] House of Lords, Official Report, 6 February 1990, col. 800.

[15] *Ibid.*, col. 789.

[16] See the Child Support Act 1991, s. 3; and Jacobs, E. and Douglas, G., *Child Support: The Legislation* (London, Sweet & Maxwell, 1999).

[17] House of Lords, Official Report, 20 March 1990, col. 210.

[18] House of Lords, Official Report, 6 March 1990, col. 1097.

[19] Or for that matter, could such actions be taken by grandparents; on the emergent legal status of grandparents, see Douglas, G. and Lowe, N., 'Becoming a Parent in English Law' (1992) 108 LQR 414; and 'Grandparents and the Legal Process' (1990) JSWFL 89.

[20] Robertson, J., *Children of Choice: Freedom and the New Reproductive Technologies* (New Jersey, Princeton University Press, 1994).

[21] House of Lords, Official Report, 6 February 1990, col. 762.

[22] But for those wishing to consider such matters, see Harris, J., *Wonderwoman and Superman* (Oxford OUP, 1992).

[23] Golombok, S., *Parenting: What Really Counts?* (London, Routledge, 2000) at 45–60.

[24] See further the arguments of Golombok, S. and Rust, J., 'The Warnock Report and Single Women: What about the Children' (1986) *Journal of Medical Ethics* 182.

[25] Freeman, M., in Kennedy, I. and Grubb, A., *Principles of Medical Law* (Oxford University Press, 1998), para. 10.60 (p. 565).

[26] Douglas, G., (1993) 'Assisted Reproduction and the Welfare of the Child' *Current Legal Problems* 46.

[27] See also Boivin, J., Scanlan, L. and Walker, S., 'Why are Infertile Couples not using Psychological Counselling?' (1999) *Human Reproduction* 1384.

[28] *Janaway* v *Salford AHA* [1988] 3 All ER 1079; and see also Kennedy and Grubb, *Principles of Medical Law* (1998).

[29] Social Services Select Committee, Tenth Report, HC 123 (17 October 1990), *Abortion Act: The Conscience Clause.*

[30] *Ibid.*, 21 March 1990, p. 22.

[31] Douglas, G., *Law, Fertility and Reproduction* (1991), at 122.

[32] Freeman, M., 'Medically Assisted Reproduction' in Kennedy and Grubb, *Principles of Medical Law* (1998) at 572.

[33] Kennedy and Grubb, *Medical Law Text with Materials* (1994), at 787–8.

Chapter 7
Consent and Counselling

CONSENT AND THE COMMON LAW

As we shall see, the 1990 Act has specific requirements relating to consent to infertility treatment. It is necessary also to consider the background law of consent to medical treatment for at least two reasons. First, it is clear that the courts will employ the common law principles relating to consent when interpreting the particular requirements of the statute. Secondly, as discussed, not all forms of infertility treatment are regulated by the Act, such that the common law retains a significance in governing these medical procedures. What follows is not a comprehensive review of the common law on consent to treatment (medical law textbooks offer ample consideration of the subject) but a reflection upon the continuing importance of the common law principles in an area of clinical practice which is now largely regulated by statute.

It is accepted law that there are certain acts to which one cannot lawfully consent (see *R* v *Brown* [1994] 1 AC 212 and the judgments of the Court of Appeal in *Re F* [1989] 2 WLR 1025, upheld on different grounds at [1989] 2 All ER 545). This doctrine has been widely criticised as paternalistic, as indeed it is, actively discouraging certain behaviour or conduct. Such conduct includes the deliberate exposure of persons to the risk of bodily harm at the hands of others. In laying down such moral rules, the courts attempt to determine matters of public interest; and because such guidelines are quite essentially moral, the courts will be slow to recognise exceptions to such rules. Nonetheless, one such exception is recognised in relation to medical interventions, allowing the patient to agree to interventions and, in some cases, injuries not otherwise within the tolerance of the law. This applies, however, only to 'proper medical treatment' on the basis of the 'propriety' of that treatment (*per* Lord Mustill in *Airedale NHS Trust* v *Bland* [1993] 1 All ER 821, at 889). This raises two issues of significance here. First, in the absence of consent, any doctor will risk the immunity which the law is prepared to allow. Secondly, that immunity extends only to proper medical treatment. In the rapidly developing area of assisted conception, it may be difficult to know what constitutes proper practice. In part, the job of the HFEA is to state exactly where the boundaries of proper practice lie. For treatment falling outside definitions of 'treatment services' under the Act,[1] these boundaries may be set in accordance with the views of bodies such as the Royal College of Obstetricians and Gynaecologists. Not all such clinical guidelines are free from controversy and the restrictions on the transfer of multiple eggs or embryos to avoid multiple births are contested. Yet physicians should be aware that the tolerance of what might be permitted in the name of proper medical practice could be stretched to breaking point in the face (say) of a return to the practice prior to the Act of the transfer of up to seven eggs.

Given that the patient might consent to such procedures in the hope of successful infertility treatment, the issue here is the therapeutic benefit in terms of both the physical and mental health of that patient. Since the courts have accepted other forms of intervention (such as sterilisation) at the behest of the patient, it is clear that they are attempting to reflect the public interest in terms of what can prove socially acceptable. This is well illustrated by the view of Lord Denning (expressed in 1954) that vasectomy was 'plainly injurious to the public interest' (in *Bravery* v *Bravery* [1954] 3 All ER 59, at 67). In an area where Parliament has laid down procedures for determining what is to be taken as acceptable, one would generally expect the courts to have regard to any statutory guidance, even when dealing with procedures lying outside the confines of the regulated regime.[2]

The first requirement of consent under the 1990 Act is that it should be in writing. There is no such requirement at common law. It follows that for those procedures falling outside the Act, oral consent will be sufficient, though clearly any clinic would be ill-advised to proceed without a written record of the patient's consent. Indeed, it is possible that consent need not be express but could be implied. This might be most likely to happen in situations in which consent to routine procedures or diagnostic tests will be inferred in the context of the treatment as a whole. As we discuss below, the courts have moved towards construing the doctor's duties in relation to explaining the course of treatment and obtaining consent in the context of the law of negligence. It seems likely, therefore, that these obligations fall upon a doctor as part of the duty of care owed by doctor to patient and arise once responsibility is assumed for the patient's treatment. (See the judgment of Lord Scarman in *Sidaway* v *Board of Governors of Bethlam Hospital* [1985] 1 All ER 643, at 652.)

It is interesting to note that English law has developed notions of negligence in preference to those of trespass. In *Chatterton* v *Gerson* [1980] 3 WLR 1003 the court refused to accept any notion of consent to treatment beyond the necessity of informing the patient in broad terms of the nature and purpose of any intended operative procedure. In that case, the patient was taken to have given effective consent to a medical intervention even though she had no knowledge of an accepted side-effect of the treatment. Any claim based on the failure of the doctor to disclose known risks lay in negligence rather than trespass. In *Chatterton*, having been informed of the broad nature of the treatment, the patient gave real consent, and the court also dismissed her claim in negligence.

This judgment was endorsed, most notably, in *Sidaway* v *Board of Governors of Bethlam Hospital* (above), where the wider point of precisely which risks ought to be disclosed by a doctor was addressed. In this case, the House of Lords subsumed the duty to offer a patient sufficient warning under the general head of the doctor's duty of care in negligence. This means that a duty is owed, in practice, to each patient treated; but in determining whether that duty has been met, the test is based much more upon what the doctor chooses to disclose rather than on what the patient might want to know. This results from the application, in determining the appropriate standards of care, of the principles in *Bolam* v *Friern Hospital Management Committee* [1957] 2 All ER 118: 'A doctor is not guilty of negligence if he has acted in accordance with a practice accepted as proper by a responsible body of medical men skilled in that particular art.' In the context of warnings and consent, the standard, once we govern these matters by negligence, therefore becomes such warnings as a responsible body of practitioners consider accepted practice, in this case in relation to infertility treatment services.

There are a number of obvious objections here, quite apart from the helplessness (not to say impotence) of the patient in controlling his or her therapeutic destiny. Implicitly, the doctrine allows the doctor to dictate the standard to the court. The House of Lords showed some consciousness of this in *Sidaway*, three of their Lordships seeming to suggest that when it came to warnings, as opposed to diagnosis or treatment, the courts would remain the final arbiters of the test to be applied. However, the basis of this qualification is unclear, Lord Templeman appearing to draw a distinction between general risks and special dangers (at 664), and Lord Bridge (with whom Lord Keith concurred) suggesting the need to disclose 'substantial risk of grave adverse consequences'. Nonetheless, Lord Scarman (dissenting) took the view that the standard should be based upon risks which the prudent patient would wish to be disclosed as significant.

In the case of *Gold* v *Haringey Health Authority* [1987] 2 All ER 888, which involved the absence of warning of the risk of failure of a sterilisation operation, the court seemed to favour the unrestrained application of the *Bolam* principle as expressed only by Lord Diplock in *Sidaway*. The question arose in this case as to what might be expected of a doctor in advising contraceptive services. Lloyd LJ said (at 894):

The [*Bolam*] principle does not depend on the context in which any act is performed, or any advice given. It depends on a man professing skill or competence in a field beyond that possessed by the man on the Clapham omnibus. If the giving of contraceptive advice required no special skill, then I could see an argument that the *Bolam* test should not apply. But that was not, and could not have been suggested. The fact (if it be the fact) that giving contraceptive advice involves a different sort of skill and competence from carrying out a surgical operation does not mean that the *Bolam* test ceases to be applicable. It is clear from Lord Diplock's speech in *Sidaway* that a doctor's duty of care in relation to diagnosis, treatment and advice, whether the doctor be a specialist or a general practitioner, is not to be dissected into its component parts. To dissect a doctor's advice into that given in a therapeutic context and that given in a contraceptive context would be to go against the whole thrust of the majority of the House of Lords in that case. So I would reject the argument of counsel for the plaintiff under this head, and hold that the judge was not free, as he thought, to form his own view of what warning and information ought to have been given, irrespective of any body of responsible medical opinion to the contrary.

In more recent cases, some doubt has been cast upon this principle, primarily because of a changed interpretation of the *Bolam* principle following the House of Lords' judgment in *Bolitho* v *City & Hackney Health Authority* [1998] AC 232.

In this case their Lordships stressed that the principle was based upon a *responsible* body of medical opinion reflecting a *reasonable* body of opinion. Lord Browne-Wilkinson expressed the view that there could be rare cases in which a body of medical opinion has no 'logical basis'. Notwithstanding the difficulties of this expression, and the disclaimer by Lord Browne-Wilkinson that his remarks were confined to cases of diagnosis and treatment rather than 'disclosure of risk', the undeniable logic of a challenge to the previously unassailable *Bolam* principle is to cast doubt on its use as the basis for *Sidaway*. It follows that in future considerations of whether risks attaching to treatment should be disclosed, it will be open to the courts to take a 'hard look' at any claim that such risks would not be ordinarily disclosed (see the judgment of Farquharson LJ in *Joyce v Merton, Sutton and Wandsworth HA* [1996] 7 Med LR 1). This is to allow the court to remain free to determine that there has been a failure to disclose amounting to negligence (*per* Roch LJ, at 13).

In the context of infertility treatment, with the attendant risks of multiple order birth, this might imply a duty to warn of the intention to transfer more than one egg with the possibility of more than one child.[3] Although these medical risks might need to be disclosed, this would not extend to, for example, the social or financial consequences of twins, triplets or quads. It should be borne in mind, however, that this is the position at common law, and the counselling requirements of the legislation might envisage just this sort of information. The possibility of superovulation or infertility treatment giving rise to a multiple pregnancy and birth would not be something, in the words of Lloyd LJ in *Gold* (above), within the common understanding of the passenger on the Clapham omnibus. The social, physical and financial (and possibly the psychological) costs of caring for several children might be thought to be so.

All of this, however, assumes that a responsible body of medical opinion would warn of particular risks attaching to assisted conception. Even ignoring the recent inroads made by *Bolitho* into the *Bolam* principle, the majority of the House of Lords in *Sidaway* seemed to accept that at some point the risk would be sufficiently substantial to require disclosure. Both Lords Bridge and Templeman in *Sidaway* were of a view that certain risks were of such a magnitude that there could be no doubt that they must be disclosed to the patient. In the words of Lord Bridge (at 663), the court 'might in certain circumstances come to the conclusion that disclosure of a particular risk was so obviously necessary to an informed choice on the part of the patient that no reasonably prudent medical man would fail to make it'. The kind of risk which he had in mind was one such as 'an operation involving a substantial risk of grave adverse consequences'. The example then given is interesting: a 10% risk of grave adverse consequences would be 'substantial', such that the risk ought to be disclosed. This is apparently irrespective of whether disclosure was the commonly accepted practice within the profession or not.

It is fascinating to consider such a yardstick as against crucial information such as the risks of disability or mortality in the resulting foetus or child, or indeed the success rate of the procedures as a whole given their capacity for both distress and discomfort. To protect against liability in negligence for non-disclosure, time is needed for discussion, reflection and judgment. That is precisely what the counselling opportunity demanded by the 1990 Act seeks to provide. Increasingly it will form the bench-mark against which the activity in non-licensed centres will be judged. In a situation in which counselling becomes the norm for assisted conception, some of the post-*Gold* cases may require re-evaluation. For example, and in the light of *Bolitho*, it might be necessary to revisit cases such as *Blyth* v *Bloomsbury HA* [1993] 4 Med LR 151 which suggested that a doctor is under no duty to answer questions truthfully provided *Bolam* standards are met.

One last point of some importance is that very often in relation to assisted conception the doctor will be offering treatment to a couple rather than to a single patient. Precisely which party is the recipient of treatment services will depend on the nature of the services provided. Nonetheless, it will be common for both the couple to attend the clinic together. If consent is to be valid, it should be given freely by a person with the requisite capacity. It is important, therefore, to establish that each party subject to treatment consents on a voluntary basis to it. In other contexts, such as financial transactions (see *Barclays Bank* v *O'Brien* [1994] 4 All ER 417), the courts have been ready to invoke concepts of undue influence to set aside agreements apparently made freely. This concept has now been invoked in medical law, by the Court of Appeal, in the case of *Re T* [1992] 4 All ER 649. There the woman's apparent refusal of consent was said to be the subject of undue influence on the part of her mother. Nonetheless, the opportunity for a patient to challenge the voluntary nature of consent on the basis of undue influence by a partner now exists, and doctors may wish to be especially careful that both parties undergoing treatment consent to assisted conception in real terms and free from undue influence.

POSTHUMOUS TREATMENTS

It will be clear from what is written above that a cornerstone provision of the legislation is the principle of 'effective consent'. This concept had itself been emerging through the 1970s and 1980s as a bench-mark for the negotiation of the proper relationship between health care professionals and the people who became their patients. But assisted conception, rightly or wrongly, was felt to give rise to special and sensitive questions such that certain absolute prohibitions or restrictions were written into the Act and the HFEA was given further regulatory powers. Some of these are relevant to the question of access to assisted conception following the death of a partner.

It sometimes happens that gametes, or embryos derived from gametes, remain in storage at the death of one or (rarely) both of the genitors. The surviving party might then nonetheless seek to make use of the stored gametes or embryos. The Warnock Committee wished to see the posthumous use of gametes 'actively discouraged'.[4] The Committee believed that birth in such circumstances might give rise to profound psychological problems for child and mother, and was worried about the lack of finality in the administration of estates which would be engendered by the possibility of such births.[5] It would have been open to the legislature to provide that no such use could be contemplated, but it did not. Instead, the Act provided that if posthumous use of gametes is to be made, the provider has to have given a clear *written* indication that that conformed with, and certainly did not go against, any specific wishes or views that he or she held. Not surprisingly the mechanism used to ensure this outcome was consent. One exception to the requirement of formal written consent is where sperm are being used in a treatment service for the benefit of the woman and the sperm provider *together* (s. 4(1)). Use of gametes in contravention of the consent provision carries a number of consequences; it may breach the licence issued by the HFEA to the 'person responsible' for the clinic where the treatment services are offered; it may amount to a criminal offence: and it may affect the status of any child born of those treatment services.

These provisions and other matters relating to post-mortem treatment fell to be considered most famously in *R v Human Fertilisation & Embryology Authority, ex parte Blood* [1997] 2 All ER 687 (CA), (1997) 35 BMLR 1. The case of Diane Blood has assumed a place of its own in discussions of English medical law and ethics. One striking feature is its relative novelty.[6] Although parallels do exist in the United States and France,[7] *Blood* is the first litigated case which tests the application of domestic legislation to post-mortem insemination where there is no written consent to the taking of the sperm.[8] Additionally, it exposed the HFEA for the first time to the particularly harsh glare of judicial review.

Mr and Mrs Blood had been married for four years before his death in 1995; they had had a long courtship of nine years before they had married 'according to the rights of the Anglican church using the traditional service contained in the 1662 Book of Common Prayer'. Beginning at the end of 1994, they 'actively decided to try for a family' (*per* Lord Woolf, [1997] 2 All ER 687, at 690) and, according to Mrs Blood's evidence, had discussed what Stephen Blood would want to happen should he die before they could complete their plans. Three months later Stephen Blood was pronounced clinically dead, on 2 March 1995, four days after contracting bacterial meningitis. Shortly before, Mrs Blood had raised with doctors the question of taking 'a sample of sperm by electro ejaculation from her husband who by that time was in a coma'.[9] Two samples were recovered and entrusted to the Infertility Research Trust at a second hospital for storage. The second sample was taken 'shortly before' Stephen Blood was certified clinically dead. Mrs Blood wanted to use the samples of the semen to have her husband's child.

In these 'sad circumstances' the propriety of the doctors' response to Mrs Blood's request to recover sperm from her dying husband was, for Lord Woolf, clear: 'humanity dictated that the sperm was taken and preserved first, and the legal argument followed.' The HFEA when contacted by the Infertility Trust, advised that the recovery, storage and use of the sperm was unlawful. It was this advice and later decisions of the Authority which 'frustrated . . . this desire' of Diane Blood 'to have her husband's child' and led to her challenge.

The courts agreed that the storage of the sperm was 'technically' an offence. Storage of gametes otherwise than in accordance with a licence is an offence under s. 4(1)(a) of the 1990 Act. Section 12 makes it a condition of every licence that the consent provisions of sch. 3 are met. In the absence of Stephen Blood's written consent, there could be no doubt that the provisions of the consent schedule had been breached. Further, s. 4(1)(b) provides that no person shall as part of treatment services use the sperm of any man except in pursuance of a licence unless the services are provided for the man and the woman together. Given that Mr Blood was dead, and given the strictures explained above on the use of sperm post-mortem, it was also clear that the insemination of Mrs Blood would breach the provisions of the Act.

Diane Blood wanted to become pregnant. She wanted to be able to use the process of artificial insemination to achieve this. Neither desire is particularly unusual. Biologically speaking, she had all the necessary ingredients, and there was no physical impediment to her plans. Stephen Blood's *intent* to share children with his wife appears to have been clearly established.[10] What was missing was his *consent* – specifically, and crucially, his written consent – and in the absence of such consent there was a major barrier in the form of the HFEA charged with the job of policing the Act in a situation in which its provisions had already been breached.

If the law thus far was clear, however, following consultation with Mrs Blood's lawyers, what also fell to be considered was the HFEA's powers to make what are called in ss. 23 and 24 'directions' to clinics about specific matters. Section 24(4) of the Act deals with what was to become one of the major vessels of Blood's argument in the Court of Appeal, the import and export of gametes and embryos. Section 24(4) gives to the HFEA a broad discretion to give directions on the export of gametes, and general directions under that section were made in 1991.[11] Faced with the restriction upon lawful use of the sperm within the jurisdiction, Mrs Blood wished to seek treatment overseas, and she sought judicial review of the HFEA's decision not to make *specific* directions under s. 24(4) of the Act in order to allow her access to and use of the sperm. For the application to proceed, it was necessary for the court to put aside what would seem to be the unlawful recovery and storage of the sperm. Storage of the sperm without consent, Lord Woolf admits, means that an offence was committed, but that 'there is no question of any prosecution being brought in the circumstances' (at 695 and 697).[12] In addition, 'the question of the lawfulness of the storage is quite separate from the lawfulness of taking the sperm from Mr Blood as he lay unconscious'. However, the Court did not hear argument on the propriety of these actions and 'it is therefore not necessary to make any comment about this'.

Mrs Blood's desire to use the sperm of her dead husband collected from him specifically for this purpose appeared to have fallen irredeemably against the barrier of the express intentions of Parliament. The Court of Appeal, however, was ready to assist Mrs Blood in her 'agonising situation'. This it did in accepting argument that the HFEA's decision refusing to make specific directions allowing access to the sperm for export was an interference with her rights under Arts 59 and 60 (now 49 and 50) of the Treaty of Rome (see also *U v W (Attorney General intervening)* [1997] 1 FLR 282). These Articles provide that restrictions on one of the Union's four freedoms – here the right to receive services (as a concomitant of the guarantee of freedom of movement) – have at least to be justified by some imperative public interest requirement. Since the HFEA had not given an adequate account of such considerations, it was required to reconsider its decision, taking into account principles of EU law and, in the light of the Court's judgment on the legality of preserving sperm without consent, the unlikely possibility of such a case recurring. Most unusually, while stressing the HFEA's dominion of the substantive issue, the Court opined that Mrs Blood's position was 'much stronger' than when the Authority last considered the matter, 'the legal position having received further clarification'. Moreover, although not ruling on whether the reasons given by the HFEA could pass European scrutiny, Lord Woolf thought this 'unlikely'. Unsurprisingly, in view of this judgment, a direction allowed Diane Blood access to the sperm and permission for its export. Following treatment abroad she gave birth to a son, called Liam, in December 1998.

The potential consequences and significance of *Blood* go much further than the Court of Appeal's apparently deceptively simple finding that the provision of infertility treatment services is an economic activity provided for remuneration, and hence a 'service', within the terms of Art. 59 (now 49) of the Treaty of Rome. It is difficult to overestimate the importance of the jurisprudence which is emerging under the freedoms supported by the EC Treaty. Articles 49 and 50 (ex 59 and 60) come into play only once four criteria have been satisfied[13]:

(a)   Article 50 provides that the provisions on free movement of services will apply only where a particular restriction is not covered by the provisions on free movement of goods, persons, or capital.

(b)   There must be an interstate element to the provision.

(c)   The services provided must be economic in nature, in that they are provided for remuneration, whether the remuneration comes from one party to the transaction or from a party other than the intended service recipient.[14]

(d)   The burden is on the member state to show legitimate public policy requirements – 'the imperative requirements of public interest' – which justify a restriction on the freedom to provide or to receive services involving a 'fundamental ethical judgment'. (See Advocate General Van Gerven, in *Society for the Protection of the Unborn Child* v *Grogan* (Case C-159/90) [1991] ECR I-4685, at 4715 (the Irish 'abortion information' case).) Such considerations of public interest are particularly relevant in cases of assisted conception.

If one asks where in *Blood* any expression of or judgment on the public morality of Mrs Blood's intended course of conduct is to be found, this can only be within the Warnock Report and its expression in the legislative form of the 1990 Act. Whatever is said of the merits of the choices made there in relation to post-mortem usage of sperm in the absence of consent, it is difficult to find *alternative* expressions of public policy and morality. Even if one accepts the necessity for the HFEA to reconsider its position on freedom to benefit from services, it is hard to accept the view of the Court of Appeal that the Authority should consider the 'much stronger' position of Mrs Blood. Whether or not her position is stronger necessarily involves the very 'fundamental ethical value judgment' which is said to be part of the 'process in the application of Community Law'.[15]

Moreover, in deciding that infertility treatment services unequivocally fall within the scope of Arts 49 and 50 (ex 59 and 60), the Court of Appeal has opened a number of other important lines of inquiry. For example, is the United Kingdom's strict licensing scheme for clinicians who wish to offer regulated infertility treatment services, established by the 1990 Act, fundamentally in contravention of Art. 28 (ex 30) (free movement of goods) and Arts 49 and 50 (ex 59 and 60) (free movement of services)? *Blood* indicates the potential of EU trade law as a mechanism for review of national laws not seen as immediately connected with trade, which might, of course, include the entire licensing regime of the 1990 Act.[16] While considerations of public morality might be weighed in the defence of such legislative provisions, there is something troubling about the very requirement to justify rules framed to protect social and moral values in order to satisfy an economic imperative.

In reality, Mrs Blood's desire to gain access to the gametes for export in order
to seek treatment services tells us nothing about her enforceable Community rights.
The HFEA decision prevented Mrs Blood from taking the means by which she
might do something unlawful in the UK to another member state; but did it thereby
restrict the freedom to provide or to receive services? At first instance, Lord Lester,
as counsel for Mrs Blood, submitted in the High Court that the then Arts 59 and
60 entailed that an individual's freedom from restriction to *receive* services (itself
a right derived from the freedom to provide services) implied freedom from
restriction on the export of resources necessary to secure those services. In this he
relied upon *Society for the Protection of the Unborn Child* v *Grogan* above and
Luisi and Carbone v *Ministero del Tesoro* [1984] ECR 377.[17] This latter case had
been brought by two Italian nationals who claimed that restrictions placed on the
export of Italian currency infringed their rights to receive services (tourism) in
another member state. The European Court of Justice held that:

> . . . the freedom to provide services includes the freedom, for the recipients of
> services, to go to another Member State in order to receive a service there,
> without being obstructed by restrictions, even in relation to payments and that
> tourists, persons receiving medical treatment and persons travelling for the
> purposes of education or business are to be regarded as recipients of services.

Of this argument, Sir Stephen Brown P commented in the High Court that the
complaint, if correct, would lead to the 'very surprising' conclusion that EU law
would require the United Kingdom to permit the export of gametes. This would be
so even where this would conflict with the protective measures which Parliament
has thought necessary, 'merely because these sensitive issues are less extensively
regulated in Greece and Belgium'. However, in the Court of Appeal, Lord Woolf
argued that 'it is artificial to treat the refusal of permission to export the sperm as
not withholding the provision of fertilisation treatment in another Member State',
and concluded that from a functional point of view the ability to provide those
services 'is not only substantially impeded but made impossible'. The HFEA's
original refusal to permit the export of Mr Blood's sperm 'prevents Mrs Blood
having the only treatment which she wants' ([1997] 2 All ER 687, at 700 and 698).

Lord Lester may indeed be correct that member states cannot imperil the right
of access to services by making its exercise impossible; in many cases a right to
export the necessary resources must be appended to the right to receive services.
But that does not mean that in a particular case the export of those resources must
be allowed. This is where a reference back to the lawfulness of the initial recovery
of the sperm could have been crucial. However far the 'right' to receive services
is to be made to extend, surely it cannot be made to encompass access to services
with the export of the necessary resources which may have been unlawfully
obtained. Certainly it should not be allowed to do so without much more careful
consideration of the consequences.

Warnock offered a clear lead against the use by a widow of her dead husband's
sperm. It was a lead that the legislation chose not to follow. The effect of
ss. 14(1)(b) and 4(1)(b) is that where a clinic decides, or where a contract for
treatment services provides, that the death of a partner is to terminate the provision
of treatment, the surviving partner has no right to insist upon the clinic making

available the stored gametes or embryos. Many clinics do indeed take the view that they will not assist in the conception of a child after the death of a partner in such circumstances.[18] If, however, a clinic decides that it will honour the wishes of the deceased partner, that partner will have had to give express written consent to the use of stored gametes or embryos governing 'what is to be done . . . if the person giving their consent dies' (sch. 3, para. 2(2)(b)). If the written consent permits post-mortem use of the gametes/embryo, problems then arise in relation to the status of any child born following treatment services. This unnecessary confusion seems to arise because the legislation failed to follow the Warnock proposal not 'actively [to] discourage' post-mortem treatment other than by the curious route of leaving the status and rights of the child in a hopelessly unsatisfactory state. These status issues are dealt with in detail in Chapter 9.

It is possible, but not certain, that the child born as a result of post-mortem use of a husband's sperm is presently legally fatherless. In any event the father has died. In such circumstances, the clinic will be charged with considering the welfare of any child born as a result of treatment, including specifically the need of that child for a father. This controversial provision takes on an additional dimension in circumstances in which there has been a father, the progenitor of the child, who will never be known to the child but whose life that child may celebrate. Warnock felt that profound psychological problems could result both for child and mother. Certainly a number of jurisdictions have thought that there are sufficient arguments to bar posthumous assisted conception.[19] Ironically, the use of an embryo by a man following the death of his wife would call for no specific consideration of the need for a mother, but the welfare of the child would remain a factor to be taken into account. Given that this would involve the use of a surrogate mother, one might expect that clinics would consider more carefully still this type of arrangement.

The case of Diane Blood certainly led to a flurry of legislative activity and, it is now clear, will lead eventually – 'when Parliamentary time permits' – to a change in the law. As Diane Blood's case was being considered by the courts, Lord Winston published in the House of Lords a Human Fertilisation and Embryology (Amendment) Bill, to provider for the waiver of the need for written consent in exceptional circumstances. That Bill provided for the amendment of Schedule 3 of the 1990 Act by making that paragraph 1 of the schedule subject to a new provision, to be inserted as paragraph 1A. The amendment read:

> When it appears to the Human Fertilisation and Embryology Authority reason-
> able in all the circumstances, including in particular the welfare of any child that
> might be born as a result of the treatment or the death or incapacity of the person
> providing the gametes, consent under this Schedule to the provision or use of
> gametes need not be in writing.

The Bill did not proceed further, because the then Minister of Public Health, Tessa Jowell, announced at the conclusion of the *Blood* case that she was to establish a review of the Consents requirements of the Act. That review was undertaken by Professor Sheila McLean of the Institute of Law and Ethics in Medicine at Glasgow University whose report was published in July 1998. In paragraphs 1.13 and 2.15 of her report, Professor McLean advised that the case for a change in the legal position on consent and removal of gametes had not been made out and that the 1990 Act's provisions in this respect should remain unchanged. Yvette Cooper, the Department of Health's Minister for Public Health announced in late August 2000 that the Government had accepted these recommendations.

At the same time, she announced the acceptance of another of Professor McLean's recommendations which stemmed from the case of Diane Blood. When Mrs Blood's son Liam was born after successful treatment with her deceased husband's sperm at a clinic in Belgium, her 'elation' was dampened by knowledge that her son's birth certificate could not carry his father's name. The case of another woman, Marion Jordan, whose husband had died leaving sperm in storage, was taken up by her MP, Debra Shipley. Shipley moved a 10 Minute Rule Bill in the House of Commons, the Human Fertilisation and Embryology (Amendment) Bill 2000. This Bill provided for an amendment to section 28 of the Act:

> Section 28 of the Human Fertilisation and Embryology Act 1990 (meaning of 'father') is amended, by inserting after subsection (6) the following new subsection—
>
> '(6A)   Paragraph (b) of subsection (6) does not apply where at the time of the man's death the woman and the man—
> (a)   were married to each other,
> (b)   were otherwise living as man and wife, or
> (c)   had been receiving treatment services together from a person to whom a licence applies.'

Effectively, that Bill was an attempt to pre-empt or encourage a Government response to Professor McLean's conclusion that special provision should be made for births to be regularised and registerable following 'posthumous treatment'. As McLean had recommended in paragraph 3.7 that there should be no consequential changes to the law of succession in such a case, she had advocated this as a recognition of the symbolic rather than practical value to the child of its mother being able to name her former husband on the birth certificate. As with most 10-Minute Rule Bills, the Amendment Bill fell in June, doubtless informed by the knowledge that in a forthcoming Government response McLean's views were to be adopted. The August announcement indicated that section 28 would be amended in due course, and indeed that in one important respect any such amendment would go further than McLean had envisaged. Yvette Cooper's statement said that because of the 'considerable importance of this provision to the small number of people who are affected by the existing restriction, we have decided to make the amendment retrospective in effect'. This highly unusual concession will, therefore, benefit the dozen or so women and their children believed to have been involved in such births since 1990, and an anomalous category of 'fatherless children' will be closed.

COUNSELLING AND ASSISTING CONCEPTION

In a 1990 Report surveying the work of 121 health authorities, Harriet Harman stated that there was, prior to the Act, 'very little specific counselling for those who are embarking on infertility tests for treatment'.[20] The majority of responses to the survey reported that counselling was done informally by the consultant at the time of appointment, although some district health authorities undertook some counselling within the Family Planning Clinics. At the time of this Report, the British Infertility Counselling Association reported that in practice few infertility clinics had professionally trained counsellors available. This was in spite of guidelines by the ILA that centres should have 'appropriate counselling services with access to properly trained independent counselling staff'.[21] Moreover, by this time, other jurisdictions had adopted the notion of counselling. For example, in Victoria, Australia, the original Infertility (Medical Procedures) Act 1984 had placed a duty upon doctors providing treatment services to ensure that the woman and the man seeking treatment had been counselled, and that there was further counselling upon completion of the procedures.

The 1990 Act made provision under s. 25 for the HFEA to deal with matters such as counselling arrangements at licensed centres within a Code of Practice. As is shown below, matters of counselling are regulated by this Code. Elsewhere within the Act, s. 13(6) provides that treatment services which involve the use of donated gametes or a donated embryo (either obtained by lavage or brought about *in vitro*) should not be provided to a woman unless she has been given 'a suitable opportunity to receive counselling'. However, it is impossible to discern from the Act alone what might amount to 'a suitable opportunity'. One reason for this might be that it is no more than a one-off chance to discuss proposed treatment prior to its commencement. Note, then, that the Act does not make counselling mandatory but envisages that it will be available and directed towards the implications of following the proposed treatment. Where a woman is being treated together with a man, this same opportunity should be afforded to both of them. Beyond this, nowhere in the Act is it clear what counselling might comprise, and within the framework of the Act itself major questions in terms of when and where it should take place go unanswered. In debates at the time of the Act, it was envisaged that some persons might go for treatment but following counselling might reconsider whether or not they should proceed with treatment services, and it was thought that some might choose not to go ahead.[22]

These types of questions are largely answered by Part 6 of the Code of Practice, which over 26 paragraphs details the type of counselling to be made available and its broad content. Prior to reviewing this material, it is worth also stating that issues of counselling form part of more general matters within the Code itself. For example, at the very outset of the Code, in relation to staff, it is made clear that within the skill mix for any licence centre, there should be expertise in counselling. This means that, other than four centres engaged only in research, a centre should ensure that it has at least one recognised and qualified social worker or person accredited by the British Association of Counsellors, or a chartered psychologist. Where this is not the case, however, the Code seems to dilute the counselling requirement by stating that such a person should be available as an adviser to other (presumably non-qualified) counselling staff (see paras 1.2 and 1.10). In relation to the facilities to be made available, under the heading 'maintaining and improving standards' centres are told that they should monitor counselling practice to ensure that what is done is satisfactory by the standards of professional colleagues in relevant disciplines. Moreover, there should be procedures for keeping counselling practice under review in order to achieve optimum standards.

The above provisions apply not only to counselling, since in relation to quality issues, similar assurance of adequate standards will be expected for laboratory and clinical practices. Elsewhere, too, there are general provisions of the Code (e.g., on confidentiality) which can be taken to have a particular relevance in relation to counselling services. Lastly, it should be noted that, while there is a general duty under the Act to provide an opportunity for counselling, the Code of Practice chooses to emphasise the need to offer counselling in relation to particular treatments. For example, in relation to gametes taken from women over 35 and men over 55 to be used in their own treatment or the treatment of their partner, counselling is advised prior to deciding whether to proceed with treatment services. Another example arises in relation to genetic testing and screening, where both pre- and post-testing counselling is specifically recommended.

This raises the question concerning the scope of the requirements of the Act in demanding a suitable opportunity for proper counselling in relation to treatment services. In so far as genetic testing is a service provided for the purposes of assisting women to carry children, it would fall within the requirements of s. 13(6). Thus, in certain situations, complex patterns of counselling may be required. For example, the Code of Practice recommends in relation to cystic fibrosis that centres should normally screen donors, especially from population groups with high frequencies as carriers. Thus where a clinic is using unscreened donors, the patient should be informed of this and offered counselling. On the other hand, if the centre has screened donors, patients should be cautioned in relation to the limitations of the test and the risk that the screened donor could nonetheless be a carrier. Note that the Code does not bar the possibility that the donor may be known to be a carrier in exceptional circumstances. Again, here, it will be necessary to explain risk to patients and to offer counselling (see para. 3.50).

This also raises the possibility that a licensed centre may decide that a potential donor is unsuitable. The Code demands that centres should present an explanation for this 'sensitively' and that they should 'encourage the person to seek further information'. The clinic may take the view that the donor has physical or psychological problems which may require treatment or the skills of a counselling service. In such a situation the centre would not be required to provide such counselling, but the Code does state that clinics should provide 'all reasonable assistance' to help the person obtain it.

It may be the case that a centre discovers that a person is a carrier of some inherited condition, or has (unknowingly) some genetic disease. This may occur after treatment services have been provided using that donor's sperm and may become known through the birth of the child with that particular condition. Obviously, in such circumstances there is a requirement to inform the supplying centre and the Authority. Thereafter, the supplying centre should inform any treatment centre which has received the sperm concerning the donor's status as a carrier. However, in relation to further counselling to the parties involved, the Code takes a questionable approach. Those patients whose treatment, with the donor's sperm, has resulted in a live birth should be informed and should be then offered counselling. However, if a woman is merely pregnant as a result of treatment with the donor's sperm, centres are required only to 'consider carefully when and how' the pregnant woman should be informed of the donor's carrier status. This approach is presumably justified on the basis that worst fears may not be realised following the birth of a healthy child. More curiously, however, the supplying centre is under no absolute duty to inform the donor of his or her condition as either a carrier or someone with an existing genetic disorder. The supplying centre is asked only to 'consider' informing the donor, but where it does so then it should offer him or her counselling and further testing. There are similar provisions for egg donation. It seems rather curious, not to place the demand on the centre to inform the donor of the problem. It is accepted that there may be certain circumstances in which this would not be vital, but in general it would seem more appropriate that the donor be informed, and offered counselling, in such situations.

Although much of what is written above relates to the provision of information, the Code of Practice expressly states that the need for counselling should be clearly distinguished from and is in addition to the provision of such information. Similarly, the Code states that counselling as referred to in the Act goes beyond the types of professional advice and the development of a client relationship as would ordinarily occur between clinician and patient, client or donor. The development of this relationship will entail some process of assessing the suitability of people prepared to make a donation of gametes or seeking infertility treatment. Again, the Code stresses that counselling goes beyond such forms of assessment.

The Code of Practice distinguishes three forms of counselling which centres should consider (see para. 6.4). These are as follows:

(a) *Implications counselling*. This is said to be directed at enabling persons to understand the implications of the course of action proposed. It covers the implications both for those persons and also for the family and any children born as a result of treatment services. It may include genetic counselling.

(b) *Support counselling*. This aims to provide emotional support at times of stress. The example given is on failure to achieve a pregnancy.

(c) *Therapeutic counselling*. This aims to assist people to cope with the consequences of infertility and infertility treatment. Specifically mentioned here is assistance to people in managing expectations, or accepting the nature of their situation.

In line with the Act, the Code, although supporting counselling as beneficial, states that no one is obliged to accept it. Nonetheless, it then makes a distinction between implications counselling, which must be made available to everyone, and support or therapeutic counselling, which should be provided only in appropriate cases. This provision of the Code is a strict interpretation of the wording of the Act which refers to 'proper counselling about the implications of taking proposed steps' and it seems that counselling to provide (say) emotional support is not seen as part of the mandatory requirements of s. 13 of the Act. On the other hand, the wording of the Act is not seen by the Code as referring only to counselling at the outset of treatment. The Code demands that people should be able to seek counselling at any stage of their investigation or treatment, although it recommends that counselling takes place after oral and written explanations of the proposed steps have been provided. This is thought to aid a discussion centering upon the meaning and consequences of the action rather than the practical explanation of what it involves. One interpretation of the Act and the notion that counselling is available while a patient is 'being treated' is that it might be suggested on every clinic visit. This is unlikely to be the case and the Code does not seem to demand it.

It is known that counselling has a low take-up rate.[23] Only 18–21 per cent of patients offered counselling decide to attend sessions when these are made available. Although the Code recognises counselling as beneficial, it does relatively little to promote its uptake. The Code states that there should be no pressure to accept counselling, and that it should be presented as an offer which is 'part of normal routine'. Time should be allowed to consider the offer of counselling, but it may be that this delay will do little to aid the acceptance of the counselling opportunity. Moreover, because time should be allowed for adequate counselling, it may be that acceptance of counselling will be seen to entail yet another visit to the treatment centre. Clinics are told that while group counselling sessions may be run, they alone do not provide an adequate counselling opportunity. Indeed, people should have the chance to be counselled individually, as well as with their treatment partner if they have one.

In relation to implications counselling, the Code of Practice suggests a number of issues which counsellors might invite potential clients or providers of gametes and embryos to consider. These are as follows (para. 6.10):

(a)   the social responsibilities which centres and providers of genetic material bear to ensure the best possible outcome for all concerned, including the child;

(b)   the implications of the procedure for themselves, their family and social circle, and for any resulting children;

(c)   their feelings about the use and possible disposal of any embryos derived from their gametes;

(d)   the possibility that these implications and feelings may change over time, as personal circumstances change;

(e)   the advantages and disadvantages of openness about the procedures envisaged, and how they might be explained to relatives and friends.

There is a similar list of issues which counsellors should invite potential donors of gametes and embryos to consider. These are as follows (para. 6.16):

(a)   their reasons for wanting to become a donor;

(b)   their attitudes to any resulting children, and their willingness to forgo knowledge of and responsibility for such children in the future;

(c)   the possibility of their own childlessness;

(d)   their perception of the needs of any children born as a result of their donation;

(e)   their attitudes to the prospective legal parents of their genetic offspring;

(f)   their attitudes to allowing embryos which have been produced from their *gametes* to be used for research.

Where a person seeking to donate genetic material is married or in a long-term relationship, the centre may counsel the potential donors and their partners together if they so desire.

In addition to the above issues, counsellors are directed to the specific issues which they should invite their clients to consider. These begin with clients' attitudes towards infertility, either their own or that of their partners, together with recognition of the possibility that treatment might fail. There is also a wide range of issues where the use of donated gametes or embryos is likely. Here counsellors may raise issues concerning the feelings of the clients in not being the genetic parents of the child, and the perception of the clients in relation to the needs of the child during childhood and adolescence. Although something is now known of this, a mutual friend who has always been open with his children born following sperm donation, relates that on being asked to draw a family tree at school his six-year-old daughter's resultant map included a branch for her 'sperm daddy'.

The Code of Practice envisages that a woman may already be undergoing infertility treatment when the question of the donation of gametes or embryos is raised. Here it is suggested that separate counselling should be available concerning the use of donated material, and that this should be offered quite separately from counselling concerning the implications of treatment. Indeed, the Code of Practice suggests that treatment with donated material should not proceed unless a woman (and when necessary her partner) have been given a suitable opportunity of counselling. Lastly, the Code recognises that persons involved in infertility treatment may become donors. Here, again, it is said that counselling about the implications of donation should be conducted quite separately from counselling concerning the implications of treatment. Again a woman and, as appropriate, her partner should be given a suitable opportunity to receive counselling prior to any donation taking place. Counselling in relation to donation or storage of genetic material may be undertaken with the man and the woman together, or there can be separate counselling where that is the wish of a particular partner.

Although the Act is vague concerning the time and place of counselling and the treatment cycle, the Code suggests that there should be opportunities for counselling throughout treatment, after consent has been given, and even where someone who has previously been a donor or a client returns to the centre with a request for further counselling. The type of implication counselling referred to here can include genetic counselling, both for patients and for donors. For some reason, the Code stresses particularly in relation to genetic counselling the confidentiality provisions of the Act. This may be a somewhat oblique reference to the provisions of s. 35(1) indicating the possible need for disclosure in the interests of justice where an action is taken under s. 1 of the Congenital Disabilities (Civil Liability) Act 1976 (see Chapter 10). However, as phrased in the Code, it seems to suggest that confidentiality requirements should be particularly to the fore in genetic counselling over and above counselling more generally.

Under s. 33(5), no person to whom a licence applies or to whom directions have been given shall disclose information falling within s. 31(2) of the Act. Such information includes the provision of treatment services for any identifiable individual. This raises the question whether counselling is included within the notion of treatment services. Since it is a requirement that an opportunity for counselling be given in the course of treatment, it would not seem too far-fetched to suggest that counselling falls as part of the provision of treatment services. In such a case, irrespective of any professional responsibilities, there will be a restriction on disclosure of information gained during the course of counselling by virtue of s. 33 of the Act. For the avoidance of any doubt, para. 3.29 of the Code demands that all information obtained in the course of counselling should be kept confidential.

For support counselling, the Code suggests that centres should take 'all practicable steps' to offer support to those denied treatment, whose treatment has failed, who are found to be unsuitable as donors, or in whom a previously unsuspected defect is found. The purpose of the counselling is said to be to 'help them come to terms with their situation'. Measures can include references to or the establishment of support groups. Centres are advised to train staff in such emotional support, not merely within counselling itself but also during the course of treatment. In order to allow for therapeutic counselling it is necessary to have in place procedures to identify people who suffer particular distress as a result of their situation. The Code demands that such procedures should be established within a centre. The Code recognises that certain forms of mental ill health, or psychological disorders, may not be related simply to the question of infertility. Nonetheless, in such situations the centre should take 'all practicable steps' to help clients obtain the necessary help and advice in some appropriate place outside the centre.

Note that because the Code demands that a record be kept of all counselling offered, and also whether or not the offer is accepted, the Authority is able to form a clear picture of how many patients and donors choose to accept counselling, and also the stage at which such counselling is taken up. The HFEA ought to be concerned with the low take-up of counselling if it serves as important a purpose as suggested in the Code. Although patients should 'be encouraged to ask for further information and their questions should be answered in a straightforward way' (para. 4.2 of the Code), the availability of counselling is part of a significant amount of information which needs to be passed over to the patient. Without further direction one must question how far centres will go to promote counselling. After all, they are in the business of selling treatment services and counselling might be seen as a process in which doubts are expressed or fears raised.

NOTES

[1]   See pp. 134–36.

[2]   Although it must be admitted that doubt is cast on this proposition by the decision of the Court of Appeal in *R v HFEA, ex parte Blood* [1997] 2 WLR 806, in which a clear flouting of statutory requirements seems to have counted for little.

[3]   *Cf.* the experience of Helen Pusey, *New Statesman and Society*, 11 May 1990, p. 12.

[4]   Cm 9314, para. 4.4.

[5]   *Ibid.*, paras 10.9 and 10.15. For resolution of precisely this point under the Tasmanian Administration and Probate Act 1936, s. 46(1), see *In the Matter of the Estate of the Late K and in the Matter of the Administration and Probate Act 1935, ex parte The Public Trustee* [1996] 5 Tas LR 365. Considered in Atherton, R., 'Posthumous Children in the Succession Context' (1999) 19 LS 139, and Morgan, D., 'Rights and Legal Status of Embryos' (1996) 4(7) *Australian Health Law Bulletin* 61.

[6]   Mrs Blood's was not the first attempt to make post-mortem use of her partner's sperm which has given rise to public difficulties. In 1985, Sonia Palmer's desire to use the frozen sperm of her deceased husband was referred to the Infertility Services Ethical Committee of Central Manchester District Health Authority. The Committee refused her request to use the sperm at the hospital which had

previously been treating her in an infertility programme, but said that she should be allowed to take the frozen sperm elsewhere if she could find a clinic which would treat her; see the *Guardian*, 25 September 1985, p. 19. Neither is this the first time clinicians have knowingly agreed to assist in the posthumous use of sperm; for an example pre-dating the 1990 Act of the use of the procedure in England & Wales see the affidavit of Professor Lord Winston, Professor of Fertility Studies at the Royal Post Graduate Medical School, Hammersmith Hospital, referred to by Sir Stephen Brown in the High Court in *Blood* ((1997) 35 BMLR 1, at 14), which averred that to withhold the sperm here would be 'cruel and unnatural'. Shortly before the Court of Appeal's judgment in *Blood*, the *Guardian* (25 February 1997, p. 4) reported that a woman whose husband had died three years previously was soon expecting to give birth to twins. Described as the first case of its kind, the woman had been inseminated with sperm stored with her husband's 'effective consent' under the Human Fertilisation and Embryology Act 1990.

[7]   *Hecht v Superior Court of the State of California for the County of Los Angeles (W.E. Kane, real Party in Interest)* (1993) 20 Cal Rptr 2d 275 (California Court of Appeals) (Supreme Court of California; petition for review denied and Court of Appeal judgment de-authorised for use as a precedent, 15 January 1997, Case No. S057498); *Pires v Centre Hospitalier Regional de la Grave (Tribunal de Grande Instance de Toulouse*, 11 May 1993); *Parpalaix v CECOS (Centre d'Etudes et de Conservation de Sperme)* (*Gazette du Palais*, 15 September 1984; Cour de Cassation, 9 January 1996, Dict. Perm. Bioethic, bull, no. 30; JCP 1996, edition G. II 22666); (see Garay, J., 'Recent aspects concerning medically assisted procreation in France,' paper presented to the Council of Europe, Third Symposium on Bioethics, Medically Assisted Procreation and the Protection of the Human Embryo, Strasbourg, 15–18 December 1996, (dealing with posthumous use of embryos and the French Laws of 29 July 1994 and 5 July 1996)). For other examples of attempted post-mortem recovery of sperm, see the *Guardian* (21 October 1995, p. 7), 'Dead Men Can Still Have Children'; the *Independent* (26 October 1995, p. 10); and of eggs see the *Guardian*, 12 January 1995, p. 11. For a brief consideration of other jurisdictional approaches, see Law Reform Commission of Canada, Working Paper 65, *Medically Assisted Procreation* (Ottawa, Minister of Supply and Services, 1992), at 186–87.

[8]   For discussion of some of the issues raised by posthumous use of gametes and embryos see John Robertson, 'Posthumous Reproduction' (1994) 69 *Indiana Law Journal* 1027–66 and Douglas Cuisine, 'Artificial Insemination with the Husband's Sperm after the Husband's Death' (1977) 3 *J Med Ethics* 163.

[9]   One wonders why the Trust or its advisers did not at this stage take advantage of the recently fashioned declaratory jurisdiction of the Family Division to address questions of the legality of such a procedure.

[10]   This much, at least, was accepted by Sir Stephen Brown: (1997) 35 BMLR 1, at 8.

[11]   *Export of Gametes*, Directions made under the Human Fertilisation and Embryology Act 1990, s. 24(4), D1991/8 (London, HFEA, 1991).

[12]   The offence is one created under s. 41(2)(b).

[13]   Craig, P. and de Burca, G., *EC Law: Text, Cases & Materials* (Oxford, Clarendon Press, 1995), at 752 and generally their excellent discussion of free movement of services at 750–76.

[14] Although if the service is provided by the state, and hence is free at the point of consumption, the position is quite different; see *Gravier* v *City of Liege* (case 293/83) [1985] ECR 593, opinion of Advocate-General Slynn at 603, and *Belgium* v *Humber* (case 263/86) [1988] ECR 5365, discussed by Craig and de Burca, *op. cit.* n. 13, at 759 *et seq.*

[15] In *Customs and Excise Commissioners* v *Schindler* [1994] QB 610, the European Court of Justice held that member states were entitled in deciding whether and how to regulate the provision of lotteries, to have regard to 'the moral, religious or cultural aspects' of gambling. Thus economic freedoms may be restricted having regard to their wider social consequences.

[16] Human Fertilisation and Embryology Act 1990, esp. ss. 4, 11–22. It is clear from cases such as *Van Binsbergen* v *Bestuur van de Bedrijfsvereniging voor de Metaalnijverheid* (case C-33/74) [1974] ECR 1299, that while the public good ground will normally be sufficient to support licensing or registration requirements imposed on a profession, those which inhibit the provision of services will be permissible only if they are: (a) non-discriminatory; (b) objectively justified; and (c) proportionate.

[17] For an analysis of this case law in the context of the *Blood* case, see Hervey, T., 'Buy Baby: The European Union and Regulation of Human Reproduction' (1998) 18 OJLS 207.

[18] Corrigan, A., *et al.* 'Posthumous storage and use of sperm and embryos: Survey of opinion of treatment centres' (1996) 313 *British Medical Journal* 24.

[19] Including Canada, Germany, France and Sweden: see McLean, S., *Consent and the Law: Consultation Document and Questionnaire*, September 1997, DoH.

[20] Harman, H., *Trying for a baby: a report on the inadequacy of NHS infertility services* (1990).

[21] See the ILA Guidelines, para. 13(g).

[22] See the words of Lord Mackay, House of Lords, Official Report, 6 February 1990, col. 800.

[23] Boivin, J., *et al.*, 'Why are Infertile Patients not using Psycho-Social Counselling' (1999) 14 *Human Reproduction* 1384.

Chapter 8
Surrogacy

'I would strongly advise you, Mr Worthing, to try to acquire some relations as soon as possible, and to a definite effort to produce at any rate one parent of either sex before the season is quite over.'[1]

'SENSITIVE SUBJECTS OF HUMAN ENDEAVOUR'

Introduction

There are passages in the history of events which outrank time and place, circumstance and people. Surrogacy is not one of those. But the symbolic crusade which it has attracted might occasionally persuade us to accept that a counterfeit of those judgments on events is justified.

There are in the history of ethical turmoil, stigmata events. They might be cases, they may be legislation, or they might be scientific discoveries or the reworking of old problems and questions possible only through the analytical and philosophical devices of modernity, such as Fermat's Last Theorem.[2] They are defining moments of a culture and part of its psyche. Surrogacy is not one of those either. But in the theatre of identity, in the morality play in which the personal is theoretical, surrogacy has a small part, a cameo role, an illustrative montage to fulfil; a side-show at the moral jamboree of reproductive technologies more generally.

There is much in the surrogacy story – or the surrogacy stories as we would argue they should be regarded – which is illustrative and emblematic of our thesis that medical law is in (large) part about declaiming the values and virtues of a society. In the case of surrogacy, it is almost entirely concerned with that. Surrogacy does not necessarily demand the most technologically sophisticated contribution to conception; neither is it thought to be statistically the most significant response to problems of fertility. Yet, at least perhaps temporarily, it has emerged at the eye of the storm over the 'reproduction revolution'. It has become the whipping post for the moral backlash against the brave new world of technological rationality and scientific finality. Philosopher Roger Scruton has demanded that surrogacy be seen as the revision of moral perceptions; the bond between the mother and child is severed from the experience of incarnation, it is 'demystified, made clear, intelligible, scientific'. Surrogacy contracts touch upon one of the (if not the) most sensitive subjects of human endeavour. (See *Johnson* v *Calvert* 851 P 2d 776 (1993), at 787 *per* Arabian J (Supreme Court of California, concurring opinion).)

Surrogacy is one of those sorts of ethical problem on which everyone appears to have a view, defending it strongly and indeed passionately, and on which hardly anyone seems neutral. It is at the heartland of the ethical divide in which we also find subjects such as abortion, research and experimentation on human embryos, genetic engineering, and cloning. And yet, as the Chairman of the HFEA has observed, writing in a personal capacity, when surrogacy runs smoothly there are no objections; but if the arrangement breaks down, the surrogacy is disapproved of by the media and the general public, and the disposition of sympathy is dependent almost entirely on the facts of the individual case.[3]

We have chosen here to consider the treatment of surrogacy arrangements at law for a number of reasons. In a work on assisted conception it would be wrong to ignore what is for many a treatment of last resort. Moreover, it is an area which the law has chosen to regulate in however a limited fashion, and regulate in part through the vehicle of the 1990 Act. Some of the roots of that regulation lie in the Warnock Report along with much of the rest of assisted conception. Lastly, as the quotation from Ruth Deech above indicates, this is one area of regulation which the HFEA would wish to avoid, and indeed, the Brazier Report does not suggest that the HFEA should be the regulatory body. But that only raises the issue as to why it should fall outside the Authority's portfolio.

Surrogacy stories

We observed in Chapter 2 that Anne Maclean identified surrogacy as complex and difficult because it raises not one issue but a cluster of issues, and issues of different sorts at that: 'It is easy to confuse considerations relevant to one of these issues with considerations relevant to another, or to misunderstand the character of a particular claim or a particular objection.'[4] She has suggested that there is no single moral issue called surrogacy. In much the same way, people's moral worries about surrogacy arrangements will vary greatly depending on the type of surrogacy in question, the relationships of the parties involved to one another, and whether it is a commercial transaction. And this moral concern will engage a variety of wider concerns too; not just about the family and parenthood, but 'about one's whole attitude to what life brings'. The sorts of worries, or objections, the 'issues of different sorts' as Maclean puts it, will carry different force in different circumstances. Thus, worries about resource implications (which can of course involve ethical concerns) are very different sorts of worries from those deep, inarticulated worries about the basic legitimacy of an action or of a general attitude exemplified in an action.

There are questions such as whether it is more desirable that the relationship be established and maintained solely at arm's length, with the participants' identities known only to a third party. Or whether it is preferable, as is sometimes suggested, that if surrogacy is to take place it should be only between close friends or sisters.[5] Should commercial surrogacy be prohibited or preferred? And on what plane should surrogacy be tolerated, if at all – the vertical or the horizontal? If vertical, in which direction?

'Surrogacy stories' disclose some of the complexities that Maclean is concerned to identify and distinguish. We present a selection of them here for illustrative purposes; they show graphically the moral and legal webs which can be woven with surrogacy:

- A 17-year-old woman in Lancashire, England, gave birth to a child for her own mother who had been unable to conceive the child she desired in a new marriage.[6]
- Pat Anthony, a 48-year-old woman, gave birth in a Johannesburg hospital to triplets. The intended mother of the children was her daughter, who had had her womb removed following the delivery of her first child.[7]
- Lori Jasso, who was regarded by her sisters, all of whom were successful professional women without children, as little more than 'a baby making machine' and who had four young children, was asked by her eldest sister, the vice-president of a large bank, to carry a child for her. She agreed, despite her own and her husband's misgivings, because it made her feel powerful and important in her family's life. She inseminated herself with sperm from her sister's husband and, engulfed by a sense of foreboding, rather hoped that it would not work: 'I did it out of obligation. . . . I felt raped by sisterly love.'[8] Eight years later she had not seen the child, Tiana, since her birth, immediately after which the baby was taken away by her sister.[9]
- A couple who arranged for a surrogate to carry a child for them became the first couple to be granted full parental rights without adoption procedures using the 'parental order' under s. 30 of the Human Fertilisation and Embryology Act 1990, which was granted by two magistrates sitting in the Family Court in Manchester. Their solicitor, Christine Buchan, was quoted as having said that 'This procedure is much less time consuming than adoption. Adoption also tended to emphasise that a couple *were in some way out of the ordinary*'.[10]
- A baby girl was born from the egg of a woman who had died in a car accident two years earlier;[11] the surrogate was the dead woman's husband's married sister. Dr Pasquale Bilotta is quoted as having said to Italian newspapers that 'It was strange and very sweet to see two men suffering as they waited the birth of the same daughter. . . . This isn't a case of incest, but of a child adopted by one of its relations. . . . The baby is not an orphan, but, if you like, a child with a bigger family than normal.'
- In *Johnson* v *Calvert* the surrogacy dispute was complicated somewhat by the conclusion that *both* women adduced evidence of a mother-child relationship, as contemplated by the relevant legislation.[12] In terms, this provides that maternity may be established either through the fact of giving birth – the equivalent of the *mater est quam gestatio demonstrat* presumption – or genetic consanguinity, based on evidence derived from blood testing. Lacking Solomon's belief that the best way of winnowing out an acceptable solution to this dilemma was to chop the child in two, the court concluded that there were two ways forward: that it should attempt to discern the 'best interests of the child'; or that the intentions of the parties as initially expressed in the contract should dispose of the case, whether that amounted to a fully enforceable contract or not.

- Another Californian couple arranged to have a child with a surrogate following the death of their unmarried daughter who had left frozen embryos in storage.[13]
- '. . . Video Baby [is] a tape just produced in the States for those who fancy being parents but in the abstract. A pair of delightful infants crawl around, take baths and all the rest of it. But they never have to be changed, and if you get bored, you can always switch them to fast-forward for a while.'[14]

Thus, a woman has given birth to her sister, to her grandchildren, and to her niece. The Italian case was condemned by Cardinal Ersilio Tonini: 'we have reached the point of producing human beings as if they were boxes', he said, in terms reminiscent of Lady Bracknell's admonishment to Mr Worthing in Oscar Wilde's incomparable play, *The Importance of Being Earnest*.[15] Recall that Jack Worthing, whom Lady Bracknell is interrogating about his suitability and standing for engagement to her daughter Gwendoline, has just revealed that he was abandoned at birth by his parents and found in a handbag in the cloakroom at Victoria Station on the Brighton line. Lady Bracknell fulminates:

> The line is immaterial Mr Worthing. I confess I feel somewhat bewildered by what you have just told me. To be born, or at any rate bred, in a handbag, whether it has handles or not, seems to me to display a contempt for the ordinary decencies of family life that reminds one of the worst excesses of the French revolution. And I presume you know what that unfortunate movement led to. . . .
>
> I would strongly advise you, Mr Worthing, to try to acquire some relations as soon as possible, and to a definite effort to produce at any rate one parent of either sex, before the season is quite over. . . . You can hardly imagine that I and Lord Bracknell would dream of allowing our only daughter – a girl brought up with the utmost care – to marry into a cloakroom, and form an alliance with a parcel?

INCIDENCE OF SURROGACY

There are a few anecdotal incidences of surrogacy arrangements being undertaken on an informal basis prior to the 1980s, but beyond this, an informal history of the economy of surrogacy is difficult to construct. Biblical examples, wet-nursing, anthropological examples and those from other jurisdictions, all routinely trotted out, can be melded together to form a partial skeleton, but no full anatomy emerges: the body of the surrogacy story that we see is a warped and incomplete one. We can hazard a guess that surrogacy did not, however, emerge hydra-headed and fully formed in 1984 when the national newspapers appeared to announce its birth with Kim Cotton. Indeed, the banns had already been read on a number of occasions.

Although various ways of estimating the extent of surrogacy in Britain have been tried, it is currently impossible to know the real incidence of surrogacy arrangements in the absence of any central registry of data; doubtless some arrangements are made secretly between family members or friends. Section 30 of the Human Fertilisation and Embryology Act 1990, which came into effect on 1 November 1994, allows intended parents to apply to a competent court to transfer the parentage of the child in surrogacy cases. Measuring the number of such applications might have provided a means of assessing the extent of some types of surrogacy at a particular time.

From November 1994 until April 1995, thanks to the 'Jopling amendment', the Act opened a window for couples whose child was born at any time in the past following a surrogacy arrangement. Any married couple caring for a child born under such an arrangement, provided they met the other criteria, could apply for a parental order. After April 1995, the application must be made within six months of the child's birth. In 1995, a study of applications lodged for parental orders in the immediate six-month period from 1 November 1994 to 30 April 1995 was undertaken for the British Medical Association's report, *Changing Conceptions of Motherhood*. It tried to gauge the incidence of surrogacy, based on the assumption that parents who had had a surrogate-born child at any time in the past might use this 'retrospective window' to formalise the relationship, as contemplated by s. 30. Few couples took this opportunity. A number of reasons might account for this.

An initial problem was whether potential applicants were aware of the existence of s. 30 and their chance to apply. Some solicitors experienced in working with parties involved in surrogacy cases reported that the different responses of court-appointed guardians *ad litem*, required under the provisions of s. 30 to report on the suitability of the intended parents, and the delays experienced by some applicants, had persuaded some of them and their clients that the alternative route of the adoption procedure was a more valuable way to proceed, extinguishing as it does all previous parental rights and responsibility.

The benefits of s. 30 are afforded to 'the parties to a marriage'; in at least one case a parental order had been made in favour of an individual applicant whose spouse had died since the birth of the child (in circumstances unrelated to the surrogacy). The legal effect of such an order therefore seems to us to be worthless; the order as made is void. The surrogate could at any time seek rectification of the Parental Orders Register and seek to recover custody of the child. Concomitantly, the child could, until majority, seek support from the surrogate and, if she is married, her husband. The only avenue now open would, it seems to us, be for the surviving spouse to seek an adoption order.

Lastly, some couples who in the past have had a child born as a consequence of a surrogacy arrangement may have already successfully applied for adoption, or may have never revealed the fact of the surrogacy and registered the child at birth as though it was their child. The Brazier Report[16] – which we review below – has made recommendations which in part should enable us to paint a more accurate picture of the extent of surrogate births.

SURROGACY: THE STANDARD ARGUMENTS

We do not propose extensively to review the ethical debate which has raged around surrogacy since its public appearance in the 1980s. The main arguments can, however, be summarised as set out in Table 8.1.

The possible breadth and depth of the legal complications which might flow from the translation of animal studies to humans was remarked upon at the end of the 1950s:

> . . . the transplantation of fertilised ova from one female to another, or even of complete ovaries [in cattle enables] the foster-mother [to bear] a child which is

Table 8.1　Arguments for and against surrogacy

For	Against
• it is the only chance for some couples to have a child	• surrogacy is an assault on the marital relationship
• carrying a child for another is an act of generosity or virtue	• it is inconsistent with human dignity that a woman should use her uterus for profit
• women can and should decide for themselves how to use their own bodies	• the relationship between mother and child is distorted by surrogacy
• true voluntariness excludes exploitation	• surrogacy is potentially damaging to both (a) the child and (b) the mother
• those who feel surrogacy compromises the marital relationship should not impose this view on others	• the risks of pregnancy should not be run for money
• there is no firm evidence to support 'bonding' between mother and child during pregnancy	• a woman should not be forced to part with a child against her will

biologically the child of the donor and has no characteristics of the foster-mother. Hence the opportunity may be given for women to have children without bearing them. . . . when it becomes an established practice it will assuredly set the legal profession by the ears. It will raise the profound and (in terms of established concepts) almost insoluble problem whether a child born from the ovum of A in the womb of B is legally A or B's. . . . But this problem may be left to care for itself.[17]

SURROGACY AND THE 1985 ACT

Surrogacy trespassed upon reproductive redevelopments in 1985 with the announcement that a British woman, Kim Cotton, was to give birth to a child with the intention that it should be brought up by another woman and her husband in their native America. The debates which accompanied the passage of the hastily drafted Surrogacy Arrangements Act 1985 were replete with the language of moral panic and outrage. The tenor of the Parliamentary debates which prefaced the legislation recalls the abhorrence and reluctance which English courts reserved for their preliminary dealings with surrogacy.

In the first of the two cases which had commanded their attention, *A v C* [1905] FLR 445, the judges did not stand accused of moral ambivalence. In *A v C*, a man and his wife paid £3,000 to a woman who decided on birth to keep the child. The woman had been introduced to the couple by a friend, who had been approached by them after she had appeared in court on a prostitution charge. The Appeal Court set itself steadfastly against the contract: Ormrod LJ complained that it was 'a quite deplorable story . . . a bizarre and unnatural agreement . . . a sordid commercial bargain'; Cumming-Bruce LJ described it as 'a baby farming operation of a wholly distasteful and lamentable kind . . . a guilty bargain'; while Stamp LJ characterised it as an 'ugly little drama'.

Adopting a more pragmatic approach in *Re C (A Minor)* [1985] FLR 846, Latey J, while remarking that 'the moral, ethical and social considerations are for others and not for this court in its wardship jurisdiction', decided that it was first of all important to establish that the commissioning couple still wanted the child and that the surrogate mother did not. Following that, the court should consider the commissioners' ages, their marital status and the state of their relationship, and their employment and residential circumstances. These factors would enable the court to assess their ability to provide for the child's material and emotional well-being compared with any other source.[18]

The Surrogacy (Arrangements) Bill was introduced shortly afterwards, and passed smoothly through its legislative process with almost universal blessing. Surrogacy and surrogate mothers[19] were condemned as 'sick, as is any form of womb leasing';[20] 'totally immoral';[21] 'repugnant';[22] 'the sale of children';[23] 'trafficking in human beings';[24] 'this extremely distasteful matter';[25] 'a well defined evil';[26] 'sheer effrontery';[27] and as making 'reproduction as marketable for women as sexuality has always been historically',[28] resulting in 'widespread abhorrence'.[29] Fears were expressed for women who agreed to act as surrogates, for commissioning parents, surrogate-born children, family life, the 'whole of our country'[30] and 'the nation and humanity'.[31] The responsibility of Parliamentarians was clear: 'the eyes of the world will be upon us'.[32] The Bill was heralded because it would 'preserve family life, stabilise society and do away with this unnatural and unfortunate practice which has sickened so many decent and family-loving people'[33] and 'rightly outlaw the hell and wickedness which exists in America'.[34] Surrogacy, or at least its fully commercialised variant, was not welcome. Clearly, the world as we had known it was about to come to an end.

In fact, the 1985 Bill had more modest aims than those proclaimed for it. And life, perhaps eccentrically, progressed much as usual. An attempt was made in the House of Lords later in 1985 to expand the criminal prohibitions of the Act to render all manifestations and aspects of surrogacy unlawful, but this failed. Surrogacy became not quite as invisible as it had been hitherto,[35] but it functioned as a more or less acceptable subterranean reproductive alternative for some couples. Indeed, the anecdotal evidence available in the UK suggests that there is an increase in the numbers of people embarking on a surrogacy arrangement: Blyth reports communications from COTS, the self-help group, which would suggest 98 recent or ongoing arrangements within the past few years, with 55 out of 57 surrogacy arrangements resulting in live births that have been regarded as a satisfactory outcome; COTS' own data suggest that more than 200 children have been born following a surrogacy agreement in the past 15 years.[36]

The core of the Surrogacy Arrangements Act 1985 is directed towards commercial agencies. The recruitment of surrogate mothers (extensively defined in s. 1) is prohibited, as is the negotiation of surrogacy arrangements by agencies acting on a commercial basis (s. 2(1), (4)). The Act was drafted in such a way as to try to catch anything in which there is the underlying possibility of payment, extending to 'a promise or understanding that payment will or may be made to the [surrogate mother] or for her benefit' (s. 1(4)). However, the Act does not attempt to deal with 'altruistic'[37] or family arrangements, or with those in which the offices of a charitable organisation have assisted the establishment of the contract. To underline the fact that the thrust of this legislation is directed towards commercial agencies, the surrogate herself is exempted from the prohibitions of s. 2(1), which encompass the initiation or participation in pre-arrangement negotiations, an offer or undertaking to negotiate such an agreement, or even the compilation of 'any information' with a view to using it in making or negotiating surrogacy agreements. A similar dispensation is given in s. 2(2)(b) for somebody who commissions a surrogate to carry a child. The expressed reasoning behind these exemptions is to avoid the birth of a child whose mother or family are 'subject to the taint of criminality'.[38]

Even though 'altruistic' surrogacy, or even surrogacy for which the surrogate is paid without agency involvement, is not prohibited, the restraints on advertising surrogacy services attempt to ensure that to all intents and purposes surrogacy will be kept 'within the family'. As Kenneth Clarke, the then Health Minister, put it in the Standing Committee debate, 'an agreement between sisters [is] the least harmful of all'.[39] Section 3 makes it an offence to advertise to act as a surrogate mother, to advertise in the search for a surrogate mother, or to say that one is willing to set up a surrogacy agreement. The prohibition is exhaustive, making it clear that it is not only newspaper or periodical advertising that is caught, but also advertising which uses telecommunication systems or through putting a card in the local corner shop (s. 3(3), (4)). Contravention of these provisions, which can only be prosecuted by or with the consent of the DPP, attracts a fine not in excess of level 5 on the standard scale,[40] while offences under s. 2 may be visited with the additional sanction of up to three months' imprisonment.

In enacting the 1985 Act, Parliament has combined elements of a 'prohibitory' state regulation model with facets of private ordering. Yet the decision to legislate on this basis, even if as an interim measure, distressed some members of Parliament. One felt 'either that the practice of surrogacy is undesirable and anti-social, and carries considerable risks for the children concerned, or it does not, or does not in any substantial measure'.[41] If surrogacy is undesirable, it should have been prohibited altogether. Settling for the 1985 Act's approach might be thought to legitimate some forms of agreement. Indeed, these sentiments informed the introduction, late in 1985, of the Surrogacy Arrangements (Amendment) Bill. That initiative sought to extend the 1985 Act in three important ways. First, it would have introduced an offence committed by any person assisting or taking part in the establishment of a pregnancy knowing that it is in pursuance of a surrogate motherhood agreement. Secondly, it would have brought within the ambit of the legislation non-commercial bodies or agencies which have as their function the negotiation or establishment of surrogacy arrangements. Lastly, and perhaps of most significance, it would have removed the immunity from prosecution which the main Act had established in favour of the surrogate mother and any person commissioning her. The Bill fell.

SURROGACY AND THE 1990 ACT

The Human Fertilisation and Embryology Act 1990 established the HFEA to regulate certain types of infertility treatment and research. It is a statutory requirement for any centre undertaking activities covered by the Act to have a licence from the Authority which specifies the activities covered by the licence, the premises in which the activities may be performed and the name of a 'person responsible' under whose supervision the work must be carried out (ss. 12–15). Licensed activities include the creation or use of an embryo outside the body and the use of donated eggs, sperm or embryos. Any medical treatment used as part of a surrogacy arrangement will involve the donation of sperm, eggs or embryos and thus must be carried out in a licensed centre. Under the Act's requirements, details of every treatment carried out must be lodged with the HFEA. Thus, although the Authority does not directly regulate surrogacy, licensed treatment services provided to establish a surrogate pregnancy will be carried out under its auspices.

HFEA Code of Practice

The HFEA issues licences to centres carrying out certain activities. One aspect of the Authority's supervisory role is the publication of a Code of Practice which provides guidance concerning the proper conduct of licensed activities. All centres providing treatment services for the purpose of establishing a surrogate pregnancy must be licensed by the HFEA and abide by the Code of Practice.

Section 13(5) of the 1990 Act makes it a condition of all treatment licences that 'A woman shall not be provided with treatment services unless account has been taken of the welfare of any child who may be born as a result of the treatment (including the need of that child for a father), and of any other child who may be affected by the birth'. Thus all centres providing treatment services as part of a surrogacy arrangement are legally obliged to take account of the welfare of the child. This requirement is complicated by the fact that either the surrogate mother and her partner, if she has one, or the intended parents could take on the role of social parents; the centre is therefore obliged to make inquiries of both parties. The HFEA's Code of Practice advises consideration of the following factors:

(a)   the commitment of the woman, and her husband/partner to having and bringing up a child or children;

(b)   their ages and medical histories and the medical histories of their families;

(c)   the needs of any child or children who may be born as a result of treatment, including the implications of any possible multiple birth and the ability of the prospective parents (or parent) to meet those needs;

(d)   any risk of harm to the child or children who may be born, including the risk of inherited disorders, problems during pregnancy and of neglect or abuse; and

(e)   the effect of a new baby on any existing child of the family (Code, para. 3.17).

The HFEA also advises in its Code of Practice that all people seeking treatment are entitled to a fair and unprejudiced assessment of their situation and needs, which should be conducted with the skill and sensitivity appropriate to the delicacy of the case and the wishes and feelings of those involved (Code, para. 3.16).

Enforceability of surrogacy arrangements

Those participating in a surrogacy arrangement must reach agreement between themselves as to how the arrangement will proceed. Nevertheless, regardless of whether the agreement is detailed in writing or whether expenses have been paid,

s. 36 of the Human Fertilisation and Embryology Act 1990 renders surrogacy contracts unenforceable.[42] This means that if the surrogate mother wishes to keep the child, she is entitled to do so. Equally, if the intended parents decide they do not want the child, the surrogate mother, as the legal mother of the child (which we have considered in Chapter 9), is responsible in law for its welfare. In practice, a child rejected by its birth mother and the intended parents is likely to be placed for fostering or adoption.

Birth registration

A child born to a surrogate mother must be registered as her child and, if applicable, that of her partner or the person treated as the father under the Act. Where a parental order has been granted under s. 30 by a court, the Registrar General will make an entry in a separate Parental Order Register registering the child and cross-referencing to the entry in the existing Register of Births. There is no public Parental Order Register. It is not possible to 'abolish' the original record of birth, and at the age of 18 a person who was the subject of a parental order may be supplied with information enabling him or her to obtain a certified copy of the original record of his or her birth. This certificate will include the name of the surrogate mother. Prior to being given access to the information, the person is to be advised of the counselling services available. This is an exception to the general rule (which we discuss in Chapter 9) that children born of assisted conception may not discover the identity of the people party to their conception.

The Parental Orders (Human Fertilisation and Embryology) Regulations 1994 (SI 1994 No. 2767) (made under the provisions of the Human Fertilisation and Embryology Act 1990, ss. 30(9), 45(1) and (3)) are intended to achieve the same effect as an adoption order. The relevant provisions of those Regulations are Paragraph 1(1), (2) and Paragraph 2, column 1, sch. 1, para. 1(b), which adopts (under s. 30(9) of the 1990 Act) amended provisions of the Adoption Act 1976, s. 12(1)–(3). As amended, the relevant part of that section reads:

(1)   A parental order is an order giving parental responsibility for a child to the husband and wife, made on their application by an authorised court.
. . .
(3)   The making of a parental order operates to extinguish—
    (a)   the parental responsibility which any person has for the child immediately before the making of the order;
    (aa)   any order under the Children Act 1989;
    (b)   any duty arising by virtue of an agreement or the order of a court to make payments, so far as the payments are in respect of the child's maintenance or upbringing for any period after the making of the order.

Concerns, however, have arisen with the s. 30 procedure.[43] Some couples are reported to have believed that s. 30 would substantially modify the adoption procedure, yet wanted to ensure that in formalising their relationship with the child, the surrogate mother and any of her parental rights would be excluded. This is indeed the case with the adoption procedure, but not with s. 30. In England and Wales the terms of the Adoption Act 1976, ss. 12 and 39 provide that adoption is the process whereby a court irrevocably extinguishes the legal ties between a child and his or her natural parents and creates analogous ties between the child and the adopters. Section 30 only has the effect that the intending social parents are registered as the child's legal parents; two birth certificates will be issued, one accessible to the public naming the commissioning parents as the child's parents if they have completed the parental orders procedure. A second register, not open to the public, will list the surrogate mother.

The 1990 Act thus does not explicitly extinguish the legal responsibilities of the surrogate mother but gives additional rights to the intending social parents. It is therefore possible that the surrogate mother could apply for access to the child under the Children Act 1989, and for a court to be required to consider whether to admit such a claim.

Regulations made under s. 30(9) provide for the court to be satisfied that the welfare of the child is being prioritised throughout the proceedings. Some solicitors have argued that by the time a social worker has been appointed as guardian *ad litem* (under the Children Act 1989, s. 41(1)) for these purposes, and assuming only a first hearing, the time involved could be as that usually involved in obtaining an adoption order. Section 30(5) further requires the consent of the surrogate mother to the making of the orders, and s. 30(6) that that consent is ineffective if given within the first six weeks after the child's birth. Compared with the adoption process, in which any refusal of consent is open to review after consultation with social work staff, including whether any consent is being unreasonably withheld, s. 30 has clear and present dangers or limitations.

The limitation of s. 30 to married couples caused predictable disappointment to some people, but the limitation has gone further than some could have anticipated. Section 30(1) provides that 'The court may make an order providing for a child to be treated in law as the child of the parties to a marriage' if the further conditions of the section and subsequent regulations are satisfied. The phrase 'parties to a marriage' has for lawyers, of course, a particular significance. Death is one of the incidents which brings a marriage to an end. In separate cases reported to the surrogacy self-help group COTS within the same week in December 1994, two women who had intended to apply with their respective husbands for parental orders under s. 30 died. One woman was killed in a road accident and the other died of natural causes. In both cases their husbands were deprived by the death of, amongst other things, the ability to apply for a s. 30 order. In the first case the child had been living with the couple for several years, while in the latter the child was only 12 weeks old. The father would face uncertainty in establishing a good case under the Adoption Act that he is the most fitting person to care for the child, because he has, by definition, little parenting experience.

THE METAMORPHOSIS OF SURROGACY

Since 1985, surrogacy has undergone a metamorphosis, or more accurately, a series of metamorphoses, from: (i) the sexual to the medical; (ii) the private and invisible to the public and intermittently visible; (iii) the altruistic to the commercial and back again; and (iv) the contested and controversial to the accepted and clinically mediated, and back again. The 'medicalisation of surrogacy' has occurred in parallel with the remarkable turnaround in the legal approach to surrogacy in the

1990 Act and in the decisions in cases brought before the High Court which have been almost universally pragmatic and usually sympathetic. These developments need brief consideration; together they represent the enclosure of surrogacy from the common wealth to the private purse.

Technology transfers

Two interrelated themes of change are evident in the developments within the *practice* of surrogacy. Surrogacy may be seen as a form of 'collaborative conception',[44] in which the medical profession has to be involved in creating a symmetry between the intending social parents. Here the man and the woman (facilitated by clinicians) collaborate to enable the woman's fertilised egg to be transferred to a woman who has agreed to attempt to become pregnant using their genetic material. The total medicalisation of surrogacy which this implies may have profound consequences.[45] Edgar Page anticipated this question.[46] His argument was this:

> When the woman who gestates the child receives the embryo by donation, she has a strong claim to the child *because* the embryo was donated to her. But surely if the embryo transferred to her uterus was *not* donated to her, her claim to the child would not be the same, especially if those who supplied the embryo did so on the explicit understanding that the resulting child would be *returned* to them and if they would not have supplied the embryo otherwise.[47]

The importance which might be attached to Page's distinction must not be overlooked, for it has persuaded at least one court in the United States that the genetic link in 'gestational surrogacy' is sufficiently important that the wishes of the surrogate to retain the child after birth should be set aside. In *Johnson* v *Calvert*, Anna Johnson agreed to *in vitro* fertilisation with the sperm and egg from Mark and Crispina Calvert. Midway through the pregnancy, she decided that she wanted to keep the resulting child, and the Calverts sought custody. When the child was five weeks old, the California Court Judge Parslow decided that the Calverts would keep the child; he likened Johnson's role to that of a foster-mother who cares for a child for a period when the 'true parents' are unable to. He decided also that the surrogacy contract between the parties was legal and enforceable.[48]

Ethical evolution: the views of the BMA

The British Medical Association (BMA) originally vacillated in its views on surrogacy. A 1984 statement cautioned that 'the Council . . . considers that it is unethical for a doctor to become involved in techniques and procedures leading to surrogate motherhood', while the Annual Representative Meeting the following year 'agree[d] with the principle of surrogate births in selected cases with careful controls'. A BMA Board of Science Report in 1987, *Surrogate Motherhood*, advised that the 'interests of childless couples were outweighed by legitimate social considerations opposing surrogacy', which provoked the 1987 Annual Representative Meeting to conclude that 'This meeting advises that, until ARM has agreed appropriate ethical safeguards and controls, doctors should not participate in any surrogacy agreement'. Thereafter, the BMA *Report of the Working Party on*

Human Infertility Services (1988) concluded that 'it would not be possible or desirable to seek to prevent all involvement of doctors in surrogacy arrangements especially as the government does not intend to make the practice illegal'.

In a second report, *Surrogacy: Ethical Considerations*,[49] the BMA advocated that surrogacy should be an option of last resort, in which the interests of the child should be paramount. The BMA's conclusions and recommendations provide that surrogacy should be used only 'where the commissioning couple suffers from infertility due to a medically recognised disorder, and where all other appropriate means for enabling them to have a child have been tried, and failed'.[50] Lastly, the Association suggested that it is 'inadvisable for the commissioning couple and the surrogate to be aware of each other's identity'.[51]

While these recommendations were couched in the language of caution, the BMA effectively assisted in making the case for 'medicalised versions of surrogacy' which have been increasingly insistent.[52] The BMA returned to consider surrogacy for a third time in *Changing Conceptions of Motherhood: A Report on Surrogacy*,[53] which effectively liberalised the profession's stance a little further. The Report observed that it was now believed that 'surrogacy is an acceptable option of last resort in cases where it is impossible or highly undesirable for medical reasons for the intended mother to carry a child herself. In all cases the interests of the potential child must be paramount and the risks to the surrogate mother must be kept to a minimum'.[54] Doctors who were approached by patients considering self-insemination were advised that they should encourage those concerned to take account of the issues and implications very carefully, and should ensure that they were aware of how to obtain accurate information about the medical, psychological, emotional and legal issues involved with surrogacy. Once a pregnancy was established, however, it was imperative that the pregnant woman was given the same level of appropriate care as any other expectant mother. The Report concluded that

. . . in itself, the fact of being born following a surrogacy arrangement is not sufficient disadvantage to the child to justify refusing the request of the intended parents for assistance with conception. Although little evidence is available, the risk of serious psychological harm to the child is considered low if open acknowledgement is made from an early stage in the child's life.[55]

Before agreeing to provide treatment services aimed at establishing a surrogate pregnancy, for example through *in vitro* fertilisation or insemination, the healthcare team must take all reasonable steps to ensure that the medical, emotional and legal issues have been carefully considered and must, in all cases, take account of the welfare of the child who may be born as a result of the treatment. Such treatment services may be provided only in clinics licensed by the HFEA and in compliance with the HFEA's Code of Practice. In contrast to the 1990 Report's stress on anonymity, the 1995 Report recommended that openness and honestly between parents and children was generally to be encouraged.

Regulating reproduction: changing the template

Section 30 was a late amendment to the 1990 Bill, and, it has been claimed, has the effect of reducing 'parenthood to its constituent parts'. It recognises that 'combined with recent developments in clinical technology, genetic, gestational, nurturing and legal parenthood may be performed by a variety of adults'.[56] The MP who was largely responsible for securing the introduction of the section, Michael Jopling, did so following specific concerns which had been raised with him by a couple who lived in his constituency. The clause on which the section is based was introduced following the well-publicised case of *Cumbria CC* v *X, The Times*, 25 June 1990.[57] The effect of this local affair was to complete the most important metamorphosis of surrogacy, from being cast at the eye of the storm which the whirlwind of publicity had generated in the mid-1980s, to its reception in the harbours of reproductive regulation only five years later.

Jopling's constituents had been challenged by their local social services department when they applied formally to adopt twin children who had been living with them since their birth following a 'full' surrogacy arrangement. They were the children's genetic parents, but the social services department argued that they should fulfil the full legal criteria for adoption before the children were allowed to remain with them. In an extraordinary procedural manoeuvre, Jopling succeeded in having the legislation amended so that it could apply retrospectively to the benefit of couples such as his constituents.

As we explained above, s. 30 introduced the 'parental orders' provisions as an 'acceptable face of surrogacy'. However, a technical drafting flaw rendered the implementation of this provision more complex and circumspect than first intended. It was provided in s. 30(2) that 'the husband and the wife must apply for the order within six months of the birth of the child', or, in what may be called the Jopling amendment, 'in the case of a child born before the coming into force of this Act, within six months of such coming into force'. The intended effect of that provision was to make retrospective the application of the provisions of the section, as long as the 'parents' of any surrogate-born child (however long ago the birth took place) applied to the court for recognition as the child's legal parents within the specified six months. Unfortunately, different sections of the Act were to be brought into force on different days, and there was no one date which could be identified as the apposite date.

THE BRAZIER REVIEW

In parallel with the reviews by the BMA have come two major Government reviews: first the Warnock Report of 1984, and latterly the Brazier Committee Report of 1998. Just after election in 1997, the Labour Administration was galvanised into action by a number of events which came together to push surrogacy back on to and up the public policy agenda. The Brazier Review was commissioned immediately following the publicity in May attracted by Karen Roche and Sonja and Clemens Peters, a Dutch couple for whom Roche had agreed to act as a surrogate mother for payment of 'expenses' of £12,000.[58] The agreement proceeded to unravel before an entirely delighted press corps as accusations about the arrangements grew more rancorous; revelations that Roche had terminated the pregnancy were swiftly followed by retraction and an announcement that she would in fact keep the child herself. This appeared to confirm an impression of the UK as the surrogacy capital of western Europe.[59] It was coupled with headlines earlier in 1997 proclaiming that '£35,000 Gets You the Perfect Baby', as newspapers previewed a London seminar by Bill Handel of the Centre for Surrogate Parenting and Egg Donation in Los Angeles, aimed at intending parents from the United Kingdom.[60]

These were but the most celebrated of a number of 'difficult' cases, as the Public Health Minister Tessa Jowell called them. A year previously, *Re Q* [1996] 1 FLR 369, further complicated what understanding there might have been of payments made on a 'commercial basis' within the 1985 Act and was thought by many to demonstrate the benign, if not relaxed, attitude of a number of judges to the question of expenses properly allowable to a surrogate mother under s. 30. In that case Johnson J was asked retrospectively to authorise, and did authorise, receipt by a surrogate mother of over £8,000 in respect of a child which she had carried on behalf of intending parents who subsequently applied for a 'parental order' under s. 30. This approach reflected that which had been established by Latey J in hearing the surrogacy cases which came before the High Court in the 1980s. He instituted the highly pragmatic solutions to cases such as the Cotton case (*Re C* [1985] FLR 445), and in *Re An Adoption Application (Surrogacy)* [1987] 2 All ER 826, he held that payments made to a surrogate were to recompense her for her time and inconvenience. Hence, he said, they were not payments in contravention of s. 57(3) of the Adoption Act 1976 which renders it unlawful to make or give any payment or reward in consideration of the adoption of a child.

The announcement of a Committee of Inquiry to review developments in the law of surrogacy enjoyed widespread assent. The terms of reference for the review required the Committee to consider whether in the caring, compassionate 1990s (compared with the grasping, greedy 1980s), payments should continue to be allowed[61] and whether there was a case for the 'regulation of surrogacy arrangements through a recognised body or bodies'. The Committee was charged to advise on the scope and operation of any such arrangements that it recommended, and in both cases to consider whether reforms of the Surrogacy Arrangements Act 1985 and s. 30 of the Human Fertilisation and Embryology Act 1990 were required.

The Committee was chaired by Professor Margaret Brazier, and its Report was published in October 1998.[62] The Committee recommended that:

(a)   payments to surrogate mothers should cover only genuine expenses associated with pregnancy and that the surrogate should be required to provide documentary evidence of the expenses incurred;

(b)   any additional payments should be prohibited in order to prevent surrogacy arrangements being entered into for financial benefit;

(c)   legislation should define such expenses in terms of broad principle;

(d)   agencies involved in establishing surrogate pregnancies and supporting participants in the process should be required to register with the Department of Health and conform to a Code of Practice drawn up by the Department, with a voluntary Code put in place as an interim measure;

(e)   Health Departments should take the opportunity to establish full record-keeping mechanisms to discover the incidence of surrogacy and to facilitate research into the outcomes of surrogacy arrangements.

The review team recommended that a new Surrogacy Act should replace the 1985 Act and s. 30 of the 1990 Act. This new Act should continue to provide for the continuing non-enforceability of surrogacy contracts, a prohibition on advertising and profiting from surrogacy arrangements,[63] and should introduce new provisions to define and limit lawful payments. Other consequential amendments to establish a Code of Practice should be included, as should reform of s. 30. Under the Brazier proposals, parental orders applications should henceforth go only to the High Court (and not as now to any court with family jurisdiction) and the guardian *ad litem* should have power to review records of criminal convictions before an order is issued.

Brazier proceeded on the basis that public concern had moved on from Warnock, from regarding surrogacy as being an almost offensive offering on the reproductive menu to being a legitimate service after all other courses have been sampled and found wanting. As we have tried to show, the metamorphosis of surrogacy is an extraordinary incident of the development of assisted conception. For Brazier, the fundamental concerns were now with safeguarding the welfare of the child born of the surrogacy arrangement and ensuring protection of the interests of the surrogate. But perhaps pre-eminent was the one question that clearly troubled Brazier personally above all others: is the payment in surrogacy distinguishable from the buying and selling of children? She has elsewhere publicly declared her view that it is not:

> If an infertile couple can buy an egg, and rent a womb, why should they not buy the finished product? It will be argued of course that in purchasing gametes and/or the services of a surrogate, they are *not* buying a baby. I hope to demonstrate that that argument is specious. If, in the UK we wish to sustain objections to trade in babies, payments to surrogates should continue to be outlawed, and continuing payments to gamete donors must be, at least, a cause for concern.[64]

There are those who have argued that it is possible to distinguish between the payment for the reproductive services of a surrogate which we should permit and 'baby selling' which we should not, including philosophers such as Dickenson[65] and lawyers such as Mason[66] and Freeman,[67] who suggests that 'Brazier is too readily dismissive of the distinction between payment for the purchase of a child and payment for a potentially risky, time-consuming and uncomfortable service', although the reasoning that supports that conclusion is largely of a consequentialist kind.

We briefly consider these two forms of argument, from Brazier and Freeman, of what we call the 'exploitation' and the 'consequences' argument.

Commodification and exploitation

It is widely agreed that:

> The evils of baby bartering are loathsome for a variety of reasons . . . [including that] the child is sold without regard for whether the purchasers will be suitable parents. . . . The profit motive predominates, permeates, and ultimately governs the transaction. . . . There are, in a civilised society, some things that money cannot buy. . . . There are . . . values that society deems more important than granting to wealth whatever it can buy, be it labor, love or life.[68]

But, as Sandra Marshall has suggested, the really interesting questions with surrogacy may lie elsewhere. They are not just the questions about surrogacy but the ones which we need to see as part of the background to surrogacy: in particular, the question about what sort of problem we take infertility to be, such that biotechnology seems a suitable way of dealing with it:

> . . . there is no reason that I can see why surrogacy should be limited to the alleviation of infertility; this is to say that I can see no reason why infertility should be taken as the only serious reason.[69]

Of course, this was written in response to the Warnock Committee's exhortation that surrogacy arrangements entered into on the grounds of convenience alone are 'totally ethically unacceptable':

> Even in compelling medical circumstances the danger of exploitation of one human being by another appears to the majority of us to far outweigh the potential benefits in almost every case.[70]

As Marshall in her commentary on this passage makes clear, it is possible that one or more of three different objections is being raised: (i) that surrogacy is itself exploitative; (ii) that in some circumstances it might be; (iii) commercial surrogacy is necessarily exploitative. The burden of Marshall's argument is that 'contract pregnancy corrupts or distorts women's reproductive labour in such a way as to alienate that labour'. For Marshall, the application of economic norms:

(a) requires the surrogate mother to repress whatever parental love she feels for the child (notice the interesting use of language here – not foetus but child) (and thus alienates her (reproductive) labour);

(b) denies the legitimacy of the surrogate's evolving perspective of her own pregnancy (and thus degrades her); and

(c) leaves the surrogate open to exploitation in taking advantage of her non-commercial motivations.

As Freeman has suggested, properly read these objections focus on the claim that surrogacy exploits because it involves 'a transaction in which one party is as a result of circumstances (such as poverty, unemployment) subjected to the demands of another more powerful party'.[71] Exploitation thus takes the form of coercing one person into doing something which otherwise she would not have done because she has less power than the exploiter, and when the exploiter uses his advantage of power to force her to do as he wishes. Thus the surrogate's basic claims to liberty and equality are being undermined.

Most surrogates already have children of their own (and there may be concern at the emotional costs on these children) and few are poor, in the sense of needing money as opposed to needing more money. Indeed, it might be thought that one of the concerns which motivated the couple would be a concern for the health and welfare of any future child which might not necessarily be secured in an environment of poverty and destitution. This is not, of course, an argument for celebration of destitution and poverty, but an observation which challenges at least some of the assumptions commonly made in respect of exploitation.

Martha Field has responded to those who suggest that it is patronising to women not to enforce surrogacy contracts by arguing that this is to misconstrue the argument. It does not, she suggests, entail the view that women (or those who contemplate surrogacy contracts) are weak, rather that

> ... there are certain subject matters that are so important and so deeply personal that we as a society do not want the state to intervene to bind people – men *or* women – by their previous promises. .... Society also has an interest in keeping certain contracts outside of the market economy – and the transfer of children is one of them. Sometimes this objection is called an objection to commodifying children – to treating them as objects subject to barter and exchange.[72]

Of course, as Field herself readily recognises, this is an argument not so much about exploitation but about commodification: 'an advantage of simple non-enforcement, in comparison with criminalisation of surrogacy arrangements, is that it does respect a right of women to do with as they wish with their bodies'.[73]

In framing the present surrogacy laws in the way that Parliament has done and providing that surrogacy contracts are unenforceable,[74] it has opted for a compromise on whether surrogacy is demeaning or liberating – perhaps permissive would be more neutral here – for women. It allows women to enter into reproductive pre-conception contracts, to be paid, and does not dictate what work women may and may not be allowed to do. As Field argues, 'non-enforcement allows women to enter into these arrangements and to go through with them on whatever terms they choose . . . All non-enforcement does is to protect the woman who herself decides that she does not want to go through with the arrangement after all'.[75]

Carmel Shalev has argued strongly a contrary view. She holds that women capable of bearing children should be allowed freely to agree to be paid to do so by infertile couples who want to form a family; establishing a 'free market in reproduction' would allow the 'reproducing woman' to operate as an 'autonomous moral and economic agent'.[76] It would follow from this that if her 'autonomous reproductive decision' is voluntary, 'she should be held responsible for it so as to fulfil the expectations of the other parties'.[77] Alan Wertheimer has pointed to further limitations to the optional performance model. While it may well be the preferred public policy option, it fails in two ways to address questions of autonomy. First, a crucial dimension of one's autonomy is the ability to enter into *binding* agreements; if B wants to enter into an agreement with A but A will not do so unless B's agreement is enforceable, a decision not to enforce such agreements 'constrains *B*'s ability to make the decision she prefers – a justifiable restraint, but a restraint nonetheless'.[78] And secondly, echoing Shalev, he writes that in trying to protect a woman from coming later to regret her decision 'we are refusing to treat her as an autonomous and responsible person'.[79]

It does not follow that in doing this we are refusing to treat people as less than full citizens, for there may be social benefits to a limited state paternalism or protectionism which serves to benefit the state; as Freeman has said of both the Warnock and the Brazier Reports, they are shot through with an ample injection of paternalism when it comes to surrogacy.[80] It might be quite a defensible public policy to seek to prevent as much distress and anguish as possible – real psychic costs – so as to release medical treatment and care for others who need it. If the unenforceability of certain types of contract contributes to that goal then it may be an appropriate one for a state to pursue, even if it looks as though it is treating people less than autonomously.[81] It also contributes, as we have suggested, to the symbolic representation of surrogacy as part of a world which we would prefer to live without, an important part of saying who we are and who we do not want to become.

The consequences

> We may live to rue the consequences of removing remuneration from surrogates. . . . The Report fails to appreciate that withdrawing remuneration from surrogates will only drive potential surrogates away from regulated surrogacy and into an invisible and socially controlled world where the regulators will be more like pimps than adoption agencies.[82]

There are difficulties with this argument. Of course, we might make this prediction from historical evidence; prohibiting something – alcohol, prostitution, abortion – has always had the effect of driving it 'underground' or into the back streets, even though the reasons behind the prohibition may be as much (or more) symbolic as instrumental.[83] Leave aside for the moment the belief that underground or back-street 'illegal' activities are the price, and the price worth paying, for the initial prohibition. There are some who would honestly and reasonably hold this belief and happily and wholeheartedly defend it. Rather, we think that there are several arguments which need to be addressed in a more sympathetic response to the 'simple' prohibition argument. First, the *direct* evidence which would be needed to support this argument in respect of surrogacy is difficult to garner, although there are few examples of outright prohibition and even fewer of prosecution following such a prohibition. In fact, because we know so little about surrogacy, because we are still so hazy after all these years, we can have little *predictive* confidence in knowing what would happen if surrogacy were prohibited under pain of severe criminal penalty. But how secure is the analogy between, say, abortion and surrogacy?

There is a difference between termination of an unwanted, unlooked for or even inconvenient pregnancy and the involvement of a third party in a desperately wanted pregnancy. Of course it is not the involvement of the third party in itself that makes the difference; a third party, the abortionist, is concerned with the termination too. It is true, also, that both the termination and the reproductive assistance might attract criminal penalty and the lure of lucre for both might be great. But the *concealment* of the fact of the termination by a third party in abortion might be thought to be rather easier than the involvement of a third party in surrogacy. The appearance and later disappearance of the resultant child in surrogacy would be less easy to explain than that, and if prohibition were thought to be a serious need then laws on registration of birth, production of birth certificates and facilities of genetic diagnosis could be turned to much greater use in the scrutiny of lineage. The argument that if we prohibit surrogacy we will *necessarily* drive it underground needs more evidence than that suggested by analogy to make a convincing case.

And so we might be driven to the conclusion that *some form of regulation* is now the only acceptable or viable reform option. Then the question is properly put: regulation of whom or of what, and at what moral and financial cost? Brazier advocates the introduction of a regulatory regime for surrogacy because it 'might reduce the more obvious hazards to the child and the others involved. . . . The risks of not having a regulatory framework are greater than any entailed by introducing one'.[84] Here, we can see only two realistic possibilities: (i) registration and supervision of surrogacy agencies, support groups and hospitals which offer IVF (or host) surrogacy; or (ii) the registration and regulation of each and every surrogacy arrangement.

What of regulating the agencies? One problem here is that we have set our face against this, at least as far as commercial agencies are concerned, in the 1985 Act and in language sufficiently unequivocal to make revision of that policy only 15 years later unlikely. The mixture of commerce, commodity and children is not yet ready for much, let alone that degree of, revisionism. So then one might turn from commercial agencies to support groups, 'introductory' agencies and help lines. But here a difficulty of a drafting nature occurs; who, precisely, is to be regulated? One introduction and support agency which operates on a non-profit-making basis – COTS – which enjoys at least informal and tacit recognition if not approval from the Department of Health (it was asked to contribute information to the recent surrogacy review team's work and officials of the Department are known to refer people to COTS, information packs and help lines), has been refused charitable status several times so that that avenue of regulation is closed off.

Hospitals providing IVF surrogacy and IVF (host) surrogacies undertaken there are already subject to HFEA review and licence. The question which then arises concerns the extent to which surrogacy – already metamorphosed from BMA 'no' to BMA 'yes' – should become an *exclusively* medical procedure, and highly technology driven one at that. There might be some in the IVF profession (or business) who would welcome such a move – it would be good for business to have the back-bedroom procreationists out of the surrogacy domain altogether. But we suspect there would be something repellent about moving from the counterpane to the laboratory altogether in this small corner of the reproductive close.

Alternatively, we might say – despite the criticisms that this would evoke about further state regulation of reproduction and motherhood – that surrogacy agencies (if not the arrangements themselves) should be subject (at least) to some form of scrutiny, if not registration and regulation. Yet again, surrogacy arrangements might themselves be required to be registrable. And this is what Brazier concluded.

The questions then become: Who should do the regulating? What would be the consequences of non-registration? Who should think through the administration and adumbration of the principles on which such a scheme might work? Who should pay for it? There is a ready-made template upon which some of the answers to these questions could be forged in the model proposed for Ontario by the Ontario Law Reform Commission in 1984, and widely thought to be the work of the Commission's Consultant, Bernard Dickens.[85] There are problems with this, though: freedom of reproductive choice and personal autonomy are sacrificed to the imprimatur of a state body and, as we reviewed in Chapter 2, there are many who would object to this model on that ground.

Rather more mundanely, but we suspect more sensibly, the HFEA could be mandated to establish a system of review and report over the activities of surrogacy arrangements agencies. And that of course raises the thorny issue of costs and subventions; cover for substitutes. Here a fairly stark public policy issue presents itself: providing public funding for assisted conception services risks positioning the state as pimp, purser, patriarch or protector. The irony here is that while private money is deemed to be the root of the problem – altruistic surrogacy attracts almost universal sympathy and praise rather than criticism and condemnation – we are singularly reluctant to offer public money in finding a way through the moral maze.

The HFEA made it reasonably clear throughout the Brazier Committee's work that it did not see itself as the ideal home for the re-fashioned surrogacy arrangements, and it wanted to see any regulation or supervision of such arrangements undertaken by a new body. For the most part, surrogacy probably does not take place in licensed clinics or under their supervision, so there would arise the difficult question of funding the review process and the enforcement of the new Code of Practice; and regulation raises its own issues, some ethical, some legal, some psychological, with which the Authority, with its work based firmly at the IVF end of the reproduction revolution, was inexperienced and ill-equipped to deal with. Surrogacy was more akin to adoption than IVF, and this should be recognised in the way any *new* regulatory body was structured and staffed. Brazier's option, then, is for the Department of Health to operate a loosely structured review forum, with rather minimal consequences for non-compliance. But as Freeman has pointed out, 'regulation is not, however, an easy answer and regulated surrogacy will continue to throw up problems. Decentralised regulation . . . is likely to create more and greater problems'.[86]

By 'decentralised regulation' Freeman means the model which has commended itself to Brazier, the statutory obligation of voluntary surrogacy agencies to register with the Department of Health and to operate in compliance with a Code of Practice drawn up by the Department. The medical and scientific expertise of the HFEA would, it was thought, be wasted on the general run of surrogacy cases, although with IVF surrogacy the clinics and the HFEA are already involved anyway. But unless surrogacy is set to experience a major surge of popularity as the assisted conception option of choice, what little evidence there is suggests the value of a coherent, centralised approach.

NOTES

[1] Oscar Wilde, *The Importance of being Earnest*, Act 1, Lady Bracknell (Collins, 1948).
[2] Singh, S., *Fermat's Enigma* (London, Fourth Estate, 1998).
[3] Deech, R., 'Family Law and Genetics' (1998) 61 MLR 697.
[4] Maclean, A., *The Elimination of Morality* (London, Routledge, 1993), 202.
[5] This suggestion was made by the then Health Minister Kenneth Clarke in Standing Committee debate in the Surrogacy Arrangements Act 1985: Official Report, House of Commons, Standing Committee B, 25 April 1985, col. 7. See also Singer, P. and Wells, D., *The Reproduction Revolution* (Oxford, Oxford University Press), p. 124 for details of the Crozier case in France, where a woman carried a baby for her infertile twin sister: (*Guardian*, 29 September 1984, *The Times*, 23 November 1984, p. 11, *Woman*, 2 June 1984, p. 21 and the BBC 'Day to Day' programme, 13 January 1987, for comparable English examples. On egg donation between sisters, see *Independent*, 29 September 1987, p. 13.

[6] *Star*, 1 October 1987, pp. 1–4.

[7] *Mail on Sunday*, 4 October 1987, pp. 1, 2.

[8] *Daily Telegraph*, 23 February 1994.

[9] This example certainly casts a shadow over the opinion expressed by the then Health Minister (Kenneth Clarke) at the time of the 1985 Act that surrogacy between sisters was the most acceptable.

[10] *Guardian*, 25 February 1995, p. 5.

[11] *Guardian*, 12 January 1995, p. 11.

[12] Supreme Court of California interpreting the Californian Civil Code, ss. 7003, subd. (1), 7004, subd. (a), 7015 and Californian Evidence Code, ss. 621, 892.

[13] *Sunday Times*, 30 November 1997.

[14] *Independent on Sunday*, 17 June 1995, p. 7.

[15] In *The Plays of Oscar Wilde* (London, Collins, 1948), Act 1, 462–63.

[16] *Surrogacy: Review for Health Ministers of Current Arrangements for Payments and Regulation* (Cm 4068) (London, 1998).

[17] Glanville Williams, *Sanctity of Life* (London, Faber & Faber, 1958), at 114–15.

[18] Consequent upon this judgment was advice issued by the Department of Health and Social Security, *Responsibilities of Local Authority Social Service Departments in Surrogacy Cases* (LAC(85)12/HC(85)21), which reminded responsible departments of their ability to seek a place of safety order under s. 28(1) of the Children and Young Persons Act 1969 in such cases. Paragraph 55 of the circular indicated that 'The Court is likely to want as much information as possible about the persons seeking custody of the child. The authority should also report wherever possible on whether the arrangement between the parties provides for any payments to the surrogate mother or to any agency or third party involved in the arrangements.'

[19] Following a remark by Miriam David to this effect in correspondence, see a discussion of the problems associated with the use of the term 'surrogate mother' when, in truth, the surrogate is a surrogate for maternity, not motherhood, in 'Surrogacy: An Introductory Essay' in Robert Lee and Derek Morgan (eds), *Birthrights: Law and Ethics at the Beginnings of Life*, (London, Routledge, 1989), at 56–60. It is fair to say that these views have not passed without criticism. The descriptions 'full' and 'partial' surrogacy which have more recently entered the lexicons of assisted conception are really misnomers: it is not the surrogacy that is partial, it is the contribution of the commissioning couple that genetically is partial or full. The work done by the surrogate, a difficult term to which we shall return, is in both (and indeed all) cases quite unique and cannot properly be subdivided according to the genesis of the gametes. Both forms of surrogacy are full, and in this sense, full-time work for at least nine months: the differences between them, if they are in any way determinative, are that in one the surrogate makes a genetic contribution to the resulting child, in the other she does not. In this way, to describe surrogacy in full and partial terms is like the debate between nature and nurture: it does not really get us very far because it addresses the wrong sets of issue. If descriptions are to be accurate and operational, it may be better to recognise the force of the distinctions suggested by the Canadian Royal Commission between genetic-gestational and gestational: see *2 Final Report of the [Baird] Royal Commission on New Reproductive Technologies, Proceed with Care* (Ottawa, Minister of Government Services, Canada, 1993).

[20] Peter Bruinvels, *Hansard*, vol. 77, col. 42.

[21] Ian Paisley, *Hansard*, vol. 68, col. 555.

[22] William Benyon, *ibid.*, col. 582.

[23] Jill Knight, *ibid.*, col. 565.

[24] Patrick Cormack, *Hansard*, vol. 74, col. 1193.

[25] Roger Sims, *ibid.*, col. 1189.

[26] Norman Fowler, *ibid.*, col. 1193.

[27] Alan Beith, *Hansard*, vol. 77, col. 33.

[28] Michael Meacher, *Hansard*, vol. 68, col. 537.

[29] Michael Meacher, *Hansard*, vol. 77, col. 28.

[30] Ann Winterton, *Hansard*, vol. 68, col. 577.

[31] John Ward, *ibid.*, col. 578.

[32] William Cash, *ibid.*, col. 575.

[33] Peter Bruinvels, *Hansard*, vol. 77, col. 43. There is little evidence that these empirical claims have been fulfilled.

[34] Harry Greenaway, *ibid.*, col. 45.

[35] There have been various attempts to chart the history of surrogacy arrangements in the UK in the 20th century – see, for example Morgan, D., 'Surrogacy: An Introductory Essay' in Robert Lee and Derek Morgan (eds), *Birthrights: Law and Ethics at the Beginnings of Life* (London, Routledge, 1989), at 55–84 – but the reported prevalence has remained small; a variety of reasons could be given for this.

[36] Blyth, E., 'Section 30 – The Acceptable Face of Surrogacy' [1993] JSWFL 249, at 258.

[37] The term 'altruistic' surrogacy is that suggested by Singer and Wells, *op. cit.* n. 5, at 124, in discussing the Crozier case in France of a twin who bore a child for her infertile sister.

[38] Warnock Report, para. 8.2.

[39] Official Report, House of Commons, Standing Committee B, 25 April 1985, col. 7.

[40] Presently £2,500: Criminal Justice Act 1982, s. 37, and SI 1984 No. 447, sch. 4.

[41] Bernard Braine, Official Report, House of Commons, vol. 77, col. 32. And see to similar effect vol. 68, col. 578.

[42] The Human Fertilisation and Embryology Act 1990, s. 36 inserts s. 1A into the Surrogacy Arrangements Act 1985 and provides that 'No surrogacy arrangement is enforceable by or against any of the persons making it'.

[43] These following paragraphs are based on the evidence presented to and marshalled in the British Medical Association's report, *Changing Conceptions of Motherhood* (London, BMA, 1995).

[44] John Robertson, J., 'Embryos, Families and Procreative Liberty: The Legal Structure of the New Reproduction' (1986) 59 *Southern California Law Review*, at 939–1041.

[45] The difference between the two types of surrogacy are neatly illustrated in the experiences of Kim Cotton, and her retelling of them; see Cotton, K., *Baby Cotton: For Love and Money* (London, Dorling Kindersley, 1985) and Cotton, K., *Second Time Around: the full story of my second surrogate pregnancy* (London, Kim Cotton, 1992). At p. 5 of the latter she observes that 'host surrogacy is not for the faint hearted or for the squeamish'; and at p. 9, 'being a surrogate mother was a hard act to follow job-wise'.

[46] Page, E., (1985) 2 *Journal of Applied Philosophy* 162, reprinted in Brenda Almond and Donald Hill (eds), *Applied Philosophy: Morals and Metaphysics in Contemporary Debate* (London, Routledge 1991), at 272–83.

[47] *Ibid.*, at 163; second emphasis added. As Jennifer Trusted points out ((1985) 2 *Journal of Applied Philosophy* 331), the view that such donation should be accompanied by legal forfeit of rights is better supported by analogy with donation of other living bodily tissues, such as kidneys. But after donation in these and closely related gametes cases, the donor has done her or his part. In any case of surrogacy this is not so. And in this way, it is submitted that the analogy of donation, or spare parts, does not get us any further; there is, if you like, no further to go. There is no appropriate analogy for the work that a woman does in pregnancy. Thus Pages analogy between the soufflé and surrogacy is simply implausible; the child is not a soufflé, the gametes are more than eggs and milk and to try to treat them as the same – or analogous – is what we may call a recipe for disaster.

[48] On appeal, the Supreme Court of California Appeals Court affirmed this outcome, but not on the grounds of the enforceability of the contract (851 P.2d 776 (1993)); see Morgan, D., 'A Surrogacy Issue: Who is the Other Mother?' [1994] *International Journal of Law and the Family* 386–412.

[49] (BMA, London, 1990), following the report of a committee chaired by Sir Callum McNaughton.

[50] The British Medical Association, *Medical Ethics Today: Its Practice and Philosophy* (London, BMJ Publishing Group, 1993), at 122.

[51] *Ibid.*

[52] Blyth, *op. cit.* n. 36, at 257.

[53] (London, BMJ Publishing Group, 1995).

[54] Chapter 7, recommendation 1.

[55] At 23.

[56] Blyth, *op. cit.* n. 36, at 248.

[57] See also *Re W* [1991] 1 FLR 385; see [1990] Fam Law 118 and 232, and Morgan, D. and Lee, R., *Blackstone's Guide to the Human Fertilisation and Embryology Act 1990* (London, Blackstone Press, 1991), at 153–54.

[58] Reported, for example, in *The Times*, 15 May 1997.

[59] As Brazier has elsewhere noted, surrogacy is effectively prohibited in Austria Germany and Sweden and payments to surrogates prohibited in France, Denmark and The Netherlands. Payments for gametes are prohibited in Germany, Switzerland, Italy, Denmark, France and Spain.

[60] *Independent Tabloid*, 31 January 1997, at 1–3; in a nice example of cheque-book journalism (you can pay two journalists the same money from the same cheque-book to cover the same story and they will still come up with different detail), the *Daily Telegraph*, 3 February 1997, at 3, had bid this up to 'around £40,000'.

[61] As Freeman has noted, 'surprisingly, neither the Warnock report nor the 1985 Act addressed the question of payment to surrogate mothers': Freeman, M., 'Does Surrogacy Have a Future After Brazier?' (1999) 7 Med LR 1, at 3.

[62] *Op. cit.* n. 16.

[63] Although it has been reported that Ministers intend to relax this prohibition to the extent that lawyers would be able to charge for services such as advice in arranging a surrogacy agreement; see *Independent on Sunday*, 14 November 1999, at 12.

[64] 'Can you Buy Children?' (1999) 11 CFLQ 345, at 345.

[65] Dickenson, D., *Property, Women and Politics* (Cambridge, Polity Press, 1997), at 160 *et seq.*

[66] Mason, K., *Medico-Legal Aspects of Reproduction and Parenthood*, 2nd ed. (Aldershot, Ashgate, 1998), at 259.

[67] *Op. cit.* n. 61, at 9.

[68] *In the Matter of Baby M*, 525 A. 2d 1127 (1988), at 1241, 1249. On the confusions implicit in this rhetoric, see Arneson, R., 'Commodification and Commercial Surrogacy' (1992) 21 *Philosophy & Public Affairs* 132.

[69] 'Whose Child is it Anyway?', in Morgan, D. and Douglas, G. (eds), *Constituting Families* (Stuttgart, Franz Steiner Verlag, 1994).

[70] Warnock Report, para. 8.17.

[71] Freeman at 168.

[72] Field, M., 'Surrogate Motherhood' in John Eekelaar and Petar Sarcevic (eds), *Parenthood in Modern Society: Legal and Social Issues for the Twenty First Century* (Dordrecht, Martinus Nijhoff, 1993), at 225.

[73] *Ibid.*, at 226.

[74] Human Fertilisation and Embryology Act 1990, s. 36, inserting s. 1A into the Surrogacy Arrangements Act 1985: 'No surrogacy arrangement is enforceable by or against any of the persons making it.'

[75] Field, *op. cit.* n. 72 at 227; to the same effect see Bartlett, K., 'Re-Expressing Parenthood' (1988) 98 *Yale LJ* 293, 'declining to enforce surrogacy agreements would also disaffirm the notion of "convenient" childbearing' (at 335). *Cf.* Dolgin, J., 'Status and Contract in Feminist Legal Theory of the Family: A Reply to Bartlett' (1990) 12 *Women's Rights Law Reporter* 103. For an argument that a woman cannot make a genuinely autonomous decision to become a surrogate because she cannot have adequate information about her future emotional responses to pregnancy and relinquishment of the child, see Dodds, S. and Jones, K., 'Surrogacy and Autonomy' (1989) 3 *Bioethics* 9, and the response by Oakley, J., 'Altruistic Surrogacy' (1992) 6 *Bioethics* 269, 'making an autonomous decision may . . . sometimes *require* ignorance of the actual material, emotional or other consequences of this decision for me' (at 272, n. 5). The 'theoretical opacity of experience', deriving from Thomas Nagel's seminal paper, 'What is it Like to be a Bat?' in *Mortal Questions* (Cambridge, Cambridge University Press, 1979) and familiar from the philosophy of the mind, has, as Oakley notes at 278, an interesting contribution here.

[76] *Birth Power: The Case for Surrogacy* (New Haven, Yale University Press, (1989), at 145.

[77] *Ibid.*, at 96.

[78] Wertheimer, A., 'Two Questions about Surrogacy and Exploitation' (1992) 21 *Philosophy and Public Affairs* 211, *op. cit.*, 237.

[79] *Ibid.*

[80] *Op. cit.* n. 61, at 5.

[81] Compare the state's policy on compulsory motor-accident insurance. That too could be seen as a form of state paternalism (indeed, that argument is advanced by writers such as Robert Nozick in his *Anarchy, State and Utopia* (Oxford, Basil Blackwell, 1974)), albeit for the particular benefit of third parties. But it nonetheless detracts from our being autonomous and responsible persons as much as

refusing to enforce certain types of contract, although in both cases we might disagree whether this truly characterises what it would mean to be an autonomous and responsible person.

[82] Freeman, *op. cit.*, n. 61, at 8, 10.

[83] See Ericson, K., *Wayward Puritans: A Study in the Sociology of Deviance* (New York, John Wiley, 1966).

[84] Brazier Report, at paras 6.3, 6.5.

[85] See Morgan, D., 'Making Motherhood Male: Surrogacy and the Moral Economy of Women' (1985) 12 J Law Soc 219.

[86] Freeman, *op. cit.*, n. 61, at 20.

Chapter 9
Children of the Reproduction Revolution

STATUS PROVISIONS

The question of genetic status and personal identity is a complex, intermeshing construct of psychological, philosophical, historical, cultural, ethical and legal matrices. That said, the reader may be relieved that we shall not attempt here to unravel them all, but will concentrate primarily on the legal provisions that deal with the status of children following assisted conception. This is a significant matter since it overturns previous common law assumptions that the genetic link was determinative of parentage.[1] Moreover, at the time of the passage of the Act, it was said that an estimated 1 in 20, or 5%, of the population have a genetic parent who is other than the one or two named on their birth certificate.[2] The problem of 'designer genes' raised by assisted conception is insignificant compared with the 'genetic passing off' which appears widespread.

The 1990 Act was passed at a time of change in terms of societal reactions to family structures. This was not only to do with the rising rates of divorce, but marital breakdown and the growth of relationships outside marriage are not irrelevant to the issues considered below in relation to the status of the child. More and more children had found themselves, in the second half of the 20th century, effectively victimised by the attempts of the law to discourage their parents from extra-marital relationships. Much of what is written below will reinforce just how significant marriage remains, and how it can crucially determine notions of parentage and family. Nonetheless, the statute was enacted at a time when law reform agencies had recognised finally the injustice and anomaly inherent in labelling the status of certain children as illegitimate.

These developments had little to do with the emergence of techniques of assisted conception, and more to do with the simple recognition of changing family structures and the futility of seeking to use the law as a mechanism to express disapproval of personal choices about relationships. Nonetheless, the ability to alleviate infertility, though sometimes with dependency on the assistance of other parties as donors and surrogates, emphasised the dated and rigid nature of much within family law. This is not to say that the description of the provisions of the 1990 Act that follows presents a model of consistency and enlightenment. Neither is it always clear, notwithstanding the significance that must inevitably attach to the questions of identity which are raised. Allowing for this, however, one can say that the 1990 Act was an important milestone in recognising and (for the most part) accepting the diversity of family patterns that would follow not only the techno-logical possibility of addressing problems of infertility, but also the changing mood towards seizing such opportunity.

The Act contains four important sections on the status of the various participants in assisted conception procedures: s. 27 deals with mothers; s. 30 with the special position of children born to a surrogate mother; s. 28 deals with fatherhood; and s. 29 states the effect of these provisions.

Mothers

As is stated above, the provisions of the Act override the common law rules to allow the presumption of parenthood in spite of the genetic link. (See *Re B (Parentage)* [1996] 2 FLR 15, for the view that in the absence of statutory intervention, paternity is governed by the genetic link.) The 1990 Act was not the first legislation to do so. The Family Law Reform Act 1987 stated that the husband of a wife giving birth following artificial insemination should be taken to be the father of the child.[3] However, the provisions of the 1990 Act, which repeal those of the 1987 Act, offer a more comprehensive set of measures, not least because they deal with egg and embryo donation. Section 27 provides that a woman who has carried a child as a result of the placing in her of an embryo or sperm and eggs shall be the mother of that child, whatever its genetic make-up. A potential difficulty in the wording of the section is the use of the phrase 'sperm and eggs'. Obviously, in the case only of sperm donation, the patient will remain the mother. Suppose, however, that donated eggs only are implanted so that they can then be fertilised. If we read the section as demanding that both sperm and eggs be placed then its status provisions do not extend in this case, even though IVF generally and GIFT and ZIFT fall squarely within the provision. This would appear to be an oversight, and in consequence common law rules would apply to govern the status of any child.

At this point it may be worth considering the somewhat confused common law. The problem arises through an absence of case law precisely on the point. However, in California, in *Johnson* v *Calvert* 851 P 2d 776 (1993), the legal mother of a child born from the gametes of a couple who involved another woman in a surrogacy arrangement, was said to be the genetic, not the gestational, mother. This was on the basis of the commissioning couple's intention to procreate. However, in so far as one can determine the position under the English common law, it would be principles of consanguinity rather than questions of intention that will determine parentage.[4] Thus, in the situation of egg (only) donation envisaged above, the effect of invoking common law principles would be to deny the intended social mother, and to deny even the recognition of gestational motherhood. The only recourse for the woman bearing the child would be to seek a parental order under s. 30 (below).

The effect of the provisions in s. 27 is significant in the context of surrogacy. Under the Act, the decision in *Johnson* would not apply in the UK; the gestational mother would be recognised as the legal mother. This is in spite of the clear intentions of the parties relating to social motherhood. It seems clear from the background to the legislative provisions that this is deliberate in providing a disincentive towards surrogacy arrangements. It is in the parental order provisions of s. 30 that some allowance is made. Section 30 also introduces a saving where a parental order may be made in respect of gamete donors. In addition, there is a saving in s. 27(2) for adoption. Section 27(3) provides that s. 27 applies whether the woman was within the UK or not when the embryo or sperm and eggs were placed within her (and see s. 49(3) and *Re M (Child Support: Parentage)* [1997] 2 FLR 90).

Saving surrogacy

Section 30 was a late amendment to the Bill. It provides limited circumstances in which a 'parental order' in respect of gamete donors can be sought. Where a woman (a 'surrogate mother') has carried a child on behalf of another couple both of whom were both that child's genetic parents (full surrogacy), or where one of the couple is the child's genetic parent, having donated sperm or an egg, the couple may apply for an order to be treated legally as the child's parents. The section can be used wherever the procedure effecting the surrogacy arrangement was agreed (s. 30(11)). Section 30(2) provides that the application for the 'intending' parents to be treated as the child's lawful parents must be made within six months of the child's birth.[5]

Without this provision, or where the order is not sought in time, there might be a curious disparity between the status of the man and that of the woman. In a situation involving full surrogacy, the genetic mother would appear to have no legal rights whatsoever in her own children. In contrast, her partner, the genetic father, would have the right to apply under the guardianship legislation to have himself recognised as the father of the child (and presumably might then seek some custody of the child).[6] At the very least, therefore, the section accords to genetic mothers some of the rights exercisable by genetic fathers.

Clearly, there are a number of assumptions and controversial arguments which could be joined here, but the principal question is a relatively simple one: should surrogacy arrangements, generally disfavoured by the legislation, be given this apparent encouragement, even in the marginal case? That it is a simple question does not, of course, mean that it admits of a simple answer. Indeed, we would maintain that it is highly complex. But the answer to it, and the route by which we arrive at it, discloses much about our underlying approach to the field of reproductive technology more generally. We do not have space here to rehearse those arguments. Section 30 is itself a formal admission that there are no easy answers to the riddles of reproductive assistance. Almost every case is a hard case.

The s. 30 procedure applies in cases of assisted conception,[7] and where the following conditions are satisfied. Broadly, these require that:

(a) the child's home is with the applicant husband and wife (s. 30(3)(a)) (the section applies only for the benefit of married couples (s. 30(1));
(b) the husband, the wife, or both of them must be domiciled in the United Kingdom, the Channel Islands or the Isle of Man (s. 30(3)(b));
(c) both husband and wife must be at least 18 years old (s. 30(4));
(d) the court must be satisfied that the child's father (where he is not the husband) and the surrogate mother freely agree to the making of the order; that

agreement must be freely and unconditionally given with full understanding of what is involved (s. 30(5)), unless either the father or the surrogate mother cannot be found or is incapable of giving agreement (s. 30(6));

(e)   there is a minimum 'thinking period' for the woman who gave birth to the child; hence, a surrogate mother's agreement is ineffective if given less than six weeks after the birth (s. 30(6));

(f)   the court must be satisfied that no money or other benefit has changed hands in consideration of:

(i)   the making of the parental order,
(ii)   the agreement to relinquish the child to the 'parents',
(iii) the handing over of the child to the applicants,
(iv)   the making of the arrangements prior to the making of the parental order (s. 30(7)).

There are two exceptions to this prohibition: the court may authorise any such payments; and it does not prohibit the payment to the surrogate mother of reasonable expenses.

In *Re Q (Parental Order)* [1996] 2 FCR 345 the courts were required to decide precisely whose consent was required for a parental order. In that case the surrogacy arrangement involved sperm donation to fertilise an egg following treatment at a licensed clinic. The outcome of this treatment was that an unmarried surrogate mother gave birth to a child, but the intending father was neither the husband of the 'surrogate' mother such that the common law presumption of paternity could apply, nor, in the view of the court, was he treated together with his wife for the purposes of s. 28(3) (considered below). In such circumstances there was no man available to fulfil the requirements of s. 30(5), and the intending father's consent to the s. 30 order was not required.

Applications for a s. 30 order can presently be made to the High Court, a county court or a magistrates' court. By virtue of the Parental Orders (Human Fertilisation and Embryology) Regulations 1994 (SI 1994 No. 2767), the provisions of the Adoption Act 1976 apply in terms of the tests to be used in determining applications and the procedures to be followed. Similarly, the 1994 Regulations (rather than the Act) regulate the effects of a parental order under s. 30, generally by applying relevant provisions of the Adoption Act 1976. This means that the child is to be treated as if he or she had been born a child of the marriage, and not as the child of any other person. An exception to this is with regard to prohibited degrees of relationship in relation to marriage and incest as against the genetic relations of the child. In part to allow for this there is a register of parental orders. This is open to inspection, including by the person subject to the order upon attaining the age of 18 years, following the availability of counselling.

It may be necessary to consider the question of what might happen if the s. 30 procedure is not open to a couple for some reason (e.g., they did not have the child living with them in the first six months of its life so that they were in no position to make an application). As is explained above, it may well be that the man could seek to establish that he is the father, and could even seek a declaration to this effect. This might lead to the adoption of the child, since the genetic relationship to the child makes the father a relative and as such there is a much easier route to an adoption order. However, the marital status of both the intending parents and the surrogate mother may be relevant. A joint adoption order can be made only in favour of a married couple (Adoption Act 1976, ss. 15–16). Thus if the intending parents were unmarried, this might prove an obstacle (but equally they would face an obstacle to a parental order under s. 30(1)). However, all is not lost, because it is possible to issue an adoption order to one of the couple (say the man) and a residence order alongside this (see *Re AB (Adoption: Joint Residence)* [1996] 1 FLR 27).

The marital status of the surrogate mother is rather more problematic. If she is married then the putative father will be her husband, complicating any application for adoption by a 'genetic' father. In an early surrogacy case, and in advance of the Children Act 1989, the surrogate mother left the child in hospital to be collected by the intending parents who successfully applied for care and control under the inherent jurisdiction of the High Court (*Re C (A Minor) (Wardship: Surrogacy)* [1985] FLR 846). In the case of a married surrogate mother, however, although it may be possible to adopt the child, ordinarily the couple will need to have had the child living with them for at least 12 months. But where a surrogate mother places the child with the commissioning couple, and there is to be no s. 30 order, placement for adoption should be with the approval of the court, at least where there is no familial relationship between surrogate mother and either of the intending parents. It is possible for the court to sanction a placement retroactively (*Re G (Adoption: Illegal Placement)* [1995] 1 FLR 403), but beginning from a position in which the rules on placements have been broken is not ideal. It follows that it makes sense for intending parents to take advantage of the s. 30 parental order procedure when and where they can do so.

Fathers

Section 28 defines 'father' for the purposes of the Act. It is a complex and difficult provision, but one of great significance creating, as it did, a new class of child, the (legally) 'fatherless child'.[8] Section 28 proceeds by providing a saving in certain circumstances for any child treated as the legitimate child of the parties to a marriage or of any person, whether by virtue of statute or common law. So, where a woman is married, s. 28(2) provides that if she becomes pregnant following embryo transfer, or GIFT or similar procedure, or following artificial insemination, her husband is to be treated as the father of any resulting child. However, if he can show that he did not consent to the treatment service, he is not to be treated as father under s. 28(2), although he will remain the child's presumed father by virtue of s. 28(5). This saves the common law presumption of paternity that a child is the child of a marriage, unless the husband shows otherwise. It will also deal with the husband who changes his mind about accepting his wife's child as his own.

Section 28(2) provides that the lack of consent must be shown to have been at the time of the treatment of his wife, and not at some later time. Thus, a man who has not consented to his wife's treatment (and there is no requirement in the Act that it be sought, although it is almost invariable practice) may later accept that the child is his. As s. 28(2) is drafted, his lack of consent at the time of treatment would have been enough for him later to disown the child. The common law presumption will operate to secure the continuing link between the child and its presumed father. The man could, if he so wished, then seek to rebut the common law presumption. Presumptions of paternity can be rebutted applying a balance of probabilities test to the evidence presented. This would ordinarily be done by way of blood tests, or any other method of DNA testing. The scheme of s. 28(2) extends that introduced by the Family Law Reform Act 1987, s. 27 for artificial insemination to the other treatments here discussed, and, by saving the common law presumption, refines the earlier provision, which had made the question of the husband's consent conclusive as to paternity. In *Re CH (Contact: Parentage)* [1996] 1 FCR 768 a married couple had a child following assisted conception using donor sperm. After the child was born the couple separated and the mother sought to deny access to the child on the basis that her ex-husband had no genetic link to the child. Unsurprisingly, the court ruled that the man having consented to the assisted conception was the father under the Act, and should not be barred from contact with the child in the absence of some pressing reason against such contact.

Section 28(3) applies in a similar way to an unmarried woman who seeks infertility treatment together with a man who is not the sperm donor. Note that where the man is the sperm donor, the ordinary common law presumptions of paternity would apply. A man seeking treatment together with the unmarried woman, and no other person, is to be treated as the father of the child subject to the s. 28(5) presumptions. There was disquiet and confusion throughout the Parliamentary debates about access to treatment of what are sometimes called 'unconventional' families, despite evidence that the 'conventional' family of the advertisements of the 1940s and 1950s has disappeared. Section 13(5) provides that before a woman is provided with treatment services regard is to be paid to the welfare of the child, including the need of that child for a father. This is an odd provision (discussed in greater detail at p. 159) for, *ex hypothesi*, the child has a father. The section is not making special provision for parthenogenesis. What the section means to provide for, of course, is that the woman seeking treatment should have a male partner. That is rather different. Given this, it is extraordinary that, as we shall see, s. 28 goes on to create categories of 'legally fatherless' children and to prevent some children from ever discovering their genetic origins. However, the policy behind the legislation is actively to discourage treatment for those infertile people who live outside the umbrella of the nuclear family. This was made clear in one contribution to the debate by the then Lord Chancellor, Lord Mackay:

> . . . if it is to remain possible for unmarried couples to receive the benefit of treatment to bring a child into being, both should have imposed upon them the responsibility for the child. I was most concerned that this proposal [to amend the Bill] should not be seen as encouraging unmarried people to use infertility treatments thus undermining marriage or leading to children having unsuitable fathers because of the difficulty in distinguishing partners to stable relationships from more transitory ones.[9]

Where a married woman seeks treatment services together with a man other than her husband, her husband will nonetheless be treated as, or be presumed to be, the father, unless he can defeat both the statutory provision and the common law presumption. This indicates also the woolly nature of the concept of treatment 'together', for it seems (probably correctly) that the woman cannot be seeking treatment together with a man simply because they attend the clinic together. Kennedy and Grubb suggest that what is important here is their joint intention to bring up a child together.[10] In *Re B (Parentage)* [1996] FLR 15 Bracewell J expressed the view that simply living with the mother at the time that she receives the treatment was not likely to fulfil this formulation (*cf. Re Q* (above) which suggested that the man ought also to be receiving treatment), although providing sperm and attending the treatment centre probably would. *Re B* makes it clear that whether or not persons seek treatment together is a matter of fact for the courts to decide. In *R v HFEA, ex parte Blood* [1997] 2 All ER 687, the approach taken in *Re B* was largely endorsed, and it was said that the use of sperm taken from the husband while he was in a coma did not amount to 'treatment together'.

Because of the unique provisions of s. 28(3), problems may arise in relation to treatment outside the jurisdiction, as they did in *U v W* [1997] 2 FLR 282. In that case a woman (U) and a man (W) sought treatment in Rome, having previously received infertility treatment in the UK. Following this treatment, U became pregnant and became the genetic and gestational mother of twins, neither of whom was genetically related to W. However, by this time U and W, who had never been married, had parted. U brought an application under s. 27 of the Child Support Act 1991 for a declaration that W was the father of her twins. W had signed a form at the clinic in Rome acknowledging paternity of any resulting children, and U and W had attended the clinic together.

In giving judgment, Wilson J concluded that s. 28(3) applied in practice only in the UK since it referred to treatment in a clinic licensed by the HFEA. Although the section did nothing to prevent couples seeking infertility treatment outside the UK, the effect of its provisions was that the extension of paternity to the man seeking treatment by donated sperm would not apply where that treatment took place outside the jurisdiction. In so far as this might apply to other jurisdictions within the European Union, this might be seen as a restriction on the freedom to provide infertility services, since the withholding of paternity would be likely to deter couples from seeking access to infertility treatment services in other member states. However, in the view of the court, such a restriction could be capable of objective justification under principles of Community Law.

All of these justifications lay in the legislative framework in the UK. It may have assisted the court that, in comparison, infertility services in Italy had no statutory regulation. This allowed Wilson J to point to the requirements of the Act and the Code on matters such as information, written consent and acknowledgement of paternity, and record-keeping. In relation to the last, Wilson J read from the speeches of Lord Mackay in the House of Lords to the effect that:

> . . . the unsupervised use of artificial insemination techniques outside the statutory scheme, including treatment outside the jurisdiction of the United Kingdom, will not be covered by the new provisions. Without the regulation provided by the Bill, it would be extremely difficult to be certain about who is the mother's partner and who is to be treated . . . as the father.[11]

For all of these reasons, in so far as the refusal of acknowledgement of paternity amounted to a restriction of Art. 59 (now 49) of the European Union Treaty, it lay within the margin of discretion allowed to member states and was proportionate.

One final argument concerned whether the provisions of s. 28(3) contravened the principles laid down in Art. 8 of the European Convention on Human Rights. This was on the basis that the twin boys had been denied W as a father. However, the court expressed the view that the background facts did little to establish any element of family life or relationship. Whether this might mean that in other circumstances Art. 8 might apply remains to be seen. The status of the twins is not fully considered in *U* v *W*. Presumably, however, they were not legally fatherless but had an unknown father, somewhere in Italy perhaps. This does not resolve the problem of how the creation of children who are at the outset legally fatherless squares with the provisions of the Convention. Lastly, it is difficult to assess in this case the significance of the lack of any regulation of assisted conception in Italy. It may not have been so easy to produce the justifications used if treatment services had been obtained in another member state with a regulatory system equivalent to that of the UK.

Where a man is by virtue of s. 28(2) or s. 28(3) treated as a child's father, s. 28(4) provides that no other man is to be so regarded. Also, in this case, the unmarried man seems to be unable to disclaim paternity in a way that a married man might do. It might be open to him to show a lack of consent, but then the difficulty would be the consent form in the clinic, assuming the centre has met its obligations under the Code. Section 28(6)(a) provides that where a donor's gametes are used in accordance with the consents required under sch. 3, para. 5, the donor is not to be treated as the father of the child. An attempt to ensure that the birth certificate of a child born following treatment services should have this fact endorsed upon it was defeated in the House of Commons during the passage of the Bill.

Section 28(6) is intended to provide 'protection' to a donor whose sperm is used in accordance with his consent to establish a pregnancy to which a married woman's husband has not consented. Two conclusions seem to follow. First, that a child born in such circumstances will be one of the new legally 'fatherless children'. Secondly, where sperm is used without the effective consents given under sch. 3, para. 5, a donor may not be protected by s. 28(6)(a), and may indeed be treated as the father of a child produced without his consent. This produces, intentionally or otherwise, a disincentive to assisting single women with DIY treatment through sperm donation, given the increasingly tough child support provisions. It has also been suggested that because of the provisions of s. 13(5) and the requirement of the clinic to consider the need of the child for a father, married women will be denied access to treatment services without their husbands' consent, since if those husbands disproved paternity then the child would be left legally fatherless.[12]

It may occur to readers that the above provisions create some confusion in that the answer to status questions may depend upon birth dates. Thus, for a child born in England and Wales on or after 4 April 1988 up to (and including) 31 July 1991 as a result of artificial insemination, a man will be treated as the legal father if married to the mother of the child. It is open, however, to the man to show that he never gave consent to the procedure. This is the effect of the (now repealed) provisions of s. 27 of the Family Law Reform Act 1987.

Prior to this provision, i.e. for a child born before 4 April 1988, paternity depends on genetic links, so that the sperm donor will be the father of the child. However, it is likely that the donor will be unknown, and the presumption of paternity will mean that the husband of a child of a marriage will be assumed to be the father. Otherwise it would have been necessary to use an adoption order to secure status as the father.

Where a child was born on or after 1 August 1991 then, by virtue of s. 28(2) of the Act, the husband of a married woman will be treated as the father subject to his proving the absence of consent, or, in the case of an unmarried couple, the man will be considered the father where he sought licensed infertility treatment together with his partner.

One final date that might prove significant in the case of a surrogacy arrangement is 1 November 1994, when the parental order procedure under s. 30 took effect. After this date the procedure would be available to establish parentage as outlined above. In fact 30 April 1995 may have been a date of more practical importance for certain commissioning couples where births took place prior to the coming into force of the 1990 Act, as a result of a surrogacy arrangement. Such persons would have had until 30 April 1995 to make an application for a parental order.

Posthumous children

The second category of legally 'fatherless child' is created by s. 28(6)(b). This provides that where an embryo is created with a man's sperm following his death, or where a woman is allowed access to frozen sperm (whether for the purposes of artificial insemination or for a procedure such as GIFT) after a man's death then he is 'not [posthumously] to be treated as the father of the [resulting] child'. This will be the case whether the woman becoming pregnant is using her deceased husband's frozen sperm in accordance with his express consent given under sch. 3, para. 2(2)(b), or that of an unknown donor. The *Blood* case also raises the possibility of using the sperm of the dead husband even though there was no express consent, though the Master of the Rolls in that case was insistent that this was an isolated event that ought not to be repeated. Famously in that case, the HFEA found itself subject to judicial review when, in line with the Act, it declined to allow treatment to proceed in the UK, or to make directions that would have allowed treatment outside the UK (see the discussion of this case in Chapter 7). Given that death ends the marriage, the child in such situations will be born not only legally fatherless, but also illegitimate, unless the woman has remarried prior to the insemination, in which case s. 28(5) and (2) will operate, as above, to treat the new husband as the child's father.

This provision is inserted, as the Warnock Report recommended, to ensure that estates can be administered with some degree of finality (see Warnock Report, paras 10.9 and 10.15) and to give effect to Warnock's expressed desire that fertilisation of a woman following the death of her partner (or husband, as Warnock would have limited it) 'should be actively discouraged'. This was recommended by the Committee because it might give rise to profound psychological problems for the child and the mother (para. 4.4). They did recommend, however, that where one of a couple who has stored an embryo dies, the right to use or dispose of that embryo should pass to the survivor. Whether that is to be the case will depend on the consent given under sch. 3, para. 2(2)(b) and whether the surviving spouse is seen to have a right to demand treatment with the stored sperm.

There is one case in which the section as drafted renders the position complex. This is where an embryo created legitimately becomes illegitimate on its use following its genetic father's death. Where during a man's lifetime his sperm is used to create an embryo which is then frozen, the embryo is clearly then the legitimate offspring of the marriage. He subsequently dies, and his widow later uses the frozen embryo to establish a pregnancy. The created embryo is 'used after his death' within s. 28(6)(b) and is legally fatherless and illegitimate. This assumes, of course, that the woman has not remarried, for the s. 28 presumptions would then apply so that the husband of her remarriage would again be treated as the father of the child.

The widespread apparent sympathy for Diane Blood, both in the courts and amongst the general public, led to the McLean review of the Warnock policy of actively discouraging post-mortem insemination remains to be seen. Nonetheless, the policy behind these sections is clearly to discourage posthumous pregnancies. But the instrument which is used is that of punishing the child for what are seen as 'the sins of its mother'. This was an odd, not to say indefensible, way of proceeding. First, it seems inconsistent with the general legislative mood of recent years which has sought to minimise or mitigate the differential statuses of children (and the adults they will become) based solely on the conduct of their parents (e.g., Family Law Reform Act 1987, s. 1). Indeed, it offends against the judgment of the European Court of Human Rights in *Johnston* v *Ireland* (1987) 9 ECHR 203, which condemned such distinctions between children. Secondly, it seems to fly in the face of the approach taken under legislation such as the Surrogacy Arrangements Act 1985. The specific reason why the surrogate and the intending parents were exempted from the criminal provisions of that Act was to give effect to Warnock's anxiety to 'avoid children being born to mothers subject to the taint of criminality' (para. 8.19). It seems unfortunate, to say the least, that that philosophy did not inform the drafting of these important status provisions.

In relation to the post-mortem inseminations of s. 28(6)(b), clearly, the 'legitimacy' and paternity of the child are not protected by the common law presumptions which are specifically saved by s. 28(5). The effect of those rules of common law is: (i) a child conceived before marriage but born after her father's death would be presumed to be and be treated as legitimate; (ii) a child born to a married woman during the subsistence of her marriage is presumed also to be the child of her husband – this presumption is given a very wide scope and can be shifted only by discharging a heavy burden of rebuttal; it arises even though the child must have been conceived before marriage, because in marriage the man is prima facie taken to have acknowledged the child as his own. To rebut the presumption, it must either be shown that blood tests establish no genetic link, or that no sexual intercourse took place between the spouses during the possible time when the child must have been conceived, which can be achieved by showing that: (i) sexual intercourse was impossible because the parties were physically absent from one another – which presumably includes the fact that one of them was dead – or that at least one of them was impotent; or (ii) that the circumstances were such as to render it highly improbable that sexual intercourse took place.

The litigation which these grounds, and especially the second, have spawned need not detain us here. In the case of a man who has died, the death terminates the marriage and reliance on the common law presumption will be insufficient to 'save' the paternity and the legitimacy of the child of the marriage. However, the possibility arises that s. 1(1) of the Legitimacy Act 1976 (as amended by the Family Law Reform Act 1987, s. 28(1)), which creates a form of statutory legitimacy, might apply. Section 1(1), which is derived from s. 2 of the Legitimacy Act 1959, applies to the children of a void marriage. (Section 28(7)(b) of the 1990 Act 'saves' void marriages if one of the parties reasonably believed that the marriage was valid.) It provides for the legitimacy of the child of a void marriage if at the time of insemination resulting in the birth, or at the time of the child's conception, or at the time of the celebration of the marriage if later, both or either of the partners reasonably believed that the marriage was valid. The debates on the Family Law Reform Act 1987 made it clear that for the purposes of conception *in vitro*, conception takes place when the ovum is fertilised and not when the resulting zygote or embryo is replaced in the uterus.[13] As the leading commentator Bevan observed, this raises the possibility that if at the time of *in vitro* fertilisation, both or either of the parties reasonably believe that the marriage is valid, but the fertilised egg is then frozen and later inserted into the woman, even some years later (perhaps after the man has died), the child would be legitimate.[14]

If this is correct in respect of void marriages, and s. 28(7)(b) and sch. 3 give no indication that that provision is to be repealed or amended in any way, it appears to place the child born posthumously following conception during a void marriage in a better position than one of a marriage where all the formalities had properly been attended to. While the courts might not look favourably upon such an argument, it means generally that children of marriages declared void are consistently advantaged in the legitimacy stakes as against children of the post-mortem births which we have described.

Under s. 28(2), the husband of the marriage will not be treated as father at all (subject to s. 28(5)) if he can show that he did not consent to the infertility treatment. However, in the case of a void marriage not 'saved' by s. 28(7)(b), arguably the Legitimacy Act 1976 provisions prevail. In such a case, the provisions of the 1976 Act would mean that it would avail the man nothing to plead an absence of consent, for the legitimacy of the child would be preserved.

Returning to post-mortem births, the presumption under s. 28(5) applies where the child is born within the possible period of gestation after the marriage has been terminated by the husband's death. (For the modern authorities, see *Re Leman's Will Trusts* (1945) 115 LJ Ch 89 and *Knowles v Knowles* [1962] P 161; although Cohen J in *Re Heath, Stacey v Baird* [1945] Ch 417 declined to decide definitely whether the presumption applied to the posthumous child.) This might raise the distasteful possibility of the bereaved woman seeking the thawing and implantation of the frozen embryo at the earliest opportunity after her deceased husband's death, in order to save the legitimacy and parentage of the child under the common law presumption. However, the statutory language militates against this course of action. The language of s. 28(6) is too unambiguous to allow the common law presumption to arise. Unlike s. 28(2), s. 28(6) is not made subject to the common law presumption, as it was in the first draft of the Bill published in November 1989.

But suppose that, if the man and woman were not married, while the man was still alive and the embryos were frozen he declared himself as father of the child, and the woman later applied to register the parentage under the Family Law Reform Act. Section 22 of the Family Law Reform Act 1987 (substituting s. 56,

Family Law Act 1986) enables a county court or the High Court to grant declarations of parentage, legitimacy or legitimation, though at the instance of the child only. Difficult questions arise as to whether a child born posthumously could use this section for a declaration of parentage. Section 28(6) seems to preclude this, although there must be some doubt about the meaning of 'not to be treated' in that section. Where the embryo was brought about before his death, the man is not being *treated as* the child's father, because he *was* the child's father at conception, and is now her *deceased* father. It might be argued that no question of 'treating' him as such arises.

As we have seen, however, the policy of the Act is that the genetic father is not necessarily to be taken as the father. A parallel question arises under s. 24 of the Family Law Reform Act 1987, which substitutes a new s. 10 in the Births and Deaths Registration Act 1953. This provides that an unmarried father can obtain registration of his name as the father on the child's birth certificate at the joint request of the mother and himself; at the request of the mother and on production of declarations by her and him to the effect that he is the father; at his own request and on production of similar declarations; or at the written request either of himself or the mother and on production of a parental rights order made under various provisions. The entry of a man's name in the register as the father of a child is prima facie evidence that he is the father (s. 34, Births and Deaths Registration Act 1953). Could the father make the request and produce the declaration before his death and the child's birth, or must the evidence supporting the acquisition of the declaration necessary to found the mother's request for registration be adduced only after the child's birth?[15]

These questions are vital since they surround the possible creation of a new category of child: those *prohibited by law* from establishing their paternity. The late addition of what is now s. 31(5) manufactures a similar difficulty for children born following anonymous donation; short of primary legislation they too are hostages to the 'reproduction revolution'. One lesson is clear from this benighted policy and complex mesh of statute and common law. Any married couple contemplating the freezing of the gametes before the man undergoes major surgery with a risk of death (which risk occurs in almost any operative procedure under general anaesthetic), or treatment which may render him sterile, such as chemo-therapy, and where there is in any case a real risk of early death, must be advised that if they wish to have any possibility of circumventing these rules on posthumously conceived children they must have fertilised ova – embryos – frozen, and not just their unmixed gametes. Statutory legitimacy might just apply to save the former, but could not operate on the latter.

GENERAL PROVISIONS

Section 28(8) applies the provisions of the section wherever the treatments took place. For example, if an English couple domiciled in the UK live abroad for a while, where they obtain infertility treatment and later return to the UK, where the child is born, by virtue of s. 27(1) and s. 28(2) they are treated as that child's parents. In the absence of the section, the donor of sperm would have been the child's father. In more than one sense, the Act gives us the opportunity to determine what sort of children we want.

Section 29 provides that the legal effect of ss. 27 and 28 is to apply for all purposes, such as incest and prohibited degrees of marriage (s. 29(1), (2)), except succession to and transmission of succession rights to dignities or titles of honour (s. 29(4) and (5)). The effect of s. 29(1) and (2) in respect of inheritance is that children born following assisted conception will take under a will, a trust or deed as would a blood relative. A donor child whom, for example, the testator (maybe long ago) could not have had in contemplation and of whose existence she or he may have even disapproved, will take, perhaps to the exclusion of others. But that is much how life is. Trusts or deeds made after the coming into force of the Act can be framed so as to give effect to a contrary intention and exclude donor children. If the testator is still alive, they can be redrawn at any time to take account of children born as a result of infertility treatment. But where the testator is dead, there is no chance to vary the trust. It will remain open to any person to demonstrate that the terms of a past will, trust or deed show a contrary intention to s. 29(3), so as to exclude children born following treatment services.

Section 29(4) and (5) reintroduce provisions which took up a great deal of time and emotional energy in the House of Lords' debates. They represent a major derogation from the scheme of the provisions which we have just been considering. When the Bill passed to the Commons, the clauses (as they then were) were thrown out almost peremptorily: 'I heard on the radio the debates in another place about the inheritance of clan chieftainships and titles. I could not believe that such a debate was taking place in the late twentieth century.'[16] It was always clear, however, that this could provoke a major clash between the two Houses, and when Government ministers and business managers were working hard to get the Act passed before the summer recess in 1990, this was one of the hostages which the Lords were able to liberate. Accordingly, these provisions were reinserted in the Bill in an attempt to ensure that it reached the statute book in July 1990.

The effect of s. 29(4) and (5) is that succession in England, Wales and Northern Ireland to any dignity or title of honour and property limited to devolve with it will remain with the blood line only. In other words, donor children will not be able to succeed to such titles and property as though they were children conceived 'in the usual manner'. The law of arms, with which we are here concerned, comes under the jurisdiction of the High Court of Chivalry, a civilian court, which last sat in 1954 (see *Manchester Corporation* v *The Manchester Palace of Varieties* [1955] P 133). There was much discussion in the House of Lords' debates on the present legislation of whether a coat of arms is included within a dignity or title of honour (and hence was not a property right), which are matters of common law. Earlier statutes referring to dignities, such as the Adoption and Legitimacy Acts of 1976 and the Family Law Reform Act 1987, have adopted the wording preferred here, relying on the *dictum* of Lord Goddard (sitting as the surrogate for the Earl Marshal) in the *Manchester Corporation* case, that a coat of arms was so protected. But as Lord Mackay confessed, this is a point 'not free from difficulty'.[17] The College of Arms and the Lord Lyon King of Arms are already charged with the problems of succession in disputed parentage cases, including ones in which assisted conception is alleged. The Act does not affect that present position.

The law of arms in Scotland is quite different, with the Scots law of peerages, dignities and offices having its own difficulties and niceties. In that jurisdiction, it is taken as settled that a title, honour or dignity does not include a coat of arms

(Succession (Scotland) Act 1964, s. 37(1)). A separate Scottish provision had originally been included in the Bill only on amendment, when it was disclosed that the original draft, of November 1989, had not taken account of these differences. Of particular concern to the Scottish peers and peeresses was that, as drafted, the Bill appeared to be separating clan chieftainships and hereditary offices from associated peerages, dignities or other titles. The reason for this concern is that such 'hereditary offices' are viewed as incorporeal heritable property like land, rather than as a title or dignity, and are often closely linked to the landed estate which is granted with them and with which they descend. The rights to these offices can be and are recorded in the General Register of Sasines or Land Register of Scotland.

In Scotland, there are five heritable offices (England has only two) and each is associated with a specific peerage carrying with it associated lands. The offices are those of the Lord High Constable (attached to the Earl of Errol); Hereditary Banner Bearer (the Earl of Dundee); Hereditary Bearer of St Andrew's Flag (the Earl of Lauderdale); Hereditary Master of the Household (the Duke of Argyll); and Hereditary Keeper of the Palace of Holyrood House (the Duke of Hamilton). The effect of s. 29(4) and (5) is that these nobles can once again rest peacefully in their beds, thanks to the efforts of Lady Saltoun of Abernathy, a Scottish chief and member of the Standing Council of Scottish Chiefs.[18]

Sections 27–29 apply only to births occurring after the coming into force of the sections on 1 November 1994. Section 27 of the Family Law Reform Act 1987, which dealt with questions of status of children born following AID only, ceased to have effect after the commencement of those sections.

ACCESS TO INFORMATION

In *Gaskin* v *United Kingdom* [1990] 1 FLR 167, the European Court of Human Rights held that Art. 8 of the European Convention on Human Rights, demanding respect for the private life of an individual, requires that 'everyone should be able to establish details of their identity as individual human beings'. This judgment was relied upon in debate as the source of a right to receive information about the genetic and personal identity of donors whose gametes were used in the provision of treatment services. As we shall see, whether these provisions amount to knowing one's identity in the sense used in *Gaskin* is open to doubt.

In respect of treatment licences, s. 13 of the 1990 Act provides that by directions issued under s. 23 or s. 24, the Authority may direct licence holders to record information about the recipients of treatment, the services provided, the identity of gamete donors and of any child apparently born following treatment services. A gamete donor may be paid for his or her donation in accordance with directions made by the HFEA (s. 12(e)). We deal with the payment debate in Chapter 5, but it may be worth recording here that work by Lui *et al.*[19] found that the vast majority of donors (96 per cent) said that they felt sorry for the infertile couple, and over two-thirds of donors (69 per cent) said that payment was irrelevant to their intention to assist.

If the licensee does not know whether a child has been born following treatment, all this information must be stored for at least 50 years (s. 24(1)). Section 31 requires the Authority to keep a register of information acquired from licensed centres, and s. 31(3) gives an applicant aged over 18 the power to obtain specified and limited information. Information to be kept on the register includes that showing that an identifiable individual may have been born following treatment services, as defined. Thus where an applicant seeking information has been given a 'suitable' opportunity for counselling, the Authority must comply with the request.

Information concerning gametes donation could identify the donor or could be restricted to non-identifying information. Section 31(5) allows that regulations could spell out the type of non-identifying information to be given – presumably about matters of ethnic origin and genetic health.[20] However, ten years on, precisely what form that information will take is not known since no regulations have been forthcoming. It is clear that only non-identifying information is likely to be disclosed, and that the position will be kept under review. A late safeguard was written into the Act by s. 31(5). That provides that the HFEA cannot be required to give information about the *identity* of a donor if acquired by a licence holder at any time when the HFEA could not have been required to give the information. One consequence of this is that even if regulations are introduced allowing the disclosure of some identifying information, children already born through assisted conception will not benefit. These provisions could be repealed, but the section was inserted to ensure that a full Parliamentary debate and primary legislation would be necessary to achieve that result.

There are four positions with regard to releasing information: (i) that no identifying information be provided; (ii) that identification may be made with the consent of the donor; and (iii) that all identifying information be given. A fourth possibility, that adopted by the Act, is that some non-identifying information should be provided. An amendment proposed during the Report stage of the House of Commons, to add to s. 13(2)(c) that the HFEA should require information to be stored about the physical characteristics, family background, education, skills and interests and the health history of donors, was defeated. Regulations will need to provide for an applicant requiring the Authority to disclose if she or he is genetically related to a person whom he or she proposes to marry. A minor who intends to marry (i.e. someone between the ages of 16 and 18) may acquire similar information about his or her intended partner, but not the more widely ranging information that may be available from the age of 18.

Maclean and Maclean[21] have reviewed the evidence base for suggestions that donor anonymity is crucial in maintaining an adequate level of gamete donations. A survey by Schover et al.[22] suggests that 69 per cent of donors would not donate without some assurance of anonymity. Lui et al.[23] found that 87 per cent had no wish to meet the resulting children, though 82 per cent were happy to provide non-identifying information about themselves. This suggests a hardening of attitudes since a limited survey conducted at the King's College Hospital Unit in London.[24] This revealed that only one-third of donors there were opposed to identification, while the other two-thirds were in favour or reserved their position. However, it should be noted that there was some decline in donations once the 1990 Act came into force. This might be the result of more careful regulation and better health checking.

At the time of the Act, the British Association of Adoption and Fostering, the British Association of Social Workers, the Association of Directors of Social

Services and the British Infertility Counselling Association were all in favour of moving away from anonymity and towards counselling. Counsellors working with infertile couples receiving treatment have found that a lack of information about the donors is frequently the cause of much disquiet and distress. Moreover, studies in 1993 and 1994 found that more than 70 per cent of couples do not inform the children of their genetic origins.[25] Both the HFEA and the Government are in favour of greater openness so that parents share more openly with their children information concerning such origins, yet it is difficult to maintain this position while little information is actually available. In Sweden, the Act on Artificial Information of 1985 allows identifying information to be kept for up to 70 years and disclosed to applicants when they are sufficiently mature.

It is of interest to observe here that the Glover Report[26] concluded that there should be a presumption that children born through semen donation should have access to knowledge of the identity of their biological fathers when they reach adulthood. Because of worries about a resulting reduction in the supply of donors, the Report advocated a trial period of experiment following Swedish law.[27] The Swedish experience is illuminating, because there are many forceful opponents of anonymity who argue for the child's (or later adult's) right to know of his or her genetic heritage. Following the abolition of anonymity in Sweden, there was an initial decline not only in donors, but also in couples seeking AID and physicians prepared to continue AID practice under the new decree. Since then, in centres continuing to offer assistance (before the law was introduced there were 12; now there are nine, with others starting up continuously), the numbers of donors have returned to their previous levels, although with two marked changes. The donors now tend to be older men, and also more often to be married men.[28] The general experience, shared even by those who were most forceful in their opposition to the law, is that it has been and is working most successfully, and that the similarity to the experience with adopted children seeking to discover their genetic identity is so strong that the denial of that interest to children of reproductive technology would be mistaken.[29]

The decision of what to tell the children born of assisted conception has long stood as one of the most problematic aspects of technological creation. The balance between preserving the identity of the donor and fracturing the identity of the resulting child has produced one of the deepest of philosophical and pragmatic tensions. With artificial insemination and gamete donation there arises not just the possibility of anonymity for the donor, but of secrecy surrounding the circumstances of the person's conception. In a parallel case, adoption, the law in England and Wales has moved towards that in Scotland where, since the inception of adoption regulation in 1930, adoptees have had access to their original birth certificates from the age of 17. Section 26 of the Children Act 1975 introduced the entitlement of a person of the age of 18 to a copy of his or her original birth certificate (see now Adoption Act 1976, s. 51; but see also *R* v *Registrar General, ex parte Smith* [1991] 2 QB 393). In 1992, a review of adoption supported both pre- and post-adoption openness in relation to contact between the birth parents and adopting parents as in the interests of the child. However, this is in a climate in which the shortage of babies for adoption has generally led to older children being placed for adoption. To that extent the comparison between children whose family ties depend upon adoption and those whose ties depend upon assisted conception is of limited value. The principle may remain the same, though, and openness must be worth pursuing.

Having said that, Katherine O'Donovan has argued[30] that the need to know one's genetic ancestry is socially induced, and that we should concentrate on changing society's attitude to the importance of the blood relationship rather than undermining the protection presently given to anonymous gamete donors. She has further questioned the notion of a 'search for identity' said to characterise people who have been adopted; the empirical evidence is lacking which would substantiate the claim that there is an overwhelming urge on the part of adoptees to seek out their genitors.[31] In reply, Don Evans has questioned whether the need of the infertile person or couple, and the accompanying demands for secrecy expressed by many, should require the deployment of medicine at the price of denying another need, that of any resulting child to know its genetic parents. And of the 'constructed' need to know one's genetic parentage, he has argued that the 'needs' of the infertile, for treatment or for secrecy, may themselves be thought of as socially constructed. If the importance of socially induced needs for the provision of medical treatment are to be denied, he writes, then we shall have to deny treatments for longevity, physical grace and beauty and the avoidance of, or palliation of, pain.[32]

The Act makes limited provision for rights of access to genetic information for those born of assisted conception, or for those who think they may have been. Section 31 provides that the HFEA shall maintain a register of information supplied to it by clinics providing treatment services within the Act. On attaining the age of 18 an applicant may require the HFEA to furnish certain information. If the HFEA's information shows that the applicant was or may have been born following assisted conception, and the applicant has been given the opportunity to receive suitable counselling about the implications of receiving the information, the Authority is placed under a duty to furnish it. This information will not enable the applicant to identify any gamete or embryo donor involved, i.e. the applicant will not be able to trace her or his genetic parent unless he or she has already been told of his or her identity. The Act in making provision for an extraordinary case may require reconsideration. An applicant may require the HFEA to disclose if she or he is genetically related to a person whom he or she proposes to marry. It is submitted that at least this provision should be amended, such that it is only on the application of both intending marriage partners that the HFEA will be able to disclose if the joint applicants are genetically related.

Section 31 makes provision for a register of information relating to the provision of treatment services, the keeping or use of gametes or embryos and births resulting from treatment services. There are then a number of procedures (outlined above) allowing access to that information. Section 33 then limits the disclosure of both registered information under s. 31 and also of any other information obtained in confidence by the HFEA and its staff. This was achieved by a strict prima facie rule against disclosure by HFEA members and employees of such information, albeit with exemptions from the rule such as that allowing for disclosure to another member, or to the Registrar General or to a court which, by virtue of s. 32 or 34 of the Act, may demand the assistance of the HFEA in determining paternity claims. Note in the last case that the court can only do so on an application by a party to the proceedings, where the court then determines that it is in the interests of justice to do so having taken into account representations of other parties and issues concerning the welfare of the child.

At a very early stage following the passage of the Act, it was said that the wording of the limitations was too harsh, not only restricting the work of clinicians but also exposing them to criminal liability.[33] At this point we sought to argue that these fears were largely unfounded.[34] There is not a great deal of point revisiting these arguments now, as amending legislation was secured in the light of the views expressed by other commentators and the HFEA itself.[35] The legislation, the Human Fertilisation and Embryology (Disclosure of Information) Act 1992, redefines the circumstances in which information can be disclosed and, to avoid problems in the future of needing to secure primary legislation, creates enabling powers to extend possible disclosure by regulation (see now s. 33(6G) of the Act).

Registered information may also be disclosed (s. 33(3)):

(a) to members and staff of the HFEA, acting as such;
(b) to licence holders where necessary to discharge relevant functions;
(c) to the Registrar General;
(d) for statistical or other purposes where no individual can be identified;
(e) as allowed for in s. 31 (above);
(f) on the order of a court, in favour of a child seeking to bring an action under the Congenital Disabilities (Civil Liability) Act 1976, or a child in Scotland seeking to pursue an action for damages consisting of or including damages or soliatum for personal injury;
(g) on the order of a court (usually *in camera*) in the interests of justice during any proceedings before that court. This will accommodate orders such as those which may be made, for example, on an application for a maintenance order for a child where paternity is disputed.

In both cases, (f) and (g), the court is enjoined strictly in the way it must determine whether or not to make the orders requested (see above).

Non-registered information of a nonetheless confidential nature may be disclosed (s. 33(4)):

(a) to members and staff of the HFEA, acting as such;
(b) with the consent of the person whose confidence would otherwise be protected;
(c) where lawful public disclosure has previously been made.

In the last category, it is possible to argue that the information has already lost the necessary quality of confidence anyway.

Existing and previous licence holders are also bound by non-disclosure rules similar to those under s. 33(1). It is this body of restrictions that the 1992 Act relaxed by the extension of exceptions already written into the 1990 Act. Three additions to the list are added in s. 33(6). As originally drafted this mirrored the exceptions in s. 33(3), with the additional requirement only that such licences can be required to disclose if directed to do so under s. 24(5) or (6) (see s. 33(6)(e)). The three further exceptions now allow that:

(a)   doctors can reveal otherwise confidential information when defending themselves in proceedings (including formal complaints – see s. 33(9) as added by s. 1(4) of the 1992 Act), but subject to maintaining the confidentiality of the donor of gametes (see s. 33(6A));[36]

(b)   disclosure may be made where the information provided is to support an application for a parental order under s. 30 of the 1990 Act;

(c)   disclosure may be made to support an application for information where there is a right of access to health records, generally by someone other than the patient (e.g., a relative of a deceased patient) since the patient would already have rights of access under s. 33(7).

The last of these amendments came about because the Access to Health Records Act was passed alongside and at the same time as the 1990 Act, and insufficient attention was given as to how the two relate to each other. In general, the Access to Health Records Act could not apply to the HFEA, but could apply to treatment centres.[37] However, this in turn was subject to an amendment in the Access to Health Records (Control of Access) Regulations (SI 1993 No. 746), in order to prevent disclosure of an identifiable individual who was, or may have been, born as a result of the provision of treatment services (see reg. 2).

Other new provisions introduced by the 1992 Act allow disclosure with the consent of the patient(s). This may be express or (in some senses) implied, since although consent to disclosure should be addressed to a specific person, the 'need to know principle' applies such that disclosure to one member of the team is assumed to allow disclosure within the team. Here the principle is taken to apply not only to treatment services, but also to other 'medical, surgical or obstetric' services, and for clinical audit purposes (s. 33(6C)). In order to allow this, patients must be informed of the consequences of consenting to disclosure (or at least the clinician should take 'reasonable steps' to ensure such counselling: s. 33(6D)). In order to avert imminent danger to health, and where it is not reasonably practical to obtain consent, disclosure is permitted (s. 33(6E)), and this may cover incidental disclosures where the first disclosure may allow disclosure of the possibility that another person was born as a result of assisted conception. In these emergency situations, the consent of that person is not required (s. 33(6F)).

In addition to the above rules, information under s. 31(2)(a) and (b) – namely, information about the provision of treatment services, or the keeping or use of gametes of any identifiable individual, or of an embryo taken from an identifiable woman – can be disclosed if it relates only to that individual, or, if he or she is being treated with another, if it relates only to that person and that other. Notice that s. 33(7)(b) excludes the provision of information to a person who was, or might have been, born as a result of treatment services. It provides that only information falling within s. 31(2)(a) or (b) is not protected by the relaxation of the prohibition on disclosure.

Difficulty surrounds the interpretation of the phrase 'and that other', which occurs at the end of s. 33(7)(b). It would have been clearer if the section had provided that information about A and B could have been disclosed to A or B. But that is not what it says. The difficulty that this creates may be illustrated by the following example: A and B are being provided with treatment services. In the course of so doing, the clinic discovers that B has recently come under suspicion by the local social services department of child abuse, or chronic alcohol abuse, such that the clinic now fears for the welfare of any child to be born as a result of the treatment services. Taking such factors into account under s. 13(5), the clinic decides to suspend the provision of the treatment services provided to A and B. May the clinic lawfully disclose the reason for the discontinuance to A?

It is necessary to consider the disclosure provisions in conjunction with those of the Data Protection Act 1998.[38] This Act regulates the processing of personal data. Doctors may be taken to be 'data controllers' within the meaning of the Act, and 'processing' can include the obtaining, storage and use of such data. It is important to be aware that the 1998 Act is broader than its predecessor, the Data Protection Act 1984, in that it covers all health records whether held electronically or in written form. The Data Protection Act 1998 entitles a data subject (patient) to serve notice on a data controller (doctor) to stop the processing of personal data, allowing the data controller to rectify or erase inaccurate data, and giving individuals the right to seek compensation for damage. Under s. 30(1), the Secretary of State is empowered to exempt certain categories of data, one of which is personal data concerning the physical or mental health or condition of the data subject.

From an early stage in the life of the Data Protection Act 1984, the forerunner to the 1998 Act, it was made known that these powers would be used to restrict the disclosure of certain personal health data. This was done in the Data Protection (Subject Access Modification) (Health) Order 1987 (SI 1987 No. 1903). Under this statutory instrument, permission was given to withhold data which might otherwise have to be disclosed in line with the Act. In consequence, it has been possible to refuse to disclose personal data on the physical and/or mental health of the data subject which is held by a health professional. This exemption also applied to any other person, provided that the information constituting the data was first recorded by, or on behalf of, a health professional. The 1998 Act also makes provision for exempting information from access (see s. 38(1)).

The withholding of information under the 1987 Order is permissible only on two grounds. These are that the data will be likely to:

(a)   cause serious harm to the physical or mental health of the data subject; or
(b)   lead the data subject to identify another person (other than a health professional who has been involved in the care of the data subject) who has not consented to the disclosure of his or her identity.

This latter ground, which does not apply to health professionals involved in the care of the particular patient, will presumably mean that a data subject cannot, by searching his or her own health records, discover information relating to the health records of any other person (e.g., as to whether serious harm is likely to result). In each case the decision on disclosure is that of the health professional, a non-health professional being required under the Order to consult the medical practitioner responsible for the clinical data ('an appropriate health professional') before deciding whether or not to supply the health data required. Similar categories of non-disclosure apply under the Access to Health Records Act 1990 (see ss. 4 and 5 of that Act).

These subject access provisions were generally exempted by s. 33(8) of the 1990 Act (which added a new s. 35A to the Data Protection Act 1984), except in so far as disclosure accorded with the s. 31 rules. However, the Data Protection Act 1998 repeals s. 33(8) of the 1990 Act, thereby eliminating specific exemption relating to information covered by the Human Fertilisation and Embryology Act 1990. This is on the basis that new orders will be made under the 1998 Act.[39] This will apparently allow the opportunity to widen the scope of the exemption to cover all information within s. 31(2) of the 1990 Act. However, at the time of writing the powers to make further exemption under s. 38 of the Data Protection Act 1998 have yet to be brought into force.

CONCLUSION

On the whole, in the first ten years of the Act, questions of status and identity have proved remarkably uncontroversial. This may reflect the fact that such issues are significantly less contested within society as a whole. Indeed, ten years on, the Act does not appear to be widely criticised as too liberal in its view as much as too cautious in places. Chief amongst these may be donor identity where, whatever the practical difficulties, the withholding of information, and probably detailed identifying information at that, may prove to be as unsustainable in practice as it is in all conscience. The present stance in terms of anonymity does little to encourage openness within the new family units that the legislation facilitates.

NOTES

[1] This most strongly applied to the sperm donor as father since, as Freeman points out (Freeman, M., 'The Unscrambling of Egg Donation' in S. McLean (ed.), *Law Reform and Human Reproduction* (Aldershot, Dartmouth, 1992), at 273) there was little consideration of egg donation prior to the Act, and it may have been that whatever the theoretical common law position, the gestational mother was regarded as the parent.

[2] Baroness Hooper, House of Lords, Official Report, 7 December 1989, col. 1112.

[3] At least unless the absence of any consent on his part to the insemination could be shown – see s. 27 of the 1987 Act.

[4] For an analysis, see Douglas, G., 'The Intention to be a Parent and the Making of Mothers' (1994) 57 MLR 636.

[5] In an extraordinary procedural manoeuvre, MP Michael Jopling secured a retrospective application of this section, almost literally at the last minute in the Parliamentary voting. The section thus applies to the birth of children born before the Act came into force where the parents then applied for the parental order within six months of the Act's commencement (s. 30(2)).

[6] For background to this type of problem, see *Re W (Minors) (Surrogacy)* [1991] 1 FLR 385, and a letter to *The Times* by the solicitor involved (D.B. Forrest, *The Times,* 28 February 1990).

[7] This means that there is no room for the procedure to apply in the case of a father having sexual intercourse with a woman on the understanding that she will hand over any resulting child to the father and his partner.

[8] See Lee, R. and Morgan, D., 'Children of the Reproduction Revolution' (1990) 87(18) LS Gaz 2.

[9] House of Lords, Official Report, 20 March 1990, coll. 1209–10.

[10] Kennedy, I. and Grubb, A., *Medical Law: Text with Materials*, 2nd ed. (London, Butterworths, 1994), at 818.

[11] *Ibid.*, at 71–72. For arguments concerning the reference to this debate and the use of *Hansard*, see *U v W (Admissibility of Hansard)* [1997] Fam Law 403.

[12] Stern, K., 'The Regulation of Assisted Conception in England' (1994) 1 *European Journal of Health Law* 53, at 63.

[13] House of Lords, Official Report, 10 February 1987, coll. 519–22.

[14] Bevan, H., *Child Law* (London, Butterworths, 1987), at 67.

[15] On this particular point, the Law Commission Report, *Family Law: Illegitimacy* (Law Com. No. 118, 20 December 1982), observed that where the father dies before the child's birth, a declaration of parentage will be available for the child once born.

[16] House of Commons, Standing Committee B, 15 May 1990, coll. 191–98.

[17] House of Lords, Official Report, 6 March 1990, col. 1156.

[18] See House of Lords, Official Report, 7 December 1990, coll. 1089–91 for her most belligerent intervention.

[19] Lui, Weaver, Robinson, Debano, Neiland, Killick and Hay, 'A Survey of Semen Donor Attitudes' (1995) 10 (1) *Human Reproduction* 234.

[20] *Human Fertilisation and Embryology: A Framework for Legislation* (Cm 259), 1987, paras 79–86.

[21] Maclean, S. and Maclean, M., 'Keeping Secrets in Assisted Reproduction' (1996) 8 (3) *Child and Family Law Quarterly* 243.

[22] Schover, Rothman and Collins, 'The Personality and Motivation of Semen Donors: A Comparison with Oocyte Donors' (1992) 7 *Human Reproduction* 575.

[23] *Op. cit.* n. 19.

[24] Quoted by Peter Thurnham, House of Commons, Official Report, 20 June 1990, col. 985.

[25] See Lui (*op. cit.*), and Kovacs, Mushin, Kane and Baker, 'A Controlled Study of the Psychosocial Development of Children Conceived Following Insemination with Donor Semen' (1993) 8 *Human Reproduction* 778.

[26] *Fertility and the Family* (London Fourth Estate, 1989).

[27] See generally the work of McWhinnie, A.; especially McWhinnie, A., 'Creating Children – The Medical and Social Dilemmas of Assisted Reproduction' (1992) 81 *Early Child Development and Review* 39; McWhinnie, A., 'A Study of Parenting of IVF and DI Children: The Social, Medical and Legal Dilemmas' (1995) 13 (2) *Medicine & Law* 501; McWhinnie, A., 'Ethical Dilemmas in the Use of Donor Gametes' (1998) 17 (3) *Medicine & Law* 311.

[28] Glover, *op. cit.* n. 26, at 36.

[29] See Haimes, E., 'Recreating the Family? Policy Considerations Relating to the ''New'' Reproductive Technologies' in Maureen McNeil, Ian Varcoe and Steven Yearley, *The New Reproductive Technologies* (1990) p. 154, at 158–59; for a contrary argument and view, see Braude *et al.*, 'Editorial' (1990) 330 *British Medical Journal* 1410.

[30] O'Donovan, K., 'What Shall We Tell The Children?' in Robert Lee and Derek Morgan (eds), *Birthrights, Law and Ethics at the Beginnings of Life* (1989).

[31] *Ibid.*, and see Haimes, E., 'Secrecy: What Can Artificial Insemination Learn From Adoption?' (1988) *International Journal of Law and the Family* 46.

[32] Evans, D., 'Government Legislation and Medical Practice' (1990) 55 *Bulletin of the Institute of Medical Ethics* 13.

[33] Brahms, D., (1991) 338 *Lancet* 1449.

[34] Morgan, D. and Lee, R., 'Disclosure is possible under the Human Fertilisation and Embryology Act' (1992) 75 *Bulletin of Medical Ethics* 25.

[35] See the response to our paper by Leigh and Barker in (1992) 77 *Bulletin of Medical Ethics* 10, and the first Annual Report of the HFEA.

[36] Kennedy and Grubb, *op. cit.*, n. 10 at 814 point out that in cases that concern inadequate testing or screening of gametes, this may remain a problematic restriction.

[37] This results from the definition of a 'holder' of records in s. 1(2) of the Access to Health Records Act 1990.

[38] Readers should be aware, however, that at the time of writing, a Bill to amend the Data Protection Act 1998, the Freedom of Information Bill, is before Parliament.

[39] See *Data Protection Act 1998: Consultation Paper on Subordinate Legislation* Home Office, 1998).

Chapter 10
Liability and Responsibility

In Chapter 3 on embryo research, we considered the many questions surrounding the status of the embryo. On the whole we do not intend to revisit those arguments here. This chapter considers the liability issues which surround assisted conception, both in criminal and civil law. In a book on assisted conception it is not obvious that there should be some discussion of abortion. However, quite apart from the treatment of so-called 'selective reduction', which may continue to be an adjunct to certain types of infertility treatment, avoidance of the issue is not so easy. If we ban experiments on embryos from 14 days, why allow abortion up to (say) 24 weeks? Or why allow abortion at all if we are to allow recompense for disability consequent on acts prior to birth? Thus an examination of the liabilities of clinics under congenital disabilities legislation is better informed by an examination of what the criminal law does to protect (or not, as the case may be) the foetus.

The foetus is not invested with legal personality. This is clear at least from those cases in which a putative father has intervened in the hope of preventing abortion (see for example: *Paton v Trustees of BPAS* [1978] 2 All ER 987; and *C v S* [1987] 1 All ER 1230). In a case considered in greater detail below, *C v S* [1988] QB 135, at 140, it was said that a child will attain the status of a legal person at birth and that in certain circumstances certain rights, including the right to pursue a claim in damages, crystallise on the birth (see also the similar action in *Paton v British Pregnancy Advisory Service Trustees* [1979] QB 276, at 279). This was endorsed more directly in *Burton v Islington Health Authority* [1993] QB 204, which seems to be the first and only case on the status of the foetus in English common law, and in which it was said (at 219):

> In law and logic no damage can have been caused to the plaintiff before the plaintiff existed. The damage was suffered by the plaintiff at the moment that, in law, the plaintiff achieved legal personality and inherited the damaged body for which the Health Authority . . . was responsible.[1]

Although, as we shall see, the common law in this area has been superseded by statute (i.e., the Congenital Disabilities (Civil Liability) Act 1976), the common law solution that a child injured by a pre-natal act or omission may treat that injury as occurring and capable of remedy when at birth that child reaches personhood, broadly accords with that adopted by statute. We shall see that similar public policy-based solutions have been adopted in criminal law, such that a foetus harmed by the activity of a person towards the mother might upon being born be the subject of the criminal conduct (*Attorney-General's Reference (No. 3 of 1994)* [1996] QB 581; [1997] 3 All ER 936).

THE LAW OF ABORTION: THE 1861 ACT AND THE 1929 ACT

Historical background

There is much dispute about the attitude of the common law to abortion, whether performed pre- or post-quickening. We cannot review that dispute here,[2] but a brief historical sketch will assist in understanding the present law.

In an Act of 1803, Lord Ellenborough's Act, Parliament provided that the abortion of a quick foetus (one which has passed the first recognisable movement *in utero*, usually about the 16th to 18th week of pregnancy) was to be a capital offence. In addition, lesser penalties were provided for abortion before quickening. In 1837, the distinction between pre- and post-quickening abortions was dropped, and capital punishment removed by an Act on which the Offences Against the Person Act 1861 is modelled. Thus, since 1803 Parliament has laid out prohibited areas of conduct in respect of the developing foetus, and has sanctioned abortion only where the life of the mother was at risk.

The law which establishes the offence commonly referred to as 'abortion' remains as stated in the Offences Against the Person Act 1861. Section 58 of that Act provides that:

> Every woman, being with child, who, with intent to procure her own miscarriage, shall unlawfully administer to herself any poison or other noxious thing, or shall unlawfully use any instrument or other means whatsoever with the like intent and whosoever, with intent to procure the miscarriage of any woman, whether she be or not with child, shall unlawfully administer to her or cause to be taken by her any poison or other noxious thing, or shall unlawfully use any instrument or other means whatsoever with the like intent, shall be guilty of an offence, and being convicted thereof shall be liable to imprisonment.

That section was buttressed by s. 59, which provides:

> Whosoever shall unlawfully supply or procure any poison or other noxious thing, or any instrument or thing whatsoever, knowing that the same is intended to be unlawfully used or employed with intent to procure the miscarriage of any woman, whether she be or not be with child, shall be guilty of an offence, and being convicted thereof shall be liable to imprisonment for a term not exceeding five years.

That legislation was supplemented in 1929 by the Infant Life (Preservation) Act which had two functions. First, it attempted to close a perceived lacuna in the protection which the 1861 Act gave to the developing foetus. This followed from the common law distinction between the status of a foetus and that of a child born alive. In *R* v *Poulton* (1832) 5 C & P 329, Littledale J had directed a jury that 'with respect to birth, the being born must mean that the whole body is brought into the world; it is not sufficient that the child respores in the progress of birth'. It followed from this that the killing of a child in the process of birth was not the procurement of a miscarriage, nor murder or manslaughter of a child born alive, because the child was not yet a 'reasonable creature in being' as required by the law of homicide. This lacuna had been exploited, for example, in a trial and acquittal at the Liverpool Assizes in June 1928, where Talbot J in charging the Grand Jury had observed that 'the law upon this matter is unsatisfactory and it is right that every appropriate opportunity should be taken to call public attention to it. It is a felony to procure abortion and it is murder to take the life of a child when it is fully born, but to take the life of a child while it is being born and before it is fully born is no offence whatever'.[3] The following session, Parliament considered but failed to pass a Child Destruction Bill 1928, which was the immediate precursor to the Infant Life (Preservation) Act 1929. Secondly, as Mason[4] points out, this Act was designed to legalise the operation of craniotomy – the crushing of an impacted foetal head which inevitably causes foetal death – which was widely practised before Caesarean section became commonplace.

'Capable of being born alive'?

Section 1 of the Infant Life (Preservation) Act 1929 created the offence of 'child destruction', punishable with life imprisonment. That section provides:

(1)   Subject as hereinafter in this subsection provided, any person who, with intent to destroy the life of a child capable of being born alive, by any wilful act causes a child to die before it has an existence independent of its mother, shall be guilty of a felony, to wit, of child destruction, and shall be liable on conviction thereof on indictment to penal servitude for life:
Provided that no person shall be found guilty of an offence under this section unless it is proved that the act which caused the death of the child was not done in good faith for the purpose only of preserving the life of the mother.
(2)   For the purposes of this Act, evidence that a woman had at any material time been pregnant for a period of twenty-eight weeks or more shall be prima facie proof that she was at that time pregnant of a child capable of being born alive.

Parliament thus closed the loophole by adopting the concept of a child 'born alive' and extending it back to any child *in utero* which was 'capable of being born alive', up to the moment when it was in fact born alive. In other words, the phrase adopted by Parliament in 1929 extended to cover not only the process of birth, but also that period when the foetus capable of being born alive was still in its mother's womb. The policy of the Act when introduced in 1929 had been to fill a lacuna in the legislation through which, since 1803, Parliament had regulated women's access to abortion services. In 1929 Parliament declared the policy of the law to be that the taking of a potential human life at a stage of gestation when it was capable of independent existence but before it had that existence independent of its mother was unlawful, unless the mother's life was in danger. It is unclear from the face of the statute whether the 28th week there referred to is the 'real' 28th week or the 'medical' count, which would make it the 26th week. This point is noted by Williams.[5] He suggests that the medical practice of counting pregnancy as commencing from the beginning of the woman's period before conception, whereas the conception probably occurs about two weeks thereafter in the middle of the menstrual cycle, would mean that the week there referred to would be the 'medical' week, when the woman was likely to have been pregnant for about 26 weeks. He argues that the 'actual' 28 weeks should be taken to have been intended here, as, in favour of the defendant on a charge, being the latest date on which a pregnancy could have commenced.

It is important to note that the 28-week prima-facie presumption of a child 'capable of being born alive' is merely that; it could be displaced by evidence to the contrary. The Abortion Act 1967, s. 5(1) saved the provisions of the Infant Life (Preservation) Act 1929 which it described as 'protecting the life of the viable foetus'. What the 1967 Act did was to protect a registered medical practitioner and a pregnant woman in certain specified circumstances from committing the offence of 'procuring a miscarriage' under the 1861 Act. What the 1967 Act did *not* do (quite the opposite) was to introduce any protection in respect of killing a 'child capable of being born alive'. Hence, there was great importance attached to knowing which foetuses were protected by that Act.

In Scotland, where the 1929 Act never applied, child destruction was a crime at common law; but because no time limit ever appeared in statute there has been said to be a much greater degree of flexibility, and in theory abortions had until the 1990 Act been available up to term. However, in practice a notional limit of 28 weeks had been adhered to by most authorities and medical practitioners, and even before the introduction of the Abortion Act 1967 controversy in that jurisdiction had been fierce about the limits for lawful abortion. The Lord Advocate had circulated advice to consultants in Scotland that they risked prosecution for carrying out abortions, and this led directly to the inclusion by the newly returned MP David Steele of an extension of his Bill to Scotland. In 1987 there were only two abortions carried out in Scotland after 24 weeks, and in 1988 only one. So, although Scots law appeared to be more liberal, in fact the 24-week limit was more honoured than breached.[6] The time limits in the 1990 Act now extend explicitly to Scotland.

This body of criminal law remained the bedrock of abortion law until 1967. Even a cursory examination of these provisions discloses some of the difficulties of interpretation to which the law was subject. Immediately it is clear that the offence stated in 1861 consists of the unlawful procurement of a miscarriage, but there are three elements which need brief elucidation.

First, the offence is defined by reference to miscarriage, and is committed by one who unlawfully procures a miscarriage. We discuss the importance of what constitutes a miscarriage below when we consider the legality of what has come to be called 'selective reduction' of multiple pregnancy.

Secondly, there arises the question of which foetuses are 'capable of being born alive' such that the procurement of their miscarriage would be an offence under the 1929 Act. Dunn and Sirratt, from the Bristol Maternity Hospital, in an article reviewing their understanding of the legal position under the 1929 Act, added in a footnote: 'at the time of writing two infants of 23 weeks gestation are in our care, one now being $2\frac{1}{2}$ weeks old the other one week old'.[7] The difficulty in this area was that the exception might tend towards the norm. There was, in the Bristol case, no doubt that the baby born at $20\frac{1}{2}$ weeks was capable not only of being born alive but also of surviving. However, the article did not indicate whether either child survived beyond that time, nor indeed what significance their survival would have had for the interpretation of the law. Indeed, it was not until 13 years later that the courts were drawn to make a formal ruling on the meaning of 'capable of being born alive' and its relationship with the concept of 'viability' introduced by the Abortion Act in 1967.

In *C* v *S* [1987] 1 All ER 1230, Lord Donaldson MR said that a child was capable of being born alive if it was capable of independent or assisted breathing; if '[the foetus] has reached the normal stage of development and . . . is incapable of breathing, it is not in our judgment "a child capable of being born alive" within the meaning of the 1929 Act' (at p. 1241). Earlier he had said that a foetus of 18–21 weeks' gestation, while demonstrating 'real and discernible signs of life' – in that the cardiac muscle is contracting and a primitive circulation developing – 'even if then delivered by hysterectomy, would be incapable ever of breathing either naturally or with the aid of a ventilator. It is not a case of the foetus requiring a stimulus or assistance.'

This appears to settle that the 1929 Act protects only the 'viable' foetus, and not the wider category of foetuses described by the common law as those of live birth – infants, however premature, alive at the moment of birth.[8] As Williams suggests, this accords with the view apparently adopted by Parliament in the Abortion Act 1967, s. 5(1), which refers to the 1929 Act as protecting viable foetuses.[9] The use of the word 'viable' in the 1967 Act (which saved the operation of the 1929 provisions alongside the Abortion Act) has been accepted as shorthand for 'capable of being born alive' and as not effecting any change in the foetuses which were subject of the 1929 Act's protection (*per* Brooke J in *Rance*, below). But Donaldson's *dictum*, that the child must be 'capable of breathing', does not examine the meaning of viability in the sense of describing how long such survival must be in order to have satisfied the requirement of the child possessing the capacity to survive. It substitutes for one formulation (that in the 1929 Act) another (that of capacity to breathe, with or without assistance).

In her first-instance judgment in *C* v *S* Heilbron J observed that 'viability . . . embraces not only being born alive but surviving, for however short a time' (p. 1238). She added, however (at p. 1239), that:

'capable of being born alive' does not have a clear and plain meaning. It is ambiguous. It is a phrase which is capable of different interpretations, and probably for the reason that it is also a medical concept and . . . the expertise of doctors may well be required and gratefully received to assist the court.

Brooke J had to consider the meaning of this phrase in *Rance* v *Mid-Downs Health Authority* [1991] QB 587. Here parents claimed that a hospital's medical staff had negligently failed to discover a foetal abnormality and hence deprived the woman of the opportunity of having an abortion. They sought damages for the shock, trauma, distress and pain associated with the subsequent birth and consequent cost of bringing up a severely handicapped child. The Health Authority defended the negligence action by arguing that the scan which would have disclosed the abnormality was carried out at 26 weeks. They argued that the foetus would then have been 'capable of being born alive' and hence that an abortion, even if carried out within the period of 28 weeks, would have been unlawful. They contended that it would be contrary to public policy to award damages for the negligent failure to carry out an unlawful act. In holding that the foetus was capable of being born alive within the meaning of the 1929 Act, Brooke J stated that:

> the words 'born alive' are clear, and the meaning of the words 'capable of being born alive' are also clear. . . . [A child is] born alive if, after birth, it exists as a live child, that is to say breathing and living by reason of its breathing through its own lungs alone, without deriving any of its living or power to live by or through any connection with its mother. . . . Once the foetus has reached a state of development in the womb that it is capable, if born, of possessing those attributes, it is capable of being born within the meaning of the 1929 Act.

Brooke J's stress on the child's unaided survival introduces an ambiguity which he had claimed not to discover on the face of s. 1(1) itself. His judgment is open to two interpretations: (i) that to be capable of being born alive a child must be capable of breathing through its own lungs alone without assistance; or (ii) alternatively, that the independence which the child must possess is that of its mother and independence of any other assistance, mechanical or otherwise, which may be necessary or available. It is, however, consistent with the *dictum* of Lord Donaldson MR in *C* v *S* that the breathing must take place other than by or through connection with its mother. That necessary dependence must have been overcome, whether in fact the umbilical link has been broken or not. It is not necessary that the child be able to sustain its lung function without mechanical ventilation. To require otherwise would mean that all the varied circumstances in which neonates might require ventilation would involve children who were not capable of being born alive, and failure to attend to them or render medical assistance would not be culpable. Indeed, Brooke J went on to consider the submission of counsel for the plaintiffs that 'capable of being born alive' meant viable in the sense of 'being born alive and surviving into old age in the normal way without intensive care or surgical intervention'. This argument was underlined by arguing that, when the Act was passed in 1929, Parliament can only have had in mind the capacity of a neonate to survive naturally and without artificial ventilation or other assistance. This approach would have avoided the uncertainties introduced by having to specify for how long the survival must be to count as a capacity to be born alive. But Brooke J rejected that interpretation. It would, he said, entail the view that Parliament intended that the phrase it had adopted in the 1929 Act was for individual juries to accord substance, with the result that some children in the course of being born would be denied protection because their expectation of life was not assured at the moment of birth.

Lastly, the 1861 statute clearly contemplated that there were circumstances in which an abortion could be lawfully performed, even before the Abortion Act 1967 introduced statutory defences to the offence. The grounds for such action were considered in the leading case of *R* v *Bourne* [1939] 1 KB 687.

There, Macnaughten J examined the meaning of the word 'unlawfully' in s. 58, in light of the wording of the 1929 Act. He concluded that:

> . . . the word unlawfully [in s. 58] is not . . . a meaningless word. I think it imports the meaning expressed by the proviso [the 1929 Act] . . . and that section 58 of the Offences Against the Person Act 1861, must be read as if the words making it an offence to use an instrument with intent to procure a miscarriage were qualified by a similar proviso.

He went on to say that if the act was done for the purpose of saving the life of the woman, or for preserving her health – later clarified to be physical or mental health – then it would not have been done unlawfully there. (*Cf.* the critical examination of *Bourne* by Keown,[10] the thrust of which is that the understanding of 'unlawfully' had been long debated before 1939 and that the interpretation given to it by Macnaughten J was much narrower than authorities preceding the case and than that adopted in two subsequent but little cited cases, of *Bergmann* (1948) and *Newton* (1958).)

THE LAW OF ABORTION: THE 1967 ACT AND THE 1990 ACT

Until the late 1960s, the *Bourne* interpretation remained the only source of defence for a person charged with the unlawful procurement of a miscarriage. In 1967 a Private Member's Bill was introduced to provide a limited statutory defence to a charge of unlawful procurement. That Bill became the Abortion Act 1967. It withstood numerous challenges[11] before the Human Fertilisation and Embryology Act 1990 recast the law in several important ways. Section 37 of the 1990 Act amended s. 1 of the 1967 Act. That section provided for the first time a statutory time limit for abortion, a limit of 24 weeks now being specified in the 1967 Act itself. In England and Wales, the previous 'limit' of 28 weeks was derived only from the presumption provided for in the 1929 Act that a child was 'capable of being born alive' after a woman's continuous pregnancy of 28 weeks. Procurement of a miscarriage after this time would amount to the offence of child destruction, unless within the provisio to s. 1(1) of that Act, that the miscarriage was procured with the sole intent of saving the life of the mother. The other fundamental change is that in respect of three of the four grounds for statutory lawful abortion, no time limit is specified at all, and abortion is lawful if carried out on these grounds up to term. Under the law as amended by the 1990 Act there are now five separate grounds for a lawful abortion within the terms of the 1967 Act (see below).

The grounds of abortion

There are a number of preliminary points to make on the manner in which abortion legislation operates. First, the legislation identifies separately grounds for abortion which at one time were run together under the 1967 Act; the grounds are now set out in s. 1(1)(a), (b), (c) and (d), and s. 1(4). Secondly, the way in which two of these grounds have been worded has given rise to doubts as to their precise scope and application. Thirdly, and of most importance, in respect of the four initial grounds, the protection given to the pregnant woman and the doctor performing the abortion arises only where the pregnancy is terminated by a registered medical practitioner, following certification by two registered medical practitioners acting in good faith that the ground for abortion exists. Lastly, an abortion performed on any of the specified grounds in s. 1 is lawful, whether carried out on a child incapable of being born alive or on one capable of being born alive. This follows s. 37(4) of the 1990 Act which 'uncoupled' the Abortion Act from the Infant Life (Preservation) Act. It is in this sense that the explicit nature of the underlying eugenic philosophy of the reforms may be most clearly seen.

The first ground (s. 1(1)(a)) relates to the relative risk to the pregnant woman or her existing children of continuing the pregnancy. This ground is subject to the 24-week time limit. The 'unlimited' grounds are:

(a)   that the termination of the pregnancy is necessary to prevent grave permanent injury to the physical or mental health of the pregnant woman (s. 1(1)(b));

(b)   that the continuance of the pregnancy would involve risk to the life of the pregnant woman, greater than if the pregnancy were terminated (s. 1(1)(c));

(c)   that there is a substantial risk that if the child were born it would suffer from such physical or mental abnormalities as to be seriously handicapped (s. 1(1)(d)).

Each of the grounds in (a) to (c) above, which may be invoked at any stage of the pregnancy until birth, needs separate attention. But two preliminary notes may be entered. Each of these 'unlimited' grounds may be used to justify termination of the pregnancy between the end of the 24th week and term. But each is restricted by specific wording. They are open-textured, in the sense that they will justify all abortions after 24 weeks as long as one of the grounds can be presented. In each case, it will be necessary for the medical practitioners to certify that the proper conditions of the grounds have been satisfied. Otherwise, practitioners will remain open to prosecution under the Offences Against the Person Act 1861. They may also remain vulnerable to prosecution under the 1929 Act where the foetus aborted was 'capable of being born alive'. However, the revised s. 5(1) of the 1967 Act (referred to above) provides that: 'No offence under the Infant Life (Preservation) Act 1929 shall be committed by a registered medical practitioner who terminates a pregnancy in accordance with the provisions of this Act.' Accordingly, a practitioner who terminates a pregnancy believing, in all good faith, that the foetus if born would suffer from 'such physical or mental abnormalities as to be seriously handicapped' is protected from prosecution. This is so even if it later transpires that he or she has made a mistake and aborted a perfectly healthy foetus. The question of good faith here is one for the jury to decide on the totality of the evidence. *R* v *Smith* [1974] 1 All ER 376 is the only reported case in which a conviction has followed the questioning of the bona fides of the doctor. In this case, when a doctor accepted a cash payment to carry out a termination with an inadequate medical history of the patient and without any consultation with a second doctor, the Court of Appeal held that the jury were entitled to find a lack of good faith.

One interesting, and perhaps controversial, question is the relationship of the HFEA to abortion legislation. Section 8 of the Human Fertilisation and

Embryology Act 1990 lays upon the HFEA a duty to 'keep under review information about embryos and any subsequent development of embryos'. The long title of the 1990 Act includes the latter phrase: 'An Act to make provision in connection with embryos and any subsequent development of embryos . . .'. Talk of 'subsequent development' became necessary at the point at which the Bill was adopted as a vehicle for the reform of the law of abortion. To a large extent, that provision is made through the establishment of the HFEA, although, of course, the HFEA would have only those responsibilities in relation to abortion that the Act placed upon it. For the most part there are no such responsibilities except for two areas. The first is in relation to selective abortion (which is dealt with later in this chapter and which may be adopted in the course of treatment services). The second arises out of s. 8 of the Act and the duty to review the subsequent development of embryos. However, it seems that the HFEA does not feel itself to be bound by this duty. There is no evidence of any monitoring of abortion, and nothing about this duty, or about abortion more generally, appears in the Annual Reports of the HFEA.

Risk to the pregnant woman or her existing children: s. 1(1)(a) Where the continuance of the pregnancy would involve risk greater than if the pregnancy were terminated, of injury to the physical or mental health of the pregnant woman or any existing children of her family, a lawful abortion may be performed up to the end of the 24th week of pregnancy. Historically this has been the primary ground for terminations.

The 1990 Act amendments introduced for the first time a specific time limit which has been written into the Abortion Act. Under the 1967 legislation, the time limit was taken to be 28 weeks (following from the presumption in the 1929 Act), although it had become very rare indeed for any abortions to be performed after 24 weeks (see above) and, according to specialists who gave evidence in *Rance*, unusual for abortions to be performed after 20 weeks. The effect of introducing a limit into the legislation is to create an overlapping pair of offences under the Offences Against the Person Act 1861 and the Infant Life (Preservation) Act 1929 after 24 weeks. The terms of s. 1(1)(a) are wide, particularly because the injury that would be risked by continuation of the pregnancy is not qualified in any way. Simple risk of injury is a sufficient ground. Indeed, it may be possible to argue that the risk of carrying a baby to term will always involve a greater risk than an early termination.[12]

Grave permanent injury: s. 1(1)(b) Prior to the 1990 Act, s. 1(4) of the Abortion Act 1967 (which was not affected in any case by the changes in the 1990 Act) provided that a pregnancy may be terminated following determination by one medical practitioner alone where it is 'immediately necessary to save the life or to prevent grave permanent injury to the physical or mental health of the pregnant woman'. Examples of such causes would be conditions such as pre-eclampsia, abruption and placenta praevia. Section 1(1)(b) introduces another ground based upon grave permanent injury to the woman, but the difference is that this ground requires two medical practitioners to be of the opinion that the termination is necessary (and not immediately necessary) to prevent 'grave permanent injury' to the woman's physical or mental health, falling short of being an immediate threat to her life (provided for in s. 1(4)).

There is no need on this ground to balance the risk to the woman against that posed by the continuance of the pregnancy, as in s. 1(1)(a). It is necessary to show that the woman would suffer 'grave permanent injury', and not simply 'injury' as in the previous case. The effect of this is to put into statutory form the reading given to the Infant Life (Preservation) Act 1929 by *R* v *Bourne* [1939] 1 KB 687. Recall that Macnaughten J opined that 'the word "unlawfully" is not [in s. 58 of the 1861 Act] a meaningless word'. He held that it imported a meaning similar to that expressed legislatively in 1929, and that the statutory offence of s. 58 should be read as if subject to a defence of acting in good faith solely for the purpose of saving the life of the pregnant woman. And, he continued, it is not necessary to wait until the woman is in peril of immediate or instant death (separately provided for in s. 1(4)). Indeed, he went so far as to suggest that a doctor was not merely entitled, but was enjoined by a common law duty, to intervene to save the life of the pregnant woman.

This would include cases where the doctor (and a second registered medical practitioner under abortion law other than in s. 1(4)) is of the opinion, formed in good faith and on the basis of her or his clinical experience, that the woman is in danger of grave permanent injury to her physical or mental health. In such a case, the doctors are justified in proceeding to the termination without having to wait for the events that put the life of the woman at immediate risk. Examples here might include: mild pre-eclampsia; breast or cervical cancer in which the risk to the woman increases during pregnancy because of the hormonal changes which increase with the growth of the foetus; uncontrolled diabetes; conditions that may improve or deteriorate during pregnancy, such as asthma and epilepsy; and conditions such as hypertension, where the woman may run the risk of severe permanent damage to her brain, heart or kidneys. It does appear that although this ground gives access to a lawful abortion after 24 weeks, it does so in such a way that most practitioners would attempt to save the life of a viable foetus if possible.

This goes some way to helping understand what would be necessary to prevent 'grave permanent injury' to the pregnant woman's physical or mental health such as to justify termination at any stage. The wording speaks of a grave (not a serious) risk. It is possible that a jury would be invited to give these expressions a similar, if not an identical, meaning. It is suggested that this provision will enable immediate termination in such cases as discussed where the continuation of the pregnancy might seriously accentuate or exacerbate the illness to the point at which the woman's health would be permanently affected.

Risk to the life of the pregnant woman: s. 1(1)(c) This ground overlaps with that considered under s. 1(1)(b), and is a restatement of a provision previously tied into s. 1(1)(a). However, abortion on this ground is available at any time during the course of the pregnancy where it can be shown that the continuation of the pregnancy would entail a risk to the life of the woman greater than that posed by termination. With the sophistication of abortion technology and the increasing skill of health care practitioners performing abortions, most terminations up to 12 weeks carry less risk to the life of the mother than continuing with the pregnancy, which always carries with it degrees of risk. As term and birth approaches, those risks increase, but so do the obstetric risks associated with termination. A similar effect had been provided for in the Infant Life (Preservation) Act 1929, s. 1(1), with a saving for an abortion at any stage of the pregnancy to preserve the life of the woman.

There is an important similarity, however, which can be adduced between this and the previous ground. It concerns the notion of 'termination'. Recall that s. 1(1)(b) provides for cases in which the termination is necessary to prevent grave permanent injury to the physical or mental health of the woman, where her actual or reasonably foreseeable circumstances may be taken into account. Such a termination may take place, up to term, on a healthy foetus capable of being born alive. Section 1(1)(b) thus provides for the case in which it can be foreseen that termination will be necessary for the benefit of the woman, but which is not at the time that the termination is carried out immediately necessary to save her life (since this is separately provided for, see s. 1(4)). Neither is it a pregnancy the continuance of which would put her life more at risk than if it were terminated – that is provided for in s. 1(1)(c). As with s. 1(1)(c), s. 1(1)(b) may be thought of as a 'sacrifice' ground. But the statute does not say in what sense that sacrifice must be effected. It does not say, for example, that the termination must be carried out in such a way as to kill the foetus. What the statute now provides is that there will be a lawful defence to a charge under the Offences Against the Person Act 1861 when that course is chosen.

Where the termination is carried out very close to term, it may be possible to argue that the pregnancy may be terminated in such a way as to maximise the possibilities of producing a live birth, consistent with achieving the objectives which the termination grounds set out. (It is unlikely that this argument would be applied to the serious foetal handicap ground (s. 1(1)(d), below), where the whole purpose of the ground is to relieve the mother or parents of the foetus from the responsibility of caring for it.) This novel argument was indeed proposed by one commentator during the Bill's legislative passage. In a striking essay,[13] Sheila McLean recalled that the time at which viability occurs is a mobile one and foetuses at the lower end of the scale may develop sufficiently to become not just potentially but actually salvageable in greater numbers and with greater frequency. It is at this point that the interests of the developing relatively mature foetus and the rights of the woman who is carrying it are seldom so clearly in conflict. Indeed, some philosophers suggest that a proper understanding of sacrifice would entail that it is in circumstances such as this that the woman should be prepared to 'lay down her life' for that of her foetus. McLean's proposal is different, however, in that it seeks to challenge two routinely made assumptions: (i) that this last, post-viability period of pregnancy is sacrosanct and that termination should not be routinely available in the third trimester; and (ii) that pregnancy termination automatically equates to foetal death.

As we have seen, the 1990 reforms swept away the first of the assumptions above, but left the second, perhaps equally controversial, suggestion open for review. McLean observed:

> What is sacroscant for many about the final stage of pregnancy is, primarily, the fact that the foetus is recognisably 'human' at this stage, that is, it could be born in the shape of a human baby and kept alive. To anti-abortion protagonists, therefore, the well developed foetus should be saved. At no stage has this lobby argued for any concessions because the anticipated outcome of pregnancy termination at this stage is the destruction of the foetus. . . . On the other hand,

the pro-choice lobby, if consistent, would have to argue that pregnancy termination at this stage should be permissible, since the issue is not the development of the foetus but the rights of the woman.

However logical it may be, this last position is counter-intuitive for many people. This is because, as the anti-abortion lobby has stressed, it entails the destruction of something which at the moment of destruction could have been saved. . . . this situation is another very clear example of a case where the very evidence used by the anti-abortion lobby can facilitate women's rights, without harming the interests of foetuses. . . . late pregnancy termination is not, and need not be, synonymous with foetal destruction. Indeed, induction, the method commonly used to terminate such pregnancies, is a technique also in wanted pregnancies.

Interestingly, a House of Lords amendment to the effect that where an abortion involved a child capable of being born alive, the doctor should be placed under a duty to use 'all reasonable steps to secure that the child is born alive', was defeated.[14] It is also worth noting that there was no suggestion that it should apply to the following ground under s. 1(1)(d).

It may be arguable that the doctor is under a legal duty to assist a living abortus. To make out this case it is necessary to consider the facts of *Attorney-General's Reference (No. 3 of 1994)* [1996] QB 581. A pregnant woman was stabbed, and while there was no direct harm to the foetus, as a result of the stabbing, at 26 weeks, the child was born prematurely. She died some weeks later of complications relating to the premature birth. The man was charged with murder, but acquitted on the direction of the judge that the facts could not give rise to a charge of murder or manslaughter. However, the Court of Appeal held that the *actus reus* could be found in the injury to the mother of whom the foetus was, at that stage, a part and that the direction was mistaken. The Court stressed that the *mens rea* was found through the doctrine of transferred malice, with the intention of the accused towards the mother transferred to the child on its birth. The House of Lords ([1997] 3 All ER 936) ruled both that the Court of Appeal had overstretched the concept of transferred malice, and that it was wrong to treat the foetus as part of the mother rather than as a unique organism. Their Lordships suggested that it would be open to the jury to find the accused guilty of manslaughter, on the basis that the required *mens rea* for manslaughter was an intention to do an unlawful and dangerous act. Thus it was possible to establish the necessary *mens rea* in stabbing the mother, and that the child on birth could fall within the scope of that *mens rea*:

> For the foetus life lies in the future, not in the past. It is not sensible to say that it cannot be harmed, or that nothing can be done to it that can never be dangerous. Once it is born it is exposed like all living persons to the risk of injury. It may also carry with it the effects of things done to it before birth which, after birth, may prove to be harmful . . . (*per* Lord Hope, at 957)

Mason expresses the view that if a child born alive is a person, then it is not open to someone to kill that child intentionally. 'Thus the problems surrounding the living abortus are by no means closed, and, essentially can be distilled into a discussion of the doctor's duty to keep the child alive in so far as he or she is able'.[15]

Serious foetal handicap: s. 1(1)(d)   Prior to the 1990 amendments, the Brightman Committee[16] had argued that if an unborn child were diagnosed as 'grossly abnormal and unable to lead any meaningful life, there is in the opinion of the Committee no logic in requiring the mother to carry her unborn child to full term merely because the diagnosis was too late to enable an operation for abortion to be carried out before the 28th completed week'. We may abstain for the moment from a detailed examination of the philosophical and ethical assumptions lying behind this statement. It suffices to remark that this sentiment was one which was eventually to commend itself to MPs. However, the time limit of 28 weeks disappeared consequent upon references to the Infant Life (Preservation) Act 1929, with its presumption of foetal survivability at 28 weeks, being removed from the Abortion Act 1967 and the introduction of a specific 24-week limit for abortions on all grounds other than foetal handicap.[17]

This is the most difficult of the abortion grounds to interpret, although it is probably that which has the most widespread public support. Curiously, it is also the one ground under the abortion legislation of 1967 which has not been subject to sustained analysis.[18] Foetal handicap may not be diagnosable until fairly late in the pregnancy, although medical techniques such as Chorion Villi Sampling, Fluorescence Activated Cell Sorting and DNA sampling techniques using PCR (Polymerase Chain Reaction) are making the amniocentesis technology less burdensome.[19] The problem with s. 1(1)(d), and the cause of the controversy, is how one might interpret words such as 'substantial risk' and 'seriously handicapped'. In an amendment that was not taken in the House of Commons debates[20] there was a proposal that the foetal handicap ground should be more clearly delineated by providing that abortion could be justified only where 'there is a foetal abnormality with a strong possibility that the child would suffer a condition both incurable and wholly destructive of the quality of life'. The unease felt by some at the operation of the section is not assisted by its availability without limit of time. One suspects that whatever moral arguments are employed, views as to the serious nature of the handicap may be influenced by the time at which termination is suggested.

Selective reduction of multiple pregnancy

At the time of the passage of the 1990 Act, one of the late amendments to the Bill in the House of Commons dealt with the legality of the procedure which has become known as 'selective reduction' of multiple pregnancy. The Third Report of the ILA described the use of this procedure 'whereby one or more embryos in a multiple pregnancy are selectively killed to allow others to develop'. The technique was developed in response to discordant twinned pregnancies following diagnosis of severe abnormality or genetic anomaly to stop the development of the abnormal foetus.[21] It involves the injection of potassium chloride into the amniotic sac or into the heart of the selected foetus, or foetal exsanguination or aspiration.[22] The nature of the Parliamentary concern was captured by Kenneth Clarke:

> The best advice that we can obtain is that selective reduction is subject to the Abortion Act 1967 but that there is considerable doubt about the matter . . . The difficulty of deciding exactly what selective reduction is, when the foetus is killed inside the womb, makes the position different from that of ordinary abortion. Therefore, miscarriage is regarded as the legally correct description.[23]

'Selective' reduction is, in fact, a misnomer in all but very few cases. Usually, in a higher order pregnancy where a decision is taken to reduce the number of implanted foetuses, the 'reduction' is of those most easily accessible to the clinician. No question of medical judgment is involved and hence the procedure is more properly regarded as completely random. Very occasionally, and not usually in assisted conception work, a foetus higher up the placenta is aborted rather than one closer to the neck of the uterus on grounds of clinical judgment. This might properly be termed 'selective' reduction.

Commentators have suggested that this procedure is unlawful unless performed in compliance with the provisions of the Abortion Act 1967,[24] or further, that the nature of the offence and the limited parameters of the exclusions created by the 1967 Act are such that there are no circumstances in which the reduction may be performed lawfully. On this point John Keown[25] has argued that while the offence created in the 1861 Act of 'procuring a miscarriage' has been committed, the requirement for the protection afforded by the Abortion Act 1967, of the 'termination of a pregnancy', has not been satisfied.

There is some confusion in this legal literature which has discussed selective reduction. John Keown[26] set out to rebut the argument that s. 58 of the Offences Against the Person Act 1861 does not apply because there has been no miscarriage. He argues that the understanding of miscarriage on which the contrary analysis is based – that it implies an expulsion from the uterus – incorrectly perceives the ingredients of the offence of procuring a miscarriage. His careful argument is that, properly understood, miscarriage does not require the expulsion of foetal remains from the uterus, but speaks rather to the failure of gestation.[27] Price reaches a broadly similar conclusion: 'it is the causing of foetal death which is the essence of the crime of abortion and not simply the expulsion of the foetus from the mother.'[28] Kennedy and Grubb[29] introduce their discussion of selective reduction by observing that 'the potentially crucial factual distinction between this procedure and other abortions is that when selective reduction is performed the destroyed foetus is absorbed into the mother's body and is not expelled'. There appears to be no discussion of whether or when the products of conception which have been reduced are expelled from the uterus.

Section 37(5), which amends s. 5(2) of the 1967 Act, again refers to the procurement of a miscarriage, or 'in the case of a woman carrying more than one foetus, her miscarriage of any foetus'. In about 1 in 50 reductions, the attempt to reduce the number of viable foetuses causes the spontaneous abortion of all of the foetuses. Almost all reductions will be justifiable on the grounds that there is a substantial risk that each infant will be born with 'such physical or mental abnormalities as to be seriously handicapped' within s. 1(1)(d), because multiple pregnancy carries with it a significant risk of prematurity with the associated birth risks. If Keown and Price are correct in their interpretation of the notion of miscarriage, then any difficulties of interpretation are lessened. But if the better view is that expulsion of the products of conception from the womb is an essential ingredient of miscarriage then prima facie there remain difficulties.

Selective reduction cannot be performed until after ultrasonic visualisation of a foetal heartbeat. When such a heartbeat is detectable, other foetal organs have begun their process of development. This cannot be earlier than about six weeks following conception. Most reductions are performed between eight and 14 weeks of pregnancy, although it is common to wait until at least the 11th week to see how many of the foetuses are viable, because one or more of the foetuses may have died spontaneously. In such cases, or in those in which reduction is performed, the foetal sac collapses and is squashed to the side of the uterus by the pressure of the growth of the remaining foetal sac(s). The remains of the aborted foetus may be visible as an attachment to the placenta; the selective reduction does not sever the umbilical connection, and the foetal remains will be expelled from the uterus with the placenta at the time of the delivery of the remaining foetuses. Alternatively, if the reduction is performed at an early stage, and the foetal fluid has dispersed, the remaining tissue cells will have been absorbed into the placenta. Similarly, if a foetus dies naturally very early in a pregnancy, the tissue remains gradually degenerate and become absorbed into the placenta. Pathological section of the placenta at delivery can detect these remains, but visual inspection cannot. Where a death or abortion occurs at about 20 weeks, the tissues will not disintegrate but the foetus will lose its fluid and will become a foetus papyraceous of up to two centimetres and paper-like, which can be discerned on the placenta to which it has retained its umbilical connection when the woman delivers any remaining normal babies. The form of the foetus will be visible, but it will appear as paper thin. Where a death occurs at 30 weeks, the fluid loss will be such that on delivery of a remaining baby several weeks later, there will be some maceration and skin peeling, but the foetal form will be maintained. Thus, with reduction, it is apparent that the later in the pregnancy that it is performed, the more the likelihood that the foetal remains will be expelled at the time of the delivery of the placenta. It is then that the miscarriage is completed, in so far as the legal understanding of the term requires expulsion (see the authorities reviewed, only to be challenged, by Keown, in his 1987 article). Neither Keown, nor Price nor Kennedy and Grubb take this point. In a way this is perhaps not surprising, as this facet of selective reduction appears not to have been written up in any of the medical literature which discusses the procedure, although in illustrated presentations the remains of the aborted foetuses are shown clearly. But in early reductions, the concept of miscarriage which relies on expulsion from the womb will remain of dubious validity.

Such was the concern about the health of women and foetuses in higher order births (triplets or more, of which there were 299 sets in the two and a half years of the study's life; 275 sets of triplets, 24 sets of quads and quins) that the Department of Health commissioned a research study into the effects of such pregnancies. This report[30] was published during the Parliamentary recess after the Bill had failed to gain assent in July. Its disturbing conclusions included the finding that in 6% of triplet cases and 16% of quads and above, the correct number of foetuses in the pregnancy became clear only at birth. In addition, and not surprisingly, the mortality rates of such babies have not fallen as steeply as other pre-term births and foetuses are at increased risk of cerebral palsy, especially spastic diplegia.[31]

Against such a background, and with no public knowledge of how many reductions are performed annually, it was perhaps not surprising (although again it illustrated the fluid way in which the Department of Health approached the Bill) that the abortion section was amended at a very late stage to bring such reductions within the ambit of the Abortion Act 1967. Section 37(5) of the 1990 Act inserts a new wording into s. 5(2) of the 1967 Act. That section now reads as follows:

(2)   For the purposes of the law relating to abortion, anything done with intent to procure a woman's miscarriage (or, in the case of a woman carrying more than one foetus, her miscarriage of any foetus) is unlawfully done unless authorised by section 1 of this Act and, in the case of a woman carrying more than one foetus, anything done with intent to procure her miscarriage of any foetus is authorised by that section if—

(a)   the ground for termination of the pregnancy specified in subsection (1)(d) of that section applies in relation to any foetus and the thing is done for the purposes of procuring the miscarriage of that foetus, or

(b)   any of the other grounds for termination of the pregnancy specified in that section applies.

This new provision introduces the reformulated grounds of abortion to selective reduction. Such a procedure must now be legally related to one of the grounds for lawful abortion, thus mere numbers alone will apparently not suffice. While the practical effect of such a rewording may be less real than apparent, it is important, nonetheless, to examine this ground in a little more detail.

One ground for 'reduction' is of course s. 1(1)(d) (physical or mental abnormality amounting to serious handicap of any child born). Selective reduction properly so termed – selective foeticide – will fall within this ground. As we have seen, however, usually there is random reduction and the doctor will not be able to show that the one or more foetuses terminated would have suffered handicap. This is not the end of the argument, though, for multiple order birth will carry with it attendant risks of abnormality. It may be likely, therefore, that there is a greater risk that however healthy tests may show the embryos to be, the fact of the multiple order pregnancy may mean that there is a greater risk that, at birth, some of the children will be handicapped. Nevertheless, the new s. 5(2) of the 1967 Act speaks of the application of s. 1(1)(d) of that Act to 'any foetus', while s. 1(1)(d) addresses the handicap to 'the child'. It might be argued that these provisions apply to the specific risk of handicap to a particular child, and that a general risk of handicap to some children of a multiple order pregnancy or birth is insufficient. Alternatively, it might be argued that the attendant risks of such handicap are not 'substantial'.

Such arguments may prove academic. Random reduction would seem to be permissible on the other three grounds of s. 1 by virtue of s. 5(2). As reduction is usually carried out early in the pregnancy, and most usually in the first trimester, the first ground under s. 1(1)(a) – that the pregnancy has not exceeded its 24th week and that its continuation gives rise to the risk of injury to the woman's physical or mental health which outweighs that of the termination – might apply. In general, foetal reduction will reduce the risk of injury to the pregnant woman. In any multiple pregnancy, the threat to the mother's continued welfare will be relieved by each successive miscarriage procured, in the same way that the termination of any pregnancy sufficiently early removes a growing health threat (the foetus) which increases as the pregnancy moves towards term and childbirth. In a higher order pregnancy the risks to the pregnant woman include hyperemesis (excessive vomiting); high blood pressure, which may produce fits, cerebral haemorrhage or placental bleeding; and hydramnios (excessive fluid accumulation in the uterus), which may result in long-term bed confinement and bring associated risks of thrombosis in the leg or pelvic veins. The risk of a pulmonary embolism, the passage of a blood clot to the lungs, which endangers the woman's life, is also increased in these circumstances.[32] One problem here, however, is that the risk of the injury to the woman must arise from the continuation of the pregnancy. But if pregnancy means 'the state of being with child', or 'the status of the uterus in being pregnant', then following 'reduction' the woman will remain pregnant. Only a definition of pregnancy which relates to the gestation of a foetus would permit random reduction under s. 1(1)(a); the pregnancy (gestation) of certain foetuses is discontinued. Here we use the word 'pregnancy' to refer to the foetus, yet in more common usage the word describes the state of the woman. This is reflected in the way MP Ann Widdecombe put her understanding of the point in debate:

> I am not sure that the amendment is technically viable, because it refers to a miscarriage. A miscarriage is not an abortion and it is not a selective reduction or a stillbirth. When a woman has a miscarriage she loses her child. In a selective reduction, the child is left in the womb until birth occurs naturally . . .[33]

This point would refer equally to the ground under s. 1(1)(c), which speaks also of the continuance of the pregnancy. This would leave only the ground under s. 1(1)(b) (which uses the word 'termination') as clearly available. It is clear that multiple order pregnancy may pose threats of grave permanent injury to the health of the woman. But it remains then problematic to discuss what is 'necessary' under this ground. Would reduction from three to two foetuses be necessary prevention? Or from eight to three? Triplets are without doubt less risky than a much higher multiple order birth, but would the doctor be able to defend such reduction if it still left the attendant risks to the woman's health that the birth of triplets must pose?

Medicinal terminations

A second late amendment which was accepted (by 233 votes to 141) introduces a change to s. 1(3) of the 1967 Act. That section provides that an abortion ('any treatment for the termination of pregnancy') is lawful under the Act only if carried out in a hospital vested in the Minister of Health or Secretary of State under the National Health Service Acts, or in a place approved by the Minister or Secretary. To this is now added a rider, a new s. 1(3A), which enables the Secretary or Minister to limit approval to a class of places, where the 'treatment for termination' consists of specified medicinal treatment. In addition, it may be required that the termination be carried out only in a specified manner:

> (3A) The power under subsection (3) of this section to approve a place includes power, in relation to treatment consisting primarily in the use of such medicines as may be specified in the approval and carried out in such manner as may be so specified, to approve a class of places.

The purpose in introducing this section was quite specific. It anticipates the marketing in the United Kingdom of the French manufactured 'abortion pill' RU486, or mifepristone. The administration of the drug involves no surgery or anaesthetic, and yet without the amendment it would have been necessary for the drug to have been administered in a hospital or an approved clinic. The change was introduced to reflect the fact that there was no medical reason for that to be necessary, certainly with RU486, and possibly with other 'medicinal terminations'. The new section, extraordinarily, does not take the opportunity to clarify the legality of such methods which, essentially, operate so as to prevent the implantation of the fertilised egg. It has been suggested that such destruction amounts to a criminal offence unless done within the terms of the Abortion Act 1967.[34] In a forceful reply, Kenneth Norrie has observed that the phrase 'termination of a pregnancy' is not synonymous with 'abortion'. 'Abortion in the sense of the law requires something more.' Norrie suggests that that requirement is the intention to destroy potential human life by the termination of pregnancy:

> There are (at least) three elements: destruction, intention to destroy, and the termination of pregnancy. Destruction is a purely factual matter and causes no real problems for the law (except in trying to define what a 'potential human life' is). Intention does cause problems, because it is often very difficult to prove . . . The real difficulties for the law come about when we try to define termination of pregnancy.[35]

Norrie argues that British courts have a long history of deference to the practices and understandings of the medical profession, and that 'medically speaking, pregnancy begins on implantation, that is the completion of the process whereby the fertilised egg attaches itself to the wall of the uterus'. From this he concludes that 'any anti-pregnancy technique that prevents implantation does not terminate pregnancy, because there is no pregnancy, and therefore cannot be abortion'.[36] However, with RU486 there is a further complication. Mifepristone can dislodge the implanted egg at a later stage, as can the IUD. Hence, a medical practitioner who administers RU486 knowing that a woman is pregnant and with intent to end the pregnancy, clearly intends to procure a miscarriage within the terms of the 1861 Act, and will do so lawfully only if within the terms of the Abortion Act 1967.

It is a truism, sometimes shot across the bows of counsel in argument by more belligerent judges, that 'doctors do not write the common law'. And yet Norrie's observation will find general accord amongst medico-legal commentators. Whether in an individual case that would be persuasive, however, is more open to doubt.

CIVIL LIABILITY: CONGENITAL DISABILITY

The Congenital Disabilities (Civil Liability) Act 1976 provides for civil liability in the case of children born disabled in consequence of the intentional act, negligence, or breach of statutory duty of some person prior to the birth of the child. In so doing, it implemented the Law Commission's recommendations.[37] The Act covers liability for children born alive, 'born' here meaning reaching the point at which the child has life separate from its mother (s. 4(2) of the 1976 Act, and see *Rance*, above). The defendant is answerable to the child if the defendant would have been liable in tort to one or both of the parents in respect of the matters which gave rise to the disability at birth. Such matters could arise either before conception, or during the pregnancy of the mother or in the process of childbirth. In relation to matters arising before conception, this would clearly cover an injury to the parent which, at the time of conception, was transmitted to the child. Under the 1976 Act, liability on the part of the mother to her own child is excluded, but the liability of the father is not. Our interest in this legislation here arises out of the extension of the Act to disabilities which may result from infertility treatments (see s. 44 of the 1990 Act which adds a new s. 1A to the 1976 Act).

As stated earlier, the common law position in relation to the duties owed in the English law of tort to an unborn child does not seem to have been resolved until the case of *Burton* v *Islington Health Authority* [1993] QB 204. The Law Commission chose to recommend statutory intervention in this area in advance of any lead case that might emerge. It was thought that this would reduce uncertainty and allow certain ancillary questions to be addressed – such as the liability of the mother – on which the authors of the Report had firm views. The 1976 Act provides a number of defences to an action. A significant one is that if the parents, or either of them, knew of a risk of the child being born disabled and accepted that risk, the creator of the occurrence carrying that risk is excused liability. Clearly, this applies only to matters which precede conception (s. 1(4)). This defence is not available to the father acting as defendant, where he but not the mother had no knowledge of the risk. For present purposes, however, s. 1(5) also provides a significant defence:

> (5) The defendant is not answerable to the child, for anything he did or omitted to do when responsible in a professional capacity for treating or advising the parent, if he took reasonable care having due regard to then received professional opinion applicable to the particular class of case; but this does not mean that he is answerable only because he departed from received opinion.

This implements para. 96 of the Law Commission Report, but probably does little more than to enshrine, within the statute, standards which would be applicable in the law of negligence under the principles laid down in *Bolam* v *Friern Hospital Management Committee* [1957] 2 All ER 118 (see discussion above in relation to consent to treatment, Chapter 7).

The 1990 Act, by s. 44, introduces a new s. 1A into the 1976 Act specifically to provide for actions which might arise in the course of providing assisted conception. It follows the scheme of the 1976 Act, and introduces for children born as a result of assisted conception the same sort of regime in respect of statutory conditions for liability as that Act did for natural conception. It applies to any case where:

> (a) a child has been born disabled following the placing in a woman of an embryo, or sperm and eggs, or following her artificial insemination;
> (b) the disability results from an act or omission in the course of the selection of the embryo or the gametes used to bring about the embryo; or
> (c) the disability results from some act or omission in the keeping or use of the embryo or gametes outside the body; and
> (d) the defendant is (or would if sued in time have been) liable for negligence or breach of statutory duty to one or both of the parents, irrespective of whether

they suffered actionable injury, as long as there was a breach of duty which if injury had occurred would have given rise to liability.

Section 1A(3) provides a defence to an action by a child where at the time of the treatment either or both of the parents knew the risk of their child being born disabled created by the particular act or omission (we discuss this further below). The other defences available under the 1976 Act are also available in this extended action (s. 1A(4)).

Section 1A of the 1976 Act clearly covers damage caused by the keeping or storage of the embryos or gametes, whether they have been frozen or not. It also applies to the procedure of selection of the embryos for implantation, although so little is known about this process that it is more of a morphological check than a scientific screening procedure. There are on the face of the section some difficulties. For example, it is not clear that it applies to an act or omission which causes damage to an embryo being recovered from a woman by lavage for subsequent implantation in another woman who gestates the child subsequently born injured. It is arguable that the recovery of the embryo could be regarded as a 'selection', but it is probable that that wording would be more strictly confined to the selection of one rather than another embryo for transfer to the woman's uterus.

Where a surrogacy arrangement has taken place and the genetic parent(s) apply for a parental order under s. 30 of the 1990 Act, the provisions of s. 1A of the 1976 Act will still apply for the benefit of the child. Section 1A(2) provides that it is a condition of a successful action that the defendant was liable in tort to one or both of the 'parents'. Prima facie, where a parental order in favour of the gamete donors is later made, they are not the parents referred to in that section and hence the basis for the child's claim fails. Section 30(1) of the 1990 Act provides for 'a child to be treated in law as the child of the parties to a marriage'. If this is applied in the same way as, say, s. 29(1) and (2) (person to be treated in law as the mother or father of a child for all purposes) then this may give rise to difficulty in this one case of surrogacy. This argument can be assailed, however, in that s. 30 speaks not of the parental order ensuring that that person or couple is to be regarded as the child's parents for all purposes, as does s. 29, but of 'an order providing for a child to be treated in law as the child of the parties to a marriage'. It might be argued that the difference in wording is significant, and that it should be interpreted so as to save, rather than defeat, the introduction of a scheme for the benefit of that child.

Section 1A(3) of the 1976 Act provides the same defence in respect of parental knowledge as in the Act. Thus, where at the time the embryo, or sperm and eggs were placed in the woman, or at the time she was inseminated, either or both of the parents knew the particular risk created by the act or omission of their child being born disabled, then the defendant (a 'person answerable to the child' under s. 1A(2)) is not answerable to the child. Since the HFEA Code of Practice demands that information be given on such matters as 'possible outcomes of the treatment proposed' and 'variations of effectiveness over time', the parents ought not to be ignorant of possible risks. Indeed the Code goes much further in suggesting disclosure of known side-effects, medical risks to the woman of hyperstimulation and multiple pregnancy, and the social consequences of treatment. Whether such broad-based coverage of attendant risks is sufficient may at some point be tested.

In the light of the speeches of Lords Bridge and Keith in *Sidaway* v *Board of Governors of Bethlem Royal Hospital* [1985] 1 All ER 643 about the disclosures of risk, it may well be that such a blanket attempt to provide 'information' would be insufficient for the parents to be satisfactorily appraised, as a matter of law, of the 'particular risk created by the act or omission' of which s. 1A(3) speaks.[38] Recall that Lord Bridge had said (at 663):

> . . . even where, as here, no expert witness in the relevant medical field condemns the practice of non-disclosure as being in conflict with accepted and responsible medical practice, I am of the opinion that the judge might in certain circumstances come to the conclusion that disclosure of a particular risk was so obviously necessary to an informed choice on the part of the patient that no reasonably prudent medical man would fail to make it. The kind of case I have in mind would be an operation involving substantial risk of grave adverse consequences . . .

When this is coupled with Lord Diplock's assertion (at 657) that this general duty 'is not subject to dissection into a number of component parts to which different criteria of what satisfy the duty of care apply, such as diagnosis, treatment and advice (including warning of risks of something going wrong however skilfully the treatment has been carried out . . .)' the basis for understanding s. 1A(3) in a more comprehensive light is laid out. There will be some risks of congenital disability which are so grave and adverse that specific disclosure of them and the consequences to which they may give rise if they materialise will be necessary to escape liability under s. 1A.

It is clear that, in a number of instances, for the purpose of instituting proceedings under s. 1 of the 1976 Act, it would be necessary to identify the genetic father or mother of the child. Suppose, for example, that a complete failure of genetic screening at a treatment centre resulted in the birth of a child disabled within the meaning of the 1976 Act. If a mother were then to make a claim that the failure of genetic screening at the centre 'affected . . . her ability to have a normal, healthy child' since she was introduced to a donor whose sperm was always likely to give rise to a disabled child, it might be necessary for evidential purposes to trace that donor. Similarly, the donor himself might be liable where, knowing that he was HIV positive, he nonetheless allowed his sperm to be used for infertility treatment. As the Act places liability upon 'a person (other than the child's own mother)', it is clear that there is nothing in the 1976 Act itself which would exempt the donor, even if considered as father, from liability.[39] Again, however, the problem would lie in identifying the donor. Lastly, the state of the father's knowledge may be relevant to the s. 1(4) defence considered above. But who is the 'father' for these purposes?

An amended s. 4(4) of the Congenital Disabilities Act 1976 now provides that where as the result of assisted conception a child carried by a woman is born disabled, references within the 1976 Act to a 'parent' will include a reference to a person who would be a parent but for ss. 27–29 of the 1990 Act. Also, in an attempt to resolve some of the difficulties of identifying parents, s. 35(1) of the 1990 Act states that where for the purposes of initiating proceedings under the 1976 Act, it is necessary to identify a person who would or might be the parent of a child (*cf.* the wording in s. 4(A) of the 1976 Act) 'but for sections 27 to 29 of this Act, the court may, on the application of the child, make an order requiring the Authority to disclose' registered information under s. 30 of the Act such that the person could be identified. Most importantly, this will include sections such as 27(1) and 28(6) which provide that donors of gametes other than the couple receiving treatment are not to be treated ordinarily as either the mother or the father of the child in question. Note that this is only available on a court order which requires the Authority to disclose such information.

CONGENITAL DISABILITY: PRODUCT LIABILITY

The Consumer Protection Act 1987 introduces strict product liability into English law, implementing the EU Product Liability Directive.[40] Section 6(3) of the 1987 Act extends this strict liability regime such that the unborn child is to have the benefit of it. Since it does so by restating the way in which s. 1 of the Congenital Disabilities Act 1976 will have effect, the rights of any child born are dependent upon there being a liability to the parent arising out of the defective product. This raises the problem of whether gametes or embryos could ever amount to a 'product' within the meaning of the Consumer Protection Act 1987. This raises the odd possibility of the child suing on the basis of a defect in the very genetic material which brought it into being, so that there will be some who regard the asking of the question as itself evidence of the moral bankruptcy of this whole area. Nonetheless, it is one to which we now turn.

The 1987 Act places upon producers strict liability for products which prove to be defective and which cause damage or personal injury. 'Producer' in this context generally means the manufacturer of the product, but it can also encompass a person who is responsible for extracting a non-manufactured product. Liability may attach to a person who is not a producer if that person imports a product into the European Community. The Act gives a very broad meaning to the word 'products'; it includes 'goods' (s. 1(2)), which is itself deemed to include substances. 'Substances' for the purposes of the Act 'means any natural or artificial solid, vaporous or liquid substance' (s. 45(1)). A product is considered to contain a 'defect' when 'the safety of the product is not such as persons are generally entitled to expect' (s. 3(1)). In determining whether or not a product has lived up to its expectations of safety, regard must be paid to the manner of the marketing of the product, including any instructions or warnings provided at the time of its supply. Looking at the operation of the product liability law under the 1987 Act, there is no reason in principle why gametes and embryos may not be 'products' within the meaning of that Act. They are clearly 'substances', and it is interesting to recall that the Pearson Commission[41] recommended that 'human blood and organs should be regarded as 'products' and authorities responsible for distributing them as their "producers" for the purposes of product liability'. The argument against this might be that the provision of infertility treatment is the provision of services which ought not to be encompassed within the Consumer Protection Act 1987.[42]

Provided causation can be shown, physical damage, including personal injury, is recoverable. Physical injury here includes disease and the impairment of mental as well as physical health (s. 45(1)). As we have said, s. 6(3) of the 1987 Act gives effect to s. 1 of the Congenital Disabilities Act 1976, thereby incorporating the provisions of this legislation into the strict liability regime. This is done by providing that where a parent has a right to sue for an occurrence arising out of a defect in a product, the defendant faces the same liability towards a child suffering from disability following the parent's exposure to that occurrence. This provision clearly addresses matters such as the Thalidomide litigation, which in part inspired the implementation of this form of product liability measure. There are a number of defences under the Consumer Protection Act, but the most significant one is that at the time of supply the state of scientific knowledge was not such that a producer of products of the same description might be expected to have discovered the defect if it had existed in the product while it was under the producer's control (the 'state of the art' defence, s. 49(1)(e); *cf.* Art. 7(e) of the Directive).

Although s. 6(3) of the 1987 Act specifically incorporates claims for congenital disability, it is likely that it had in mind claims based on pharmaceutical products. It is a rather different matter to consider claims where the 'product' which was alleged to be defective is the very stuff which gave rise to the life of the litigant herself or himself. Courts might prove highly reluctant to allow such claims, especially in view of the rejection of such matters as wrongful life claims (see *McKay* v *Essex Area Health Authority* [1982] QB 1166).[43] Issues of liability might also founder on the question of 'damage'. 'Damage' means 'death or personal injury or any loss of or damage to property' (s. 5(1)), but liability is excluded when the defect in the product causes loss of or damage to the product itself or to 'the whole or any part of any product which has been supplied with the product in question comprised in it' (s. 5(2)). It is a difficult question of British jurisprudence whether a person can properly be described as a 'product supplied', even where he or she comprises the gametes or embryos from which he or she is derived. On the other hand, would the courts find it so difficult if in the course of offering infertility treatment, the embryo which was implanted into the woman caused the woman to become seriously ill?

In many ways the whole tone of the 1987 Act seems inappropriate for this body of law. Consider the defence under s. 4(1)(f). This applies where the product was a component in some other product and the defect causing damage is wholly attributable either to the design of the other product or to specifications given by the designer of the other product, to the producer of the component or to inadequate installation. One can see arguments arising as to whether the sperm was a defective component, or whether the actual problem was the adequate installation of the fertilised egg. It seems to make 'genetic engineering' a most appropriate term. On the other hand, are there reasons in principle why, if the persons engaged in such activities, they ought not to be liable for the damage which may result?

NOTES

[1]   This judgment of Phillips J was endorsed in the Court of Appeal, see the note at (1993) 1 Med LR 103.

[2]   For an introduction, see Keown, J., *Abortion, Doctors and the Law*, 1988 (Cambridge, Cambridge University Press, Mason, J.K., *Medico Legal Aspects of Reproduction and Parenthood*, 2nd ed. (Aldershot, Ashgate, 1998); and Kennedy, I. and Grubb, A., *Principles of Medical Law* (London, Butterworths, 1994), ch. 11.

[3] Cited in Brightman Committee Report, HLC 50, para. 8; and see the consideration of a similar point in Atkinson, S.B., 'Life, Birth and Live-Birth' (1904) 20 LQR 157.

[4] *Op. cit.* n. 2, at 112.

[5] *Textbook of Criminal Law*, 2nd ed. (London, Stevens, 1982), p. 291, n. 1.

[6] Indeed Mason makes the point that the subject has never attracted the interest in Scotland that it has in England (*op. cit.* n. 2, at 114), but then see Russell, E.J., 'Abortion Law in Scotland and the *Kelly* Foetus' (1997) 24 *Scots LT* 187.

[7] In *The Lancet* for 10 March 1984, entitled 'Capable of Being Born Alive'.

[8] de Cruz, S.P., 'Abortion, *C* v *S* and the Law' (1987) 17 *Fam Law* 319.

[9] *Op. cit.* n. 5, at 303–04.

[10] In his book *Abortion, Doctors and the Law, op. cit.* n. 2, at 49–59.

[11] See further Clarke, L., in Lee and Morgan, *Birthrights, Law and Ethics at the Beginnings of Life* (London, Routledge, 1989), at 155; and Keown (*op. cit.* n. 10 above).

[12] Mason, *op. cit.* n. 2, at 117.

[13] McLean, S., 'Abortion Law: Is Consensual Reform Possible?' in Len Doyal and Lesley Doyal (eds), *Legal and Moral Dilemmas in Modern Medicine* (1990) 17 *Journal of Law and Society Special Issue* 106, at 116.

[14] Official Report, House of Lords, 18 October 1990, coll. 1043–87.

[15] Mason, *op. cit.* n. 2, at 166.

[16] The Select Committee of the House of Lords on the Infant Life (Preservation) Bill (1987–8), at 18.

[17] House of Commons, Official Report, 24 April 1990, coll. 273–304, and note that an attempt to reinstate a 28-week limit was defeated, see House of Commons, Official Report, 24 April 1990, coll. 273–304.

[18] See Morgan, 'Abortion – The Unexamined Ground' [1990] Crim LR 687; Mason, J.K., *Medico-Legal Aspects of Reproduction and Parenthood, op. cit.* n. 2, at 105 *et seq.*

[19] For a discussion of the legal implications, see Morgan, 'Legal and Ethical Dilemmas of Fetal Sex Identification and Gender Selection' in A.A. Templeman and D. Cusine, *Reproductive Medicine and the Law* (Edinburgh Churchill Livingstone, 1990), at 53–77.

[20] House of Commons Official Report, 24 February 1990, col 169.

[21] See, for example, A. Aberg *et. al.*, 'Cardiac puncture of fetus with Hurler's disease avoiding abortion of unaffected co-twin' (1978) *Lancet* 990; Howie suggests that this might properly be regarded as 'selective feticide' Howie, P.W., 'Selective Reduction – Medical Aspects' in A.A. Templeton and D. Cusine, *op. cit.* n. 19, at 25.

[22] For a consideration of the methods of reduction see Howie, P.W., *op. cit.* n. 21, at 30–31; for a review of some of the issues, see Price, F., 'Establishing Guidelines: Regulation and the Clinical Management of Infertility' in Robert Lee and Derek Morgan (eds), *Birthrights: Law and Ethics at the Beginnings of Life, op. cit.* n. 11, at 44–45.

[23] House of Commons Official Report, 21 June 1990, col. 1198.

[24] Price, D., 'Selective Reduction and Feticide: The Parameters of Abortion' [1988] Crim LR 199; Pickup, Z., 'Selective reduction, abortion and the law' at 33–39.

[25] 'Selective Reduction of Multiple Pregnancy' (1987) NLJ 1165 (see also his opinion at VLA Third Report, appendix 4, and the reply by Ian Kennedy and Andrew Grubb to this latter point in their *Medical Law, Text and Materials*, *op. cit.* n. 2, at 796.

[26] *Ibid.*

[27] Citing his own close examination, 'Miscarriage – a Medico-Legal analysis' [1984] Crim LR 604.

[28] *Op. cit.* n. 24, at 200.

[29] Kennedy and Grubb.

[30] *Three, Four or More* (London, HMSO, 1990).

[31] The limited data is reviewed in Howie, *op. cit.* n. 21, at 26–27.

[32] *Ibid.*, at 27–28.

[33] House of Commons Official Report, 21 June 1990, col. 1192.

[34] Tunkel, V., 'Modern Anti-Pregnancy Techniques and the Criminal Law' [1974] Crim LR 461 and 'Abortion: How Early, How Late and How Legal' (1979) *British Medical Journal* 253; Keown, J., *op. cit.* n. 27.

[35] Norrie, K., 'Post Coital Anti-Pregnancy Techniques and the Law' in A.A. Templeton and D. Cusine, *op. cit.* n. 19, at 12.

[36] *Ibid.*, at 13.

[37] *Report on Injuries to Unborn Children*, Law Com. No. 60 (1974).

[38] It may in any case be open to the court to review the practice of clinics in this respect, see *Bolitho* [1998] AC 232.

[39] A possibility recognised when the 1990 reforms were introduced (see House of Commons Official Report, 20 June 1990, coll. 993 *et seq.*).

[40] Council Directive on Product Liability (85/374/EEC).

[41] Commission on Civil Liability and Compensation for Personal Injury (Cmnd 7054, 1978), para. 1276.

[42] See Whittaker, S. (1989) 105 LQR 125, who argues that professional liability should remain fault-based.

[43] See also Lee, R., 'To Be or Not to Be: Is That the Question?' in Lee, R. and Morgan, D. (eds), *Birthrights*, *op. cit.* n. 11.

Chapter 11
Assisted Conception: The International Response

INTRODUCTION

James Watson, writing in 1971, suggested of the possible developments in human reproductive research that:

> Different societies are likely to view the matter differently and it would be surprising if all came to the same conclusion. We must, therefore, assume that techniques for the *in vitro* manipulation of human eggs are likely to be of general medical practice, capable of routine performance in many major nations within some 10 to 20 years. . . . [Yet] a sufficient international consciousness might be apparent to make possible some forms of international agreement before the cat is totally out of the bag.[1]

The statutory regulation of assisted conception – that, for example, now adopted in the United Kingdom and said by many commentators to provide a model for other jurisdictions, and one which is indeed appealed to by many – is only one of a number of possible models of regulation. Here, we examine the different sorts of judgment that must be made in deciding whether and then how to regulate innovative health technologies and the challenges that this poses for what might be called 'biomedical diplomacy'. Then we review some of the responses which have been made to the burgeoning science of reproduction and infertility services around the globe. We consider briefly the terms of the recent and significant Council of Europe Convention on Human Rights and Biomedicine[2] and offer some preliminary observations on the difficulties of harmonisation or approximation of laws at a time of developing global business of assisted conception in the shadow of subsidiarity.

THE CHALLENGES OF REGULATING MEDICAL PRACTICES

The existence of a few specialist clinics has revealed a global market for assisted conception services.[3] The techniques and trappings of assisted conception, AID, IVF, GIFT, cryopreservation of gametes, eggs and embryos, gamete and embryo donation, surrogacy, and other developments in assisted conception challenge our traditional views of procreation and parenthood. This challenge has legal as well as ethical implications.

A variety of different instruments can be and are employed to regulate the activities of scientific and technical societies, each of which requires us to examine what is meant by 'regulation'. Thus, one might distinguish at least between:

(a)   formal (state) law, that is specially formulated legal principles and norms applied to the subject matter in question, or to the processes which are the subject matter;
(b)   formal (state) law which is of general applicability;
(c)   informal, general or specific law, such as professional codes of practice or discipline, which may either be promulgated under a general state law which regulates professions (or professionals of a particular kind, or subject to special and specific qualifications), or which may be adopted voluntarily by the professional body concerned and which may be either of a general directive kind or specific mandatory provisions which covers certain defined activities rather than (say) providing only the conditions of good professional practice;
(d)   moral suasion; and
(e)   the market.[4]

In respect of each type of approach, we may ask to whom or to what are 'the rules' of the regulation directed? In each case, again, it is necessary to consider the relationship between:

• the international community;
• the nation state;
• 'individual' patients or consumers;
• scientific and technical practitioners; and
• resulting 'social practices' with respect to relationships between people.

And when assessing novel medical technologies – such as assisted conception – and their judicious introduction into therapeutic practice and the applicable form or nature of regulation, it is appropriate to distinguish a number of 'phases'. These include:

• the developmental phase;
• the human subjects trial phase;
• the incorporation of the technology into health care; and
• the diffusion phase.[5]

Part of the reason why it is commonly said that assisted conception techniques and medical technology generally outstrip ethical and legal debate is that there exists no consensus about the complex ethical issues which arise: the challenge is to obtain all the advantages of the reproduction revolution and avoid the disadvantages; to avoid becoming prisoners of progress, but to control the development and guide it in the directions we want. One of the problems is trying to foresee unwarranted consequences; another is to agree upon which consequences are unwarranted and how they are best avoided or minimised. One cause of the apparent despair is that society has chosen, for a variety of reasons, to avoid attempts at reaching a moral consensus. In such a field, then, government sometimes acts wisely in refusing or failing to regulate (by law) in order to allow debate and discussion to proceed, and perhaps to encourage some moral consensus to emerge.

And yet, as European countries increasingly debate questions arising from *in vitro* fertilisation and embryo research, it is apparent that general agreement is emerging, both within the scientific community and in European institutions, that common, core approaches are desirable.[6] Differences in legislative response, differences in the extent to which questions such as those arising from the advent and adventure of reproductive technology constitute items on public, social and legal policy agendas, will depend on permutations and nuances in tradition, religion, culture, economics and wealth. Throughout the European Union and the member states of the Council of Europe, moral and legal pluralism reflecting these variations is evident. Yet it is sometimes overlooked that this pluralism typically operates at the margins of what might be called the ethical stationery. The depth and breadth of agreement far outweighs and outpaces moral disagreement, whether the supporting reasoning is of a broadly consequentialist or a deontological kind. However, it is at the margins of this ethical page that the lines become less clear, the text blurred and the meanings most ambiguous, oppositional and most evidently contextual. It is in these margins that legal script becomes most branded with national trademarks, and yet in the commonality of responses there are some common themes to be pursued.

In analysing this Europeanisation of ethical responses to reproductive technologies, two sorts of foundational work driving deep into the bedrock of ethical debate need to be surveyed, excavated, reinforced and reconstructed. First, an attempt to declare and understand differing philosophical approaches needs to identify the background cultural theories implicated in the analysis; this is an essentially epistemological question. Secondly, the way in which these views have been translated into legal regulation or its functional equivalent, legislative quiescence, needs to be carefully constructed and explored. Assumptions and expectations, intentions and outcomes need to be documented and analysed.

The differences (real or perceived) in the domestic approach to questions of regulation are nowhere better parodied than by Wayland Kennet, in his essay 'Legislation and Regulation in Europe':

> There is in human nature a scale of different possible reactions to the slogan 'from ethics to law.' At one extreme is the temperament which feels, 'if it's wrong, we must legislate at once. Let us forbid it in the Penal Code, or at least write it into the Civil Code, and if we can't do either of those, then let us outlaw it in some other code or body of law, such as the Public Health Code.' The British think that is the French way.
>
> At the other extreme is the temperament which feels: 'if it's wrong, let us educate everybody to know that it is wrong, and that will surely solve the problem. At the very most, let us hope that the professionals will regulate it in their codes of practice; medical, nursing, and so on. Above all, no new law.' The French think that is the British way.[7]

We can, in fact, identify several discrete approaches adopted in the international responses to assisted conception which have so far emerged – what we might call different 'models' – which might variously be described as:

- the United Kingdom's Human Fertilisation and Embryology Act 1990, which exhibits what may be thought of as a 'radical *laissez-faire*' approach; a system of regulated private ordering;
- the Danish legislation of 1987 and 1992, which embodies a 'cautious regulatory system';
- the Austrian Act on Procreative Medicine, which exemplifies a 'prohibitive licensing system'; and
- the proposals of the Law Reform Commission of Canada, 'Medically Assisted Procreation', which may be characterised as a form of 'liberal constitutional approach'.

Of course, there will remain the difficulty of whether harmonisation, approximation or convergence is desirable; and even if it is judged that it is, whether it should gravitate towards a more restrictive, or more liberal or radical approach – which is the polar position to which plural systems should be magnetised, and what are the active critical masses?

Bartha Knoppers and Sonia Le Bris[8] have identified a range of emergent assumptions about the necessary forms of limitation and prohibition of assisted conception, and a narrower area in which disagreement or national difference is more pronounced. They suggest that a general consensus exists such that:

(a)   access to assisted conception should be limited to married heterosexual couples or those in stable unions;

(b)   clinicians offering treatment services should be supervised or regulated, at least by medical colleagues;

(c)   legal considerations of paternity and maternity should be addressed;

(d)   confidential medical records of donors and children should be established;

(e)   research on or experimentation with embryonic life *in utero* should be limited to 14 days;

(f)   time limits on storage should be established;

(g)   posthumous implantation or insemination should be discouraged or prohibited;

(h)   participant consent and common conditions of donation should be established;

(i)   reproductive technologies should be free from commercialisation;

(j)   sex selection of embryos for other than genetic disease should be prohibited, as should forms of eugenic selection; and

(k)   controls and prohibitions on extreme forms of genetic engineering, such as cloning, parthenogenesis, inter-species fertilisation and the creation of chimeras, should be established.

As Deryck Beyleveld and Shaun Pattinson more recently comment:

> Where legislation exists, it typically prohibits reproductive cloning and germline gene therapy, either prohibits non-therapeutic embryo research or subjects it to conditions (such as a 14 day cut-off point), permits abortion and PND, and regulates those assisted reproductive techniques that involve the storage or use of embryos outside the body. However, there is far less convergence on issues

such as the permissibility of PGD, and the use of medically assisted reproduction by single women and homosexual couples.[9]

In other areas there is less or no agreement. For social, cultural, economic or religious reasons there is lack of unanimity on questions such as the remuneration of donors; access to information by children born following assisted conception; the maintenance of information registers; the donation and conservation of and experimentation with human embryos; limitation on the number of children by donor; and on the genetic diagnosis of embryos. On these differences, Knoppers and Le Bris comment:

> These differences are fundamental. Thus, the possibility of a comprehensive policy, or of legislation encompassing all of these new technologies in each state, may never be forthcoming and may not even be desirable where it would run contrary to basic human rights and freedoms. Furthermore, even if internal domestic agreements were to be achieved, today's modern 'global village', with its means of transportation and communication, would allow citizens to practise 'procreative tourism' in order to exercise their personal reproductive choices in other less restrictive states.[10]

Against this background of difference and similarity, Knoppers and Le Bris suggest that five basic principles may be identified as needing to be safeguarded: the respect for human dignity; the security of human genetic material; the quality of services; the inviolability of the human person; and the inalienability of the human body.

We have reviewed Eser's suggestion that legal initiatives may be required for one or more of four reasons[11]: *a symbolic function of law; a protective function; a regulative or declarative function;* and *a technical function of law.* Donald Chalmers has more concretely argued that the most salient arguments for regulation of some kind are, first, that science and technology frequently call for the expenditure of public monies, which itself justifies the introduction of a regulatory framework if the community so chooses.[12] Other important reasons are the prevention of harm, particularly in connection with community safety and public health, the welfare of children born of assisted conception technology, the disclosure of information in a democratic society and, because assisted conception involves the medical profession in the creation of children within modern family units, the development and deployment of family law.[13]

There are, of course, serious doubts which may be expressed about the 'externalities' involved in different types of regulation. For example, suppose that the Danish legislation were to propose (as the German Embryo Protection Act 1990 has done) that research using human (pre-) embryos is prohibited unless for the therapeutic benefit of that individual embryo. Would that mean that citizens or inhabitants of Denmark would or should be disentitled from reaping the benefits (if any appear) of subsequent scientific work which has traded specifically on such research?[14] This is a variant of an argument much canvassed since the Third Reich when experiments or torture were performed on human beings without their consent. Is such 'knowledge' so morally tainted that to draw any benefit from it whatsoever is similarly profane and perverted?

The Danish Council of Ethics perceptively observes:

> . . . this relationship between ethics and legislation makes it necessary to pose
> two questions in connection with concrete legislation: Does the legislation live
> up to that minimum of humanity which the society wishes to preserve and does
> it allow real freedom for the individual to observe stricter standards than those
> contained in the law?[15]

In addition, the Danish Council of Ethics believes that the legislation concerning
these problems must take its point of departure in Danish conditions. This means
that there may be deviations in relation to the legislation of other countries. The
acquisition of knowledge can in some instances raise ethical questions, and it is
important that such questions be discussed internationally in order, if possible, to
create consensus. But this does not exclude a national regulation. Indeed, the
adoption by (say) Denmark of its own legislation, may mean a greater possibility
of influencing the supranational law.

It is true that wise government does not always legislate at the first opportunity,[16]
and the global nature of the reproduction revolution makes the lack of attention to
concerted international legislation perhaps more surprising than would be its
presence.[17] For lawyers, as much as for anyone else, the present dilemmas
surrounding the international regulation of assisted conception technologies and
services have nowhere been better encapsulated than in the following quotations:

> When people face what nothing in their past has prepared them for they grope
> for words to name the unknown, even when they can neither define nor
> understand it.[18]

> . . . we lack a perspective for judgments that go so deep . . . Everything around
> us is new and different – our concerns, our working habits, our relations with
> one another. Our very psychology has been shaken to its foundations, to its most
> secret recesses. Our notions of separation, absence, distance, return, are reflec-
> tions of a new set of realities, though the words remain unchanged. To grasp the
> meaning of the world of today, we use a language created to express the world
> of yesterday.[19]

There is a temptation to believe that legislative attempts to secure recognition of
one particular view at the expense of others would be the enforcement of moral
majoritarianism. Thus legislation is sometimes asked to portray or reflect a
weakened and expansive ethical or moral conception. Ethically based legislation
must seek the fulcrum which will ensure a proper balance between a minimum
level of humanity and moral standards and freedom for individual women and men
to live according to the dictates of their own consciences, which may, of course,
entail stricter demands than those contained in law. Law, on this view, is naturally
seen as part of what might be understood to be comparative public policy-making
and responses to the forces of globalisation.

In each country of Europe, including Eastern Europe,[20] similar questions arise
with respect to law, medicine and bioethics. But, as we have already suggested,

there are differences of a philosophical, economic and social nature which are not easily (even if desirably) bridged. The parallel between explosive political change within and across Europe and the rapid developments in biomedical sciences and their impacts on the fields of law, ethics and human rights gives rise to challenges at at least three levels:[21]

(a) *Human rights* – What is the meaning, for example, of a 'fundamental right to human life', and in what way(s) is this question metamorphosed by biotechnology? What is meant by the European Convention on Human Rights' guarantee (in Art. 12) of the right to 'marry and found a family', and how do substantive and procedural barriers to access to biotechnology impinge on that 'right'? Reconciliation of advances in medicine and science with values expressed through human rights is necessary to preserve the bioethical balance; to ensure that the risks to patients, providers and the subjects of biotechnology are minimised. Laws, administrative regulations and professional codes of conduct must be carefully scrutinised to elaborate the effects they set out to achieve, whether they achieve those and only those ends, and whether there are other, unintended, unforeseen or unforeseeable effects.[22]

(b) *Democracy and public choice* – How should these difficult issues be mediated? Towards consensus, a toleration of moral pluralism, or within the dictates of one dominant philosophical approach? What is the fulcrum of the bioethical balance? What institutional structures are used, proposed or necessary to articulate and effect these determinations of public choice?

(c) *The rule of law* – A fundamental question which arises for any jurisdiction is whether there is any existing law which regulates biomedical practice, research and development, and whether it is satisfactory in assisting our responses to ethical dilemmas posed by biotechnology. Is it too accommodating or too antagonistic?

Possible responses to these challenges, an understanding of intellectual forces which have produced them, and the mediation of differences of form and substance comprise what one of the authors has elsewhere called *biomedical diplomacy*.[23] This concept can be located within a wider theoretical construct, identifying shifts in the nature of philosophical practices, and the development and deployment of new forms of regulation which both supplement and represent a challenge to the increasing juridification (the danger of the uncritical and unreflective appeal to and of law)[24] of social and technical practices.

Biomedical diplomacy attempts to identify and negotiate 'tragic choices'[25] which have to be constantly (re-) negotiated. It examines how modern biomedicine requires the re-negotiation and regulation of existing boundaries of risk, technology and power, and how it attempts to achieve this at the level of the individual state. This it does at a time of enormous geopolitical, economic and epistemological upheaval; a global concern with ethics appears to have become the defining stigmata of the late 20th century,[26] pluralism is replacing old certainties and the generic 'patient' is disappearing.[27] Biomedical diplomacy, negotiating the tragic choices, is part of ensuring that societies collectively will be privy to and retain a belief in influencing what the outcomes of individual choices will be.

The clearest example of an attempt to articulate the necessary dialogue and broker the deals of biomedical diplomacy is found in the Council of Europe's

Convention on Human Rights and Biomedicine. For over a decade the Council of Europe had been working, through the Parliamentary Assembly and the *ad hoc* Committee of Experts on Bioethics (CAHBI; later renamed the CDBI – the Steering Committee on Bioethics), with responses to the advances in medicine and biology. At the seventh Meeting of the Ministers of Justice of the Council of Europe, in Istanbul in 1990, the CAHBI was instructed to examine the possibility of preparing a framework convention which would set out 'common general standards for the protection of the human person in the context of the development of the biomedical sciences'.[28] A first version of the draft Convention was submitted to public consultation and for the opinion of the Parliamentary Assembly of the Council of Europe in 1994. The Convention was adopted by the Committee of Ministers on 19 November 1996 and opened for signature on 4 April 1997.[29]

The Convention sets out only the most important principles; additional safe-guards and more detailed questions will be spelled out in protocols, of which the first, on the Prohibition of Cloning[30] was opened on 12 January 1998. The Convention requires signatories to ensure that their law provides for:

(a)   the priority of the interests and welfare of the human being over those of society (Art. 2);

(b)   equitable access to health care (Art. 3);

(c)   health interventions, including research, to be carried out in accordance with professional obligations and standards (Art. 4);

(d)   free and informed consent by a person before an 'intervention in the health field' (Art. 5);

(e)   respect for a person's private life in relation to health information (Art. 10);

(f)   no discrimination on the grounds of genetic heritage (Art. 11);

(g)   protection against human genome modification unless for therapeutic purposes (Art. 13);

(h)   a prohibition on sex selection, unless for preventing the transmission of a serious sex-linked disease (Art. 14);

(i)   only limited research on the human embryo, ensuring where the law permits research 'adequate protection of the embryo' (Art. 18) and a prohibition on the creation of an embryo only for the purposes of research (Art. 19); and

(j)   a prohibition on the use of the human body and its parts for financial gain (Art. 21).

Article 36 provides for states to enter a reservation to their signature to the Convention if law already in force in that state is not in conformity with a provision of the Convention. This, if the question arose of UK accession to the Convention (which does not look likely in the near future[31]), would be the instrument used to excuse the Human Fertilisation and Embryology Act's sanction of embryo research in the UK. Article 29 of the Convention provides that the European Court of Human Rights in Strasbourg may give Advisory Opinions on the interpretation of the Convention, thus beginning the process of tying the Convention to European human rights jurisprudence.

We now turn to look more specifically at the way member states of the European Union and other countries have addressed the conundrums of assisted conception and the technologies of the reproduction revolution.

INTERNATIONAL APPROACHES TO ASSISTED CONCEPTION

This section explores the ways in which European and international legal systems have responded to the challenges of reproductive medicine. The aim of this review, as with all comparative law, is not just to suggest that we should strive for (or can arrive at) a consensus with regard to regulating assisted conception by seeing what the majority of states which have addressed these questions have done and then opting for what seems to be the most popular as a template for international harmonisation. As Lord Steyn has recently observed in *McFarlane* v *Tayside Health Board* [1999] 4 All ER 961, at 976:

> . . . the discipline of comparative law does not aim at a poll of the solutions adopted in different countries. It has the different and inestimable value of sharpening our focus on the weight of competing considerations. And it reminds us that the law is part of the world of competing ideas markedly influenced by cultural differences.

But that there may be good reason to explore the possibilities of international consensus is remarked by Margot Brazier:

> Another nightmare awaits the HFEA and its counterparts in continental Europe. Each national jurisdiction has sought to fashion a scheme of regulation accept-able to its own culture and community. However, those wealthy enough to participate in reproduction markets can readily evade their domestic constraints. If I can order sperm on the internet, or hire a surrogate mother from Bolivia, are British regulators wasting their time? The international ramifications of the reproductive business may prove to be a more stringent test of the strength of British law than all the difficult ethical dilemmas that have gone before.[32]

This is a brochure from the regulators of the businesses of 'procreative tourism'.[33]

Scandinavia

In the Scandinavian countries, artificial procreation is not generally seen as a matter of individual rights. While an individual's strong desire to have a child may indeed help ensure a secure basis for the child's later development, it is not sufficient to outweigh the interests of the child in later life. The differences among the Scandinavian countries concerning entitlement to access to reproductive technology may reflect differing attitudes to marriage and perhaps variations in the degree of religious influence.[34]

Denmark[35]   In Denmark, IVF in public hospitals is offered only to spouses or cohabiting couples who have been living together for at least three years. It is an additional precondition that there are no children already living in the family. Lastly, there are conditions as to age. The Danish Council of Ethics records that artificial insemination and *in vitro* fertilisation should be placed on an equal footing with intercourse, at least when semen and unfertilised ova from the interested couple are used and the woman herself becomes pregnant. Here, the family relationship is not changed by the use of assisted conception techniques. Majorities of the Council, however, then proceed to make two different findings. First, one group holds that it is desirable for a child to have parents of the opposite sex. A different group holds, however, that it is not crucial that a child is secured a father from the outset of the treatment services. It ought not to be a prerequisite, they write, for artificial insemination or IVF that it concerns married or established cohabiting couples. There are many single women with children; this family form is becoming more recognised and accepted and, they conclude, single women ought also to have access to artificial insemination and IVF. Secondly, by a different majority, the Danish Council of Ethics go further, however, and comment that

> Danish society today has given lesbian couples the possibility of a marital status; from this point of view, lesbian couples ought also to have the possibility of artificial fertilisation. Furthermore, there ought to be no differential treatment of single women and two women who live together.[36]

The Danish Act, however, does not address this point; there was no pressure for this to be included in the legislation so policy will be decided in individual hospitals and clinics. This effectively leaves this important question of medical jurisprudence solely to clinical discretion. It would have been better to have made provision in the legislation to address this issue rather than for it to have been left to individual clinicians.

There are interesting comparisons to be drawn between the ways in which Scandinavian countries, especially Sweden, have responded to the particular problem of donation and anonymity. Egg-donation is allowed in Denmark according to the 1992 legislation, while embryo-donation is banned. The Act does not give a reason for making this distinction. In the *traveaux préparatoires* it is merely stated that this will be a problem only for very few couples. In Norway and Sweden egg-donation and embryo-donation are presently prohibited by law, on grounds both of the interest of the child and human values. Donation would deprive the child of a link which is fundamental to its identity. Also, procreation is seen as a single process which takes place inside the woman, and egg-donation would break the natural link between uterus and egg. Donation is characterised as a technical problem-solving method which could have damaging repercussions for human values. Lastly, ethical considerations are linked to the risks of conflict over the identity of the mother, unethical selection and commercialisation. These risks are considered to outweigh the right of personal freedom and autonomy for the parents.

In all of the Scandinavian countries artificial insemination by donor is accepted. The practice is not regulated by law in Denmark, but donor anonymity is secured by administrative fiat, through the way in which the public donor bank functions; the child is not entitled to be informed of the identity of the father, nor of the fact that donor insemination has taken place. The Ethical Council Report of 1990 was quite forthright on this issue. Anonymity is seen as essential. However, there has been a debate in Denmark as to the right of the child to know the donor, once the child has reached sufficient maturity. In Norway anonymity is established by law. In Sweden it is considered a basic right of a child to know its origin. Without such knowledge, the child will be deprived of the ability to develop an accurate self-image.

Lastly, surrogacy has been prohibited in all of the Scandinavian countries; contracts are not valid and surrogacy arrangements are generally considered to be unwarranted.

The Danish legislation does not aim to be as comprehensive or wide-ranging as the British; and in neither case does the legislation present itself as a code covering all questions of assisted conception. In practice, publicly-funded treatment services are restricted to women who are:

(a) married or have been cohabiting for three years;
(b) under 37 years at the time of entry on to the waiting list;
(c) without children; and

who have a medical need for treatment.

Some private clinics are emerging in Denmark, although earlier incarnations struggled to gain social acceptability.

In the Act establishing the Council of Ethics a temporary prohibition concerning embryo research was laid down. This 'interim' approach to regulation is in itself worthy of comment. When issues of reproductive technology came initially to be discussed in Denmark, the view was taken that they were of such importance that a legal vacuum was quite inappropriate, and the Law of 1987 was enacted to provide what in effect amounted to a moratorium on embryo research and a restriction on the uses of assisted conception. The Danish Council of Ethics which was established at the same time was charged with addressing the social, legal and ethical questions which it was believed that these developments disclosed.

In 1991 a draft Danish Bill was published and the resulting legislation – Act No. 503 of 24 June 1992 – came into force in October 1992, with a statutory obligation to undertake review and revision if necessary by 1995–96.

The 1992 Act sanctions embryo research up to 14 days after fertilisation. The proviso is that the object of the research, sanctioned by a regional as well as the central committee, must be the improvement of techniques of *in vitro* fertilisation with a view to promoting pregnancy. Removing and fertilising eggs or embryos for any other purpose is prohibited. The legal motives (explanatory memorandum) appended to the Bill make it clear that the main reason for accepting research but restricting it in this way is that IVF is a recognised treatment and that research is accepted internationally as an integrated part of the development of treatment; prohibiting all research would mean consciously offering less optimal treatment than possible.

Chapter 2, Section 5 of the legislation provides that any biomedical research project which includes research on living human individuals, human gametes which are intended for use in fertilisation, fertilised human eggs and pre-embryos or embryos should be reported to regional ethical committees. There are presently seven such committees, established according to local government boundaries, and they comprise nine or 11 members, three of whom are nominated by the state-authorised scientific committee. A central ethical committee is established by the Minister of Education and Research, who appoints two members. In addition, two members are appointed by the Minister of Health and two members are appointed by each of the regional committees. The central and regional committees are charged to oversee and (where appropriate) approve research.

Section 9 provides that fertilised eggs may be kept outside the woman's womb for only 14 days from conception, excluding any period of cryopreservation. Fertilised human eggs which have been subjected to research must not be implanted into a woman's womb unless this can be done without risk of transmitting hereditary disease, defects, abnormalities or deformities. The purpose of this provision appears to be to permit the diagnostic biopsy of embryonic material *ex utero* without thereby attracting the prohibition on transfer to the uterus of embryos which have been the subject of research.

Additionally, Chapter 4, Section 14 prohibits cloning, the production of individuals by fusion of genetically different embryos or parts of embryos prior to implantation (nucleus substitution) and experiments the objective of which is to make possible the production of living human individuals which are hybrids with a genome containing constituent parts of other species (cross-species fertilisation).

The Danish legislation establishes that it will be permissible to cryopreserve eggs, but according to the legal motives only for a maximum of one year. Donation of fertilised eggs is prohibited, although by virtue of Section 13 the Minister of Health may make further rules regarding cryopreservation and donation of human eggs, and further regulations securing donor anonymity. The legal motives specify that it is a precondition that the donation of unfertilised human eggs is undertaken anonymously. The Danish Act does not deal with sperm donation, although administrative provisions operated through the central Danish cryopreservation facility for sperm ensure that this will also only be undertaken anonymously. Neither does the law address the question of access to assisted conception. Civil law questions of family rights will not be affected by this legislation because those questions are deemed to lie within the domain of the Ministry of Justice. A Law Reform Commission has been charged with the task of considering the rules regarding paternity and other questions arising from the extended use of assisted reproduction.[37]

Norway   In Norway, Act No. 68 of 12 June 1987 concerning artificial fertilisation, established[38] that this may be carried out only in institutions specially approved for this purpose by the Ministry of Social Affairs. This Act was repealed and its provisions incorporated into Act No. 56 of 1994, which itself was subject to review in 1999.

The freezing of unfertilised eggs is prohibited. Only establishments which are authorised to carry out artificial fertilisation or IVF may freeze or store sperm or fertilised eggs. The latter may be utilised for implantation only in women from whom they are derived, and embryos may be implanted only in women from whom the eggs to create the embryo were derived (section 2-11). Research on embryos is prohibited (section 3-1).

The decision to undertake treatment to bring about artificial fertilisation must be taken by a physician. The decision must be made on the basis of medical and psychological assessment of the couple. Artificial fertilisation may be carried out only in married women. Artificial insemination may be carried out only when the husband is sterile or the carrier of a serious hereditary disease (section 2-9). The attending physician shall select a suitable semen donor. The identity of the donor is to be kept secret (section 2-7). Fertilisation outside the body may be carried out only if the woman is sterile. Such treatment may be effected only with the gametes of the couples themselves.

In Norway it is emphasised in the *traveaux préparatoires* that the involvement of medical science in the creation of human life and the allocation of technical, medical and economic resources from society means that there is an opportunity to take into account the interests of the child. That opportunity should be taken. While the creation of one-parent families cannot be averted, the deliberate use of assisted conception services in such circumstances offends against the rights of the individual child who will result.

Sweden   The Swedish legislation is that of 1984, 1988 and 1991. According to Law No. 1140 of 20 December 1984 on insemination, this may take place only where the woman is married or has been cohabiting with the relevant man under marriage-like conditions for at least two years. Donor insemination may take place only in a public hospital under the supervision of a physician qualified in gynaecology and obstetrics. The physician shall determine whether insemination is appropriate, having taken into consideration the medical, psychological and social circumstances of the couple. Insemination may take place only if it is probable that the resulting child will be brought up under favourable conditions. The physician shall select an appropriate donor of the sperm.

In Sweden there is no longer the principle of donor anonymity. Information concerning donors is to be registered and the record kept for at least 70 years. A child conceived as a result of insemination is entitled to be advised of the contents of the record, provided the child has reached sufficient maturity. The local Social Welfare Committee shall assist the child in obtaining this information when he or she so desires.

According to Law No. 711 of 14 June 1988 on fertilisation outside the human body, this may be carried out only in a general hospital, unless the authorisation of the National Board of Health and Welfare is obtained. An egg which has been fertilised outside the body of a woman may not be introduced into her body, unless the woman is married or cohabiting and the egg is the woman's own and has been fertilised with the sperm of her husband or cohabitant.

In 1991, Law No. 115 concerning embryo research was enacted. Research is forbidden if it takes place later than two weeks after fertilisation. In addition, the research must not have the intention of developing methods of creating genetic effects which can be hereditary. A fertilised egg which has been subject to research must be destroyed without delay after the expiration of the two weeks.

A fertilised cryopreserved egg must not be kept for more than one year. However, the National Board may allow a longer period if there are special reasons for it. If a (fertilised) egg (or sperm) has been subject to research, the egg must not be introduced into a woman's body. Egg-donation is still prohibited (although the National Council on Medical Ethics presented a report in 1995, recommending that it should be allowed).

The same Act from 1991 regulating the use of human embryos in research, permitting research during the first 14 days (although frozen fertilised ova may now be stored for five years). There have been debates on whether the Act needs to be amended to make it completely clear that cloning of human beings is not allowed.

Finland[39]   An Act on Assisted Reproduction and an Amendment to the Paternity Act have been foreshadowed for some time, but at present legislative proposals have not been brought before the Parliament. Medical practitioners presently offer AIH, AID, different techniques of IVF and surrogate motherhood arrangements. When the child is born in a marriage, the husband will be the father of the child. As services may be made available to unmarried women, the law provides that if the child is born outside a marriage, the companion of the mother can declare that the child is his. If there is no biological link between the father and the child, there is always a possibility that the court, upon petition of the man, the mother or the child, will rule that the man is not the father of the child.[40] The identity of the donor of the gametes is usually anonymous.

An Act on Medical Research[41] came into force on 1 November 1999. According to this Act, an embryo may be used for research purposes subject to the following conditions:

(a)   the research institution has been approved by the National Authority on Medicolegal Affairs;

(b)   the embryo may not be older than 14 days, not counting the days when it has been frozen;

(c)   the donors of the gametes have given their consent to the research;

(d)   the donors have received information about the research before giving their consent;

(e)   no embryo may be used after the donors have withdrawn their consent;

(f)   embryos may not be produced for research purposes;

(g)   an embryo which has been an object for research may not be used in assisted reproduction;

(h)   an embryo may not be kept alive for a longer time than 14 days, not counting the days when it has been frozen;

(i)   embryos may be kept frozen for 15 years, after which they must be destroyed.

Research on embryos with the purpose of learning how to influence hereditary characteristics is not permitted, unless the research has as a purpose increased possibilities to treat or prevent difficult hereditary diseases. A precondition for a research project on embryos is that is has received a favourable opinion from the District Board on Health Care Ethics, or in some cases from the National Advisory Board on Health Care Ethics.

Mainland Europe

Belgium   There is an embryonic proposal for a law being brought through the Belgian Parliamentary system. In practice, assisted reproduction is available for single and lesbian women at more than five Flemish centres.

France[42]   There are now approximately 150 assisted conception centres in France performing some 40,000 treatment cycles.[43] According to Law 94-654 of 29 July 1994, assisted conception may take place only where a couple consists of a man and a woman, both of whom

(a)   are alive;[44]
(b)   are married or able to prove at least two years' cohabitation; and
(c)   are of reproductive age;

and where the treatment is to be provided solely to alleviate infertility, or to avoid the transmission of a particularly serious disease (Ch. II, Art. 152-2). Before the treatment services, the couple must be interviewed by members of a multi-disciplinary team at the treatment centre who must:

(a)   establish the couple's motives for assisted conception;
(b)   inform them of the chances of success and failure of assisted conception, as well as its risks; and
(c)   allow a month for reflection to pass after this before carrying out the treatment service.

Further provisions of the law determine how and from whom gametes may be recovered, how often donor gametes may be used (not more than five times), and where and how storage and treatment services may be offered and carried out.

An embryo may be conceived *in vitro* in order to achieve medically assisted procreation, as defined in Art. 152-2. Gametes must come from one of the couple to be treated. Embryos may be stored for five years with the consents of both gamete providers or both of the couple who intend to use the embryo in treatments services, and both must be consulted every five years to determine whether they consent to further storage. The law makes no provision for couples who do not address the question of continued storage, who divorce, or one of whom dies. Consequently, there are some 6,000 frozen 'orphan' embryos awaiting a decision as to disposal, and this has the hallmarks of a gathering ethical and social storm.[45] Exceptionally, and where both genitors consent in writing, stored embryos may be used for the treatment of another couple. To receive an embryo where the conditions of Art. 152-2 are fulfilled, a couple must seek and obtain judicial approval, and the donation must be effected anonymously and without payment.

The *in vitro* creation of embryos for research is prohibited (Art. 152-8), as is embryo research (Art. 152-8), unless and exceptionally both members of a couple express their consent in writing for an embryo to be used in research.

Germany[46]   The Embryo Protection Act 1990[47] lays down some of the most restrictive provisions in Europe for the protection of embryonic life. This is supplemented by guidelines from the Federal Physicians' Chambers on the circumstances in which IVF might be offered, and indications for IVF and embryo transfer and regulations for the payment for assisted conception treatment services. These guidelines require physicians to ensure that the couple are in a stable relationship and that, in principle, access should be restricted to married couples. A special committee has the power to consider the case of unmarried persons.

It is an offence to under the Act:

(a)   to fertilise a human egg for any purpose other than to start a pregnancy in the woman who produced the egg (Art. 1(2));

(b)   to use an embryo for any purpose other than its maintenance and healthy development (Art. 2(1)); and

(c)   to separate and use totipotent cells of an embryo for research and diagnosis.

Thus, non-therapeutic embryo research is prohibited, as are oocyte donation, embryo donation and surrogate motherhood, and posthumous use of sperm. Violation of the law is sanctioned by imprisonment for up to three years or a fine (art. 2).

The newly elected Minister of Health, Andrea Fischer from the Green Party, is said to be planing a new Reproduction Medicine Act. While little is presently clear, it is proposed to hold a federal conference in May 2000 to promote public discussion of a review of the 1990 Act. After this conference several committees were established to conduct a wholesale review and to consider new legislation which might include the regulations of the Embryo Protection Act. Furthermore, the new Act will address areas not presently well regulated in Germany, such as germ cell donation. The Minister of Health intends to maintain the strict prohibition of pre-implantation genetic diagnosis, but it is not clear if this will be successful. In late 1999 an ethics committee of the federal state of Nordrhein Westfalen published a report in favour of pre-implantation genetic diagnosis, and a working group of the German Physicians Society has also published a report favouring this procedure.

Ireland   Ireland has no specific law which addresses assisted conception, although it is believed that Art. 40.3.3 of the Constitution implicitly prohibits embryo research. Any assisted conception services are carried out under guidelines of the Medical Council. Under these guidelines, IVF may be offered only to married couples.

Luxembourg   In practice, no assisted reproduction services are available in Luxembourg.

The Netherlands   Under the Hospitals Act, a decree on IVF Planning was issued in 1989. In practice, most IVF centres adopt an age limit of 40 for the woman.

Portugal   The National Council for the Life Sciences, established by the Law of June 1990[48] under the Chairmanship of the Ombudsman, is charged to address the matter of assisted procreation and embryo research. A *Report on Medically Assisted Procreation* (3/CNE/93) was issued by the Conselho Nacional de Etica para as Ciencias da Viva (Chairman Mario Raposo) in February 1993. The Council is to consider a White Paper on medically assisted procreation drawn up by the Centro de Estudos de Medico, University of Coimbra. In practice, there is currently only limited provision for donor insemination, IVF and GIFT, and again, in practice, offered to stable heterosexual couples.

A draft Bill to regulate assisted conception was approved by Parliament but vetoed by the President in 1999.

Spain[49]   Law 35 of November 1988[50] remained unimplemented until 1999, due to a constitutional challenge. Therefore, the provision of assisted reproduction in Spain has been subject to professional self-regulation. Under s. 6 of the 1988 Law, 'every woman' is eligible for treatment as long as she provides her written consent, is at least 18 years old and is mentally competent. The law covers IVF, GIFT, artificial insemination, and related techniques.

Under the Law, research is permitted on non-viable embryos up to 14 days after fertilisation, provided the parties concerned give their written consent (s. 15(1) and (3) and s. 20). Research can be conducted on viable embryos only if it is applied research of a diagnostic character, or if it has a therapeutic or prophylactic purpose, and the non-pathological genetic patrimony is not modified (s. 15(2)). A review committee must consider and review each research proposal. Research must address one of the purposes laid down in s. 16, such as the improvement of the techniques of assisted reproduction, or increasing knowledge about infertility, gene and chromosome structure, contraception, or the origin of genetic and hereditary diseases.

The constitutional challenge to the 1988 Act was made by the Partido Popular, then the opposition party now the party of government. The challenge, launched on 13 March 1989, was resolved by the Spanish Constitutional Court in July 1999. The object of the challenge was that the Law had been enacted as a *Ley ordinaria* and not (as it was claimed it should have been) as a *Ley orgánica*, in other words that it had been enacted procedurally *ultra vires*. The objectors claimed that the Law should have been an 'organic' and not an 'ordinary' law because it had the effect of infringing or impacting on fundamental rights and human dignity under the Constitution. These are reserved and protected areas which call for the particular Parliamentary procedure engaged by the *Ley orgánica* (i.e. requires qualified majority of the Congress) before a law abridging such rights can be validly enacted (Art. 53 of the Constitution). The fundamental rights which it was claimed the Law infringed were the 'right to life' (under Art. 1.1 of the Spanish Constitution) and the dignity of the human being (under Art. 1.2).

The Constitutional Court held that the right to life does not recognise the unborn[51] and that this law deals with unborns. The dignity of the human being need not be regulated by a *Ley orgánica* – only the limited rights of Arts 14–30 require this treatment. One of the judges dissented and thought that dignity is a fundamental right that must be regulated by a *Ley orgánica*. Secondly, the Court held that embryos before implantation do not have the right to life. There is a constitutional right to experimentation. The distinction made in the Law between viable and non-viable embryos, affording stronger protection of the viable embryo, is enough to satisfy the protection of the 'process of this new being'.

Italy A National Bioethics Committee was established in 1990, but reports on biotechnology, gene therapy, and the collection and testing of human sperm have not been paralleled with one on assisted reproduction. However, in May 1999 a proposed law was introduced into and approved by the Camera of Deputies. It was sent for consideration and examination by the Senato.[52] If passed, the law, which contains provisions as to paternity and maternity following assisted conception, would be much more restrictive than the regulations Italian clinicians have been accustomed to working with. For example, Art. 4 permits recourse to assisted conception only on showing the impossibility of resolving infertility in any other way; Art. 4(3) prohibits the use of donated gametes; Art. 13 prohibits embryo experimentation unless it is for the therapeutic (i.e. nondestructive) benefit of the individual embryo; and selective reduction of multiple pregnancies would be prohibited under Art. 13(5). Fierce opposition to the proposed law from the clinicians most closely involved ensued, and for the present has foundered.

Greece[53]   The Law on the Modernisation and Organisation of the Health System[54] makes provision for Presidential decrees which will regulate the conditions for the establishment and functioning of units for assisted procreation services and the ethical, deontological, legal and economic aspects of the techniques.[55]

Insemination with sperm from a woman's husband poses no significant legal problems according to the Greek law, because the decision of the couple to proceed with artificial insemination is protected under the civil right to obtain natural descendants. Although the Greek Constitution attributes no reproductive rights to individuals, such rights are implicitly protected as part of the free development of personality (Art. 5 I). Procreation is seen as a specific manifestation of the right to the free development of personality.[56] Problems do, however, arise when sperm from the partner has been taken and conserved for the purpose of future insemination, and the partner dies before such insemination takes place. Although the Greek courts have not yet faced such questions, current constitutional literature addresses this as an aspect of the right to procreate. However, such right cannot be activated after the subject's death, because only living persons can be subjects of fundamental rights. The right to procreate is closely linked to the responsibility that parenthood implies, and such responsibility can be assumed only by living persons.[57]

Similar problems arise when an embryo created from a fertilised ovum remains in storage, and before it can be transferred to the woman her husband dies. The question in this case is whether the *in vitro* conceived embryo should be transferred to its mother or not. The embryo enjoys limited, but autonomous, constitutional protection. The cumbersome question of whether the respect of the natural parental relationship should always prevail over the right of a third couple faced with serious sterility problems to acquire and use the embryo has not yet been resolved.[58]

Insemination with donor semen poses no difficult problems with regard to the Constitution. The Greek constitutional literature accepts that assisted conception does not offend the human dignity of the partners, when based on their mutual agreement and consent.

Surrogacy is considered in the Greek constitutional literature as an aspect of the right to procreation. Such a right constitutes a particular expression of the right to free development of personality according to Art. 5 I of the Constitution. However Art. 5 I of the Constitution provides that the free development of personality is limited by the prevailing customs, which have to be defined in accordance with the general moral opinions of Greek society. The institution of surrogate motherhood, it has been argued, does not conform with such moral opinions.[59] Consequently, although no specific provision prohibits surrogate motherhood, such contractual obligations cannot be enforced and are not legally binding as they violate the prevailing moral opinions.[60]

The Greek Council of State recently addressed a case of surrogate motherhood. It refused to acknowledge a distinction between natural and social motherhood and ruled that, consequently, the natural mother cannot lose her parental rights after the child's birth and the respective acknowledgement of paternity.[61]

The protection of the human genotype (genome) and the general questions referring to the protection of the human being against any development by the genetic technology, are related to the legal recognition of the value of the human being. Such recognition is a fundamental obligation assumed by the state and one of its principal missions is provided for by Art. 2 I of the Constitution. This constitutional norm is activated against any third-party intervention in the sphere of human self-determination and self-definition.[62]

Austria[63]   On 14 May 1992 the Austrian Act on Procreative Medicine was enacted and the legislation came into force on 1 July 1992.

The Act – which defines assisted conception as a medical procedure – has three main aims: (i) to introduce a range of prohibitions in relation both to assisted conception treatment services and research; (ii) to establish a system of regulation of those limited treatment services which are to remain lawful after 1 July 1992 and to introduce penalties for contravention of either the prohibited or regulated activities; (iii) to deal with what may be called the status and relationship considerations of assisted conception.

A wide spectrum of prohibitions, backed with administrative penalty, disclosed the essential antipathy with which assisted conception is viewed in Austria. All forms of assisted conception using donated gametes are prohibited, with the exception of donor insemination *in vivo*. Artikel I, s. 3(3) prohibits embryo transfer or embryo donation and provides that ova and embryos may be used only for women from whom they are genetically derived. This ensures that donated embryos or gametes may not be used to establish a surrogate pregnancy. Assisted conception is confined to married or stable heterosexual cohabitations, thus ensuring that single women may not benefit from medically assisted conception. Storage may not exceed one year, after which any stored embryos or gametes must be allowed to perish (Artikel I, s. 17(1)). Artikel I, s. 10 provides that a doctor may only cause as many eggs to be fertilised as are to be used in that treatment cycle. This is an important provision; within a regime of limited access to assisted conception services it will ensure that treatment procedures are even more closely circumscribed. A final pair of prohibitions in Artikel I, s. 9 address the question of research. Destructive embryo research is forbidden under the terms of s. 9(1), while s. 9(2) prohibits any interference with the germ cell line. Section 9(1) provides that *in vitro* embryos may not be used for purposes other than medically assisted reproduction and, hence, may be examined and treated only as far as this is necessary in accordance with clinical practice. The same applies to eggs and semen to be used in treatment services.

The main thrust of the regulatory provisions of the Act is that any assisted conception procedure which remains lawful after 1 July may be practised only by obstetricians and gynaecologists, whereas previously no clinical or other restrictions existed. AIH may be administered in the private practices of such gynaecologists. All other assisted conception treatments (DI, IVF and GIFT using the couple's own gametes) may, under the provisions of s. 5, be conducted only in specially licensed hospitals loosely supervised by one of the nine provincial Governor's Offices. Section 17(2) of Artikel I restricts the ability of couples in an assisted conception treatment programme to direct what may be done with their own gametes.

Section 14 provides that the semen of any given donor may be used for medically assisted reproduction in up to three marriages or cohabitant relationships. Semen donors will not enjoy rights of anonymity, although this was earnestly discussed in the Judiciary Committee. In the event, s. 13(1) emerged as the compromise; on donation, the semen donor must record his consent that any child who may be born following the use of his sperm may, from the age of 14, request information regarding his identity. Clinics have a duty to keep records showing the names of donors, their birth date, birthplace, nationality, residence and the names of the donors' parents. The purpose of this last requirement is to ensure that where a doctor or clinic uses semen, there is no inadvertent insemination of a woman with semen donated by, for example, her brother.

Turkey The In Vitro Fertilisation and Embryo Transfer Centres Law[64] established an IVF and ET Scientific Committee in the Ministry of Health and outlined the principles on which it is to work. Use of sperm, ova and embryos for any purpose other than the treatment of the person(s) from whom they are recovered is unlawful. This prohibits not only research, but also use of donated gametes or embryos in treatment services. Storage and transfer outside the terms of the Law are prohibited, as is the sale of gametes or embryos. IVF and ET are limited to married couples, who must complete a standardised consent form and information sheet. One copy of the completed form is retained by the Centre, the other must be sent to the centralised Scientific Committee.

North America

Canada[65] There is presently no specific legislation in an area in which the Federal Government clearly has jurisdiction. The Human Reproductive and Genetic Technologies Act[66] would have enacted, if passed, a national, comprehensive scheme of regulation which would replace existing family, health, contract, commercial and related legal regimes which 'apply to new reproductive technologies largely by inference, if at all [where] few or no court cases have been decided'.[67] It fell, although it is thought likely that the new Bill will, when published, include both a more limited prohibitions section than did the original Bill and the regulatory portion. As a result of this, Canadian law presently provides no definitive guidance on issues such as status, liabilities and responsibilities of participants; access to treatment; informed consent; privacy and confidentiality; and the boundaries between acceptable and unacceptable practices, procedures and treatments.

The Law Reform Commission of Canada's Working Paper No. 65, *Medically Assisted Procreation* (1992), contained a draft Bill which would have established a national regulatory agency empowered to establish a system of certification for clinics offering medically assisted procreation services and gametes and embryo banks. The 1996 Bill proposed to introduce a licensing scheme, which is thought likely to survive in the new version and which envisaged the establishment of a regulatory agency for reproductive medicine.

As originally proposed, the Act contained no provisions in respect of access, although it may be envisaged that these will in time be formulated. For the present, each province which has either considered the questions of assisted procreation or

Table 11.1   Access to treatment services

Province	Unmarried heterosexual couple	Single woman	Women in homosexual relationship
British Columbia	Yes	Not excluded	Not excluded
Ontario	Yes	Yes	Not excluded
Quebec	Yes	No	No

Table 11.2   Conditions for access

Province	Medical cause	Welfare of child	Partner consent	Other
British Columbia			Yes	
Ontario	Infertile			Decision by physician
Quebec	Infertile			

has been advised on such by reform bodies has its own position. These are summarised in Tables 11.1 and 11.2.

United States   Much of what would be regarded as health law is, as in Australia (see below), reserved to the state not the federal governments. Although the US has signed the International Covenant on Civil and Political Rights, the International Covenant on Economic, Social and Cultural Rights (1966) and the Universal Declaration of Human Rights, each bringing with it some obligations in international law, the US is not party to any European regional agreements and has not ratified the UN Convention on the Rights of the Child or the UN Educational, Scientific and Cultural Organisation (UNESCO) Universal Declaration on Human Genome and Human Rights. Accordingly, there is no legislation or national system of formal legal regulation of assisted conception similar to that in the UK or in other individual European countries. There is no federal legislation requiring doctors and clinics to collect genetic information about gamete donors; and only five states require the information (for example, New Hampshire) and there is no uniformity amongst those states that have enacted legislation. This despite over 20,000 conceptions following IVF treatment each year.[68]

Under the Uniform Laws provisions proposed by the American Law Institute, a number of draft laws have been promulgated. Until the legislature of a particular state enacts a uniform law, however, it is of no legal effect in that state. The four most important laws with potential effects on assisted conception are:

(a)   the Uniform Act on Paternity (UAP), proposed in 1960 and adopted by six states. This addresses the paternity and support obligations of fathers of children born outside marriage;

(b)   the Uniform Parentage Act (UPA), promulgated in 1973 and adopted by 17 states. This carries the same obligations as for the UAP;

(c)   the Uniform Putative and Unknown Fathers Act (UPUFA), proposed in 1988. This would confer greater parental rights on fathers of children born outside marriage. However, excluded from protection as a father is a 'donor of semen used in artificial insemination or *in vitro* fertilisation whose identity is not known to the mother of the resulting child or whose semen was donated in circumstances indicating that the donor did not anticipate having any interest in the resulting child'. This Act has not been adopted by any state;

(d)   the Uniform Status of Children of Assisted Conception Act (USCACA), promulgated in 1988. Under this Act, a husband who gave consent in assisted conception is the father of the child; donors for assisted conception are not the parents. A dead person is not a parent of a child born following assisted conception. The USCACA provides for court-approved surrogacy agreements. The Act has been adopted in two states.

It is only in the instance of surrogacy that there has been sustained legislative intervention. Almost half the states have legislation dealing with surrogacy, some criminalising participation in arrangements and/or in brokering, some explicitly permitting 'altruistic surrogacy' and a few (e.g., Florida, New Hampshire, Nevada and Virginia) either expressly allowing commercial surrogacy or (while forbidding 'payments' to surrogates) permitting payment of broadly defined 'expenses'.[69]

The most advanced congressional intervention in assisted conception has been the Fertility Clinic Success Rate and Certification Act 1992,[70] the product of collaboration between the American Fertility Society and the Society for Assisted Reproductive Technology (now called the American Society of Reproductive Medicine) and the initiative of Democrat Senator Ron Wyden. The Act calls for the submission of annual reports to the Centers for Disease Control of pregnancy success rates achieved in 'assisted reproductive technology' programmes and for the development of a model programme for certification of embryo laboratories. 'Assisted reproductive technology' was defined to include 'all treatments or procedures which include the handling of human embryos or oocytes or embryos, including *in vitro* fertilisation, gamete intrafallopian transfer, zygote intrafallopian transfer' and whatever other methods the Secretary of Health and Human Services might include.[71]

In 1993, Congress enacted the National Institutes of Health Revitalization Act,[72] and therein provided for the creation of research centres with respect to contraception and infertility, estimated at the beginning of the 1990s to affect 1:6 Americans and to have generated a service industry worth over $1 billion.[73] The American Fertility Society and American Society of Reproductive Medicine developed many of the features of the legislation on a voluntary basis, in a way that mirrors the response of the Royal College of Obstetricians and the Medical Research Council following the publication of the Warnock Report in the UK a decade earlier. The Wyden Bill promoted the establishment of the In Vitro Fertilisation Registry under the wing of the American Society of Reproductive Medicine, enabling the submission of clinic specific data. Few states have, however, adopted the provisions of the Act, largely because of the financial and administrative burdens which it would impose upon them, and the comprehensiveness and comprehensibility of the position on assisted conception in the US is flawed.

Havins and Dalessio suggest several reasons why there has been no unified federal government response to assisted conception. These include the speed at which the technologies arise, proliferate and mutate, the 'entrepreneurial' spirit of American medicine and the absence of a health care payment system.[74] Robert Stenger has additionally drawn attention to the linkage between issues of regulating reproductive technologies and the acrimonious debate in the United States concerning abortion.[75] Ronald Dworkin has characterised the 'war' between anti-abortion groups and their opponents in the United States as 'America's new version of the terrible seventeenth-century European civil wars of religion'.[76]

Opposing armies march down streets or pack themselves into protests at abortion clinics, courthouses, and the White House, screaming at and spitting on and loathing one another. Abortion is tearing America apart.

The metamorphosis of the Supreme Court's position on the interest of the state from *Roe* v *Wade* to *Casey* has also had a dramatic, 'chilling' effect on the development of any more 'permissive' federal regulation. *Roe* v *Wade* 410 US 113 (1973) is, of course, the American Supreme Court's seminal decision addressing and recognising the constitutional status of a woman's decision to seek a termination of pregnancy. There, the Supreme Court delineated the (now famous) trimester approach to the state's legitimate interest in the developing foetus – the three different time periods which marked the development from the earliest stage, when the state lacks a compelling interest, through to the third period, in which it might legitimately intervene to protect the life of a viable foetus. While *Planned Parenthood* v *Casey* 112 S Ct 2791 (1992) affirmed the holding that a pregnant woman could choose whether to continue with her pregnancy, the majority rejected Roe's trimester analysis 'and recognized the state's substantial interest, throughout the pregnancy, in potential life'.[77] It is perhaps small wonder that assisted conception has remained at best a shadowy presence on the federal public policy agenda.

IVF is largely unregulated by federal government and state regulation is similarly sparse; most states let the 'industry' regulate itself. 'It is probably fair to say that the guidelines promulgated by the American Fertility Society represent the only American ethical standards which can guide programs of assisted reproductive technology in the USA.'[78] Groups traditionally opposing abortion have ensured the denial of federal funding to research involving human embryos or assisted conception and that such activities are forbidden in governmentally funded hospitals (which include most medical schools where such research would otherwise have been most likely able to take place).[79] The effect of such prohibitions is that research and treatment services (where they do take place) are private sector, market driven and market provided, where the 'entrepreneurial' activities of American scientists and reproductive specialists become more difficult to regulate at a federal level. In the absence of legislation, the American Bar Association, amongst other organisations, is drafting codes in the hope that they will generate guidance to state legislatures.

But infertility's engagement with law is far from undeveloped in the United States, as we shall briefly show. Perhaps most clearly demonstrating this is a ruling of the Federal Equal Opportunities Commission that infertility is a disability for the purposes of the Americans with Disabilities Act 1994 and Title VII of the Civil

Rights Act 1964 (which includes the Pregnancy Discrimination Act). The Supreme Court in *Bragdon* v *Abbott* US 524 (1998) 624 held that 'reproduction is a major life activity under the Americans with Disabilities Act, and that those who have an impairment that substantially limits their ability to reproduce qualify for protection from discrimination on the basis of their infertility'. On this basis an equal opportunities claim had been filed against a company because a health insurance policy covered some male infertility treatments but excluded many that would be regarded as female treatments. The Commission ruled that the female employee qualified as having a disability under the Americans with Disabilities Act, and that she also suffered from a pregnancy-related condition deserving of protection under the Pregnancy Discrimination Act when requiring assisted conception services that were excluded from her employer's health insurance plan.[80]

Perhaps the most important consequence that this lacuna has generated is the many parentage controversies that have arisen because the system is highly unregulated. Parentage is established by three presumptions:

(a) Presumption of maternity of the woman who gave birth.
(b) Presumption of the paternity of the husband if the woman is married.
(c) Presumption of paternity by open acknowledgement and/or cohabitation.

Similarly, the fate of the embryo in the absence of the parties' express intentions or the death of the genitors has generated conflict. In general, the people who donated the constituent genetic material are the people who have control over the destiny of the embryo. Contracts usually provide that where the parties fail to act, the IVF clinic has the authority. Several disputes have reached the courts, and their response has been within fairly well-established paradigms. Marsha Garrison suggests that this should provoke little surprise:

> Given that technological conception, for all its novelty and glitter, ultimately produces altogether familiar family forms and problems, it should come as no surprise that courts have typically dealt with questions of parental rights and responsibilities in these cases using very traditional lines of attack.[81]

The most prominent disputes have included *Davis* v *Davis* 842 SW2d 588 (1992), where a husband and wife had had embryos frozen but they subsequently divorced. The wife wanted to donate embryos to another woman, but her husband refused his consent. The court held that the husband had a right not to become an unwilling parent and that this outweighed the wife's right to donate the zygotes. In *Kass* v *Kass* 91 NY 2d 554 (1998), a pre-conception contract provided that there had to be the consent of both parties before use; if there was no agreement the clinic had permission to donate the IVF-generated embryos for research. On divorce, the former wife wanted the embryos without her former husband's consent. The court held that the consent form was so badly drafted that it was unenforceable and awarded in favour of the wife – a decision reversed on appeal. Garrison applauds these emblematic approaches: 'because families that come into being through technological conception are not markedly different from those that come into being in other ways, it makes sense for courts to utilise traditional family law doctrine when resolving claims about parental status and obligation.'[82]

The American Society of Reproductive Medicine has developed a Protocol to govern posthumous reproduction. In January 1999, legislation was introduced banning posthumous sperm collection in the absence of prior written consent. Doctors are left to their consciences as to whether or not to perform operations.

Australasia

Australia[83]   The regulation of assisted reproduction technologies in Australia has since 1982 been a complex matter. Infertility treatment services are presently a matter for the states, and three of them have passed legislation; in the others, legal questions are an amalgam of the common law and ethical guidelines. But these guidelines also form the backdrop to the legislation which has been enacted. In addition to guidelines issued in 1982 by the National Health & Medical Research Council (NHMRC) in Supplementary Note 4 (SN4) to the Statement on Human Experimentation (soon to be updated; see below), there is a well-established system of self-regulation and accreditation, comprising the Reproductive Technology Accreditation Committee (RTAC) and its Code of Practice for the 22 units practising IVF and related technologies in 53 different centres. To date, only three states have responded with specific statutory provisions (Victoria, South Australia and Western Australia) and those states have done so in different ways. Surrogacy is regulated in five states (Victoria, Queensland, South Australia, Tasmania, Australian Capital Territory (ACT)): in all a surrogacy contract is illegal and unenforceable; in four states IVF surrogacy is prohibited, but in the ACT it may be allowed in the absence of commercial arrangements.

The Commonwealth Family Law Act 1975 (as amended by the Family law (Amendment) Act 1987) and various states' legislation provide that where a woman gives birth to a child as the result of assisted conception, the child is the child of that woman and her spouse (which includes a *de facto* husband) if he has given consent to the procedure. A person donating sperm and (in most states) eggs has no legal connection with the child whatsoever. Where the spouse does not consent, or there is no spouse, the genetic father does not become the legal father of the child. A donor of gametes has no legal claim whatsoever on the child born as a result of an assisted conception procedure and the child has no right to the parentage of that person, even where the donors are known (1975 Act, ss. 60, 60A, 60B).

The regulation of treatment services in the individual Australian states is discussed in further detail below.

(1) Victoria   The Infertility (Medical Procedures) Act 1984 (as amended by the Infertility (Medical Procedures) (Amendment) Act 1987) and the Infertility (Medical Procedures) Regulations 1988 are now consolidated in the Infertility Treatment Act 1995.

The 1984 Act established a Hospital Approval Advisory Panel which has the task of carrying out inspections of hospitals, supervising RTAC accreditation, and recommending to the Minister of Health for approval hospitals and research protocols. Approval is not, however, based on RTAC accreditation (neither is it determined by RTAC), but lies with the Minister (s. 7). When the 1995 Act is fully implemented, that function will be undertaken by the Infertility

Treatment Authority; similarly, when introduced, the Standing Review and Advisory Committee in Infertility (SRACI) will advise the Minister and make recommendations to the Authority on research matters.

Section 3 of the 1984 Act defines, *inter alia*, 'fertilisation procedure', 'relevant procedure', 'married woman' and 'husband', for the purposes of the Act, and s. 6 establishes certain absolute prohibitions.

(i)   Storage and use of gametes   The use of gametes produced by a person who has not attained the age of 18 and is not married (s. 25), and the use of semen produced by more than one man in a procedure of artificial insemination (s. 26) are prohibited. Regulations make further provision.

(ii)   Storage and use of embryos   Procedures involving the freezing of embryos are prohibited, except where such a procedure is conducted in an approved hospital for the purpose of implantation in a woman at a later date. Regulations make further provision.

(iii)   Access to treatment   A fertilisation procedure may not be carried out unless in accordance with the specific provisions of the Act. The permitted fertilisation procedures are as follows:

(a)   *IVF no donors (s. 10)*   The strict conditions for IVF are that:

(i)   It is only to be carried out in an approved hospital.

(ii)   The woman must be married (subject to a transitional provision, s. 3(2), now of limited, if any, applicability) or in a stable *de facto* relationship.

(iii)   Both the woman and her husband must have consented in writing to the procedure.

(iv)   At least 12 months before the procedure is undertaken, a medical practitioner, not being the one to carry out the procedure, has examined or treated the woman and her husband or begun to do so, in such a manner as might reasonably be expected to establish whether or not pregnancy would be possible by a means other than a fertilisation procedure.

(v)   As a result, that medical practitioner is satisfied that the woman is unlikely to become pregnant other than by the use of a fertilisation procedure.

(vi)   The medical practitioner who is to perform the procedure must be satisfied that both parties have received counselling from an approved counsellor and that an approved counsellor will be available to give further counselling to them after the procedure is carried out. Regulations prescribe the matters concerning which counselling must be given.

(b)   *IVF with male donor (s. 11)*   The requirements are as under s. 10 above, with the following additional matters:

(vii)   With respect to (iv) and (v) above, an alternative justification for undertaking the procedure is that the medical practitioner is satisfied that should fertilisation by the husband's semen be permitted, an undesirable hereditary disorder may be transmitted to the child born.

(viii) The document containing the consent of the woman and her husband must be retained by the hospital in which the procedure is being carried out and a copy given to both the woman and her husband.

(ix) Both the sperm donor and his spouse (if any) must have received counselling from an approved counsellor and provide written consent to the use of the semen in the procedure.

(x) Apart from the reimbursement of expenses, the semen donor is not to receive payment.

(c) *IVF female donor (s. 12)* The requirements are as for male donors, with the necessary changes being made to take account of the fact that the procedure contemplated involves the use of donated ova and not sperm.

(d) *IVF with male and female donors (s. 13)* Again, the requirements are similar to those for sperm donation alone, with the necessary changes being made to take account of the fact that the procedure contemplated involves the use of donated ova and sperm. In addition, where more than one embryo is to be used in the procedure, the gametes used must have been produced by the same two persons. A couple's excess embryos may be donated to another woman, provided that, prior to the gamete removal, both the woman and her husband are counselled with respect to, and gave their consent to, this possibility.

(e) *GIFT (s. 13A)* The requirements are similar to those for IVF with male donation, with the necessary changes being made to take account of the fact that GIFT and related procedures involve differing techniques.

(f) *Artificial insemination* AI is to be carried out only by a medical practitioner or in an approved hospital. It is prohibited to carry out AI unless both the woman and her husband have received counselling in prescribed matters from an approved counsellor.

(2) South Australia The Reproductive Technology Act 1991 introduced a licensing scheme, and current RTAC accreditation is a condition of licence under the Reproductive Technology Act 1987, which, as in Victoria, establishes a licensing regimen for the practice of all infertility techniques which are defined for the purposes of the Act (s. 3). The 1987 Act does not apply to GIFT. There is no need for a licence to practise AI in certain circumstances (s. 13(7)), i.e. where the AI is carried out by a registered medical practitioner who has submitted his or her name for registration by the South Australian Health Commission and has made an undertaking to the Commission to observe the code of ethical practice formulated by the Council under the Act, or where the AI is carried out gratuitously.

(i) Storage and use of gametes and embryos Unlike the legislation in Victoria, the South Australian legislation does not contain an extensive set of provisions purporting to regulate each fertilisation procedure. That task is delegated to the South Australian Council on Reproductive Technology, established by the Act (s. 10(1)), which from time to time updates a code of ethical practice.

The principle on which the Code is to be based is that the welfare of any child to be born as the result of a procedure is of paramount importance (s. 10(2)) and the Code must (and does) contain provisions which:

(a)   prohibit embryo flushing;

(b)   provide that those on whose behalf embryos are stored have the right to decide on their disposition and to review decisions every 12 months;

(c)   provide that embryo storage does not exceed 10 years;

(d)   provide that embryos must not be cultured beyond the stage of development at which implantation would normally occur.

(ii)   Access to treatment   There are similar restrictions under the South Australian legislation as to the type of persons who can benefit from infertility treatment. These are similar to the South Australia's adoption criteria – the welfare of the potential child is paramount. Only married couples (or *de facto* couples who have lived together for five years) who are infertile or in danger of producing a genetically defective child are eligible for treatment. Treatment may be denied:

(a)   to couples suffering from any illness or disability which could interfere with their capacity to care for a child;

(b)   to couples one of whom has been convicted of an offence;

(c)   to couples convicted of child abuse;

(d)   to couples who have had children removed from their care by community welfare authorities.

(3)   Western Australia   The Human Reproductive Technology Act 1991 requires continuing compliance with the RTAC standards (rather than actual RTAC accreditation) and is the basis of the standards of practice established under the 1991 Act. Otherwise, the licensing scheme is similar to that under the South Australian Act, placing its supervision under the auspices of the Western Australia Reproductive Technology Council. The Council has produced a Code of Practice to cover services provided by licensees, storage and dealing with gametes and embryos, inspection facilities, privacy, limitations and conditions of research and the recognition of institutional ethics committees.

The Act prohibits:

(a)   human cloning;

(b)   embryo flushing or production of chimeras;

(c)   replacement of a nucleus of an embryo cell;

(d)   alteration of the genetic structure of an embryo cell;

(e)   payment for supplying gametes or embryos.

(i)   Storage and use of gametes and embryos   Embryos were initially to be stored for a maximum of three years; the Human Reproductive Technology (Amendment Act) 1996 extends that period to five years.

(ii)   Access to treatment   The Act sets out provisions for consent, generally restricts services to married or *de facto* couples of at least five years' standing and requires consideration of the welfare of any child likely to be born as a result of a proposed procedure. However, unlike Victoria, Western Australia permits the treatment of a single woman by artificial insemination if the donor consents to this use of his semen (Western Australian Reproductive Technology Council Guidelines 1994).

(4)   Other states and territories   Other jurisdictions in Australia rely on ethical principles which have been established by the Australian Medical Association and the National Health & Medical Research Council (NHMRC); and (as shown by the Supreme Court of Tasmania decision in *In the Estate of the late K, ex parte The Public Trustee* [1996] 5 Tas LR 365) in default, on the operation of the common law and the interpretation of legislation in hitherto unimagined cases.

Briefly, the NHMRC's present guidelines provide that:

(a)   all aspects of IVF should be approved by an institutional ethics committee which should keep full records of all attempted pregnancies, including parentage;

(b)   registers should be confidential;

(c)   special restrictions should apply to ovum donation;

(d)   there should be no element of commerce;

(e)   married couples only should be recipients of IVF treatment;

(f)   research with sperm, ova or fertilised ova is inseparable from development of safe and effective IVF, but embryos should nonetheless not be developed *in vitro* beyond the stage at which implantation would occur;

(g)   sperm and ova belong to donors, and their wishes as to use, storage and disposition should be respected; where there is a difference between joint donors, the institutions should decide the course of action;

(h)   storage of human embryos may carry biological and social risks and should be subject to restriction, i.e. for no more than 10 years and not beyond the time of conventional reproductive need or competence of the female donor;

(i)   cloning is unacceptable.

In 1996, the NHMRC's Australian Health Ethics Committee Reproductive Technology Working Group published 'Guidelines on Assisted Reproductive Technology' which will soon replace the NHMRC's 1982 guidelines. The governing principles of the Guidelines provide that the following principles or axioms should underpin clinical and research practices of assisted reproductive technology: respect for and protection of the interests, rights, dignity and welfare of all the individuals involved in ART, in particular those of any children who may be born as a result of the technology and those of the couples and in particular the women; the principle of social justice and the promotion of the common good; the principle of protection of the human subjects of experimentation. The Guidelines then deal with specific questions:

(a)   regulation and licensing, whether a particular state has legislation or not;

(b)   eligibility criteria for access to assisted reproductive technology;

(c)   surrogacy;

(d)   informed decision-making;

(e)   consent;

(f)   counselling and the role of the clinic counsellor;

(g)   research, monitoring and the dissemination of results;

(h)   research on embryos;

(i)   genetic diagnosis, therapy and selection;

(j)   sources of gametes and embryos for research;

(k)   clinical issues;

(l)   storage of gametes and embryos;
(m) record-keeping and access to information;
(n)   quality assurance and risk management;
(o)   complaints and appeals;
(p)   conscientious objection and public interest disclosures;
(q)   prohibited or unacceptable practices.

New Zealand[84]   There continues to exist a legislative vacuum in New Zealand regarding reproductive technology. The Ministry of Justice established an Interdepartmental Monitoring Committee on Assisted Reproductive Technology (IMCART) in 1987, and the latest series of recommendations, in a report entitled *Biotechnology Revisited* (prepared by the Otago University Bioethics Research Centre) for the licensing body for doctors, the Medical Council of New Zealand, called for more decisive government action. The Minister of Health responded in 1993 to calls from clinics providing infertility treatments by establishing the Interim National Ethics Committee on Assisted Reproductive Technology (INECART). Presently, such clinics participate in a voluntary licensing scheme which requires ethical approval for new treatment or research initiatives.

The Status of Children Amendment Act 1987 is thus the only relevant legislation in New Zealand. This deals with the status of children conceived by: artificial insemination by donor (ss. 4, 5); use of donor semen in an implantation procedure (ss. 6, 7); use of donor ovum or donor embryo in an implantation procedure (ss. 8, 9); use of donor semen in an intra-fallopian transfer procedure (ss. 10, 11); use of donor ovum in an intra-fallopian transfer procedure (ss. 12, 13); and use of embryos in an intra-fallopian transfer procedure (ss. 14, 15). There are general provisions which deal with evidence of paternity (s. 16), the presumption of a husband's consent (s. 17), and the rights and liabilities of child and donor where the donor marries the mother of the child (s. 18). In this last case, unless there is an agreement to the contrary, the child has no rights and liabilities to the man and the man no rights and liabilities to the child before the marriage, but following marriage each has rights and liabilities as father and child (s. 18(2)(a) and (b)).

The provisions of the Act apply to *de facto* relationships and to the status of children born following assisted reproductive technology to such couples (s. 2(1)). The Act applies to relevant treatments whether the pregnancy occurred before or after the commencement of the Act, and whether or not the pregnancy resulted from a procedure carried out in New Zealand or elsewhere (s. 3).

The scheme of the legislation provides, throughout, that where a married woman has become pregnant as the result of an infertility treatment with the consent of her husband, he shall be treated for all purposes as the father of that child and any donor shall not be treated for any purposes as the father of that child. Where the woman is not married, or where a married woman becomes pregnant with the use of a fertility treatment without the consent of her husband, her husband shall not have the rights and liabilities to that child which a father would usually have, unless he subsequently marries the woman. But, similarly, the donor of any sperm shall not have any rights or liabilities towards the child, unless he subsequently marries the child's mother.

Where a woman becomes pregnant as a result of a donor ovum or donor embryo implantation procedure, she shall for all purposes be the mother of any resulting

TABLE 11.3 GUIDELINES AND LEGISLATION – ASSISTED REPRODUCTIVE TECHNOLOGY AUSTRALIA, APRIL 1999

Legislation	NHMRC	NSW	Victoria	Queensland	South Australia	West Australia	ACT	Northern Territory	Tasmania	RTAC
Specific Legislation	National Guidelines produced for Institutional Ethics Committees	NIL	Infertility Treatment Act 1995	NIL, except for Surrogate Parenthood Act 1988	Reproductive Technology Act 1988	Reproductive Technology Act 1991. This Act is silent on Donor Insemination.	NIL, except for Substitute Parent Agreement Act 1994	Guided by South Australian Reproductive Technology Act 1988	Surrogacy Contracts Act 1994	RTAC Guidelines 1985
Access to Services	No specific guidelines.	IEC Decision. Access by de facto couples and legally married couples. Increasingly access to services by single women and same-sex couples.	Heterosexual, de facto and legally married couples only (Infertility Treatment (Amendment) Act 1997).	IEC decision. Woman in stable lesbian relationship successfully brought proceedings to have services available to her.	De facto and legally married. Single women and same sex couples must be infertile to be eligible for access.	Heterosexual, de facto and legally married couples for IVF and GIFT. Access to DI procedures is not specified.	IEC decision	SA legislation	IEC decision	N/A
Selection Criteria for Access to Services	None specified.	None specified.	Evidence that a woman is unlikely to become pregnant other than by a treatment procedure; or to prevent the transfer of a genetic abnormality or disease.	None specified.	Husband or wife appear to be infertile; or prevention of a genetic defect being transferred to child; and requirements of parenting code to be met.	Infertile; or prevent risk of transfer of genetic abnormality.	None specified.	SA Legislation	None specified.	N/A
Storage of Embryos	10-year limit recommended.	NHMRC Guidelines	Gametes 10-year limit, embryos 5 year limit; can apply for extension of storage period.	NHMRC Guidelines	10-year limit for embryos. No provision for extension required to contact couples every 12 months.	Consents to be renewed every 3 years for embryos and 5 years for gametes. Can apply for extensions. Maximum of 15 years' storage overall.	NHMRC Guidelines	SA Legislation	NHMRC Guidelines	10-year storage limit

child and the woman who produced the ovum or the embryo used in the procedure shall for all purposes not be the mother of the child (s. 9(3)). The same is the case where the woman becomes pregnant following a donor ovum intra-fallopian transfer procedure, (s. 13(3)) or a donor embryo or an embryo intra-fallopian transfer procedure (s. 15(3)).

The Middle East and Far East[85]

Only Taiwan has specific legislation dealing with assisted conception, although Ministerial regulations also exist in Singapore, Malaysia, Israel, Hong Kong and Saudi Arabia. Some form of licensing of the provision of assisted conception services also exists, whether by government authorities or by medical councils, in Indonesia, Thailand, Japan and Lebanon.

In most Asian countries, where some form of assisted reproductive technology provision is made there is no central state registry; these exist only in Taiwan, Singapore, Korea, Japan and Israel.

In almost all Moslem countries, any kind of gamete donation is banned, while in most of the eastern (Sinic) countries it is practised. Table 11.4 shows which types of donation are permitted in the countries listed. Donation of any kind is not permitted in Indonesia, Japan, Iran, Jordan, Malaysia, Lebanon, Pakistan and Saudi Arabia.

Where donation is permitted, the child is treated under the law for all purposes as the legitimate child of the recipients, but they are not entitled to know the identity of the genetic father. Singapore, Korea and India permit non-anonymous oocyte donation.

Where services are provided they are usually provided to married couples alone. Table 11.5 indicates which countries offer treatment services to other recipients.

Israel   One of the most liberal legislative regimes is that in Israel, contained in the Public Health (In Vitro Fertilisation) Regulations 1987[86] and in the Public Health (Semen Banks) Regulations 1979.[87]

The Director General of the Ministry of Health has power under the 1987 Regulations to ensure that IVF procedures are carried out only in a recognised hospital or clinic. An ovum may only be recovered from a woman, or fertilised or frozen, and a fertilised ovum may only be implanted in a woman in such a hospital or clinic; and an ovum may only be removed for the purposes of IVF and

Table 11.4   Permitted forms of gamete donation

Sperm donation	Ovum donation	Embryo donation
China	Hong Kong	India
Hong Kong	India	Singapore
India	Israel	Taiwan
Israel	Korea	Thailand
Korea	Singapore	
Singapore	Taiwan	
Thailand	Thailand	

Table 11.5   Permitted recipients of treatment services

Married couples	Cohabitants	Single women
China	China	Israel
Hong Kong	Hong Kong	
India	India	
Indonesia	Israel	
Iran		
Israel		
Japan		
Jordan		
Korea		
Lebanon		
Malaysia		
Pakistan		
Saudi Arabia		
Singapore		
Taiwan		
Thailand		

implantation following fertilisation (reg. 3). An ovum may only be removed if the woman is undergoing infertility treatment and the physician in charge determines that it will be advantageous to her treatment (reg. 4), and may only be implanted in a woman who intends to be the mother of that child; there is to be no surrogacy arrangement (reg. 11).

The sperm to be used in a fertilisation procedure must be sperm which has been recovered from:

(a)   the woman's husband;

(b)   an anonymous donor who has consented to the use of his sperm in accordance with the directions of the Director General;

(c)   a donor whose sperm is held at a semen bank recognised by the Director General in accordance with the Semen Bank Regulations of 1979 (reg. 5).

All necessary measures must be taken to preserve the identity of donors of semen or ova (reg. 15). Before an ovum recovered from a married woman is fertilised with donated semen, she and her husband must give written consent to the fertilisation (reg. 6), as they must have done in respect of a donated ovum which is to be fertilised with the woman's husband's sperm (reg. 7). A fertilised ovum must not be implanted in a married woman unless it has been provided by that woman or the donor and is fertilised in accordance with the Regulations. There are three exceptions to this:

(a)   Where the woman is unmarried, only her ovum may be used, and only after a social work report which supports such use.

(b)   In any posthumous procedure, where the woman's husband has died, one year has elapsed since the ovum was removed and fertilised and there is a social work report.

(c)   Where the woman in whom the ovum fertilised by her former husband is to be replaced has since divorced, implantation may be carried out only with the consent of her former husband (reg. 8).

Ova, including fertilised ova, may be cryopreserved for up to five years, unless the woman and her husband make a specific written request, when the ova may be stored for up to an additional five years (reg. 9). An ovum may not be recovered for use from a deceased woman (reg. 10(a)), but an ovum recovered from a married woman whose husband has died may be donated with her consent (reg. 10(b)). A fertilised ovum recovered from a couple one of whom has died may be used in accordance with reg. 8(b)(2) if the man has died, but may not be used at all if the woman has died. An ovum, including a fertilised ovum, taken from a single woman who has died may be used for another woman if the single woman consented to donation (reg. 10(c) and (d)).

Before any procedure is undertaken, the physician in charge of the hospital or clinic must explain to each participant the significance of the procedure, and each person must have given their consent to involvement in the procedure (reg. 14(a)). Any IVF procedure with a married woman must have the consent of her husband (reg. 14(b)). Under the Prohibition of Genetic Intervention (Human Cloning and Genetic Manipulation of Reproductive Cells) Law 5759 of 1999, there is a five-year moritorium on genetic intervention on human beings. This is said to be in order to examine the moral, legal, social and scientific aspects of such interventions. The prohibition covers human cloning and 'causing the creation of a person by the use of reproductive cells that have undergone a permanent intentional genetic modification' (Germ Line Gene Therapy).

Japan   In Japan there is no legal or administrative regulation of medically assisted procreation or pre-natal diagnosis, although their use is widespread. Germ line gene therapy is covered by a moratorium established by Ministry of Health guidelines issued in 1994. A Bill to prohibit the creation of human clones, chimeras and hybrids was presented to the Japanese Diet in spring 2000, and resultant legislation is expected.

Japanese physicians are not regulated by a professional disciplinary body such as the General Medical Council (UK), the Aerztekammer (Germany) or the Ordre des Medecins (France). The Japanese Society of Obstetrics and Gynaecology has published guidelines on some aspects of medically assisted procreation, but it is widely thought that they are interpreted generously by individual clinicians. There is no Society guideline on gamete donation, and AI is carried out in clinics under the auspices of the medical schools to which they are attached.

In 1994, over 17,000 IVF/ET procedures using fresh eggs/embryos were carried out in 232 centres. Over 1,100 IVF/ET procedures using cryopreserved eggs/embryos were undertaken in 62 clinics.

For IVF/ET, the Committee on Registration of Reproductive Medicine of the Japanese Association of Obstetrics and Gynaecology guidelines provide that they should be carried out for the treatment of a legally married couple. Cryopreservation of an embryo is permitted only while the couple are married and the woman is of 'procreative age'. Donation of embryos to other couples is not permitted.

In 1991, the Association of Obstetrics and Gynaecology approved clinical application of micro-insemination. Any member obstetrician wishing to perform the insemination must register in advance with the Association and must report on each case to the Association. The Association has taken steps to regulate selective reduction of multiple pregnancies, and has disfavoured surrogacy. Pre-implantation diagnosis using human ova remaining from embryo transfer may be carried out with the prior permission of the gamete donors, but only for research, not clinical, purposes.

Hong Kong The Parent and Child Ordinance No. 17 of 1993 deals with three specific issues:

(a) questions of legitimacy (ss. 3, 4, which are in terms those of the United Kingdom's Family Law Reform Act 1987, s. 27);
(b) presumptions as to paternity and legitimacy (s. 5) and declarations as to parentage and paternity (ss. 6, 7); and
(c) the legal consequences of assisted conception (ss. 9–15).

There is presently no licensing scheme for assisted conception services. There is a draft Reproductive Technology Bill under active discussion, following the production of a Final Report by a government-appointed Committee on Scientifically Assisted Human Reproduction (SAHR) in 1993. The Bill, based upon the Committee's recommendations, would:

(a) establish a statutory body to license medical institutions to carry out reproductive technology procedures;
(b) permit artificial insemination by a husband without specific statutory control, if administered by a general practitioner, and hence subject to professional rules of conduct and ethics;
(c) provide for the anonymity of a semen donor's identity, while allowing all people over 18 the right to ascertain whether they were born following a reproductive technology procedure and, if so, to have access to certain non-identifying information;
(d) actively discourage surrogacy, especially commercial surrogacy, while permitting genetic *in vitro* fertilisation (IVF) surrogacy.

A Consultation Paper on the Draft Reproductive Technology Bill and the accompanying Code of Practice which is to be drawn up make it evident that the Hong Kong Act, if it comes to fruition, will be very substantially based on the United Kingdom model in the Human Fertilisation and Embryology Act 1990.

Sections 9 and 10 of the 1993 Ordinance define who is to be regarded as 'mother' and 'father' respectively in the birth of a child following assisted conception services. The terms of the Ordinance's provisions are virtually identical to those of the United Kingdom's 1990 Act, ss. 27, 28, 29 and 30 (the 'parental orders' sections, providing for cases of surrogate births), with necessary amendments as to jurisdiction and some minor variances of local Hong Kong law.

Sections 13–15 make provision for the court to give directions for the use of scientific tests in the civil determination of parentage, including, for the consent of the person who has the care and control of a person under the age of 16 years (s. 14(3)), and for the taking of a bodily sample who is suffering from a mental disorder as defined within the Mental Health Ordinance (s. 14(4)).

In the Philippines, the Family Code (effective from August 1988, repealing and replacing several provisions of the Civil Code (Book I) of 1950), provides in Art. 164 that

> Children conceived or born during the marriage of parents are legitimate. Children conceived as a result of artificial insemination of the wife with the sperm of the husband or that of a donor or both are likewise legitimate children of the husband and wife, provided that both of them authorised or ratified such insemination in a written instrument executed and signed by them before the birth of the child. The instrument shall be recorded in the civil registry together with the birth certificate of the child.

Art. 166 also provides that the legitimacy of a child may be impugned only on limited grounds. In respect of children conceived through artificial insemination, where it is shown that 'written authorisation or ratification of either parent was obtained through mistake, fraud, violence, intimidation or undue influence'.[88]

NOTES

[1]   Watson, J., *The Double Helix* (Harmondsworth, Penguin, 1970).

[2]   Council of Europe Convention for the Protection of Human Rights and Dignity of the Human Being with Regard to the Application of Biology and Medicine (DIR/JUR(96/14), Strasbourg, 1996); see also the Council of Europe, Directorate of Legal Affairs, *Explanatory Report to the Convention for the Protection of Human Rights and Dignity of the Human Being with Regard to the Application of Biology and Medicine* (DIR/JUR (97(1) Strasbourg, 1997).

[3]   Lee Silver has noted that, by 1994, more than 38 countries had established IVF programmes; see his *Remaking Eden* at 335, deriving this information from data compiled by pharmaceutical company Organon at http://www.bris.ac.uk/Depts/ObysGyn/crm/ivf.94.html.

The Secretary General of the Society of Gynaecology and Obstetrics of Nigeria, Friday Okonofua, has called for a moratorium on the establishment of IVF clinics in developing countries (see 'The case against the development of reproductive technology in developing countries' (1996) 103 *British Journal of Obstetrics & Gynaecology* 957) and indicated in correspondence that as of February 2000 no legal provisions regulating the practice of assisted conception exist in Nigeria or most parts of sub-Saharan Africa.

[4]   The most comprehensive consideration of a market in reproductive services has been suggested by Posner, R.A., *Sex and Reason* (Cambridge, Mass., Harvard University Press, 1992), at 404–34. The belief that Posner, or any other 'law and economics' analysis, thereby posits an *unregulated market* is examined and corrected by Neil Duxbury in 'Do Markets Degrade?' (1996) 59 MLR 331.

[5]   After Health Council of The Netherlands, Committee on *in vitro* fertilisation, *IVF-Related Research* (Rijswijk, 1998), at 66.

[6]   Knoppers, B.M. and Le Bris, S., 'Recent Advances in Medically Assisted Conception: Legal, Ethical and Social Issues' (1991) 17 *American Journal of Law & Medicine* 329.

[7]   *Parliaments and Screening* (London, John Libby, 1995).

[8]   *Op. cit.* n. 6. Although now somewhat dated, the fundamentals of the approach which they adopt are still illuminating.

[9]   *The Ethics of Genetics in Human Procreation* (Aldershot, Ashgate, 2000).

[10]   *Op. cit.* n. 6, at 341.

[11]   After Eser, A., 'Legal Aspects of Bioethics' in *Europe and Bioethics*, Proceedings of the First Symposium of the Council of Europe on Bioethics (Strasbourg, 1989), at 42.

[12]   It is interesting in this context to recall that fewer than 10% of licences for basic research granted by the HFEA are registered in private clinics; i.e. most useful innovation comes in the scientifically more prolific public (and especially university) sector.

[13]   Chalmers, D., 'Government's Role in Human Sexuality and Reproduction', paper at Monash University, Melbourne, Symposium, *Reproductive Medicine: Beyond 2000*, November 1994, at 26–27.

[14]   See Danish Council on Ethics Second Report, at 75–76, acknowledging this difficulty.

[15]   *Assisted Reproduction – A Report* (Copenhagen, Danish Council of Ethics, 8th Annual Report, 1995).

[16]   Caplan, A., 'Introduction' in Dianne Bartels, Reinhard Priester, Dorothy Vawter and Arthur Caplan (eds), *Beyond Baby M; Ethical Issues in New Reproductive Technologies* (Clifton, New Jersey, Humana Press, 1990), at 5–6: 'Where matters of morality and medicine are concerned, society is best served not by policies based on fear, ignorance, prejudice, or raw emotion, but by the emergence of moral consensus.'

[17]   Cook, R. and Dickens, B., *Considerations for Formulating Reproductive Health Laws* (Geneva, World Health Organisation, 1998).

[18]   Hobsbawm, E., *Age of Extremes: The Short Twentieth Century* 1914–1991 (London, Michael Joseph, 1994), 287.

[19]   de Saint Exupery, A., *Wind, Sand and Stars* (London, Pan, 1975) 39–40.

[20]   On the recent Hungarian law on medically assisted procreation, for example, see Judit Sandor, 'The Hungarian Legislative Approach' in Jenny Gunning (ed.), *Assisted Conception: Research Ethics and Law* (Aldershot, Ashgate, 2000).

[21]   Following Mme Catherine Lalumiere, 'Allocutions D'Ouverture' in *Europe and Bioethics*, Proceedings of the First Symposium of the Council of Europe on Bioethics, (Strasbourg, 1989), at 12–14.

[22]   See Griffiths, J., 'Is Law Important?' (1979) 54 *New York University Law Review* 339.

[23]   Morgan, D., 'What does Biomedical Diplomacy Mean? Law, Ethics and the Regulation of Modern Medicine' (IV World Congress of Bioethics, Tokyo, Japan, 1998) and 'Law & Medicine Colloquium' (University College, London, July 1999). The theme is established and explored in Morgan, D., *Explorations in Medical Law and Ethics* (London, Cavendish, 2000), chapter 3.

[24]   Galanter, M. G., 'Law Abounding' (1992) 55 MLR 1; Teubner, 'Juridification: Concepts, Aspects, Limits, Solutions' in Teubner (ed.), *Juridification of Social Spheres* (Berlin, Walter de Gruyter, 1987), at 3–48.

[25]   Calabresi, G. (with Bobbit, P.), *Tragic Choices* (New York, W.W. Norton, 1978).

[26]   Hobsbawm, *op. cit.* n. 18; Fujiki, N. and Macer, D., *Bioethics in Asia* (Tskuba Science City, Eubios, E., Ethics Institute, 1998); Kumar, K., 'Legal Implications

of Medical Advancement' in P. Leelakrishan and G. Sadasivan Nair (eds), *New Horizons of Law* (Cochin, Cochin University of Science and Technology, 1987), at 199–212, esp. at 199–204 and 210–12; Manga, P., 'New Reproductive Technologies in the Third World: Heightened Human Rights and Ethical Controversies', paper delivered to the Third International Conference on Health Law and Ethics, Toronto, July 1992.

[27] Wolf, S., 'The Rise of the New Pragmatism' (1994) 20 *American Journal of Law & Medicine* 211; Doyal, L., *What Makes Women Sick?* (New Brunswick, Rutgers University Press, 1995).

[28] This brief historical note is drawn from the Council of Europe, Directorate of Legal Affairs, *Explanatory Report to the Convention for the Protection of Human Rights and Dignity of the Human Being with Regard to the Application of Biology and Medicine* (DIR/JUR (97(1), Strasbourg, 1997), at 4–5.

[29] To January 2000, ten states had signed the Convention: Denmark, Finland, France, Greece, Italy, Luxembourg, The Netherlands, Portugal, Spain and Sweden; see Deryck Beyleveld and Shaun Pattinson, *op. cit.* n. 9, at 267, n. 133.

[30] Protocol on the Prohibition of Human Cloning (Strasbourg, Council of Europe, 1998).

[31] In April 1997, 21 member states of the Council of Europe (but not the UK) signed the Convention at Oviedo in Spain.

[32] Brazier, M., 'Regulating the Reproduction Business?' (1999) 7 *Medical Law Review* 166, at 193.

[33] We have drawn from and built on, where information has come later to hand, the survey reported in Deryck Beyleveld and Shaun Pattinson, *op. cit.* n. 9.

[34] This summary of Scandinavian jurisdictions draws from Linda Nielsen's essay, 'Artificial Reproductive Technology and Genetics: The Scandinavian Approach', in Ruth Deech and Therese Mulders-Klein (eds), *Artificial Reproductive Technology and Genetics* (The Hague, Kluwer International, 2000).

[35] Law No. 460 of 1997 on Medically Assisted Reproduction. A further Bill was due to have been published at the end of 1999.

[36] *Op. cit.* n. 15.

[37] This account also builds on Morgan, D. and Nielsen, L., 'Dangerous Liaisons: Law, Technology, Reproduction and European Ethics – An Anglo-Danish Comparison' in Sean McVeigh and Sally Wheeler (eds), *Medicine, Law and Regulation* (Aldershot: Dartmouth Press, 1992), at 52–74.

[38] The Act Relating to the Application of Biotechnology in Medicine.

[39] We are grateful to Desirée Sonderlund, Counsellor of Legislation at the Ministry of Justice, Helsinki, for an English language copy of this recent legislation, and for her comments on the present position.

[40] Paternity Act 700/1975.

[41] 488/1999.

[42] There is an excellent account and examination of the origins and functioning of the French sperm bank system – CECOS – in Noaves, S., *Les Passeurs de Gametes* (Nancy, Presses Universitaires de Nancy, 1994).

[43] Cohen, J., 'The French Experience' in Peter Brinsden (ed.), *A Textbook of In Vitro Fertilisation & Assisted Reproduction*, 2nd edn, 1999, at 428.

[44] Posthumous insemination is now prohibited, after several well-publicised cases in which wives sought access to their deceased husbands' sperm. One case, *Pires*

v *Centre Hospitalier de la Grave* (Jugment du 11 mai 1993, Tribunal de Grande Instance de Toulouse, Première Chambre), forms the basis of the thoughtful and thought-provoking essay by Bateman Noaves, S. and Salem, T., 'Embedding the Embryo' in John Harris and Soren Holm (eds), *The Future of Human Reproduction* (Oxford, Clarendon Press, 1998), at 101.

[45] Cohen, *op. cit.*, n. 43 at 429.

[46] See Ludwig, M. and Diedrich, K., 'The German Experience' in Brinsden, *op. cit.* n. 43, at 431. We are grateful to Sigrid Graumann of the University of Tubingen for information on further developments in Germany.

[47] Gesetz zum Schutz von Embryonen – Embryonenschutzgesetz (EschG) (Bundesgesetzblatt, 13 December 1990).

[48] Diario da Republica, Series I, 9 June 1990, No. 133, 2516–17.

[49] The most accessible English language review of the Spanish law is provided in an overview by one of the country's leading academic commentators who has written extensively on the law in Spanish, Jamie Vidal Martinez. See his 'Main Aspects of the Regulation Concerning Some Important Bioethical Issues in the Spanish Law' (trans. B. Vidal Villasur), in *Bioethics: From Ethics to Law, From Law to Ethics* (International Colloquium, Lausanne, Schultess Polygraphischer Verlag Zurich, 1997), at 79–107. We were provided with a translation of the decision of the Tribunal Constitucional (Spanish Constitutional Court) (July, 1999) by Itziar Alkorta, PhD student of Professor Adela Asua of the University of the Basque Country, to whom we are most grateful.

[50] Ley 35/1988, de 22 de noviembre, que regula las técnicas de reproducción asistida humana.

[51] STC 212/1996, that deals with abortion.

[52] Draft law 4048. We have been assisted by Gilda Ferrando of the University of Genoa in reviewing this Act and by our colleague Thomas Watkin who generously undertook to translate a copy of the Bill for us to work with. She has previously commented on various decisions of the Italian courts in questions arising from the use of assisted conception technologies in Italy; see, for example, 'Interesse del minore e status del figlio' (1999) *Estratto dalla Giurisprudenza italiana* 1110, 'L'Interesse del Minore Nella Procreazione Assista' (1994) *Materiali per una Storia Della Cultura Giuridica* 119, 'Consenso del Marito, Fecondazione Eterologa e Disconoscimento di Paternita' (1997) *La Nuova Giurisprudenza Civile Commenta* 167.

[53] We are grateful to our former colleague, Akas Manolkidis, and to Katerina Iliadou of the Ministry of Justice, Athens, for information on which this section is based.

[54] Law 2071/192; Act No. 123, 15 July 1992.

[55] Greece, with Act 2619/1998 (Official Gazette A' 132) has ratified the European Convention for the Protection of Human Rights and Dignity of the Human Being with regard to the Application of Biology and Medicine: Convention on Human Rights and Biomedicine (ETS No. 164), and has recently established a National Bioethics Committee. Such Committee has the mission to address the problems pertaining to the applications of genetic technology and to investigate their moral, legal and social aspects and impacts (Art. 10 IV of the Act 2667/1998, Official Gazette A' 281).

[56] Is. Kriari-Katrani, *Biomedical Developments and Constitutional Law* (in Greek) (Thessaloniki, 1994), at 70 *et seq.*

[57] *Ibid.*, at 95 *et seq.*

[58] *Ibid.*, at 98 *et seq.*

[59] *Ibid.*, at 127.

[60] *Cf.* Art. 178 of the Civil Code, according to which immoral contracts are not valid.

[61] Council of State, Judgment No. 157/1999, in EDDDD 1999, at 555 *et seq.* (557).

[62] Kriari-Katrani, *op. cit.* n. 56, at 109 *et seq.*

[63] This section draws from Morgan, D. and Bernat, E., 'The Reproductive Waltz: The Austrian Medically Assisted Procreation Act 1992' [1992] JSWFL 420.

[64] 21 August 1987.

[65] This section is drawn from Morgan, D. and Lee, R.G., 'Artificial Reproductive Technology and Genetics: The Common Law Report' in Ruth Deech, P. Vlaardingerbroek and Therese Mulders-Klein (eds), *Artificial Reproductive Technology and Genetics* (The Hague, Kluwer International, 2000). In turn, the report on the Canadian provinces was prepared by Bernard Dickens of the University of Toronto. We are grateful to Roxanne Mykitiuk of Osgoode Hall Law School for additional information on the progress of proposed legislation. Bill C47, first published in 1996, has recently returned to the Federal Parliament for consideration. There is a good account of the main provisions of the original Bill, which the 1999 version replicates, and a commentary on its possible impact in the Canadian Fertility and Andrology Society, 'Response to Bill C47; Human Reproductive and Genetic Technologies Act' (Montreal, 1996).

[66] First reading of Bill, 14 June 1996.

[67] *Final Report of the [Baird] Royal Commission on New Reproductive Technologies*, at 16.

[68] Garrison, M., 'The Technological Family: What's New and What's Not' (1999) 33 FLQ 691, at 692–93; although only 1,100 of these were conceptions involving donated eggs.

[69] For a recent review, see Garrison, at 701–02 and accompanying notes.

[70] 42 USC ## 263a (1)–(4) (Supp. V 1993) (the Wyden Bill).

[71] See Stenger, R., 'Law and Assisted Conception in the United Kingdom and the United States' (1995) 9 *Journal of Law & Health* 135 for a careful and detailed examination both of that Act and its relationship with the Human Fertilisation and Embryology Act 1990.

[72] 42 USC ## 285g(5), 289g(1)–(2) (Supp. V 1993).

[73] Stenger, *op. cit.* n. 71, at 135, 136.

[74] Havins, W. and Dalessio, J., 'The Ever-Widening Gap Between the Science of Artificial Reproductive Technology and the Laws which Govern that Technology' (1999) 48 Depaul Law Review 825.

[75] Stenger, *op. cit.* n. 71.

[76] *Life's Dominion: An Argument about Abortion and Euthanasia* (London, Harper Collins, 1993), at 4.

[77] Stenger, *op. cit.* n. 71, at 137.

[78] Jones, H., 'The USA Experience' in Brinsden, *op. cit.* n. 43, at 442.

[79] Stenger, *op. cit.* n. 71.

[80] See www.resolve.org.adveeoc.htm; 'EOC Ruling: Infertility as a Disability'.

[81] *Op. cit.* n. 68, at 697; also reviewing much of the leading litigation involving assisted conception.

[82] *Op. cit.* n. 68, at 700.

[83] This section is drawn from Morgan and Lee, *op. cit.* n. 65. In turn, the report on the Australian jurisdictions was prepared by Loane Skene.

[84] This section is drawn from Morgan and Lee, *op. cit.* n. 65. The report on New Zealand was prepared by Ken Daniels of Canterbury University, New Zealand.

[85] This section is drawn from Morgan and Lee, *op. cit.* n. 65. The report on Japan was prepared by Keiko Irako. This has been supplemented in various ways, particularly with the assistance of our former colleague, Carol Jones, now of the City University, Hong Kong. There is a very helpful discussion of the law in that jurisdiction in Chiu Man Chung, *A Report on the Study of Artificial Reproduction Law in Hong Kong* (City University of Hong Kong 1999). A Human Reproductive Technology Bill is presently under consideration.

[86] Ministry of Health (27 April 1987) (Kovetz Ha-Takkanot, 11 June 1987).

[87] Int. D. Health leg. 1980, 31, 333.

[88] We are grateful to Attorney Eduardo Victor J Valdez of Quezon City for this information.

Appendix 1
Human Fertilisation and Embryology Act 1990

Principal terms used

1 Meaning of 'embryo', 'gamete' and associated expressions

(1) In this Act, except where otherwise stated—

(a) embryo means a live human embryo where fertilisation is complete, and

(b) references to an embryo include an egg in the process of fertilisation,

and, for this purpose, fertilisation is not complete until the appearance of a two cell zygote.

(2) This Act, so far as it governs bringing about the creation of an embryo, applies only to bringing about the creation of an embryo outside the human body; and in this Act—

(a) references to embryos the creation of which was brought about *in vitro* (in their application to those where fertilisation is complete) are to those where fertilisation began outside the human body whether or not it was completed there, and

(b) references to embryos taken from a woman do not include embryos whose creation was brought about *in vitro*.

(3) This Act, so far as it governs the keeping or use of an embryo, applies only to keeping or using an embryo outside the human body.

(4) References in this Act to gametes, eggs or sperm, except where otherwise stated, are to live human gametes, eggs or sperm but references below in this Act to gametes or eggs do not include eggs in the process of fertilisation.

2 Other terms

(1) In this Act—

'the Authority' means the Human Fertilisation and Embryology Authority established under section 5 of this Act,

'directions' means directions under section 23 of this Act,

'licence' means a licence under Schedule 2 to this Act and, in relation to a licence, 'the person responsible' has the meaning given by section 17 of this Act, and

'treatment services' means medical, surgical or obstetric services provided to the public or a section of the public for the purpose of assisting women to carry children.

(2)   References in this Act to keeping, in relation to embryos or gametes, include keeping while preserved, whether preserved by cryopreservation or in any other way; and embryos or gametes so kept are referred to in this Act as 'stored' (and 'store' and 'storage' are to be interpreted accordingly).

(3)   For the purposes of this Act, a woman is not to be treated as carrying a child until the embryo has become implanted.

Activities governed by the Act

3   Prohibitions in connection with embryos

(1)   No person shall—
(a)   bring about the creation of an embryo, or
(b)   keep or use an embryo,
except in pursuance of a licence.

(2)   No person shall place in a woman—
(a)   a live embryo other than a human embryo, or
(b)   any live gametes other than human gametes.

(3)   A licence cannot authorise—
(a)   keeping or using an embryo after the appearance of the primitive streak,
(b)   placing an embryo in any animal,
(c)   keeping or using an embryo in any circumstances in which regulations prohibit its keeping or use, or
(d)   replacing a nucleus of a cell of an embryo with a nucleus taken from a cell of any person, embryo or subsequent development of an embryo.

(4)   For the purposes of subsection (3)(a) above, the primitive streak is to be taken to have appeared in an embryo not later than the end of the period of 14 days beginning with the day when the gametes are mixed, not counting any time during which the embryo is stored.

3A   Prohibition in connection with germ cells

(1)   No person shall, for the purpose of providing fertility services for any woman, use female germ cells taken or derived from an embryo or a foetus or use embryos created by using such cells.

(2)   In this section—
'female germ cells' means cells of the female germ line and includes such cells at any stage of maturity and accordingly includes eggs; and
'fertility services' means medical, surgical or obstetric services provided for the purpose of assisting women to carry children.

4   Prohibitions in connection with gametes

(1)   No person shall—
(a)   store any gametes, or
(b)   in the course of providing treatment services for any woman, use the sperm of any man unless the services are being provided for the woman and the man together or use the eggs of any other woman, or
(c)   mix gametes with the live gametes of any animal,
except in pursuance of a licence.

(2)   A licence cannot authorise storing or using gametes in any circumstances in which regulations prohibit their storage or use.

(3)   No person shall place sperm and eggs in a woman in any circumstances specified in regulations except in pursuance of a licence.

(4)   Regulations made by virtue of subsection (3) above may provide that, in relation to licences only to place sperm and eggs in a woman in such circumstances, sections 12 to 22 of this Act shall have effect with such modifications as may be specified in the regulations.

(5)   Activities regulated by this section or section 3 of this Act are referred to in this Act as 'activities governed by this Act'.

The Human Fertilisation and Embryology Authority,
its functions and procedure

5   The Human Fertilisation and Embryology Authority

(1)   There shall be a body corporate called the Human Fertilisation and Embryology Authority.

(2)   The Authority shall consist of—

(a)   a chairman and deputy chairman, and

(b)   such number of other members as the Secretary of State appoints.

(3)   Schedule 1 to this Act (which deals with the membership of the Authority, etc) shall have effect.

6   Accounts and audit

(1)   The Authority shall keep proper accounts and proper records in relation to the accounts and shall prepare for each accounting year a statement of accounts.

(2)   The annual statement of accounts shall comply with any direction given by the Secretary of State, with the approval of the Treasury, as to the information to be contained in the statement, the way in which the information is to be presented or the methods and principles according to which the statement is to be prepared.

(3)   Not later than five months after the end of an accounting year, the Authority shall send a copy of the statement of accounts for that year to the Secretary of State and to the Comptroller and Auditor General.

(4)   The Comptroller and Auditor General shall examine, certify and report on every statement of accounts received by him under subsection (3) above and shall lay a copy of the statement and of his report before each House of Parliament.

(5)   The Secretary of State and the Comptroller and Auditor General may inspect any records relating to the accounts.

(6)   In this section 'accounting year' means the period beginning with the day when the Authority is established and ending with the following 31st March, or any later period of twelve months ending with the 31st March.

7   Reports to Secretary of State

(1)   The Authority shall prepare a report for the first twelve months of its existence, and a report for each succeeding period of twelve months, and shall send each report to the Secretary of State as soon as practicable after the end of the period for which it is prepared.

(2)   A report prepared under this section for any period shall deal with the activities of the Authority in the period and the activities the Authority proposes to undertake in the succeeding period of twelve months.

(3)   The Secretary of State shall lay before each House of Parliament a copy of every report received by him under this section.

8   General functions of the Authority

The Authority shall—

(a)   keep under review information about embryos and any subsequent development of embryos and about the provision of treatment services and activities governed by this Act, and advise the Secretary of State, if he asks it to do so, about those matters,

(b)   publicise the services provided to the public by the Authority or provided in pursuance of licences,

(c)   provide, to such extent as it considers appropriate advice and information for persons to whom licences apply or who are receiving treatment services or providing gametes or embryos for use for the purposes of activities governed by this Act, or may wish to do so, and

(d)   perform such other functions as may be specified in regulations.

9   Licence committees and other committees

(1)   The Authority shall maintain one or more committees to discharge the Authority's functions relating to the grant, variation, suspension and revocation of licences, and a committee discharging those functions is referred to in this Act as a 'licence committee'.

(2)   The Authority may provide for the discharge of any of its other functions by committees or by members or employees of the Authority.

(3)   A committee (other than a licence committee) may appoint sub-committees.

(4)   Persons, committees or sub-committees discharging functions of the Authority shall do so in accordance with any general directions of the Authority.

(5)   A licence committee shall consist of such number of persons as may be specified in or determined in accordance with regulations, all being members of the Authority, and shall include at least one person who is not authorised to carry on or participate in any activity under the authority of a licence and would not be so authorised if outstanding applications were granted.

(6)   A committee (other than a licence committee) or a sub-committee may include a minority of persons who are not members of the Authority.

(7)   Subject to subsection (10) below, a licence committee, before considering an application for authority—

(a)   for a person to carry on an activity governed by this Act which he is not then authorised to carry on, or

(b)   for a person to carry on any such activity on premises where he is not then authorised to carry it on,

shall arrange for the premises where the activity is to be carried on to be inspected on its behalf, and for a report on the inspection to be made to it.

(8)   Subject to subsection (9) below, a licence committee shall arrange for any premises to which a licence relates to be inspected on its behalf once in each calendar year, and for a report on the inspection to be made to it.

(9)   Any particular premises need not be inspected in any particular year if the licence committee considers an inspection in that year unnecessary.

(10)   A licence committee need not comply with subsection (7) above where the premises in question have been inspected in pursuance of that subsection or subsection (8) above at some time during the period of one year ending with the

date of the application, and the licence committee considers that a further inspection is not necessary.

(11)   An inspection in pursuance of subsection (7) or (8) above may be carried out by a person who is not a member of a licence committee.

10   Licensing procedure

(1)   Regulations may make such provision as appears to the Secretary of State to be necessary or desirable about the proceedings of licence committees and of the Authority on any appeal from such a committee.

(2)   The regulations may in particular include provision—

(a)   for requiring persons to give evidence or to produce documents, and

(b)   about the admissibility of evidence.

Scope of licences

11   Licences for treatment, storage and research

(1)   The Authority may grant the following and no other licences—

(a)   licences under paragraph 1 of Schedule 2 to this Act authorising activities in the course of providing treatment services,

(b)   licences under that Schedule authorising the storage of gametes and embryos, and

(c)   licences under paragraph 3 of that Schedule authorising activities for the purposes of a project of research.

(2)   Paragraph 4 of that Schedule has effect in the case of all licences.

Licence conditions

12   General conditions

The following shall be conditions of every licence granted under this Act—

(a)   that the activities authorised by the licence shall be carried on only on the premises to which the licence relates and under the supervision of the person responsible,

(b)   that any member or employee of the Authority, on production if so required, of a document identifying the person as such, shall at all reasonable times be permitted to enter those premises and inspect them (which includes inspecting any equipment or records and observing any activity),

(c)   that the provisions of Schedule 3 to this Act shall be complied with,

(d)   that proper records shall be maintained in such form as the Authority may specify in directions,

(e)   that no money or other benefit shall be given or received in respect of any supply of gametes or embryos unless authorised by directions,

(f)   that, where gametes or embryos are supplied to a person to whom another licence applies, that person shall also be provided with such information as the Authority may specify in directions, and

(g)   that the Authority shall be provided, in such form and at such intervals as it may specify in directions, with such copies of or extracts from the records, or such other information, as the directions may specify.

13   Conditions of licences for treatment

(1)   The following shall be conditions of every licence under paragraph 1 of Schedule 2 to this Act.

(2) Such information shall be recorded as the Authority may specify in directions about the following—

(a) the persons for whom services are provided in pursuance of the licence,

(b) the services provided for them,

(c) the persons whose gametes are kept or used for the purposes of services provided in pursuance of the licence or whose gametes have been used in bringing about the creation of embryos so kept or used,

(d) any child appearing to the person responsible to have been born as a result of treatment in pursuance of the licence,

(e) any mixing of egg and sperm and any taking of an embryo from a woman or other acquisition of an embryo, and

(f) such other matters as the Authority may specify in directions.

(3) The records maintained in pursuance of the licence shall include any information recorded in pursuance of subsection (2) above and any consent of a person whose consent is required under Schedule 3 to this Act.

(4) No information shall be removed from any records maintained in pursuance of the licence before the expiry of such period as may be specified in directions for records of the class in question.

(5) A woman shall not be provided with treatment services unless account has been taken of the welfare of any child who may be born as a result of the treatment (including the need of that child for a father), and of any other child who may he affected by the birth.

(6) A woman shall not be provided with any treatment services involving—

(a) the use of any gametes of any person, if that person's consent is required under paragraph 5 of Schedule 3 to this Act for the use in question,

(b) the use of any embryo the creation of which was brought about *in vitro*, or

(c) the use of any embryo taken from a woman, if the consent of the woman from whom it was taken is required under paragraph 7 of that Schedule for the use in question,

unless the woman being treated and, where she is being treated together with a man, the man have been given a suitable opportunity to receive proper counselling about the implications of taking the proposed steps, and have been provided with such relevant information as is proper.

(7) Suitable procedures shall be maintained—

(a) for determining the persons providing gametes or from whom embryos are taken for use in pursuance of the licence, and

(b) for the purpose of securing that consideration is given to the use of practices not requiring the authority of a licence as well as those requiring such authority.

14 Conditions of storage licences

(1) The following shall be conditions of every licence authorising the storage of gametes or embryos—

(a) that gametes of a person or an embryo taken from a woman shall be placed in storage only if received from that person or woman or acquired from a person to whom a licence applies and that an embryo the creation of which has been brought about *in vitro* otherwise than in pursuance of that licence shall be placed in storage only if acquired from a person to whom a licence applies,

(b) that gametes or embryos which are or have been stored shall not be supplied to a person otherwise than in the course of providing treatment services unless that person is a person to whom a licence applies,

(c) that no gametes or embryos shall be kept in storage for longer than the statutory storage period and, if stored at the end of the period, shall be allowed to perish, and

(d) that such information as the Authority may specify in directions as to the persons whose consent is required under Schedule 3 to this Act, the terms of their consent and the circumstances of the storage and as to such other matters as the Authority may specify in directions shall be included in the records maintained in pursuance of the licence.

(2) No information shall be removed from any records maintained in pursuance of such a licence before the expiry of such period as may be specified in directions for records of the class in question.

(3) The statutory storage period in respect of gametes is such period not exceeding ten years as the licence may specify.

(4) The statutory storage period in respect of embryos is such period not exceeding five years as the licence may specify.

(5) Regulations may provide that subsection (3) or (4) above shall have effect as if for ten years or, as the case may be, five years there were substituted—

(a) such shorter period, or

(b) in such circumstances as may be specified in the regulations, such longer period,

as may be specified in the regulations.

15   Conditions of research licences

(1) The following shall be conditions of every licence under paragraph 3 of Schedule 2 to this Act.

(2) The records maintained in pursuance of the licence shall include such information as the Authority may specify in directions about such matters as the Authority may so specify.

(3) No information shall be removed from any records maintained in pursuance of the licence before the expiry of such period as may be specified in directions for records of the class in question.

(4) No embryo appropriated for the purposes of any project of research shall be kept or used otherwise than for the purposes of such a project.

Grant, revocation and suspension of licences

16   Grant of licence

(1) Where application is made to the Authority in a form approved for the purpose by it accompanied by the initial fee, a licence may be granted to any person by a licence committee if the requirements of subsection (2) below are met and any additional fee is paid.

(2) The requirements mentioned in subsection (1) above are—

(a) that the application is for a licence designating an individual as the person under whose supervision the activities to be authorised by the licence are to be carried on,

(b) that either that individual is the applicant or—

(i)   the application is made with the consent of that individual, and

(ii)   the licence committee is satisfied that the applicant is a suitable person to hold a licence,

(c)   that the licence committee is satisfied that the character, qualifications and experience of that individual are such as are required for the supervision of the activities and that the individual will discharge the duty under section 17 of this Act,

(d)   that the licence committee is satisfied that the premises in respect of which the licence is to be granted are suitable for the activities, and

(e)   that all the other requirements of this Act in relation to the granting of the licence are satisfied.

(3)   The grant of a licence to any person may be by way of renewal of a licence granted to that person, whether on the same or different terms.

(4)   Where the licence committee is of the opinion that the information provided in the application is insufficient to enable it to determine the application, it need not consider the application until the applicant has provided it with such further information as it may require him to provide.

(5)   The licence committee shall not grant a licence unless a copy of the conditions to be imposed by the licence has been shown to, and acknowledged in writing by, the applicant and (where different) the person under whose supervision the activities are to be carried on.

(6)   In subsection (1) above 'initial fee' and 'additional fee' mean a fee of such amount as may be fixed from time to time by the Authority with the approval of the Secretary of State and the Treasury, and in determining any such amount, the Authority may have regard to the costs of performing all its functions.

(7)   Different fees may be fixed for different circumstances and fees paid under this section are not repayable.

17   The person responsible

(1)   It shall be the duty of the individual under whose supervision the activities authorised by a licence are carried on (referred to in this Act as the 'person responsible') to secure—

(a)   that the other persons to whom the licence applies are of such character, and are so qualified by training and experience, as to be suitable persons to participate in the activities authorised by the licence,

(b)   that proper equipment is used,

(c)   that proper arrangements are made for the keeping of gametes and embryos and for the disposal of gametes or embryos that have been allowed to perish,

(d)   that suitable practices are used in the course of the activities, and

(e)   that the conditions of the licence are complied with.

(2)   References in this Act to the persons to whom a licence applies are to—

(a)   the person responsible,

(b)   any person designated in the licence, or in a notice given to the Authority by the person who holds the licence or the person responsible, as a person to whom the licence applies, and

(c)   any person acting under the direction of the person responsible or of any person so designated.

(3)   References below in this Act to the nominal licensee are to a person who holds a licence under which a different person is the person responsible.

18   Revocation and variation of licence

(1)   A licence committee may revoke a licence if it is satisfied—

(a)   that any information given for the purposes of the application for the grant of the licence was in any material respect false or misleading,

(b)   that the premises to which the licence relates are no longer suitable for the activities authorised by the licence,

(c)   that the person responsible has failed to discharge, or is unable because of incapacity to discharge, the duty under section 17 of this Act or has failed to comply with directions given in connection with any licence, or

(d)   that there has been any other material change of circumstances since the licence was granted.

(2)   A licence committee may also revoke a licence if—

(a)   it ceases to be satisfied that the character of the person responsible is such as is required for the supervision of those activities or that the nominal licensee is a suitable person to hold a licence, or

(b)   the person responsible dies or is convicted of an offence under this Act.

(3)   Where a licence committee has power to revoke a licence under subsection (1) above it may instead vary any terms of the licence.

(4)   A licence committee may, on an application by the person responsible or the nominal licensee, vary or revoke a licence.

(5)   A licence committee may, on an application by the nominal licensee, vary the licence so as to designate another individual in place of the person responsible if—

(a)   the committee is satisfied that the character, qualifications and experience of the other individual are such as are required for the supervision of the activities authorised by the licence and that the individual will discharge the duty under section 17 of this Act, and

(b)   the application is made with the consent of the other individual.

(6)   Except on an application under subsection (5) above, a licence can only be varied under this section—

(a)   so far as it relates to the activities authorised by the licence, the manner in which they are conducted or the conditions of the licence, or

(b)   so as to extend or restrict the premises to which the licence relates.

19   Procedure for refusal, variation or revocation of licence

(1)   Where a licence committee proposes to refuse a licence or to refuse to vary a licence so as to designate another individual in place of the person responsible, the committee shall give notice of the proposal, the reasons for it and the effect of subsection (3) below to the applicant.

(2)   Where a licence committee proposes to vary or revoke a licence, the committee shall give notice of the proposal, the reasons for it and the effect of subsection (3) below to the person responsible and the nominal licensee (but not to any person who has applied for the variation or revocation).

(3)   If, within the period of twenty-eight days beginning with the day on which notice of the proposal is given, any person to whom notice was given under subsection (1) or (2) above gives notice to the committee of a wish to make to the

committee representations about the proposal in any way mentioned in subsection (4) below, the Committee shall, before making its determination, give the person an opportunity to make representations in that way.

(4)   The representations may be—

(a)   oral representations made by the person, or another acting on behalf of the person, at a meeting of the Committee, and

(b)   written representations made by the person.

(5)   A licence committee shall—

(a)   in the case of a determination to grant a licence, give notice of the determination to the person responsible and the nominal licensee,

(b)   in the case of a determination to refuse a licence, or to refuse to vary a licence so as to designate another individual in place of the person responsible, give such notice to the applicant, and

(c)   in the case of a determination to vary or revoke a licence, give such notice to the person responsible and the nominal licensee.

(6)   A licence committee giving notice of a determination to refuse a licence or to refuse to vary a licence so as to designate another individual in place of the person responsible, or of a determination to vary or revoke a licence otherwise than on an application by the person responsible or the nominal licensee, shall give in the notice the reasons for its decision.

20   Appeal to Authority against determinations of licence committee

(1)   Where a licence committee determines to refuse a licence or to refuse to vary a licence so as to designate another individual in place of the person responsible, the applicant may appeal to the Authority if notice has been given to the committee and to the Authority before the end of the period of twenty-eight days beginning with the date on which notice of the committee's determination was served on the applicant.

(2)   Where a licence committee determines to vary or revoke a licence, any person on whom notice of the determination was served (other than a person who applied for the variation or revocation) may appeal to the Authority if notice has been given to the committee and to the Authority before the end of the period of twenty-eight days beginning with the date on which notice of the committee's determination was served.

(3)   An appeal under this section shall be by way of rehearing by the Authority and no member of the Authority who took any part in the proceedings resulting in the determination appealed against shall take any part in the proceedings on appeal.

(4)   On the appeal—

(a)   the appellant shall be entitled to appear or be represented,

(b)   the members of the licence committee shall be entitled to appear, or the committee shall be entitled to be represented, and

(c)   the Authority shall consider any written representations received from the appellant or any member of the committee and may take into account any matter that could be taken into account by a licence committee,

and the Authority may make such determination on the appeal as it thinks fit.

(5)   The Authority shall give notice of its determination to the appellant and, if it is a determination to refuse a licence or to refuse to vary a licence so as to designate another individual in place of the person responsible or a determination to vary or revoke a licence, shall include in the notice the reasons for the decision.

(6)   The functions of the Authority on an appeal under this section cannot be discharged by any committee, member or employee of the Authority and, for the purposes of the appeal, the quorum shall not be less than five.

21   Appeals to High Court or Court of Session

Where the Authority determines under section 20 of this Act—

(a)   to refuse a licence or to refuse to vary a licence so as to designate another individual in place of the person responsible, or

(b)   to vary or revoke a licence,

any person on whom notice of the determination was served may appeal to the High Court or, in Scotland, the Court of Session on a point of law.

22   Temporary suspension of licence

(1)   Where a licence committee—

(a)   has reasonable grounds to suspect that there are grounds for revoking the licence under section 18 of this Act, and

(b)   is of the opinion that the licence should immediately be suspended,

it may by notice suspend the licence for such period not exceeding three months as may be specified in the notice.

(2)   Notice under subsection (1) above shall be given to the person responsible or, where the person responsible has died or appears to the licence committee to be unable because of incapacity to discharge the duty under section 17 of this Act, to some other person to whom the licence applies or the nominal licensee and a licence committee may, by a further notice to that person, renew or further renew the notice under subsection (1) above for such further period not exceeding three months as may be specified in the renewal notice.

(3)   While suspended under this section a licence shall be of no effect, but application may be made under section 18(5) of this Act by the nominal licensee to designate another individual as the person responsible.

Directions and guidance

23   Directions: general

(1)   The Authority may from time to time give directions for any purpose for which directions may be given under this Act or directions varying or revoking such directions.

(2)   A person to whom any requirement contained in directions is applicable shall comply with the requirement.

(3)   Anything done by a person in pursuance of directions is to be treated for the purposes of this Act as done in pursuance of a licence.

(4)   Where directions are to be given to a particular person, they shall be given by serving notice of the directions on the person.

(5)   In any other case, directions may be given—

(a)   in respect of any licence (including a licence which has ceased to have effect), by serving notice of the directions on the person who is or was the person responsible or the nominal licensee, or

(b)   if the directions appear to the Authority to be general directions or it appears to the Authority that it is not practicable to give notice in pursuance of paragraph (a) above, by publishing the directions in such way as, in the opinion of the Authority, is likely to bring the directions to the attention of the persons to whom they are applicable.

(6)   This section does not apply to directions under section 9(4) of this Act.

24   Directions as to particular matters

(1)   If, in the case of any information about persons for whom treatment services were provided, the person responsible does not know that any child was born following the treatment, the period specified in directions by virtue of section 13(4) of this Act shall not expire less than 50 years after the information was first recorded.

(2)   In the case of every licence under paragraph 1 of Schedule 2 to this Act, directions shall require information to be recorded and given to the Authority about each of the matters referred to in section 13(2)(a) to (e) of this Act.

(3)   Directions may authorise, in such circumstances and subject to such conditions as may be specified in the directions, the keeping, by or on behalf of a person to whom a licence applies, of gametes or embryos in the course of their carriage to or from any premises.

(4)   Directions may authorise any person to whom a licence applies to receive gametes or embryos from outside the United Kingdom or to send gametes or embryos outside the United Kingdom in such circumstances and subject to such conditions as may be specified in the directions, and directions made by virtue of this subsection may provide for sections 12 to 14 of this Act to have effect with such modifications as may be specified in the directions.

(5)   A licence committee may from time to time give such directions as are mentioned in subsection (7) below where a licence has been varied or has ceased to have effect (whether by expiry, suspension, revocation or otherwise).

(6)   A licence committee proposing to suspend, revoke or vary a licence may give such directions as are mentioned in subsection (7) below.

(7)   The directions referred to in subsections (5) and (6) above are directions given for the purpose of securing the continued discharge of the duties of the person responsible under the licence concerned ('the old licence'), and such directions may, in particular—

(a)   require anything kept or information held in pursuance of the old licence to be transferred to the Authority or any other person, or

(b)   provide for the discharge of the duties in question by any individual, being an individual whose character, qualifications and experience are, in the opinion of the committee, such as are required for the supervision of the activities authorised by the old licence, and authorise those activities to be carried on under the supervision of that individual,

but cannot require any individual to discharge any of those duties unless the individual has consented in writing to do so.

(8)   Directions for the purpose referred to in subsection (7)(a) above shall be given to the person responsible under the old licence or, where that person has died or appears to the licence committee to have become unable because of incapacity to discharge the duties in question, to some other person to whom the old licence applies or applied or to the nominal licensee.

(9)   Directions for the purpose referred to in subsection (7)(b) above shall be given to the individual who under the directions is to discharge the duty.

(10)   Where a person who holds a licence dies, anything done subsequently by an individual which that individual would have been authorised to do if the licence had continued in force shall, until directions are given by virtue of this section, be treated as authorised by a licence.

(11)   Where the Authority proposes to give directions specifying any animal for the purposes of paragraph 1(1)(f) or 3(5) of Schedule 2 to this Act, it shall report the proposal to the Secretary of State; and the directions shall not be given until the Secretary of State has laid a copy of the report before each House of Parliament.

25   Code of practice

(1)   The Authority shall maintain a code of practice giving guidance about the proper conduct of activities carried on in pursuance of a licence under this Act and the proper discharge of the functions of the person responsible and other persons to whom the licence applies.

(2)   The guidance given by the code shall include guidance for those providing treatment services about the account to be taken of the welfare of children who may be born as a result of treatment services (including a child's need for a father), and of other children who may be affected by such births.

(3)   The code may also give guidance about the use of any technique involving the placing of sperm and eggs in a woman.

(4)   The Authority may from time to time revise the whole or any part of the code.

(5)   The Authority shall publish the code as for the time being in force.

(6)   A failure on the part of any person to observe any provision of the code shall not of itself render the person liable to any proceedings, but—

(a)   a licence committee shall, in considering whether there has been any failure to comply with any conditions of a licence and, in particular, conditions requiring anything to be 'proper' or 'suitable', take account of any relevant provision of the code, and

(b)   a licence committee may, in considering, where it has power to do so, whether or not to vary or revoke a licence, take into account any observance of or failure to observe the provisions of the code.

26   Procedure for approval of code

(1)   The Authority shall send a draft of the proposed first code of practice under section 25 of this Act to the Secretary of State within twelve months of the commencement of section 5 of this Act.

(2)   If the Authority proposes to revise the code or, if the Secretary of State does not approve a draft of the proposed first code, to submit a further draft, the Authority shall send a draft of the revised code or, as the case may be, a further draft of the proposed first code to the Secretary of State.

(3)   Before preparing any draft, the Authority shall consult such persons as the Secretary of State may requite it to consult and such other persons (if any) as it considers appropriate.

(4)   If the Secretary of State approves a draft, he shall lay it before Parliament and, if he does not approve it, he shall give reasons to the Authority.

(5)   A draft approved by the Secretary of State shall come into force in accordance with directions.

Status

27   Meaning of 'mother'

(1)   The woman who is carrying or has carried a child as a result of the placing in her of an embryo or of sperm and eggs, and no other woman, is to be treated as the mother of the child.

(2)   Subsection (1) above does not apply to any child to the extent that the child is treated by virtue of adoption as not being the child of any person other than the adopter or adopters.

(3)   Subsection (1) above applies whether the woman was in the United Kingdom or elsewhere at the time of the placing in her of the embryo or the sperm and eggs.

28   Meaning of 'father'

(1)   This section applies in the case of a child who is being or has been carried by a woman as the result of the placing in her of an embryo or of sperm and eggs or her artificial insemination.

(2)   If—

(a)   at the time of the placing in her of the embryo or the sperm and eggs or of her insemination, the woman was a party to a marriage, and

(b)   the creation of the embryo carried by her was not brought about with the sperm of the other party to the marriage,

then, subject to subsection (5) below, the other party to the marriage shall be treated as the father of the child unless it is shown that he did not consent to the placing in her of the embryo or the sperm and eggs or to her insemination (as the case may be).

(3)   If no man is treated, by virtue of subsection (2) above, as the father of the child but—

(a)   the embryo or the sperm and eggs were placed in the woman, or she was artificially inseminated, in the course of treatment services provided for her and a man together by a person to whom a licence applies, and

(b)   the creation of the embryo carried by her was not brought about with the sperm of that man,

then, subject to subsection (5) below, that man shall be treated as the father of the child.

(4)   Where a person is treated as the father of the child by virtue of subsection (2) or (3) above, no other person is to be treated as the father of the child.

(5)   Subsections (2) and (3) above do not apply—

(a)   in relation to England and Wales and Northern Ireland, to any child who, by virtue of the rules of common law, is treated as the legitimate child of the parties to a marriage,

(b)   in relation to Scotland, to any child who, by virtue of any enactment or other rule of law, is treated as the child of the parties to a marriage, or

(c)   to any child to the extent that the child is treated by virtue of adoption as not being the child of any person other than the adopter or adopters.

(6)   Where—

(a)   the sperm of a man who had given such consent as is required by paragraph 5 of Schedule 3 to this Act was used for a purpose for which such consent was required, or

(b)   the sperm of a man, or any embryo the creation of which was brought about with his sperm, was used after his death,
he is not to be treated as the father of the child.

(7)   The references in subsection (2) above to the parties to a marriage at the time there referred to—

(a)   are to the parties to a marriage subsisting at that time, unless a judicial separation was then in force, but

(b)   include the parties to a void marriage if either or both of them reasonably believed at that time that the marriage was valid; and for the purposes of this subsection it shall be presumed, unless the contrary is shown, that one of them reasonably believed at that time that the marriage was valid.

(8)   This section applies whether the woman was in the United Kingdom or elsewhere at the time of the placing in her of the embryo or the sperm and eggs or her artificial insemination.

(9)   In subsection (7)(a) above, 'judicial separation' includes a legal separation obtained in a country outside the British Islands and recognised in the United Kingdom.

29   Effect of sections 27 and 28

(1)   Where by virtue of section 27 or 28 of this Act a person is to be treated as the mother or father of a child, that person is to be treated in law as the mother or, as the case may be, father of the child for all purposes.

(2)   Whereby virtue of section 27 or 28 of this Act a person is not to be treated as the mother or father of a child, that person is to be treated in law as not being the mother or, as the case may be, father of the child for any purpose.

(3)   Where subsection (1) or (2) above has effect, references to any relationship between two people in any enactment, deed or other instrument or document (whenever passed or made) are to be read accordingly.

(4)   In relation to England and Wales and Northern Ireland, nothing in the provisions of section 27(1) or 28(2) to (4), read with this section, affects—

(a)   the succession to any dignity or title of honour or renders any person capable of succeeding to or transmitting a right to succeed to any such dignity or title, or

(b)   the devolution of any property limited (expressly or not) to devolve (as nearly as the law permits) along with any dignity or title of honour.

(5)   In relation to Scotland—

(a)   those provisions do not apply to any title, coat of arms, honour or dignity transmissible on the death of the holder thereof or affect the succession thereto or the devolution thereof, and

(b)   where the terms of any deed provide that any property or interest in property shall devolve along with a title, coat of arms, honour or dignity, nothing in those provisions shall prevent that property or interest from so devolving.

30   Parental orders in favour of gamete donors

(1)   The court may make an order providing for a child to be treated in law as the child of the parties to a marriage (referred to in this section as 'the husband' and 'the wife') if—

(a)   the child has been carried by a woman other than the wife as the result of the placing in her of an embryo or sperm and eggs or her artificial insemination,

(b)   the gametes of the husband or the wife, or both, were used to bring about the creation of the embryo, and

(c)   the conditions in subsections (2) to (7) below are satisfied.

(2)   The husband and the wife must apply for the order within six months of the birth of the child or, in the case of a child born before the coming into force of this Act, within six months of such coming into force.

(3)   At the time of the application and of the making of the order—

(a)   the child's home must be with the husband and the wife, and

(b)   the husband or the wife, of both of them, must be domiciled in a part of the United Kingdom or in the Channel Islands or the Isle of Man.

(4)   At the time of the making of the order both the husband and the wife must have attained the age of eighteen.

(5)   The court must be satisfied that both the father of the child (including a person who is the father by virtue of section 28 of this Act), where he is not the husband, and the woman who carried the child have freely, and with full understanding of what is involved, agreed unconditionally to the making of the order.

(6)   Subsection (5) above does not require the agreement of a person who cannot be found or is incapable of giving agreement and the agreement of the woman who carried the child is ineffective for the purposes of that subsection if given by her less than six weeks after the child's birth.

(7)   The court must be satisfied that no money or other benefit (other than for expenses reasonably incurred) has been given or received by the husband or the wife for or in consideration of—

(a)   the making of the order,

(b)   any agreement required by subsection (5) above,

(c)   the handing over of the child to the husband and the wife, or

(d)   the making of any arrangements with a view to the making of the order, unless authorised by the court.

(8)   For the purposes of an application under this section—

(a)   in relation to England and Wales, section 92(7) to (10) of, and Part I of Schedule 11 to, the Children Act 1989 (jurisdiction of courts) shall apply for the purposes of this section to determine the meaning of 'the court' as they apply for the purposes of that Act and proceedings on the application shall be 'family proceedings' for the purposes of that Act,

(b)   in relation to Scotland, 'the court' means the Courts of Session or the sheriff court within whose division the child is, and

(c)   in relation to Northern Ireland, 'the court' means the High Court or any county court within whose division the child is.

(9)   Regulations may provide—

(a)   for any provision of the enactments about adoption to have effect, with such modifications (if any) as may be specified in the regulations, in relation to orders under this section, and applications for such orders, as it has effect in relation to adoption, and applications for adoption orders, and

(b)   for references in any enactment to adoption, an adopted child or an adoptive relationship to be read (respectively) as references to the effect of an order under this section, a child to whom such an order applies and a relationship arising by virtue of the enactments about adoption, as applied by the regulations, and for similar expressions in connection with adoption to be read accordingly, and the regulations may include such incidental or supplemental provision as appears to the Secretary of State necessary or desirable in consequence of any provision made by virtue of paragraph (a) or (b) above.

(10)   In this section 'the enactments about adoption' means the Adoption Act 1976, the Adoption (Scotland) Act 1978 and the Adoption (Northern Ireland) Order 1987.

(11)   Subsection (1)(a) above applies whether the woman was in the United Kingdom or elsewhere at the time of the placing in her of the embryo or the sperm and eggs or her artificial insemination.

Information

31   The Authority's register of information

(1)   The Authority shall keep a register which shall contain any information obtained by the Authority which falls within subsection (2) below.

(2)   Information falls within this subsection if it relates to—

(a)   the provision of treatment services for any identifiable individual, or

(b)   the keeping or use of the gametes of any identifiable individual or of an embryo taken from any identifiable woman,

or if it shows that any identifiable individual was, or may have been, born in consequence of treatment services.

(3)   A person who has attained the age of eighteen ('the applicant') may by notice to the Authority require the Authority to comply with a request under subsection (4) below, and the Authority shall do so if—

(a)   the information contained in the register shows that the applicant was, or may have been, born in consequence of treatment services, and

(b)   the applicant has been given a suitable opportunity to receive proper counselling about the implications of compliance with the request.

(4)   The applicant may request the Authority to give the applicant notice stating whether or not the information contained in the register shows that a person other than a parent of the applicant would or might, but for sections 27 to 29 of this Act, be a parent of the applicant and, if it does show that—

(a)   giving the applicant so much of that information as relates to the person concerned as the Authority is required by regulations to give (but no other information), or

(b)   stating whether or not that information shows that, but for sections 27 to 29 of this Act, the applicant, and a person specified in the request as a person whom the applicant proposes to marry, would or might be related.

(5)   Regulations cannot require the Authority to give any information as to the identity of a person whose gametes have been used or from whom an embryo has been taken if a person to whom a licence applied was provided with the information at a time when the Authority could not have been required to give information of the kind in question.

(6)   A person who has not attained the age of eighteen ('the minor') may by notice to the Authority specifying another person ('the intended spouse') as a person whom the minor proposes to marry require the Authority to comply with a request under subsection (7) below, and the Authority shall do so if—

(a)   the information contained in the register shows that the minor was, or may have been, born in consequence of treatment services, and

(b)   the minor has been given a suitable opportunity to receive proper counselling about the implications of compliance with the request.

(7)   The minor may request the Authority to give the minor notice stating whether or not the information contained in the register shows that, but for sections 27 to 29 of this Act, the minor and the intended spouse would or might be related.

32   Information to be provided to Registrar General

(1)   This section applies where a claim is made before the Registrar General that a man is or is not the father of a child and it is necessary or desirable for the purpose of any function of the Registrar General to determine whether the claim is or may be well-founded.

(2)   The Authority shall comply with any request made by the Registrar General by notice to the Authority to disclose whether any information on the register kept in pursuance of section 31 of this Act tends to show that the man may be the father of the child by virtue of section 28 of this Act and, if it does, disclose that information.

(3)   In this section and section 33 of this Act, 'the Registrar General' means the Registrar General for England and Wales, the Registrar General of Births, Deaths and Marriages for Scotland or the Registrar General for Northern Ireland, as the case may be.

33   Restrictions on disclosure of information

(1)   No person who is or has been a member or employee of the Authority shall disclose any information mentioned in subsection (2) below which he holds or has held as such a member or employee.

(2)   The information referred to in subsection (1) above is—

(a)   any information contained or required to be contained in the register kept in pursuance of section 31 of this Act, and

(b)   any other information obtained by any member or employee of the Authority on terms or in circumstances requiring it to be held in confidence.

(3)   Subsection (1) above does not apply to any disclosure of information mentioned in subsection (2)(a) above made—

(a)   to a person as a member or employee of the Authority,

(b)   to a person to whom a licence applies for the purposes of his functions as such,

(c)   so that no individual to whom the information relates can be identified,

(d)   in pursuance of an order of a court under section 34 or 35 of this Act,

(e)   to the Registrar General in pursuance of a request under section 32 of this Act, or

(f)   in accordance with section 31 of this Act.

(4)   Subsection (1) above does not apply to any disclosure of information mentioned in subsection (2)(b) above—

(a)   made to a person as a member or employee of the Authority,

(b)   made with the consent of the person or persons whose confidence would otherwise be protected, or

(c)   which has been lawfully made available to the public before the disclosure is made.

(5)   No person who is or has been a person to whom a licence applies and no person to whom directions have been given shall disclose any information falling within section 31(2) of this Act which he holds or has held as such a person.

(6)   Subsection (5) above does not apply to any disclosure of information made—

(a)   to a person as a member or employee of the Authority,

(b)   to a person to whom a licence applies for the purposes of his functions as such,

(c)   so far as it identifies a person who, but for sections 27 to 29 of this Act, would or might be a parent of a person who instituted proceedings under section 1A of the Congenital Disabilities (Civil Liability) Act 1976, but only for the purpose of defending such proceedings, or instituting connected proceedings for compensation against that parent,

(d)   so that no individual to whom the information relates can be identified,

. . .

(e)   in pursuance of directions given by virtue of section 24(5) or (6) of this Act

(f)   necessarily—

(i)   for any purpose preliminary to proceedings, or

(ii)   for the purposes of, or in connection with, any proceedings,

(g)   for the purpose of establishing, in any proceedings relating to an application for an order under subsection (1) of section 30 of this Act. whether the condition specified in paragraph (a) or (b) of that subsection is met, *or*

(h)   under section 3 of the Access to Health Records Act 1990 (right of access to health records).

(6A)   Paragraph (f) of subsection (6) above, so far as relating to disclosure for the purposes of, or in connection with, any proceedings, does not apply—

(a)   to disclosure of information enabling a person to be identified as a person whose gametes were used, in accordance with consent given under paragraph 5 of Schedule 3 to this Act, for the purposes of treatment services in consequence of which an identifiable individual was, or may have been, born, or

(b)   to disclosure, in circumstances in which subsection (1) of section 34 of this Act applies, of information relevant to the determination of the question mentioned in that subsection.

(6B)   In the case of information relating to the provision of treatment services for any identifiable individual—

(a)   where one individual is identifiable, subsection (5) above does not apply to disclosure with the consent of that individual;

(b)   where both a woman and a man treated together with her are identifiable, subsection (5) above does not apply—

(i)   to disclosure with the consent of them both, or

(ii)   if disclosure is made for the purpose of disclosing information about the provision of treatment services for one of them, to disclosure with the consent of that individual.

(6C)   For the purposes of subsection (6B) above, consent must be to disclosure to a specific person, except where disclosure is to a person who needs to know—

(a)   in connection with the provision of treatment services, or any other description of medical, surgical or obstetric services, for the individual giving the consent,

(b)   in connection with the carrying out of an audit of clinical practice, or

(c)   in connection with the auditing of accounts.

(6D)   For the purposes of subsection (6B) above, consent to disclosure given at the request of another shall be disregarded unless, before it is given, the person requesting it takes reasonable steps to explain to the individual from whom it is requested the implications of compliance with the request.

(6E)   In the case of information which relates to the provision of treatment services for any identifiable individual, subsection (5) above does not apply to disclosure in an emergency, that is to say, to disclosure made—

(a)   by a person who is satisfied that it is necessary to make the disclosure to avert an imminent danger to the health of an individual with whose consent the information could be disclosed under subsection (6B) above, and

(b)   in circumstances where it is not reasonably practicable to obtain that individual's consent.

(6F)   In the case of information which shows that any identifiable individual was, or may have been, born in consequence of treatment services, subsection (5) above does not apply to any disclosure which is necessarily incidental to disclosure under subsection (6B) or (6E) above.

(6G)   Regulations may provide for additional exceptions from subsection (5) above, but no exception may be made under this subsection—

(a)   for disclosure of a kind mentioned in paragraph (a) or (b) of subsection (6A) above, or

(b)   for disclosure, in circumstances in which section 32 of this Act applies, of information having the tendency mentioned in subsection (2) of that section.

(7)   This section does not apply to the disclosure to any individual of information which—

(a)   falls within section 31(2) of this Act by virtue of paragraph (a) or (b) of that subsection, and

(b)   relates only to that individual or, in the case of an individual treated together with another, only to that individual and that other.

(8)   At the end of Part IV of the Data Protection Act 1984 (Exemptions) there is inserted—

'35A.   Information about human embryos, etc.

Personal data consisting of information showing that an identifiable individual was, or may have been born in consequence of treatment services (within the meaning of the Human Fertilisation and Embryology Act 1990) are exempt from the subject access provisions except so far as their disclosure under those provisions is made in accordance with section 31 of that Act (the Authority's register of information).'

(9)   In subsection (6)(f) above, references to proceedings include any formal procedure for dealing with a complaint.

34   Disclosure in interests of justice

(1)   Where in any proceedings before a court the question whether a person is or is not the parent of a child by virtue of sections 27 to 29 of this Act falls to be determined, the court may on the application of any party to the proceedings make an order requiring the Authority—

(a)   to disclose whether or not any information relevant to that question is contained in the register kept in pursuance of section 31 of this Act, and

(b)   if it is, to disclose so much of it as is specified in the order,

but such an order may not require the Authority to disclose any information falling within section 31(2)(b) of this Act.

(2)   The court must not make an order under subsection (1) above unless it is satisfied that the interests of justice require it to do so, taking into account—

(a)   any representations made by any individual who may be affected by the disclosure, and

(b)   the welfare of the child, if under 18 years old, and of any other person under that age who may be affected by the disclosure.

(3)   If the proceedings before the court are civil proceedings, it—

(a)   may direct that the whole or any part of the proceedings on the application for an order under subsection (2) above shall be heard in camera, and

(b)   if it makes such an order, may then or later direct that the whole or any part of any later stage of the proceedings shall be heard in camera.

(4)   An application for a direction under subsection (3) above shall be heard in camera unless the court otherwise directs.

35   Disclosure in interests of justice: congenital disabilities, etc

(1)   Where for the purpose of instituting proceedings under section 1 of the Congenital Disabilities (Civil Liability) Act 1976 (civil liability to child born disabled) it is necessary to identify a person who would or might be the parent of a child but for sections 27 to 29 of this Act, the court may, on the application of the child, make an order requiting the Authority to disclose any information contained in the register kept in pursuance of section 31 of this Act identifying that person.

(2)   Where, for the purposes of any action for damages in Scotland (including any such action which is likely to be brought) in which the damages claimed consist of or include damages or solatium in respect of personal injury (including any disease and any impairment of physical or mental condition), it is necessary to identify a person who would or might be the parent of a child but for sections 27 to 29 of this Act, the court may, on the application of any party to the action or, if the proceedings have not been commenced, the prospective pursuer, make an order requiring the Authority to disclose any information contained in the register kept in pursuance of section 31 of this Act identifying that person.

(3)   Subsections (2) to (4) of section 34 of this Act apply for the purposes of this section as they apply for the purposes of that.

(4)   After section 4(4) of the Congenital Disabilities (Civil Liability) Act 1976 there is inserted—

> '(4A)   In any case where a child carried by a woman as the result of the placing in her of an embryo or of sperm and eggs or her artificial insemination is born disabled, any reference in section 1 of this Act to a parent includes a reference to a person who would be a parent but for sections 27 to 29 of the Human Fertilisation and Embryology Act 1990.'.

Surrogacy

36   Amendment of Surrogacy Arrangements Act 1985

(1)   After section 1 of the Surrogacy Arrangements Act 1985 there is inserted—

'1A   Surrogacy arrangements unenforceable

No surrogacy arrangement is enforceable by or against any of the persons making it.'

(2)   In section 1 of that Act (meaning of 'surrogate mother', etc.)—

(a)   in subsection (6), for 'or, as the case may be, embryo insertion' there is substituted 'or of the placing in her of an embryo, of an egg in the process of fertilisation or of sperm and eggs, as the case may be,', and

(b)   in subsection (9), the words from 'and whether' to the end are repealed.

Abortion

37   Amendment of law relating to termination of pregnancy

(1)   For paragraphs (a) and (b) of section 1(1) of the Abortion Act 1967 (grounds for medical termination of pregnancy) there is substituted—

'(a)   that the pregnancy has not exceeded its twenty-fourth week and that the continuance of the pregnancy would involve risk, greater than if the pregnancy were terminated, of injury to the physical or mental health of the pregnant woman or any existing children of her family; or

(b)   that the termination is necessary to prevent grave permanent injury to the physical or mental health of the pregnant woman; or

(c)   that the continuance of the pregnancy would involve risk to the life of the pregnant woman, greater than if the pregnancy were terminated; or

(d)   that there is a substantial risk that if the child were born it would suffer from such physical or mental abnormalities as to be seriously handicapped.'

(2)   In section 1(2) of that Act, after '(a)' there is inserted 'or (b)'.

(3)   After section 1(3) of that Act there is inserted—

'(3A)   The power under subsection (3) of this section to approve a place includes power, in relation to treatment consisting primarily in the use of such medicines as may be specified in the approval and carried out in such manner as may be so specified, to approve a class of places.'

(4)   For section 5(1) of that Act (effect on Infant Life (Preservation) Act 1929) there is substituted—

'(1)   No offence under the Infant Life (Preservation) Act 1929 shall be committed by a registered medical practitioner who terminates a pregnancy in accordance with the provisions of this Act.'

(5)   In section 5(2) of that Act, for the words from 'the miscarriage' to the end there is substituted 'a woman's miscarriage (or, in the case of a woman carrying more than one foetus, her miscarriage of any foetus) is unlawfully done unless authorised by section 1 of this Act and, in the case of a woman carrying more than one foetus, anything done with intent to procure her miscarriage of any foetus is authorised by that section if—

(a)   the ground for termination of the pregnancy specified in subsection (1)(d) of that section applies in relation to any foetus and the thing is done for the purpose of procuring the miscarriage of that foetus, or

(b)   any of the other grounds for termination of the pregnancy specified in that section applies'.

Conscientious objection

38   Conscientious objection

(1)   No person who has a conscientious objection to participating in any activity governed by this Act shall be under any duty, however arising, to do so.

(2)   In any legal proceedings the burden of proof of conscientious objection shall rest on the person claiming to rely on it.

(3)   In any proceedings before a court in Scotland, a statement on oath by any person to the effect that he has a conscientious objection to participating in a particular activity governed by this Act shall be sufficient evidence of that fact for the purpose of discharging the burden of proof imposed by subsection (2) above.

Enforcement

39   Powers of members and employees of Authority

(1)   Any member or employee of the authority entering and inspecting premises to which a licence relates may—

(a)   take possession of anything which he has reasonable grounds to believe may be required—

(i)   for the purpose of the functions of the Authority relating to the grant, variation, suspension and revocation of licences, or

(ii)   for the purpose of being used in evidence in any proceedings for an offence under this Act,

and retain it for so long as it may be required for the purpose in question, and

(b)   for the purpose in question, take such steps as appear to be necessary for preserving any such thing or preventing interference with it, including requiring any person having the power to do so to give such assistance as may reasonably be required.

(2)   In subsection (1) above—

(a)   the references to things include information recorded in any form, and

(b)   the reference to taking possession of anything includes, in the case of information recorded otherwise than in legible form, requiring any person having the power to do so to produce a copy of the information in legible form and taking possession of the copy.

(3)   Nothing in this Act makes it unlawful for a member or employee of the Authority to keep any embryo or gametes in pursuance of that person's functions as such.

40   Power to enter premises

(1)   A justice of the peace (including, in Scotland, a sheriff) may issue a warrant under this section if satisfied by the evidence on oath of a member or employee of the Authority that there are reasonable grounds for suspecting that an offence under this Act is being, or has been, committed on any premises.

(2)   A warrant under this section shall authorise any named member or employee of the Authority (who must, if so required, produce a document identifying himself), together with any constables—

(a)   to enter the premises specified in the warrant, using such force as is reasonably necessary for the purpose, and

(b)   to search the premises and—

(i)   take possession of anything which he has reasonable grounds to believe may be required to be used in evidence in any proceedings for an offence under this Act, or

(ii)   take such steps as appear to be necessary for preserving any such thing or preventing interference with it, including requiring any person having the power to do so to give such assistance as may reasonably be required.

(3)   A warrant under this section shall continue in force until the end of the period of one month beginning with the day on which it is issued.

(4)   Anything of which possession is taken under this section may be retained—

(a)   for a period of six months, or

(b)   if within that period proceedings to which the thing is relevant are commenced against any person for an offence under this Act, until the conclusion of those proceedings.

(5)   In this section—

(a)   the references to things include information recorded in any form, and

(b)   the reference in subsection (2)(b)(i) above to taking possession of anything includes, in the case of information recorded otherwise than in legible form, requiring any person having the power to do so to produce a copy of the information in legible form and taking possession of the copy.

Offences

41   Offences

(1)   A person who—

(a)   contravenes section 3(2)[, 3A] or 4(1)(c) of this Act, or

(b)   does anything which, by virtue of section 3(3) of this Act, cannot be authorised by a licence,

is guilty of an offence and liable on conviction on indictment to imprisonment for a term not exceeding ten years or a fine or both.

(2)   A person who—

(a)   contravenes section 3(1) of this Act, otherwise than by doing something which, by virtue of section 3(3) of this Act, cannot be authorised by a licence,

(b)   keeps or uses any gametes in contravention of section 4(1)(a) or (b) of this Act,

(c)   contravenes section 4(3) of this Act, or

(d)   fails to comply with any directions given by virtue of section 24(7)(a) of this Act,

is guilty of an offence.

(3)   If a person—

(a)   provides any information for the purposes of the grant of a licence, being information which is false or misleading in a material particular, and

(b)   either he knows the information to be false or misleading in a material particular or he provides the information recklessly,

he is guilty of an offence.

(4)   A person guilty of an offence under subsection (2) or (3) above is liable—

(a)   on conviction on indictment, to imprisonment for a term not exceeding two years or a fine or both, and

(b)   on summary conviction, to imprisonment for a term not exceeding six months or a fine not exceeding the statutory maximum or both.

(5)   A person who discloses any information in contravention of section 33 of this Act is guilty of an offence and liable—

(a)   on conviction on indictment, to imprisonment for a term not exceeding two years or a fine or both, and

(b)   on summary conviction, to imprisonment for a term not exceeding six months or a fine not exceeding the statutory maximum or both.

(6)   A person who—

(a)   fails to comply with a requirement made by virtue of section 39(1)(b) or (2)(b) or 40(2)(b)(ii) or (5)(b) of this Act, or

(b)   intentionally obstructs the exercise of any rights conferred by a warrant issued under section 40 of this Act,

is guilty of an offence.

(7)   A person who without reasonable excuse fails to comply with a requirement imposed by regulations made by virtue of section 10(2)(a) of this Act is guilty of an offence.

(8)   Where a person to whom a licence applies or the nominal licensee gives or receives any money or other benefit, not authorised by directions, in respect of any supply of gametes or embryos, he is guilty of an offence.

(9)   A person guilty of an offence under subsection (6), (7) or (8) above is liable on summary conviction to imprisonment for a term not exceeding six months or a fine not exceeding level five on the standard scale or both.

(10)   It is a defence for a person ('the defendant') charged with an offence of doing anything which, under section 3(1) or 4(1) of this Act, cannot be done except in pursuance of a licence to prove—

(a)   that the defendant was acting under the direction of another, and

(b)   that the defendant believed on reasonable grounds—

(i)   that the other person was at the material time the person responsible under a licence, a person designated by virtue of section 17(2)(b) of this Act as a person to whom a licence applied, or a person to whom directions had been given by virtue of section 24(9) of this Act, and

(ii)   that the defendant was authorised by virtue of the licence or directions to do the thing in question.

(11)   It is a defence for a person charged with an offence under this Act to prove—

(a)   that at the material time he was a person to whom a licence applied or to whom directions had been given, and

(b)   that he took all such steps as were reasonable and exercised all due diligence to avoid committing the offence.

42   Consent to prosecution

No proceedings for an offence under this Act shall be instituted—

(a)   in England and Wales, except by or with the consent of the Director of Public Prosecutions, and

(b)   in Northern Ireland, except by or with the consent of the Director of Public Prosecutions for Northern Ireland.

Miscellaneous and General

43   Keeping and examining gametes and embryos in connection with crime, etc

(1)   Regulations may provide—

(a)   for the keeping and examination of gametes or embryos, in such manner and on such conditions (if any) as may be specified in regulations, in connection with the investigation of, or proceedings for, an offence (wherever committed), or

(b) for the storage of gametes, in such manner and on such conditions (if any) as may be specified in regulations, where they are to be used only for such purposes, other than treatment services, as may be specified in regulations.

(2) Nothing in this Act makes unlawful the keeping or examination of any gametes or embryos in pursuance of regulations made by virtue of this section.

(3) In this section 'examination' includes use for the purposes of any test.

44   *(Inserts the Congenital Disabilities (Civil Liability) Act 1976, s. 1A and amends s. 4(2)–(4) of that Act, Vol. 45, title* Tort.)

45   Regulations

(1) The Secretary of State may make regulations for any purpose for which regulations may be made under this Act.

(2) The power to make regulations shall be exercisable by statutory instrument.

(3) Regulations may make different provision for different cases.

(4) The Secretary of State shall not make regulations by virtue of section 3(3)(c), 4(2) or (3), 30, 31(4)(a), 33(6G), or 43 of this Act or paragraph 1(1)(g) or 3 of Schedule 2 to this Act unless a draft has been laid before and approved by resolution of each House of Parliament.

(5) A statutory instrument containing regulations shall, if made without a draft having been approved by resolution of each House of Parliament, be subject to annulment in pursuance of a resolution of either House of Parliament.

(6) In this Act 'regulations' means regulations under this section.

46   Notices

(1) This section has effect in relation to any notice required or authorised by this Act to be given to or served on any person.

(2) The notice may be given to or served on the person—

(a) by delivering it to the person,

(b) by leaving it at the person's proper address, or

(c) by sending it by post to the person at that address.

(3) The notice may—

(a) in the case of a body corporate, be given to or served on the secretary or clerk of the body,

(b) in the case of a partnership, be given to or served on any partner, and

(c) in the case of an unincorporated association other than a partnership, be given to or served on any member of the governing body of the association.

(4) For the purposes of this section and section 7 of the Interpretation Act 1978 (service of documents by post) in its application to this section, the proper address of any person is the person's last known address and also—

(a) in the case of a body corporate, its secretary or its clerk, the address of its registered or principal office, and

(b) in the case of an unincorporated association or a member of its governing body, its principal office.

(5) Where a person has notified the Authority of an address or a new address at which notices may be given to or served on him under this Act, that address shall also be his proper address for the purposes mentioned in subsection (4) above or, as the case may be, his proper address for those purposes in substitution for that previously notified.

47   Index

The expressions listed in the left-hand column below are respectively defined or (as the case may be) are to be interpreted in accordance with the provisions of this Act listed in the right-hand column in relation to those expressions.

Expression	*Relevant provision*
Activities governed by this Act	Section 4(5)
Authority	Section 2(1)
Carry, in relation to a child	Section 2(3)
Directions	Section 2(1)
Embryo	Section 1
Gametes, eggs or sperm	Section 1
Keeping, in relation to embryos or gametes	Section 2(2)
Licence	Section 2(1)
Licence committee	Section 9(1)
Nominal licensee	Section 17(3)
Person responsible	Section 17(1)
Person to whom a licence applies	Section 17(2)
Statutory storage period	Section 14(3) to (5)
Store, and similar expressions, in relation to embryos or gametes	Section 2(2)
Treatment services	Section 2(1)

48   Northern Ireland

(1)   This Act (except sections 33(6)(h) and 37) extends to Northern Ireland.

49   Short title, commencement, etc

(1)   This Act may be cited as the Human Fertilisation and Embryology Act 1990.

(2)   This Act shall come into force on such day as the Secretary of State may by order made by statutory instrument appoint and different days may be appointed for different provisions and for different purposes.

(3)   Sections 27 to 29 of this Act shall have effect only in relation to children carried by women as a result of the placing in them of embryos or of sperm and eggs, or of their artificial insemination (as the case may be), after the commencement of those sections.

(4)   Section 27 of the Family Law Reform Act 1987 (artificial insemination) does not have effect in relation to children carried by women as the result of their artificial insemination after the commencement of sections 27 to 29 of this Act.

(5)   Schedule 4 to this Act (which makes minor and consequential amendments) shall have effect.

(6)   An order under this section may make such transitional provision as the Secretary of State considers necessary or desirable and, in particular, may provide that where activities are carried on under the supervision of a particular individual, being activities which are carried on under the supervision of that individual at the commencement of sections 3 and 4 of this Act, those activities are to be treated, during such period as may be specified in or determined in accordance with the

order, as authorised by a licence (having, in addition to the conditions required by this Act, such conditions as may be so specified or determined) under which that individual is the person responsible.

(7)   Her Majesty may by Order in Council direct that any of the provisions of this Act shall extend, with such exceptions, adaptations and modifications (if any) as may be specified in the Order, to any of the Channel Islands.

SCHEDULES

Section 5

SCHEDULE 1
THE AUTHORITY: SUPPLEMENTARY PROVISIONS

Status and capacity

1.   The Authority shall not be regarded as the servant or agent of the Crown, or as enjoying any status, privilege or immunity of the Crown; and its property shall not be regarded as property of, or property held on behalf of, the Crown.

2.   The Authority shall have power to do anything which is calculated to facilitate the discharge of its functions, or is incidental or conducive to their discharge, except the power to borrow money.

Expenses

3.   The Secretary of State may, with the consent of the Treasury, pay the Authority out of money provided by Parliament such sums as he thinks fit towards its expenses.

Appointment of members

4.—(1)   All the members of the Authority (including the chairman and deputy chairman who shall be appointed as such) shall be appointed by the Secretary of State.

(2)   In making appointments the Secretary of State shall have regard to the desirability of ensuring that the proceedings of the Authority, and the discharge of its functions, are informed by the views of both men and women.

(3)   The following persons are disqualified for being appointed as chairman or deputy chairman of the Authority—

(a)   any person who is, or has been, a medical practitioner registered under the Medical Act 1983 (whether fully, provisionally or with limited registration), or under any repealed enactment from which a provision of that Act is derived,

(b)   any person who is, or has been, concerned with keeping or using gametes or embryos outside the body, and

(c)   any person who is, or has been, directly concerned with commissioning or funding any research involving such keeping or use, or who has actively participated in any decision to do so.

(4)   The Secretary of State shall secure that at least one-third but fewer than half of the other members of the Authority fall within sub-paragraph (3)(a), (b) or (c) above, and that at least one member falls within each of paragraphs (a) and (b).

Tenure of office

5.—(1)   Subject to the following provisions of this paragraph, a person shall hold and vacate office as a member of the Authority in accordance with the terms of his appointment.

(2)   A person shall not be appointed as a member of the Authority for more than three years at a time.

(3)   A member may at any time resign his office by giving notice to the Secretary of State.

(4)   A person who ceases to be a member of the Authority shall be eligible for reappointment (whether or not in the same capacity).

(5)   If the Secretary of State is satisfied that a member of the Authority—

(a)   has been absent from meetings of the Authority for six consecutive months or longer without the permission of the Authority, or

(b)   has become bankrupt or made an arrangement with his creditors, or, in Scotland, has had his estate sequestrated or has granted a trust deed for or entered into an arrangement with his creditors, or

(c)   is unable or unfit to discharge the functions of a member,

the Secretary of State may declare his office as a member of the Authority vacant, and notify the declaration in such manner as he thinks fit; and thereupon the office shall become vacant.

6.   . . .

Remuneration and pensions of members

7.—(1)   The Authority may—

(a)   pay to the chairman such remuneration, and

(b)   pay or make provision for paying to or in respect of the chairman or any other member such pensions, allowances, fees, expenses or gratuities,

as the Secretary of State may, with the approval of the Treasury, determine.

(2)   Where a person ceases to be a member of the Authority otherwise than on the expiry of his term of office and it appears to the Secretary of State that there are special circumstances which make it right for him to receive compensation, the Authority may make to him a payment of such amount as the Secretary of State may, with the consent of the Treasury, determine.

Staff

8.—(1)   The Authority may appoint such employees as it thinks fit, upon such terms and conditions as the Authority, with the approval of the Secretary of State and the consent of the Treasury, may determine.

(2)   The Authority shall secure that any employee whose function is, or whose functions include, the inspection of premises is of such character, and is so qualified by training and experience, as to be a suitable person to perform that function.

(3)   The Authority shall, as regards such of its employees as with the approval of the Secretary of State it may determine, pay to or in respect of them such pensions, allowances or gratuities (including pensions, allowances or gratuities by way of compensation for loss of employment), or provide and maintain for them such pension schemes (whether contributory or not), as may be so determined.

(4)   If an employee of the Authority—

(a)   is a participant in any pension scheme applicable to that employment, and

(b)   becomes a member of the Authority,

he may, if the Secretary of State so determines, be treated for the purposes of the pension scheme as if his service as a member of the Authority were service as employee of the Authority, whether or not any benefits are to be payable to or in respect of him by virtue of paragraph 7 above.

Proceedings

9.—(1)   The Authority may regulate its own proceedings, and make such arrangements as it thinks appropriate for the discharge of its functions.

(2)   The Authority may pay to the members of any committee or sub-committee such fees and allowances as the Secretary of State may, with the consent of the Treasury, determine.

10.—(1)   A member of the Authority who is in any way directly or indirectly interested in a licence granted or proposed to be granted by the Authority shall, as soon as possible after the relevant circumstances have come to his knowledge, disclose the nature of his interest to the Authority.

(2)   Any disclosure under sub-paragraph (1) above shall be recorded by the Authority.

(3)   Except in such circumstances (if any) as may be determined by the Authority under paragraph 9(1) above, the member shall not participate after the disclosure in any deliberation or decision of the Authority or any licence committee with respect to the licence, and if he does so the deliberation or decision shall be of no effect.

11.   The validity of any proceedings of the Authority, or of any committee or sub-committee, shall not be affected by any vacancy among the members or by any defect in the appointment of a member.

Instruments

12.   The fixing of the seal of the Authority shall be authenticated by the signature of the chairman or deputy chairman of the Authority or some other member of the Authority authorised by the Authority to act for that purpose.

13.   A document purporting to be duly executed under the seal of the Authority, or to be signed on the Authority's behalf, shall be received in evidence and shall be deemed to be so executed or signed unless the contrary is proved.

Investigation by Parliamentary Commissioner

14.   The Authority shall be subject to investigation by the Parliamentary Commissioner . . .

Section 11 etc.   SCHEDULE 2
ACTIVITIES FOR WHICH LICENCES MAY BE GRANTED

Licences for treatment

1.—(1)   A licence under this paragraph may authorise any of the following in the course of providing treatment services—

    (a)   bringing about the creation of embryos *in vitro*,

    (b)   keeping embryos,

    (c)   using gametes,

    (d)   practices designed to secure that embryos are in a suitable condition to be placed in a woman or to determine whether embryos are suitable for that purpose,

    (e)   placing any embryo in a woman,

    (f)   mixing sperm with the egg of a hamster, or other animal specified in directions, for the purpose of testing the fertility or normality of the sperm, but only where anything which forms is destroyed when the test is complete and, in any event, not later than the two cell stage, and

    (g)   such other practices as may be specified in, or determined in accordance with, regulations.

    (2)   Subject to the provisions of this Act, a licence under this paragraph may be granted subject to such conditions as may be specified in the licence and may authorise the performance of any of the activities referred to in sub-paragraph (1) above in such manner as may be so specified.

    (3)   A licence under this paragraph cannot authorise any activity unless it appears to time Authority to be necessary or desirable for the purpose of providing treatment services.

    (4)   A licence under this paragraph cannot authorise altering the genetic structure of any cell while it forms part of an embryo.

    (5)   A licence under this paragraph shall be granted for such period not exceeding five years as may be specified in the licence.

Licences for storage

2.—(1)   A licence under this paragraph or paragraph 1 or 3 of this Schedule may authorise the storage of gametes or embryos or both.

    (2)   Subject to the provisions of this Act, a licence authorising such storage may be granted subject to such conditions as may be specified in the licence and may authorise storage in such manner as may be so specified.

    (3)   A licence under this paragraph shall be granted for such period not exceeding five years as may be specified in the licence.

Licences for research

3.—(1)   A licence under this paragraph may authorise any of the following—

    (a)   bringing about the creation of embryos *in vitro*, and

    (b)   keeping or using embryos,

for the purposes of a project of research specified in the licence.

    (2)   A licence under this paragraph cannot authorise any activity unless it appears to the Authority to be necessary or desirable for the purpose of—

    (a)   promoting advances in the treatment of infertility,

    (b)   increasing knowledge about the causes of congenital disease,

    (c)   increasing knowledge about the causes of miscarriages,

    (d)   developing more effective techniques of contraception, or

    (e)   developing methods for detecting the presence of gene or chromosome abnormalities in embryos before implantation,

or for such other purposes as may be specified in regulations.

    (3)   Purposes may only be so specified with a view to the authorisation of projects of research which increase knowledge about the creation and development of embryos, or about disease, or enable such knowledge to be applied.

    (4)   A licence under this paragraph cannot authorise altering the genetic structure of any cell while it forms part of an embryo, except in such circumstances (if any) as may be specified in or determined in pursuance of regulations.

(5)   A licence under this paragraph may authorise mixing sperm with the egg of a hamster, or other animal specified in directions, for the purpose of developing more effective techniques for determining the fertility or normality of sperm, but only where anything which forms is destroyed when the research is complete and, in any event, not later than the two cell stage.

(6)   No licence under this paragraph shall be granted unless the Authority is satisfied that any proposed use of embryos is necessary for the purposes of the research.

(7)   Subject to the provisions of this Act, a licence under this paragraph may be granted subject to such conditions as may be specified in the licence.

(8)   A licence under this paragraph may authorise the performance of any of the activities referred to in sub-paragraph (1) or (5) above in such manner as may be so specified.

(9)   A licence under this paragraph shall be granted for such period not exceeding three years as may be specified in the licence.

General

4.—(1)   A licence under this Schedule can only authorise activities to be carried on on premises specified in the licence and under the supervision of an individual designated in the licence.

(2)   A licence cannot—

(a)   authorise activities falling within both paragraph 1 and paragraph 3 above,

(b)   apply to more than one project of research,

(c)   authorise activities to be carried on under the supervision of more than one individual, or

(d)   apply to premises in different places.

Section 12 etc.   SCHEDULE 3
CONSENTS TO USE OF GAMETES OR EMBRYOS

Consent

1.   A consent under this Schedule must be given in writing and, in this Schedule, 'effective consent' means a consent under this Schedule which has not been withdrawn.

2.—(1)   A consent to the use of any embryo must specify one or more of the following purposes—

(a)   use in providing treatment services to the person giving consent, or that person and another specified person together,

(b)   use in providing treatment services to persons not including the person giving consent, or

(c)   use for the purposes of any project of research,
and may specify conditions subject to which the embryo may be so used.

(2)   A consent to the storage of any gametes or any embryo must—

(a)   specify the maximum period of storage (if less than the statutory storage period), and

(b)   state what is to be done with the gametes or embryo if the person who gave the consent dies or is unable because of incapacity to vary the terms of the consent or to revoke it, and may specify conditions subject to which the gametes or embryo may remain in storage.

(3)   A consent under this Schedule must provide for such other matters as the Authority may specify in directions.

(4)   A consent under this Schedule may apply—

(a)   to the use or storage of a particular embryo, or

(b)   in the case of a person providing gametes, to the use or storage of any embryo whose creation may be brought about using those gametes,

and in the paragraph (b) case the terms of the consent may be varied, or the consent may be withdrawn, in accordance with this Schedule either generally or in relation to a particular embryo or particular embryos.

Procedure for giving consent

3.—(1)   Before a person gives consent under this Schedule—

(a)   he must be given a suitable opportunity to receive proper counselling about the implications of taking the proposed steps, and

(b)   he must be provided with such relevant information as is proper.

(2)   Before a person gives consent under this Schedule he must be informed of the effect of paragraph 4 below.

Variation and withdrawal of consent

4.—(1)   The terms of any consent under this Schedule may from time to time be varied, and the consent may be withdrawn, by notice given by the person who gave the consent to the person keeping the gametes or embryo to which the consent is relevant.

(2)   The terms of any consent to the use of any embryo cannot be varied, and such consent cannot be withdrawn, once the embryo has been used—

(a)   in providing treatment services, or

(b)   for the purposes of any project of research.

Use of gametes for treatment of others

5.—(1)   A person's gametes must not be used for the purposes of treatment services unless there is an effective consent by that person to their being so used and they are used in accordance with the terms of the consent.

(2)   A person's gametes must not be received for use for those purposes unless there is an effective consent by that person to their being so used.

(3)   This paragraph does not apply to the use of a person's gametes for the purpose of that person, or that person and another together, receiving treatment services.

In vitro fertilisation and subsequent use of embryo

6.—(1)   A person's gametes must not be used to bring about the creation of any embryo in vitro unless there is an effective consent by that person to any embryo the creation of which may be brought about with the use of those gametes being used for one or more of the purposes mentioned in paragraph 2(1) above.

(2)   An embryo the creation of which was brought about in vitro must not be received by any person unless there is an effective consent by each person whose gametes were used to bring about the creation of the embryo to the use for one or more of the purposes mentioned in paragraph 2(1) above of the embryo.

(3)   An embryo the creation of which was brought about *in vitro* must not be used for any purpose unless there is an effective consent by each person whose gametes were used to bring about the creation of the embryo to the use for that purpose of the embryo and the embryo is used in accordance with those consents.

(4)   Any consent required by this paragraph is in addition to any consent that may be required by paragraph 5 above.

Embryos obtained by lavage, etc

7.—(1)   An embryo taken from a woman must not be used for any purpose unless there is an effective consent by her to the use of the embryo for that purpose and it is used in accordance with the consent.

(2)   An embryo taken from a woman must not be received by any person for use for any purpose unless there is an effective consent by her to the use of the embryo for that purpose.

(3)   This paragraph does not apply to the use, for the purpose of providing a woman with treatment services, of an embryo taken from her.

Storage of gametes and embryos

8.—(1)   A person's gametes must not be kept in storage unless there is an effective consent by that person to their storage and they are stored in accordance with the consent.

(2)   An embryo the creation of which was brought about *in vitro* must not be kept in storage unless there is an effective consent, by each person whose gametes were used to bring about the creation of the embryo, to the storage of the embryo and the embryo is stored in accordance with those consents.

(3)   An embryo taken from a woman must not be kept in storage unless there is an effective consent by her to its storage and it is stored in accordance with the consent.

Section 49   SCHEDULE 4
              MINOR AND CONSEQUENTIAL AMENDMENTS

1–4.   . . .

Family Law Reform (Northern Ireland) Order 1977 (SI 1977/1250 (NI 17))

5.   In Article 13 of the Family Law Reform (Northern Ireland) Order 1977 (interpretation), at the end of the definition of 'excluded' there is added 'and to sections 27 to 29 of the Human Fertilisation and Embryology Act 1990'.

6.   (*Applies to Scotland only.*)

Adoption (Northern Ireland) Order 1987 (SI 1987/2203 (NI 22))

7.   In Article 15 of the Adoption (Northern Ireland) Order 1987 (adoption by one person), in paragraph (3)(a) (conditions for making an adoption order on the application of one parent), after 'found' there is inserted 'or, by virtue of section 28 of the Human Fertilisation and Embryology Act 1990, there is no other parent'.

Human Organ Transplants Act 1989 (c 31)

8.   Sections 27 to 29 of this Act do not apply for the purposes of section 2 of the Human Organ Transplants Act 1989 (restrictions on transplants between persons not genetically related).

Human Organ Transplants (Northern Ireland) Order 1989 (SI 1989/2408 (NI 21))

9.   Sections 27 to 29 of this Act do not apply for the purposes of Article 4 of the Human Organ Transplants (Northern Ireland) Order 1989 (restrictions on transplants between persons not genetically related).

Appendix 2
Human Fertilisation and Embryology Authority
Code of Practice (Fourth Edition)

INTRODUCTION

Medical intervention or research which aims to alleviate infertility or reduce the risk of inherited abnormality intrudes upon the most private and sensitive aspects of our existence and relationships. The Human Fertilisation and Embryology Authority (HFEA) was established in response to deep public concern about the implications which the new techniques might have for the perception and valuing of human life and family relationships.

The HFEA's principal task is to regulate, by means of a licensing system, any research or treatment which involves the creation, keeping and using of human embryos outside the body, or the storage or donation of human eggs and sperm. It must also maintain a Code of Practice giving guidance about the proper conduct of the licensed activities.

The object of the Code is wider than to secure the safety or efficacy of particular clinical or scientific practices. It is concerned with areas of practice which raise fundamental ethical and social questions. In framing it, we have been guided both by the requirements of the Human Fertilisation and Embryology Act and by:

- the respect which is due to human life at all stages in its development;
- the right of people who are or may be infertile to the proper consideration of their request for treatment;
- a concern for the welfare of children, which cannot always be adequately protected by concern for the interests of the adults involved; and
- a recognition of the benefits, both to individuals and to society which can flow from the responsible pursuit of medical and scientific knowledge.

We recognise that these considerations may sometimes conflict and have sought to reconcile them in a way which is both practicable and in accordance with the spirit and intentions of the Act. Our aim is to support the best clinical and scientific practice, while guarding against the undoubted risk of exploitation of people at a time when they may be particularly vulnerable.

The Code assumes that all those involved in providing treatment or conducting research will observe the standards and requirements of good clinical and scientific practice. It also adopts the guidance given by other authorities or professional bodies on particular points.

The Act covers both *in vitro* fertilisation and donor insemination, and imposes obligations upon centres to give information, provide counselling and take account of the welfare of children. It recognises that, while infertile people deserve and can expect proper consideration of their medical and social needs, licensed treatments may result in children who would not otherwise have been born and whose needs must also be taken into account.

The Act also allows the HFEA to give guidance on any procedure involving the placing of eggs and sperm in a woman. A basic guideline appears at paragraph 7.9 which is of general application.

The Code is regularly reviewed and amended in the light of experience and to keep abreast of the latest developments in both clinical practice and public concerns. This third revision of the Code contains guidance on matters which have been brought to the HFEA's attention since the Code was last revised in December 1995. There are three major additions. New guidance has been included on the genetic testing of donors and patients. Although the testing of gamete donors for cystic fibrosis has not been made mandatory, it is strongly recommended, and clinics are required to make genetic counselling available to patients and donors in order that the implications of genetic testing are properly understood following the principles set out by the Advisory Committee on Genetic Testing. General guidance has been included on the statutory storage period for embryos following on from the Regulations introduced in 1996 and this reflects the guidance that was issued to clinics on 15 April 1996. Finally, the guidelines on the welfare of the child were reviewed following concerns about the treatment of HIV positive patients.

This revised Code of Practice has been approved by the Secretary of State and laid before Parliament in accordance with section 26 of the Human Fertilisation and Embryology Act 1990.

PART 1 – STAFF

General standards

1.1   In order to protect the interests and privacy of donors and clients, and to guard against the misuse of genetic material, it is essential that all those responsible for or taking part in licensed activities have high standards of integrity and responsibility.

1.2   The skill mix of clinical, nursing, counselling and scientific staff should reflect the requirements of the work undertaken in the centre.

The person responsible

1.3   A licence application **must** name the person under whose supervision the licensed activities will be carried on ('the person responsible').[1]

1.4   The person responsible **must** ensure:[2]

- that the character, qualifications and experience of anyone carrying out licensed activities are suitable for those activities;

- that proper equipment is used;
- that proper arrangements are made for the keeping and disposal of genetic material;
- that suitable practices are used in carrying out the licensed activities; and
- that the centre complies with the conditions of its licence.

1.5   The person responsible will need to have sufficient insight into the scientific, medical, legal and other aspects of the centre's work to enable them to supervise its activities properly, but the qualities of integrity, responsibility and managerial capability are more important than any particular professional qualification. The Authority will expect the person responsible to take whatever specialist advice is necessary.

Staff engaged in clinical services

1.6   Overall clinical responsibility for treatment services using *in vitro* fertilisation should be held by someone with accredited consultant status or an equivalent appropriate training recognised by the Royal College of Obstetricians and Gynaecologists.

1.7   Medical staff engaged in treatment services using *in vitro* fertilisation who do not have overall clinical responsibility should be fully registered Medical Practitioners with a sufficient period of experience under supervision in *in vitro* fertilisation to qualify them to take part in that activity. Medical staff engaged in laparoscopy should also be Fellows or Members of the Royal College of Obstetricians and Gynaecologists. Medical staff in a training capacity are exempt from this requirement but should only carry out these activities under proper supervision.

1.8   If the centre is licensed to provide donor insemination but not *in vitro* fertilisation, the person with overall clinical responsibility should be a fully registered Medical Practitioner with a sufficient period of experience in an established infertility clinic to qualify them to take full charge of the centre's treatment services.

Nursing staff

1.9   All nursing staff must be appropriately qualified and effectively registered by the United Kingdom Central Council for Nursing, Midwifery and Health Visiting (UKCC), for the duties they carry out.

Counselling staff

1.10   Unless it is engaged only in research, a centre should ensure *either* that at least one of its staff has a Certificate of Qualification in Social Work or an equivalent qualification recognised by the Central Council for Education and Training in Social Work, or is accredited by the British Association of Counsellors, or is a Chartered Psychologist, *or* that a person with such a qualification is available as an advisor to counselling staff and as a counsellor to clients as required.

Staff engaged in scientific services

1.11   The person in charge of an embryology laboratory should have an appropriate scientific or medical degree, plus a period of experience in an embryology laboratory sufficient to qualify the person to take full charge of the laboratory. Where clinics undertake the genetic testing of patient and donors, centres should ensure that a person is available who understands the nature of the tests used, their scope and limitations, and the accuracy, implications and use of the result.

1.12   The person in charge of a seminology laboratory should have a degree or an HND in a relevant discipline, plus a period of experience in a seminology laboratory sufficient to qualify the person to take full charge of the laboratory.

1.13   The person in charge of an endocrinology laboratory should have a degree or an HND in a relevant discipline, plus a period of experience in an endocrinology laboratory sufficient to qualify the person to take full charge of the laboratory.

In-service training

1.14   Centres should arrange relevant training for all staff taking part in specialist scientific, clinical or counselling activities for which existing formal qualifications are not entirely sufficient. Centres with too few staff to provide adequate training themselves should make arrangements for staff to be trained where there are such facilities. All staff taking part in specialist activities should also receive regular updating.

Conscientious objection

1.15   Anyone who can show a conscientious objection to any of the activities governed by the Act is not obliged to participate in them.[3]

1.16   Prospective employees should be provided with a full description of all the activities carried out at the centre. Interviewers should raise the issue of conscientious objection during the recruitment process and explain the right of staff to object.

Criminal convictions

1.17   When deciding whether a person is suitable to take part in a licensed activity, the person responsible should take account of any relevant criminal convictions. Applicants who have such convictions should not be appointed to posts in which they will have access to donors, clients, genetic material or records about these, unless the person responsible is satisfied that the applicant is suitable for the post in question.

1.18   Relevant convictions will depend upon the particular post and the gravity of the particular offence, but may include any offence of violence or dishonesty, blackmail, sexual offences and offences against children, drugs offences and breaches of regulatory machinery.

PART 2 – FACILITIES

General

2.1   The person responsible **must** ensure that proper equipment and suitable practices are used.[4]

2.2   If a centre decides to use outside facilities, the person responsible should be satisfied that those facilities comply with any relevant provisions of this Code. Licensed activities **must** only take place on the licensed premises.[5]

Clinical facilities

2.3   Backup and emergency clinical facilities for each technique practised should be available at the centre, equivalent to those which are standard practice in other specialties and appropriate to the degree of risk involved.

2.4   Further emergency facilities should be available locally to cater for all reasonably foreseeable eventualities.

2.5   Centres should be sensitive to their clients' and donors' needs for comfort and privacy, and take all reasonable steps to ensure that facilities are acceptable to them. In particular:

- centres should provide a private and comfortable room for the examination and treatment of clients, out of the sight and hearing of others, and not subject to unannounced and uninvited entry by staff or others;
- similar facilities should be provided in which semen specimens can be produced.

2.6   If the centre is licensed to provide treatment services using *in vitro* fertilisation, a member of staff should be available to clients at all times.

Laboratory facilities

2.7   It is essential that centres follow good laboratory practice, whether their laboratories are used for research or for clinical services.

2.8   All blood products, other than those of the woman receiving treatment, with which gametes or embryos might come into contact should be pre-tested for HIV, Hepatitis B and Hepatitis C.

2.9   The room where eggs are collected for *in vitro* fertilisation should be as close as practicable to the laboratory where fertilisation is to take place.

Counselling facilities

2.10   People seeking licensed treatment (i.e. *in vitro* fertilisation or involving donated gametes) or consenting to the use or storage of embryos, or to the donation or storage of gametes **must** be given a suitable opportunity to receive proper counselling.[6] Detailed guidance is given in Part 6.

2.11   Centres should provide a private and comfortable room for counselling, where discussion can take place undisturbed.

2.12   Centres should so far as practicable maintain an up-to-date list of different types of counselling which are available locally and of national organisations which can provide local information. They should make the list available to clients who wish to seek counselling outside the centre.

2.13 Centres should so far as practicable establish and maintain good relationships with independent counselling organisations, so that donors and clients may be given the maximum help in obtaining the counselling they need.

2.14 Centres should designate an individual responsible for ensuring that counselling facilities are provided as described above and in Part 6.

Secure storage for gametes and embryos

2.15 Centres should provide secure storage for gametes and embryos, access to which is controlled. Detailed guidance is given in Part 8.

Maintaining and improving standards

2.16 Centres should inform the Authority as soon as possible of any breach of the Code of Practice or of any serious problem that has occurred at that centre.

2.17 Centres should have an effective system for monitoring and assessing laboratory, clinical and counselling practice, to ensure that both the procedures and the outcomes are and can be shown to be satisfactory by the standards of professional colleagues in relevant disciplines elsewhere. This system should include obtaining feedback from clients, donors and people seeking storage of gametes and embryos.

2.18 Centres should have procedures for improving and updating laboratory, clinical and counselling practice, so that every effort is made to achieve optimum procedures and outcomes by the standards of professional colleagues elsewhere. These procedures should include obtaining feedback as in paragraph 2.17, above.

Advertising

2.19 Centres may wish to circulate information about the kinds of treatment which they provide. All publicity material should conform to the guidelines of the General Medical Council and the Code of Professional Conduct of the United Kingdom Central Council for Nursing, Midwifery and Health Visiting. To the extent that these permit centres or their services to be publicised to the general public, their material should conform to the guidelines of the Advertising Standards Authority.

PART 3 – ASSESSING CLIENTS, DONORS AND THE WELFARE OF THE CHILD

INTRODUCTION

General obligations

3.1 Centres should take all reasonable steps to ensure that people receiving treatment and any children resulting from it have the best possible protection from harm to their health. Before providing any woman with treatment, centres **must** also take account of the welfare of any child who may be born or who may be affected as a result of the treatment.[7]

3.2   Centres should therefore ensure that clients' medical needs are fully assessed, and that any treatment offered is the most suitable to meet their needs and that donors and gametes are properly screened in accordance with the guidance given below.

3.3   In addition, in deciding whether or not to offer treatment, centres should take account both of the wishes and needs of the people seeking treatment and of the needs of any children who may be involved. Neither consideration is paramount over the other, and the subject should be approached with great care and sensitivity. Centres should avoid adopting any policy or criteria which may appear arbitrary or discriminatory. Further guidance is given in paragraphs 3.12 to 3.32 below.

Confidentiality

3.4   Any information which centres obtain from potential donors or clients **must** be kept confidential unless disclosure is authorised by law.[8] Certain types of information may only be disclosed in the circumstances authorised in the Act (see paragraph 11.8, below). If a centre is in doubt about whether or not it should disclose information, it should refer to the Authority.

3.5   The Act states that information about the provision of treatment services for, or the keeping or use of the gametes of any identifiable individual can, in general, only be disclosed either to the Authority or to another person covered by a licence or to the individual concerned. However, identifying information about the provision of treatment services can be disclosed *either*:

(a)   with the consent of the person to whom the information relates; *or*

(b)   in an emergency, i.e. where disclosure is necessary to avert an imminent danger to the health of the person to whom the information relates *and* it is not reasonably practicable to obtain that person's consent. It follows that if it is practicable to obtain consent in an emergency, and that consent is refused or not requested, then the information must not be disclosed.

Also, if disclosing the identity of any resulting child cannot be avoided as a result of disclosing the client's name with consent or in an emergency, this is not against the law.

3.6   Where information is disclosed with consent, the following conditions must be met:

(a)   before this consent is given, reasonable steps must have been taken to explain the implications of disclosure to the person whose consent is requested; *and*

(b)   the person(s) to whom the information is to be disclosed must either:

(i)   be specified in the consent, e.g. a solicitor or interpreter; or,

(ii)   be someone who needs to know in connection with providing treatment services or other medical, surgical or obstetric services for the person giving consent (for the other circumstances in which information can be disclosed see paragraph 11.8, below).

3.7   It is generally in the interests of the person concerned that relevant information be passed on to other clinicians involved in their treatment or diagnosis. But, except in an emergency, it is that person's right to decide what information will be passed on and to whom. In seeking consent, therefore, centres should:

(a)   obtain the client's consent in writing. The consent of each person whose identity is to be disclosed should be obtained. Where a woman and a man are being treated together it is desirable to use the same form. A model consent form is at Annex A;

(b)   tell the client whose consent is requested what information is to be disclosed;

(c)   give a full explanation of the reasons for wanting to disclose the information (for example so that a GP can be kept informed of a client's fertility treatment), and the implications of disclosing this information, so that the client can make an informed judgment about consent. Implications will include the fact that once disclosed, the information will no longer be covered by the special provisions of the Act, but only by the ordinary law on confidentiality (see paragraph 11.10, below);

(d)   so far as possible specify the person to whom the information is to be disclosed and, if that is not possible, to identify the unit or clinic concerned;

(e)   renew the consent of the client(s) if treatment which has not initially involved consent subsequently does so.

3.8   Wherever consent is given for information to be disclosed to an unspecified person, particular care should be taken to ensure that any person to whom the information is disclosed does indeed need to know the information in connection with the provision of treatment services or other medical, surgical or obstetric services, (for disclosure in connection with medical and financial audit, see paragraph 11.8 below).

3.9   When passing on information with consent, centres should also make clear to the recipient(s) the terms of the consent given.

3.10   Centres should as far as possible ensure that those receiving information record details of treatment services only on the client's medical record and not on that of any resulting child.

3.11   If a centre refers a client to another centre for licensed infertility treatment, the requirements of good clinical practice should be followed in supplying any relevant information to that centre. Any information relevant to the welfare of the child should always be supplied.

PROSPECTIVE PARENTS AND THE WELFARE OF THE CHILD

Welfare of the child

3.12   One of the conditions of a treatment licence is that 'a woman shall not be provided with treatment services unless account has been taken of the welfare of any child who may be born as a result of the treatment (including the need of that child for a father), and of any other child who may be affected by the birth'.[9]

This applies to every woman whether or not she is resident in or a citizen of the United Kingdom. 'Any other child' includes children who already exist within the client's household or family.

3.13 The condition applies only to centres with a treatment licence, but it covers any of the services they offer to assist conception or pregnancy, whether or not these require a licence. However, the degree of consideration necessary will be greater if the treatment is required to be licensed under the Act and particularly if it involves the use of donated gametes.

3.14 Centres should have clear written procedures to follow for assessing the welfare of the potential child and of any other child who may be affected. The HFE Act does not exclude any category of woman from being considered for treatment. Centres should take note in their procedures of the importance of a stable and supportive environment for any child produced as a result of treatment.

Factors to be considered

3.15 Centres should take all reasonable steps to ascertain who would be legally responsible for any child born as a result of the procedure and who it is intended will be bringing up the child. When clients come from abroad, centres should not assume that the law of that country relating to the parentage of a child born as a result of donated gametes is the same as that of the United Kingdom.

3.16 People seeking treatment are entitled to a fair and unprejudiced assessment of their situation and needs, which should be conducted with the skill and sensitivity appropriate to the delicacy of the case and the wishes and feelings of those involved.

3.17 Where people seek licensed treatment, centres should bear in mind the following factors:

(a) their commitment to having and bringing up a child or children;

(b) their ability to provide a stable and supportive environment for any child produced as a result of treatment;

(c) their medical histories and the medical histories of their families;

(d) their health and consequent future ability to look after or provide for a child's needs;

(e) their ages and likely future ability to look after or provide for a child's needs;

(f) their ability to meet the needs of any child or children who may be born as a result of treatment, including the implications of any possible multiple births;

(g) any risk of harm to the child or children who may be born, including the risk of inherited disorders or transmissible diseases, problems during pregnancy and of neglect or abuse; and

(h) the effect of a new baby or babies upon any existing child of the family.

3.18 Where people seek treatment using donated gametes, centres should also take the following factors into account:

(a) a child's potential need to know about their origins and whether or not the prospective parents are prepared for the questions which may arise while the child is growing up;

(b)   the possible attitudes of other members of the family towards the child, and towards their status in the family;

(c)   the implications for the welfare of the child if the donor is personally known within the child's family and social circle; and

(d)   any possibility known to the centre of a dispute about the legal fatherhood of the child (see paragraphs 5.6 to 5.8, below).

3.19   Further factors will require consideration in the following cases:

(a)   where the child will have no legal father. Centres are required to have regard to the child's need for a father and should pay particular attention to the prospective mother's ability to meet the child's needs throughout their childhood. Where appropriate, centres should consider particularly whether there is anyone else within the prospective mother's family and social circle willing and able to share the responsibility for meeting those needs, and for bringing up, maintaining and caring for the child;

(b)   where it is the intention that the child will not be brought up by the carrying mother. In this case, centres should bear in mind that *either* the carrying mother and in certain circumstances her husband or partner, *or* the commissioning parents may become the child's legal parents. Centres should therefore consider the factors listed in paragraphs 3.17 and 3.18 as applicable in relation to all those involved, and any risk of disruption to the child's early care and upbringing should there be a dispute between them. Centres should also take into account the effect of the proposed arrangement on any child of the carrying mother's family as well as its effect on any child of the commissioning parent's family.

3.20   The application of assisted conception techniques to initiate a surrogate pregnancy should only be considered where it is physically impossible or highly undesirable for medical reasons for the commissioning mother to carry the child.

3.21   Centres should be aware of the Parental Orders (Human Fertilisation and Embryology) Regulations 1994 and the Parental Orders (Human Fertilisation and Embryology) (Scotland) Regulations 1994 which came into effect on 1 November 1994. Under these Regulations, parental rights and obligations relating to a child born from a surrogacy arrangement may be transferred from the birth parents to the commissioning parents. The conditions that must be fulfilled before an application can be made are set out in Annex B. Annex B also contains information about birth registration of children born through surrogacy arrangements.

3.22   When selecting donated gametes for treatment, centres should take into account each prospective parent's preferences in relation to the general physical characteristics of the donor. This does not allow the prospective parents to choose, for social reasons alone, a donor of different ethnic origin(s) from themselves. Clients should be advised that the result of any attempt at matching physical characteristics cannot be guaranteed.

Inquiries to be made

3.23   Centres should take a medical and social history from each prospective parent. They should be seen together and separately. This should include all the information relevant to paragraphs 3.12 to 3.19 above.

3.24 Centres should seek to satisfy themselves that the GP of each prospective parent knows of no reason why either of them might not be suitable for the treatment to be offered. This would include anything which might adversely affect the welfare of any resulting child.

3.25 Centres should obtain the client's consent before approaching the GP. However, failure to give consent should be taken into account in considering whether or not to offer treatment.

3.26 If any of these particulars or inquiries give cause for concern, e.g., evidence that prospective parents have had children removed from their care, or evidence of a previous relevant conviction, the centre should make such further inquiries of any relevant individual, authority or agency as it can.

3.27 Centres should obtain the client's consent before approaching any individual, authority or agency for information. However, failure to give consent should be taken into account in deciding whether or not to offer treatment.

Multidisciplinary assessment

3.28 The views of all those at the centre who have been involved with the prospective parents should be taken into account when deciding whether or not to offer treatment. Prospective parents should be given a fair opportunity to state their views before any decision is made and to meet any objections raised to providing them with treatment.

3.29 If a member of the team has a cause for concern as a result of information given to them in confidence, they should obtain the consent of the person concerned before discussing it with the rest of the team. If a member of the team receives information which is of such gravity that confidentiality *cannot* be maintained, they should use their own discretion, based on good professional practice, in deciding in what circumstances it should be discussed with the rest of the team.

3.30 The decision to provide treatment should be taken in the light of all the available information. Treatment may be refused on clinical grounds. Treatment should also be refused if the centre believes that it would not be in the interests of any resulting child, or any child already existing, to provide treatment, or is unable to obtain sufficient information or advice to reach a proper conclusion.

3.31 If treatment is refused for any reason, the centre should explain to the woman and, where appropriate, her husband or partner, the reasons for this and the factors, if any, which might persuade the centre to reverse its decision. It should also explain the options which remain open and tell clients where they can obtain counselling.

3.32 Centres should record in detail the information which has been taken into account when considering the welfare of the child or children. The record should reflect the views of all those who were consulted in reaching the decision, including those of potential parents.

Prospective donors and people seeking storage of gametes and embryos

3.33 Centres should draw the screening procedure to the attention of potential donors at the outset and ensure that they understand which tests will be carried out and that the procedure may reveal previously unsuspected defects, including genetic anomalies and HIV infection. Centres should ask a prospective donor whether they have ever provided gametes at another centre. If they have, the centre should satisfy itself that the limit of 10 offspring per donor will not be exceeded (see paragraphs 7.18 and 7.19, below).

3.34   Payment may only be made, or benefits given, in exchange for gametes or embryos in accordance with directions made by the Authority.[10] This includes payments or benefits that a centre knows have been given, or will be given, through the involvement of an agency or intermediary.

3.35   If an egg donor becomes ill as a direct result of making a donation, centres should reimburse any direct expenses that the donor incurs.

Age and mental capacity

3.36   Gametes should not be taken for the treatment of others from female donors over the age of 35, and from male donors over the age of 55, unless there are exceptional reasons for doing so. If there are exceptional reasons, these should be explained in the treatment records.

3.37   Gametes taken from women over 35 and men over 55 may be used for their own treatment, or the treatment of their partner. They should be offered clinical advice and counselling before deciding whether to proceed with treatment.

3.38   Gametes should not be taken for the treatment of others from anyone under the age of 18.

3.39   Gametes **must not** be taken from anyone who is not capable of giving a valid consent or who has not given a valid consent to examination and treatment *and* an effective consent to the use or storage of those gametes.[11]

3.40   In exceptional circumstances, gametes may be taken from people under the age of 18 if it is the intention to use them for their own treatment or that of their partner, provided that the centre is satisfied that the person from whom the gametes are taken is capable of giving an effective consent to the use or storage of those gametes and has done so. Effective consent to the use or storage of gametes and embryos may only be given by the person who provides the gametes.[12]

3.41   Sperm taken from a male under 18 may only be stored for the purpose of research if he is capable of giving an effective consent, and that consent has been obtained.

3.42   Eggs should not be taken from females under 18 either to be stored for the purpose of research or to be used for research requiring a licence without first referring to the Authority.

History

3.43   A medical and family history should be taken before any gametes are provided. This should include details of any donations which the potential provider of gametes has made elsewhere. Donors should also be encouraged to provide as much other non-identifying biographical information about themselves as they wish, to be made available to prospective parents and any resulting child.

3.44   Centres should wherever practicable ask a potential donor's GP whether they know of any reason why the potential donor might not be suitable to donate gametes for the treatment of others.

3.45   Centres should wherever practicable ask the GP of any person seeking storage of gametes or embryos for their own or partner's use whether the GP has any relevant information.

3.46   Centres should obtain the person's consent before approaching the GP. Failure to give such consent should be taken into account in deciding whether or not to accept the gametes or embryos for research or treatment.

Suitability as donors

3.47   Centres should give careful consideration to the suitability of individual donors before accepting or using their gametes for the treatment of others. The views of all those at the centre who have been involved with the potential donor should be taken into account. Centres should consider in particular:

(a)   any personal or family history of heritable disorders;
(b)   any personal history of transmissible infection;
(c)   the level of potential fertility indicated by semen analysis;
(d)   whether the donor has children of their own; and
(e)   the attitude of the donor towards the donation.

Scientific tests

3.48   Centres should adopt whatever is current best practice in the scientific testing of semen samples and of donors of gametes and embryos.

3.49   All reasonable steps to prevent transmission of a serious genetic disorder should be taken. In most situations this will be served by taking a thorough family history from the prospective gamete donor. Genetic testing should be limited to the determination of carrier status for inherited recessive disorders in which an abnormal result carries no significant direct health implications for the donor. The use of genetic tests other than in the setting of the doctor/patient relationship raises a number of issues that will be the subject of review and guidance from the Advisory Committee on Genetic Testing (ACGT). Centres should ensure that where genetic testing of gamete donors is carried out it is with the same level of support and counselling as for recipients. This means that gamete donors should be informed of the result of their test and offered post-test counselling.

3.50   In relation to cystic fibrosis, centres should normally screen donors especially those from population groups with high frequencies of cystic fibrosis carriers. If a centre uses unscreened donors, the centre should inform the patient and offer screening and counselling. If a centre uses screened donors, the centre should caution the patient about the limits of the test, and the likelihood of a screened donor being a cystic fibrosis carrier. In exceptional circumstances such as where a donor would be difficult to replace, centres may use a donor who is known to be a cystic fibrosis carrier. When this is necessary the patients should be made aware of the risks involved and be offered screening and counselling.

3.51   For other common recessive disorders, centres should follow the BAS guidelines which already specify screening for Tay-Sachs, thalassaemia and sickle cell anaemia in appropriate population groups. The screening of egg donors for recessive diseases should be the same as that carried out for sperm donors.

3.52 In relation to HIV testing, centres should adopt as a minimum the procedure set out in 'HIV Screening for Gamete Donors' by the Human Fertilisation and Embryology Authority and the Department of Health, (Annex C).

3.53 In relation to the testing of donors for other infections and of semen samples, centres should as a minimum follow the guidelines of the British Andrology Society. It is for centres to ensure that the most up-to-date guidance is followed.

3.54 Centres should also re-screen potential donors where appropriate, and adopt any other test which may come to be regarded as a matter of good practice by the standards of professional colleagues in relevant specialties or may be indicated in a particular case while this Code is in force.

Potential donors who are undergoing treatment

3.55 The possibility of donating gametes or embryos should not be raised during the potential donor's treatment cycle. The possibility should be raised by someone other than the staff involved in the treatment.

People unsuitable as donors

3.56 If a centre decides that someone is unsuitable as a donor, it should record the reasons for the decision and explain these to the person concerned. Centres should present the explanation sensitively, encourage the person to seek further information, and answer questions in a straightforward, comprehensive and open way.

3.57 If a centre refuses to accept someone as a donor because of a physical or psychological problem which requires separate treatment or specialised counselling, the centre should give the person all reasonable assistance in obtaining this.

3.58 If information suggesting that someone might not be suitable as a donor becomes available after the selection process is complete, the centre should review the donor's suitability in the light of that information and take any necessary action.

3.59 Where a centre becomes aware that a sperm donor has a previously unsuspected genetic disease or is a carrier of a deleterious recessively inherited condition through the birth of a child with that condition (rather than from a genetic test) the centre should immediately inform both the supplying centre and the Authority. The supplying centre should inform any centre that has received sperm from that donor of his carrier status. The supplying centre should also consider informing the donor that he may be a carrier and, if they do so, should offer him counselling and testing. Centres should inform patients who have received treatment at their centre using that donor's sperm and whose treatment has resulted in a live birth. They should also offer the patients counselling. If a woman is pregnant as a result of treatment with that donor's sperm, centres should consider carefully when and how she should be informed of the donor's carrier status.

3.60 Where a centre becomes aware that an egg donor has a previously unsuspected genetic disease or is a carrier of a deleterious recessively inherited condition through the birth of a child with that condition (rather than from a genetic test) the centre should inform the Authority immediately. The centre should inform any centre that has received embryos created from the eggs of the donor of the donor's carrier status. The centre who recruited her should also consider informing the egg donor that she may be a carrier and, if they do so, should offer her counselling and testing. Centres should inform patients who have received treatment using that donor's eggs and whose treatment has resulted in a live birth of the donor's carrier status. They should also offer patients counselling. If a woman is pregnant as a result of treatment with that donor's eggs, centres should consider carefully when and how she should be informed of the donor's carrier status.

PART 4 – INFORMATION

General obligation

4.1   Before anyone is given licensed treatment (i.e., *in vitro* fertilisation or treatment using donated gametes) or consents to the use or storage of embryos, or to the donation or storage of gametes, they **must** be given 'such relevant information as is proper'.[13] This should be distinguished from the requirement to offer counselling, which clients and donors need not accept.

4.2   Clients and donors should be given oral explanations supported by relevant written material. They should be encouraged to ask for further information and their questions should be answered in a straightforward, comprehensive and open way.

4.3   Centres should devise a system to ensure that:

(a)   the right information is given;

(b)   the person who is to give the information is clearly identified, and has been given sufficient training and guidance to enable them to do so; and

(c)   a record is kept of the information given.

Information to be given to clients

4.4   Information should be given to people seeking treatment on the following points:

(a)   the limitations and possible outcomes of the treatment proposed, and variations of effectiveness over time. This should include the centre's own live birth rate per treatment cycle and the national live birth rate per treatment cycle;

(b)   the possible side effects and risks of the treatment to the woman and any resulting child. This should include:

(i)   the possible side effects and risks of ovarian stimulation (where relevant) for the women, including the risks associated with ovarian hyperstimulation syndrome (OHSS)

(ii)   the risks to the women and fetus associated with multiple pregnancy and the possible practical, financial and emotional impact of a multiple birth on the family unit;

(c)   the genetic and other screening that donors at that centre undergo. This should include the sensitivity of the tests that are carried out and the likelihood that a screened donor will be a carrier;

(d)   the availability of genetic testing, especially if the donors that are used at the centre are not screened for cystic fibrosis;

(e)   the possible disruption of the client's domestic life which treatment will cause, and the length of time he or she will have to wait for treatment;

(f)   the techniques involved, including (where relevant) the possible deterioration of gametes or embryos associated with storage, and the possible pain and discomfort;

(g)   the availability of embryo freezing facilities, including the likelihood of success of embryo freezing, thawing, transfer and implications of storage;

(h)   any other infertility treatments which are available, including those for which a licence is not necessary;

(i)   that counselling is available;

(j)   the cost to the client of the treatment proposed and of any alternative treatments;

(k)   the importance of telling the treatment centre about any resulting birth;

(l)   who will be the child's parent or parents under the Act. Clients who are nationals or residents of other countries, or who have been treated with gametes obtained from a foreign donor should understand that the law in other countries may be different from that of the United Kingdom (see paragraph 3.15, above);

(m)   the child's right to seek information about their origins on reaching 18 or on contemplating earlier marriage;

(n)   the information which centres must collect and register with the HFEA and the extent to which that information may be disclosed to people born as a result of the donation;

(o)   a child's potential need to know about their origins;

(p)   the centre's statutory duty to take account of the welfare of any resulting or affected child; and

(q)   (where relevant) the advantages and disadvantages of continued treatment after a certain number of attempts.

Information to be given to people providing gametes and embryos

4.5   Information should be given to people consenting to the use or storage of embryos, or to the donation or storage of gametes, on the following points:

(a)   the procedures involved in collecting gametes, the degree of pain and discomfort and any risks to that person, e.g., from the use of superovulatory drugs;

(b)   the screening which will be carried out, and the practical implications of having an HIV antibody test, even if it proves negative;

(c)   the genetic testing that will be carried out, its scope and limitations and the implications of the result for the donor and their family;

(d)   the purposes for which their gametes might be used;

(e)   whether or not they will be regarded under the Act as the parents of any child born as a result;

(f)   that the Act generally permits donors to preserve their anonymity;

(g)   the information which centres must collect and register with the HFEA and the extent to which that information may be disclosed to people born as a result of the donation;

(h)   that they are free to withdraw or vary the terms of their consent at any time, unless the gametes or embryos have already been used;

(i)   the possibility that a child born disabled as a result of a donor's failure to disclose defects, about which they knew or ought reasonably to have known, may be able to sue the donor for damages;

(j)   in the case of egg donation, that the woman will not incur any financial or other penalty if she withdraws her consent after preparation for egg recovery has begun;

(k)   that donated gametes and embryos created from them will not normally be used for treatment once the number of children believed to have been born from them has reached 10, or any lower figure specified by the donor; and

(l)   that counselling is available.

PART 5 – CONSENT

Consent to examination and treatment

5.1   People generally have the right to give or withhold consent to examination and treatment. Centres' attention is drawn to the general guidance given in 'A Guide to Consent for Examination and Treatment' by the Department of Health.

5.2   No licensed treatment should be given to any woman without her written consent to that particular treatment. The written consent should explain the nature of the treatment and the steps which are to be taken, and indicate that she has been given all the information referred to in paragraph 4.4 above. The woman should be given the opportunity to decide whether she wishes to consent to all stages of her IVF and GIFT treatment before it begins, or whether she would prefer to consider the number of eggs or embryos to be replaced after they have been retrieved. If she is to undergo frozen embryo replacement she should be asked to consider the number of embryos to be replaced at that stage. Examples of consent forms appear in Annex D. A copy of the consent form should be given to the person giving consent.

5.3   If it is possible that the question of treatment with donated gametes or embryos derived from them may arise, the centre should raise the matter with the client or clients beforehand. The centre should allow clients sufficient time to reflect before asking for consent to treatment with donated material.

Treatment without consent

5.4   Centres may examine or treat people without first obtaining their consent only in exceptional circumstances.[14] The only circumstances likely to arise in the course of infertility treatment services are where the procedure is necessary to save the patient's life, cannot be postponed, and she is unconscious and cannot indicate her wishes.

Consent to the presence of observers

5.5   If a member of the centre's team wishes an observer to be present when a client is being examined, treated or counselled, they should explain, preferably beforehand, who the observer is and why this is desirable, and ask the client whether there is any objection. If the client objects, the observer should not attend.

Consent of the husband or male partner and legal fatherhood

5.6   Centres should adopt the procedures described in the following paragraphs in the interests of preventing or resolving a dispute at a later stage about the fatherhood of a child. (Centres are also referred to paragraph 3.17(a), above.)

5.7   A woman's husband will be the legal father of a child born as a result of treatment using donated sperm, unless they are judicially separated or he can prove that he did not consent to the treatment. If a married woman is being treated with donated sperm, centres should explain the position and ask her whether her husband consents to the treatment. If he does, the centre should take all practicable steps to obtain his written consent. If the woman does not know, or he does not consent, centres should, if she agrees, take all practicable steps to ascertain the position and (if this is the case) obtain written evidence that he does not consent.

5.8   If a woman is being treated together with a male partner, using donated sperm, and she is unmarried *or* judicially separated *or* her husband does not consent to the treatment, her male partner will be the legal father of any resulting child. Centres should explain this to them both and record at each appointment whether or not the man was present. Centres should try to obtain the written acknowledgement of the man both that they are being treated together and that donated sperm is to be used. Centres should also explain that when a child is born to an unmarried couple the male partner may not have parental responsibility for that child.[15] Unmarried couples concerned about how parental responsibility affects their legal rights should seek their own legal advice.

CONSENT TO THE STORAGE AND USE OF GAMETES AND EMBRYOS

Consent to storage

5.9   Anyone consenting to the storage of their gametes, or of embryos produced from them, **must**:[16]

(a)   specify the maximum period of storage (if this is to be less than the statutory storage period);
(b)   state what is to be done with the gametes or embryos if they die, or become incapable of varying or revoking their consent.

5.10   Centres should ensure that anyone wanting to store an embryo for more than 5 years satisfies the conditions for an extended storage period before their consent is obtained.

5.11   In the case of sperm which was already in store on 1 August 1991, the written consent of the person who provided the sperm is not needed in order for storage to continue legally. However, there is no obligation on a centre to continue to store sperm where there is no written agreement to do so.

Consent to use

5.12   If the intention is to donate gametes for the treatment of others, including the creation of an embryo for that purpose, the donor **must** consent in writing to their use for that purpose.[17]

5.13   If the intention is to create an embryo outside the body, the person giving consent to the use of an embryo produced from their gametes **must** specify the purpose or purposes for which it may be used, namely one or more of:[18]

   (a)   to provide treatment for themselves, or themselves and a named partner;
   (b)   to provide treatment for others;
   (c)   for research.

5.14   If consent to use sperm was given before 1 August 1991, that consent must be in writing and remain effective (i.e. not have been subsequently withdrawn).

5.15   If no written consent has been given before or after 1 August 1991, no use can be made of the sperm unless and until a consent to use is obtained. It follows that where a person providing sperm has died and there is no written consent in existence no use can be made of the sperm.

General consent

5.16   In all cases, people giving consent may specify additional conditions subject to which their gametes or embryos produced from them may be used or stored, and may vary or withdraw their consent at any time provided that the genetic material has not already been used.

5.17   Centres should ensure that people do not feel under any pressure to give their consent.

5.18   Centres should allow potential donors and those seeking storage sufficient time to reflect on their decision, before obtaining written consent. A copy of the consent form should be given to the person giving consent.

5.19   The centre does not have to obtain the consent of a donor's partner to the donation of their gametes. However, if the donated gametes are to be used for treatment, and the donor is married or has a long-term partner, centres should encourage donors to ask their partner to consent in writing to the use of the gametes for treatment.

5.20   The centre should be prepared to accept the financial loss if the woman withdraws after preparation for egg recovery has begun.

Consent to export

5.21   The specific consent of people providing gametes must be obtained to the export of those gametes or of embryos produced using them (see also paragraph 7.23, below).

PART 6 – COUNSELLING

General

6.1   People seeking licensed treatment (i.e. *in vitro* fertilisation or treatment using donated gametes) or consenting to the use or storage of embryos, or to the donation or storage of gametes, **must** be given 'a suitable opportunity to receive proper counselling about the implications of taking the proposed steps', before they consent.[19]

6.2   Counselling should be clearly distinguished from:

(a)   the information which is to be given to everyone, in accordance with the guidance in Part 4;

(b)   the normal relationship between the clinician and the person offering donation or seeking storage or treatment, which includes giving professional advice; and

(c)   the process of assessing people in order to decide whether to accept them as a client or donor, or to accept their gametes and embryos for storage, in accordance with the guidance given in Part 3.

6.3   No-one is obliged to accept counselling. However, it is generally recognised as beneficial.

6.4   Three distinct types of counselling should be made available in appropriate cases:

(a)   **implications counselling:** this aims to enable the person concerned to understand the implications of the proposed course of action for themselves, for their family, and for any children born as a result. It may include genetic counselling;

(b)   **support counselling:** this aims to give emotional support at times of particular stress, e.g. when there is a failure to achieve a pregnancy;

(c)   **therapeutic counselling:** this aims to help people to cope with the consequences of infertility and treatment, and to help them to resolve the problems which these may cause. It includes helping people to adjust their expectations and to accept their situation.

Centres **must** make implications counselling available to everyone.[20] They should also provide support or therapeutic counselling in appropriate cases or refer people to sources of more specialist counselling outside the centre.

6.5   Centres should present the offer of counselling as part of normal routine, without implying either that the person concerned is in any way deficient or abnormal, or that there is any pressure to accept. Centres should allow them sufficient time to consider the offer.

6.6   Centres should allow sufficient time for counselling to be conducted sensitively, in an atmosphere which is conducive to discussion. The length and content of counselling, and the pace at which it is conducted, should be determined by the needs of the individual concerned.

6.7   Centres should offer people the opportunity to be counselled by someone other than the clinician responsible for their treatment, donation or storage. Such counselling should be independent of the clinical decision-making process.

6.8   Centres should offer people the opportunity to be counselled individually and with their partner if they have one. Group counselling sessions may also be offered, but it is not acceptable for a centre to offer only group sessions.

6.9   People should be able to seek counselling at any stage of their investigation or treatment. However, counselling should normally be made available after the person seeking treatment or providing the gametes or embryos has received the oral and written explanations described in paragraphs 4.4 and 4.5, above. Discussion may then focus on the meaning and consequences of the decision, rather than on its practical aspects.

Implications counselling

6.10   Counsellors should invite potential clients or providers of gametes and embryos to consider the following issues:

(a)   the social responsibilities which centres and providers of genetic material bear to ensure the best possible outcome for all concerned, including the child;

(b)   the implications of the procedure for themselves, their family and social circle, and for any resulting children;

(c)   their feelings about the use and possible disposal of any embryos derived from their gametes;

(d)   the possibility that these implications and feelings may change over time, as personal circumstances change;

(e)   the advantages and disadvantages of openness about the procedures envisaged, and how they might be explained to relatives and friends.

6.11   Counsellors should invite **clients** to consider in particular:

(a)   the client's attitude to their own, or partner's infertility;

(b)   the possibility that treatment will fail.

6.12   Where treatment using donated gametes or embryos is contemplated, clients should also be invited to consider:

(a)   their feelings about not being the genetic parents of the child;

(b)   their perceptions of the needs of the child throughout their childhood and adolescence.

6.13   If a woman is already undergoing infertility treatment when the question of treatment with donated gametes or embryos derived from them arises, counselling about the implications of receiving donated material should be offered separately from counselling about the other implications of treatment. Treatment with donated material should not proceed unless the woman and, where appropriate, her partner have been given a suitable opportunity to receive counselling about it.

6.14   If a woman is undergoing infertility treatment and the possibility of her or her partner becoming a donor also arises, counselling about the implications of donation should be undertaken separately from counselling about the implications of treatment in the first instance. If the possibility of donation arises at a later stage in the treatment, donation should not proceed unless the woman and, where appropriate, her partner have been given a suitable opportunity to receive counselling about it.

6.15   Counselling about the implications of donation may be combined with counselling about the other implications of treatment at a later stage, if this is advisable in the light of the initial counselling sessions and the client's or potential donor's wishes.

6.16   Counsellors should invite potential *donors* of gametes and embryos to consider in particular:

(a)   their reasons for wanting to become a donor;

(b)   their attitudes to any resulting children, and their willingness to forego knowledge of and responsibility for such children in the future;

(c)   the possibility of their own childlessness;

(d)   their perception of the needs of any children born as a result of their donation;

(e)   their attitudes to the prospective legal parents of their genetic offspring;

(f)   their attitudes to allowing embryos which have been produced from their gametes to be used for research.

6.17   If a person seeking to donate or store genetic material is married or has a long-term partner, the centre should counsel them together if they so wish. If a partner wishes to be counselled separately about the implications of donation or storage, centres should take all practicable steps to offer counselling at the centre, or to assist them in contacting an external counselling organisation.

Genetic counselling

6.18   Centres should have arrangements in place to make genetic counselling available for patients and donors. Centres should ensure that when patients and donors are referred for genetic counselling the confidentiality provisions of the HFE Act are taken into account.

Later counselling

6.19   Centres should take all practicable steps to provide further opportunities for counselling about the implications of treatment, donation or storage after consent has been given, and throughout the period in which the person is providing gametes, or receiving treatment, if this is requested. If someone who has previously been a donor or client returns to the centre asking for further counselling, the centre should take all practicable steps to help them obtain it.

Support counselling

6.20   Centres should also take all practicable steps to offer support to people who are not suitable for treatment, whose treatment has failed, prospective donors who are found to be unsuitable and people who have previously unsuspected defects, to help them come to terms with their situation.

6.21   These steps should include, wherever practicable, reasonable assistance in contacting or establishing a support group.

6.22   Centres should ensure that, as part of their training, all staff are prepared to offer appropriate emotional support at all stages of their investigation, counselling and treatment to clients who are suffering distress.

Therapeutic counselling

6.23   Procedures should be in place to identify people who suffer particular distress and to offer them, as far as is practicable, therapeutic counselling, with the aim of helping them to come to terms with their situation.

6.24   If a client experiences mental ill-health or a severe psychological problem which may or may not be related to infertility, for which it would be more appropriate to seek help and advice outside the centre, the centre should take all practicable steps to help them to obtain it.

Records

6.25   A record should be kept of all counselling offered and whether or not the offer is accepted.

6.26   All information obtained in the course of counselling should be kept confidential, subject to paragraph 3.29, above.

PART 7 – USE OF GAMETES AND EMBRYOS

Obtaining gametes and embryos

7.1   Centres may only import and export gametes and embryos in accordance with directions made by the HFEA.[21]

7.2   Centres may only transport gametes and embryos between licensed premises in accordance with directions made by the HFEA.[22]

7.3   Centres should only allow a donor to provide sperm produced at home in exceptional circumstances. If a centre does allow a donor to provide sperm produced at home the centre should take all reasonable steps to satisfy itself that the sperm has been produced by that man, not more than two hours previously, and that it has not subsequently been interfered with (so as to ensure that the screening procedures outlined in paragraphs 3.48 and 3.52 remain effective).

7.4   Where any part of treatment services is to take place in premises not covered by a licence (a satellite centre), the law requires the licensed centre intending to carry out the subsequent embryo transfer to ensure that all the requirements of the Act and the Code of Practice are complied with before any part of the treatment begins. These requirements cover information, counselling, the welfare of the child and confidentiality. Copies of the Act and the Code of Practice should be supplied by the licensed centre to the satellite centre.

Clinical use

7.5 Eggs or sperm which have been subjected to procedures which carry an actual or reasonable theoretical risk of harm to their developmental potential, and embryos created from them, should not be used for treatment. Treatment centres should satisfy the Authority that sufficient scientific evidence is available to establish that any procedures used do not prejudice the developmental potential of the gametes or embryos.

7.6 Similarly, embryos which have themselves been subject to procedures which carry an actual or reasonable theoretical risk of harm to their developmental potential should not be used for treatment. Treatment centres should satisfy the HFEA that sufficient scientific evidence is available to establish that any procedures used do not prejudice the developmental potential of the embryos.

7.7 Attempts to produce embryos *in vitro* should not be made if there is no intention to store or use the resulting embryo(s), unless there is a specific reason why it is necessary to do so in connection with the provision of treatment services for a particular woman. On each such occasion, the reason should be explained to the woman, implications counselling should be offered and the written consent of each person providing the gametes must have been obtained.[23]

7.8 Gametes or embryos which have been exposed to a material risk of contamination which might cause harm to recipients or to any resulting children should not be used for treatment. If there is any doubt, centres should seek expert advice.

7.9 No more than three eggs or embryos should be placed in a woman in any one cycle, regardless of the procedure used.

7.10 Women should not be treated with the gametes or with embryos derived from the gametes of more than one man or woman during any treatment cycle.

7.11 Before donor insemination treatment begins, there should be discussion with the client about the number of treatment cycles to be attempted before further investigation into the causes of lack of success (if this arises). This matter should be reviewed at regular intervals.

7.12 Centres may supply sperm for home insemination if, but only if, there are exceptional circumstances making it impracticable or undesirable for the woman to be inseminated at the centre, and the procedures set out in paragraphs 7.13–7.17 below are followed.

7.13 Where sperm is supplied for home insemination this should always be noted and the exceptional circumstances explained in the treatment records.

7.14 As with all other donor insemination treatment, the giving of information, assessment of the client, consideration of the welfare of the child and an offer of counselling are required in accordance with the Human Fertilisation and Embryology Act and other Code of Practice guidelines. If it is decided to offer home insemination, centres should obtain an undertaking in writing from the woman to be offered treatment that the sperm will be used by her alone.

7.15 Before supplying sperm for home insemination a centre should obtain an undertaking in writing from the woman to supply information to the centre about the outcome of the treatment.

7.16 The Act forbids the supply of frozen sperm[24] to a person not covered by a licence, and centres may therefore only supply sperm in the process of thawing.

Provided that the woman has attended the clinic for assessment purposes, this may be supplied in a dry shipper, either to her in person, or by post or courier.

7.17   Centres should complete DI treatment cycle form (96)2 in the normal way, entering the date of supply or posting as the date of insemination and noting on the form that the sperm was supplied for home insemination.

7.18   Donated gametes or embryos should not be used for treatment once the number of live children believed to have been born as a result of donations from that donor has reached 10. It is the responsibility of the supplier and of the user to agree an appropriate procedure for ensuring that the limit is not exceeded.

7.19   This limit of 10 may be exceeded only in exceptional cases, e.g. where a recipient wishes to have a subsequent child from the same donor. The HFEA should be notified whenever the limit is exceeded. If the donor has specified a limit, this must never be exceeded.[25]

7.20   Centres should not select the sex of embryos for social reasons.

7.21   Centres should not use sperm sorting techniques in sex selection.

7.22   Centres **must not** attempt to produce embryos *in vitro* by embryo splitting for treatment purposes (see paragraph 10.5, below).[26]

7.23   Centres **must not** export gametes from donors who have produced ten live children in the UK (see paragraphs 5.21 and 7.18, above).[27]

Termination and disposal

7.24   The special status of the human embryo is fundamental to the provisions of the Act. The termination of the development of a human embryo and the disposal of the remaining material are sensitive and delicate issues. Centres should take full account of this when considering how the development of an embryo is to be brought to an end, and what is to happen thereafter. The approach to be adopted will depend on whether the embryos are being stored for treatment or to be used for research.

7.25   Where an embryo is no longer to be kept for treatment, the centre should decide how it is to be allowed to perish, and what is to happen to the perished material. The procedure should be sensitively devised and described, and should be communicated to the people for whom the embryo was being stored if they so wish.

7.26   In the case of embryos used for research, the centre should decide at the outset the duration of the culture period, the method which is to be used to terminate development, and the procedure which will ensure that embryos do not continue to develop after fourteen days or (if earlier) the appearance of the primitive streak.

PART 8 – STORAGE AND HANDLING OF GAMETE AND EMBRYOS

General

8.1   Centres should ensure that the highest possible standards are maintained in the storage and handling of gametes and embryos.

Security

8.2   Gametes and embryos should be stored in a designated security area, access to which is controlled.

8.3   The person responsible should allow access only to named individuals in the centre, for whom such access is essential to their work. No other person should have access to gametes and embryos.

8.4   The location of gametes and embryos in storage should be recorded in detail, in order to minimise the amount of handling required in retrieving them. Each occasion on which gametes or embryos are handled should be recorded.

8.5   There should be an effective monitoring system to ensure high standards of security wherever gametes and embryos are handled or stored.

Identification

8.6   The source of gametes and embryos should be accurately recorded and labelled in a manner which is not susceptible to unauthorised or undetectable alteration.

8.7   Records should enable authorised staff to trace what happens to an individual embryo, egg or sperm sample from the date of collection.

Storage review

8.8   Centres should carry out a periodic review of the status of stored gametes and embryos at least once a year. The purpose of this review is two-fold. The first is to reconcile the centre's records with the genetic material actually in storage. The second is to review the purpose and duration of storage and to identify any action which needs to be taken.

8.9   Centres should also operate a 'bring forward' system, which will alert the centre in good time that particular gametes or embryos are about to reach the end of the statutory storage period specified in the centre's licence, or any shorter period specified by the donor.

8.10   Centres should make efforts to maintain contact with couples so that they can be reminded when the storage period for their gametes or embryos is due to expire. Couples should be contacted in good time to give them a reasonable period in which to consider the options available to them. For couples who placed embryos in storage before 1 May 1996 this will include informing them of the possibility of extending the storage period beyond 5 years.

8.11   When embryos placed in storage before 1 May 1996 have been created from donor sperm or eggs or both the renewed consent of the donor(s) is required for storage of more than 5 years. Centres should attempt to contact the donors where it is reasonable to do so. Centres should consider carefully the interests of both the couple and the donor before attempting to contact the donor. Centres should approach each case on an individual basis and take appropriate advice if necessary. Centres should keep a full record of the reasons for the decision and any action taken in each case.

Contamination

8.12   Gametes and embryos which may in future be used for treatment should not be placed in close proximity to any radioactive material or any potential source of infection or chemical or atmospheric contamination.

Transfer of gametes and embryos

8.13   It is the responsibility of the receiving centre to ensure that effective consents have been given to the use and storage of any gametes or embryos that are transferred to their centre. This includes consent to the creation of embryos *in vitro* where donor sperm is being provided for use in IVF treatment.

8.14   Centres are responsible for ensuring that the standards of quality and security of genetic material are maintained, wherever the material happens to be on the premises. This includes material being transferred from the laboratory for treatment or preparation for treatment.

8.15   Gametes and embryos may not leave licensed premises except in accordance with the HFEA's directions. If gametes or embryos are transferred from one site to another, adequate arrangements should also be made to protect their quality and security. Centres should operate a fail-safe mechanism to ensure that the correct gametes or embryos are transferred.

PART 9 – STORAGE OF GAMETES OR EMBRYOS FOR CANCER PATIENTS

Introduction

9.1   The following section draws together guidance which is relevant to the storage of sperm for male cancer patients and of embryos produced using the eggs of female cancer patients. The advice assumes that the cancer patient will wish to store gametes or embryos only for their own or partner's use in the future.

9.2   A patient presenting for oncology treatment who wishes to store gametes or embryos may have different immediate and future priorities. Provision should be made for supplying appropriate information and counselling as the health needs of the patient change.

Information to be given to cancer patients storing gametes or embryos

9.3   Before anyone consents to the storage of gametes or embryos they **must** be given 'such relevant information as is proper'.[28] Explanations should be oral and supported by relevant written information. Patients should be encouraged to ask for further information and their questions should be answered in a straight-forward, comprehensive and open way.

9.4   Centres should devise a system to ensure that:

(a)   the right information is given;

(b)   the person who is to give the information is clearly identified, and has been given sufficient training and guidance to enable them to do so; and

(c) a record is kept of the information given.

9.5   Information should be given to cancer patients consenting to the storage of gametes or embryos on the following points:

(a) the procedures involved in collecting gametes, the degree of pain and discomfort and any risks to that person, e.g. from the use of superovulatory drugs;

(b) the purposes for which their gametes may be used;

(c) whether or not they will be regarded under the Act as the parents of any child born as a result of using the stored gametes or embryos;

(d) that they are free to withdraw or vary the terms of their consent at any time, unless the gametes or embryos have already been used;

(e) that counselling is available;

(f) that the normal storage period for sperm is 10 years, although sperm may be stored for more than 10 years where the patient was under 45 years of age when the sperm was placed in storage;

(g) that the normal storage period for embryos is 5 years, although embryos may be stored for more than 5 years where the woman who would be treated by the embryos was under 50 years when the embryos were placed in storage.

Counselling

9.6   People consenting to the use or storage of embryos and to the storage of gametes, **must** be given 'a suitable opportunity to receive proper counselling about the implications of taking the proposed steps' before they consent.[29] Although not obligatory, counselling is generally recognised as beneficial.

9.7   Counselling should be distinguished from:

(a) the information which is to be given to everyone;

(b) the normal relationship between the clinician and the person seeking storage, which includes giving professional advice; and

(c) the process of assessing people in order to decide whether to accept their gametes or embryos for storage.

9.8   Centres **must** make implications counselling available to everyone.[30] This aims to enable the person concerned to understand the implications of the proposed course of action for themselves, for their family, and for any children born as a result.

9.9   Centres should present the offer of counselling as part of normal routine. The patient should be allowed sufficient time to consider the offer. Centres should allow sufficient time for counselling to be conducted sensitively at the pace determined by the needs of the person concerned. Counselling should normally be made available after the patient has received the explanations described in paragraph 9.4.

9.10   Centres should offer people the opportunity to be counselled by someone other than the clinician responsible for storage.

9.11   Centres should take all practical steps to provide support and further opportunities for counselling about the implications of storage after consent has been given.

9.12   A record should be kept of all counselling offered and whether or not the offer is accepted. All information obtained in the course of counselling should be kept confidential.

Consent to the storage and use of gametes and embryos

9.13   Anyone consenting to the storage of their gametes, or of embryos produced from them, **must**:

(a)   specify the maximum period of storage (if this is to be less than the statutory storage period);[31]
(b)   state what is to be done with the gametes or embryos if they die, or become incapable of varying or revoking their consent.[32]

9.14   Cancer patients storing sperm may give consent to storage separately from consent to use.

9.15   Cancer patients storing embryos produced using their eggs **must** specify the purpose for which they may be used, namely to provide treatment for themselves, or themselves and a named partner.[33]

9.16   The terms of the consent of a cancer patient storing embryos produced using her eggs **must** be compatible with the consent of the man who provided the sperm.[34]

9.17   Centres should allow those seeking storage sufficient time to reflect on their decision before obtaining written consent. Consent should be obtained on a consent form provided by the HFEA for the purpose. A copy of the consent form should be given to the person(s) giving consent.

Storage review

9.18   Centres should carry out a periodic review of the status of stored gametes and embryos at least once a year. The purpose is two-fold. The first is to reconcile the centre's records with the genetic material actually in storage. The second is to review the purpose and duration of storage and to identify any action which needs to be taken.

9.19   Centres should operate a 'bring forward' system, which will alert the centre in good time that particular gametes or embryos are about to reach the end of the statutory storage period specified in the centre's licence, or any shorter period specified by the donor.

Subsequent use of the stored gametes or embryos

9.20   Insemination of a woman at a licensed centre using her late husband's or partner's sperm is regulated under the Act. For this to take place the man **must** have given written consent to the posthumous use of his sperm to treat the woman.[35] The treatment centre **must** take account of the welfare of the potential child in considering whether to treat the woman.

9.21   People seeking treatment should be informed that the Human Fertilisation and Embryology Act states that if the sperm of a man is used after his death in treatment services i.e. for insemination, IVF or embryo transfer, he is not to be regarded in law as the father of any offspring produced from that treatment.

9.22 Similarly, if an embryo produced using the egg of a woman who has since died is used in treatment, the woman who provided the egg is not to be regarded in law as the mother of the child.

9.23 Frozen embryo transfer is a regulated activity. When a woman who has stored an embryo as a cancer patient wishes to have the embryo transferred in treatment the centre must consider her for treatment in the normal way, taking into account the welfare of the potential child.

Confidentiality

9.24 The attention of centres undertaking storage for cancer patients is drawn to the need for confidentiality of identifying information about people providing gametes (see Part 11, below).

PART 10 – RESEARCH

10.1 All research which involves the creation, keeping or using of human embryos outside the body **must** be licensed by the HFEA.[36] A centre **must** apply to the HFEA for a separate licence for each research project.[37]

10.2 The HFEA may grant licences for research projects for the following purposes only:

    (a)   to promote advances in the treatment of infertility;

    (b)   to increase knowledge about the causes of congenital disease;

    (c)   to increase knowledge about the causes of miscarriages;

    (d)   to develop more effective techniques of contraception;

    (e)   to develop methods for detecting the presence of gene or chromosome abnormalities in embryos before implantation.

10.3 The HFEA cannot grant a licence unless it is satisfied that the use of human embryos is essential for the purposes of the research.

10.4 The following activities are prohibited by law:

    (a)   keeping or using an embryo after the appearance of the primitive streak or after 14 days, whichever is the earlier;

    (b)   placing an embryo in a non-human animal;

    (c)   replacing a nucleus of a cell of an embryo with a nucleus taken from the cell of another person, another embryo, or a subsequent development of an embryo;

    (d)   altering the genetic structure of any cell while it forms part of an embryo.

10.5 The HFEA will not license research projects involving embryo splitting with the intention of increasing the number of embryos for transfer (see paragraph 7.22, above).

10.6 Embryos which have been appropriated for a research project **must not** be used for any other purposes.[38]

10.7 Centres should refer each research project to a properly constituted ethics committee for approval before applying for a research licence.

10.8 Centres within the NHS should refer research projects to the Local Research Ethics Committee (LREC) of the relevant District Health Authority. Centres outside the NHS may also refer projects to the LREC by prior arrangement, or may wish to set up their own committee. If so this should be an independent body of not fewer than 5 members. The chairman should be independent of the centre. No more than one third of its members should be employed by or have a financial interest in the centre. Membership of the ethics committee should be approved by the HFEA. For further information on the establishment and operation of a research ethics committee, centres should contact the Department of Health.

10.9 Proposals for research projects involving the use of embryos will be submitted for peer review to appropriate academic referees chosen by the HFEA.

10.10 Centres' attention is drawn to paragraphs 5.9 to 5.20 on consent to storage and use of gametes and embryos, paragraphs 7.5 and 7.6 on the use of gametes and embryos which have been subject to procedures which might prejudice their developmental potential, and paragraphs 7.24 to 7.26 on the termination and disposal of embryos which have been used for research.

PART 11 – RECORDS

Accuracy

11.1 All information which centres are required to keep by directions should be accurately recorded with proper cross references where this is required.

11.2 Centres' attention is drawn to paragraphs 3.36, 3.41, 3.56, 4.3(c), 5.2, 5.7, 5.8, 6.25, 8.4, 8.6, 8.7, 8.9, 8.11 and 12.1 of this Code, which set out additional matters about which records should be kept.

Access to Records

11.3 There should be a clearly identified individual in each centre whose responsibility it is to receive, check and arrange authorised access to confidential records. Apart from the access described in paragraphs 11.4, 11.5, 11.8 and 11.11, access to records must be limited to those covered by a licence.

11.4 Data to which the Data Protection Act 1984 applies and records to which the Access to Health Records Act 1990 applies will, unless exempted, be subject to the rights of access provided by those Acts. Centres with computerised records **must** ensure that they are registered with the Data Protection Registrar.[39]

11.5 Centres should allow all donors and clients who provide information about themselves to the centre access to the record of that information and an opportunity to correct it, even if it does not fall within the scope of the 1984 and 1990 Acts.

Access to Health Records Act 1990

11.6 Centres should be aware that under the Access to Health Records Act 1990, patients, or their agents authorised in writing, are normally entitled to have access to their own health records. The person seeking access must apply in writing to the holder of the record and may choose either to see the record or be supplied with a copy. An explanation of unintelligible terms must be given. If the records were made within 40 days proceeding the application, access must be allowed within 21 days. No charge is payable except the cost of making a copy and postage. Where records were made more than 40 days before the application, the record holder must allow access within 40 days. In this case a fee not exceeding £10 may be charged and the cost of copying and postage.

Confidentiality

11.7   Centres **must** ensure that information provided in confidence is kept confidential and only disclosed in the circumstances permitted by law.[40] People should not have access to any other person's records (including those of their spouse or partner) without their consent.

11.8   The Act puts strict limits on the disclosure of certain information by centres.[41] Information about any identifiable person who receives treatment services, provides gametes or is born as a result of treatment services can generally only be disclosed to members and staff of the HFEA or to someone else who is covered by a licence for the purpose of licensed activities. This general rule is subject to the following exceptions:

(a)   information about an identifiable person who receives treatment services or provides gametes can be disclosed to that person;

(b)   information about an identifiable person who receives treatment services can also be disclosed:

(i)   with that person's consent to specified people, or to unspecified people who need to know in connection with medical treatment or carrying out a medical or financial audit. The procedure for obtaining consent is set out in paragraphs 3.5–3.8. The consent should be in writing and thoroughly discussed beforehand with the person to whom the information relates. In the case of consent to disclosure to unspecified people, centres should always satisfy themselves that the information is disclosed only to someone who really needs to know the client/patient's identity;

(ii)   in an emergency, i.e. where it is necessary to avert imminent danger to the health of the person to whom the information relates, and where it is not reasonably practicable to obtain that person's consent. If it is practicable to obtain consent in an emergency, and that consent is refused or not requested, then the information must not be disclosed;

(c)   information about an identifiable person may be disclosed if it is necessary for any purpose preliminary to, or in connection with, legal proceedings or formal complaints procedures. However, no information may be disclosed in these cases which links a donor's identity to an individual who was, or may have been, born as a result of treatment with that donor's gametes;

(d)   identifying information may be disclosed in connection with formal court proceedings for the purpose of establishing the genetic parentage of a child who is subject to an application for a parental order in a surrogacy case;

(e)   information potentially identifying a donor can be disclosed to enable a centre or person covered by a licence to defend proceedings in England and Wales under the Congenital Disabilities (Civil Liability) Act 1976, and to enable them to bring connected proceedings for compensation against that donor;

(f)   under the Access to Health Records Act 1990 information held on health records about a patient may be disclosed subject to certain safeguards to that patient, or to certain persons authorised to act on their behalf (applies only in Great Britain).

11.9   Information can also be disclosed if it cannot lead to the identification of anyone to whom the information relates.

11.10   Centres should ensure that people to whom they disclose identifying information are aware that the information remains protected by the existing common law on confidentiality. Those receiving information should also be advised that if it is not kept confidential, a child might learn in an inappropriate way that they were born as a result of treatment services (see paragraphs 3.8–3.10).

11.11   Centres should have clear security procedures which will prevent unauthorised access to records, and particular care should be taken where records are kept outside the licensed premises, e.g. when counselling takes place outside the centre. If confidentiality is breached, the centre should investigate and deal with the breach and submit a full explanation to the HFEA. If it appears that a criminal offence has been committed the centre should inform the police but where the centre is in any doubt it should consult the HFEA.

PART 12 – COMPLAINTS

General

12.1   All centres should ensure that procedures are in place for acknowledging and investigating complaints. These should include the following:

(a)   centres should nominate one of their senior staff as a complaints officer. The complaints officer should be responsible for the effective operation of the complaints procedure and the investigation of complaints, and should be the first point of contact to whom all complaints are referred;

(b)   the complaints officer (or someone whom they nominate) should keep an accurate log of complaints, including an explanation of the steps taken, records of any oral or written communication with the complainant and a record of the outcome. Centres should inform the HFEA annually of the number of all written complaints made in that year, and the number which remain unresolved;

(c)   centres should ensure that all their staff are fully conversant with people's rights to make complaints, and with the procedure to be followed if a complaint is made;

(d)   notices drawing attention to the complaints procedure should be displayed prominently in reception areas. The notices should give the name and location of the complaints officer.

12.2   Minor complaints and matters of immediate concern can often be dealt with as they arise, without the need for a formal complaint. Staff should deal promptly with issues which can be addressed in a short time, in a way which reassures the person concerned.

12.3   Nevertheless, complaints which may seem trivial to members of staff may be of great concern to the person complaining. Staff should not deter people from making a formal complaint about any matter if they wish to do so.

12.4   If someone is unable to discuss their grievance with the member of staff directly concerned, another member of staff of approximately equivalent seniority should be available to assist.

12.5   If someone has difficulty in formulating their complaint, centres should give them all reasonable assistance to do so.

Investigation of complaints

12.6   Subject to paragraph 12.2 above, complaints should be given thorough consideration, and should be investigated and processed as swiftly as possible. An independent element should be included in the investigation where appropriate. Complainants should be kept informed of progress.

12.7   When an investigation has been completed, the centre should write a letter to the person who made the complaint, giving a full explanation of the outcome. If there has been any failure on the centre's part, the explanation should include the reasons, any steps to be taken to prevent it recurring, and an apology where appropriate. The letter should also inform the person complaining about any further action which remains open to them.

ANNEX A

Consent to disclosure of identifying information about my/our fertility treatment to another person who is not covered by a licence

1. The implications of consenting to the disclosure of identifying information about my/our treatment have been explained to me/us, I/we understand that I/we do not have to consent to all or any of the following.

2. I/we consent to disclosure of identifying information about my/our fertility treatment:

to (specify name) ....
for the purpose of ....

<u>but</u>

I/we do not consent to the following information being disclosed:

....

3. I/we consent to disclosure of identifying information about my/our fertility treatment to other people (unspecified) who need to know for the purposes of (tick as applicable):

[   ]   *my/our fertility treatment or other medical, surgical or obstetric treatment;*

[   ]   *a medical audit (monitoring the unit's performance);*

[   ]   *auditing the unit's accounts.*

<u>but</u>

I/we do not consent to disclosure to the following people for the following purposes:

....

and, I/we do not consent to the following information being disclosed:

....

Signed (wife/female partner) .... Date ....

Signed (husband/male partner) .... Date ....

ANNEX B

Parental orders in surrogacy cases

Conditions which must be fulfilled before a parental order can be granted

  (i) The child must be genetically related to at least one of the commissioning couple;

  (ii) The surrogate parents must have consented to the making of the order (unless incapable of giving consent or are untraceable) no earlier than six weeks after the birth of the child;

  (iii) The commissioning couple must be married to each other, and both must have attained the age of 18;

  (iv) The commissioning couple must have applied for an order within six months of the child's birth;

  (v) No money, other than expenses, must have been paid in respect of the surrogacy arrangement, unless authorised by a court;

  (vi) The child must be living with the commissioning couple;

  (vii) The commissioning couple must be domiciled in the United Kingdom, the Channel Islands, or the Isle of Man.

Application forms for parental orders will be available from Family Proceedings Courts (magistrates' courts) in the commissioning couple's home area. Legal aid may be available to cover parental order proceedings.

Registration of birth in surrogacy cases

Surrogate parents (birth mother and her partner/husband) are the legal parents of a child born through a surrogacy arrangement until legal parentage is transferred to the commissioning couple. The surrogate mother must therefore register the baby to which she has given birth in the normal way. Her husband or partner should normally be registered as the father.

  When a parental order has been granted by a court the Registrar General will make an entry in a separate Parental Order Register re-registering the child. This will be cross-referenced with the entry in the Register of Births. It will not be possible for the public to make a link between entries in the Register of Births and the Parental Order Register. It will be possible for adults who are the subject of parental orders to gain access, after being offered counselling, to their original birth certificates.

  Further advice on parental orders is available from the Department of Health. Please contact:— Department of Health

         Health Promotion Division

         Rm 417

         Wellington House

         133–155 Waterloo Road

         London SE1 8UG   Tel: 020 7972 2000

ANNEX C

HIV screening for gamete donors

Guidance on screening for HIV infection for licensed centres produced by the Human Fertilisation and Embryology Authority in co-operation with the Department of Health.

As with all organs and tissues for transplantation donors of gametes (semen and eggs) must be shown to be free of infection with HIV. This entails testing the blood of donors for HIV antibody at the time donations are made. Antibodies may not appear in the blood for up to 3 or possibly 6 months after infection. In order to avoid transplanting gametes collected during this 'window' period of infection, donors of gametes which can be stored before use (semen) should be tested a second time for HIV antibody at least 180 days after the first test. When the donation must be used immediately (eggs) there is a slight risk that donor infection will not be identified.

Centres should assess the suitability of individual donors including any possible history of transmissible infection. The informed consent of the person concerned should be obtained before any HIV test is carried out. Donors should be advised of the practical implications of having an HIV test, even if it proves negative. The centre should offer to arrange specialist HIV counselling for anyone whose behaviour has put them at high risk or whose test proves positive.

Semen should only be used for others when immediate and 180 day tests for HIV antibody are negative. In no circumstances should donated semen be used which has been collected less than 180 days before the most recent negative HIV antibody test.

At the beginning of the treatment and collection cycle of a woman whose eggs are to be taken for the treatment of others, her blood should be tested for the presence of HIV antibodies. If treatment and collection are to take place some time after the initial assessment, a preliminary sample should also be tested at the time of the initial assessment. The eggs should only be used if the HIV antibody test is negative. The small risk of HIV infection should be explained to recipients of donated eggs.

The blood of both people whose gametes were used to produce an embryo should be tested for HIV antibodies if and when they decide to make the embryo available for the treatment of others. Stored embryos should not be used if they have been created less than 180 days before the most recent negative antibody tests on both donors.

Centres should adopt any additional guidance on HIV testing which is given by the Health Departments.

ANNEX D

Consent to treatment involving egg retrieval and/or egg or embryo replacement

Name of Centre: ....

Address: ....

Full Name of Woman: ....

Address: ....

This consent form is in two parts. These may be signed separately. When frozen embryos are being replaced they should be signed separately.

Part I

1. I consent to [delete/complete as applicable]:

i. be prepared for egg retrieval;

ii. the removal of eggs from my ovaries with the aid of:
(a) laparoscopy
(b) ultrasound

iii. the administration of any drugs and anaesthetics which may be found necessary in the course of the procedure(s);

iv. the mixing of the following [tick each column as required]:

[ ] my egg(s)   *[ ] with the sperm of my husband/partner*

[ ] eggs donated by   *[ ] with sperm donated by*
....   *.........................*

[ ] an anonymous donor's egg(s)   *[ ] with an anonymous donor's sperm*

2. I understand that if the donor has given effective consent under the Human Fertilisation and Embryology Act 1990, the donor will not be the legal parent of any resulting child.

3. I have discussed with .... the procedures outlined above. I have been given information orally and in writing about them.

4. I have been given a suitable opportunity to take part in counselling about the implications of the proposed treatment. (For GIFT using donated sperm or eggs, or any IVF treatment.)

Patient's Signature: .... *Date:* ....

Part II

1. I consent to:

i. the placing in my uterus or fallopian tube[s], as may be appropriate, of not more than (tick as applicable):

(a) 1[   ] *egg(s) mixed with sperm*   *(b)* 1[   ] *embryo(s)*
      2[   ]   2[   ]
      3[   ]   3[   ]

ii. the administration of any drugs and anaesthetics which may be found necessary in the course of the procedure(s);

2. I understand that only the egg[s] from one woman and sperm from one man will be used in any one treatment cycle.

3. I have discussed with .... the procedures outlined above. I have been given information orally and in writing about them.

4. Other remarks (if required): ....

...

Patient's Signature: .... Date: ....

5. All the information listed in paragraph 4.4 of the Human Fertilisation and Embryology Authority's Code of Practice has been given to the patient. The patient has been offered a suitable opportunity to take part in counselling about the implications of the proposed treatment.

Doctor's Signature: .... Date: ....

HUSBAND'S CONSENT

6. I am the husband of .... and I consent to the course of treatment outlined above. I understand that I will become the legal father of any resulting child.

7. Any other remarks: ....

...

Signature of husband: .... Date: ....

Full name in block capitals: ....

Address: ....

....

[NOTE: the centre is not required to obtain a husband's consent in order to make the treatment lawful, but where donated sperm is used it is advisable in the interests of establishing the legal parenthood of the child. See paragraphs 5.6–5.8 of the Code of Practice.]

MALE PARTNER'S ACKNOWLEDGEMENT

8. *I am not married to ...., but I acknowledge that she and I are being treated together, and that I will become the legal father of any resulting child.*

9. *Any other remarks:*..

....

Signature of male partner: .... *Date:* ....

Full name in block capitals: ....

Address: ....

....

[NOTE: the centre is not required to obtain a partner's acknowledgement in order to make the treatment lawful, but where donated sperm is used it is advisable in the interests of establishing the legal parenthood of the child. See paragraphs 5.6–5.8 of the Code of Practice.]

CONSENT TO DONOR INSEMINATION

Name of centre: ....

Address: ....

Full name of woman: ....

Address: ....

1. *I have asked the centre named above to provide me with treatment services to help me to bear a child. I consent to (delete/complete as applicable):*

    i.   *the administration as necessary of the drugs described in the attached schedule;*

    ii. *be inseminated with:*

(a)   the sperm of ....

(b)   the sperm of an anonymous donor.

2.   *I understand that if the donor has given effective consent under the Human Fertilisation and Embryology Act 1990, he will not be the legal father of any resulting child.*

3.   *I understand that I will not be treated with the sperm of more than one man during any one treatment cycle.*

4.   *I have discussed in full with* .... *the procedures outlined above. I have been given information orally and in writing about them.*

5.   *I have been given a suitable opportunity to take part in counselling about the implications of the proposed treatment.*

6.   *Other remarks (if required):* ....

....

Patient's   Signature: ....   *Date:* ....

7.   *All the information listed in paragraph 4.4 of the Human Fertilisation and Embryology Authority's Code of Practice has been given to the patient. The patient has been given a suitable opportunity to take part in counselling about the implications of the proposed treatment.*

Doctor's   Signature: ....   *Date:* ....

HUSBAND'S CONSENT

I am the husband of .... *and I consent to the course of treatment outlined above. I understand that I will become the legal father of any resulting child.*

Any   other   remarks: ....

....

Signature   of   husband: ....   *Date:* ....

Full   name   in   block   capitals: ....

Address: ....

....

[NOTE: the centre is not required to obtain a husband's consent in order to make the treatment lawful but it is advisable in the interests of establishing the legal parenthood of the child. See paragraphs 5.6–5.8 of the Code of Practice.]

MALE PARTNER'S ACKNOWLEDGEMENT

I am not married to ...., but I acknowledge that she and I are being treated together, and that I will become the legal father of any resulting child.

Signature of male partner .... Date: ....

Full name in block capitals: ....

Address: ....

...

[NOTE: the centre is not required to obtain a partner's acknowledgement in order to make the treatment lawful but it is advisable in the interests of establishing the legal parenthood of the child. See paragraphs 5.6–5.8 of the Code of Practice.]

NOTES

[1] Human Fertilisation and Embryology Act 1990 section 16(2)(a)
[2] HF&E Act 1990 s. 17(1)
[3] HF&E Act 1990 s. 38
[4] HF&E Act 1990 s. 17(1)(b) and (d)
[5] HF&E Act 1990 s. 12(a)
[6] HF&E Act 1990 s. 13(6); Schedule 3 para. 3(1)(a)
[7] HF&E Act 1990 s. 13(5)
[8] HF&E Act 1990 s. 33(5)
[9] HF&E Act 1990 s. 13(5)
[10] HF&E Act 1990 s. 12(e)
[11] This is an obligation under the general law and Schedule 3 of the HFE Act 1990, respectively. When obtaining consent to examination and treatment centres should follow Department of Health guidelines.
[12] HF&E Act 1990 Schedule 3
[13] HF&E Act 1990 s. 13(b); Schedule 3 para. 3(1)(b)
[14] This is an obligation under the general law.
[15] Children Act 1989
[16] HF&E Act 1990 Schedule 3 para. 2(2)
[17] HF&E Act 1990 Schedule 3 paras 2(1)(a) and (b), 5(1), 6(1) and (3)
[18] HF&E Act 1990 Schedule 3 para. 2(1)
[19] HF&E Act 1990 s. 13(6); Schedule 3 para. 3(1)(a)
[20] HF&E Act 1990 s. 13(6); Schedule 3 para. 3(1)(a)
[21] HF&E Act 1990 s. 24(4)
[22] HF&E Act 1990 s. 24(3)
[23] HF&E Act 1990 Schedule 3 paras 3 and 6
[24] HF&E Act 1990 s. 2(2) and s. 4(1)(a)
[25] HF&E Act 1990 Schedule 3 paras 2(1) and 2(2)
[26] HF&E Act 1990 Schedule 2 para. 3
[27] HF&E Act 1990 s. 24(4)

Index